AF605957

Looking with Robert Gardner

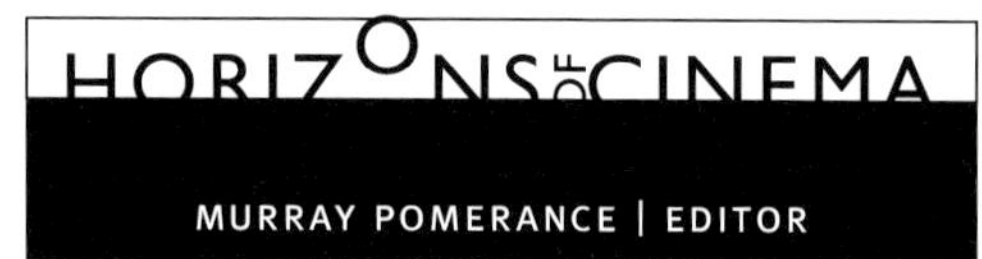

Also in the series

William Rothman, editor, *Cavell on Film*

J. David Slocum, editor, *Rebel Without a Cause*

Joe McElhaney, *The Death of Classical Cinema*

Kirsten Moana Thompson, *Apocalyptic Dread*

Frances Gateward, editor, *Seoul Searching*

Michael Atkinson, editor, *Exile Cinema*

Paul S. Moore, *Now Playing*

Robin L. Murray and Joseph K. Heumann, *Ecology and Popular Film*

William Rothman, editor, *Three Documentary Filmmakers*

Sean Griffin, editor, *Hetero*

Jean-Michel Frodon, editor, *Cinema and the Shoah*

Carolyn Jess-Cooke and Constantine Verevis, editors, *Second Takes*

Matthew Solomon, editor, *Fantastic Voyages of the Cinematic Imagination*

R. Barton Palmer and David Boyd, editors, *Hitchcock at the Source*

William Rothman, *Hitchcock, Second Edition*

Joanna Hearne, *Native Recognition*

Marc Raymond, *Hollywood's New Yorker*

Steven Rybin and Will Scheibel, editors, *Lonely Places, Dangerous Ground*

Claire Perkins and Constantine Verevis, editors, *B Is for Bad Cinema*

Dominic Lennard, *Bad Seeds and Holy Terrors*

Rosie Thomas, *Bombay before Bollywood*

Scott M. MacDonald, *Binghamton Babylon*

Sudhir Mahadevan, *A Very Old Machine*

David Greven, *Ghost Faces*

James S. Williams, *Encounters with Godard*

William H. Epstein and R. Barton Palmer, editors, *Invented Lives, Imagined Communities*

Lee Carruthers, *Doing Time*

Opposite page: Robert Gardner and Dani Tribe, Baliem Valley. Gardner returns after twenty-eight years and shows the Dani his photographs taken during the filming of *Dead Birds* in 1961. Irian Jaya, Indonesia, 1989. Photograph by Susan Meiselas.

Looking with Robert Gardner

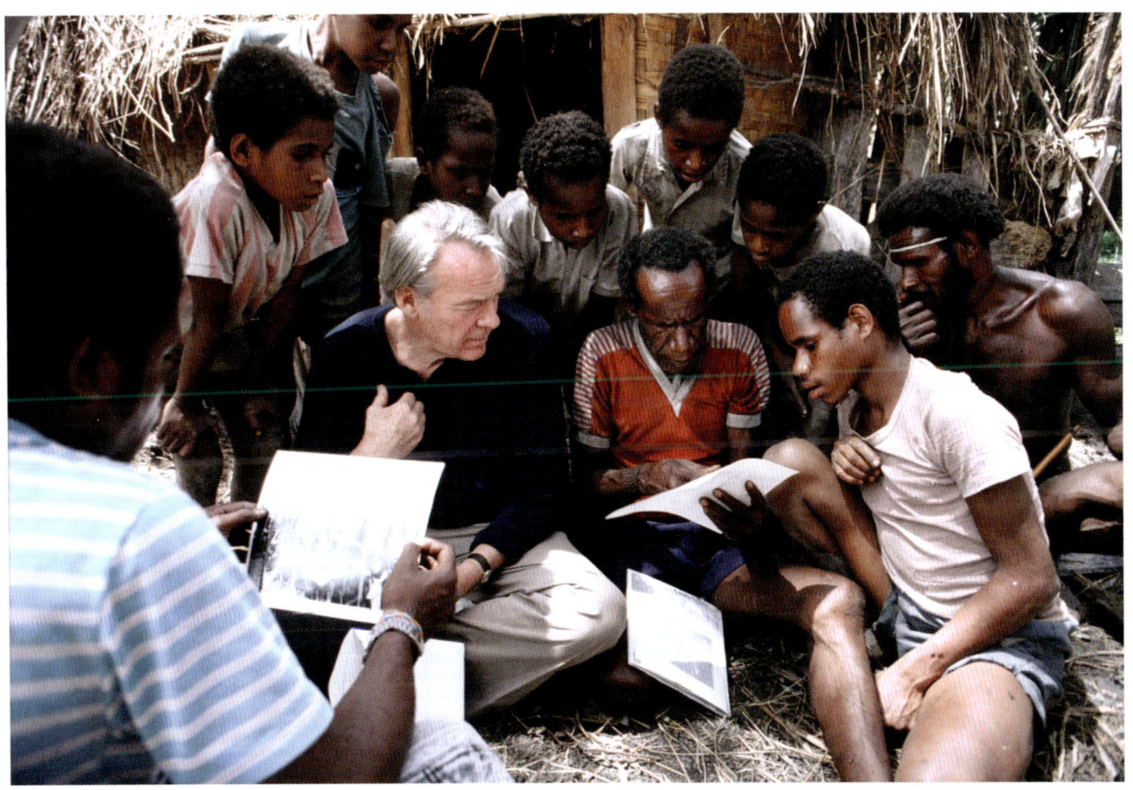

Edited by Rebecca Meyers, William Rothman, and Charles Warren

State University of New York Press

Published by State University of New York Press, Albany

Printed in the United States of America

For information, contact State University of New York Press, Albany, NY
www.sunypress.edu

Production, Laurie D. Searl
Marketing, Fran Keneston
Text and cover design, Peter Blaiwas Graphic Design

Library of Congress Cataloging-in-Publication Data

Looking with Robert Gardner / edited by Rebecca Meyers, William Rothman, and Charles Warren.
pages cm. — (SUNY series, horizons of cinema)
Includes bibliographical references and index.
ISBN 978-1-4384-6051-2 (hardcover : alk. paper) — ISBN 978-1-4384-6050-5 (pbk. : alk. paper) — ISBN 978-1-4384-6052-9 (e-book) 1. Motion pictures in ethnology. 2. Gardner, Robert, 1925–2014 — Criticism and interpretation. 3. Ethnographic films. 4. Indigenous peoples in motion pictures. I. Meyers, Rebecca, [date] editor. II. Rothman, William, editor. III. Warren, Charles, [date]
GN347.L66 2016
305.8—dc23

2015019494

10 9 8 7 6 5 4 3 2 1

Contents

Introduction
Robert Gardner

Rebecca Meyers, William Rothman, and Charles Warren

Caleb Gardner concludes his introduction to *Just Representations* (2010), a diverse collection of Robert Gardner's journals, essays, and other writings, by citing one of his father's earliest journal entries, which "describes how servants in Johannesburg bow and cup their hands around whatever money they have been given, while also trying to see just how much it is."[1] While noting that some version of this behavior will be found wherever there are people, he imagines it as having special relevance to his father's life—"a life spent looking at oneself by watching other people," as he puts it. "I can almost see the writer as a younger man, in possession, like all of us, of something still not completely known to him, eager, but also a little afraid to open his hand and find out exactly what it is."[2]

When Gayatri Chatterjee invokes this little parable near the end of her chapter in this volume, she sagely observes, "Perhaps this is a 'possession' one does not ultimately possess." For what Caleb Gardner imagines cupped in his father's hand, as he was beginning the journey of discovery that was to bring us the remarkable body of work *Looking with Robert Gardner* looks at and celebrates, can only be the gift (it can feel like a curse) of humanity. This is what he had in common with the "others" he was to watch in the course of his long career, and with us.

Because human beings are subjects as well as objects of self-knowledge, we can never know ourselves objectively. And because we are free to change, to become other than we have been, we cannot know ourselves completely. Robert Gardner's films, as Fanny Howe eloquently observes in her chapter here, "reflect on the strangeness of being ourselves." She adds, "Emmanuel Levinas, Paul Ricoeur, Richard Kearney and Julia Kristeva are just a few of those who have tackled the question of the stranger, sometimes called Other, who is finally ourselves." A philosopher closer to home who tackled this question is Stanley Cavell, Gardner's longtime Harvard colleague and friend, who in *The World Viewed* writes, "Apart from the wish for selfhood (and the always simultaneous granting of otherness as well), I do not understand the value of art."[3] Another kindred spirit was Ralph Waldo Emerson, Gardner's great New England progenitor, who begins his essay "Experience" by saying that when we awaken to our human condition, we find ourselves in no place we know. We are strangers to ourselves.

Robert Gardner overcame his fear of what he might discover about himself by watching other people, and strove tirelessly to express what he *did* discover. He opened his hand to create —he opened his hand *by* creating—the films, photographs, and writings he gave the world. (To this list should be added the Film Study Center he founded at Harvard and *Screening Room*, the weekly television show he created and hosted to promote the work and ideas of independent film and video artists.) In opening his hand, Gardner found in the human condition the painful difference between what we must be and what we might want to be, to paraphrase his narration in *Rivers of Sand* (1974). But in creating the works he gave to the world, he also found the freedom to "walk in the direction of the unattained but attainable self," as Emerson put it, despite being shackled by society's conventions, as all human beings are.

Tom Conley compares and contrasts what he calls the "aerial view" in Gardner's journals and films with the intimate view of his camera when it "touches down" and would become "the appendage of a human attending to everyday life in the milieu he or she inhabits." We have divided the book into two parts that more or less correspond to this division between Gardner's reflections on seeing the world from the air—he piloted his own private plane—and his accounts of travel and encounter when he "touched down."

The chapter by Eliot Weinberger that opens the first part of *Looking with Robert* Gardner is the only piece not written especially for the book. Although it has previously been published, we have included it, and placed it first, because it serves so admirably as a general statement about Gardner's work, and so effectively introduces themes developed in the chapters that follow.[4] The eleven pieces in Part I address general topics (but not without "touching down" at times to look closely at particular examples): Tom Conley on Gardner's geographic sensibility; Fanny Howe on color and Gardner's relation to races other than his own; Daniel Morgan on Gardner's achievement of valid ethnographic knowledge; Maxime Scheinfeigel on Gardner's striking points of comparison with and difference from his somewhat older contemporary (and friend) Jean Rouch; Charles Warren on Gardner's intellectual relationship with Stanley Cavell and an understanding of filmic reality they seem to develop between them; Gayatri Chatterjee on Gardner's self-questioning and on reaction to him in India; Kathryn Ramey on Gardner's relation to experimental film; and Brian Frye on *Screening Room*. We also bring Gardner's own voice into the mix by including a 2008 interview conducted in Mexico City by Carlos Flores and Antonio Zirión. This part of the book concludes with images photographer and close Gardner friend Susan Meiselas took on her visit with him to New Guinea in 1988–1989, many years after he had shot *Dead Birds* (1963) there.

The chapters in Part II, ordered chronologically, focus primarily on individual Gardner films (but not without offering aerial views at times): Charles Musser on *Dead Birds*; Mario Bucci and Irina Leimbacher on *Rivers of Sand*; Murray Pomerance and Ricardo Zulueta on *Deep Hearts* (1981); Richard Allen and Julia Yezbick on *Forest of Bliss* (1986); Richard Deming on Gardner's films about artists and their art; Bruce Jenkins on *2 Sons of Catalonia: Josep Lluís Sert & Joan Miró* (2013), and William Rothman on *Dead Birds Re-Encountered* (2013).

We do not claim that this book presents a complete account of Gardner's work. How could it? But the authors who have accepted our invitation to contribute represent several nationalities and a diversity of approaches, sensibilities, intellectual concerns, and disciplinary affiliations. The multiplicity of their voices helps give the book a monumental quality. It takes a monumental book to begin to do justice to the magnitude of this artist's aspirations and achievements. Yet in writing about Robert Gardner, these authors all begin from the same starting point: the conviction that the works he has placed in our hands are gifts of great value. They also share the same goal: to discover exactly what these gifts are and where their value lies. And in pursuit of this goal, they have all had the courage to open their own hands.

Too often, Gardner has been pigeonholed as an ethnographic filmmaker, then pilloried for failing to conform to the constricting conventions some take that term to imply. Undeniably, his best-known films—*Dead Birds*, *Rivers of Sand*, *Deep Hearts*, *Forest of Bliss*—have an ethnographic dimension. All his films do; far from denying the value of ethnographic knowledge, his films pursue it. Daniel Morgan mounts a powerful argument to demonstrate that, some anthropologists' claims to the contrary notwithstanding, Gardner's films *succeed* in attaining, and communicating, what can legitimately be called "ethnographic knowledge." But they challenge conventional ethnographic filmmaking, and anthropology more generally, to change—as to a degree they have, in ways Kathryn Ramey and Julia Yezbick reflect on in their chapters. Even though the value of Gardner's films cannot be separated from their poetic quality and cinematic artistry, his champions make a serious mistake, as Morgan argues, whenever they concede, rather than contest, the charge that his films make no significant contribution to anthropology.

The contributors to this volume do not make that mistake. They recognize that there is no conflict between art and science in Gardner's work. Kathryn Ramey, for example, writes, approvingly, "Although Gardner's primary motivation has been a cinematic engagement with real people in the real world, he has approached this task as an artist and a poet." Charles Warren puts it this way:

> Gardner's films make clear, as do his considerable writings on film, now collected in several volumes, that he has always seen himself as scrupulously trying to render the world as he finds it, to keep faithful to it—and at the same time as making, fashioning, working poetically, from a basis in his own sensibility. . . . Gardner believes, or finds, that the engagement of sensibility with the world—an artistic, a poetic engagement—finds out reality.

Gardner himself speaks to the point in the Mexico City interview:

> If the goal of anthropology is to try to reveal the meanings of our behavior, how can it dispense with the aesthetic dimension? I sometimes feel as though critics on warring sides of these matters make the mistake of thinking science is opposed to or incompatible with art and *vice versa*. In my view, they coexist with no difficulty at all. I would submit my own work as examples of why "aesthetics" should not be ignored.

The fact that Gardner's films are works of art does not mean they are unconcerned with attaining, and communicating, knowledge of the kind that moves anthropology closer to its goal—or what *should* be its goal, in Gardner's view—of "revealing the meanings of our behavior." Gardner believed that it was a mistake for anthropology to take itself to be—or to aspire to become—an "objective," value-free science no different in principle from chemistry or physics. Insofar as they are works of art, Gardner's films cannot but be concerned with aesthetic matters (and with moral matters as well). But so must they be concerned with aesthetic and moral matters if they are to be of real value to anthropology. To reveal the meanings of the behavior of the people he filmed, which in Gardner's view is anthropology's proper goal, his filmmaking had to be, as he put it, "of a kind that makes the humanity of others accessible," a kind that "depends as much on empathy as craft." For Gardner, in other words, ethnographic knowledge—knowledge that genuinely advances anthropology—is a kind of knowledge that is also self-knowledge, the kind of knowledge that art alone is capable of granting us. That is why the fusion of art and anthropology Gardner aspired to and achieved is not only possible but necessary—necessary *morally* as well as aesthetically, as Richard Deming argues:

> Gardner's world is an art world. His very mode of perception is that of an artist, and so the world he lives in is determined by its capability to be art, and is thus constituted by his aesthetic responses. Moreover—and this is important—such artistic perception is predicated on the sense that the phenomenal world makes moral claims upon our attention. "I propose that in film's very nature," Gardner has written, "somewhere embedded in its formal attributes as a mediator of the phenomenal world, there arises a capacity for evoking moral responses in those who come in contact with it." Such a formulation suggests that in his role as filmmaker, he is the shaper of a moral possibility occurring in response to—indeed, as part of—aesthetic experience.

Mauro Bucci concurs that it is an important feature of what he calls Gardner's "poetics" that his art has a moral dimension:

> *Rivers of Sand* allows us to draw a moral from the representation of Hamar life: it invites us to become aware of the constraints imposed by social standards and the inequalities that roles can give rise to—the way they seem obvious and inevitable because of their deep roots in

> everybody's life. The knowledge that the existence of the individual is not shaped by immutable or natural laws, but, rather, by cultural patterns—that is, possible options in the way human beings live, as Gardner reminds us in his film *Ika Hands* (1988)—allows us to confront the restrictions imposed by social models with a more critical attitude, and to consider them amenable to change.

In Gardner's own words: "Films like mine, I have hoped, would act in some manner or other, as a mirror of the viewer's own soul, that is to say, life experience. To the extent this occurs, I am confident that a viewer will examine his or her own life, which seems to me the most desirable goal of all." The chapters in this volume explore in concrete detail strategies Gardner employs in his striving to achieve this goal.

Richard Allen offers a key insight when he suggests, in his compelling reading of *Forest of Bliss*, that the film "brings to bear the full stylistic arsenal of film upon elements of actuality in order to create an experience for the spectator that is akin to ritual, where banal facts of quotidian life are perceived as expressions of spirit, or of a higher transcendent time." In this way, as Allen argues, *Forest of Bliss* "enacts, as a film, the ways of being that it strives to represent."

Maxine Scheinfeigel offers another key insight when she observes that Gardner's work, in contrast to the films of his Jean Rouch, "is traversed by a conception of images more *figural* than figurative: sails of phantom ships, undulations of human faces, rolling of the feet of camels." And yet, as she observes, "beyond the forms actualized in the images," the films express ideas—ideas that "surge forth" from the depths of the films' images and sounds, emerging "less from the decoding of meaning than by the aesthetic perception of lines and forms, of movements and sounds, of vibrations and the visual and auditory echoes that these vibrations simultaneously engender."

Irina Leimbacher illustrates how ideas "surge forth" from Gardner's images and sounds by beginning her chapter on *Rivers of Sand* with the simple evocation of what viewers see and hear in the first few moments of the film: "First just a bush, a thorn bush. Next a woman's hands pick some thorns from a branch. We hear the sound of repeated scraping accompanied by images of the up and down motion of a hand. Something is being rhythmically brushed against the metal leg rings adorning a woman's ankle and calf."

Murray Pomerance, too, illustrates this feature of Gardner's cinematic style, while at the same time making an important point about the kind of critical writing his films call for, by concluding his provocative chapter about *Deep Hearts* with a poetic evocation of his experience of the film's closing sequence. Pomerance's passage begins this way: "Day and night and night and day. The purple sky and the green sky. The bodies singing 'Aiahhhhhhhhh.' The hands gesticulating, speaking to space. The lips pulled back and marked, the flashing teeth. The flashing eyes." And it ends with this:

> The patient camels, the camels attendant, a face painted oxblood red, the long line, the blue sky, fingers touching up the eyebrows, a face as orange as yams, the blue burnoose, the blue sky, the long line,

> the smile of victory, the sharp teeth, the prize teeth, the blue sky, the multicolored umbrella. The hands, the clapping hands, the open hands, the trading hands, the open hands, the camels' feet sliding away.

The ethnographic cinema Gardner developed is based entirely on such "telling details and oblique images," as Eliot Weinberger puts it. That is why the contributors to this book have all felt the need for their prose to become evocative—to be expressive of their own experience of those film moments—whenever they "touched down" to look at particular cinematic passages. And they all recognized that their prose had to "touch down" at certain points if they were to discover the intimate secrets those "telling moments" tell, and to convey how Gardner's art enables those secrets to be told.

In the films Gardner made about artists and their art, which comprise an important but relatively neglected part of his oeuvre, the "ways of being" he strove to represent are, explicitly, ways of creating—ways of creating that are also ways of looking. Such a film as *Mark Tobey* (1952), *Mark Tobey Abroad* (1973), or *Passenger* (1997), a film he made about the painter Sean Scully, becomes "a vision of another's way of envisioning," as Richard Deming puts it, in a manner analogous to the way the chapters in this book present "visions of another's way"—Robert Gardner's way—"of envisioning."

As a filmmaker, Deming writes, Gardner attempts in these films "to represent artistic processes intimately, personally, and in such a way as to create a cinematic dialogue between his work and the work with which the artists onscreen are engaged." His camera's gaze "forges a connection between the perceived and the perceiver," just as the authors of these chapters do. But this connection isn't solely between the filmmaker and the subject. "The intersubjectivity that a film makes possible flows in two directions—towards the subject and towards the viewer." Thus in these films "cinema, as an art, *encounters* art, and the results, as Gardner suggests, have ethical implications because they are the intertwining of personal responses, which viewers must then respond to."

In the chapter on *Dead Birds Re-Encountered* that concludes this book, William Rothman extends Deming's point, in effect, by suggesting that Deming's insightful observations about Gardner's artist films apply to most—perhaps all—his other films as well. Those films, too, become "visions of another's way of envisioning." In those films, too, "cinema, as an art, encounters art" insofar as it is a characteristic feature of a Gardner film that it builds toward a climactic passage in which its own art dialogues—Rothman's word is *fuses*—with the art of the people in the film:

> In *Blunden Harbour* (1951), *Dead Birds* and *Rivers of Sand*, for example, Gardner's art fuses with dance. In *Deep Hearts*, it fuses with the performance art, as we might think of it, of the men who are participating in the "beauty contest" that provides the film with its grand finale. In *Ika Hands*, it is the chanting of the holy man called Mama Marco as he walks into the clouds, the culmination of his meditation, the fusing of song and nothingness, that is at once captured and affected, cinematically, by the camera. *Forest of Bliss* climaxes not with the sequence in which we finally see a dead body

being cremated, but with the subsequent performance of the healer, whose ecstatic chanting at once possesses, and is possessed by, Gardner's rapturous camera.

And, as Rothman argues, *Dead Birds Re-Encountered* completes the cycle when it climaxes, and concludes, by fusing with Gardner's own breakthrough film, *Dead Birds*.

In writing about *2 Sons of Catalonia: Josep Lluís Sert & Joan Miró* (2013), a short film that was more than four decades in the making, Bruce Jenkins proposes that Gardner found in the modernist architect Sert a "brother in arms," a "compelling analogue for his own attempts to create works that utilize the aesthetic interplay of space and light to mediate the realms of nature and culture" so as to discover the "spiritual dimension" that animates art and life. Like *Dead Birds Re-Encountered*, *2 Sons of Catalonia* has what Jenkins describes as "a valedictory feel, a palpable sense of looking back at the past, of chronicling the achievements of a lifetime of work." And yet, as he observes, "the two titled protagonists of the film, joined at times by the filmmaker, seem to actively challenge this reading." Like the artists he filmed, Gardner "remains focused on the work that still has to be done." His last works, for all their valedictory quality, reveal and declare that their creator was still "journeying on." This is what Emerson called "walking in the direction of the unattained yet attainable self"—although he had reached a place, as Rothman's chapter closes by saying, at which "journeying on" also means returning home.

Mark Tobey, one of Gardner's earliest films, made immediately after *Blunden Harbour*, is an "experimental portrait" (to borrow the description in the catalog of Documentary Educational Resources, which distributes the film) of the well-known painter "which tries to show in cinematic language how this man looked at the world." The film addresses the painter's art with the kind of ethnographic interest, as we might put it, that *Blunden Harbour* manifests in the dances and myths of the Kwakiutl people of the Pacific Northwest. In creating these early films, Gardner's interest in coming to know the way the people he films look at the world went hand in hand with an interest in coming to know "cinematic language." In his subsequent work, as in these early films, Gardner approached his abiding subject, the intersection of life and art, as an anthropologist *and* as an artist. In the language of cinema, there is no distinction between anthropology *and* art; art *is* anthropology, science *is* magic, looking *is* creating, creating *is* knowing.

When Stanley Cavell introduced *Forest of Bliss* at its world premiere at Harvard's Carpenter Center, he characterized the film as acting "to burst its form, as if its maker is challenging its origins, taking his work into its own exploration of the conditions of art and of life that make it possible."[5] In Cavell's formulation, the film's "origins" are its roots in the reality of the people and places Gardner filmed, but also its roots in the reality of the world his film projects—a world transformed or transfigured by the medium of film and the singular art that medium makes possible. In Gardner's words: "Film is not simply a mirror recording our physicality, but a medium achieving a transfiguration of our ordinariness."[6]

Collectively, the chapters in this volume can be seen to make the case that every Gardner film challenges its origins, bursts its form, by exploring the conditions of art and of life that make it possible—where "art" means both Gardner's own art and the art of the people he filmed, and "life" means both his life and theirs. And every Gardner film manifests, as Cavell argues *Forest of Bliss* does, "respect for difference, for otherness, respect for the other's mystery and for its own power to communicate what it wishes known. It is a version of that respect for his or her subject or material that every true artist manifests."[7]

The academic study of film is finally emerging from a protracted period in which film criticism, like anthropology, was in the grip of the notion that it should aspire to the condition of a science like physics and chemistry, not an art. Like Gardner himself, the contributors to this book manifest respect for their subject. In so doing, they testify to the value of art—and the value of criticism when, aligning itself with Gardner's art, it strives to attain and communicate a kind of knowledge that is also self-knowledge.

All the chapters in this book acknowledge that Robert Gardner's art is grounded in his practice of looking at himself by watching other people. "Gardner has always regarded his anthropological projects as pathways to 'help me understand myself,'" Bruce Jenkins writes. Charles Musser makes the point by writing, "*Dead Birds* is about the human condition, about what the film's creator has in common with the Dani." Charles Warren puts it this way: "Gardner seeks to do away with the barrier [separating us from the "ethnographic Other"], making in his work a strong gesture of, in the Chandogya Upanishad's utterance, 'I am thou.'" And Ricardo Zulueta, writing about *Deep Hearts*, says this:

> When Gardner is behind the camera, the intuitive fluidity with which he lovingly, sensitively, and passionately films the Wodaabe suggests that he feels an intimate kinship with them. Perhaps his "natural" reserve is a façade, like their painted faces and exaggerated expressions, to keep others from looking into his "deep heart," the metaphysical space in which he hides his true feelings, as they do, from the eyes of those he fears might devour him, figuratively speaking.

The authors who have contributed to this volume have looked at Gardner's works in ways that respect, and emulate, his practice of looking at himself by watching other people. They have allowed these works to teach them how to look at them. In this sense, we can say that they have looked *at* Robert Gardner by looking *with* him. Hence the title we have given this book. In looking with Robert Gardner, they have kept faith with *his* faith—above all, his faith in the power of art to bring home to us what it means to be human.

What is most to be valued about being human, Gardner fervently believed, is the capacity to create art, which is inseparable from the capacity to be moved by art. He expressed this conviction by creating *Dead Birds*, *Rivers of Sand*, *Deep Hearts*, *Forest of Bliss*, and the other sublime and beautiful works this book looks at and celebrates, works that grant us knowledge about ourselves and our fellow human beings by moving us beyond words.

Gardner's narration for *Dead Birds* famously begins:

> There is a fable told by a mountain people living in the ancient highlands of New Guinea about a race between a snake and a bird. It tells of a contest to decide whether men would be like birds and die, or be like snakes, which shed their skins and have eternal life. The bird won, and from that time all men, like birds, must die.

Robert Gardner's art will live on.

Notes

1. Caleb Gardner, "Barren Mazes," in Robert Gardner, *Just Representations* (Cambridge, MA: Studio7Arts & Peabody Museum Press, 2010), xv.
2. Ibid.
3. Stanley Cavell, *The World Viewed: Reflections on the Ontology of Film*, enlarged ed. (Cambridge, MA: Harvard University Press, 1979), 22.
4. Weinberger's work as presented here consists of two parts: excerpts from "The Camera People," which was published in Weinberger's book *Outside Stories: 1987–1991* (New York: New Directions, 1992) and also in Charles Warren, editor, *Beyond Document: Essays on Nonfiction Film* (Hanover, NH: Wesleyan/University Press of New England, 1996); and the Preface to *Still Points*, a forthcoming collection of Robert Gardner's photographs (Cambridge, MA: Peabody Museum Press).
5. Stanley Cavell, "Words of Welcome," in *Beyond Document*, ed. Charles Warren, xvii.
6. Robert Gardner, "The Moral Nature of Film," in *Just Representations*, 244.
7. Cavell, "Words of Welcome," xxvii.

Part I
Overviews and General Topics

Chapter 1
Some Notes on Robert Gardner

Eliot Weinberger

From "The Camera People" (1990)

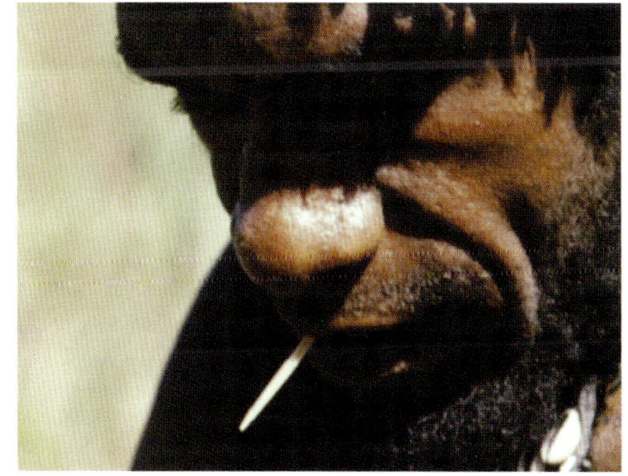

Alongside John Marshall's *The Hunters* (1957), the other celebrated ethnographic film of the era, Robert Gardner's *Dead Birds* (1963) employs many of Robert Flaherty's conventions to produce a kind of anti-*Nanook*: a film that, perhaps inadvertently, is far from ennobling. Shot among the Dani, a previously little-documented group in Western New Guinea, the film is a narrative—based, like Flaherty, on a series of archetypal anecdotes rather than the full-blown dramatic structure and developed characterizations of a "plot"—about a warrior, Weyak, and a small boy, Pua. (The boy-figure in *Moana* is named Pe'a.)

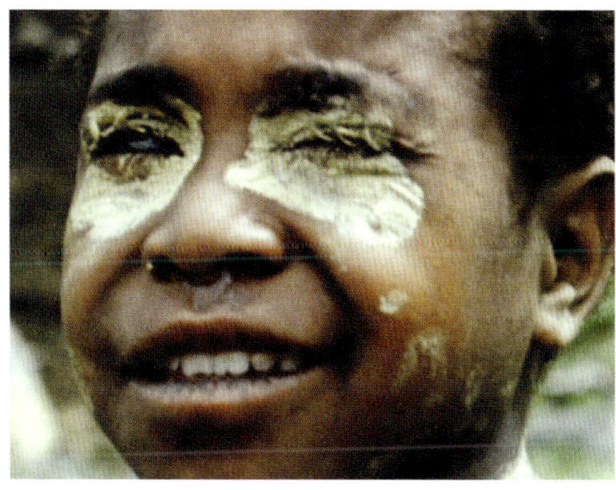

The characters do not speak; their actions (and, like *The Hunters*, thoughts) are conveyed to us by a continual narration, spoken by Gardner. Perhaps uniquely in ethnographic films, the narration is delivered in a nervous, unnaturally rapid speech: an edginess that considerably adds to the film's dramatic tensions.

Its unforgettable opening clearly announces some sort of allegory: a very long pan of a hawk flying over the treetops, and the spoken words: "There is a fable told by a mountain people living in the ancient highlands of New Guinea . . ." [It is a convention of the genre: the people are remote and as timeless as geography, but will be revealed to be, in some way, just like us. *Grass* (1925)—Merian Cooper and Ernest Schoedsack's stirring account of the annual migration by 50,000 Bakhtyari shepherds across the Zardeh Kuh mountains of Turkey and Persia—opens by promising us the "Forgotten People" who will unlock the "secrets of our own past." *Nanook of the North* (1922) opens by taking us to "mysterious barren lands" that, conversely, are "a little kingdom—nearly as large as England."] The fable is the story of the origin of human mortality: a race between a bird and a snake to determine whether people would die like birds or shed their skins and live forever like snakes. Needless to say, the bird won, and *Dead Birds*, in the Flaherty tradition of portraying man against the odds, was apparently intended as a portrayal of one culture's response to the universal destiny. Gardner writes: "I saw the Dani People, feathered and fluttering men and women, as enjoying the fate of all men and women. They dressed their lives with plumage, but faced as certain death as the rest of us drabber souls. The film attempts to say something about how we all, as humans, meet our animal fate."[1]

What the film actually shows is something quite different. With the exception of one quite powerful funeral scene, *Dead Birds* is not concerned with the effects of human destiny—rites, mourning, grief—but rather its provocation. The Dani were among the last people on earth to engage in a rigidly codified ritual war. (One that finally was ended by the local "authorities" shortly after the film was made.) The men of neighboring villages, separated only by their gardens and a strip of no man's land, would regularly adorn themselves and gather on a battlefield, fighting (theoretically) until there was one fatal casualty. Revenge for that death would provoke the next battle, and so on forever. An endless vendetta war in a land with plenty of food and no particular differences between the villages; where no territory or plunder was captured; with no mass killings and no deviation from the rules.

In fact—or at least according to the film—revenge was rarely achieved on the battlefield. In the battles themselves there is a great deal of back-and-forth feints and threats, but no hand-to-hand combat; wounds are mainly inflicted haphazardly in the shower of arrows. The two murders in the film, one for each side, occur when a group of men accidentally comes across someone from the other side: a small boy who wandered off, a man trying to steal a pig at night.

A continual, seemingly senseless war; battles where the two sides engage in menacing rhetoric but do relatively little harm; covert killings; a no man's land lined with tall watchtowers; daily life in a state of permanent dread. The allegorical import of *Dead Birds* must have been obvious to its viewers in 1963, when the Berlin Wall was still new. The film is hardly a meditation on death at all: if it were it would have presented Dani who had died from childbirth, sickness, accidents, age. Rather it is a feathered and fluttering reenactment of the Cold War that was being prolonged and endured by the drab souls of East and West.

The battle sequences in the film are extraordinary. Gardner was especially fortunate to have a mountainous terrain where he could get the aerial perspective to lay out what was, quite literally, the theater of war. A brief telephoto shot of the enemy wildly celebrating the death of the small boy becomes particularly unsettling following the moving, rapidly edited sequence of the child's funeral. (The narrator, as throughout the film, fortunately resists the temptation to editorialize.)

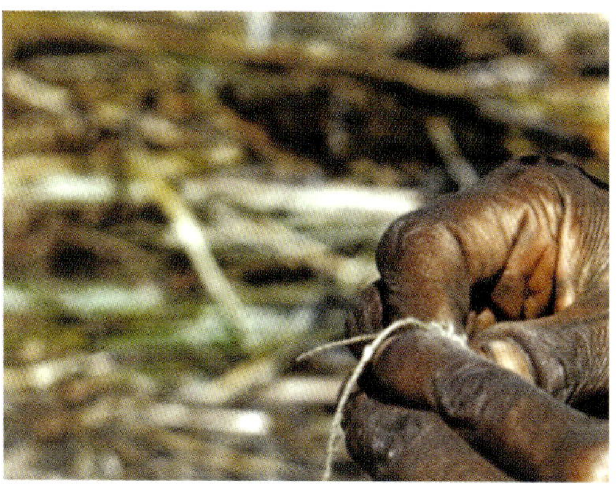

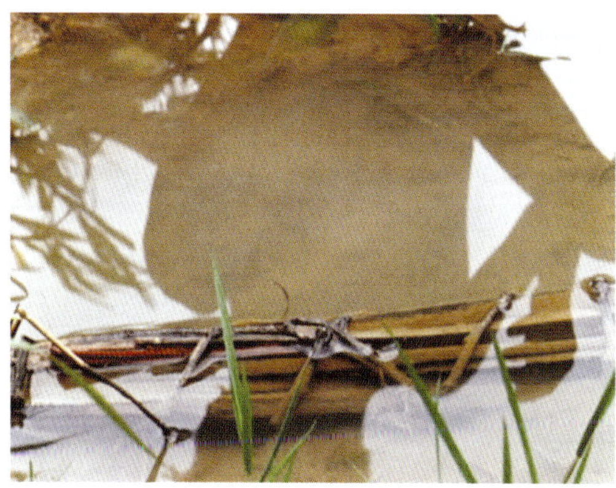

The film, in Flaherty style, occasionally concocts an artificial narrative structure: one set of battle scenes, for example, is intercut with shots of women gathering brine who are supposedly waiting for news of casualties, though there was obviously no second unit on the film. (The battles themselves are pastiches, though this is neither apparent nor explained.) And it is the Flaherty "hook"—the focus on the warrior and the boy—that seems misplaced in the film. We learn next to nothing about Weyak; and Pua, who is presented as a pathetic kid, is essentially irrelevant. Once again, women are far in the background. The cruel Dani practice of cutting off the fingers of young girls when there is a death in the village is mentioned only in passing twice. And Gardner, whose films are full of hands—(Frances Flaherty: "Simply in the beautiful movement of a hand the whole story of the race may be revealed"[2])—only gives us a split-second glimpse of the mutilated fingers of Weyak's wife.

After this, his first feature-length film, Gardner would abandon the Flaherty anecdotal narrative of the hunter/warrior, both epitome and paragon of his people, the boy who wishes to emulate him, and the Western bard who sings his praises. In *Dead Birds*, Weyak is introduced by a shot of his hands, Pua by his reflection in a puddle. In the later films, Gardner would devolve an ethnographic cinema based entirely on such telling details and oblique images, films that would pose little difficulty to general audiences accustomed to foreign imports, but which the "scientists"—those who considered film merely a form of surveillance and recording—would find incomprehensible.

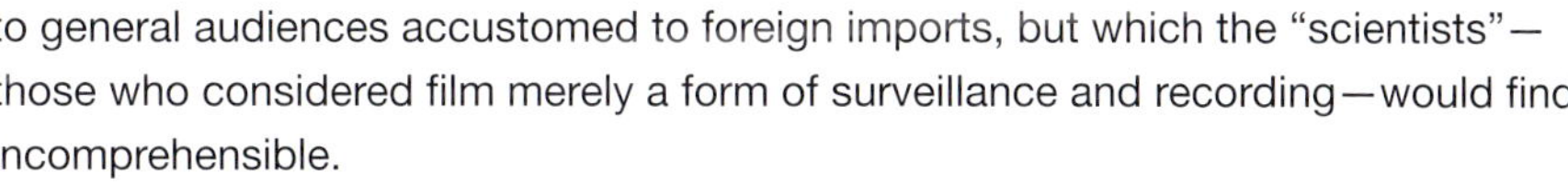

* * *

The recent literary dismantling of written anthropology (by Clifford Geertz, James Clifford, and others) has tried to demonstrate how the sober scientific professionals are no less prone to dubious generalization, manipulation of data, partial explanation, and prevailing ethnocentrism than the enthusiastic amateurs who write accounts of their travels. Similarly, the moment one erases the stylistic differences, the ethnographic differences between a research film and a made-for-television adventure travelogue are less than meets the eye.

The amateurs, in fact, often turn out to be ethnographically richer. Consider the case of an utterly "unscientific" film: *The Nuer* (1971) by Hilary Harris and George Breidenbach, with the assistance of Robert Gardner. Until Gardner's *Forest of Bliss* (1986) this was probably the film most loathed by the professionals. Karl Heider, in *Ethnographic Film*, once the standard textbook in the field, writes: "It is one of the most visually beautiful films ever made. . . . But the film is almost without ethnographic integrity. By this I mean that its principles are cinema aesthetic; its framing, cutting, and juxtaposition of images are done without regard for any ethnographic reality."[3] Throughout his book, Heider uses *The Nuer* as the classic example of how not to make an ethnographic film.

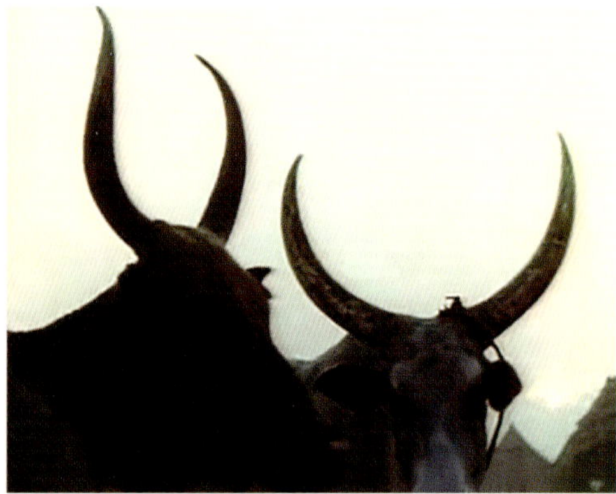

The film has no story, little narration, only one brief interview with an individual, no time frame and no events unfolded in their entirety. Most of it consists of rapidly edited shots of extraordinary beauty, accompanied by a soundtrack of local music and sounds and untranslated speech. There are galleries of close-ups—faces, tobacco pipes, jewelry, houses, corrals—and unforgettable sequences of these astonishingly elongated people merely walking through the dust and mist. Much of the film simply looks at the cows that are central to Nuer life: close-ups of cow legs and cow flanks and cow nostrils and cow horns.

Though this is one of the most "aesthetic" films in the genre, it is full of ethnographic information—far more, ironically, than many of the classics of "ethnographic reality." We see what the Nuer look like, what they make, what they eat, what their music sounds like, their leisure activities, body art, architecture, fishing and cattle-herding, local fauna, diseases, rites of exorcism, spiritual possession, and so on. Most of all, as a study of a community based on cattle, it is a startling revelation of the cow. Even an untrained urban eye finds itself immediately differentiating the cows as individuals—much as the Nuer know the personal history of each; a history that, through bride-prices and ritual exchange, is inextricably tangled with their own histories. Moreover, it becomes evident in the course of the film how an entire aesthetic could be derived from the close observation of cattle; how the shapes and textures of the herds are recapitulated in so much of what the Nuer make.

"The final goal, of which an Ethnographer should never lose sight," wrote Malinowski sixty years ago in a famous dictum, now outdated only in its gender specificity, "is, briefly, to grasp the native's point of view, his relation to life, to realize *his* vision of *his* world" (*his* emphasis).[4] Of course, the ideal is impossible—who can ever see with another's eyes, even within one's own culture? Yet *The Nuer*, rare among ethnographic films, lets us look closely at that which the Nuer look at, but which most of us do not—moreover seeing, as any of us see anything, not the "whole bodies" (insisted on by the scientists) but the telling details that set each one apart. It is one of the few instances where ethnographic film presents information that is beyond the capabilities of the written monograph. Not observed and analyzed data: it is a physical and intellectual act of seeing. Neither a recapitulation of a foreign vision nor the first-person expression of the filmmakers, it is, most exactly, an act of translation: a reading of their sensibility, recoded into our (film) language. *The Nuer*, like any film, is a metaphor for the Nuer. Its difference is that it does not pretend to be a mirror.

* * *

Surrealism introduced an aesthetic based on chance, improvisation, and the found object—an aesthetic that would seem tailored to the actual conditions of a Westerner making an ethnographic film. Yet the genre has had only one surrealist: ironically, the founder of cinema verité, Jean Rouch. (And there's a parallel to be drawn with another surrealist, the master of photojournalism, Henri Cartier-Bresson.) Robert Gardner, in *Deep Hearts* (1981) and *Forest of Bliss*, has adapted another aspect of surrealism to transform the idiosyncratic into the archetypal: he explodes time. By employing the simultaneous time of modern physics, he transforms the linear time of the unrepeatable into the cyclical time of the endlessly repeated. This has been one of the main projects of the century: through simultaneity—montage, collage, Ezra Pound's ideogrammic method—all ages become contemporaneous. It is both a criticism of Western linear time and a bridge to the mythic time that rules most traditional societies. But where the modernists sought to recapture both the formal aspects and the sheer power of so-called primitive art and oral epics, Gardner, uniquely, has employed the techniques of modernism to *represent* the tribal other. A cycle has been completed: with Gardner, James Joyce is our entry into Homer.

Deep Hearts is concerned with the annual *Gerewol* ceremony of the Bororo Fulani of Niger. The nomadic groups converge at one spot in the desert, where the young men elaborately make themselves up and, wearing women's dresses, dance for eight days in the sun as the marriageable young women look them over, until one man is selected as the most virtuous and beautiful. According to the few lines of narration in the film, the Bororo consider themselves to be "chosen people" (who doesn't?) but they are threatened by "neighbors, new ideas, disease and drought." Their combination of "excessive self-regard" and "a fear of losing what they have" makes them "easily prey to envy." So they must bury their hearts within them, for "if a heart is deep no one can see what it contains."

If this group psychological analysis is correct, then the Bororo must remain, particularly to an outsider, unreadable. Everything will remain on the surface, only, at best, inadvertently revealing what is beneath. Gardner's response to this impermeability is to turn it into a dream, a shimmering mirage. Time is scrambled and events keep repeating themselves: men dancing, people arriving, men dancing, preparations for the dance, and so on. Shots of the farewell ceremony, near the end of the film, are followed by a scene we've already seen, near the beginning, of a woman washing her enormous leg bracelets before the dance. Sounds recorded at the dance are played over scenes of preparation for it. There are strange sideways shots of milk being poured from huge bowls that recall the abstract geometries of Moholy-Nagy's films. There are freeze frames and, in one sequence, slow-motion and distortion of the sound. [Though documentary was born out of slow-motion—Eadward Muybridge's magic lantern studies of animal locomotion—it remains taboo for ethnographic film, being counter to prevailing notions of realism. Maya Deren's 1947–1951 study of voodoo in Haiti, *Divine Horsemen*, exploits both the hallucinatory quality of slow motion—which rhymes perfectly with the dance and trance possession she is filming—and its ability to let us see details we would otherwise miss in the frenetic action.]

Deep Hearts is a dream of the *Gerewol* ceremony, stolen from the sleep of an anthropologist; the woozy memory of events one has witnessed in eight days of desert sun. (Its nearest cousin is the flashbacks to Guinea-Bissau in Chris Marker's 1983 film *Sans Soleil*.) As science, it is probably as accurate a description as a more linear recreation. But, unlike science, it leaves its enigmas unsolved. Its last lines of narration are among the most abstract in the genre:

> The visitors leave as suddenly as they appeared, and, with the diminishing rains, they will resume their nomadic lives. They go knowing what they would hope to be, an ideal example having been

> selected from their midst. But this may only serve to remind them of the desires that cannot be met, and which, with the uncertainty of whether choices are really theirs, still lie at the bottom of their deep hearts.

This dream, then, becomes an expression of unfulfilled desire in an unstable society. It is interesting that we barely glimpse, and only from afar, the winner of the contest: this is a study of longing, not achievement. And, uniquely in ethnographic film—which seems to cover everything except what people really think about (other than money)—*Deep Hearts* is a study of erotic longing: the young women posed in tableaux of virginal meekness facing the men (we watch the dancers over the shoulder of one of them); the auto-eroticism of these dancing men dressed as women; the old women who, no longer in the courtship game, must ritually insult them; and the old men who, from the image of their past selves, select the most beautiful.

The film underscores what is obvious elsewhere: there are vast areas of human life to which scientific methodology is inapt; to which ethnographic description must give way to the ethnopoetic: a series of concrete and luminous images, arranged by intuition rather than prescription, and whose shifting configurations—like the points of and between the constellations—map out a piece of a world.

Simultaneous time, the babble of voices overlapping and interrupting each other, the rapid succession of images, the cacophony of programmed and random sounds: all modern art is urban art, and all film—being born with this century—is an image of the city. What then does one do with the subjects of ethnography who, with few exceptions, lead rural lives? The anthropological monograph is, as James Clifford has pointed out, this century's version of the pastoral, and its writing can and does draw on its literary antecedents. Film, however, with its short takes, shifting camera angles and multiple viewpoints is as intrinsically anti-pastoral as its filmmakers themselves. To take it (and oneself) into the countryside of the tribe, one may either deny its (and one's own) nature—as most ethnographic filmmakers have done—or somehow discover a way into one's subject.

With *Forest of Bliss*, Gardner has taken his modernist sensibility into an urban setting, however one that is uniquely archaic. The result is a panoramic "city" film in the tradition that begins with Paul Strand and Charles Sheeler's *Manhatta* (1921) and Walther Ruttmann's *Berlin: Symphony of the City* (1927), and whose latest incarnation is the first half of Wim Wenders's *Wings of Desire* (1987). And yet the nature of his subject, Benares, India, cannot help but insert the film into myth.

Benares is at least three thousand years old, and the oldest continually inhabited city on earth. Moreover, it always has had the same primary function, as the place where each day the countless dead are burned or dropped into the Ganges, and the living purified. To visit the sacred zones of the city, along the river, is like finding priests of Isis still practicing in Luxor. No other living city exists so purely in mythic time.

Similarly, the city itself is an iconographic representation of the passage from this world to the next: a labyrinth of bazaars, temples, and houses for the dying opens out onto steps that lead down to the river (at one section of steps the dead are burned); the wide river itself, cleansing all, and beyond, distantly visible, the other shore.

These are universally recognizable symbols, from which—with a host of others: the kite perched between heaven and earth, the scavenging dogs, the boats that carry the dead to the other side, the purifying fire, the flowers of veneration—Gardner has constructed a montage of the eternally repeatable. It is both a study of the mechanics of death (the organization of Benares' cremation industry) and a map of the Hindu cosmology of death—almost entirely presented through iconic images. It is surely the most tightly edited film in the genre, truly a fugue of reiterated elements, and one whose astonishing use of sound sustains the cyclical structure by carrying over the natural sounds of one scene into the next—Godard's technique adapted to a completely different purpose.

Most radically, Gardner has eliminated all verbal explanations. There is no narration, the dialogue is not subtitled, and there is only one intertitle, a single line from the Yeats translations of the Upanishads. *Forest of Bliss*, more than any other film, reinforces the outsider status of both the filmmaker and the viewer: we must look, listen, remain alert, accept confusion, draw our own tentative conclusions, find parallels from within our own experiences. Travelers confronting the exotic, we are also the living standing before the dead.

I have spent time in Benares on three separate occasions: it is curious that this, the most artistically crafted of all ethnographic films, has approached the utopian mimesis of the scientists: for me, at least, it is, as no other film I know, like being there—though there, of course, in a two-dimensional space with only two of the senses intact. This is because the film takes as its center an ultimate incomprehension: of the gods by man, of the dead by the living, of the blissful by the unenlightened, of the East by the West, of any culture by another. In Hinduism, one attempts to bridge the gap through the primary form of worship, *darshana*, the act of seeing—the eyes literally going out to touch the gods. Though I hesitate to call *Forest of Bliss* a religious experience, it, too, is dependent on a similar contemplation of iconic signs: it is an outsider's (refusing to be an insider's) seeing through Benares into the cycles of life and death.

Needless to say, the film has driven the scientists mad. The newsletter of the Society of Visual Anthropologists ran a series of polemics against it, filled with lines like "Technology has left pure imagery behind, and anthropologists ought to do so too." (The same writer commenting that, given the sanitary problems of disposing corpses in the river, an interview with a public health official would have been informative.)

These are the people who prefer a kinship chart to *Anna Karenina*, but their project is intrinsically doomed: the specificity of their brand of linear film will always subvert their attempts to generalize human behavior. It is only elaborated metaphor and complex aesthetic structures that are capable of even beginning to represent human nature and events: configurations of pure imagery will always leave technology behind.

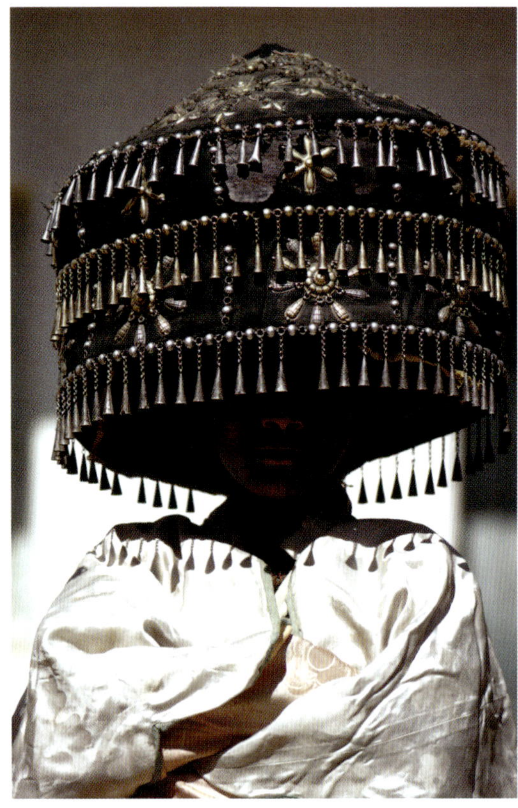

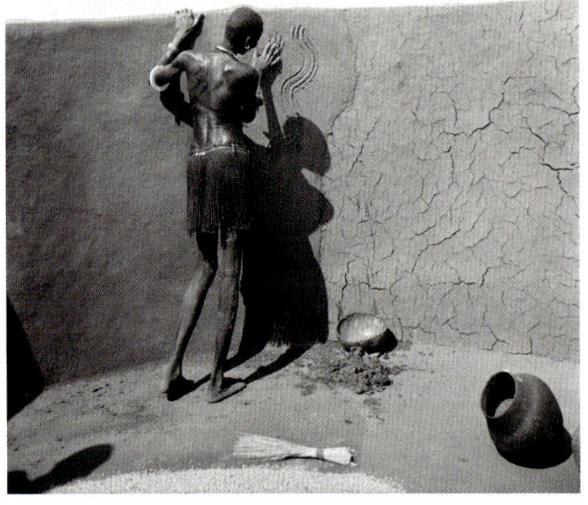

Preface to **Still Points** *(2013)*

Painters sculpt; sculptors draw; there are novels by poets and poems by novelists. Yet few photographers have made films and even fewer filmmakers are known for their photographs. To an outsider, it is a puzzle: celluloid is celluloid, and the distance from twenty-four frames of it a second to one isolated frame does not seem unbridgeable.

They are, of course, on opposite shores of motion and time. The still camera is a still center, the Confucian unwobbling pivot, an ephemeral axis around which the world turns—a world that is frozen for a fraction of a second, and then another, and then another. The film camera moves in and among the world; it is an unseen body moving among the seen bodies and the rooms and landscapes; it gives the illusion of participation. A still camera, at any given moment, cannot move. The film camera that remains motionless for more than a few moments—as is the practice of certain filmmakers, Robert Gardner among them—emphasizes a detached observation. Ozu does not pretend to be a member of the family whose story is unfolding, nor does Gardner assume he is anything but an observer of the ritually warring Dani or the dancing Bororo.

Cinema, by its nature, gives us fragments of real time. Photographs—although themselves a representation of a split-second—have tended toward two approaches to time. One is stasis: the portrait, the landscape, and (literally) the still-life. The other is the "decisive moment," essentially a scene from a narrative that the viewer supplies (or, more exactly, imagines). Its success is usually determined by the complexity of the narrative it captures or the complexity of the movement it freezes. Both kinds of photographs are the opposite of cinema. A film has no decisive moments: it presents a whole, however enigmatic, narrative scene, and its use of unmoving portraiture or still-life or landscape is always as a form of montage, the "establishing shot" where this piece of the story will take place or the succession of images that advance it.

Gardner's photographs are generally static in time; their movement is in their composition. It is possible to see them as isolated frames from a montage: the fantastic Coptic headdress; the Nuer woman drawing mud squiggles on a wall; the Bororo hands with a metaphorical empty wristwatch; the op-art stone steps in the ruins of Palenque; the "blind wisdom" of a veiled statue of Saraswati. But in this case, the montage is in a book, not a film, and the narrative is both the varieties of human experience and Gardner's extraordinary life in far-flung corners of the globe.

And yet, Gardner hints, in a koan-like statement, that these photographs may be something entirely different: "Film might be 24 frames of actuality per second but this does not account for what falls into the intervals. Maybe that is where a still wins out."[5] It sounds like Zeno's arrow: between every point in time there is another point in time, and in the infinitely smallest point, there is no motion. Time is erased: the still point.

Most of the subjects of Gardner's photographs are the subjects of his films; the photos, however beautiful they may be in isolation, cannot help but be seen in relation to the films—those masterpieces of ethnographic cinema and of cinema itself. But they are not merely addenda, or outtakes. If what Gardner says is true, they become the negative spaces of a sculpture, the silences of a poem, the holes in Taoist rocks. They are a moment between the moments in time; the moment when time is abolished.

And what could be more terrifying for a filmmaker than the abolition of time? Small wonder so few of them take photographs. Or that this would appeal to Robert Gardner, whose subjects inhabit—and whose films themselves express—another, cyclical and non-linear, order of time. There at the end of the endless cycles of time and the loops of film is stillness and these still photos.

Notes

1. Robert Gardner, "On the Making of *Dead Birds,*" in *The Dani of West Irian: An Ethnographic Companion to the Film* Dead Birds, ed. Karl G. Heider (Andover, MA: Warner, 1972), 34–35.
2. Mrs. Robert J. Flaherty, "The Camera's Eye" (1927), reprinted in *Spellbound in Darkness: A History of the Silent Film,* ed. George C. Pratt (Greenwich, CT: New York Graphic Society, 1973), 346.
3. Karl G. Heider, *Ethnographic Film* (Austin: University of Texas Press, 1976), 35.
4. Bronislaw Malinowski, *Argonauts of the Western Pacific* (New York: Dutton, 1961 [1922]), 25.
5. Gardner, letter to the author, October 11, 2012.

Chapter 2
In Flight with Robert Gardner

Tom Conley

Early on in *Pantagruel*, Rabelais's riotous fiction of 1534, the hero of the same title receives a letter from Gargantua, his father, who offers his dear son valuable counsel about future studies. After describing the virtue of learning many languages, of becoming versed in history and theology, in cosmography, and in the seven liberal arts, he tells his young son to go into the world. He ought to witness it as best he can, and above all to examine everything about him in keen detail:

> Et quand à la cognoissance des faictz de nature, je veux que tu te y adonne curieusement, qu'il n'y ayt mer, riviere, ny fontaine, dont tu ne congnoisse les poissons, tous les oyseaulx de l'air, tous les arbres, arbustes et fructices des foretz, toutes les herbes de la terre, tous les metaulx cachez au ventre des abysmes, les pierreries de tout Orient et midy, rien ne te soit incogneu.[1]
>
> [And as for the knowledge of the facts of nature, I want you to devote yourself to them curiously, so that there be no sea, river, or fountain whose fish you fail to know, all the birds of the air, all the trees, shrubs and fruit of the forest, all the grasses of the earth, all the metals hidden in the belly of abysses, precious stones of the entire Orient and southern realm, that nothing be unknown to you.]

When he was of Pantagruel's age Robert Gardner must have heard the same words. The writer and filmmaker celebrated in this volume would count among those wondrous companions Rabelais included among his *pantagruélistes*, generous souls so eager to learn all and everything about their surroundings that what they find falls into an *abyme de science*, an abyss of knowledge into which they plunge with joy. Readers of *Just Representations* and viewers of the documentary films sense that Gardner was not just a founder of visual and documentary anthropology but, in a deeper perspective, a person born of the early Renaissance, born of a moment when unrestricted travel gave rise to new relations with people, things, and places until then unknown. A living reincarnation of this individual, Gardner, like the great traveling scribes of the Renaissance, inspires us to think of what it might have been, whether in 1534 or in the early years of our century, to behold worlds of uncommon biological and cultural complexity. In the paragraphs that follow the wager is that Gardner filmed and wrote of what he encountered with a freshness and vigor akin to those of his earlier avatars. Like themselves, eager to capture the world in all of its infinite variety, Gardner begins as lofty cosmographer ("a describer of the whole world") but soon after becomes telluric topographer ("a describer of places") who relates to the locales he studies without needing to fix them into an overriding mental scheme. In seeing and reading Gardner's work, we regain a sense of the traveler's boundless curiosity, of voyagers who visualize what they reported to have encountered and whose effects draw them deeper and deeper into an abyss of knowledge.

Travelers all, the writers who took account of things other and unfathomed kept meticulous registers of their displacements. In the French tradition there stands Rabelais's *Quart livre* (1551), the aging author's narration of travel to real and imaginary islands of an endless archipelago where he records behavior of strangely familiar but oddly shaped people for whom satire is the distorting lens the author uses to account for contemporary aberration and destruction. *L'Histoire d'un voyage faict en terre de Brésil*, Jean de Léry's magnificent relation of his trip to Guanabara (today the Bay of Rio de Janeiro) with a Protestant expedition under Nicolas Durand de Villegagnon, remains what Claude Lévi-Strauss has called every modern "ethnologist's breviary," an account that looks closely and empathetically at social mores of savages and cannibals. The incipit, in fact, is close in tone and tenor to the entries Gardner inks into his logbooks:

> Chap. I.
>
> *Of the Motive and Occasion that Made Us Undertake this Distant Voyage to the Land of Brazil*
>
> A number of cosmographers and other historians of our time have already written about the length, width, beauty and fertility of that fourth part of the world called "America"—or the land of Brazil, together with the islands near it and the lands adjacent to it (lands completely unknown to the Ancients)—as well as of the various navigations in the eighty years since it was first discovered; therefore I will not pause to summarize those matters at length or in a general fashion. My intention and my subject in this history will simply be to declare what I myself have experienced, seen, heard and observed, both on the sea, coming and going, and among the American savages, with whom I visited and lived for about a year.[2]

Like Rabelais's, the vigor of Léry's account and mode of observation resonates in two of Michel de Montaigne's greatest ethnological documents, "Of Cannibals" (chapter 31 of the first volume of the *Essays* of 1580) and the "Travel Journal of a Voyage to Italy" (published posthumously). In the former, received accounts of voyages are called in question in order to launch an attack on custom and inherited belief (along with Spanish depredations of the New World) while the latter, dictated or written en route, attests to meticulous observation of the cultures he discovers while journeying from Paris to Rome via southern Germany and Switzerland in the years 1580 and 1581. In "Cannibals," as if he were rehearsing the first sentence of Léry's relation and anticipating Gardner's writings, Montaigne sums up the anthropologist's charge when he writes that in contrast to "cosmographers" who put forward erroneous views of the world in their copious compilations and descriptions, "il nous faudroit des topographes qui nous fissent narration particuliere des endroits où ils ont esté" [we ought to have topographers offering us detailed account of the places where they have been].[3]

Gardner's reflections are close to what Rabelais, Léry, and Montaigne make of the need to *experience* the ambient world—to touch and feel it with a haptic sense—and to relate it to us with words and moving images that make clear the audible, visual, and even gustatory character of that experience. All of them make the experience palpable when, one way or another, they move from a whole to part or from *cosmos* to *topos*, from a global, albeit imaginary sense of the condition of the world to what it reveals to the five senses. For the writers of the Renaissance the distinction was drawn from the first sentences of Ptolemy's *Geographia* (circa 145 CE). For the Alexandrian scientist cosmography (what he calls geography) "is a representation in picture of the whole known world together with the phenomena which are contained within. It differs from Chorography [or topography] in that Chorography, selecting certain places from the whole, treats more fully the particulars of each by themselves—even dealing with the smallest conceivable localities, such as harbors, farms, villages, river sources, and such."[4] He soon infers that those who inquire of the nature of the world are artists, since "[t]he end of Chorography is to deal separately with a part of the whole, as if one were to paint only the eye or the ear by itself," while the "task of Geography is to survey the whole in its just proportions, as one would the entire head. For as in an entire painting we must first put in the larger features, and afterward those detailed features which portraits and pictures may require, giving them proportion in relation to one another so that their correct measure apart can be seen by examining them, to note whether they form the whole or a part of the picture" (25–26). On the heels of the Columbian discoveries sixteenth-century authors of manuals of cosmography revised the *Geographia*. They provided immediate, visually arresting, and what are now surreal memory-images of the distinction. A Parisian edition of Pieter Apian's *Cosmographia* juxtaposed a world map in one circle to a portrait of a Christ-like sitter in profile in another to show how the cosmographer deals with "the entire head." Below the pair, to extend the conceit to include the topographer, he placed a city view in one circle contiguous to a drawing of an isolated eye and ear that are irrevocably detached from whatever body to which they would belong, the result being an *autopsy* of the known world.[5]

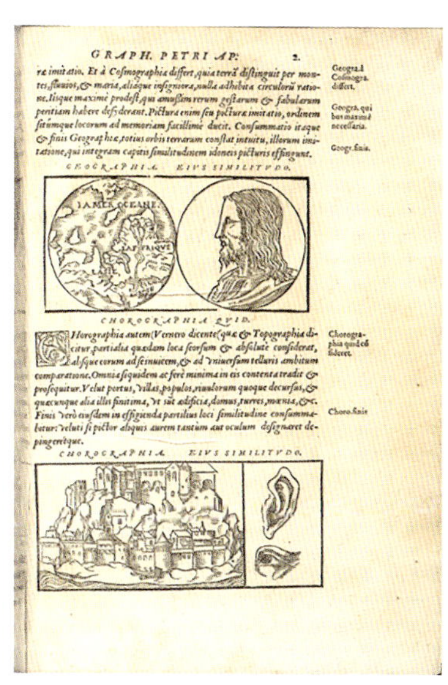

GRAPH. PETRI AP: 2.

re imitatio. Et à Cosmographia differt, quia terrã distinguit per montes, fluuios, & maria, aliaque insigniora, nulla adhibita circulorũ ratione. Iisque maximè prodest, qui amussim rerum gestarum & fabularum peritiam habere desyderant. Pictura enim seu picturæ imitatio, ordinem sitũmque locorum ad memoriam facillimè ducit. Consummatio itaque & finis Geographiæ, totius orbis terrarum constat intuitu, illorum imitatione, qui integram capitis similitudinem idoneis picturis effingunt.

Geogra. à Cosmogra. differt.

Geogra. quibus maximè necessaria.

Geogr. finis.

GEOGRAPHIA. EIVS SIMILITVDO.

CHOROGRAPHIA QVID.

Chorographia autem (Vernero dicente) quæ & Topographia dicitur, partialia quædam loca seorsum & absolutè considerat, absque eorum ad se inuicem, & ad vniuersum telluris ambitum comparatione. Omnia siquidem ac ferè minima in eis contenta tradit & prosequitur. Velut portus, villas, populos, riuulorum quoque decursus, & quæcunque alia illis finitima, vt sũt ædificia, domus, turres, mœnia, &c. Finis verò eiusdem in effigienda partilius loci similitudine consummabitur: veluti si pictor aliquis aurem tantùm aut oculum designaret depingeretque.

Chorographia quid cõsideret.

Choro. finis.

CHOROGRAPHIA. EIVS SIMILITVDO.

These writers and the tradition that informs their experience are invoked in view of a recurring topos in both *Just Representations* and some of Gardner's films. In sweeping panoramics that move to and from cosmographical to topographical perspectives Gardner brings his reader and viewer into keenly detailed accounts of fabled or unknown cultures and places. Although scripted in passing, his accounts of flight, of flying and aviation, the mode of transport that carries anthropologists to the countries where they engage their fieldwork, are decisive. And so, too, in films from *Blunden Harbour* (1951) and *The Nuer* (1971) to *Ika Hands* (1988), are cutaway shots of birds circling high above the peoples their eyes seem to be studying from afar, which indicate that what the camera witnesses in detail is not without a cosmographical counterpart when imagined from afar.[6] First looking at the world from above and before touching down, Gardner inherits a commonplace in physical and existential geography that he complicates from his first to his most recent writings. The "Kalahari Journal" (1958) begins with an uncommonly literary turn of phrase: "The aircraft is lovely, deadly, bearing me aloft with cold flexibility. I am quieted by barbiturates and lulled by the whir of miraculous propellers spinning in the darkening night."[7] Hardly coddled by the drone of the engines of a C-47, he is unmoved by what, given his view from the bubble of a cockpit of the earth below or the stars above, we anticipate to be a Pascalian meditation, à la Saint-Exupéry's little prince perhaps, on the two infinites. The subject, rather, is anesthesia and dyspepsia that come with the fear of flight. "I am all curiosity despite my compromised gut, the result of spoiled mayonnaise last night in Lisbon" (5). Through the filter of indigestion and the smell of acrid olive oil he only later gives us to visualize what we expected, "the earth's face as it changes complexion, from tropical green to lime to the brick red of what I take to be Morocco" (5). The landscape happens to be that which carries the name of Atlas, Mercator's titular emblem of the god who bears the world and its parts on his shoulders, that he sketches with figures related to drawing. "Its expression changes according to the contouring of charcoal-colored *wadis*, and the spidering of shallow runoffs and other soot-colored lineaments. It has a dry and wrinkled look. In the distance I take there to be the Atlas Mountains, habitat of orchardists and horsemen. Berbers and Tuareg on the further side. Black basins dot the nearer landscape and seem to be arranged regularly across the plain below like holes in a giant game of Chinese checkers or the craters of old boils on a previously agitated earth" (5–6).

Much like the younger Lévi-Strauss who, upon his initial voyage to Brazil in 1935 searched for natives but only encountered an isolated French elite, Gardner lands in Accra and is scurried off to meet, among others, a prepossessing British archaeologist from Oxford. The alterity of Africa is deferred before being found in a hotel in Johannesburg. Having taken flight again after repair of an engine in Leopoldville, realizing that cultures are far more proximate than they had been in the age of sea and rail travel, he manages to coordinate impressions of things far and near. On the way to South Africa, he beholds the "Transvaal, the treasure land plateau, [that] soon appears beneath us, and it is here that men have turned the most earth. Mountains of dirt are piled everywhere in this landscape, looking like great ziggurats, especially in the environs of Johannesburg. Whole minicontinents of spurned earth in which nothing will ever grow except the hate of the tormented ones who built them" (8). Irony prevails where the metaphor of the *ziggurat*, the great Babylonian pyramid of time immemorial, composed of eight staggered stages, describes the detritus of heaped waste shaped by forced labor under the yoke of Dutch colonizers. The mystical metaphor that would have been the fruit of aerial fantasy, what would convey in a figure of speech the inexpressible beauty of the relation of cosmos and earth, takes a material and political turn.[8] It is next to this view from above that he follows with one from below, when he notes, with equally searing irony, that after receiving a tip, when they "cup their hands around their tip and do a little bow or curtsey," bellboys are using the gesture to count the money while obsequiously thanking their donors. The rest of the journal reveals how the ubiquitous misery he sees among the Bushmen attests to the double bind with which the anthropologist is destined to live. As avatars of the colonizer, he notes that "[w]e are at the heart of their problem, even as we suppose we can alleviate their misery" (11). He sees destitution and beauty all about the desert whose view, he infers, if for an instant it can be detached from the effects of uneven economic development, wondrously melds sky and sand.

Air travel resumes in the Asmat journal (March 10–19, 1961) where, Gardner remarks, after marveling from high above about how stunningly the steep foothills in the central range descend precipitously to "vast rivers, plains of mud, and sago palm forests," upon landing at the Merauke airfield of New Guinea, he beholds how the landscape bears the effects of a civilian version of an aerial invasion. A blitz of Indonesian immigrants has scarred the land beyond recognition. Urban areas are repositories of human trash. Respite comes with travel by canoe into the hinterland, yet now the sight and touch of mud and earth, now of another sort, leads Gardner to conclusions similar to the observations he sketched in Africa in 1958. He notes that the Asmat "are caught in a cultural web that both supports and confines them. Stepping out of the web results in a life of helplessness and anomie" (43). In a flash he brings the reflection close to home when, suddenly, he compares the color and texture of the physiognomies of the inhabitants to the once-proud faces of Native Americans. The final image of the New Guinean landscape—the topographies both of the countryside and the faces of their inhabitants—now melds what he had seen from afar with his closer acquaintance of the contradictions. Seen first in the wrinkles of the natives' skin exposed to intense sun and rain, it is evident everywhere that the population is under the yoke of colonization and conflict. "For a long time it will be just green with foliage and red with blood" (44).

The journal of January 8 to December 6, 1995, in which commercial carriers ferry Gardner from Cambridge to Morocco and from London to Beijing and Urumchi (in the vast Xinjiang province of China), avers a spirited critique of contemporary narrative cinema. Gardner takes a hard look at feature films crafted to appeal to an international public of uninformed anthropological and historical pretension. Earlier in his notes Gardner had speculated on the relations—if relations there can be—between documentary and narrative film. The inspiration behind the unfinished projects of *Cooper's Creek* and *Isle of Dogs*, two ethnological films in narrative mantle, was to mix one tradition into the field of the other. In the preface to the chapter he recalls that if they were to be successful the films would braid a story line of adventure and of spatial displacement with close description of milieus and *terroirs* so present that they would become a matrix, and perhaps (it can be speculated) even obtain the force of a strong "conceptual personage."[9] Recounting the tribulations met in his efforts to produce an adaptation of J.M. Coetzee's *Waiting for the Barbarians*, the pages of the journal betray searing remarks about what global commercialism does both to cinema and, as Gardner had shown time and again in its integrity in the earlier entries, an enduring *art of travel*.[10] Offhanded impressions of commercial aviation go apace with frustration and annoyance about the way feature films are negotiated, budgeted, and crafted for what, varying on the mold of the Marxian formula (of x + [or hyphen: -] value), he calls their "production [-] value": not use-value, not exchange-value, but a value implied of a lesser valence. Recorded in the early heydays of deregulation, the sensory impressions in the transitional paragraphs accounting for where and how he was traveling mesh with what he finds to be the insipid character of cinema of the moment.

The aims of the voyages are simple: to meet and collaborate with a producer, to confer about casting, to seek viable actors and actresses to fill the principal roles and, above all, to find a suitable *location* for a narrative best situated at the edges of civilizations in conflict, rich in geographical traditions, living in fear of one another, far from our everyday lives. Locations are hard to find. Most of the world, like what he experiences in air travel, exudes *ennui*. On February 10 Gardner flies to London from Boston on Virgin Air in mid-class where, contrary to earlier travel in propeller-driven carriers, he is dopey under the impact of jetlag (111). A flight in a Cessna over the mountains of Morocco at 12,000 feet offers pleasure but little of the detail—from his perspective faintly viable but hardly ideal—that he soon finds when driving over rough terrain south of the Atlas (112). Return to Cambridge (March 1–March 15) affords time to reflect on cinemas where "optical experience" is a virtue and where echo of a dialogue with set designer John Boxer, in which the latter wanted his film built on "character, character, character," gnaws at the director, who is driven, it could be said, by "location, location, location." On June 6 he returns to Boston from London on an American Airlines morning flight so packed that he cannot focus on the screen on his PowerBook (117). When producer Michael Fitzgerald informs him that, for reasons of self-involvement, actor Tommy Lee Jones, for whom much of the project was destined, has backed out, he questions his own fitness for the endless negotiation and mediation and so wonders who and what a director may be for films aimed at drawing profit from an international public.

Given that Morocco is out of the picture for *Waiting for the Barbarians*, he flies to China on Lufthansa from Boston via Frankfurt. By some miracle not full, the flight allows him to stretch out and "get some fitful sleep" (122) before taking refuge in the "non-place" of a day room at the Frankfurt airport to repose during a six-hour layover.[11] He flies off to Beijing and its "small and remarkably dilapidated airport" outside of the city. He beholds the Forbidden City through memories of Bertolucci's trivialization of the same place in *The Last Emperor* (1987). Now the deferred voyage to Urumchi becomes an adventure. A tasteless breakfast (Gardner's culinary memories are pellucid) precedes travel via Xinjiang Airlines to Urumchi in "an enormous Soviet jet of unknown vintage (. . .), more a boat than an aircraft," whose entry reminds of him of "stairwells in large ocean liners" (125). On arrival he is brought to a polluted city where a Holiday Inn offers faint solace from the stench of cigarette and coal smoke. Once he drives out of the city along the edges of the Silk Road, in Tuyu he finds earthen architecture reminding him, again, of impressions from the New World of the cliff dwellers of New Mexico. The mixed blessing of dirty shirts, "an undistinguished Uighur meal," and the mess of a five-star hotel bring him closer to the "cultural bone" from which he had been insulated in Urumchi. Among other panoramas, the garbage littering the streets of the casbah in Kashgar and the "dismal ruins" about it

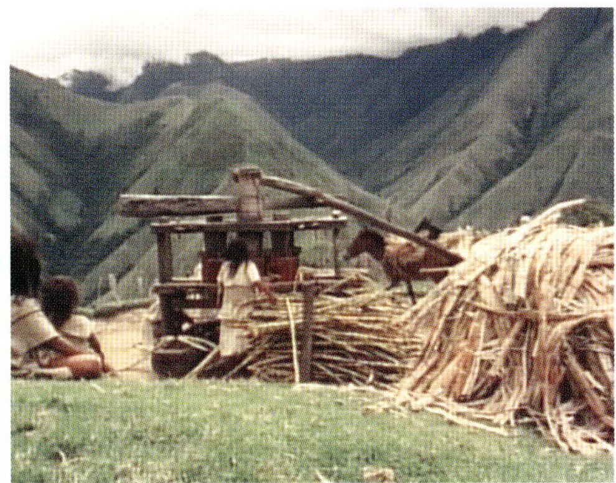

inspire him to consider abandoning the idea of having the script of the film serve as a faithful representation of Coetzee's novel. The uncommon cultural space causes him to question the pretensions of the genre in which he and his producer have been embroiled. The "authenticity of the landscape and the interest contained in its human occupation" (135) far outweigh anything that could be called cinematic fidelity to narrative. It appears as if two strands of experience—one of air travel in the commercial age and the other that of the boredom with cinema that would have story supersede the space that gives rise to it—break Gardner away from fiction film once and for all, even if a postface at the end of the pages dedicated to *Waiting for the Barbarians* would contain the promise of the conclusion to *Waiting for Godot.*

To which the compelling "Chile Journal" (February–March 1999) attests: we discover that along the spine of the Andes Gardner revives a friendship with aviator Robert Fulton, a friend who seems to be an avatar of Cary Grant in *Only Angels Have Wings* (1939). The meeting releases the passion he had known as a child for flying and filming. Viewers know that everywhere the cinema bears the traces of such passion, as it does saliently in many shots of *Ika Hands*—deep focus shots that set the human labors of everyday life in the foreground and the folds of the slopes of deep valleys in the back.

For that film Fulton and Gardner had not only flown to a base where they climbed the steep hills of Colombia, they also retained an aerial perspective within the frame of the people and the lofty locale where the culture lives within and below the clouds, especially in taking a shaman over the mountains and down to the seaside far below and away from his settlement. In Chile, however, the pair set out to film the lands extending from La Serena (north of Santiago) to the Tierra del Fuego. Time is accorded only enough for thumbnail chorography when they are on the ground. Upon departure Gardner flies in commercial aircraft from New York to Lima and then from Lima to Iquique (close to 20° southern latitude) where a stopover allows him to take a breath before flying to La Serena (circa 30° south), then Puerto Montt (42° south), then Golfo Corcovado (42.5° south), Chaiten, the Rio Polena, Lago Yulten, and Puerto Asien before landing at Punto Arenas (55° south), a bustling city set adjacent to the Tierra del Fuego. They fly over Lake Cochrane, Rio Baker, Punta Asien once again, then Puerto Natales before turning north to Torres del Paine where they see the slopes of the Sarmiento and soon after they cross the *Estrecco de Magallanes* "in search of new wildernesses" (160).

In flight the enumeration of names and description of the surface of the earth betray a love of displacement and deferred encounter. Gardner sails over vastly complex geological formations on which toponyms are glued as if to authenticate the more recent and generally romanticized histories of their discovery.[12] The long trip reveals ecstasy felt in negotiating the elements—winds, clouds, scud, frigid cold—and desolation when he and his companion find what international commerce has wrought in faraway places whose toponyms inspire imagination of the first voyages travelers had taken to lands never seen or experienced before. At the Antipodes, when they crisscross traces left by the great travelers of the sixteenth century, Fulton and Gardner find grace and solace in the Icarian perspective from the cockpit. Their illusions, predictably, are shattered when they are aground. In the midst of the Atacama Desert, a vast area that needs every drop of runoff from the Cordillera to nourish subsisting flora and fauna, the growing city of Iquique is now a "tourist resort" (141) drawing all available water to nourish pullulating hotels and golf courses. When he arrives at Torres de Paine he finds a National Park whose dioramic beauty attracts tourists who are bused through its spaces and appeals to anglers who can simulate the hunting and gathering of their forebears (150). At the Fiordo de las Montanas commercial fishermen devastate dolphins to attract king crabs whose sale, like what prevails in the North American fishing industry, yields short-term profit at risk of nefarious long-term ecological effects.

Oscillating between delight and deception, the journal negotiates two photographic projects. One, the cause for the flight, had been the commission the BBC had tendered to obtain for a British public views of a land whose breathtaking images, it can be inferred, were ordered to impose a double bind on its public, to recall and no sooner paper over lingering memories of the disaster that went with the retaking of the Falkland Islands thirteen years before. Second, closer to Gardner's vision, was the motivation to make a film about the filming itself, in which the protracted time of attending to the flight, a subject of ostensibly limited visual interest, was required to portray the mental labors the two fliers had to commit to the project—in other words, attentive and active thought that could only occasionally, if occasion allowed, mesh with the visual pleasure of the Icarian view. "It could be a film about nothing much happening, in a Warhol sort of way. I could put the camera on the ledge above the instruments and just let it run" (140).[13] While aviating Gardner reflects in ways that hark back to the first impressions he had in flight over Morocco in 1958. Paradoxically the *limitation* of being aloft is stasis rather than ecstasy, and thus the flyer, physically confined to the cockpit, is mentally limited, because he becomes a neo-Cartesian automaton who must remain in sync with the conveying agent, the craft or "metaphor" that holds him in suspension. As he puts it, "[l]ooking down on the world gives you no idea of what that world is really like. In many ways, it is an escape from such realities, and not setting foot in the country except to take taxis to and from hotels between landings and takeoffs may have the effect of never having been there" (142). And there Gardner's extraordinary sense of the *tactility* of the experience of a relation with the unknown or unforeseen is avowedly vitiated. In accord with what he sees he needs tact or touch that only his hands and feet can sense when they are on the ground.

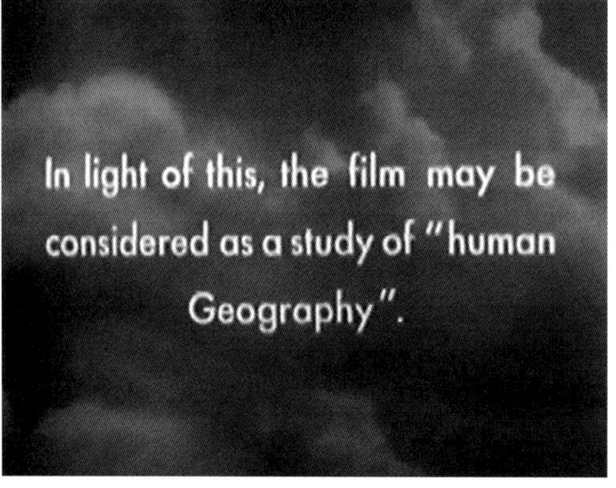

Sparse as they are, the reflections on flight that punctuate the journals belong to a rich and even fabled tradition in aviation, a key player in the resurgence of human geography. "La géographie humaine," a formula that visual anthropologists immediately recall from the credit sequence of Luis Buñuel's *Tierra sin pan* (1932), in which the words are set against a background of clouds that the viewer infers has been taken from an airplane, refers in part to Maurice Legendre's *Las Hurdes: Une étude de géographie humaine*, a study from which the director drew information vital for his groundbreaking film depicting what theorists call an originary world.[14]

The viewer notes that nowhere does the camera tilt down from an aircraft to look at the land from above, and that in the greater part of the film, at once to admire and to fetishize its subjects and the milieu, the lens closes in on the inhabitants' bare feet and hands that touch the land.[15] Contrary to the human geographer who uses aerial photography to bring a cosmic perspective to the position that "man" occupies with respect to the greater world, Buñuel remains telluric, anchored in the earth: and so does Gardner where he draws a line of divide between the aerial view, which he finds unreliable, and that of the camera that would be the appendage of a human attending to everyday life in the milieu he or she inhabits. Liable to conveying a false sense of anthropomorphic landscape, the aerial shot becomes disingenuous.[16]

Seen in the context of the establishing shots of his films, the division between Gardner's reflections on seeing the world from the air and his accounts of travel and encounter suggest that he is suspicious of the power that can be marshaled when, like the cosmographer of times past, the aerial photographer would use cinema to locate his or her subjects and thus to assign them to places that are not those in which they live. Furthermore, the mix of attraction and fear evinced in the writings suggests that his uneasiness and disquiet have much to do with the fortunes of the planet in the age in which flexible capitalism has everywhere imposed its model. The sense of adventure first felt in his flight to Morocco, or later regained now and again with his companion over Chile, gives way to awareness of a globe going to hell. In the cramped space of industrial carriers he anticipates calamity about which nothing can or is being done or, given the state of the human species in the matrix of the global economy, no individual or group is brave or strong enough to do anything. Better that we touch down, bare our feet and hands, and feel the matter of the earth much as we imagine the early explorers having done almost five centuries ago. From there perhaps, when we follow Gardner in flight, we have with us a conceptual personage who inspires us nonetheless to believe in the world.

Notes

1. François Rabelais, *Pantagruel*, in *Rabelais: Oeuvres complètes*, ed. Mireille Huchon (Paris: Gallimard/Pléiade, 1994), 244–245. Unless otherwise indicated I am responsible for all translations from the French in material that follows.
2. Jean de Léry, *History of a Voyage to the Land of Brazil, Otherwise Called America*, trans. Janet Whatley (Berkeley: University of California Press, 1990), 3. See the facsimile copy and critical edition of the second (1580) *Histoire d'un voyage faict en la terre du Bresil, autrement dite Amerique*, edition by Paul Morisot (Geneva: Librairie Droz, Coll. "Les Classiques de la pensée politique,"1975) and Frank Lestringant's carefully annotated edition of the text of the same year, which includes a lengthy interview with Claude Lévi-Strauss (Paris: Le Livre de Poche Classique, 1994). A baseline study of the work, bearing on cinema, that can be read in the context of Gardner's mode of ethnology, is Michel de Certeau, "Ethno-Graphy: Orality of the Other," chapter 5 of *The Writing of History*, translated by Tom Conley (New York: Columbia University Press, 1992).
3. Michel de Montaigne, "Des cannibales," in *Oeuvres complètes*, ed. Albert Thibaudet and Maurice Rat (Paris: Gallimard/Pléiade, 1962), 132.
4. Claudius Ptolemy, *The Geography*, trans. Edward Luther Stevenson, with an introduction by Joseph Fischer, S.J. (New York: Dover, 1932/paperback edition 1991), 25. Further page reference appears in the text.
5. Pieter Apian, *Cosmographia* (Paris: Vivant Gaultherot, 1551), f. 3 r. photograph courtesy of Houghton Library, Harvard.

6. Notes Yi-fu Tuan, in *Cosmos & Hearth: A Cosmopolite's Viewpoint*, "the life-path of a human being moves from 'home' to 'world,' from 'hearth' to cosmos.' We grow into a larger world. Not to do so is to lead a stunted life. (. . .) The judgment against patriarchal societies is that in them women are made to stay at the hearth. The judgment against hierarchical societies is that their members of the lower class are confined to a domestic work sphere (home, village, neighborhood) while the elite move on to enjoy the world. The elite can have both world *and* home. They can be cosmopolitan and yet return to the hearth for nurturance and renewal. They are privileged. Enlightened societies seek to extend the privilege to more and more people who formerly suffered constraint. . ." (Minneapolis: University of Minnesota Press, 1996), 2. In this picture, in his itineraries to and from Harvard and the world at large Gardner would be an enlightened cosmopolite who uses cinema to democratize access to the world at large. The point is often made where he shows how women, often relegated to perform domestic chores, are emblems of the hearth and men, the hunters and herders, move toward the edges of the social compact. He notes time and again the feeble force of attraction between men and women.

7. *Just Representations*, ed. Charles Warren and with an essay by Caleb Gardner (Cambridge: Studio7Arts and Peabody Museum Press, 2010), 5. All references to this work will be made in the body of the text above.

8. In the tradition in which Gardner writes, the metaphor approaches *l'indicible*, what cannot be stated in language. Noting Léry's figures, Michel de Certeau cites Michel le Guern: "metaphor effectively makes possible designation 'of realities that cannot have a term of their own,' thus to break the boundaries of language, to utter the unspeakable" *Sémantique de la métaphore* (Paris: Larousse, 1973), 72, cited in *The Writing of History*, 243, no. 70.

9. For Gilles Deleuze, in *Qu'est-ce que la philosophie?* (Paris: Éditions de Minuit, 1991) a "conceptual personage" can be a welcome stranger to ourselves within ourselves, a force of interrogation that causes us to change our positions in the milieus in which we happen to be. The conceptual personage is not just an impulsion, say, like that which leads Pascal's bettor to wager that God exists, but a force "with possibilities in movements and intensities that will bring to life even still new modes of existence, closer to animals and to rocks" (72). It is a force that causes us to recognize how the "believing in this world, in this life, might be our most difficult task" (ibid.). Earlier on Deleuze had remarked that the conceptual personage could be an animal because its activity consists in "forming *territories*, in leaving them, or in getting out of them, and even in refashioning territory upon something of another nature (the ethnologist says that the partner or friend of an animal is 'worth being-at-home,' or that the family is a 'mobile territory'). Even more the hominoid: from the moment he is born he deterritorializes his rear paw, he tears it off the ground in order to turn it into a hand, and reterritorializes it on branches and tools" (66). In the cinema Gardner's landscapes become what are constantly reterritorializing their viewers.

10. Such is the title that Morton Dauwen Zabel set above a collection of occasional pieces Henry James had sketched and published between 1870 and 1905. Time and again James takes uncanny pleasure in the effects of displacement. The incipit to "Occasional Paris" is exceptionally close to what Gardner is getting at in his impressions of global travel: "It is hard to say exactly what is the profit of comparing one race with another, and weighing in opposed groups the manners and customs of neighboring countries; but it is certain that as we move about the world we constantly indulge in this exercise. This is especially the case if we happen to be infected with the baleful spirit of the cosmopolite—that uncomfortable consequence of seeing many lands and feeling at home in none. (. . .) There comes a time when one set of customs, wherever it may be found, grows to seem to you about as provincial as another." James, *The Art of Travel*, ed. Zabel (New York: Doubleday/Anchor Books, 1962), 187.

11. Ethnologist Marc Augé qualifies the "nonplace" to be a zone of transit in international airports where experience is tepidly vanilla: redolent with the smell of plastic, illuminated under fluorescent lighting, and of aromas, be they in Munich or Manila, of the same coffee and the same fare cooked on grills and warmed over in microwaves. *Non-lieux: Introduction à la surmodernité* (Paris: Éditions du Seuil, 1992).

12. "Comme un citadin laché dans les montagnes, je m'enivrais d'espace tandis que mon oeil ébloui mesurait la richesse et la vérité des objets" [Like a city-dweller left in the mountains, I got high on space while my dazzled eye measured the richness and truth of objects]: what Lévi-Strauss (in *Tristes Tropiques* [Paris: Plon, 1955], 64), notes of the delirious delight of his first encounter with "antarctic France" in the manner of the sixteenth-century voyager, so also, albeit from the cockpit of a rickety Cessna, does Gardner behold spaces he had never known. If the ethnologist is he or she whose three formative "mistresses" are Freud, Marx, and Geology: Freud, because of the layers of the psyche that comprise a stratigraphy in every individual; Marx, because metamorphosis and upheaval comes where collective action takes place; Geology, because, as "mother and midwife of history" (63), it sets mental and physical labors in the longer duration of the telluric world—in these pages Gardner's fascination with the shape of the Tierra del Fuego shares the same force of attraction.

13. This impulse eventuated in the short film "It Could Be Good, It Could Be Bad," shot in 1997 and included in *Forsaken Fragments* (2010–2011), which documents a remarkable conversation between Gardner and fellow pilot Robert Fulton as they fly amid high peaks in the Andes.

14. Maurice Legendre, *Las Jurdes: Étude de géographie humaine* (Bordeaux: Imprimerie Gounouilhou, 1927). Prefacing a discussion of Buñuel, Gilles Deleuze notes, "the originary world does not exist independently of the geographical and historical milieu that serves as its medium. It's the milieu that receives a beginning, an ending and especially a slope," in *Cinéma 1: L'Image-mouvement* (Paris: Éditions de Minuit, 1983), 175.

15. A description of the 240-odd shots in a film of 32 minutes is provided in my *Su realismo: Lectura de 'Tierra sin pan'* (Valencia: Fundación Instituto Shakespeare/Instituto de Cine y RTV, 1988). Occasionally the camera tilts down from hillsides to record river valleys below, but more often it uses extreme close-ups of bodily members that touch the ambient earth. See also Catherine Russell, "Surrealist Ethnography: *Las Hurdes* and the Documentary Unconscious," in Alexandra Juhaz and Jesse Lerner, eds., *F is for Phony: Fake Documentary and Truth's Undoing* (Minneapolis: University of Minnesota Press, 2006), 105–115, especially 109 à propos the credits.

16. See Paula Amad's discussion of aerial photography and the tradition of human geography in *Counter-Archive: Film, the Everyday, and Albert Kahn's Archives de la planète* (New York: Columbia University Press, 2010), 170–178; also, the same author's "From God-eye to Camera-eye: Aerial Photography's Post-humanist and Neo-Humanist Visions of the World," *History of Photography* 36.1 (February 2012), 66–86, especially 74.

Chapter 3
Colors

Fanny Howe

A few years ago Robert Gardner asked if I would look at a set of photographs he had taken in 1981. I went to his studio, where he laid out the contact sheets and mildly explained their history. He didn't tell me too much about the background of his original project, so I took the work home in the spirit of a psychic looking for clues to causes and outcomes through the medium of images.

The pictures showed the people he filmed for *Ika Hands* (1988): the Ika people in the mountains of Northern Colombia who are remnants of Mayan civilization. For centuries they have been resisting absorption into the modern world by continuing to live according to traditions that link them to each other and the spirit world. In the film *Ika Hands*, we see what these traditions are, especially in relation to the men, but the earlier photographs, which I was given, are turned on the women.

These Polaroid snapshots shine on one dwelling where mothers, children, and animals hang out. Gardner's camera stayed at a remove in a fixed position and clicked every twenty seconds for half an hour. Eighty-seven of the snapshots survived after being tucked in a dark place for more than thirty years. Now they are reproduced in an art book called *In & Out*.[1]

Hens waddle in and out of the dark door that is the central image. A yellow dog, more yellow dogs, a baby and a girl, a toddler, a motherly woman with a white bulging bag, languid girls, and the eye of the camera steady as a snake. The peeling back of the Polaroid's skin to see what was captured must have been for Gardner like watching

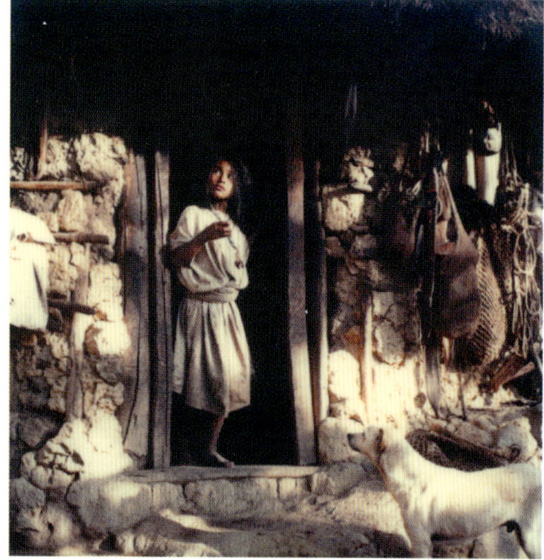

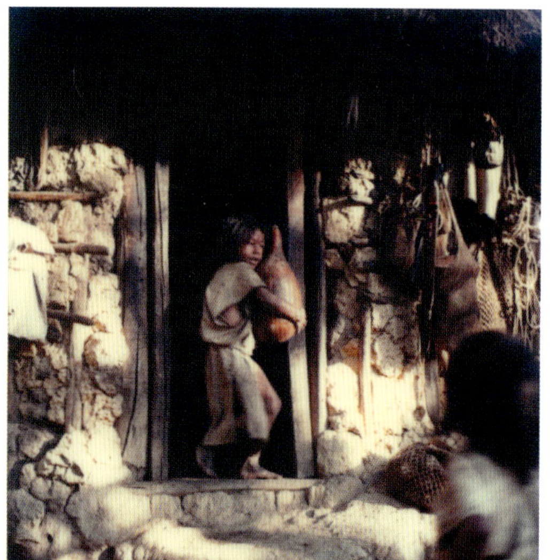

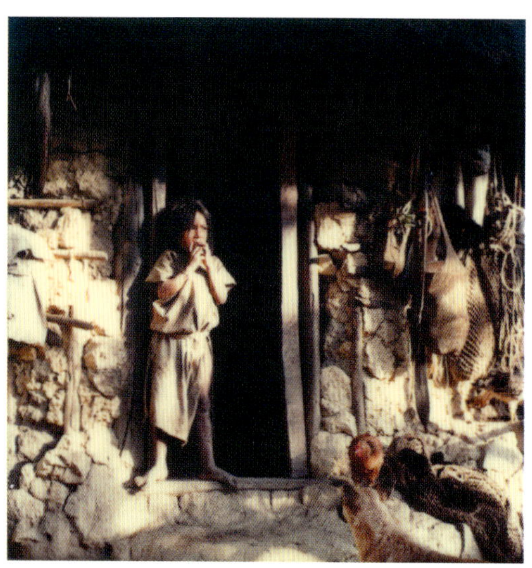

miniscule forms of life coming to light under a microscope. The colors in these Polaroids are now pale and indefinite like Italian frescoes. Each snap seems touched by the celestial.

I grew up during the experimental film era. Stan Brakhage, Yvonne Rainer, Marguerite Duras, Andy Warhol, and Chantal Akerman were out there, developing a new narrative based in fragment, long-shot, time-span, juxtaposition, and correspondence. At the same time there were experimental drugs: Timothy Leary and Carlos Castaneda. And the invention of "ethno-poetics" that collected the chants and writings of faraway cultures. All these overlapped in the region of consciousness as a new kind of mental station or paradise beyond cultural and temporal borders.

In those days the word "color" generally referred to skin tone and social caste. Gardner was filming and working on film about indigenous people (people of color) all through these decades, and even though he says he preferred the particularity of detail that is given in black and white, he turned to color film to shoot people of color.

The Ika people, in a rocky undersea mountain stratosphere, seem to have adapted to a monochrome environment. In the 1981 Polaroids I was given, the people are dressed in rough whites like the clouds in the sky. But the white, in the Polaroid pictures, is pale gold. In the film version of the Ika people, it is the same.

What is the color gold?

I guess gold is the first color because it isn't a color. It's an element and a blend of yellow and red. At the same time gold covers, as much as shade does. It works around the clock to make itself known on the surface of things.

Goethe in his *Theory of Colors* wrote: "The highest degree of light, such as that of the sun, is for the most part colorless. This light, however, seen through a medium but very slightly thickened, appears to us yellow. If the density of such a medium be increased, or if its volume becomes greater, we shall see the light gradually assume a yellow-red hue, which at last deepens to a ruby color."[2]

In the still Polaroid shot you can see the first part of this observation enacted as fact. A pale gold light suffuses the film that is weighed down equally by shadows. The posture each person assumes is stopped mid-motion and is instantly archetypal. A stunned child, a sick child, a pregnant woman, a red gourd to carry water, a girl who might be Mary at the Annunciation, animals.

In movies made at the same time as these photographs, fire turns platinum in color. The flames aren't dancing in orange and red but have an artificial platinum glow. If the sun shines on a pot, it has the same color. The Ika people are like those platinum flames.

I think color has something to do with time. We see it all day, the shifts in tone and length of shadow. Color marks time but also races us through the changing hours and heralds which night we will stand inside. It's made by something which can't be seen (our own eyes) and film chemistry.

Color appears to be stuck inside shapes and to be unable to move. Color stops time or at least slows it down—someone walking in an orange robe, or a pale painted boat cutting across a river—each is held a little back by its color.

Cast a cold eye and color suggests there is a relationship between objects that is more implicit than made. Is it part of the mystical picture? Is it inside or outside, near or far? Is color possessed by the thing or by the optic system that happens to take it in?

When there is a mute color dominating, or sepia, details blend at their edges, as if steeped in fog. But black-and-white film is another matter. Black dominates and white is silenced. Details are sharp, down to buckles and buttons and lip-shapes and lampshades. Details of stripe and circle bind the human figures to their own shadows finally.

From looking at the still photographs (and then the film) of the Ika people I had the impression that they really do not want to be discovered or be seen and they ignore the camera. It is possible to do so, because Gardner is so nonintrusive. Their shaman ("Mama") stays firmly lost in his dream world where he chants while his hands play with the living air.

The children's noses run and they cough and climb across the shaman's knees and gather around him. He has a very fine and kind face, and seems hardly present on his walks or sitting down. I had the feeling that the isolation of the people was supplemented by a communication among themselves that was nearly wordless, and telepathic. The shaman's continual mantra and his hand movements were for him as vibratory as electronics are for us. The softness of colors in their clothing served as camouflage for these hunted people.

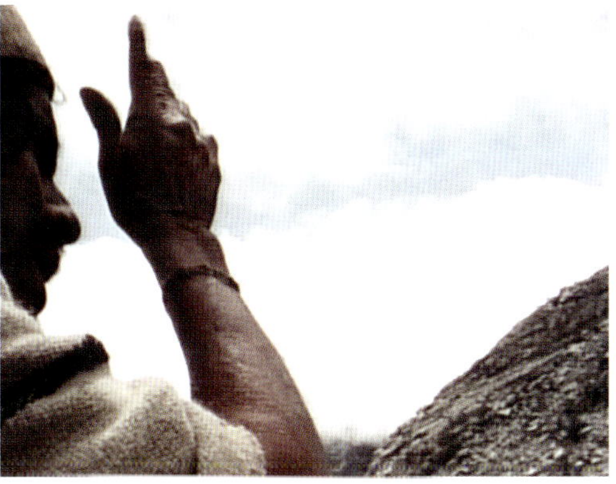

Whenever I saw other films of Robert Gardner—*Altar of Fire* (1976), *Sons of Shiva* (1985), *Forest of Bliss* (1986), *Deep Hearts* (1981), *Dead Birds* (1963)—the subject was indistinguishable from its colors, the subject again being people who live between realities, marking time by the sun's spreading, by fire, water, and religious ritual. Color slows them down or ties them into their environment.

It would be hard to make films about India without being intoxicated by more than skin color—by colors in marigolds and hibiscus, in dyes and altars. And Gardner is drawn to the liminal visions of people who love wearing colors.

Truly religious people make little distinction between manifest and unmanifest. They have idols (dolls, ideals) that they perfume, dress, feed, and let rest. This looks like fun, but such a magical relationship to objects can only be achieved in poverty, a poverty that is realized by chance sometimes in old age, sometimes in youth. It is neither voluntary nor involuntary poverty so much as an attitude to earth.

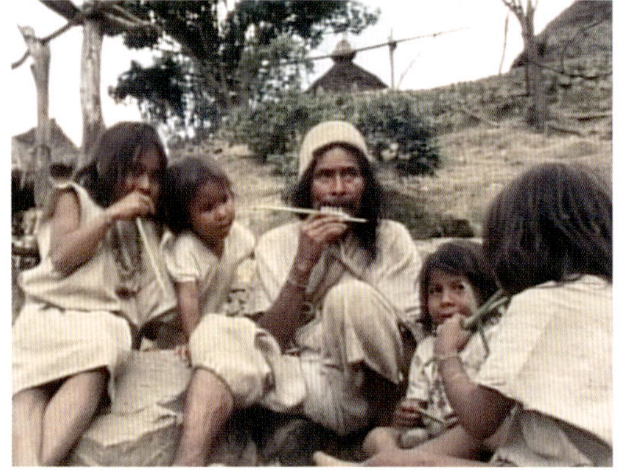

In these films labor is steady, unending, collaborative. Hands at work with needles, nails, wood, ropes, and water perform on automatic until a little bit goes off, and then the hands give it full attention to readapt. This is perhaps the moment of failure where discoveries occur.

In a money economy (as opposed to a poetic one) we rarely learn who profits from the labor, for he wears the ring of Gyges on his hand. He is the moneyman, the ultimate eater. *Forest of Bliss* is a film about a funeral economy beside the Ganges, dogs eating dogs, and the recycling of flesh. Food keeps the natural world alive until it is burned. In *Ika Hands* and *Forest of Bliss*, the hunger of the soul is inseparable from the needs of the body.

The laborer belongs to God because laborers grind themselves into earth.

I lived with the photos spread open for several months from winter into summer when my ideas became a smattering of words halfway between poems and messages.

I had studied liberation theology and heard the word "other" that took over cultural studies (not to mention the word "color") and would be applied to the people being photographed here.

I remembered playing with inanimate things as I would with the living, and even now statues of sacred ancients. It would never be foreign to me to submit to rituals that cross history and open air at the same time.

Dogs and plants and birds are animate messengers. They hover around the poor like guardians, salvaging. There are dogs in these films that echo the distress of humans. And then there are humans who have chosen the lives of birds, and there are people who work to be more beautiful than any others. They hide their feelings of envy deep in their hearts, hearts that are like pockets on the inside of the flesh. In the film *Deep Hearts* they are like runway models, genderless, yellow or red goo smeared onto their faces and eyelashes. They have delirious expressions.

This mask, the new face, is as much a stranger to its wearer as it is to the witness. Face paint in this case produces an unearthly expression, beyond the blissed-out stare of a doper, or model, a look I have never seen before.

In icons the sacred heart of Jesus is a ruby red pouch hanging outside his body. This open heart means he is giving himself to people. But why is it exposed like meat? To show that it hurts and can be eaten? It is a pagan image that hangs in the dreary quarters of parish priests to this day.

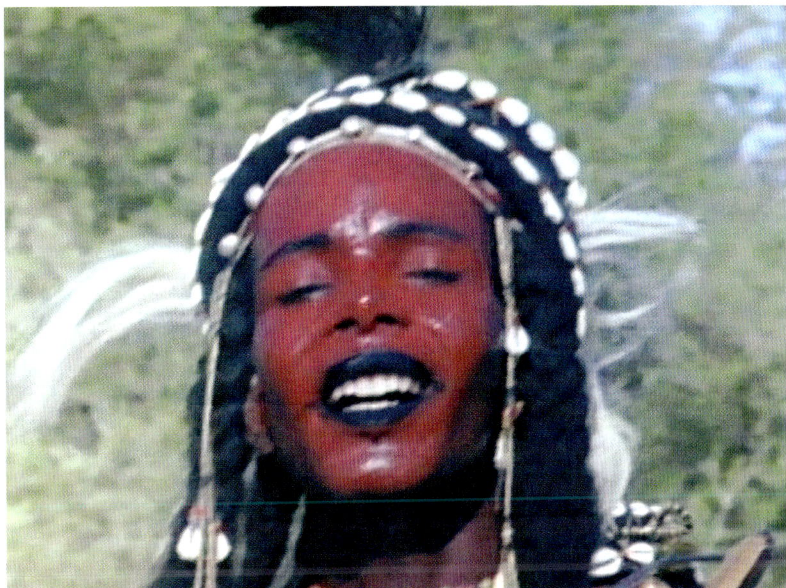

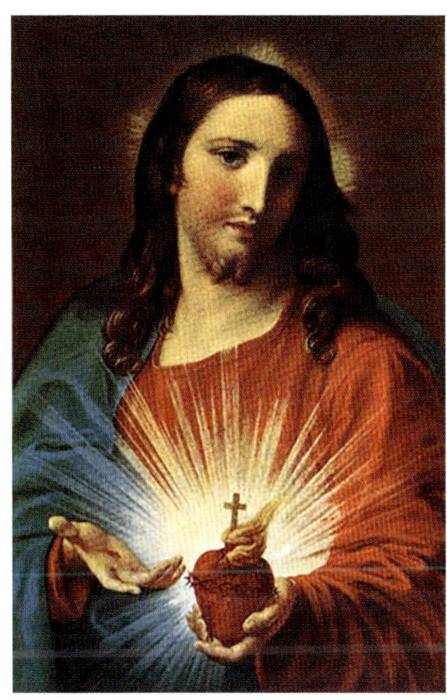

The people in Gardner's films are not pretending to be themselves. They are themselves, experienced in transmissions and dreams and poverty. They are on automatic. Can we find ourselves in them?

They might be the origin of mankind or its termination; they might be its middle. Catastrophe in the modern world could turn us into fish of Neptune, who swim through air. Fish could be trailing a glory behind them.

The Ika and the Bororo Fulani people are brilliant and imperiled; their impending annihilation draws them to the edge of the real where the next world shimmers.

Warner Brothers shows Earth floating in space as a gray ball of clay as its opening shot before *Casablanca* (1942). Some of us have grown up watching the change from this clay into color in film. It was like seeing God make the earth get up and walk. Until then film was adequate in its grays, silvers, whites, and was half in love with its own motions. Slowly colors seeped in and slowed down the objects and dyed them in emotional hues. Footsteps grew heavier and shadows denser. We know that time is measurable, and therefore it is revealed in objects and not in the wind. But behind certain very sharp black-and-white film, we could sense the color blue wanting to come through. Goethe wrote of this phenomenon outside of film:

> If on the other hand darkness is seen through a semi-transparent medium, which is itself illumined by a light striking on it, a blue color appears: this becomes lighter and paler as the density of the medium is increased, but on the contrary appears darker and deeper the more transparent the medium becomes: in the least degree of dimness short of absolute transparence, always supposing a perfectly colorless medium, this deep blue approaches the most beautiful violet.[3]

I remember the movie *Imitation of Life* (1959), whose subject was human color ("race"), and how the whole movie seemed to float in a wave of compromised silver. In the subject of passing the director Douglas Sirk presented silver as an imitation of life. White silver is glamor. Color as skin pigment is a mark of caste. The original writer of the novel, Fannie Hurst, was a close friend of Zora Neale Hurston, and a leftist Jew with a strong conscience regarding color and persecution. "White, white, white!" the girl (who is passing) cries out in anguish from her silverized false home.

The films of Robert Gardner seek out people of color for subject matter that does what most experimental artists wanted to do in the 1960s and 1970s: reflect on the strangeness of being ourselves. Now this is a central philosophical subject. Emmanuel Levinas, Paul Ricoeur, Richard Kearney, and Julia Kristeva are just a few of those who have tackled the question of the stranger, sometimes called Other, who is finally ourselves. "Neither the possession nor the unity of number nor the unity of concepts link me to the Stranger, the Stranger who disturbs the being at home with oneself. But Stranger also means the free one. Over him I have no *power*," wrote Levinas.[4]

The camera in Gardner's films is a reluctant and shy camera; it does not want to be a presence; it shuns power. It is like an insect that curls at the edges of a field. Its function is to watch and to comprehend later. After *Dead Birds* there is very little spoken commentary in a Gardner film, but supplementary conversation after the film is over.

I think he must like to see what happens rather than speak of it. The colors emerge in their relationship to each other, surprisingly relational for values that are given by chance. This is the "chance" that we all seek: the coincidence of details that indicates hidden meaning. The linguists say structure precedes grammar.

Filmmaker Ricky Leacock wanted to make films that gave you "the feeling of being there." And this is what he did. But Gardner's films do something else because of their subject matter, which involves crossing over into nowhere familiar, and the way editing has lifted parts of the nowhere into a coherent collage. The films are poetic. The great poem "Correspondences" by Baudelaire is relevant:

Nature's a temple where each living column,
At times, gives forth vague words. There Man advances
Through forest-groves of symbols, strange and solemn,
Who follow him with their familiar glances.

As long-drawn echoes mingle and transfuse
Till in a deep, dark unison they swoon,
Vast as the night or as the vault of noon—
So are commingled perfumes, sounds, and hues.[5]

The sun is our clock but it is also our painter. Stan Brakhage pointed out correspondences to Gardner in the film *Forest of Bliss* and Gardner was not impressed because he had already been surprised by what the camera revealed. In *Ika Hands*, the colors are muted and earthy. The people don't look for dyes. White is fine for cloth as it is for rope and thread and the sheets of clouds around the mountains. The skies are piled with clouds like laundry. Light is distributed with moisture, waterfalls and pools, lakes and a seaside. The Ika people who wear loose clothes are like dream figures who don't want to be found.

Notes

1. Robert Gardner and Fanny Howe, *In & Out* (Cambridge, MA: Studio7Arts, 2009).
2. Johann Wolfgang von Goethe, *Theory of Colours*, trans. Charles Lock Eastlake (1840). (Cambridge, MA: MIT Press, 1970), section 150, 61.
3. Ibid., section 151, 62.
4. Emmanuel Lévinas, *Totality and Infinity: An Essay On Exteriority*, trans. Alphonso Lingis (Dordrect/Boston/London: Kluwer, 1991), 39.
5. Charles Baudelaire, "Correspondences," in *Poems of Baudelaire: A Translation of* Les Fleurs du Mal, ed. Roy Campbell (New York: Pantheon Books, 1952), 8.

Chapter 4
Aesthetic Form and Ethnographic Discourse

Daniel Morgan

There shouldn't be any real mystery about what you've been watching.

—Robert Gardner

In one of the final scenes of Jean Rouch and Edgar Morin's *Chronicle of a Summer* (1961), the filmmakers screen the film they have made—and that we have just seen—for the people who are in it. A number of the remarks by members of the audience in the film concern the question of whether the actions of various people on screen are believable, and more precisely whether what's being said and done is "true." At one point, we hear a woman object off-screen, "What's not true? Cameras can't lie," and at that moment Rouch and Morin cut between two characters (Marilou and Jean-Pierre) in different parts of the room to establish an eyeline match between them.

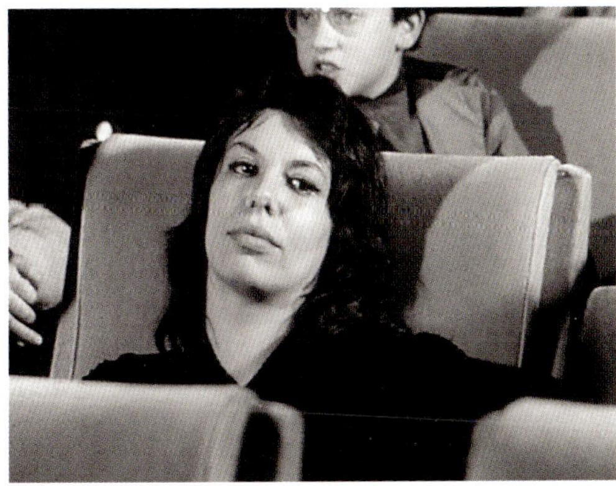

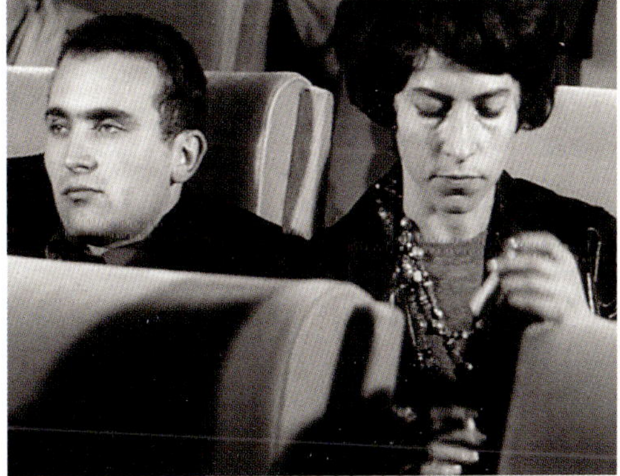

The effect of the cut, as William Rothman has argued, is to imply that they are looking at one another, a connection that, given the film we've just seen, would be fraught with emotional resonance. Indeed, the effect of the cut is to make us assume the existence of a connection even though we have no evidence outside the cut to believe it: the fact of the edit, and the associated meaning it carries, is enough.[1] This tension is key to the work of the scene. *Chronicle of a Summer* in effect produces a lie—it leads us to hold a belief that may be false—but it does so in order to make a true statement: that the words of a character are false, that cameras can and do lie. If one of the fundamental tenets of nonfiction filmmaking is that the film provides a faithful account of what was in front of the camera, *Chronicle of a Summer* argues that this recording function is not enough. The film evokes familiar assumptions about cinema in order to dispel them as illusions.

a	b
c	d
e	f

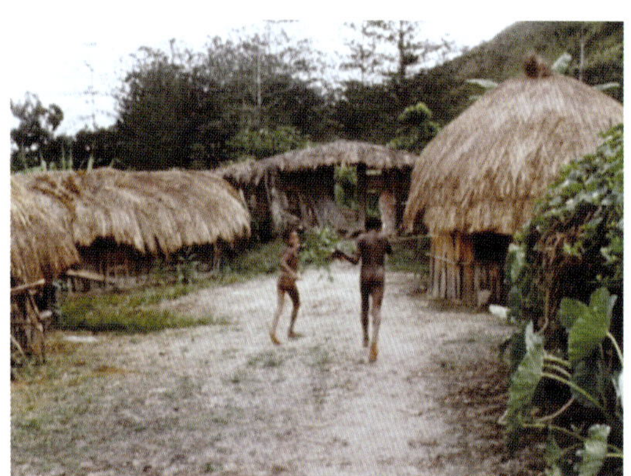

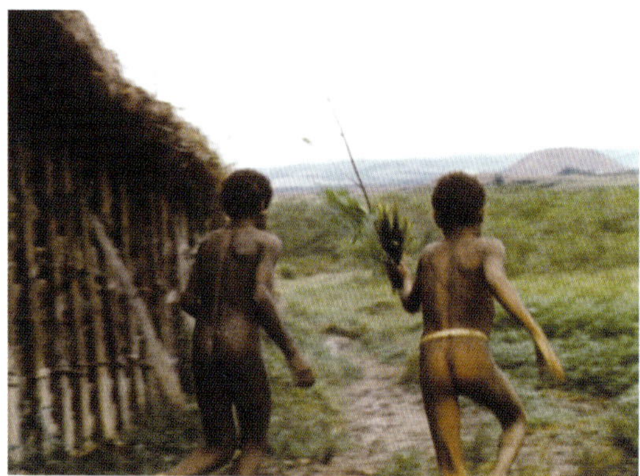

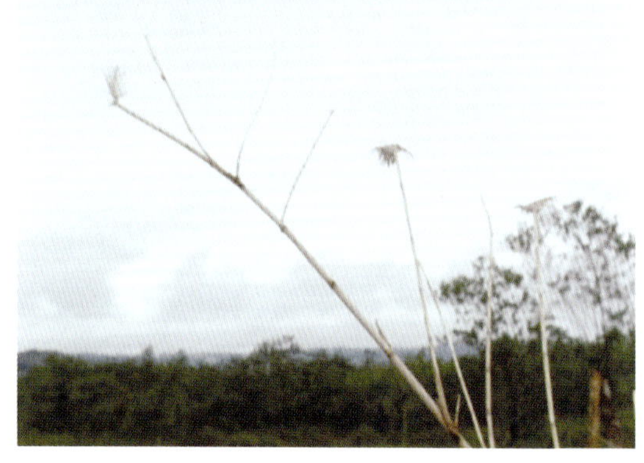

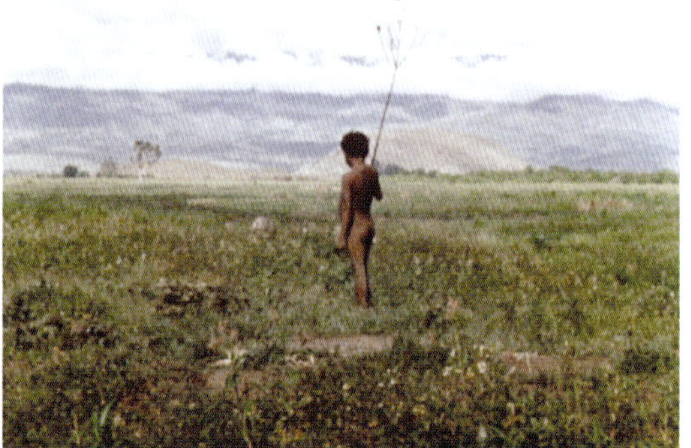

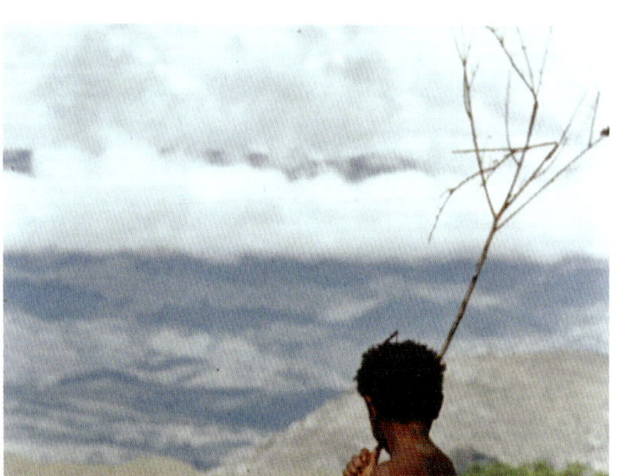

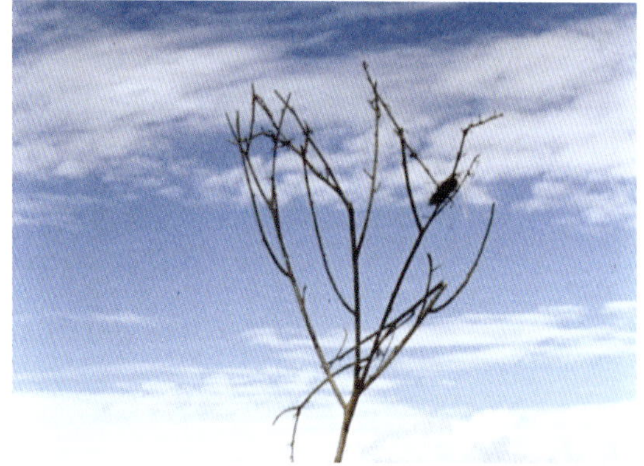

While Robert Gardner could not have seen *Chronicle of a Summer* before he began shooting what would become *Dead Birds* (1963), his first major feature-length ethnographic film, he likely saw it during the editing of the film.[2] The chronology makes it possible, but there is no direct evidence. Certainly Gardner knew of Rouch's work: in a conversation during a *Screening Room* episode, they recall meeting in 1957 at a festival in Prague, where Gardner saw *Les maîtres fous* (1955) and others of Rouch's ethnographic films, and was deeply impressed by their editing techniques, use of voice-over, and willingness to integrate documentary and fictional elements. Gardner's own films would follow broadly in these tracks, developing their own strategies within the domain of experimental ethnography, and often employing a tension similar to the one found in this scene from *Chronicle of a Summer*, where editing techniques unsettle meanings ostensibly given in the content of the film. Unlike Rouch and Morin, however, Gardner's ambitions are aimed less at the camera's truth or falsity than they are at the status of ethnographic claims themselves, and concern the ability of cinema to function as a medium for producing ethnographic knowledge.

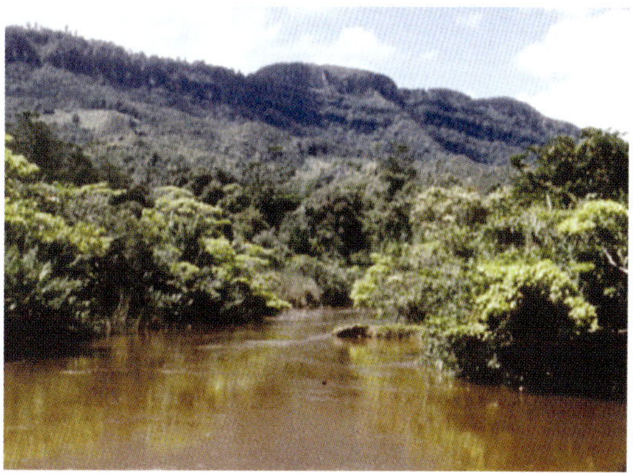

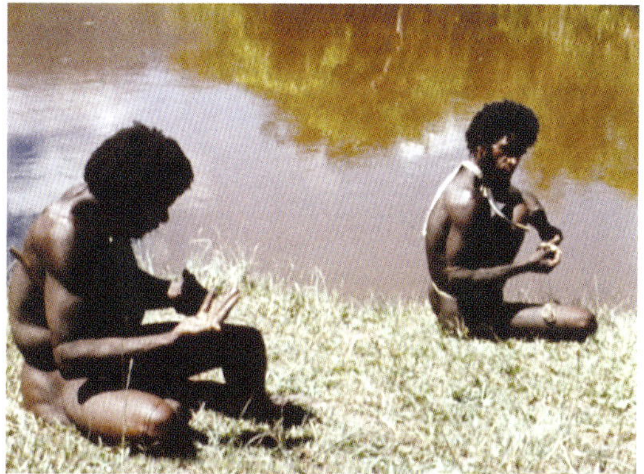

Gardner's ambition results in an unusual and complex formal style, especially within the parameters of ethnographic film. About halfway through *Dead Birds*, for example, a warrior is wounded in combat and members of his village prepare a series of spells to keep ghosts away. Gardner says, in voice-over, that young boys are instructed to run through the village to sweep it clear of ghosts; we then see two boys apparently doing just this, underneath an overcast sky. A cut shows them racing outside the village, where they plant the branches they had been using; a further cut gives us a close up of a bare branch, framed against the grey sky and held for several seconds.

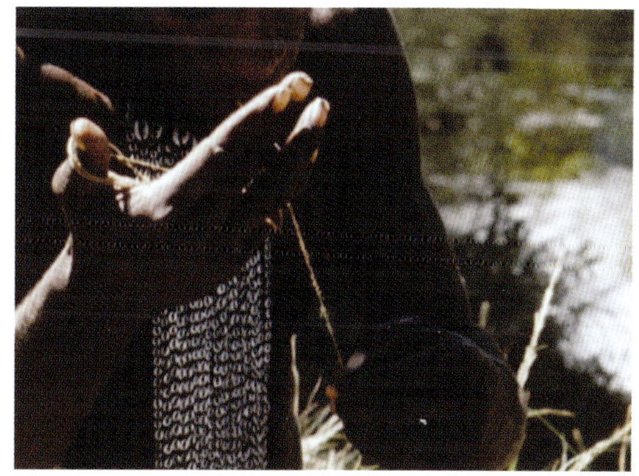

These shots function in part to establish a time and place for the sequence that follows: an account of a day in which nothing special occurs, in which the spells for a warrior's health occur against the backdrop of routine activities. The sequence begins with a shot of a small child named Pua—one of the central figures in the film—standing in a sun-drenched field; a low-angle shot of the boy and the branch he is holding; and a close-up of the branch. Over these shots, Gardner says in voice-over that the heat of the sun decreases Pua's watchfulness over the pigs he cares for.

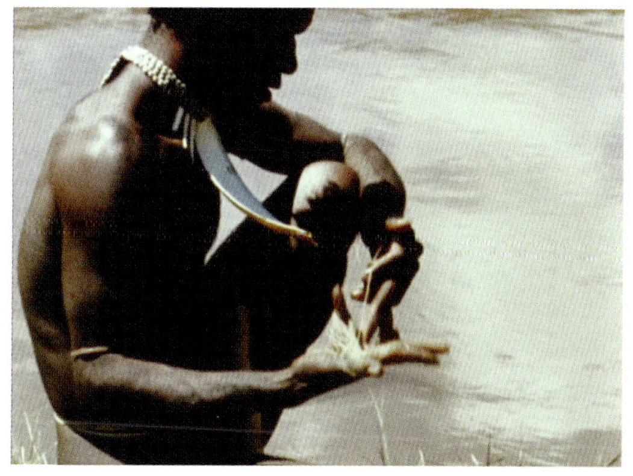

A cut takes us to the river. The camera tilts down to reveal Weyak—the other main figure in the film—and a friend sitting calmly on the bank; Gardner says that they do this knowing that there will not be a raid by the enemy village that day. Weyak is weaving, as we saw him do when he was introduced early in the film, and Gardner cuts to a close-up of his hands, then a longer shot of him.

There is a cut to a grasshopper on a bright green leaf, then a cut to Pua's hand as he picks up the grasshopper. Pulling back, the camera follows Pua as he sits and scrutinizes his find. Gardner cuts to a close shot of the insect cradled gently in the boy's hands. We learn that one of Pua's pigs is sick and has been kept at home. Gardner notes that this, too, allows Pua to be less watchful, and we see him lie down in the brush, letting the grasshopper play across his body.

Another cut brings us back to Weyak, walking into the distance to stand guard (Gardner says) over the fields until everyone has gone home. We then see Pua inside a darkened hut with the bright sun shining through door; he is visibly and audibly crying, and Gardner's voice-over tells us that "Pua, already home, weeps because his sick pig has died." Three final shots show Weyak, in his own home, weaving (a frequent activity of his), there is a fade to black, and the next scene begins by taking up the preparation of Pua's dead pig for eating.

A couple of things are striking about this sequence. First, as he often does in the film, Gardner ascribes "inner states" to the people he films, speaking about Pua's inattentiveness or Weyak's confidence about the enemy's intentions. He does this without providing testimony from the people being shown, or giving visible evidence to support his claims. Second, the sequence is organized as a parallel montage: one line takes us from the children leaving the village to Pua's time in the fields and back to the village, the other follows Weyak as he negotiates an uneventful day. The implication is that these lines of action take place simultaneously, that everything is happening on the same day—a reading established largely by the conventional meaning of parallel montage, derived from a longstanding tradition within narrative filmmaking, and by Gardner's own words, as when he notes after a shot of Weyak that Pua is "already home."

The persistent use of parallel editing is one of the most curious features of Gardner's work, part of his interest in integrating techniques of fictional narrative cinema into ethnographic film.[3] But the sequence raises questions about the claims of rough simultaneity the technique implies. We might ask: Is there any evidence, outside the editing pattern and Gardner's assertions in voice-over, that the actions take place at the same time? That what the sequence says and shows is true? We seem to be in the odd position of being unable to interrogate its claims using evidence from outside the sequence.[4]

A similar question arises with Gardner's use of voice-over. He does not step outside the immediacy of the sequence to provide factual information or to establish a stable ground of authority, speaking instead about things like emotions and other "inner states" to which we have no immediate access. And while such claims may—and often do—derive from interviews or conversations that took place at other times, no evidence of this is found within the film itself.[5] Other features of this sequence leave us unsettled as well. Gardner has stated repeatedly that he does not believe that sound has to be recorded at the same time as the image; indeed, in a conversation with Ross McElwee he acknowledges that the sound of Pua crying at the end of the sequence is in fact a recording of his own son *pretending* to cry.[6] We might also notice inconsistencies in the weather: Does the overcast sky in the first shots give way to the stultifying sunshine that tires Pua, or are they shots from different days joined together in the editing room? More broadly, we might wonder whether it is likely that Gardner was at both places on the same day, that these events just happened to coincide. Around all of this is the question of why it matters—to Gardner, to the film—to suggest that simultaneity exists, or that Pua and Weyak are feeling certain things. It's not clear what is gained from such assertions, while their risks are more evident and consequential, perhaps impacting even the truth claims of the film as a whole.

a	b	c
d	e	f
g	h	i
j		

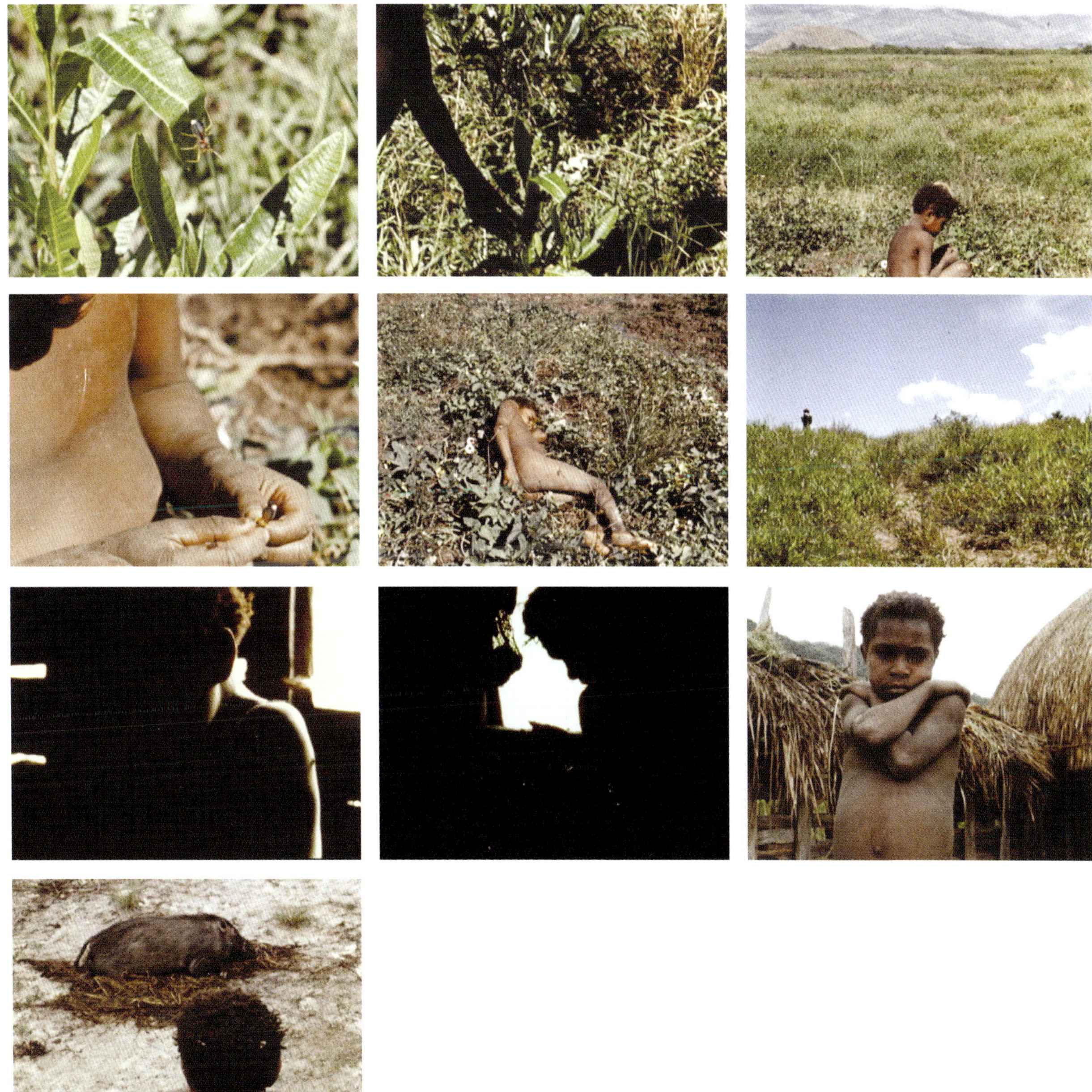

This kind of sequence is what makes Gardner unique among ethnographic filmmakers, and what makes his work so infuriating to some critics. Not only does Gardner draw central formal techniques from the resources of fictional narrative cinema, but his employment of them eschews what is generally taken to be the main attraction of film for ethnography: its ability to record, automatically and without error, what is happening in front of the camera, to preserve particular instances of a practice, ritual, or form of life for later study. Gardner seems disinclined to emphasize this function; more importantly, he appears to actively subvert it, to offer alternate perspectives through the editing and sound. All this seems to work against the type of claims that ethnographic film tries to make, and gives Gardner's films a vexed status within its domain. How can *Dead Birds* be an ethnographic film if it is so deeply invested in undermining the assumptions of that genre?[7]

This is not just a problem for Gardner's critics. Those who defend his films tend to place emphasis on their experimental nature, the way they go beyond familiar categories of ethnography. Sometimes this means labeling Gardner as a symbolist (in an aesthetic sense, not as part of the discipline of symbolic anthropology), moving toward universal claims associated with life and death; another tack describes the enigmatic features of his film style as simply subjective, based on Gardner's own personal views of the world he films; still another brings his work in line with the recent trend of "sensory ethnography," most explicitly found in *Leviathan* (Véréna Paravel and Lucien Castaing-Talyor, 2013).[8] However well-intentioned, and however successful as readings, these defenses have a basic flaw: they effectively cede the terms of the argument by implicitly agreeing with Gardner's critics that the films are not ethnographies in a familiar way. In what follows, I take Gardner's films as seriously committed to the kinds of claims that ethnographies, whether filmed or written, aim to make. The challenge of Gardner's films, I argue, is that they do so by way of those features that seem most antithetical to that very ambition.

It is important to mark a distinction between nonfiction film as a whole and ethnographic film in particular. While both are bound broadly by an imperative to be answerable to conditions in the world—that is, to be responsive to questions about what they purport to describe—ethnographic films are often aimed at a different level of generality than other kinds of nonfiction films. The latter are usually characterized as being about a specific thing—an event, a person, and so on—grounded in the camera's fidelity to whatever is placed in front of its lens. The former, however, have a broader and more general scope—what is it that a group of people do?—and so pose distinct types of problems for a filmmaker.

At stake in the specificity of ethnographic film is the form of ethnography as a whole, and the particular kinds of claims that ethnographic discourse makes. Take an early, canonical example. Marcel Mauss, in his book on magic, ranges from large declarations about magic as such to descriptions of the role of magic in individual societies. Thus, we find statements like: "Throughout its existence, magic has never forgotten its social origins. Each of its elements, agents, ties and representations not only perpetuate the memory of this original collective state, but even help in their reproduction in an attenuated form."[9] Or, on a more localized scale: "In ancient and modern India the dead, deified ancestors are invoked during magic ceremonies. In spells, however, the spirits are invoked of dead persons for whom funeral rites have not yet been appropriately performed, of those who have not been buried, of those who died a violent death, of women who died in childbirth, of the spirits of stillborn children."[10] (Although I use Mauss largely because of a close connection between his work on magic and Gardner's films, this is a kind of statement found throughout ethnographic writing.)

It's the degree of generalization in these claims that both characterizes and causes trouble for them. Mauss sometimes qualifies his judgments, noting that a particular practice is accepted only in some instances, or that it holds "only in specific cases where it is accepted." But usually the implication is that such statements apply to all members of the group they specify: all Indian people, or all people who believe in magic. These statements appear to follow the form of universal judgments (e.g., "all humans are mortal"), specifying a claim that holds true—more precisely, that *has to* hold true—for every individual who falls under the subject of the statement. For such judgments, the very existence of a counterexample (e.g., a single person who did not die) would disprove the claim.

There is an obvious problem here. It's almost certain that Mauss would not take himself to be disproved if someone in India practiced a different kind of rite, or if there were an instance in which a magical practice, agent, or representation did indeed "forget" its social origins. Ethnographic claims may look like universals, but this similarity masks a crucial difference. In a statement that follows the form, "The X do Y," the fact that an individual belonging to group X did something different—something other than Y—would not disprove the claim about the group. It's not that evidence is irrelevant to assessment: rather, ethnographic claims operate according to a form of logic in which a judgment that predicates a ritual or practice over a group holds true for that group even through every member may not observe that ritual or practice.[11] When Mauss says that people in India do a certain thing, or hold a set of beliefs, that is not meant to cover each individual living in India. The mere existence of counterexamples—presumably up to a certain proportion, after which the nature of the claim would change[12]—doesn't tell against the validity of his judgments. Mauss describes generalized, not universal, practices, and it is this form of judgment that grounds such ethnographic discourse.

In this context, film poses a particular kind of problem. While it's fairly straightforward to verbally describe a practice—the form of the statement, "The X do Y" confers a degree of generality on the claim—film seems too closely tied to the particular to achieve this kind of judgment. You film an event, not a practice; the image shows a unique set of actions, not a repeated and routinized activity. Ethnographers may have gravitated toward film because its photographic basis provides a link to the world that ensures the authenticity of what's being shown, but this basis also limits the ability of a film to move from the particular to the general: to see what's on-screen as an instance of a more general practice, and not just a specific event. Ethnographic films therefore employ a range of strategies to bridge the gap. Voice-overs are often central to this: they provide the verbal statements that elevate the particular event shown in the film into the realm of general practice, and they do so largely by employing discourse familiar to written ethnography. It's also for this reason that ethnographic films tend to function as illustrations of preexisting theories: showing, for example, what a type of ritual actually looks like, how certain objects are made, or how actions take place. Gardner's films stand out within ethnographic cinema because of his desire to use *formal* features to bridge the gap between event and practice, to make the particular into the general; this strategy constitutes both the films' originality and their difficulty. Indeed, his repeated claims that film's photographic basis is insufficient for his ends, as well as his interest in the techniques of narrative cinema, are part of this ambition.[13]

We can see how Gardner goes about this in the opening sequence of *Forest of Bliss* (1986). While *Dead Birds* uses voice-over, even if for idiosyncratic ends, in *Forest of Bliss* Gardner eschews not only any authoritative voice from outside the world being shown (both films also refuse to provide subtitles for the persons in them). Speech is wholly absent as an interpretive guide for viewers. The effect is to place full weight on the film's formal features to provide and create meaning, often by using shots whose own meaning and significance are obscure.

The film begins with a shot of a dog, the space within the frame compressed as if it were zoomed in from a great distance; the dog is running to the right and looking alternately toward the camera and straight ahead. Gardner pans to follow, then pauses to let the dog run out of the frame to the right. He cuts to a shot of a ship, almost invisible within a bank of fog, moving to the right. It slowly drifts out of the frame, and there is a cut to a bird of prey standing on the ground and looking to the right as well. Gardner holds this shot for only a few seconds, then cuts to a closer shot of another boat in the fog: two men pull oars, standing at the bow, and the boat moves across the frame to the right until it reveals a figure wrapped in white and seated at the stern. This is a haunting shot, eerie and enigmatic. Gardner then cuts to a shot of multiple boats docked at the base of a wide staircase, with people carrying loads on and around them (though the world is still shrouded in fog, the palette has subtly changed). A brief shot of a boy flying a kite leads to an image of the red sun, shrouded by mist—the sound of the boy's footsteps continues, creating a sound bridge between shots—and this in turn inaugurates the second part of the opening sequence, in which Gardner gives a series of three shots of the inhabited side of the river, before culminating in a shot of dogs fighting and squealing in pain and distress.

At one level, this sequence serves as an announcement that *Forest of Bliss* will not proceed in a familiar way by using explanatory voice-overs to provide the verbal discourse that the images and sounds then exemplify. The temptation is to say that Gardner creates an associative montage, moving between shots on the grounds that he discerns in them related elements; the terms of the connection would be personal, subjective, at best broadly thematic. As in *Dead Birds*, however, a more stable ground emerges through the way Gardner uses techniques drawn from fictional narrative cinema to articulate a path through a nonfictional world. Thus, when he begins with the alternating shots of animals and boats, the connection between them is established not least by the fact that the animals are emphasized as *looking*: they turn their heads from side to side, scanning the area around them. From these shots, the cuts to the boats suggest an eyeline match with the animals, so the connection is not just one of association but based on the conventional meanings carried by the formal structure of the eyeline match itself. As a result, the sequence is able to accomplish two larger tasks.

The first is to introduce a number of the key motifs that will run through the rest of the film (dogs, boats, kites, fire), while at the same time suggesting that there are relations between them; the second is to establish distinctions: between the two shores of the river, between life and death, between human and animal.[14] The sequence thereby establishes the basic framework for the film, the terms of its ethnographic arguments. This work emerges not despite but because of the formal features Gardner employs; we are not explicitly told the terms around which the rituals we see operate but come to realize them on our own.

a	b	c
d	e	f
g	h	i
j	k	

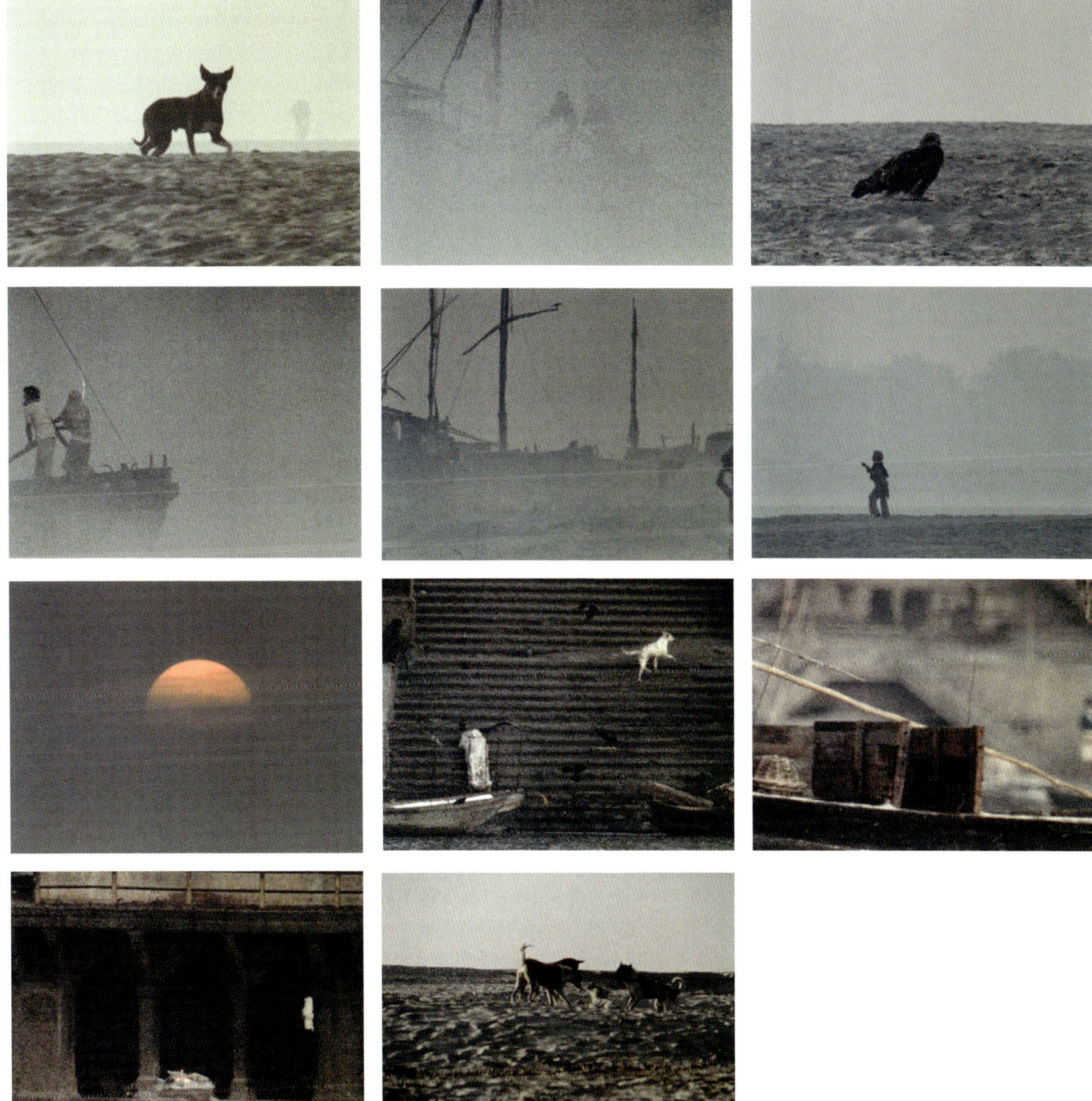

Forest of Bliss is an extreme example, one I return to below, but it illustrates the range of techniques and tools that Gardner has employed across his career in order to give his films the status of ethnographic work. One of the key features in his early films is the idiosyncratic treatment of voice-overs. In *Dead Birds*, they are frequently phrased so as to resemble, albeit in a slightly different form, familiar kinds of ethnographic statements (although their use winds up unsettling the assumption of that discourse). When he introduces the activity of farming, for example, he says: "In other gardens, men are doing the work that women cannot do as well. Most men, if they are married, will do little more in their gardens than the heaviest work. When that is done, their women come to plant, and later to harvest. Younger, unmarried men, must do a larger share of the garden labor." Or later, during one of the early combat sequences, fighting is interrupted by rain and the men take shelter: "They will stay until the rain passes, talking about the way the battle had gone. They will exaggerate what really happened, and they will be glad that, so far, it was the enemy who had failed." In these remarks, the speaker (Gardner) asserts something to hold true not for an individual or for all humans but for a group of people (the Dani). (We also note parallels to our own form of life, as in the emphasis Gardner places on the role of exaggeration.) He describes a general form of life, an activity that occurs more than once and that can be analyzed to produce useful knowledge about the group being discussed. The basic work of such voice-overs, then, is to bring the specific things we see into a relation with a more general, ongoing, and temporally extended activity.[15]

If here Gardner ostensibly follows the standard contours of ethnographic film, he also subverts and challenges them, frequently using such rhetoric to speak about individuals within the Dani rather than the group itself, creating an interpretive ambiguity and a more expansive scope for his own project. When we first see Pua, for example, Gardner says: "Usually alone, herding his foster-father's pigs, smaller and more awkward than most of his playmates, Pua waits for manhood." If the first few clauses are specific to Pua, true to the extent that they hold of him as an individual, the last clause shifts registers. "Pua waits for manhood" does not necessarily describe any particular moment, nor is it clear that at the specific instant we see Pua on screen he is doing this. However, despite the curious pitch of the words, and their poetic bent, we are still within the terms of ethnographic judgment. If it turns out that Pua is not consciously "waiting for manhood" that would not change the validity of the statement. Gardner's claim is about the kind of thing that Pua is *generally* doing; more broadly, it takes Pua to be representative of small boys in the village in order to say something about a central concern of theirs. In another instance, Gardner says, "Each morning, Weyak takes his spear or his bow and arrows and starts for his tower"; the statement is not disproved if we are able to specify a morning for which this is not the case. Or: we see Weyak climbing his watchtower to look out over the valley and Gardner remarks, "the sight never fails to please him." This makes sense not as an account of an individual moment, nor as a universal assessment of Weyak's actions (what never fails to happen), but rather as a claim about a general activity or tendency. Gardner's words speak to Weyak's appreciation of natural beauty, an indication that there is more to his life—and, insofar as he is representative of a group (an open question in the film), to the life of the Dani—than war and work alone.

Voice-overs, and verbal discourse more broadly, allow Gardner to invoke the framework of ethnographic discourse in order to work off it. But his ambitions, as we've seen, run deeper. The idea seems to be that, if he can correctly construct the form of a film, then voice-overs will be redundant; technique can do their work. A key tool for this ambition is parallel montage. In *Dead Birds*, as I argued earlier, Gardner employs a cinematic convention that implies simultaneity in order to assert a connection between events—while X happens, Y takes place—that describes not an individual occurrence but a more general situation or practice. When Gardner cuts between Pua and Weyak, or between Weyak and his wife, it is not necessarily to say that the specific actions we are watching take place at the same time. The juxtapositions tell us about a more general type of activity that *tends* to happen simultaneously: "Women go to the fields when men make war"; "Children care for animals while the adults perform other tasks." This generality is the matter of ethnography.

It is by no means new to emphasize that Gardner employs techniques from narrative film to unsettle the terms of ethnography, or that mere recording is insufficient for his purposes. Usually, such arguments proceed in two stages. The first accounts for what has been described as Gardner's "symbolist impulse,"[16] treated as a process by which he makes particular persons, objects, and actions resonate with more abstract concerns. On this reading, each particular thing that Gardner presents is imbued with deeper meaning: we are able to "read off" this meaning from the surface of the image. The second describes the content of the films as "universals," the broad truths in life that every person must confront.[17] This stage largely turns on Gardner's interest in death as an inescapable fact of human nature, a preoccupation central to both *Dead Birds* and *Forest of Bliss*.

There are deep problems with such criticisms. It is noteworthy, first, that Gardner eschews talking about his work as a kind of symbolism, largely avoiding the term except to distance himself from it.[18] More importantly, the rhetoric of symbolism tends to put weight on the meaning carried by the content of an image, a single shot, rather than the intricate patterns of montage that Gardner employs. And, while it is true that the films are explicitly attuned toward universal themes like life and death, Gardner is careful to separate those themes from the specific ritual practices he films and analyzes. Note the ending narration of *Dead Birds*:

> [Unlike birds,] men, having foreknowledge of their doom, bring a special passion to their life. They will not simply wait for death, nor will they bear it lightly when it comes; instead, they will try with measured violence to fashion fate themselves. They kill to save their souls, and, perhaps, to ease the burden of knowing what birds will never know, and what they, as men, who have forever killed each other, cannot forget.

The concern is not simply over the fact of death itself, but rather—given that inevitability—about the ways that groups of people construct repeated actions to deal with that fact. Such consciousness, Gardner suggests, results in ritual, which is the material for his films. What I argue is that Gardner's films reside between the idiosyncrasy of individual lives and the universal fact of mortality: they describe the general terms, the practices and rituals that connect the two, the middle ground through which individuals and groups negotiate their relation to death. It's in this middle ground where film moves beyond its recording function without becoming a symbol. The work of Gardner's films is to create formal structures that convey, mimic, and articulate the ritual forms of behavior. Indeed, treating his films as following the logical form of ethnographic claims is a way to avoid basic pitfalls in thinking about them.

Forest of Bliss displays Gardner's ethnographic ambitious in a particularly stark form, removing the tension between voice-over and image that drove the earlier work. It's something of a natural step, as the transitions from *Dead Birds*, to *Rivers of Sand* (1973), to *Deep Hearts* (1979), and then to *Forest of Bliss* are marked in part by the decreasing presence of voices from outside the world of the film. Indeed, some of the charges that *Forest of Bliss* does not count as an ethnographic film are based on a sense that viewers are left without a guide, hence unable to understand what they are being shown.[19] While the film certainly does pose interpretive difficulties, Gardner—as I've been arguing throughout—is careful to organize his sequences such that they lead viewers toward ethnographic knowledge. As he put it, "There shouldn't be any real mystery about what you've been watching."[20]

In a sequence fairly early in the film, Gardner introduces a motif of marigolds, flowers that will later be used to link a number of actions to each other. The sequence begins with a short transition: a shot of people carrying packages off a boat, then of a corpse floating in the water near the stone steps (the residual echo of the body will function as a reminder of the ever-present context of mortality). A cut brings us to a man walking a bicycle, a bundle loaded on its rear; the bright orange, yellow, and red colors of marigolds emerge from the top of the bundle. The camera follows for a few seconds, then there is a cut to a shot—this time taken from in front—of a different man pushing a bicycle also loaded down with marigolds. He walks past, and there is a cut to a shot from behind a third transporter of marigolds, this time on foot. A new shot shows a bicycle with a sidecar speeding past, marigolds loading it down, before Gardner changes tone and cuts to a shot of a cow eating a marigold; the shot holds, then cuts to a long shot of a cow, which

a b
c d

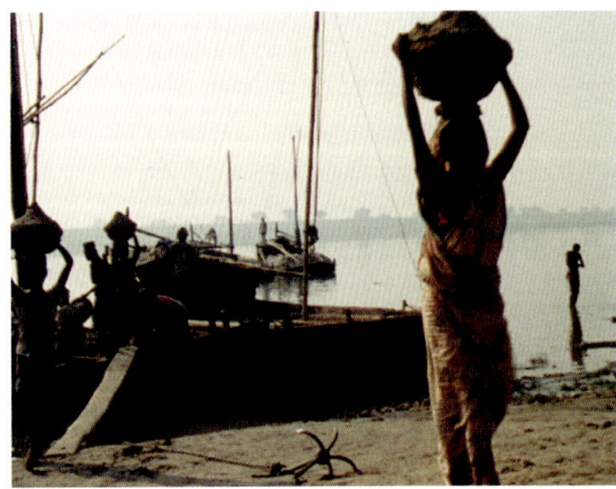

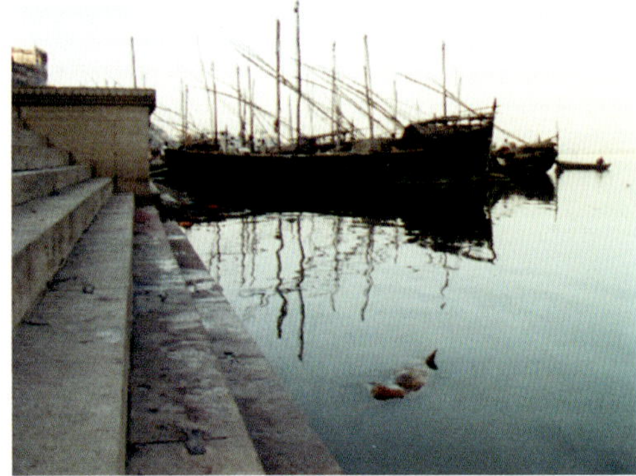

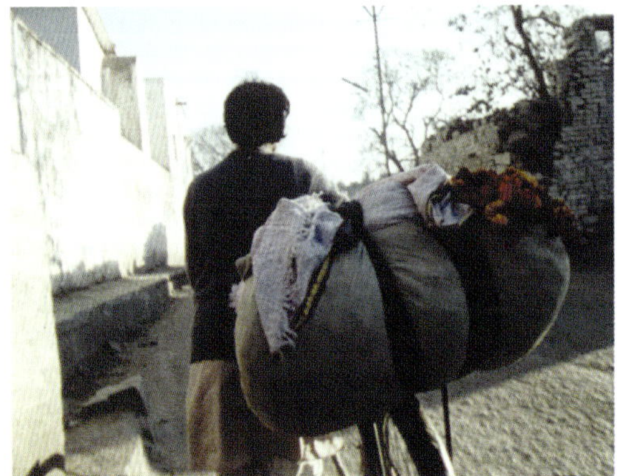

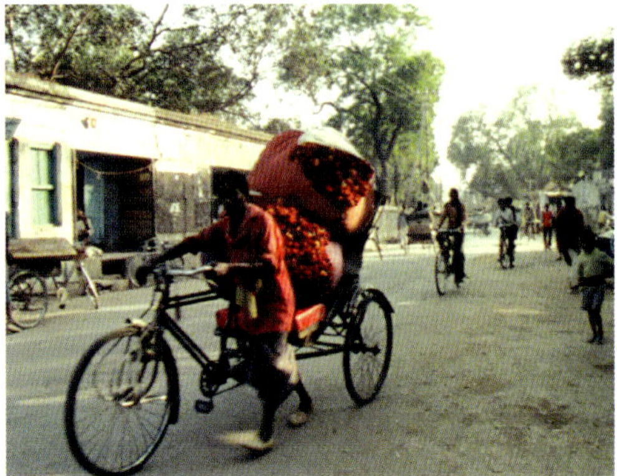

turns and runs toward the camera as a procession enters the alley behind it, a closer shot showing the procession to be organized around a litter bearing an object draped in marigolds. A final series of shots is organized around activities in a temple, as a woman bows before an altar, a priest chants and performs rituals, and two people assemble outside; throughout these shots, marigolds are present in the frame.

While the sequence is fairly clearly tied together by the presence of marigolds, its larger point is to show what Gardner describes as the "life history of a marigold," its place within the overall economy of the practices shown in the film.[21] The shots that bookend the sequence, of the boat and the temple, place the images of marigolds squarely within the context of ritual, suggesting a habitual cycle on which the marigolds are taken to the

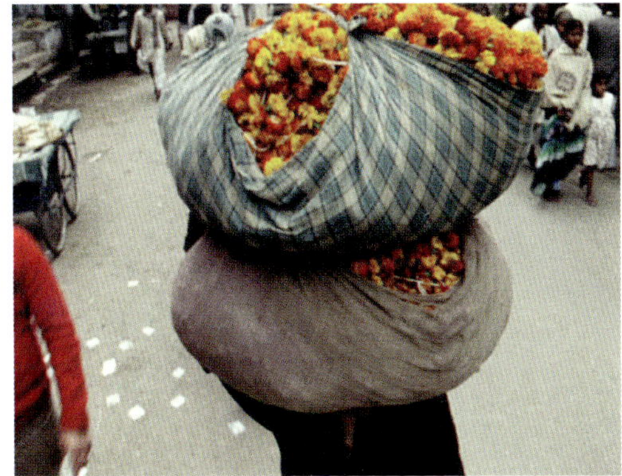
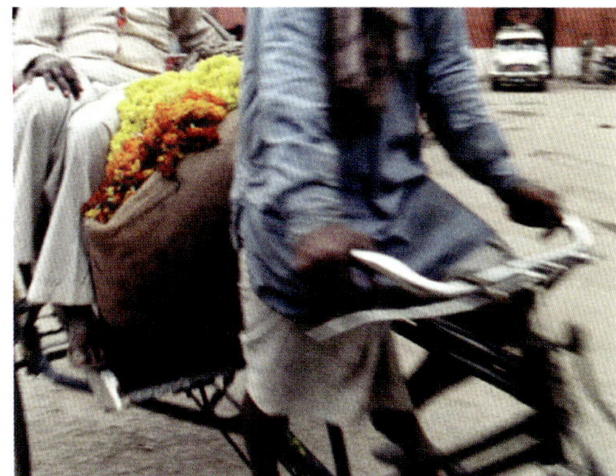
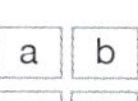

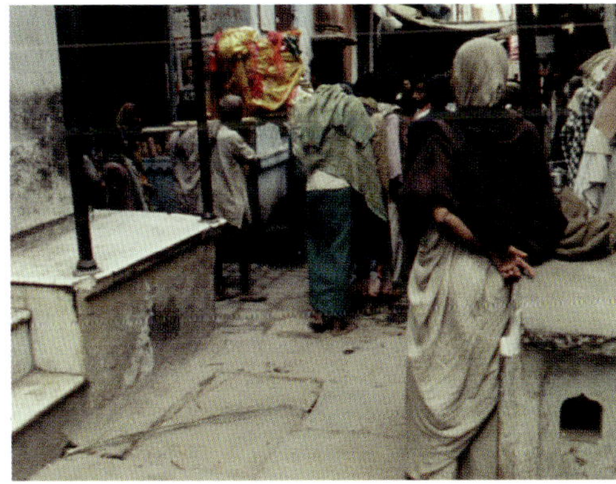
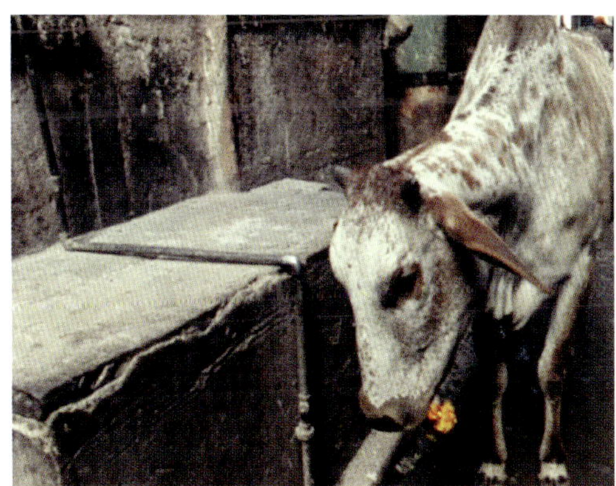
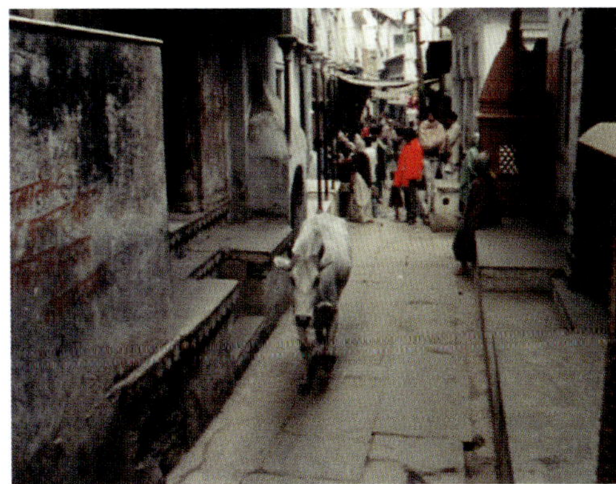

city and used in the various activities associated with death. (Even the cow eating the marigold, Gardner notes, is involved in "the whole idea of life recycling."[22]) Marigolds are everywhere, part of the basic fabric that makes up the rituals of Benares, and the editing patterns both produce the generality of the flowers—their omnipresence—and allow us to grasp their role in funereal practices.

The sense of ritual associated with the marigolds not only shapes this sequence but resonates across the film, inflecting readings of other sequences. A little more than halfway through the film, for example, we see a sequence in which a boat—an object that is everywhere in *Forest of Bliss* but which, until this point, is not the subject of any sustained treatment—is being launched. A series of shots shows a man performing a set of actions: he places handprints of yellow paint on the tools that were used to make the boat and around its circumference; pours water from a metal container onto the ground around it; and hangs rings of marigolds from its bow. Finally, the boat is dragged down steps toward the river, while another man scoops up water in his hands and pours it over the bow. Gardner then changes the direction of the sequence. First, he shows a human body floating in the water by some other steps, wrapped in a funeral shroud and covered in marigolds, mourners pouring water onto it; then he goes back to the boat being pushed into the river—but, as it floats off and men leap on board to control it, the camera pans back around to show a wide view of the steps leading down to the river, steps that are filled with clusters of people performing ritual actions of various kinds; finally there is a shot, now from on the steps and looking down, of a body covered in cloth and flowers and being taken down to the water on a litter.

In many ways, this sequence exemplifies both the difficulties and the ambitions of *Forest of Bliss*. We are given a series of shots replete with meaning—or, put differently, replete with actions that have meaning for the persons performing them—but with no overt interpretive guide to assist in understanding what we see. Again, it's the form of the sequence that gives us a way to read the actions it shows, that teaches us to recognize the kind of knowledge it's trying to produce. In this case, Gardner uses several features to ensure that we see the launching of a boat not as an idiosyncratic activity—the actions of these few individuals alone—but as a ritual practice. The marigolds are central to this, as Gardner draws on their ubiquitous involvement with ritual in order to allow the viewer to perform the right kind of abstraction toward generality; he takes a theme that has already been established and uses it to educate the viewer in a new context. Here, the marigolds prompt us to read the details of the launching as following the form of an ethnographic judgment: "When a person such as this builds a boat, he ends by putting palm prints of yellow paint around its sides, then tapping those edges with a hammer draped in marigolds." The shots that show the actual launching of the boat fill in the details of the actions—this is how the boat is sent into the water, how it is handled by the oarsman—before the pan back to the steps again draws attention to their generality: this is a ritual that holds for those who gather in Benares. The final shots of the sequence—showing the transport of the bodies; the presence of other groups on the stairs; and the body in the water—expand outward from a particular event to a general practice.

The launching of the boat is only one of a range of different activities connected with the funereal practices in Benares, occupying a place within the accepted ways of disposing bodies that Gardner shows (water, pyres, etc.). The work of the sequence is to lead us to a recognition of these claims, both their content and the scope of their application.

If this is right, and Gardner's films can be unpacked to show constructions that follow the form of ethnographic discourse, we might wonder whether his films are as radical as they have seemed. To be sure, *Forest of Bliss* lacks an explanatory voice-over, which often seems necessary for ethnographic film. But its ambition could still be construed as a fairly straightforward one: to find a cinematic form that is best able to record and present a ritual that exists independently of the act of filming. Gardner, that is, could be described as bringing his films in line with already existing ethnographic judgments, not making new ethnographic claims or providing fresh insights. A complex practice, to be sure, but one that is largely illustrative and familiar in its aims.

That's wrong, and not just for the reason that his films would not have aroused such controversy if their ambitions were less far-reaching. While it's worth bringing up the ways in which Gardner's work does fall into recognizable patterns, doing so can miss the originality of the films and their way of making arguments. One example comes toward the end of

a
b c d
e f g
h i j

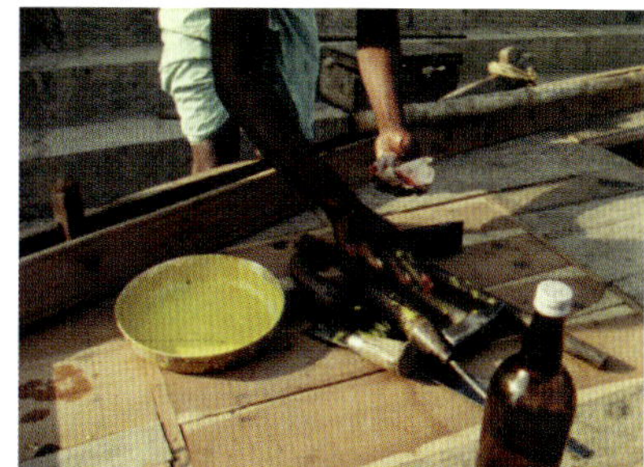

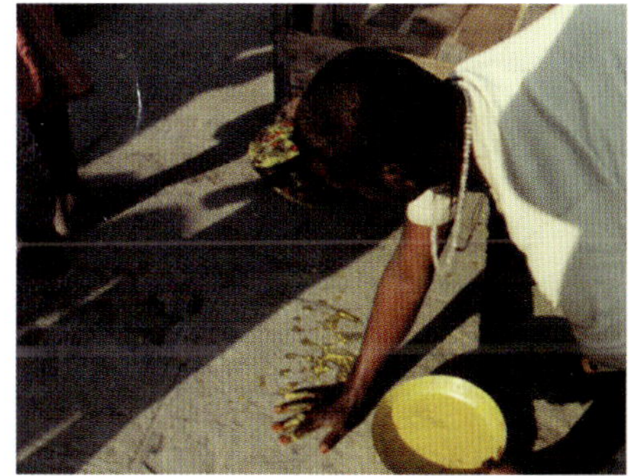

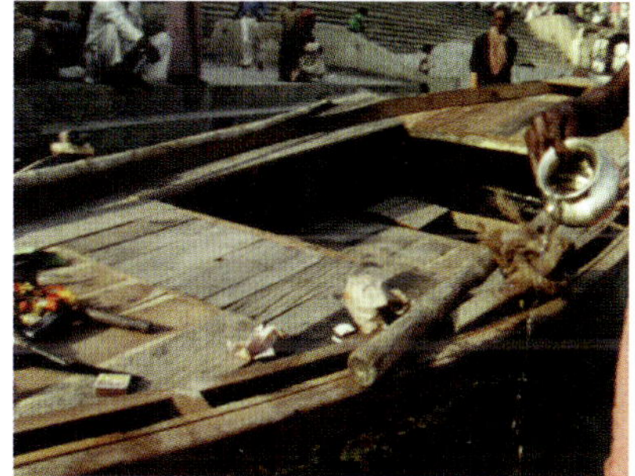

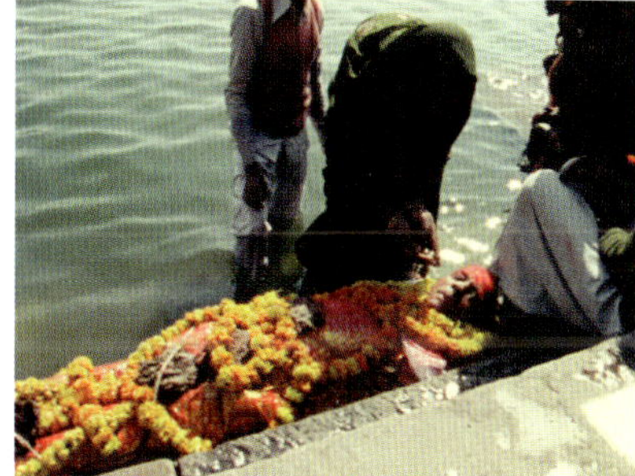

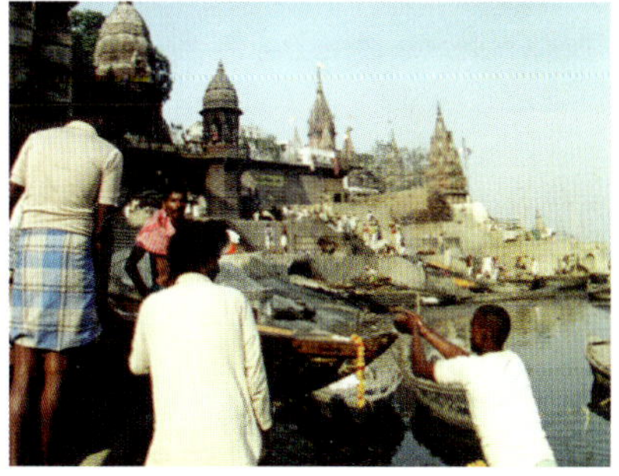

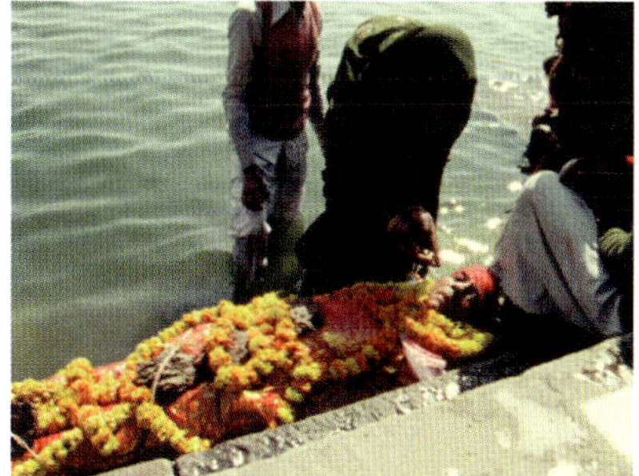

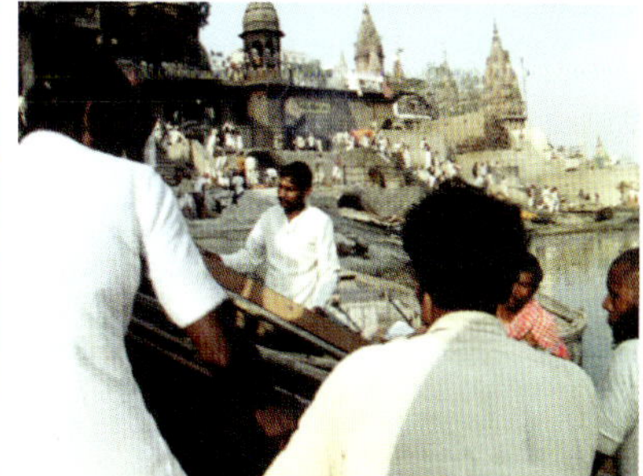

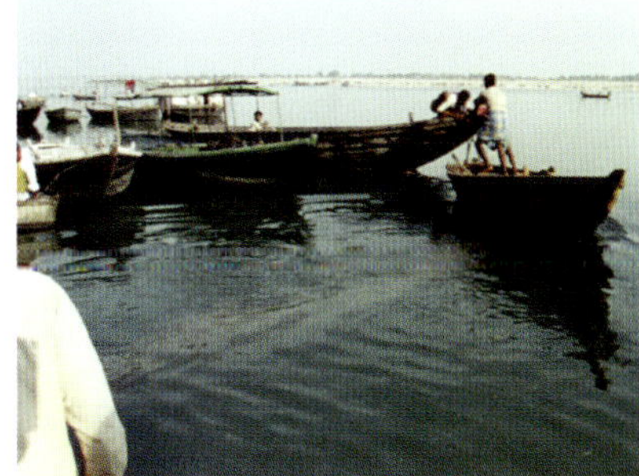

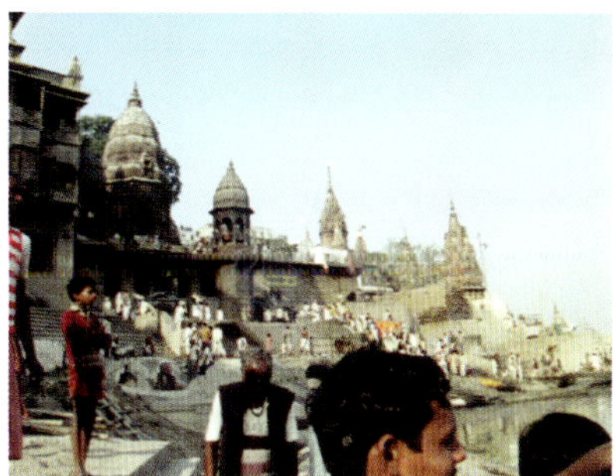

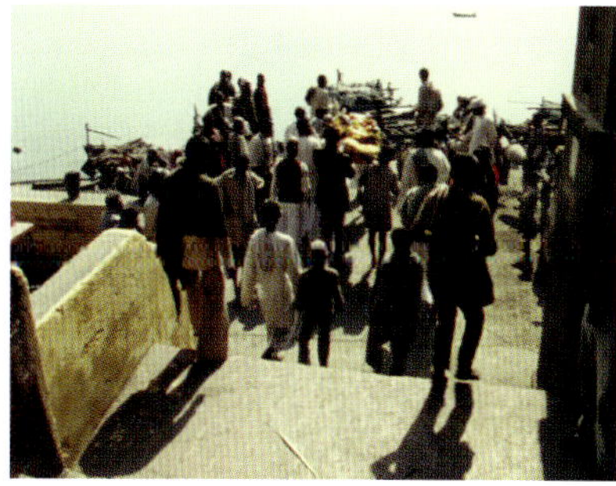

Forest of Bliss, in a sequence that brings together ostensibly unrelated activities, binding them into a broader account of the way that life and death are negotiated on the banks of the river. We see a series of shots of kids flying kites, or playing hopscotch, alongside the now familiar activities associated with the funereal rites and practices: the participants are not linked by actions, nor are they in the same space, and the activity of flying kites has no intrinsic relation to the ritual practices of cremation and mourning. What the film does is to use editing patterns—cuts on action, eyeline matches—to assert a relation between the activities, to allow each to be read in terms of the other.[23] So we might come to recognize the routinized aspects of the funereal activities, the way in which people's mundane actions are governed by a set of unspoken rules (which still allow for variation and flexibility). But, more importantly, we can see the flying of kites as having a status that is analogous to the funereal rites: Gardner suggests that the kids are part of a larger system of rituals that does not take place within the established channels. It's an astonishing gesture. Gardner is indicating that, despite the care of the rituals that we have seen and come to understand over the course of the film, the rituals that ostensibly structure the relation between life and death in Benares, there still exist a range of informal practices that are just as important in articulating that relation—and which go unnoticed by the more official activities. The play of the children, unsanctioned as it is, is part of the overall economy of ritual, even if there is no acknowledgement of it outside the film. Call it life, the counterpart to the omnipresence of death and its attendant practices. The play that Gardner shows is an activity that becomes ritual only in, and only because of, the film and its formal structures.

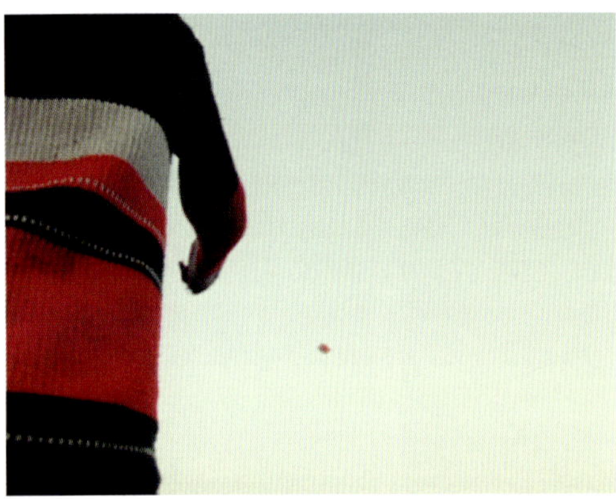

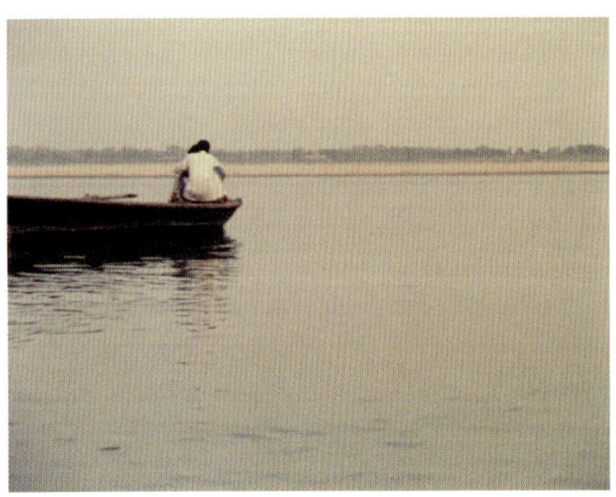

At this point, we might wonder if we are back with Rouch and Morin in *Chronicle of a Summer*, where the only evidence of a relation between events is the simple fact of the edit, the cut that joins two shots together. Rouch and Morin, though, were after something else. When they cut between people to link them, it is to create a counterpoint, a methodological lesson for the film's audience. Gardner, by contrast, uses such techniques to build a positive argument: film can provide knowledge about the place of ritual in everyday life, about the connection between the burials and the children, and it can do so in a way that makes a claim to truth within the world it shows. This project becomes explicit in one particular shot a bit earlier in *Forest of Bliss*, which is placed in the context of a series of shots that show boys flying kites. We see people on a boat, ferrying a body wrapped in white cloth into the middle of the river. As they dump the body over the side, a kite, barely visible in the background, appears within the frame and an instant later falls into the water.

Gardner has described this as one of his favorite moments in all his work: not just because there is a synchronization between the two actions, but because the connection exists independently of the filmmaker—and even went unnoticed by him at the time.[24] If much of the sequence is devoted to establishing the simple existence of a connection, this is a moment in which Gardner asserts—and does so through the recording function of the camera—that a claim has grounding in the world beyond the editing table.

In a sense, though, this moment is more of a nice flourish than a fundamental feature of Gardner's project. The point of his editing techniques is precisely that he does not have to rely on fortuitous events occurring in front of the camera, or on official and knowledgeable voice-overs. To the extent that the coincidence of body and kite aids Gardner's efforts to make ethnographic arguments, to show a social and religious world organized around the intersection between life and death, it does so because of the context that has already been established by the film. *Forest of Bliss*, like *Dead Birds*, makes ethnographic claims about groups of people through its formal techniques: claims that, while not founded on photographic reference, are nonetheless about the world the film depicts. These claims are available to interrogation, to questioning, to agreement, even to rejection. Gardner uses formal techniques to create new connections, to provide new insights that are part of the domain of ethnographic knowledge; that is to say, his films function as ethnographies by virtue of the claims they make in and through their aesthetic form.

Notes

1. See William Rothman, *Documentary Film Classics* (Cambridge: Cambridge University Press, 1997), 72.
2. *Chronicle of a Summer* was released in October 1961, and Gardner left for New Guinea in January of that year.
3. On his interest in parallel editing, see *Making* Forest of Bliss*: Intention, Circumstance, and Chance in Nonfiction Film* (Cambridge, MA: Harvard University Press, 2001), 37; on the place of fiction filmmakers as role models, see Ilisa Barbash, "Out of Words: A Conversation with Robert Gardner" in *The Cinema of Robert Gardner*, eds. Ilisa Barbash and Lucien Taylor (New York: Berg, 2007), 110.
4. Another example is the intercutting between Weyak going to his post and the sorting of the dead child's small bones: although it's possible that these events are indeed happening at the same time, there's no evidence, outside Gardner's assertion—and his use of "while" to create a connection—that this is indeed the case. On answerability to reality outside the film as a general criterion in nonfiction film, see Noël Carroll, "From Real to Reel: Entangled in Nonfiction Film" in *Theorizing the Moving Image* (Cambridge: Cambridge University Press, 1996), 223–252.
5. Peter Loizos, also drawing attention to these voice-overs, argues that Gardner "imaginatively projected himself into their thoughts and motives" because they were "characters in the story he tells"—Loizos, *Innovation in Ethnographic Film: From Innocence to Self-Consciousness, 1955–1985* (Chicago: University of Chicago Press, 1993), 151.
6. On the broader claim about the cinema verité imperative to record sound along with image, see Robert Gardner, *The Impulse to Preserve: Reflections of a Filmmaker* (New York: Other Press, 2006), 303.
7. For one version of this criticism, see Craig Mishler, "Narrativity and Metaphor in Ethnographic Film: A Critique of Robert Gardner's *Dead Birds*," *American Anthropologist* 87.3 (September 1985), 668–672.
8. For the latter case, while there are biographical and intellectual connections—not least that the Sensory Ethnography Lab at Harvard was founded a few years after Gardner's retirement and bears his legacy—Gardner's project is a different one than the more strictly immersive and experiential ambitions of sensory ethnography. Cf. Karen Nakamura, "Making Sense of Sensory Ethnography: The Sensual and the Multisensory," *American Anthropologist*, 115.1 (March 2013), 132–135.

9. Marcel Mauss, *A General Theory of Magic* [1902/1950], trans. Robert Brain (London and New York: Routledge, 2001), 171.

10. Ibid., 102.

11. In formulating this way of thinking about the kinds of claims that ethnography makes, I have been guided by arguments made by Michael Thompson about what he calls "natural-historical judgments." These judgments, he argues, function according to the form: "the wildebeest produces offspring in February"; "humans have ten fingers and ten toes." Such claims hold regardless of whether every example follows suit (e.g., some humans have different numbers of fingers and toes). To be sure, Thompson is explicit in his insistence that only natural entities involve this kind of judgment, and perhaps that's right; even so, we might say that ethnographic statements *aim* for the kind of status that judgments about species have. See the first part of Michael Thompson, *Life and Action: Elementary Structures of Practice and Practical Thought* (Cambridge, MA: Harvard University Press, 2008).

12. On this kind of argument, see Paul Horwich, *Truth*, 2nd ed. (New York: Oxford University Press, 1998), 79–81.

13. See, for example, Barbash, "Out of Words: A Conversation with Robert Gardner," 97; *Making* Forest of Bliss, 44; Gardner, *The Impulse to Preserve*, 309.

14. See *Making* Forest of Bliss, 16ff.

15. To be clear: I'm not interested in whether Gardner is right in claims about the various groups or practices he shows and describes, but rather in the form of the claims made by the film's sequences: What activities do they cover? With what generality do they hold true? What kinds of evidence could prove or disprove them? In short: what status do they have?

16. See Loizos, *Innovation in Ethnographic Film*, 140; Paul Henley, "Beyond the Burden of the Real" in *The Cinema of Robert Gardner*, 36; Marcus Banks, "The Burden of Symbols: Film and Representation in India," in *The Cinema of Robert Gardner*, 59.

17. See, for example, Roderick Coover, "Interactive Media and Construction(s) of Media in Nonfiction Film: The Case of *Dead Birds,*" in *The Cinema of Robert Gardner*, 203.

18. See Barbash, "Out of Words: A Conversation with Robert Gardner," 95. Interestingly, Karl Heider criticizes Gardner for being insufficiently attuned to the symbolism of the Dani (quoted in Coover, "Interactive Media and the Construction(s) of Memory," 210–211); cf. *Making* Forest of Bliss, 89.

19. On these charges, see Karl Heider, *Ethnographic Film*, rev. ed. (Austin: University of Texas Press, 2006), 38–42; Loizos, *Innovation in Ethnographic Film*, 139–168.

20. The full quote runs: "But even more important is the fact that there is no narrator telling you what you should know about what you are looking at. There is nobody saying: 'This is the Healer Mithai Lal, who gets up in his house in such a place and at such a time and starts down to the ghats for his morning bath in the Ganges'. . . I think it's clear that at least the pictorial style has changed; it's leading people into another way of watching so that, hopefully, they are now going to be taken up by the narrative structure implicit in certain kinds of detail. What's being depicted is pretty routine, but at the same time there is something very idiosyncratic about how this old man gets himself about. At the end of these scenes there shouldn't be any real mystery about what you've been watching" (*Making* Forest of Bliss, 26–27).

21. Gardner, *The Impulse to Preserve*, 286.

22. Ibid., 293.

23. About another part of the film, he writes: "These two shots, the birds and the corpse, are connected by editing, not at all by actuality. Still the birds are as incredibly actual as the corpse, and, of course, spliced together they're making the usual A+B=C. The corpse and the birds are put in here, when the wood is on its way up river to Manikarnika, in order to say that wood has some death-related meaning, that it is not just for keeping people warm at night. I would hope all this is fairly clear from the editing" (*Making* Forest of Bliss, 48).

24. Ibid., 110. Gardner also notes that the body being dumped in the water was that of another boy, killed when he fell from a rampart while flying a kite.

Chapter 5
Robert Gardner and Jean Rouch: *Regards Croisés*

Maxime Scheinfeigel

Translated from the French by Stefanie Goyette

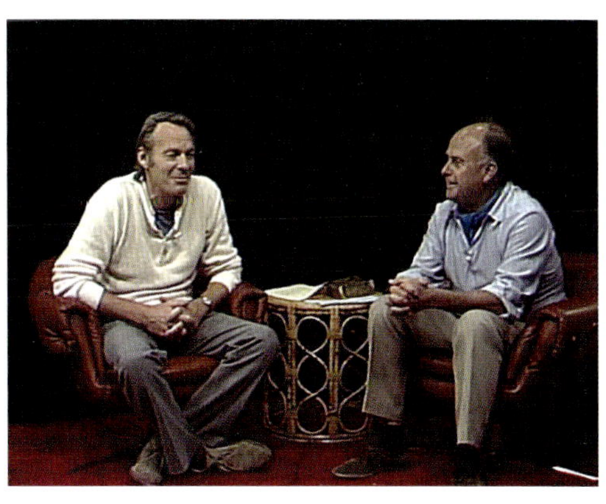

Robert Gardner with Jean Rouch on *Screening Room*

Jean Rouch made about 140 films, nearly all of them easy to find (in France, at least). In spite of this, he is not a popular director, though well known to a certain group of cinephiles, particularly those who are interested in the New Wave and have primarily seen his fiction films; and also known to interested amateurs or specialists on documentary cinema as it has progressed since the 1950s, notably with the appearance of "direct cinema." Robert Gardner was a younger (by eight years) contemporary of Rouch and, like the latter, participated in the international renaissance of ethnographic cinema. Yet, as a cinephile and documentary cinema enthusiast, and a Rouch scholar, I am not familiar with Gardner's body of work. Why? First, his films are not distributed in France, and it seems that they never have been.[1] Moreover, there is no French bibliography on Gardner.[2] I do not inquire here into this state of affairs, any more than I would speculate as to Gardner's affiliation with one school of cinema or another. I have recently had the luck to be able to see four of his films, and what I want to reflect on is how my familiarity with Rouch allows me to enter into the cinema of Gardner. The films I have seen are *Dead Birds* (1963), *Rivers of Sand* (1974), *Forest of Bliss* (1986), and *Deep Hearts* (1981), some of Gardner's most renowned work.[3] In the same time period, a few titles stand out from the abundant filmography of Rouch: *La Chasse au lion à l'arc* (1965) and *Un lion nommé l'Américain* (1969), *Gare du Nord* (1964), *Jaguar* (1967), *Petit à petit* (1970),

Cocorico, Monsieur Poulet ! (1974), and *Dionysos* (1984). Amid this list of films, a first link quickly appears between the two directors, a precise site of encounter, a singular event: accompanying the images of *Dead Birds* is the voice of Rouch, who narrates the French version of the commentary.

The Spoken Word

In this voice that serves as an entrance point for my exploration of the fabric woven between these two atypical directors, I seek something, but what? A first question poses itself to the spectator that I am, attuned to the cinema of Rouch and unfamiliar with that of Gardner: Does the voice of Rouch make *Dead Birds* a film that might be "Rouchian"? This is my initial question as I enter, with a French voice, into the universe of the American Gardner. Is it relevant? Will it be productive? At this first stage of contact with Gardner's body of work, I am not yet sure. Whatever may emerge, my question elicits an immediate response, if a qualified one: yes, Rouch's cinema rises up around his voice, even when the voice is not at home, in his own films; no, Rouch is only the mouthpiece of someone else whose cinema is not reducible to his. Let me explain.

Rouch offers his voice over Gardner's images just has he does over his own. A sweet, penetrating voice, a bit slow, elegant, the breath contained and the modulation of sounds controlled, especially when certain words point to a mystery, words that have no translation in the French language and that the commentary preserves just as they are. Rouch loves to pronounce them. He weaves in all of his films an immense, unbroken fabric that has become an unquestioned mark of his work's identity, intimately linked to that of his person, when present in the image or audible on the soundtrack. An example, among a thousand others, from the beginning of *La Chasse au lion à l'arc*, when, evoking "the story of Gaweye Gaweye," the voice-over of the demiurge director names the country of "Gandji Gamourou Gamourou," "the bush that is farther than far, the country of nowhere," this country where he is going to enter, he himself, in order to find traditional hunters. There are similar moments in *Dead Birds*, similar expressions to be heard, which the voice-over charges with an immediate poetry of the unfamiliar. And in other Gardner films that I have seen, a singular voice can also be heard, the voice of the filmmaker fashioning a world as he records images of it. The voice comes after the fact, during the postsynchronization of the films. At this moment, just as Jean Rouch narrates his films in the studio, the words that Gardner speaks over the images and the voice he uses to modulate them are not confined to the rhetorical constraint of the traditional voice-over narration of documentary films. They participate rather in a poïesis of the filmic word. The words and the voice that bears them come to establish themselves in the depths of the visual universe; they are a substantial element of it and are destined to endow it with a specific spatio-temporal dimension.

In this respect, it is possible to push further the comparison between the two filmmakers. Rouch began to narrate his own films early on, because he was dissatisfied with what happened to his first opus, *Au pays des mages noirs* (1946), a document recording a hippopotamus hunt, filmed in Niger. In the era when the film was released in theaters, short documentaries were shown as the first part of movie programs, before what was called "the big movie" (*le grand film*), and they were meant above all to entertain the public rather than instruct it. To this end, the film's distributor had arranged a voice-over narration for *Au pays des mages noirs* that seemed to mistake the endeavor for a sporting event, and misunderstood the ethnographic truth of the events that Rouch's camera had captured. Thence came his decision: from this point forward, he would narrate all of his own films, and he did so to the very end of a long and prolific career. One other trait is remarkable: aside from the technical modalities for sound recording that evolved and became increasingly faithful to the sounds of reality, Rouch's voice hardly changed between *Les Magiciens du Wanzerbé*, his second film, made in 1947, and *Dionysos*, filmed nearly forty years later. His voice is immediately recognizable, like a property inherent to his work; we might call it inalienable. The same phenomenon seems to traverse the films of Gardner. Certainly, his voice is used less than that of Rouch, but it also marks the identity of his films. The critic Alice Leroy, in remarking that Gardner is "the heir of Robert Flaherty or Jean Rouch," attributes this to the presence of the voice of these three filmmakers in their respective works. She writes that to the "recognizable voices [of Flaherty and Rouch], [Gardner] added his own, grave and preoccupied."[4]

Let us pursue the comparison. As in the work of Rouch, Gardner's voice pronounces words that incite the spectator-listener of the films to ask where their exact origin can be found, that is, to wonder about their cause (the meaning of the words) and their source (the localization of the voice in relation to represented space). How did the two directors come to pronounce the words that do not simply explain, or at least not just explain, that which is seen, but rather contribute to affirming the aesthetic of the filmic form in which they work? With regard to Rouch's speech, the origin is easy to guess, especially for the films that he made in sub-Saharan Africa, particularly in Niger and Mali. He was very familiar with these places and with their peoples; he understood and spoke a little or quite well a few of the vernacular languages of those regions. While remaining a "toubab" ("a man with white skin," as it is said in Wolof and throughout Mandingo territory), he became, in his own way, an African, such that he lived day to day with his friends from Ayorou, Niamey, and Bandiagara, and was initiated, like any good ethnologist, into the customs and rituals that he came to know on both a practical and an intellectual level. He could thus understand the people and speak with them in Bambara, Soninké, or Wolof, because these languages had permeated his thought and more or less modeled his mode of living, at least when he was on location. Rouch often functioned as the mouthpiece for his protagonists, as if their words had traversed his own body, and he could thus become his protagonists' *medium*, in the literal sense of the word. And when he spoke for himself, he used a language that was more literary than scientific, meant to account for the construction of the imagination of societies through their mythographies, their stories and legends, and their adaptation of myth to the here and now of daily life. It does not seem possible to understand Gardner's posture in the same way. It is true that on the occasion of each film, he remained for a considerable period of time on location, but from what I understand, he did not establish the same kind of durable relationship with the protagonists of his films. One does not see him as a filmmaker dedicated to immersing himself in, committing himself to, local languages and ways of life as he trekked in far-off countries.

Rouch was conscious of the powers of his voice; he knew its charm. But he also loved talk, not only his own but that of his wordy African friends, whose multiple conversations or long monologues form the primary element of the narration of many of his films, their most effective means of stimulation for audiences. Two of his African films must be mentioned, as they are essential to understanding this topic—*Moi, un noir* (1958) and *Jaguar*—as well as some of the films he made in France—*Chronique d'un été* (1961), *La Punition* (1962), *Gare du Nord*, *Petit à petit*—films in which the protagonists weave the story with their speech alone. Such empathy for the powers of speech can also be found in the work of certain notable American filmmakers, such as Shirley Clarke or John Cassavetes, but is not present in the films of Gardner. Two characteristics are worth noting in this area. Though *Dead Birds* has a fairly full commentary, Gardner tends more and more to rarify his own speech, limiting it to brief and rare comments. Then, when the protagonists of his films make themselves heard, he treats their voices in such a way that they take on a dimension that is more sonorous than verbal, more musical than narrative. The film that goes the farthest in this direction is *Forest of Bliss*. There is an important paradox: with no voice-over from Gardner, speech is nevertheless quite abundant in this film, but it does not have any meaning for spectators like us (i.e., speakers of French or English) because it is never translated. The protagonists of the film, living on the bank of the Ganges in Benares and tending to the cult of the dead, never cease to speak, to sing, to laugh, to lament, or to intone ritual chants. One among them, a mirthful old man, officiant of an unexplained ritual, distinguishes himself from the others by the extraordinarily harsh sounds of his voice, which give a particular color to the auditory atmosphere of the film. The incessant murmur of mingled or isolated voices, which is not reducible to the meaning of the words spoken, does not impose itself on the spectators as a discourse, but rather *impresses* itself on their auditory perception of the film, exactly as it is said that photographic film is "exposed" (*impressionnée*). The musical scoring of the voices, forming a keystone to the auditory architecture of the whole, becomes a fourth dimension of the image and produces a singular and unusual aesthetic. *Forest of Bliss* is a rare film, strangely experimental because the alliance of sound and image is constructed less according to the necessity of faithfully documenting what is seen and heard than to the necessity of creating a rhythmic correspondence, harmonic rather than harmonious, between the two. It seems that Robert Gardner, such a poet of cinema, seeks rhymed chords between visual and auditory forms.

At this point, a question arises that I cannot answer, as I lack specific knowledge of the realities filmed by Gardner: Is the type of audiovisual harmony that he embeds in all his films founded on chords he perceives on location, chords that would then take into account auditory conceptions and practices particular to the societies he observes? Or, are they a creative invention that the filmmaker charges with the task of distilling the image, making it relinquish its documentary character in favor of a filmic experience, of an ad-hoc audiovisual quest, of musical inspiration? The very possibility of such a question invites us to emphasize an essential trait that distinguishes the work of Gardner from that of Rouch: the voice does not have the same function. In Rouch's films, the voice bears the word and the word bears the world: it recounts the world, explains it, it exposes the time in it that constitutes the word as an element of story. It is impossible to forget that all his films, anchored in parts of the world where civilization has been passed down by oral tradition, have embraced with delight and empathy such a tradition, in order to make its functioning perceptible to Western audiences. In Gardner, the voice carries sound. It is special, but as any sound is special, in that it generates sensations, modulates vibrations, it is rhythm, it is music, and while this sound is made by human voices, this does not necessarily make it a *verbal* sound: it is and remains first and foremost a *vocal* sound. Omali Inda, the Hamar tribeswoman who speaks to us in *Rivers of Sand,* constitutes a remarkable exception. Otherwise, only the voice belonging to the filmmaker takes on the responsibility of transmitting a conception of the order of things—an abstract conception—designating things as constitutive of a more or less decipherable universe.

As a corollary, another difference marks the two filmmakers' bodies of work. Rouch is not only a voice-over in his films, he is also often present in the image, speaking with one or another of his protagonists. In *Chronique d'un été*, this occurs multiple times, and at the end he goes so far as to be filmed with Edgar Morin, the co-author of the film, while the two discuss the shooting and the results obtained so far. Thus, the audience can guess or imagine that Rouch and the subjects of the investigation led by him and Morin lived together for a certain time in the same space, crossed by one another in the area created by the film from real geographical space. On the other hand, Robert Gardner remains entirely a voice-over, a being of the off-screen, a pure "*acousmêtre*," or acoustic being, as Michel Chion would say.[5] So when the Hamar woman begins to speak in *Rivers of Sand*, she seems less to be addressing a particular listener—the filmmaker to whose questions she responds—than to be speaking to everyone and no one at the same time, that is to all of us, the spectators of the film, here and elsewhere, today, yesterday, and tomorrow.

Time

In this respect, another important characteristic distinguishes the work of Gardner from that of Rouch. In *Dead Birds* or *Forest of Bliss*, for example, the characters are not Africans, while Rouch always filmed Africans. But that is not all. Something is there, in the films of Gardner, that cannot be found in those of Rouch, and, conversely, something is found in Rouch that is not present in Gardner. This thing, present or absent, is drawn or sensed in the relationship with the Other specific to each of these filmmakers. In all of Rouch's films, documentary or fictional, there is a sense of historical contingency that allows the viewer to understand that the beings he films are people whose societies are at once traditional and determined by a context that might be called "exterior." At the beginning of the 1940s, Rouch arrived at Niamey, in the ex-French Sudan, and all of his work since that moment—whether overseeing the construction sites of bridges, as he did in those early years, or making films—inscribes itself within this colonial context. His first films, which are strict ethnographic documentaries, allow the audience to see and hear a world taking shape under the gaze of Western anthropology. But they already carry within themselves a desire to move beyond ethnocentrism even while the colonizer, if not the "toubab," is never far from the local society to which cinema had drawn near. *Les Maîtres fous* (1954) is the film that best understands this paradigm. It takes place in and just outside Accra, in Gold Coast (now Ghana). Nigerian worker émigrés, united in the sect of the Haukas, abandon themselves to a ritual of possession. Yet the spirits that "mount" or "ride" them (*chevauchent* in Rouch's commentary), that is to say, possess them, are not ancestral spirits, they are not of the same tribe, but are sent to the Nigerians by the English colonizers who then governed. Thus, the Africans filmed by Rouch, even when they perpetuate customs of their particular civilization, which is the case in all of his works from 1946 into the 1950s, are nonetheless inscribed in the history relative to a specific epoch, even a given moment. Characteristic of Rouch's work is the pregnant idea of the relativity of things, of beings, of points of view. André Labarthe was doubtless the first to remark this when he wrote in 1960, in a memorable text where he evokes the work of several French directors contemporary to the New Wave, including Rouch,[6] that "the new cinema, like the lessons of news film, of television film, and of certain neo-realist works, commits to seeking *the best possible angle* in given situations, exactly as when, in contemporary life, we crane our necks to *better* see an accident in the street even while it is impossible for us to attain the ideal viewpoint, the absolute point of view."[7] Several of Rouch's films deal with this relativity that he cherished, notably *Petit à Petit*, wherein two Nigerians come to Paris and discover French civilization and mores, just as two Persian friends did before them, imagined by Montesquieu in 1721 in *Les Lettres persanes*, where letters home evoke what constitutes for the two friends the Parisians' strangeness. Rouch claimed the book as his inspiration for *Petit à Petit*.

On the contrary, or so it seems to me, the story of *Dead Birds* and those of *Rivers of Sand* and *Deep Hearts* unfold in space-times without precise limits. *Dead Birds*, for example, orders events along a narrative modality and a simple, explicit chronology that are easy to trace. The film takes place in Papua New Guinea; on two sides of a river, two tribes are engaged in an endless war. Gardner draws close to only one of the two tribes, the other being designated in the film as the enemy. First act: an enemy is killed. Second act: his tribe takes revenge by killing a child of the first tribe. Epilogue: we see the incineration of the dead child. Yet, this story, while factual, is entirely atemporal. The three episodes are one recent link in a chain that we are given to understand as ancient, uninterrupted, "customary" (*coutumier*), we might say, if we are speaking the language of ethnology. The custom, which has the goal here of appeasing the spirits of the dead, is ordered according to a ritual determined by the animist beliefs of the two tribes. Gardner's cinema documents a custom outside of the age; he transmits a scenario belonging to eternity, unfolding in faraway Papua New Guinea, a place hardly known to Westerners. And the vision of *Rivers of Sand* confirms the a-chronological impression given by *Dead Birds*. In *Rivers of Sand*, time is also suspended in a kind of atemporal eternity, even if we have traveled from Papua New Guinea in 1961 to Ethiopia in 1974. This time, a single tribe, the Hamar, occupies the entire filmed space. In the tribe, there are two kinds of beings, men and women, and two categories, adults and children, a classification to which animals must be added. Men have one sole occupation: hunting. They reign over the women, who are responsible for all the other activities that are necessary for life: agriculture, grinding the sorghum, preparing food, collecting wood, washing, and so on. From their childhood, they are ruthlessly marked by their enslavement: the men shackle the little girls' ankles, wrists, and neck with heavy metal rings, which increase in weight and number as the girls grow. When they reach puberty, the men marry them and beat them daily, ritually. Their skin is scarified, and some of their teeth pulled. All this, whose insupportable cruelty cannot be tempered in the eyes of the Western spectator, seems to come from an immemorial past, which is recounted and which thus renders the present, documented by the film, an unchangeable *facsimile* of this past. Here, nothing is seen or heard that would allow us to believe that the future will be different. This characteristic of timelessness is more striking still because a woman, a singular protagonist, speaks to the camera, and her words are heard *as if they have been recorded in synchronous sound*.[8] A yawning chasm opens between, on the one hand, the present *hic et nunc* of the woman who evokes a suffering relative to her person and that of the other women of the tribe, a suffering that she experiences even as she speaks of it, and, on the other hand, the bottomless abyss of an impersonal and archaic time that her words call forth.

With the Hamar woman, the cinema of Gardner may recall that of Rouch. We may think of *Moi, un noir*, whose main character, the dock worker Robinson, played by Oumarou Ganda, who also sometimes speaks to the camera, describes throughout the film in voice-over the difficulties of his life as a Nigerian immigrant living in Abidjan. Yet *Moi, un noir*, a film shot according to the methods of direct cinema, had its sound nonetheless entirely recorded in studio, and is a fiction. So, no, it is probably not this film that should be compared to *Rivers of Sand*, which is a documentary. *Chronique d'été*, perhaps? Yes, despite the apparent paradox of comparing Ethiopian villagers to Parisian city dwellers. In Gardner's work in 1974, as in that of Rouch in 1960, cinema fulfills the same function: it demands from its source a voice that is original and autonomous, which could not exist without the film, but which renders the film singular, fully subjective with regard to the filmed subject. Thus, when we hear the Hamar woman denounce and deplore the cruelty of the men, we can also hear the echo of one of the most striking protagonists of *Chronique d'un éte*, Marceline Loridan, who was then a young woman. She recounts—in synchronized, live-recorded sound[9]—her deportation and that of her family to a concentration camp in Nazi Germany. The two women trace the portrait of a terrifying society, through the description of everyday treatment, for the Hamar woman, and through the story of an exceptional occurrence, for the French woman. Both evoke this lived or remembered reality with the necessary acuity and accuracy, which no scientific discourse could make so affecting, so perceptible. Nonetheless, a fundamental difference persists between the two films: the Ethiopian woman is bitter, rebellious, but nothing in her speech implies that Hamar society will change. The film is not even over when she already seems to have returned to her distant world, where we can assume that she will continue to fulfill the role that is hers and that she evokes in speaking with her interlocutor (Gardner himself?). Her condition is past, present, and future, unchangeable, almost impersonal. Marceline Loridan, on the other hand, has an individual destiny, and viewers of *Chronique d'un été* eventually learned that she became a filmmaker and married the famous documentary filmmaker Joris Ivens. Thus, the image of the sad young woman in *Chronique d'un été* goes beyond the Rouchian zone of cinema and resonates in the culture and the memory of many regular visitors to the world of documentary cinema, whether that of Rouch or others.

The Dani of Papua and the Hamar of Ethiopia seem to be alone in a world that will not exist, or not anymore, from the moment that the borders of their territory are breached and overrun. Around them and within them, as they are, a landscape is drawn. It is made of time and of space, but the two seem unfathomable, permanent, intangible. The Dani and the Hamar live as if immersed in an ocean, an ocean of time, where they swim in weightlessness, their physical bodies, their simply human presences, not leaving traces on the surface of tides that reconstruct themselves identically, or so we may believe, generation after generation. It is only in the depths to which some of them descend that there is something else to be found: their individual souls and the spirits that incarnate themselves in these people. For the Dani, it is not good to encounter the spirits or to awake them, whence the incessant quest for equilibrium between the dead of the two tribes at war, a death for a death to placate the spirits. For the Hamar, the animals that men kill—which they divide up down to the entrails, from which they drink the fresh blood—are the instruments through which men's souls draw power against the terror engendered by the presence of spirits. These spirits are always spying on them; men are their prey in the same way that the animals, raised or hunted, are the natural prey of men. In the work of Rouch we see men drink the blood of a dog they have just killed, daubing themselves with it and rejoicing in it. This scene is from *Les Maîtres fous*, mentioned earlier, the renowned documentary filmed in a single day, a film that shocked both literate Africans and European intellectuals.[10] But the Haukas filmed by Rouch celebrate a ritual that, even if it passes through the archaic process of trance, is still anchored in the contingent reality of the colonial era. It has already been said: the Haukas have embedded new gods in the modalities of an ancestral ritual, the gods given to them by colonization. There is more. The film ends with an epilogue in which the protagonists come back. They are filmed one by one, as if for a review, and each one has resumed his ordinary appearance, each gives himself over to his quotidian activities, whose details are given by Rouch. They are immersed again in the banality of the quotidian, they are again and always in the current of a time that passes for them as for the whole world, and which is tuned to the present of a single day in the year 1954, at Accra. The same cannot be said for the characters in the films of Gardner: their present is exemplarily impossible to fix in time.

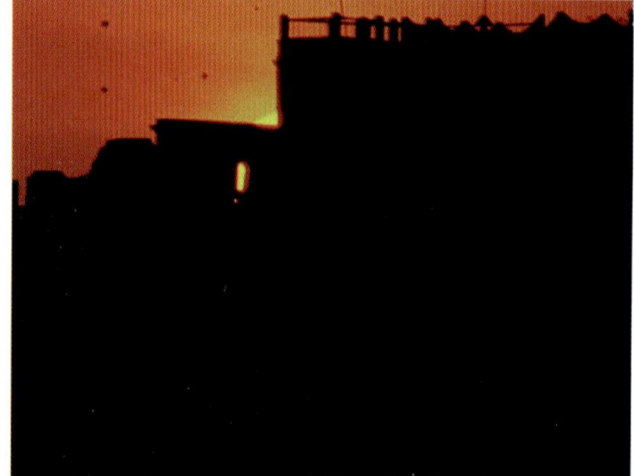

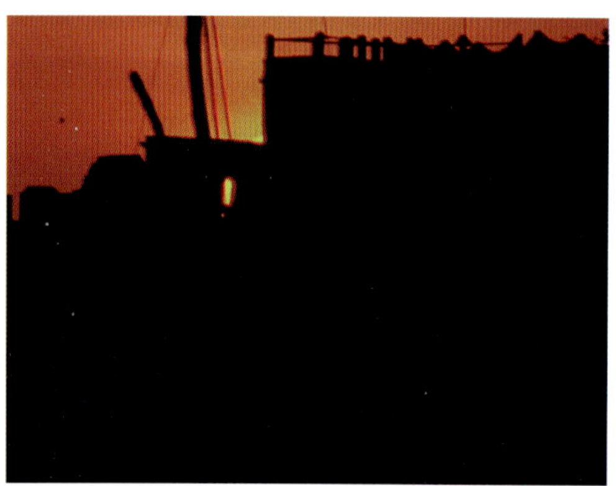

Aesthetics

Forest of Bliss and *Deep Hearts* demonstrate further differences between the work of Gardner and that of Rouch. The first film was made in India, in Benares, the second in Niger among the Peulh Bororo. Yet, in each of these films, specific and similar cinematic gestures occur that are striking, such as the contemplation of slowness or stasis, with metaphoric overtones. For example, in *Forest of Bliss* a recurring as-if slow motion rendering of boats going up and down the Ganges, and in *Deep Hearts*, slow motion on the paws of camels running in the brush. In *Forest of Bliss*, one slow shot progresses until it distills all those that came before it. The sun is setting behind a high crenellated wall, cast in deep shadow, because it is backlit. Above stretches a vast, blazing, darkening sky. It is then that behind the wall, entering from the left of the shot, a ship's mast and sail, also backlit, slowly passes, dragging in its wake the shadows of the coming night, shadows that will extinguish the fires of the setting sun.

Expressionist cinema, that of Wiene and of Murnau, could not have better rendered tangible the pressure of the forces of the night against those of the day. *Deep Hearts* contains similar moments of aesthetic bravura, for example, in the still image showing a close-up on the face of one of the Bororo dancers. Then movement returns, but in slow motion, as the face of the dancer begins to move and undulate slowly to the strangely clarifying rhythm of a smile or a wink addressed to some unknown person.

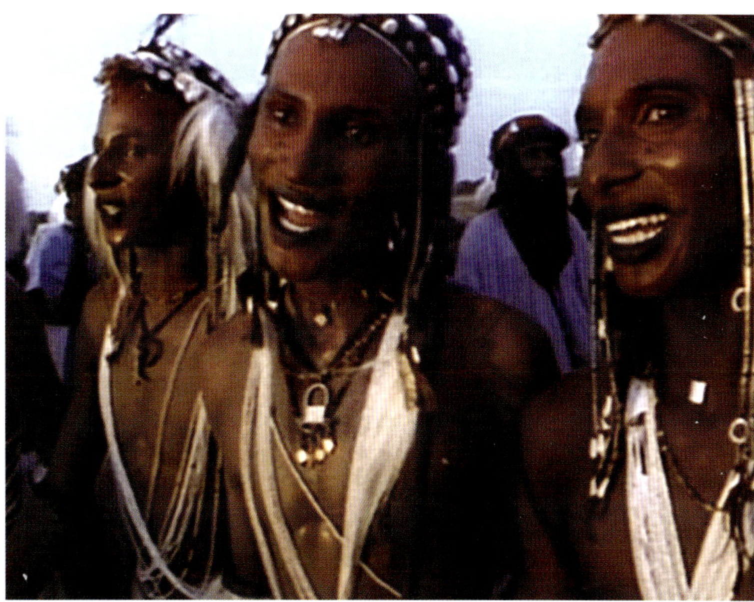

This slow-motion sequence and several others of the same type focusing on the magnificently painted faces of young men set forth their traits as if so many lines forming a drawing, or rather a figure, in the most literal sense of the word, the sense that calls on the idea of the *figura*, of the form that is suggestive *par excellence*. The image not only allows us to see the simple facial expressions, but beyond this allows a singular figure to emerge, almost abstract, that of a pure autonomous movement undulating on a surface, where it disengages from the very idea of the face that supports the undulation. A troubling de-figuration that paradoxically celebrates the beauty of these men, through a strange, indefinite alliance, that seems to be purely iconic, between the movement of their features and the very movement of the cinematograph. Gardner sets in motion a process of de-realizing the contingent facts and beings that he films. On the Ganges, the boat disappears in its aspect as boat, no longer a circumstantial mode of transport, but rather a sort of baccamerak-lit dark presence in a slow advance, the pure idea of another movement, namely that which belongs to life and its progression towards a final stasis—death. This sequence is characterized by a significant mythological theme occurring in many civilizations: the passage from one bank (life) to the other (death), made on a river that one travels down or traverses. The film that documents the uses and customs of inhabitants of a large Indian city in the twentieth century—let us remember this—takes for its motif this universal and archaic history that seems to be its true subject. Moreover, in the bush of Niger, the camels also disappear—their bodies disappear—in favor of the slow-motion shot and the narrowed frame as they are reduced to the graceful rolling of their feet. The slow-motion shot transforms the camels' feet into rapid, elegant wheels from which surges forth a perpetual movement, traced in the air where these animals seem to float, even while they are earthbound. And here, again, the film takes on a form of abstraction, which now recalls an idea widely shared and inscribed in the wisdom of Saharan voyagers for whom the camel is "the ship of the desert."[11]

Gardner's work is traversed by a conception of images more *figural* than figurative: sails of phantom ships, undulations of human faces, rolling of the feet of camels. Films that work such a plastic effect on precise objects or beings can be considered as art films or experimental films. Beyond the forms actualized in the images, the films attain an idea that they do not designate as such but that they allow to be guessed or glimpsed, like a secret that is hidden behind a door. And it is necessary that the door open so that the idea can surge forth from the depth of the image that it subtends. The manifestation of the idea emerges less from the decoding of meaning than by the aesthetic perception of lines and forms, of movements and sounds, of vibrations and the visual and auditory echoes that these vibrations simultaneously engender.

This phenomenon does not seem to mark Rouch's films. His formal mission aimed at another horizon and was achieved through other protocols. A term can summarize it: it is the *direct*, a term invented by the Italian documentary filmmaker Enrico Fulchignoni at an opportune moment to replace the expression Edgar Morin had employed in 1960 to evoke the work accomplished by the filming of *Chronique d'un été*: "*cinéma-vérité*." Rouch wanted to grasp not *the* truth of the world, but *a* truth of beings, of events, of places that he filmed, subjectively, not in complete "truth." For this reason he has become, among other things, the expert—which he was not in the beginning—of filming with a portable synch-sound camera, a practice introduced to him by the Canadian Michel Brault. He thus discovered how to better attach his gaze and that of his camera to the movements of things and of beings; at the same time he learned how to conduct the filming of his works in a discontinuous flux that foreshadowed the order of the final montage. That is to say, nothing is less "posed" than Rouch's work. The framing and the point of view are sometimes even accidental, except that, because he is often familiar with the customs, places, and people he films, Rouch had a knowledge and an experience that allowed him to anticipate his place as an observer and thus to prepare the framing and path of the camera. But the beauty of the images was not important to him; his vision did not concern itself with an aesthetic project.[12] Story was much more urgent—all stories—and words, let us repeat, were story's principal source and best ambassador. His cinema is, more than that of Gardner, a cinema of speech, of the word, the image being a vector of time that speaks in order to traverse a space or to construct the borders of a story. *Dionysos* is the most revelatory in this regard because of the significant gap between the very title of the film and what it represents. The film shows the transformation of a Citroën 2CV by an American intellectual, who has come to Paris to defend his philosophy dissertation at the Sorbonne. The procedure here is to give a name to things in order for the image to take its full shape, and it is thus that the spectator is immediately led to understand that the 2CV is a divine creation.[13] In the same vein, the protagonists of the films are not simply what they appear to be. The American Hugh Gray, the workers, and the French foremen of the factory are servants of Dionysus, the young women who dance in the workshop where this strange vehicle is being constructed are Maenads, and so on. . . . But nothing in the images of the film shows the object or the beings in some special light, no formal project transforms the prosaic nature of their appearance. Their form is realist: it is not attuned to the fantastic, legendary discourse that organizes the film. The spectator is invited to believe in this discourse, and if this belief does not come, the film runs the risk of becoming ridiculous, which certain critics have not failed to point out.

It is perhaps at this point that we can see most clearly the specific natures of the two bodies of work brought together here, as they had been earlier by the two filmmakers themselves, at their own initiative. Our starting point was the place where Robert Gardner's images vibrated with the sound of Jean Rouch's voice. It is time now to finally ask the question that we have not yet confronted: Why did Gardner ask Rouch to record the commentary for one of his films?

The Imaginary

Gardner and Rouch encountered each other and appeared together a number of times. The two filmmakers paid one another reciprocal attention and showed mutual respect. Gardner was sufficiently interested in Rouch that in 1980 he invited him to show and speak of his work on Gardner's television show, *Screening Room*, where he primarily featured experimental filmmakers. Gardner appreciated Rouch well enough to ask him to record the French commentary for one of his most important films—and Rouch complied. These facts are real, but how can we go further, beyond these signs of mutual recognition, towards an understanding of what would make possible a serious artistic encounter, indeed a collaboration, between the two?

By stepping back from the fine details of the films, it is possible to situate the two directors in a territory of cinema where the same lines of force and tension converge. Gardner and Rouch entered cinema in the same way, at the same moment. With other inventive filmmakers, they significantly eroded the walls between two filmic forms that had been rigorously distinct up to that moment, fiction and documentary. Another shared feature creates an even narrower rapport between the two: they are not only creators of documentaries, but of ethnographic films. And in these highly specialized films they both displace the rules of a well-established protocol, according to which the ethnographic filmmaker does not make "his" cinema; he is rather in the service of ethnology, for which he provides images that will feed analysis and support or undermine the theories of anthropology. Gardner and Rouch emancipate themselves from this scientific tutelage by charging their images with an expressive potential for which they are the creators and the masters. It is thus that in beginning with their interest in the same types of facts, that is, the rituals linked to animistic beliefs, they both refuse to problematize them, attempting rather to show them as they are or, for Rouch especially, to recount them not with the vocabulary of science, but rather with that of the participants in the rituals he films. And all of this occurs with them not without a neat paradox: they were early affiliated with and remained in constant contact with universities. The first spectators to whom their films were shown were their colleagues and their students in anthropology—a public with expectations and demands that are specifically linked to scientific resolutions. But the two directors were manifestly able to respond to these demands, and their work has really mattered to anthropologists over the years. At the same time, Rouch and Gardner largely surpassed the limits of the university context. Rouch made fiction films; he was friendly with New Wave filmmakers; he was a director of the Cinémathèque Française. Gardner was interested not only in far-off peoples. He also worked with artists, painters, sculptors, and photographers, to whom he consecrated a large part of his filmmaking. It is clear that his work with these artists, from Mark Tobey in 1952 to Christian Boltanski in 2011, influenced his thought and his work, which allowed him to become a filmmaker-artist while remaining a practitioner of filmic anthropology. At least this is what his films show, even when they are a priori strictly ethnographic. Further, there is a point of substantial contact in the depths of the respective bodies of work of Rouch and Gardner, which may appear most clearly where the qualities they each display, already described by me, begin to turn back on themselves.

I have remarked that Rouch's films bathe in the historical contingency of a localized space and time, relative to a constantly changing present. But I have also noted that the filmmaker was in love with a particular form of story, the fable, *La Chasse au lion à l'arc* and *Dionysos* being convincing examples of this love. But what happens in these two films? In the first, the traditional hunters put themselves in the service of shepherds and livestock farmers. They track the lions who decimate the herds. One of these lions, being more ferocious and clever than the others, is untraceable. The hunters baptize him "the American." And this lion, thus distinguished from others in the imagination of the hunters, reappears four years later. Rouch again takes up his camera and follows the lion's trail (*Un Lion nommé l'Américain*). He is still impossible to find . . . except that, a few months after the filming and notwithstanding the ancestral laws regulating lion hunting, he is prosaically felled by a shooter armed with a rifle! In *Dionysos*, part of the film shows the collision between a faraway past and a current present, as well as the immediate correspondence between improbable beings arisen from Greek mythology and the contemporaries of Jean Rouch. The amateur actors who help to make the film or who act in it "play characters in a way related to themselves (. . .) Hugh Gray is played by the anthropologist, filmmaker, and poet, Jean Monod; on his dissertation committee sit Jean Sauvy, Germaine Dieterlen, and Enrico Fulchignoni; at their side is the ethnologist Hélène Puiseux in the role of Ariadne."[14] If Rouch works more in the prose than in the poetry of cinema, his films are nonetheless capable of establishing a large gap between what is concrete in the representation, the here and now, and what takes form in the imagination, there and elsewhere. The films are conceived by the filmmaker in order to produce specific effects of the image—as with the figures of style of verbal language—across which the spectators are called to relate what they perceive on the surface of the screen to the deep or the distant in which this surface is anchored. For example, *La Chasse au lion à l'arc* is first and foremost a film that documents the practices and customs of traditional hunting. But behind the live recording of events related to the hunt, the film brings forth another dimension, one that is entirely subjective, since it accounts for the hunters' invention of a new being, a lion, traditionally considered as the king of the animals, who becomes here the representative of the most powerful conqueror of modern times, "the American," for whom the lion is an allegory. The same can be said of *Dionysos*: the god referred to in the film's title is part of the Greek pantheon. He does not live on Mount Olympus with the other gods; rather, he wanders a bit everywhere. He is the emblem of the nonsedentary, the other, the marginal. *Dionysos* is the story of the various adventures of his incessant, wine-soaked peregrinations, which are the origin of Greek theatre, where the spoken word holds the most important role. So, when the ethnologist Jean Monod, who left the university and became a poet, plays an alter ego or a realistic representative of Rouch and embodies an apprentice demiurge come from elsewhere—again, from America—we can see the image of Dionysus emerge in a kind of immediate transparency. Dionysus is the god most known for his lack of discipline, and he inspired both Rouch, the filmmaker, and Monod, the actor,[15] just as he inspired before them many authors and actors of Greek theatre. Stated differently, behind the current present of the Rouchian stories, the legendary or mythological fable is never far away. With the Africans and the Europeans filmed by Rouch, their individual, local history is traversed by a history that is more vast and more ancient, a history that each civilization retells to itself, most importantly in order to assure its own sustainability. Thus, the ethnography of Rouch's work consists less in plumbing the sociological or philosophical singularities of peoples through their ways of life or their diverse cultural productions than in recalling to their present an immaterial and yet explicit past. And through this constitution of "a singular tissue of time and space: appearance of the distant, however close it might be,"[16] something of universal anthropology is perhaps attained. It might be said that anthropology, a science that is entirely Western with its origin in Enlightenment Europe, shifts its basis here and resizes itself to a scale more planetary and more diversified.

The work of Robert Gardner sets in motion a similar process; he also permits this same "distant," something like the famous "aura" of Walter Benjamin,[17] to emerge in the present of his films. His method differs from that of Rouch. As I stated earlier, it is especially though the figural value of his plastic work on images and sounds that the ethnographic document becomes a cinematographic poem. Let us add to this the fact that unlike Rouch, who specializes in African ethnography, Gardner travels on all the continents and, as a result, there appear in his films images of a varied human type, where resemblance and dissemblance, inextricably linked, reign simultaneously. Let me explain. The Dani of Papua, the Hamar of Ethiopia, or the Indians of Benares are distant from Gardner himself, and behind him are the all the white Europeans or Americans that his culture brings along with him, even on his filming locations. For example, the Dani wage between them an incessant war that recalls those fought throughout the twentieth century in the Middle East, in South Asia, in Europe, whether for political, economic, or pseudo-"tribal" motivations.[18] The woman in *Rivers of Sand* could have been a militant in the feminist movement that arose at the end of the sixties in the United States and Europe. Thus, the images of the films of Gardner, seemingly timeless, function like mirrors that reflect more than an archaic mythography. Indeed, in the water of these mirrors we can see apparitions taking shape, ideas coming alive. They signal to us that a modernity relative to the present of the filming is there; they allow us to divine that the ancestral history of the individuals who are filmed is also inscribed in contemporary history. *Forest of Bliss* is perhaps the film that makes this phenomenon the most perceptible, as the confrontation is so abrupt between the ceaseless cycle of human existence and the contingent finitude of the life of each person. The men who tend to the dead, washing them in the river, dressing them, burning them, are at the exact intersection between the two worlds. As officiants of the cult of the dead, they are in a separate, sacred place, truly an extraordinary place. But their task is incessant; it is performed daily, under the open sky, at the bank of a river where other people walk and live, concerned with other activities. In other words, the times of the dead and the living are mixed in the same space-time, which *Forest of Bliss* defines by constructing a cycle that is less eternal than animated by the same movement as that of life, its fragility, its constant resumption or re-beginning. The distant finds an image in the near; the ritual is accomplished in the prosaic; the permanent is incarnated in the contingent. This phenomenon, already at work in the films of Rouch, but constructed according to an inverse process, allows the spectator to sense that despite its appearance to the contrary, each of Gardner's films is inspired by the actuality of the world.

I conclude this brief look at the web woven between the two bodies of work by saying that they are distinct because of their respective and irreducible singularity, but they resonate nonetheless. In fact, they can be understood in an overview as if the one was the reverse shot of the other. The two auteurs doubtless knew this, since their cinema—hybrid and prolific—is yet traversed by highly visible lines of force. The hypothesis of their complicity—which I have presumed to be real—raises a question in tune with the title of Rouch's last film, *Le Rêve plus fort que la mort* (2002). If, inversing the relation that existed between them, Rouch had asked Gardner to record the commentary for one of his films, which would have been chosen? Would they have agreed on the film? It is impossible to answer such a question. We can only imagine that the choice would have been as difficult for Jean Rouch as for Robert Gardner, because all of the films of the first could lend themselves to the voice of the second.

Notes

1. However, there are subtitled copies available in the media library of the Quai Branly museum.
2. It is for this reason that Gardner is not mentioned in Gilles Marsolais' *L'Aventure du cinéma* (Seghers éditeur, 1974). This work is still one of the most important methodical reviews of documentary filmmakers and schools that appeared in the 1950s in Europe and North America.
3. Thanks to the helpfulness of Charles Warren, Rebecca Meyers, and William Rothman, to whom I address my most keen and sincere thanks for having given me the opportunity to encounter an essential cinematic corpus in the landscape of documentary filmmaking, a corpus that was unknown to me and that has been seductive and intriguing.
4. Alice Leroy, *Cinéaste des espaces-frontières—Robert Gardner*, on the website critikat.com/Robert-Gardner.
5. Michel Chion borrowed this concept from Pierre Schaeffer, founder of the GRM (Groupe de Recherche Musicale), who coined the neologism ("acousmêtre" = "to be acousmatic") in 1965 in his famous *Traité des objets sonores*. Michel Chion, *La Voix au cinéma* (L'Etoile-Cahiers du Cinéma éditeurs, 1985).
6. Jean Rouch was, with a few other filmmakers including Chris Marker and Alain Resnais, a fellow traveler on the path of the New Wave. Jean-Luc Godard wrote two enthusiastic articles on *Moi, un Noir* in the 1950s. In 1964, Rouch contributed *Gare du Nord* to *Paris vu par*, a New Wave compendium.
7. André S. Labarthe, *Essai sur le jeune cinéma français* (Cinergon éditeur, 2010), 48, original emphasis (new edition of the original text, published in 1960 by Éditions du Terrain Vague). His remark might work as a precise description of a short sequence in *Moi, un noir*, which shows a traffic accident. The event is banal, but it marks all the better the memory of French cinema. In fact, Jean-Luc Godard reprises the scene in his own way and renders it a citation-adaption in *À bout de souffle* (1959).
8. Whatever the process used, the voice of the Hamar woman is heard as if in the present of her monologue addressed to the camera.
9. This is the first time that Rouch had the opportunity to use this sort of sound recording, thanks to a system devised by the engineer André Coutant. The latter equipped the camera with a Nagra tape recorder. Marceline Loridan wore, attached to her neck and hidden by her clothing, a microphone linked to the tape recorder. Walking down a Paris street, talking as if to herself, she narrates into the microphone this dark event from her childhood. We have entered into the fabric of live recording, which television will take up with such appetite, first with the sidewalk-microphone formula, and later with reality television.
10. Among them, the ethnologist Marcel Griaule, who advised Rouch to destroy the film. Griaule had been Rouch's thesis director, and it was on his request that Rouch filmed *Les Magiciens de Wanzerbé* in 1948.
11. In the nineteenth century, the metaphor is found in Jules Verne and describes one of his characters traveling in the south of Algeria: "Clovis Dardentor and the guide alight—a just expression, since the camel, according to the Arabs' saying, is the boat of the desert." *Clovis Dardentor* (1896) (éditions UGE, 1974), 142.
12. In this, if there is a filmmaker who is reminiscent of Rouch, it is Roberto Rossellini, who, in the name of a (neo)realist conception of cinema, worried little about aestheticizing his images. He expressed this lack of aesthetic concern in a statement that had a wide resonance and perfectly summarized and condensed his position: "Things are there. Why manipulate them?"

13. Rouch, when he was in France, drove a Citroën 2CV!
14. Maxime Scheinfeigel, *Jean Rouch* (CNRS éditions, 2008), 191.
15. Jean Monod made films and published numerous books, including *Dionysos*, which was written shortly after his participation in the film and was at once an essay and a long poem (Editeurs Evidant, 1986).
16. Walter Benjamin, "L'œuvre d'art à l'ère de sa reproduction mécanisée," *Écrits Français*, (éditions NRF Gallimard), 144.
17. Ibid.
18. An example is the "ethnic cleansing" carried out by the Serbs in Bosnia-Herzegovina in the years 1992–1995.

Chapter 6
Robert Gardner's Reality

Charles Warren

After long devotion to film and reflection on it, and some exploring of ways to teach film, Stanley Cavell published *The World Viewed* in 1971. One of the teaching experiments behind the book was a mid-1960s course co-taught with Robert Gardner, where, as Cavell writes about it in his tribute to Gardner, "Anecdote of a Season," Super-8mm cameras were made available to students, a reading list was provided, and discussions were held to relate the experience of filming, and its results, to philosophical reflection on film.[1]

Gardner at the time had recently completed *Dead Birds* (1963), shot over a period of six months amid a warring stone-age culture in the central highlands of New Guinea, and slowly edited back in Cambridge, with the provision of an elaborate voice-over commentary, written and read aloud for the film by Gardner. Gardner had studied anthropology, but did not complete the PhD, moving instead entirely into filmmaking, and the teaching of filmmaking in the setting of Harvard's Visual and Environmental Studies Department, which fostered creative work in the visual arts (and still does). As the editing and fashioning of *Dead Birds*, with its carefully written, thoughtful, poetic commentary, shows, Gardner was at the time (as he remained all his life) a filmmaker notably inclined to think, to reassess, to let creative instincts and, on the other hand, ideas, even words, feed each other—give way and give birth to each other. At the time of the co-taught course Cavell was at work on the essays on language, perception, morality, and art that would make up his epochal first book, *Must We Mean What We Say?* (1969), after which *The World Viewed: Reflections on the Ontology of Film* seemed a called-for next step.

Cavell says about the co-taught course that its ambition was to found a film studies where art and the way of thinking of artists and, on the other hand, intellectual reflection more familiar to universities, actually speak to each other and listen to each other. Film studies at Harvard and elsewhere has gone its way, or variety of ways. That is a story with its own interest. Let us just bear down a bit on the specific Gardner-Cavell interaction, which continued well beyond that early course.

In the 1970s Gardner hosted *Screening Room* (discussed by Brian Frye in this volume), a weekly 90-minute television program in Boston, where independent filmmakers showed work and talked about it with Gardner. Guests were a mix of avant-garde and documentary filmmakers and animators, among them Jean Rouch, Hollis Frampton, Yvonne Rainer, Emile De Antonio, Jan Lenica, Stan Brakhage, and Robert Fulton. In early 1973, Stanley Cavell appeared on the program with experimental filmmaker Standish Lawder (other nonfilmmakers who occasionally joined these conversations included Rudolf Arnheim and Octavio Paz). Gardner introduces Cavell by reading aloud, with the fervor of surprised discovery, a passage from early in *The World Viewed*, still then a relatively recent book: "The world of a moving picture is screened. The screen is not a support, not like a canvas; there is nothing to support, that way. It holds a projection, as light as light. A screen is a barrier. What does the silver screen screen? It screens me from the world it holds—that is, makes me invisible. And it screens that world from me. That the projected world does not exist (now) is its only difference from reality."[2] And the program moves immediately on to look at and discuss Lawder's films.

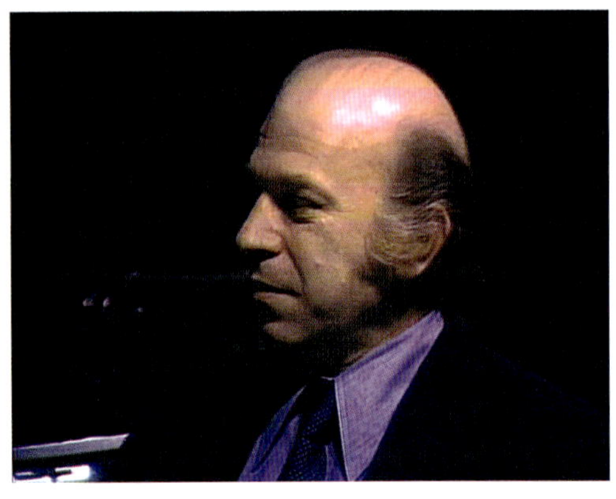

Stanley Cavell on *Screening Room*

At the time of this *Screening Room* program, Gardner had recently completed shooting and was involved in editing what would become his second large film, *Rivers of Sand* (1974), about the vanity of men and the abuse of women among the beautiful village-dwelling Hamar of southwestern Ethiopia. This film would have relatively sparse voice-over commentary, and would give considerable time, at intervals, to a Hamar woman talking to the camera about the life of women in her world. In addition to *Rivers of Sand*, Gardner was completing a short film about the painter Mark Tobey, at this point old and failing and hard to deal with, but still working, then living in Zurich. With *Dead Birds* and these current films, and indeed others, such as *The Nuer* (1971), about African herdsmen, a collaboration with Hilary Harris, Gardner had gone to enormous trouble in difficult conditions to inform himself properly and to film the actuality of life of various kinds and in various places—and had gone to enormous trouble to think how exactly to shape and present his material, one consideration being what precisely, and how much, or how little, to offer in the way of commentary. Each film is a new departure, an experiment, an *essai*. The essayist finds on each occasion a way—possibly an unprecedented way—to cope with the material of concern and to acknowledge the essayist's own stake in it. The essayist, like the poet, suggests multiple meanings at any one point, and is willing to admit the ambiguity of the world, willing not to come to a conclusion about things.

Gardner's films make clear, as do his considerable writings on film, now collected in several volumes, that he always saw himself as scrupulously trying to render the world as he found it, to keep faithful to it—and at the same time as making, fashioning, working poetically, from a basis in his own sensibility. This is what led him to break with academic anthropology, with its tendency, at least at the time Gardner broke with it, to rationalize what is observed and to depersonalize the observer. Gardner believed, or found, that the engagement of sensibility with the world—an artistic, a poetic engagement—finds out reality. His enthusiastic reading of the passage from *The World Viewed* makes clear that he takes heart and finds fascination in Cavell's discussion—throughout that book, really—of the two worlds of the light on the screen and of us who watch, where we feel, or *can* feel, depending on the film and on us, that both worlds are reality, the one reality, despite the barrier between them.

The barrier is a matter, or an issue, of time, Cavell says. The world of the screen, or of a still photograph, is "a world past," as he puts it shortly before the passage Gardner reads aloud. And later in the book, the people on film, on the screen, are said to be "*there*, all right, in your world, but to get to them you have to go where they are, and in fact, as things stand, you cannot go there *now*. Their space is not metaphysically different; it is the same human space mine is . . . The barrier . . . is time" (155). This accords with Gardner's saying repeatedly, in interviews and articles, that he is driven in his work by "the impulse to preserve"—taking the phrase from Philip Larkin: "The impulse to preserve lies at the bottom of all art." Thanks to art, thanks to film with its distinctive resources, something is not simply lost to the past. Gardner also said that an ideal "genetic inheritance cinematically speaking" would, for himself, include a large measure of Tarkovsky. Tarkovsky says in his book *Sculpting in Time* (1986) that film gives us the gift of time, meaning something like full experience, which we lack and crave.[3]

For Cavell and Gardner (and Tarkovsky) the time issue is not simple. Cavell insists in *The World Viewed* that film does not record reality, and thus capture the past, as audio equipment records sound—say, a piano performance—and then releases audible vibrations theoretically identical to the original. Film transfigures. Its reality, even in documentary, is a fiction of some kind. We can—when we do— acknowledge reality in film, eerily as of the past, because we are not sure what reality is. We exist in a state of anxiety about reality, Cavell says, invoking Heidegger, and indeed the whole compounding of epistemological skepticism since the Renaissance, which the arts keep trying to find ways to live with (159). We must be open to anxiety, and not insist on certainty, Heidegger says, and Cavell reminds us, in order for the world to manifest itself. Cavell writes in "More of *The World Viewed*" (1979), "The basis of film's drama, or the latent anxiety in viewing its drama, lies in its persistent demonstration that we do not know what our conviction in reality turns upon" (189). Film—some films—can make a claim of reality to us, to which we will, rightly, respond with acknowledgment.

Gardner, writing in 1986 on still photography, of which he was also a practiced master, quotes Cavell again, cutting two ways: "A photograph emphasizes the existence of its subject"—it points us to, challenges us to acknowledge, a reality at a distance; and, "One may also think about photography as transfiguration."[4] Transfiguration—sometimes, many times, in certain hands—is the route to reality, to emphasis on the existence of something. And Gardner writes in an essay on film also from 1986, "All films are fictive, because to exist they must be made. Their value as objects is another matter. . . . Transcribing actuality is one thing, transforming it is another, and much closer to the higher promises of film as language."[5] Reality is meaning, and language—"film as language”—finds meaning, as well as beauty, surprise, and the very challenge—bound as it is to anxiety—of existence. Gardner writing in 1995: “For a long time I have been struck by the way certain passages in fiction films have had an uncanny claim upon my credence and have had no difficulty at all convincing me of their truthfulness”—truthfulness to human behavior and impulses. He goes on to praise Teshigahara’s *Woman in the Dunes* (1964), and writes of Jean Vigo’s *Zero for Conduct* (1933),

> Vigo provides the boys with entirely unlikely means to realize their aims of righting what is wrong by empowering them through slow motion, pixilation, and other optical distortions. He is, in fact, constantly intervening with the generally perceived look of things. The children are asked to participate in a fiction that with, and perhaps because of, its absurdities justly (exactly, nicely, accurately) represents the common inner desires of all schoolboys.

Gardner is playing on Samuel Johnson’s use of the term “just” in his praise of Shakespeare—“just representations of general nature”—and going to Johnson’s *Dictionary* for the definition of the adverbial form—“exactly, nicely, accurately.” He comes to say, “the true calling of all filmmakers ought to be the employment of [film’s] fictive capabilities”—this for the sake of truthfulness, and specifically in regard to what Gardner calls “actuality filmmaking.”[6]

In “More of *The World Viewed*” (1979) Cavell has some beautiful pages on Vigo’s *L’Atalante* (1934), concluding that the power of the film comes not from the projection of characters, or character complexity and development, but rather the projection of human “types”—an important topic in the original *World Viewed*—and of what he calls the “mythical” quality of the events these types live out. Cavell speaks of Vigo’s camera eliciting this quality “with wit, with tact, with accuracy.” From this camera “we learn more than we knew of wedding processions, how they can feel like funeral processions, presumably because they commemorate the dying of the bride to her past; we know more precisely and memorably than we had known of the daze and remoteness of brides, of the innocence of grooms.” Cavell goes on enumerating things, concluding, “we realize—for the first time or the fiftieth, it makes no difference—that one’s responsibility to one’s desire is to acknowledge it, and acknowledge its object, i.e., acknowledge its object’s separateness from you. The power of these last ideas, as they find incarnation in the image of the husband searching under water for his love, is finally as inexplicable as the power of a phrase of music or of poetry. And the ideas are nothing without that power. Of course there is a sense of character explored. It is our own.” And Cavell invokes Thomas Mann’s essay on Freud, which speaks of the “point at which the psychological interest passes over into the mythical,” and asserts that “the typical is actually the mythical.” Mann goes on, “the mythical knowledge resides in the gazer and not in that at which he gazes,” resides, indeed, “in the mythically oriented artist.” Cavell finds this knowledge and gaze to be “the natural mode of revelation for film. That gaze of knowledge is the province of camera and screen.” Cavell pauses—“The mythical in the typical. I am not claiming that that is clear. I am explaining why I would like for it to be made clear” (176–178).

A few years after these words of Cavell were written, Gardner shot *Forest of Bliss* (1986), perhaps his most significant film—he always thought so—in Benares, India, rendering without any commentary, purely in images and the sounds recorded there, the daily life of this busy city, centering more and more as the film continues on care for the dying and the cremation of corpses beside the river Ganges. The film is palpably specific about Benares life and Hindu ritual, but its gaze and knowledge, to pick up Cavell's terms, readily take in how what is before the camera resonates with broader experience of death and transfiguration, death and rebirth, the earthy and even sordid passing into the sublime and re-emerging down to earth, a cycle of consumption and nourishment. We look at *ourselves* here—as we do in the picture of life being lived the more intensely for being lived in the mode of aggression and violence, in *Dead Birds*; or in the picture of the gender gap in *Rivers of Sand*. The specific is found to be typical and thus—do we want to say?—mythical.

Cavell introduced the premiere screening of *Forest of Bliss* at the Harvard Film Archive in 1985, and later published his remarks. He is very taken at this point with the film's camera finding images for itself—in wild dogs, "enchanted sails," the river, children's kites, ladders that are litters, bundles of wood weighed and then transported on human backs to feed fire, and the transfiguring fire itself. "And in each case," Cavell says, "an allegory is proposed of this camera's (perhaps not just this one's) life—of what it hungers for and would be eaten by, of its roving and floating and flowing and standing . . . of its labors of measuring and carrying that at every moment threaten to overtake the quest of transcendence . . . blessed or cursed with the fate, in the same gestures, to destroy and recreate everything it touches."[7] Benares and the Westerner's camera know each other. Are we getting closer to having it made clear how the typical is mythical?

In 2001, Gardner published *Making* Forest of Bliss*: Intention, Circumstance, and Chance in Nonfiction Film*, a conversation between himself and anthropologist Ákos Östör as they watch the film; Östör had worked with Gardner during the shooting of the film. Cavell provided an introduction to this book, where he remarks on the power of the beauty of the film's images—which include human excrement and burning corpses—that "can make one dumb about them"—make one dumb, we might say, like Vigo's reinforcement of primal, simple realizations, realizations as if they are now new. The power of this beauty, Cavell says of *Forest of Bliss*, "is not unlike the power Plato credited Socrates with bringing to philosophy, the power to make its presence felt by numbing its recipient, stopping thought, showing philosophy to begin by showing that you are unprepared for it." Cavell goes on to remark on Gardner's sensitivity to the bizarre, as challenging us to acknowledge what we ordinarily say and do as not familiar to us, but strange, acknowledge our strangeness to ourselves—a dictum Wittgenstein gives for those who would come to philosophical understanding with him. And Cavell concludes his introduction by dwelling on Gardner's discussion in the book of his sense of anticipating events that will occur within a shot, as if from a trance—as Thoreau in *Walden* speaks of assisting the sun to rise, as does Holderlin, in Heidegger's view, in the *Hymn to the Ister*—"Now come, fire."[8] There is a mystery here—a mystery about the involvement of observer and observed, which we must acknowledge but may take forever to comprehend or explain. We would like it to be made clear, because it matters, but it is hard to get clear.

Gardner writes in the book about trying to find meaning in Benares as he chose what to film and worked to make images—making meaning, in a sense, as a way to reach a meaning that wants to open out of things. He speaks, linking himself to other filmmakers, and to everybody, of being "directed by our own obscure inner thinking"—"that is what is really informing both our eyes and cameras. I probably couldn't have said at all coherently what the film was going to be like, but I always knew certain things had to be shot or I wouldn't be faithful to what I came to feel was something like a vision. Some things simply had to become images. The other thing that might be mentioned here . . . is that the sounds are terribly important"—bells, oars creaking in oarlocks, voices, animal cries . . . (18–19). "Nonfiction filmmaking is . . . more than an artifact of actuality. It has the possibility, at least, to shape a vision out of a distinct and particular awareness of actuality" (44). "Film seems to work best with simple motifs, with commonplaces . . . the idea in this film was to look for some quite ordinary realities, such as dogs, wood, kites, marigolds, etc., and to plunge into them, trusting that they will provide an evocative journey into their meaning" (45)—and Gardner speaks in the same terms of human tasks, such as loading and unloading sand, making litters, attending to the dying, dressing corpses. Shades of Cavell on *L'Atalante*.

Gardner talks about holding back from telling the viewer all about what is seen: "You might ask why all this ambiguity and mystery about these things I've called simple elements? I'm not sure, except that I thought that the audience would not simply wait for the mysteries to be dispelled but would come up with their own solutions, supply their own answers, and so, in that way, they would be doing their own anthropology. They would, in Cliff Geertz's words, be 'finding their feet'" (78). Later, "what I am trying to do in the editing is to move the meaning of the film from death in Benares to journeys to any far shore . . . persuade the audience to think in terms of other histories, mythologies, places." And he speaks of "the audience's active, meaningful synthesis of . . . fragments" (89–90). All this harks back to *The World Viewed* just before the passage Gardner read aloud on *Screening Room*, where Cavell says that we can, and need to, ask of what we see on the screen, "what lies behind it?", "what lies adjacent to that?" (23). And near the end of the original book, "I must surround [what I see on the screen] with a reality—as though the seeing of a reality is the imagining of it; and it may itself either dictate or absorb the reality with which I must surround it, or fascinate me exactly because it calls incompatible realities to itself which vie for my imagination" (158).

The mythical knowledge and gaze of the mythically oriented artist, or of film itself, calls for, calls up—like assisting the sun to rise—the mythically oriented viewer.

***

The essayist finds ways to be open to the world, to its multiplicity of meanings, its density of meaning, its real if unclear mythical dimension—and ways to bring the reader or viewer into activity, into dialogue with the work and its world. In his last years Gardner liked to think of his films as "essays" or "essay films." This was, in part, out of disgruntlement with the terms "documentary" and "ethnographic film." "Documentary" suggests a transparent and passive rendering of reality, whereas what reality is ought to be a question; rendering or finding out reality calls for cognitive and artistic activity on the filmmaker's part, and on the viewer's—calls for restlessness, calls for creativity. As for "ethnographic film," the term came to suggest for Gardner a condescending division between "them" and "us." Films made about our own familiar world, looking into its complexities, imagining directions it might go, would be simply films. Films looking at the odd culture and way of life at a distance from us, looking especially at premodern culture, are ethnographic. Gardner sought to do away with the barrier, making in his work a strong gesture of, in the Chandogya Upanishad's utterance, "I am thou."

Not all of Gardner's films look at a faraway or premodern culture, but his largest and best known films do—*Dead Birds*, *Rivers of Sand*, *Deep Hearts* (1981), *Forest of Bliss*, *Ika Hands* (1988), and his collaboration with Hilary Harris, *The Nuer* (1971). And there are a number of shorter films in this vein, going back to his very first film, *Blunden Harbour* (1951), shot in British Columbia. Why think of these—to stay just with them—as essays?

Essay—a trial, an attempt, an experiment. From the Latin *exagium*, a weighing or weighing out, rooted in the verb *agere*, to do or to make, which gives us "agent." Gardner's interest in films by Maya Deren, Luis Buñuel, Basil Wright, Georges Franju, coincided with, and to some extent antedated, his study of academic anthropology in the 1950s. Working out of the Film Study Center, which he founded in Harvard's Peabody Museum of Archaeology and Ethnology, Gardner edited *The Hunters* (1957) with John Marshall from material Marshall had shot in the Kalahari, in southern Africa, then moved on to the *Dead Birds* project in New Guinea and his further work. Inspired both by creative filmmaking and by anthropology, Gardner formed a personal/scientific/artistic way of knowing through film, a way of knowing reconceived and redeployed with each film he made—trials, attempts, experiments. Gardner and Marshall's ambition had been to film other and older ways of life with more strict accuracy than Flaherty, and at once more depth and more comprehensiveness than the fragmentary filming common among anthropologists, where film served as illustration for, or as raw data for, the kind of rational thinking-out that can be fully rendered in words, specifically in writing.[9] Knowledge was very much the point for Gardner, but a knowledge that film uniquely, in its own way, can attain. To think of Gardner's films as essays, or to ask in what ways they function as essays, is to attend to the creative way of knowledge in them.

In an influential essay from the 1990s, "In Search of the Centaur: The Essay-Film," Phillip Lopate proposes that such a film will have a reflective, meditative voice-over commentary, with which the images and other sounds of the film interact, flowering into something more than the sum of the parts. Alain Resnais's *Night and Fog* (1955) and Chris Marker's *Sans Soleil* (1982) are prime examples for Lopate. Establishment of a personal voice is essential, a questioning, even self-questioning one. But it is the *film's* voice, not a person's. Resnais collaborated with Marker on *Night and Fog*, and the film uses a commentary written by Jean Cayrol. Several minds, and the film's images and editing—and Hans Eisler's very pointed music—come together to give the *film*'s reflection. *Sans Soleil*'s commentary is read by a woman who professes to be the friend and correspondent of—and it is implied she is the film editor for—fictional cinematographer "Sandor Krasna." The reflection at the heart of this film comes through layers.[10]

Timothy Corrigan's book *The Essay Film* dwells on the dispersal of self, of voice, in the films he takes up—dispersal into plural selves, or self after self in succession—dispersal into places, into different ontologies of time, into gaps and voids in understanding. The upshot is knowledge, though, acknowledgment of and critical engagement with reality—with the world and history—and escape from blinkered fixed positions and illusions. Corrigan admits many styles and tempers of film—Ross McElwee's *Bright Leaves* (2004), where the personal dissolves into public issues; Humphrey Jennings's *Listen to Britain* (1942), with no voice-over commentary, only images and sounds; Trinh T. Minh-ha's *Surname Viet Given Name Nam* (1989), with its multiple voices; Jean-Luc Godard's *2 or 3 Things I Know About Her* (1967), with its incorporation of a fictional story; Ari Folman's animated *Waltz with Bashir* (2008).[11]

Perhaps the net might be cast wider. Perhaps any film ought to be thought of, or thought about, as an essay—any film that addresses its subject with innovation, with disruption of the expected, with, for its viewers, inducements to thought, even to worry. Is Shakespeare's *Hamlet* an essay, in its ultimate impact, its way of lingering in our thoughts, comparable to the effect of its twisting, disturbing intellectual source, Montaigne's ur-essay "Apology for Raymond Sebond"? Stanley Cavell has suggested that the 1930s and '40s comedies and melodramas he writes about restage, or stage, and rethink, the concerns of Emerson's essays.

Gardner's *Dead Birds* has a full and elaborate voice-over commentary, mainly descriptive and explanatory, with moments of reflection and a decided turn to reflection at the end.[12] In *Rivers of Sand* commentary is sparse, while the editing and structuring of the film speak volumes, drawing comparisons between men and women, humans and animals, provoking thought in the viewer, and famously taking in a local woman's testimony, fully subtitled in English. *Forest of Bliss* has no commentary of any kind, after an opening intertitle giving a sentence from W.B. Yeats's translation of Hindu scripture: "Everything in this world is eater or eaten, the seed is food and fire is eater." In each film, with different subject matter and with development on Gardner's part, the trial, the attempt, is different.

Dead Birds—which Charles Musser in this volume also wants to think about as an essay film, in terms a bit different than mine—begins with a moving shot, apparently made from high on a hill, looking down on and following the flight of a large bird through a lush green setting.

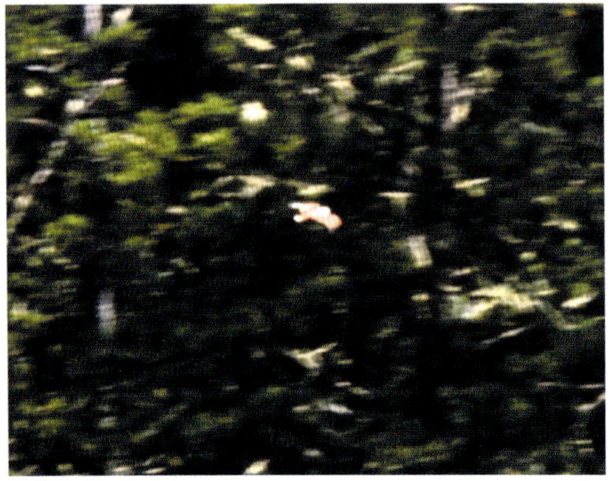

Gardner's voice tells us of "a fable told by a mountain people in the ancient highlands of New Guinea about a race between a snake and a bird." The bird—like the one flying here, one supposes—won the race, meaning that human beings must die like birds rather than live eternally like snakes, who shed their skins and renew themselves. The camera goes on and on with the bird, seemingly longer than filming from one position on a hill would allow. The camera seems to fly over the bird with supernatural ability, as if from the eternal realm beyond mortals—the realm of film, we might say, which preserves time as it transfigures the world into film. But the camera flies *with* the bird, identifying with it, realizing its own bird-ness, its kinship with what it films, kinship in mortality—just as it will realize its kinship with the whole stone-age, war-haunted, ghost-haunted world of the film in full—kinship in mortality, in violence, in humanity.

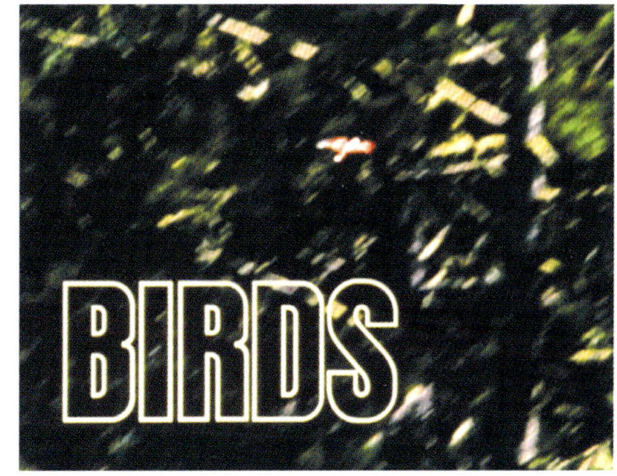

The word "birds," in large hollowed-out letters, appears over the shot, along with the sound of grieving voices, and the film quickly cuts to a view of people gathered about a corpse in a sitting position in a village compound, with the large word "dead" now showing above "birds."

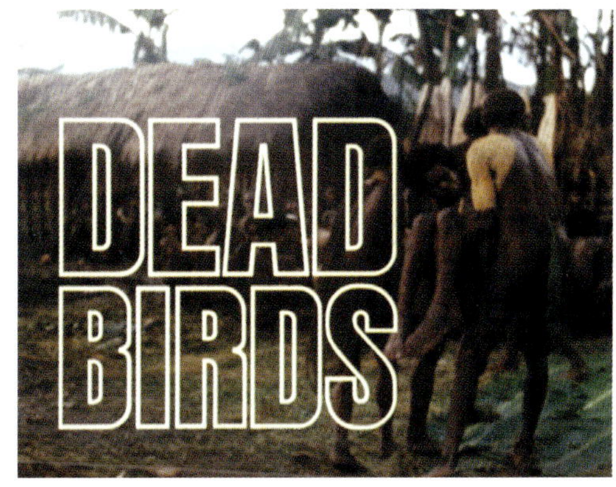

The half-chanting, half-crying voices continue, with one, a low-voiced woman or high-voiced man, prominent among them. The sounds do not match the lips of anyone we see. One might begin to tune in to the fact that Gardner accentuates and carefully controls sounds, that sounds are part of his construction, that he is not offering us synchronous-sound documentary, stretches of direct contact with reality, or as close as film can come to that, as his older contemporary and friend Jean Rouch had begun to do, notably in *Chronicle of a Summer* (1961), and as the American Direct Cinema filmmakers were beginning to do at this time (Drew Associates, Richard Leacock, D.A. Pennebaker, Albert and David Maysles, and others).

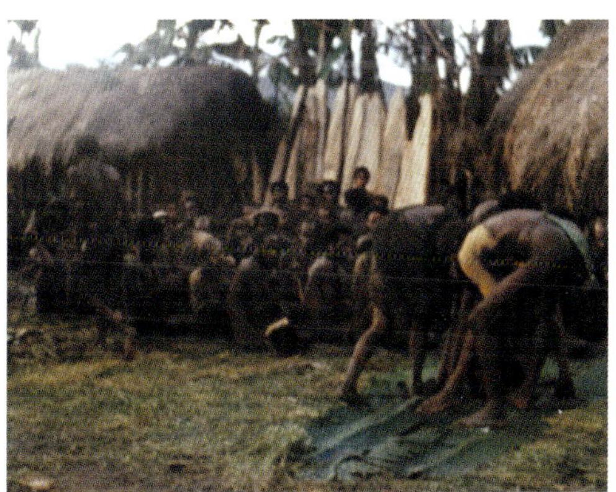

The camera turns and moves right as men carry the dead body and lay it on a bed of banana leaves. A quick dissolve gives us the corpse in a sitting position again, facing us, with a standing man well into middle age facing us just behind the body.

The dream-like, fantasy-like dissolve has moved us in time, perhaps back in time, with the position of the corpse changed—though the chanting/crying is continued over the transition. The standing man looks sobered, full of care and concern. The words "a film by Robert Gardner" show in a blank area beside the two figures, living and dead, and this turns out to be the end of the opening credits.

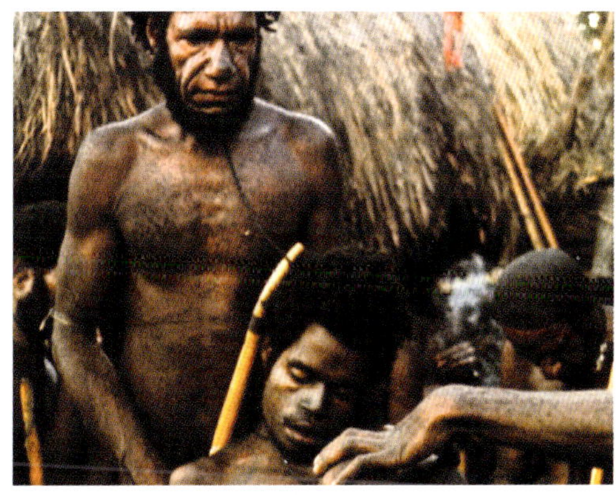

Men are said to be like birds in that they are fated to die, as we watch a bird flying, or fly with a bird—we and the bird doing as much as we can to live, to be alive, while life is ours. Then we are thrust into a world of death, where a dead man is mourned and attended to. The people are dark-skinned but not African, perfectly plausible as the "mountain people in the ancient highlands of New Guinea" referred to just before we see them. All highlands are "ancient," geologically speaking. But it soon becomes clear that the people here lead an ancient way of existence, growing sweet potatoes in gardens, keeping pigs, and working and fighting with wood and stone implements. A certain vagueness about the exact place and identity of those we see, like the bit of time-and-place confusion with the dissolve mentioned above, suggests that we are concerned with something broader than the way of life of a specific people. The words "a film by Robert Gardner" beside the sensitive standing man and the younger dead man suggest an identification of "Robert Gardner," or the source of the film, with these dark-skinned living and dead that we see, whoever they are.

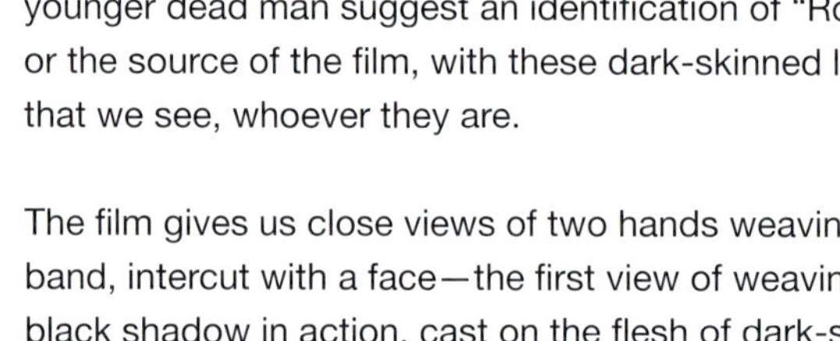

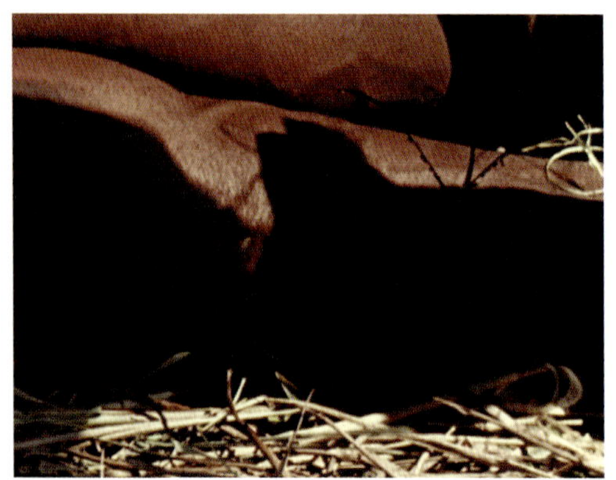

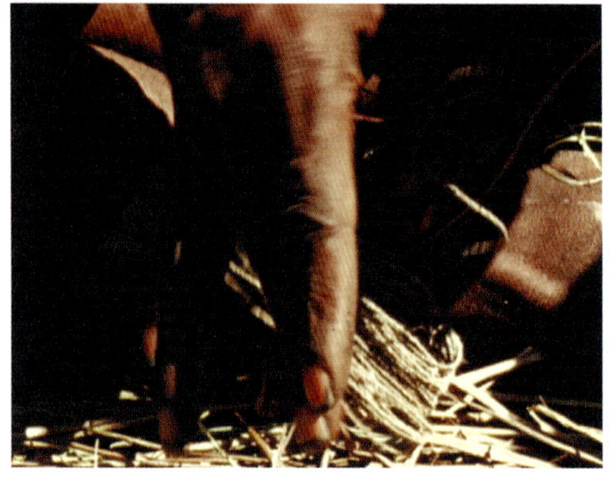

The film gives us close views of two hands weaving a long thin band, intercut with a face—the first view of weaving actually a black shadow in action, cast on the flesh of dark-skinned folded legs, suggestive of film imagery cast on a screen.

The life here—in this film—is a film, with its particular shaping and imagination. Life is knowable through film. Life is film, or indissoluble from film. The screen is flesh. Flesh enables film. Film is flesh. What is not shadow here—or the flesh/screen—is a cylinder of loosely wound string-like fiber dropped in the foreground and moved and jiggled as the weaving goes on. The threads of destiny, in many cultures traditionally woven by women—Fates or Norns—displace the shadow activity, are more present, matter more. Destiny is the prime reality.

Over all this we hear a man humming, peacefully, as people do when they work at mechanical tasks. The humming contrasts with the anguished chanting/crying heard a moment before, but suggests that that also was mechanical and usual in a way. Throughout *Dead Birds* and his other films, Gardner dwells on hands at work, suggesting, like Bresson, that people live in their hands and in their hands' tasks. Fanny Howe writes in this volume about people in Gardner's films, specifically *Ika Hands*, "They are on automatic," seeing this as a challenging, even admirable, spiritual state. In *Dead Birds* there is the destiny of daily labor, of a livable life, but also, we shall see, the destiny of a state of perpetual warfare, a destiny of grief and formalized crying out.

In counterpoint to the images and humming here, Gardner's voice-over goes on, "Among those who tell why men must die is Weyak"—so the man we see is one of those New Guinea mountain people who tell the fable of the snake and the bird. Yet Gardner himself has now told the tale as well, and the film as a whole tells it, elaborates on it fully, the film perhaps sourced in those living and dead men we have just seen along with the filmmaker's credit, blurring identities.

"[Weyak's] name means 'wrong,' for as a child he showed unreasonable rage. As a man he learned to govern his temper, and . . . has the respect of all with whom he lives." Gardner indicates a history behind this man we see "on automatic"—unreasonable rage that has been overcome. And the film, for all it shows us in its nearly ninety minutes, and for all Gardner's copious commentary, constantly points to more going on—in thoughts, histories, beliefs, activities—than the film can fully take in—more in the reality it addresses, for all the power of its take on this reality. There is the suggestion that the "automatic" is not simply a cultural inheritance, but is made and formed, is earned. Weyak had to grow up and adapt and find himself. And what has Gardner known in his own world or in himself, of impulses that had to be overcome, and of learning to govern temper? What is automatic for him, that he has earned? Perhaps, among other things, that ability to anticipate events that will occur within a shot, as if from a trance—which Cavell picked up on from *Making* Forest of Bliss. Gardner writes there, "I think after a certain amount of experience in this world of nonfiction filmmaking a kind of seeing and knowing develops that tells you something is about to happen . . . very trancelike . . . you're told by some occult knowledge, and you're riveted, absolutely riveted" (36–37).

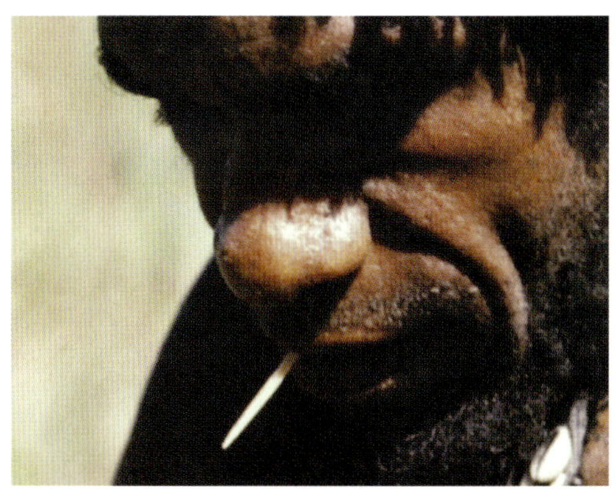

We hear that Weyak is a warrior, a farmer, and a frontier guard in a dangerous area separating his own people from their enemies. And it is on the word "enemies" that Gardner cuts to the first view of Weyak's face, half in shadow, half in light, as if to suggest that one may be double, that one's enemy is within.

The film will go on to elaborate a broad picture of these people, of whom Weyak is typical, farming, maintaining village life, engaging in almost biweekly massed battles, living under a compulsion—an enemy within—to revenge any death, a life for a life, even where this means ambushing a lonely wanderer, even a child.

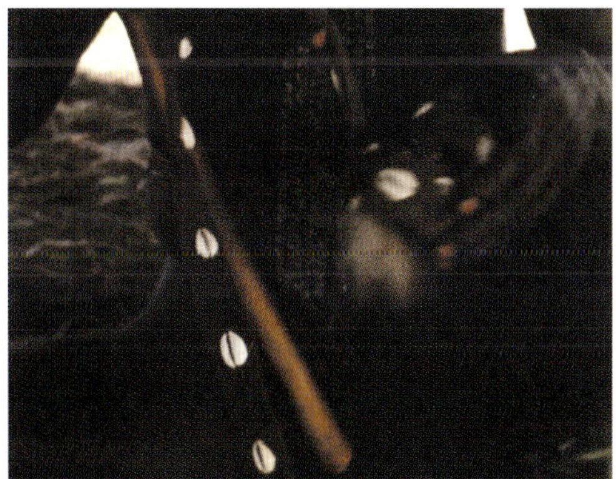

The last Gardner says here, remarking on what we have already seen, is that Weyak weaves, "a task all men perform." All men here, making the destiny of their world. All men like Gardner, who also weaves, forming his film. Weyak's woven band in progress is returned to many times in the film, a long strip decorated with bright shells, suggestive of a film.

Film is like destiny, catching its world and its people up in what Cavell calls the realm of myth, where people and the world submit and also, for good or ill, act to form the myth that catches them up. Weyak's woven band, finally finished, will find its function as a funeral decoration, as, in both Gardner's and Cavell's conception of film, it acts to preserve and honor a world separated from us in time, and to voice life, through artistic transfiguration.

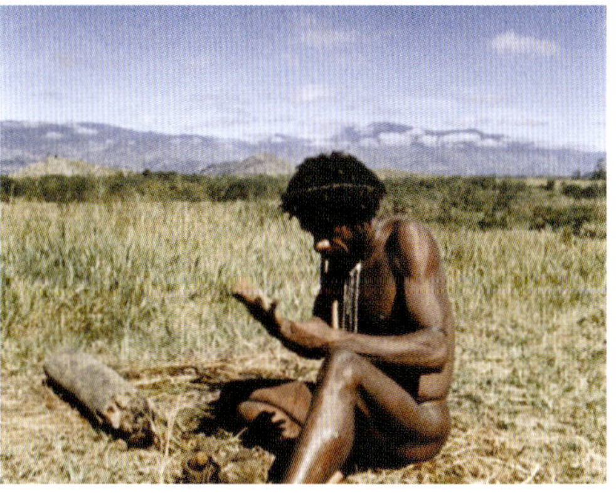

After pausing in his speech, Gardner cuts to a full view of Weyak sitting at his work, with a vast background of lush green plateau, mountains in the distance, and blue sky, all full of sunlight.

Where *are* we? The cut is a violent act, a filmmaker's manipulation, as are, we realize all the more in retrospect now, the probing close views of Weyak that we have just seen. The

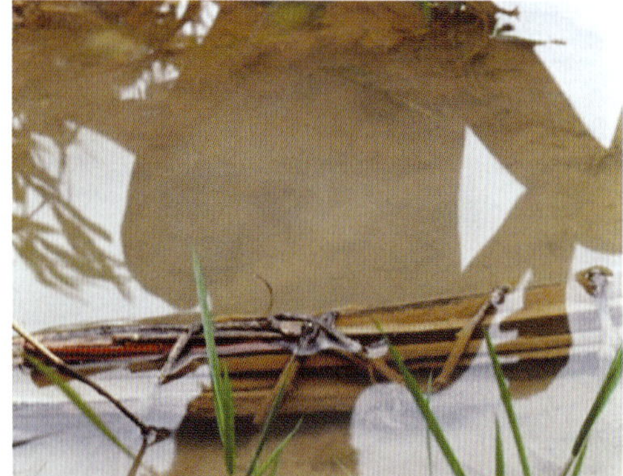

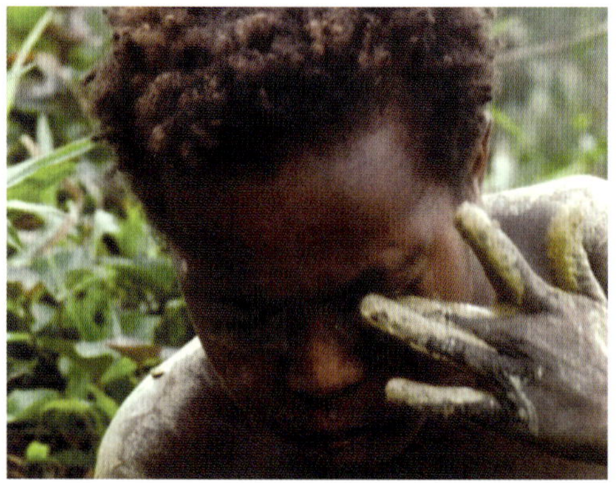

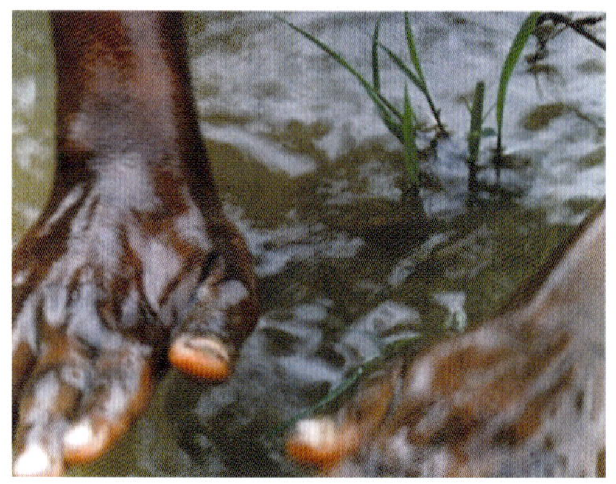

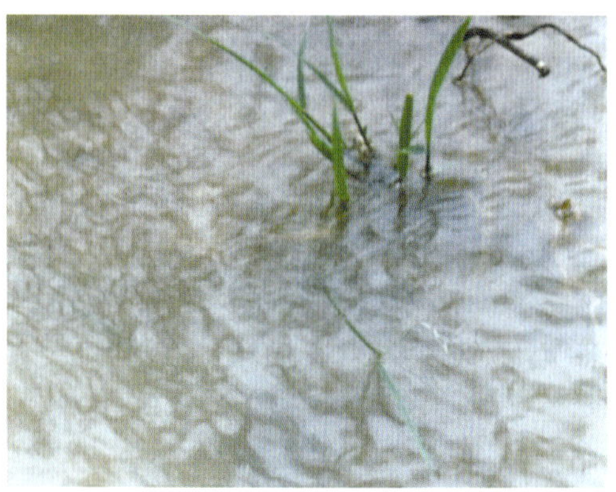

filmmaker is violent in his way, like those he studies. His violence illuminates them for him and for us. The cut is a thrust into beauty. The world seen whole and suddenly and at just the right moment, as can happen in film, is unspeakably beautiful, for all the dark shudders it entails. Perhaps Weyak's own mind shifts from time to time from his daily work to awe at his setting—later the film suggests something like this.

The film cuts now to a view down onto a yellowish puddle, which reflects the upside-down shadow of a boy doing something with his hands—another image calling attention to film itself, reflection on a surface, like the shadow cast on Weyak's skin.

And after a moment Gardner begins to introduce the second of the film's two main characters, to whom the film will come back again and again: "Pua . . . named for the yellow clay these people put on"—and we have cut to a close direct view of Pua applying the clay—"put on when a relative has been killed or dies, when an enemy has been killed, and sometimes for no reason at all. The patches of color around the eyes and shoulders help to complete their image of themselves as birds."

Death stays in consciousness, and merges with whimsicality—"no reason at all." Birds, with their fate, stay in consciousness, and the film will constantly call attention to people's adorning of themselves like birds—notably men donning feathers in preparation for battle—and the film will enter this bird-consciousness, noticing birds everywhere, cutting back and forth from human beings to birds, drawing the comparison. Putting on the clay and feathers acknowledges mortality, but also, in a sense, *aspires* to it, in a creative act where beauty is the outcome. The battle scenes later look like grand ballet, though we move in and see blood flow, and an arrowhead dug out of flesh, and all but unbearable pain on the face of a wounded man.

Gardner now cuts back to the puddle, and we see Pua's hands enter it and stir it up, washing off the clay and thus accounting for the puddle's color. Flesh—reality—enters the reflecting surface and affects it. Then the hands withdraw and we are left just with beautiful ripples on the water—what flesh has left there. The signs on the surface, all but abstract now—the film—transfigure reality but have indeed registered reality.

Gardner concludes the introduction of Pua with a close portrait shot that seems made at Gardner's request, for the film, suggesting that other things we see are done for the film—though certainly a good deal is not.

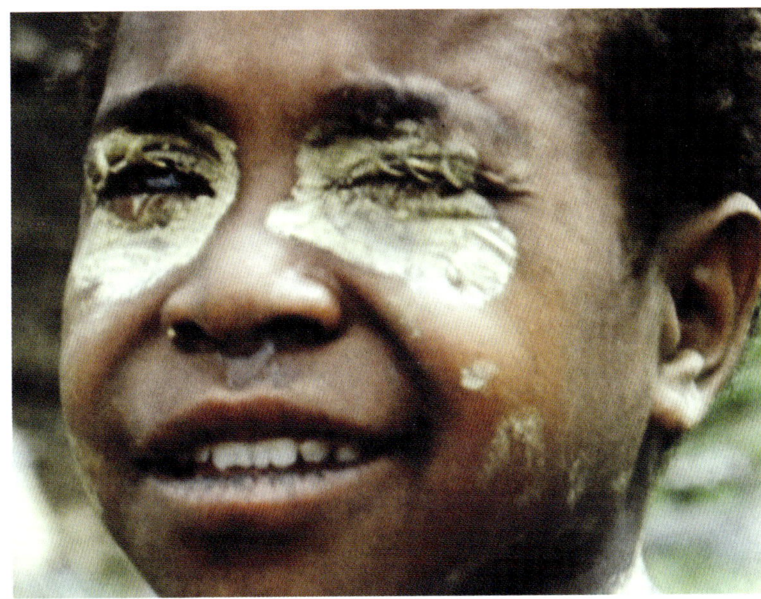

Putting on clay and feathers extends itself into participation in Gardner's film—all are acts of theater, of self-presentation, of art, that acknowledge and at the same time defy mortality, in Gardner's own spirit.

Dead Birds moves on to show the daily life of these people in their villages and gardens, the manning of watchtowers along the frontier, an incipient battle aborted due to bad weather, a full-scale battle of a day's duration yielding a wounded man who requires (local style) surgery, a religious festival where pigs are slaughtered with bow and arrow, news of a child speared to death while wandering alone, and the ensuing grief and funeral, with little girl relatives having finger joints cut off with a stone axe (we see only the aftermath), and finally news of a wandering enemy man having been speared—we see the corpse—and the ecstatic victory dance with its loud chanting which overwhelms the film and blurs with the crying and grief heard just earlier for the murdered child. The people are presented with dignity, even warmth and sympathy, despite the tragic bind in which they live—which may seem no more tragic a bind than that in which much of the world has lived of late with its hot and cold wars and decades-long standoffs.

Dead Birds moves right along, is easy to take in, and has inspired people to study anthropology, to take up filmmaking, or to take an interest in the fate of New Guinea. But a common reaction to the film, I believe, is to sense a certain jaggedness, as of realms of discourse, or of reality, that do not quite fit together—even a certain awkwardness. It is precisely in this jaggedness or awkwardness, with an overtone of self-consciousness, that the essayistic consists.

Dead Birds moves right along. But every shot, and every transition, has the feeling of loadedness, of all but endless ponderability, as in those first few moments. We know we can slow down or stop or replay, and find much provocation for thought. This is the essence of Gardner's often remarked-on "artistic" or "poetic" quality. Everything is dense, ambiguous, asking to be read—to an extent we cannot keep up with as we watch.

Gardner's commentary is very full, but proceeds relatively fast and gives the sense of itself not being able quite to keep up with the reality of the world of the film. Weyak and others speak words that are not explained or translated. Reference is made to the renewal of sacred stones for the religious gathering and pig feast that we see, and one realizes there must be a whole system of beliefs and thought that might be further filled in. Smiles and good feelings are seen on faces as people greet one another at the feast, in a departure from the usual earnestness we see—Gardner does not go into this. Men seem to exist in an erotic atmosphere of nudity and large erect penis gourds.

The camera witnesses male backsides a good deal, but nothing is said about this. The commentary seems a great effort to approach a reality it knows is bigger than itself.

The commentary is largely descriptive, with moments of reflection—notably at the end, on mortality, consciousness of mortality, and the desire to live vitally under the burden of this consciousness and the burden of fathomless tradition—the burden of ghosts. But the commentary also crafts a fiction, in a sense. There is no reason to doubt anything Gardner says, but he continually offers comments on people's thoughts, motivating and characterizing people for their place in the unfolding story of the film. Men go to war to avenge ghosts and because "they like to." The boy Pua watches his pigs until midday when "his concentration has begun to waver" and he sets out to kill a dragonfly—he fails, though, "as in so many of his enterprises." Weyak looks over empty fields at twilight, as "the sight never fails to please him, even when his thoughts concern the enemy and what they must be planning." During battle, "Weyak is worried that so many enemy arrows had found their mark, but most of the others were merely stung into more aggressive action." Weyak's wife Laklokek as a little girl had finger joints chopped off—"At first it was painful. Now it is only from time to time annoying"—as we simply watch her work with her hands. After the murder of the child Weaké ("wrong path") near Weyak's watchtower, he is "more disturbed than the others." The next morning, after the funeral day, Weyak is "stunned and angry" as he walks to the day's work at his watchtower. Days later, Pua, watching his pigs, "thinks how long his friend Weaké has been dead without revenge." And so on. There is a sense that a fiction—let us say a true fiction, summarizing what is not put into direct evidence, or speculating in good faith—comes up against a broader reality.

Then the construction of the images and sounds is fiction of another sort. There is the deliberateness of all those loaded shots and transitions. More broadly, there is cutting back and forth between the activity of boys hurling grass spears, playing at war, eventually causing hurt and serious pain, and on the other hand the work of Weyak and other men repairing his watchtower, showing that the play and development of boys occurs under the shadow of a certain destiny. Or later, scenes of the major battle are intercut with the little narrative of women climbing a mountain path miles away to work at a salt well, showing that men's and women's lives, the peaceful everyday and outbreaks of violence, are distinct but in a sense coordinated with each other, identified—war is the salt of life. There is a sense of reality, *through* the film, larger than the film, messier and more complex than the film's shapings—impossible to encompass fully—the reality of these people's lives, and the reality of what they have in common with all of us—the reality of their typicality and ours where the two merge in what might be called the mythical. The film's construction of images is, like the commentary with which it jars and interacts, a fabrication, an essaying, a means to approach and point to more than itself.

Notes

1. Stanley Cavell, "Anecdote of a Season," in *The Cinema of Robert Gardner*, eds. Ilisa Barbash and Lucien Taylor (Oxford and New York: Berg, 2007), 219–221.
2. Cavell, *The World Viewed: Reflections on the Ontology of Film*, enlarged ed. (Cambridge, MA: Harvard University Press, 1979), 24. Page references hereafter will appear in the text.

3. Robert Gardner, "The Impulse to Preserve," in *Beyond Document: Essays on Nonfiction Film*, ed. Charles Warren (Hanover, NH: Wesleyan/New England, 1996), 169–180. The remark about Tarkovsky occurs in Gardner's interview with Ilisa Barbash, "Out of Words: A Conversation with Robert Gardner," Barbash and Taylor, *The Cinema of Robert Gardner*, 110. See Andrey Tarkovsky, *Sculpting in Time*, trans. Kitty Hunter-Blair (Austin: University of Texas Press, 1986), chapter III, "Imprinted Time," 57–81.
4. Gardner, "City of Light," in his book *The Impulse to Preserve* (New York: Other Press, 2006), 307.
5. Gardner, "The Fiction of Nonfiction Film," in his book *Just Representations* (Cambridge, MA: Studio7Arts and Peabody Museum Press, 2010), 249.
6. Gardner, "Just Representing," in *The Impulse to Preserve*, 354–355.
7. Cavell, "Words of Welcome," in *Beyond Document*, ed. Warren, xxviii.
8. Cavell, "Introduction," in *Making* Forest of Bliss*: Intention, Circumstance, and Chance in Nonfiction Film*, ed. Gardner (Cambridge, MA: Harvard Film Archive/Harvard University Press, 2001), 10–13. Further page references to this book appear in the text.
9. Marshall also worked from a deeply emotional and personal connection to the Bushmen he filmed, and he continued to film and advocate for them the rest of his life. See the excellent treatment of Marshall's work and career, and indeed the work and career of Gardner, in Scott MacDonald, *American Ethnographic Film and Personal Documentary: The Cambridge Turn* (Berkeley: University of California Press, 2013).
10. Phillip Lopate, "In Search of the Centaur: The Essay-Film," in *Beyond Document*, 243–270.
11. Timothy Corrigan, *The Essay Film: From Montaigne After Marker* (Oxford and New York: Oxford University Press, 2011).
12. Lopate suggests in a later piece that *Dead Birds*, because of its commentary with information and reflection, rendered in Gardner's "grave, melancholy" voice, makes "a bridge to the essay film." "Foreword: Voyage to the Self," for Gardner, *Making* Dead Birds*: Chronicle of a Film* (Cambridge, MA: Peabody Museum Press, 2007), xvi–xvii.

Chapter 7
To Give, To Take, and To Return

Gayatri Chatterjee

To give, to take, and to return. . . .
Over many births this game has been going on between you and me.

—Rabindranath Tagore

There is a renewed interest in India today in the work of Robert Gardner. Earlier, his films were not available and few knew of him. The negative reception of *Forest of Bliss* (1986) in the North of India could not have been a factor in this lack of attention among cine enthusiasts here; there just was not much interest in documentary cinema at that time.[1] The field is much energized now, and more people are aware of Gardner's films. Recently there was a retrospective of Gardner's work in Paris, which some of my Indian filmmaker friends attended. The word spread, and I hear now about many who are watching or looking out for Gardner films. Alerted by those who were in Paris and wanting to prepare for a shoot, a young cinematographer borrowed my copy of *Forest of Bliss.* She and her filmmaker husband watched it at home with other friends. Meanwhile, the present batch of students at the Film and Television Institute of India, in Pune, have borrowed my collection and already screened them in the school. There certainly is a buzz.

Two stories form the backdrop to this chapter. One is about my first visit to the United States, when I spent four months at the Harvard Film Study Center. My conversations there with Robert Gardner laid the foundation for the thoughts I bring here. The second is about the time I started using Gardner's films for my teaching and faced a certain resistance from film students at the Institute (and some others elsewhere). The reason for this was a specific attitude among filmmakers and audiences, not only in India but across the globe, toward voice-over narration. When I spoke to Gardner, my interest largely revolved around the question of the "subjectivity of a (documentary) filmmaker." The question of narration, a nonissue then, began to take shape as I taught and faced the students' views on the subject.

A Visit to the Land of the Other

William Rothman and Vlada Petric initiated my visit to the United States in 1988. The latter was curator of the Harvard Film Archive and both taught in Harvard's Department of Visual and Environmental Studies. They had come to India in separate years with a group of American students for the International Honors Program. As a faculty member for the India section of the program, I met Rothman and Petric and engaged in intense film viewing, discussions, and dialogues with them. During my 1988 visit, I was at Harvard to study films, conduct research, benefit from talking to the scholars working and visiting there, and prepare for the writing of a book.

Circumstance had me occupying a table in the office of Robert Gardner. I needed a table at the Film Study Center and the one that anthropologist Ákos Östör had earlier occupied was vacant. Gardner very generously offered it to the visitor from India. Put in this situation of continuous proximity—Gardner did not come every day but often enough—I began with my queries, and a steady stream of conversation grew over the weeks and months.

One of first things I asked Gardner was why he begins *Forest of Bliss* with the "other side" of the river Ganga (the British had called it the Ganges) at Varanasi (this ancient-traditional nomenclature has been reinstated now, over the British-given Benares). This choice of the beginning seemed important to me as a departure from the images one normally associates with a film made in the city—images of the famous ghats. The western side of this city is crowded with numerous temples, steps leading down to the river, crematoriums by the river, and people's residences. Considered "inauspicious," the "other side" of the river is bereft of all that. One can obtain spectacular views of the ghats and the city from this side; but Gardner does not do that. He *shows* that other side, rather than merely *using* it to shoot the inhabited city of temples. The film begins with the empty desolate sand bank and a lone dog sauntering, looking for some bits of flesh, and then a boat gliding ghost-like in the early morning mist—all iconography of Death in the Indian belief system, and imagery from the epic *Mahabharata*. It isn't until much later in the film that Gardner includes a view of the city from this side.

Gardner gave me his conversations about the film with Ákos Östör to read, but also talked. Is my memory playing tricks? I can still "see" Gardner as he explained that as a white American he saw himself as a foreigner, felt himself an "other," and wanted to inscribe that fact. The entry into the film had to be from the "other side." The filmmaker had visited Varanasi prior to the making of the film and was clear about his otherness. This was my first visit to a foreign land; I was myself experiencing and learning about what was earlier for me only rhetoric and theory about *east and west* or *the self and the other*. Gardner's statement immediately put me as the other to his "otherness"—a position for observation and understanding. He had also opened up the question of "individuality" and the "self" of the filmmaker.

There are other related bits of stories that must be told in a nonchronological manner. On the first day, coming to meet with the visitor from India, Gardner had come in a *kurta* and carried a cloth bag. A few months later during the fall, I had worn my life's first Western outfit, presented to me by my Aunt. "It is getting cold. You cannot go around in your *saris* and *salwar-kurta*!" she had admonished. Gardner was happy to see me thus altered. "You look as if now you are one of us!" he had said lightly.

Dressing in clothes of a land one is traveling in is a mimetic act—it is doing something the locals do. It is also done with the desire to look like the locals and blend in. But doesn't that also change one a little, if not a lot? One does that in order to belong; but once one belongs, can one then return to becoming a pure "foreigner" by discarding the clothes? One is altered in the process.

What Gardner told me resonated strongly, bringing new insight into the film and into thoughts that anthropologists, Orientalists, and other scholars have been writing about for more than two centuries. For the first time in my life, I was learning how countries and cultures put one in the binary situation of the Self-and-Other.[2] And I felt the situation and the conversations were opening up some aspects hitherto unsaid. I was very conscious that I was going to learn something new. All this is crucial to the making of nonfiction films. I would be painfully aware of my own "otherness" when I made my first film, in 2009, in two little villages in Khajuraho in central India. But I must not race ahead.

Gardner talked about the dog that reminded him of the end of the *Mahabharata*. He was also checking whether I knew my epics. The five Pandava brothers and their wife (from their polyandrous marriage) leave home to wander around the land before their death. At the moment of departure, a dog comes and begins to walk alongside them. After traveling for several months, they make their way toward the heavens, and on the way one by one they fall down in death. The son of Dharma, the eldest brother Yudhishthir, alone walks up to the gates of heaven—with the dog.[3]

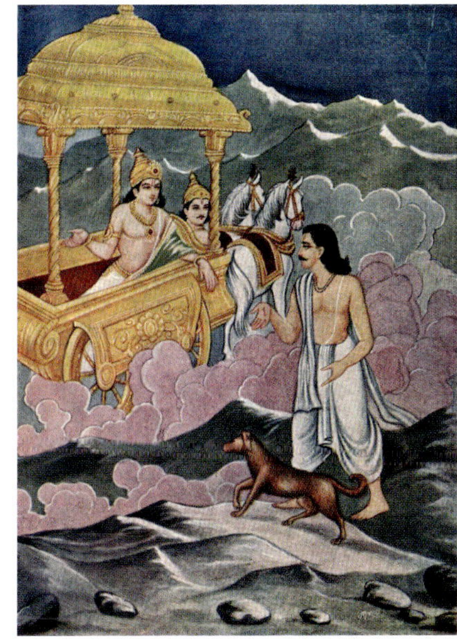

The boat, the dog, the desolation, the pall of mist covering everything, and a cadaver floating in the water, all indicate the film would be about one thing—death: the many aspects of death and various relationships people form with the inevitability and fact of death. But these motifs belong to India (a Hindu India) in general and more particularly to the Northern and Eastern parts.[4] For example, to die is to cross to the other side in a boat (and God is the ferryman). Here was a Western person who had internalized some Indian motifs while making a film in India and who was also declaring his status as an outsider. This made more sense to me than the proverbial East-West divide.

I was impressed by the constant flux of mimesis and alterity, identification, and separation that I was experiencing myself and that these conversations were explicitly bringing up.[5] I delved deeper as the notion of the Self-and-Other played out on many different fields. And my questions became pressing. One day I said, "You are like Harun-al-Rashid. People do not know you. Incognito, you go around amidst your *subjects*; and you learn and know about them—you understand many things. Then you make your films."[6]

The English language is marked by the ambiguity and interplay that exist in certain epistemological and hermeneutical situations. Is language governed by underlying processes that form human conditions? In the process of research and writing, the "object" of inquiry becomes the "subject" (matter) of the thesis. In the case of cinema, too, the subject of a film is the object at which one points the camera.

I continued, "Some of your films make me think you become invisible when you film amidst them. Or else they would be looking at you—at the camera—at the filmmaker so white and tall. And thus, you travel to different poor underdeveloped Third World countries. You make your films . . . and then . . . what happens then?" There was a flash of irritation, perhaps anger, too, in Gardner's eyes. "I have heard this before. I am not responsible for those I make films about." I quickly corrected myself: "I do not want to know what happens to them. I want to know what happens to you." Now he was surprised. (I have gone over this conversation several times in my head; this report is not verbatim but not too different from the exchange between us.)

I added, "You go and live amidst people for months; you really get to know certain aspects of their lives, their nature. You form friendships and relationships of all kinds. You feel empathy and gain deep insight. And you make your films. In the process you change a little—or much." Here I was referring to his conversation with Östör. It is customary for filmmakers to say they are going for a "take" when they go to film a shot. Gardner suggests, "When one goes for a 'take' one should stop to think what one could 'give.'"[7]

Today, the more I read Gardner's books the more I realize how strong this thought was, how intense that give and take has always been for him. Clearly, here was a filmmaker who gave much when he shot—and he took. The giving was not in any material terms. About *Dead Birds* (1963) he said at a later date, "We did not give them even a single Band-Aid. We did not interfere with the process." This giving is in terms of filmmaking.

What was the outcome of so much giving (away) of one's self! I persisted on that day, "When you make a film, you leave a bit of yourself there. And then you go to another country, another people. Do you get fragmented leaving behind a bit of yourself at every place you make a film? What happens to a filmmaker making films outside her or his own world—again and again? Can one remain 'whole'?" That day's conversation ended with Gardner saying, "No one has asked me this before. . . . When I know the answer, I will get back to you."

I left America and returned to India. A year later in a telephone conversation, Gardner talked about his plan to revisit the Dani in New Guinea. Later, on his return, he said, "The boy you see in *Dead Birds* has grown up; he is wearing a Hawaiian shirt. And there are Coca-Cola cans strewn all around. So much has changed." And in a letter Gardner wrote, "I went and shot a new film in New Guinea. I have put myself in it." (Gardner was to call that film, which he did not finish editing until 2013, *Dead Birds Re-Encountered*. It is the subject of William Rothman's essay in the present volume.)

Teaching in India: The Issue of Voice-Over Narration and Point of View

The next story begins in the late 1990s, when I brought copies of Gardner's films from America and started teaching filmmaking students. Prior to that, I had taught film appreciation courses meant for students of other disciplines and those embarking on film-related professions. These short courses paid most attention to fiction films from all over the world; there was little time for a serious look at documentary. Gradually I began teaching film students, and then for a period of five years between 2006 and 2010, I was on the faculty of the Direction Department of the Film and Television Institute in Pune. So from the 1990s onward I regularly showed Gardner's films to my students—along with the work of several other directors. A film student needs to engage with all the diverse ways of image-making and storytelling, be aware of the different ways films make meaning, become discursive and open. She might think her own way is the only way films should be made; but that narrow horizon gets broadened when exposed to different kinds of films. She does not necessarily give up her way; but there is invariably a remarkable improvement in her particular style after being thus enriched. At this time I also taught American students more regularly and intensely who were spending a semester in India under the auspices of American academic study abroad programs. I showed them *Forest of Bliss* as well as Indian films.

Following chronological order and tracing the development of Gardner's work, I would first screen *Dead Birds* for the Indian students at the Institute. However, on many occasions I saw students withdrawing from the film by looking elsewhere, whispering in class, or just walking away. The reason they gave was that the film's near total or "wall-to-wall carpet" narration did not allow them to connect with it. I would stop the film, talk a little, resume the screening, or go to another film, perhaps *Deep Hearts* (1981), and eventually *Forest of Bliss.* The former has very little voice-over narration and the second none at all. In the discussions that followed, the students would tell me how much better they liked the latter films.

The reaction of American students to *Forest of Bliss* was just the opposite. Most of them reacted uncomfortably to its lack of narration. They had only seen documentaries with voice-overs (that is how they remembered their classroom experience). Those who had attended filmmaking classes said they were "always" asked to use narration in documentary films. The comment was, "Filmmakers must have their own perception of things they want to convey to the audience. They must be clear about that and not leave us to guess." Some others thought the absence of narration was due to the fact that it was an "art" or an "experimental" film. So there was after all something in common between Indian and American students. Both groups had a certain idea about art and experimental cinema. The former wanted to make only artistic and experimental films; and the latter were divided about their allegiance—they liked something artistic, but not something too radical; a film without any narrational guidance whatsoever was too much for them. However, a couple of American students in a later year wrote very good essays on *Forest of Bliss*; one of them included discussion of the film *Nights of Prophecy* (2002) by Amar Kanwar, a filmmaker whose thoughts I draw from in this article in order to strengthen some of my own. This film, which has no narrational input from the filmmaker, strings together a series of songs and verses from oppressed people all across India.

Gradually I was learning about voice-over narration as a "problem" that deserves greater thought and discussion.

Occasionally, some of the Institute students borrowed the VHS (later DVD) copy of *Dead Birds* or *Deep Hearts* in order to see the film on his or her own. This they would do after a few days' interval, when it occurred to them that the film *is* interesting. Perhaps something would linger from the aborted screening—an image or a sequence—that they wanted to revisit. Or there was now an impulse to make better acquaintance with those unknown people the film had brought alive—people they would never meet, lives they would never get to know, except by viewing this film by Robert Gardner. So now, anthropological curiosity rather than cinematic inquiry was the motivation behind such requests. One would explain as much to me: he or she was not drawn to the film because it is a good film but because the content seemed interesting.[8]

There is nothing *wrong* in being curious about other lives. What makes a film *right* is the way a filmmaker approaches those other lives. This was a cue for me to initiate talks about filmmakers training themselves to be "rightly curious" and to look properly. There has been endless talk about the gaze: the male gaze and the Orientalist gaze. But I am not aware of books and articles on how the "right look" can produce a worthy film, one that is "good" aesthetically and politically—in terms of form as well as content. The history of colonization and the practice of white First World anthropologists' fieldwork have given rise to much academic writing. But I am not aware of books and articles that advise students on ways of checking one's own viewpoint and gaze—ways of observation, of understanding, processing, and analyzing before one goes for the shot.

Exhibiting further polarization of thought, students would insist that they were "filmmakers" and not "anthropologists" or "sociologists."[9] I would then vaguely speak of the imperative that documentary filmmakers must also be social scientists, and scurry for examples to prove my point. I was not yet mature enough to intervene in a meaningful way; I, too, was learning.

Meanwhile a similar series of questions and discussions grew around the work of Amar Kanwar, which had started with the film *The Other Side* (1987). It is about the display of highly exaggerated patriotism by the respective army personnel of India and Pakistan at the border every evening, when the national flags of the respective countries are taken down for the night. The soldiers strut like peacocks, walk up and down several times, stamp their feet, raise and lower their bayoneted rifles, pretend to charge ahead and so on, while the flags are lowered and folded ceremoniously. It is a spectacle performed with utmost gravity, but is ridiculously funny. Throughout the film, Kanwar speaks incessantly, as one possessed; he describes all that the camera observes, questions the intentions behind such a spectacle, the fascination of the people observing this day in and day out, and the repercussion of such state-sponsored shows of masculine power. He interrogates this display of national machismo by the soldiers and the hundreds of people gathering on both sides of the border—the "12-inch mythical line"—to watch and cheer their respective nations.

The film caused many to react sharply against the extensive use of voice-over. Most of those reacting recognized Kanwar's voice and asked why a filmmaker should make his presence so conspicuous. Those who did not recognize his voice simply critiqued the excess of speech. The complaint at a simple level was that the visuals were stunning but "easy to understand"; audiences needed little assistance in seeing this film. At a more serious level, it was thought that such a film could hardly be considered a "film," but was rather a "lecture" from someone wanting to "say" more than to "show."[10] There was a growing documentary movement in the country and an increasing number of filmmakers, viewers, festival organizers, students, and activists connected with issues addressed by documentary films. They were all driven, as it were, into taking sides with or against Kanwar's film—because of this heavy and polemical, but also poetic voice-over narration, combined with an acutely observational camera.

While preparing for this essay and wanting him to throw some light on what had happened in those years, I called up Kanwar. He recounted at length that history, elaborating on those debates and how they relate to contemporary filmmaking in different ways. He also sent me published articles and interviews. What he says is relevant here, because Kanwar's films have a wide global presence and his words have had resonance all over the world. On one occasion he says, "different sets of ethical dilemmas about telling and making a story coalesce and confront" a filmmaker.[11] A temporary solution necessitates a new form that might be a rearticulation of an older form. "For instance, the voice of God can be continuously subverted by the voice of a doubting God."

The "voice of god" narration in documentary films had been widespread since the early decades of the documentary, especially in films made for war and propaganda, civic instruction, or educational purposes in the 1930s and later. This was a global phenomenon that was changed gradually in different parts of the world and by different filmmakers. In India, dissatisfaction arose with films made under the aegis of the government department called Films Division, started in 1948 (one year after Indian independence). It had replaced the colonial effort called British Dominion Films that served to inform the Indians about Great Britain. In the 1960s, we saw independent filmmakers and also some working with the Films Division shed narration. For example, Sukhdev made his highly acclaimed film *India 67* (1967), in which he reveals all the anomalies of modern India, without saying what such anomalous conditions indicate. But such exceptions were few; Films Division films became examples of how films can be "boring."

Kanwar explains that the reaction to narration-heavy films eventually led many filmmakers in India to make observational films, "in which the directors make interesting and compelling observations, but without putting forward a point of view or a thesis." Kanwar elaborates on how the negative response to any authoritarian voice-over developed into the negative response to any "passionate point of view," which in time turned into a "negative response to any point of view." Soon the filmmaker would have nothing to "say," and audiences (for documentary cinema the number was very limited), too, began to prefer films that did not offer committed, if any, verbal discourse.

Some feel that films are meant to be sensual and experiential. One practitioner of cinema working in the Institute in Pune tells me in no uncertain terms that films should only be discussed and taught on the grounds of the affective stimulation they provide (or fail to provide). A filmmaker's intention is of no consequence and only the affective response determines whether a film is "good."[12] He speaks of how he must "appropriate a film and make it (his) own."

The Gods Who Walk the Earth, Make Images, and Tell Stories

It has been said that a filmmaker in a fiction film is like a god, omnipresent and omniscient. Much of the viewing pleasure of fictional cinema comes from the audience's obliviousness to the all-knowing, all-seeing narrator. We identify with a constructed world while being unaware of the construction—and the conventions behind the construction. But the gods of nonfiction films have restricted movements. They cannot be everywhere and know everything. It is possible to perceive them as such, if and when they go where few have trod, and show things of which few are aware. But in most such cases, as Kanwar pointed out, filmmakers tend to make "observational films" with no strong view. Maybe some gods can only make generalizations, because they have little time and inclination to dwell with mortals. All this ultimately comes down to the question of how much a filmmaker is invested in what they put in their films, the question of *giving* of oneself as one takes, as Gardner put it.

I have mentioned those students of mine who initially rejected Gardner films with commentary but later wanted to see them because they wanted to vicariously visit some place—they would like the filmmaker to be omnipresent and take them where they cannot go. But they do not want the filmmaker to be omniscient and tell them what they might never know—he should not make them think things they would never ponder. Having taken them to some extraordinary place, the filmmaker must be silent and unobtrusive.

Yet when I read out a draft of this paper, a student asked, citing Amar Kanwar, "So Gardner has a strong and passionate point of view; and he expresses that in his films. What is it in the case of *Dead Birds*?" I read out to them the following comments of Gardner's on "Ghosts" and "Violence," essays he wrote on the Dani of New Guinea and the time he spent there observing and filming:

> As I wrote, I was encouraged by a belief in the authenticity and relevance of those experiences. . . . For me, the proposition that ritual wars as practiced by my Dani friends had meaning for the war-likeness of other populations, including above all my own, never wavered. Their obedience to a "set of rules of engagement" (as we put it nowadays) seemed then and now to have that real usefulness to my thinking more generally about violence and even about death. . . . The title of the book containing these and other essays, *Gardens of War*, was carefully considered and ultimately chosen to convey the idea of war as something that is in many ways "cultivated" and, having a distinctly generative side, keeps getting more devastating—maybe up to a point where people will not even have an opportunity to enter a race with a snake. We will be "dead birds" the moment we are born.[13]

Dead Birds is no privileged but ordinary ethnographer's look at something peculiar and exotic on the edge of extinction. This writer/filmmaker is compelled to reflect on the authenticity of his experience; only then is it possible to delve deep into and comment on—in this case—the meaning of war in one community and race, which in turn leads him toward a universal truth: the "cultivation of war" in every human civilization. The observation folds back, encompasses the filmmaker, makes him alarmed at "his own future." Some students returned to me impressed—stunned in fact. As more wars rage all over the globe, they have worried about the state of human civilization, but had never thought it possible to see war as a cultivated cultural habit. Nor had they imagined that the genesis of cultivation of war and death could have been thus recorded in a film—a film that they had been exposed to, failed to appreciate, and then withdrew from. They wondered if they would have arrived at this point if *they* had visited the Dani tribe. They were now ready to listen to a filmmaker's voice—in words, reflections, or images achieved through "giving."[14]

The Filmmaker and His Eyes

Some are not so concerned with the question of the "voice," but rather that of the "gaze." They wonder if Gardner's *Forest of Bliss* should be critiqued in terms of a colonial or Orientalist gaze. Studying in a film school, they are introduced to that question, and the idea that the birth of Indian cinema, too, is embedded in the colonial subjects' need to cater to that gaze (in films like *The Light of Asia,* 1925; or *A Throw of Dice,* 1929, two Indo-German-Italian co-productions).[15] I tell the students what I have learned, a process that began with my conversations with Gardner. One must look and look intently . . . look *on*, if one wants to learn, feel, think and come to some understanding of what one is looking at.[16] For example, here is an account from Gardner, as he looked at an old woman in the Kalahari whom he photographed, filmed, and wrote about. (The image here is from his film "The Old Lady," 1958, included in *Forsaken Fragments*.)

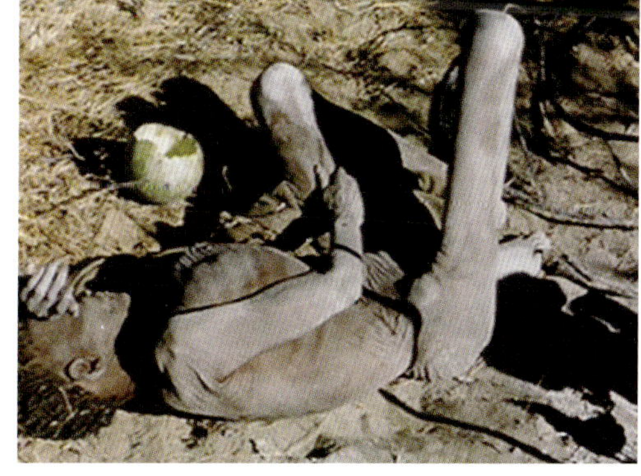

The woman, barely alive, barely moving, wanted to journey to Nyae Nyae, her native place, which her people had been forced to leave. Gardner knows intuitively that she wants to return only to die there. "To sit all day watching her was like waiting for someone to come to life." He did not, like a conventional anthropologist, look at her merely to describe her in great detail or in order to film her. As he looked, he learned something precious. It is as if the filmmaker in him had to accept defeat and die a little: "By now every visible corner, wrinkle, crack of her being had been photographed, and the camera was useless." At the end of the account he could boldly say he was looking not at someone coming to life but at someone dying. But she refused to die; and so Gardner had to "kill her" in ending his film—for he knew she would die in Nyae Nyae. She had refused to die earlier; and even after the journey she refused to die for the camera. But he could end his film and constitute her "death." He was involved.[17] And this is one instance where he also intervened—by lifting her up in a cloth bag, "as if a giant stork," and taking her on her way to her native land.

I want to at this point bring back the question of alterity. There are times when the situation goes beyond the question of the "self" and the "other"; one's ego must then totally surrender and realize there is something beyond the comprehension of "either." A film can rise to newer heights and the audience can then only feel wonderment and awe.

In his introduction to Gardner's collection *Just Representations*, his son Caleb writes about the "Kalahari Journal" and its image of servants who "cup their hands around whatever money they have been given, while also trying to see just how much it is." He says, "There is something more, I think, to this image in the context of a life spent *looking at oneself by watching other people*. In fact, I can almost see the writer as a young man, in possession, like all of us, of something still not completely known to him, eager, but also a little afraid to open his hand and find out what it is" (my italics).[18]

Perhaps this is a possession one does not ultimately possess. The filmmaker might open his palm to find incomprehensible vast nothingness. Or there may be so much that one's joined palms cannot contain it and one finds that much has spilt out and is lost. What remains are new realizations and awareness about the self and the world. In that case one changes forever—if one is willing to change. Perhaps one brings one's viewers—if they are willing and open—into this realization and change.

The last couple of times I met Gardner (in 2006 and 2009), I inquired about one film he had "put himself in"—this was to be the autobiographical *Still Journey On.* I would ask, "Is it completed? Have you ended it?" Each time his reply was very brief and said in kind of a *sotto voce*. But this one sentence remains strong in my memory: "If I end it . . . that will be the end!" I do not speculate about what he might have been thinking; at the same time, I know when he said he was putting himself in that film, he was not speaking in an ontological or literal manner. The bid to put oneself with the "other" for Gardner had been a cumulative act—the result of many years of filmmaking and living. And that statement (however he may have meant it) has, for me, deep significance. I have realized in all these years of conversations and viewing Gardner's films, that he understood much about race, gender, class, and other differences—including very abstract binaries like life and death. So many years ago, he conveyed the sense of entering into a state of being where the play of alterity is in a quick flux—so the initial differences do not matter. This is a blurring, a reaching out toward equity, a friendship and love for this world of ours that enables one to "look" and "talk" with attention, care, and wisdom. That state cannot belong to any one "self" or an "other." At the same time, there is something unalterable about reality. And so if one turns back at this very ideal scenario, one sees it is "just representation." And all that there was—one thought there was—within one's palm, head, and heart scatters into thousands of brilliant splintering pieces.

Notes

1. Upset over the content (alleging that Gardner had focused on the aspect of death and shown Varanasi as a city of death and not as "holy") and objecting to some visuals, some people organized to ban the film in the city. It could have been shown elsewhere. But there was very little of a documentary film movement at that time, nor any documentary festivals, and thus hardly any venue for screening. The International Film Festival of India only showed feature length fiction films. The Films Division, the governmental department for the making and

promotion of documentaries, was active and is mentioned later in this chapter—they did not have the habit then of showing films made by other people. Feature filmmakers occasionally made nonfiction shorts and Anand Patwardhan had just begun making political documentaries. The Film Appreciation Course conducted by the National Film Archive of India and the Film & Television Institute of India was the only venue for seeing documentaries made in the country and some from elsewhere.

2. Some years later I took my first trip to Sri Lanka (to teach in a film appreciation program). I was stunned into the realization that one has only learned about the Self as constructed according to the East/West binary; but here was a country that made me realize that there are people who are not "they" but not "us" either.

3. Yudhishthir refuses to leave the creature who has kept him company and been in his care throughout the journey. When the gods are satisfied with his adherence to his dharma, his kindness and generosity, it is revealed the dog indeed is the god Dharma.

4. I live in the Western part of India now. The imagery of the boat, the crossing over in death, and God as a boatman are rare here.

5. I had not then read *Mimesis and Alterity* by Michael Taussig (London: Routledge, 1993)—in fact, the book came out after that first visit. But today I borrow the phrase from that book, which seems apt for my thoughts and my conversations with Gardner as they flowed then.

6. I had stopped to tell Gardner about the fabulous tales of the real life Khalifa of the Abbasid dynasty in the eighth century CE. We had grown up reading stories about him. During his rule, Baghdad and other parts of the Islamic kingdom became centers of knowledge, arts, and trade. But he did not take it for granted that all his subjects were happy in his prosperous kingdom. So the popular story goes, he dressed up simply and roamed at night, mingling with and talking to people. His nightly act ended in his giving in charity or meting out justice in the morning.

7. The business of give and take could be between directors and actors. Directors ask the actor to "give a shot," and actors say when going in for shooting, "Got to go and give a shot."

8. In the final year while making their documentary, students would realize that such curiosity could be the origin of a film. Just as an image, an elaborate camera movement or an aspect of mise-en-scène could give rise to other images and even an entire film, so could something seen somewhere, something heard some time ago.

9. This reminds me of the documentary/nonfiction filmmaker Harun Farocki (and some others, too) being surprised about Indian film students' reluctance to engage verbally with their films. The tendency is to see films as art and engage with them only at an aesthetic level.

10. Voice-over narration can be a way of holding together a film, when there is not enough footage to make an argument or tell a story, and one is unable to shoot more. Many filmmakers have found themselves having recourse to narration in this situation. But here we are thinking about voice-over narration as something a director does deliberately.

11. Interview from *Fuse,* "Images of Disturbance: Richard Fung in Conversation with Amar Kanwar," fusemagazine.org/2012/05/fuse-32-4-fall-2009-3

12. A professor of the Satyajit Ray Institute of Film & Television in Kolkata recently commented, in reaction to a film I made, "documentary films should not have any narration." The film, titled *Homes for Gods and Mortals* (2013), explores the beauty of a place where people, animals, stones, trees, and bodies of water find common habitat, where things grow organically (something not found in planned walled-in housing complexes in modern cities). It is also about the government displacing people from two little villages, clearing land around the temples of Khajuraho in a bid to create "beautiful" English-style rose gardens around the temples and thus attract tourists. Several persons speak in this film—at times at length—exhibiting a rich tradition of conversation and discourse, bearing testimony to the fact that when life grows organically, language and human articulation develop richly, too. My voice-over is minimal, employed only to bind the many discourses together—but the professor could remember only that, "my voice."

13. Robert Gardner, *Just Representations* (Cambridge, Massachusetts: Studio7Arts and Peabody Museum Press, 2010), 164–65.

14. This is not an Indian problem entirely. Bill Nichols wrote way back in 1983,

> Far too many contemporary film-makers appear to have lost their voice. Politically, they forfeit their own voice for that of others (usually characters recruited to the film and interviewed). Formally, they disavow the complexities of voice, and discourse, for the apparent simplicities of faithful observation or respectful representation, the treacherous simplicities of an unquestioned empiricism (the world and its truths exist; they need only be dusted off and reported). Many documentarists would appear to believe what fiction filmmakers only feign to believe, or openly question: that filmmaking creates an objective representation of the way things really are. Such documentaries use the magical template of verisimilitude without the storyteller's open resort to artifice. Very few seem prepared to admit through the very tissue and texture of their work that all filmmaking is a form of discourse fabricating its effects, impressions, and point of view. ("The Voice of Documentary," *Film Quarterly*, 36:3 [Spring, 1983], 17–30)

Nichols in the end seems to call for such a film as *Forest of Bliss*, where a form of discourse and a point of view are fabricated "through the very tissue and texture" of images and sound.

15. Some years later, *Children of the Pyre* (2007) by Rajesh S. Jala would recall *Forest of Bliss* and raise the question of falsifying experience in order to please. Filmed at the Manikarnika ghat in Varanasi, the film shows seven boys of the Dom community working there, helping in cremation and taking part in all that happens in that inferno—sustained by their inner strength, will to survive, and continuous intake of marijuana. The film was admired for its relentless, bold and direct method of capturing every bit of the harshness and cruelty the circumstances had to offer. It was also stringently faulted for its gaze. After some words of praise, Rowena Aquino had this to say: "So let's say the obvious; the problem with most documentary films that deal with some kind of explicit content, especially when children are involved, is the impulse to contain the subject within the film—by tracing an all's-well-that-ends-well art for the drama's sake. . . . The danger, even hypocrisy, in participating in harsh living conditions when filming people and situations is that the rush to the happy ending can all but eclipse the actual everyday lives of those who, unlike the camera (because it isn't human) and unlike the filmmaker (because . . . well s/he is a filmmaker), cannot or do not move out" (*Journal of Asia Pacific Studies*, 2007). This is a very good example of what happens when one wants to observe and not go beyond; one can only "leave" then. A film cannot change the lives of people it captures; but a film can change the way of seeing and thinking for many viewers.

16. Some years later I would have similar conversations with Krzystoff Zanussi. He told me about how he looked at other people from his balcony. He lived in an apartment building. This habit produced great films like *Behind the Wall* (1971), *Camouflage* (1978) and so many others. Later when he moved into an independent house with big trees around, he could no longer pursue his habit. Once Kieslowski visited him in that house and saw the binoculars he had used for this purpose. Zanussi related to the younger filmmaker the story of the instrument and added that he now had no use for it. Kieslowski asked if he could have it—and made *A Short Film about Love* (1988). Zanussi repeatedly told me, "If one does not look, how can one help?" In *Behind the Wall*, for example, the heroine stops looking up at his balcony—she had wanted help. He begins to look down at hers, but it is too late. She will not allow him any more to help.

17. Robert Gardner, "A Human Document," in *The Impulse to Preserve: Reflections of a Filmmaker* (New York: Other Press, 2006), 1–5.

18. Caleb Gardner, "Barren Mazes," in Gardner, *Just Representations,* xv.

Chapter 8
Ethno-Cine-Poet: Robert Gardner and Experimental Film

Kathryn Ramey

In 2008 when anthropologist Peter Loizos reviewed Robert Gardner's book of journals and essays *The Impulse to Preserve*, he tried to explain the difficult time the filmmaker had received from certain quarters within the anthropological community as follows: "Those who most liked his films were not realist anthropological filmmakers but poets, painters, and the kind of people who would be found in London more often at the Institute of Contemporary Arts (ICA) than the Royal Anthropological Institute (RAI)."[1] As a friend to and a chronicler of Gardner and a well-known anthropologist and filmmaker since the mid-1960s, Loizos was in a good position to evaluate the lasting influence of Gardner. Despite detractors, Loizos maintains that Gardner made a significant contribution to anthropology.[2]

The purpose of this chapter is not to take sides in this debate as it has been conventionally framed, but rather to reconsider Gardner in terms of some late-twentieth-century developments in anthropology. These are: the exploration of connections between poetry and anthropology,[3] the development of theories of sensuous ethnography,[4] and the emerging scholarship on the interconnections between the visual and performing arts and anthropology.[5] As I work and write between the communities of practice of ethnographic film and avant-garde cinema, this chapter concludes with a look at the work of filmmakers such as Ben Russell, Ben Rivers, and filmmakers from Harvard University's Sensory Ethnography Lab who work, as Gardner did, in a place between the concerns and field sites of anthropology and the methods of production and loci of exhibition of experimental film.[6] In summary, this chapter recontextualizes Gardner's films as nonfiction poetic cinema made in an ethnographic context, and shows how his move away from linguistic comprehension as a central epistemological cinematic strategy presaged a shift within the discipline of anthropology toward a more sensuous or embodied anthropological practice, paving the way for ethnographically inspired experimental or avant-garde films to be received within anthropological contexts.[7]

In 1975, matriarch of visual anthropology Margaret Mead wrote in her preface to Paul Hocking's *Principles of Visual Anthropology* that despite gains in audio recording and photographic technology, anthropology was most stubbornly a discipline of words. Little has changed in the intervening years. Images, performance, audio collage, and other nonwritten forms of presenting ethnographically inflected information continue to be taken less seriously as scholarship, particularly in the United States. Those films that are considered most useful for teaching and adhering to anthropological precepts continue to be those that maintain certain conventions of documentary realism: long takes, wide angles, synchronous sound, no recognition of the film camera/maker within the film. Meanwhile, although anthropology has struggled with its relationship to concepts such as objectivity and realism in the ethnographic monograph and has opened itself up to alternative methods of writing such as poetry and dialogic inquiry, such experimentation has not found much purchase in disciplinarily sanctioned anthropological cinema. This is not to say that there haven't been calls for it. One of Gardner's most intense critics and my mentor, Jay Ruby, exhorts anthropologists to look at experimental cinema for strategies.[8] Nevertheless, all too often films made from within the communicative circle of anthropology that fall outside realist paradigms or the strictures of ethnographic fieldwork are found to be heretical or simply ignored.

Outside of students and historians of cinema and some filmmakers and curators, most people have very little idea about what constitutes an experimental or avant-garde film. Anthropologists are no different, exposed mostly to mainstream cinematic offerings and what comes across their radar through disciplinary conferences and film festivals. Thus, if you were to ask your average anthropologist to name an experimental ethnographic film, they would likely cite Trinh T. Minh-ha's 1982 *Reassemblage*, because it was seen widely within the community in the early 1980s and her writing is often read as a part of postcolonial and/or feminist critiques of the discipline. Trinh's film uses footage from three years of fieldwork in Senegal to critique both the economic strategies of the World Bank in West Africa and the role of the anthropologist in creating the "ethnographic other." The film is very experimental in the way it is photographed and edited and in its use of postcolonialist and feminist theory and voice, and it provoked significant outrage within the anthropological community. Some anthropologists found the film's visual style incomprehensible and faulted it for mixing disparate African cultures and not translating the "native's" voices among other offenses. I pose this work as but one example of possible experimental approaches to ethnographic cinema. Gardner's work stands in strong contrast to Trinh's. It does not rely on extra-textual or internal theoretical concepts to explain itself. In fact, at first blush Gardner's films might seem more in line with the realist documentary tradition that anthropology privileges. But this would be a misapprehension. Gardner's work has been from the very first infused with compositional artistry, visual rhythm, and free and abundant camera movement along the lines of poetic documentarist Basil Wright's *Song of Ceylon* (1935) and the dynamic experimental film style of Maya Deren. Gardner has often spoken admiringly of both Wright and Deren and said that they affected him at an early stage.[9] He was particularly entranced with Deren's cinematography and editing in *A Study in Choreography for Camera* (1945), which he eventually discussed at length with Jonas Mekas when he appeared on Gardner's 1970s television series, *Screening Room*.

Gardner's privileging of a visual aesthetic is one of the things he has been criticized for by Ruby and some other anthropologists, as though such a thing had no place in social science. Ruby critiques Gardner for privileging aesthetics over upholding the conventions of anthropological research. Of the notion that an artist's interpretation can contribute significantly to anthropology, Ruby insists that if we accept this of Gardner we must open the door to all film and literature and that doing so would completely dilute the meaning of anthropology as a discipline.[10] Here is the real crux of the argument, a contrast between the rigors of a discipline-based methodology and the interpretive strategies of the artist. For Ruby and others these realms cannot be reconciled. Ruby asks of Gardner's 1974 film *Rivers of Sand*, in reference to the criticisms of anthropologists Ivo Strecker and Jean Lydall (they were in the field with Gardner at the time of filming and are credited for translation in the film), "If someone's artistic vision is at odds with a body of ethnographically derived evidence, is it defensible to argue that the accuracy of information conveyed about a culture is less important than the artist's vision?"[11] Ruby says that a sufficient answer to this question is outside the scope of his writing, but such a question, in a slightly revised form, is central to the present essay. If films made with ethnographic intent are to embrace Ruby's (and others) call for experimentation as well as shifts within the discipline toward a more sensuous, embodied, dialogic, and/or poetic anthropology, then the practitioners must be free to make use of methods of inquiry and rationalities that fall outside of the strictly anthropological.

It is not my intention to privilege artistic interpretations over anthropological ones, but to see them both as valid epistemological and communicative strategies that can at times overlap, contradict, or complement each other in the presentation of knowledge about particular places, peoples, or events. It is not to say that specific methodological or disciplinary theories are inconsequential, rather that interesting work can be done with a myriad of approaches and the discords created in the spaces between disciplines can be as interesting and informative as the harmonies. Although written histories of either experimental or ethnographic film frequently fail to acknowledge it, there is a long history of interconnection between experimental film and anthropology.[12] And this gap in institutional knowledge, despite the practice of individuals moving between the communities, is probably why Gardner's work remains so difficult for some quarters of the anthropological world to accept. Those who have written favorably about his work, such as Loizos, Barbash, and Castaing-Taylor, have not seen their arguments influence his reception in mainstream anthropological circles. This isn't the fault of their writing but rather reflects the fact that anthropology as a discipline continues to struggle to value and comprehend aesthetic processes and artistic rationalities.

Although Gardner was a prodigious chronicler and not infrequent essayist, he rarely engaged explicitly with anthropological theory to explain his processes. In the essay "The Fiction of Nonfiction Film," Gardner asserts that *all* film is *made*, and that to see nonfiction film as being somehow more "real" is a product of it being a techno-democratic (as in anyone can do it) discipline, if a highly expensive one.[13] Gardner wants to focus on the craft and art of the made thing. If we consider nonfiction films to be those that are about a place or people or event that actually exists or once existed, then following Johannes Fabian's articulation of the difference between reality and our representation of it, "a good representation is one that works." It works well when we are able to "act on the world together."[14] Acting on the world together means developing curiosity about cultures other than our own, feeling empathy for persons imaged, breaking down preconceived notions about "the other." When this is achieved through acts of cinematic artistry, and viewers are brought into it, it involves not just the eye and the rationalities of processed language but also the body (in all its sensorium) and the emotions of the viewer.

Although interested in anthropologist Ruth Benedict's culture and personality theory in the early days of his filmmaking, Gardner mainly derived his theory of practice from artists and poets. *The Impulse to Preserve* takes its title from British poet Phillip Larkin, who says, "The impulse to preserve lies at the bottom of all art."[15] This must not be interpreted as wanting to cast the present in concrete so that it doesn't change, but rather, as Gardner suggests, to delineate and present the artist's feelings and impression of the world to others so that they can experience something new. This is not *mimesis*—or the imitation of life—but *poïesis*. The Greek word at the root of "poetry" means "to make," which Heidegger accounts for in art as a "bringing forth," a "poetical bringing into appearance and concrete imagery."[16] As anthropology moved away from positivist doctrine in the later part of the twentieth century, there was a call to experiment in the writing up of anthropological knowledge.[17] One of these strategies was to incorporate poetry either as a part of the field experience or the published monograph or both.

In discussing the work of anthropologist Paul Friedrich (father to experimental filmmaker Su Friedrich, as it happens), Stephen Tyler quotes Ernest Fenellosa to suggest why poetry is at least one cure for a perceived crisis in anthropology[18]: "The poem reveals the direct flow of thought in a non-Aristotelian pre- or postlogical consciousness in which the juxtaposition of particulars, even of opposites, does not produce a third, a synthesis, a more abstract thing, as does the dialectic; it leads instead to a non-logical transcendent complementarity, an unresolved catachresis, a thing in constant motion."[19] This *unresolved catachresis* can be understood as a paradox that opens the reader to multiple meanings and possibilities. Another way of looking at poetry as a distinct meaning-making structure was offered by Maya Deren in a 1952 roundtable on poetry and cinema with Willard Maas, Parker Tyler, Dylan Thomas, and Arthur Miller. Deren described poetry as a "*vertical* investigation of a situation, in that it probes the ramifications of the moment, and is concerned with its qualities and its depth, so that you have poetry concerned in a sense not with what is occurring, but with what it feels like or what it means."[20] She contrasts this with the "horizontal" nature of narrative, in which events progress one from the other to some kind of end. In Gardner's films and the more contemporary works discussed here, there is both this sense of verticality or layered sensoria *and* the paradox of meaning in motion. Gardner struggled with this in some of his films, inserting voice-over that attempts to direct meaning; however, in most of his work his intense visual creativity resists overdetermination and opens up the films for multiple readings.[21]

Although Gardner's primary motivation has been a cinematic engagement with real people in the real world, he has approached this task as an artist and a poet. Peter Loizos, in *Innovation in Ethnographic Film*, discusses Gardner's work in terms of the painter Gaugin and Symbolist poetry. The late-nineteenth-century Symbolist movement in art and literature eschewed positivist and scientific understandings of the natural world in favor of metaphorical representations. As Loizos describes it, "The essence of Symbolism is the belief that a complex reality can be appreciated through metaphor, or symbols, isolated from the flux of events and particulars and given emphasis by the observer."[22] Indeed, when Stan Brakhage and Gardner sit down to discuss *Forest of Bliss* (1986) for its twenty-first-century DVD rerelease, Brakhage can only speak about the film in terms of metaphors. Gardner responds sometimes in the affirmative and sometimes with resistance, because the film is not just a series of visual and aural metaphors, but the result of the filmmaker's embodied experience of Benares, India. The way the film is shot and edited draws out in the viewer an empathic and embodied response. This is beyond the comprehension of symbols and metaphors, and representative of what anthropologist Paul Stoller calls *sensuous scholarship*, which he describes, following Maurice Merleau-Ponty, as exploring the inner space in which external experiences "awaken an echo in our body."[23] In his evolving film style, Gardner calls on the viewer to empathize, not just observe.

So how does Gardner achieve this empathy? From his very first film, the 1951 *Blunden Harbour*, Gardner's work is structured more like music or verse than expository narrative. During the late 1940s and early 1950s Gardner spent some time in Seattle and British Columbia where he made his first films. *Blunden Harbour* is a short meditation on the life and environs of a Kwakiutl village. Although Gardner entrusted the cinematography to William Heick, he directed and edited the piece. Like Wright's *Ceylon*, the black-and-white film uses dramatic voice-over, in this case written by Gardner—telling a story from the history of the people who are represented. There is never the explanation, "I am telling you a story about the Kwakiutl"; rather, the myth that opens the film is the only exposition, and it is a spare tale about the founding of the village by a man who was once a whale. The tale is told in a sonorous voice with a rhythmic clicking from the motor of a small boat in the background. The words are spoken over a boat ride into the town and then images of the villagers going about their work, drying seaweed, gathering mollusks. When the tale is finished, a male voice begins singing in his native tongue, while the women continue to gather fruits of the sea.

The photography in these sequences features close-ups of faces, hands, and tools. As the people return to the village, the man's singing voice is joined by a woman's and then others. There are images of both men and women working, as excerpts from the poetic passage from the beginning are repeated: "From water food, from wood a way of life." Although there are sequences of work and play, these are not presented as complete actions with beginning, middle, and end; they are woven together as a tapestry of village life. About fourteen minutes into the twenty-two-minute film there is an extended sequence of a man painting a mask. Still the only sound is of native chanting, until the voice-over intones, "A way of life, a way of death, a way of dreams, and a way to remember." This introduces the most dramatic sequence of the film, in which the villagers dance in elaborate costumes and play music and sing. At the end of this sequence we return to the man painting masks, then cut to a child swinging, women gossiping, a man in a boat in the harbor, and then the scooping of water out of a rain barrel—and the movie ends.

a	b
c	d
e	f

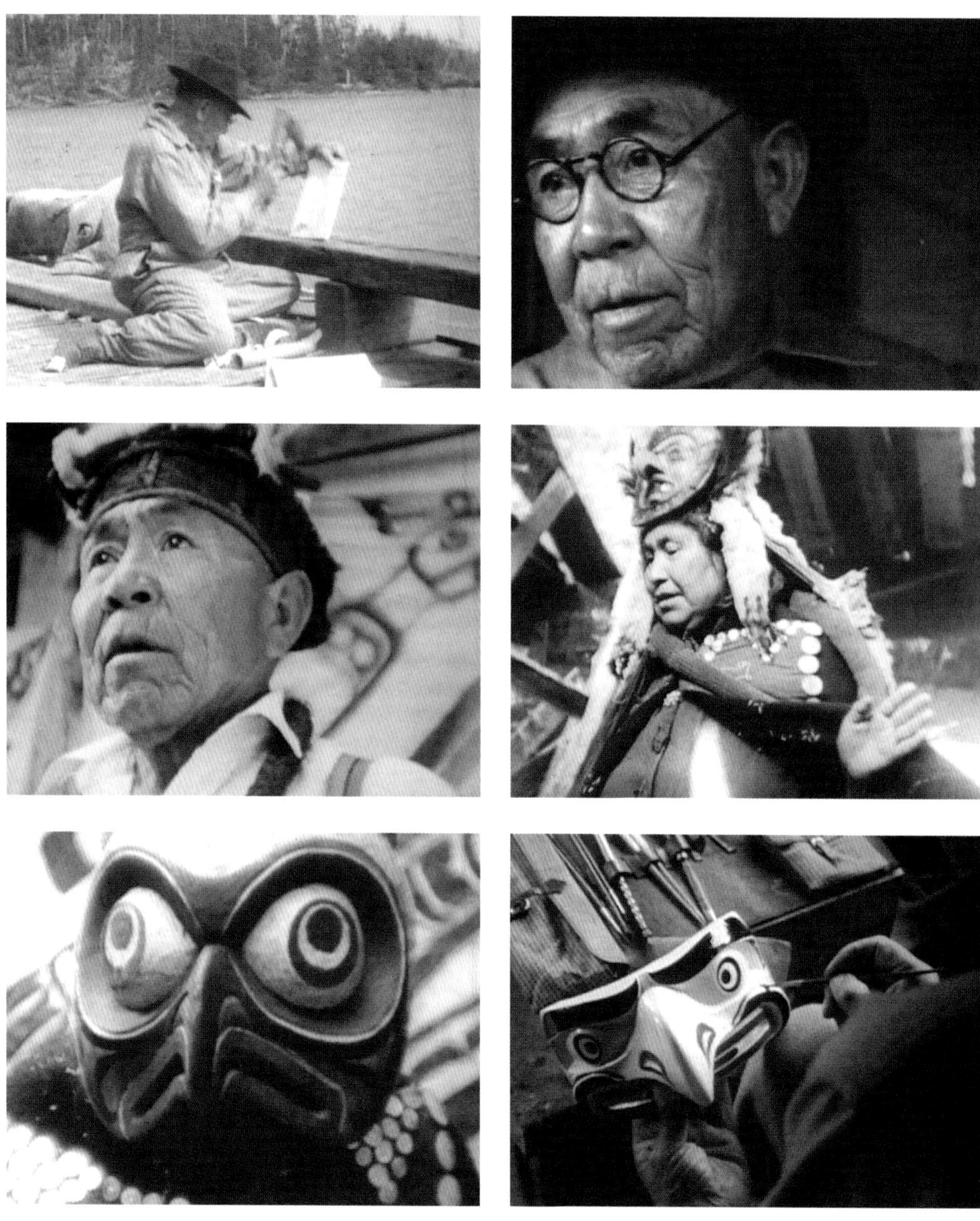

This final montage is almost identical to a sequence that precedes the mask painting/performance segment, and creates what I have come to think of as a "stanza," with opening and concluding "lines" that have the same meter and in a sense rhyme with each other, creating a kind of poetic logic to end the film. The effect that this editing, the sound collages, and the poetic voice-over have is to turn the film into a kind of song that is to be experienced rather than an informational film that is telling you something specific.

This movie stands in dramatic contrast to the then-emerging field of anthropological film, which emphasized a positivist realism with wide framing, long unbroken shots, and spare editing, summarized by Karl Heider's dictum to show "whole people, whole bodies, whole lives." Gardner's film also contrasts with the documentarian advocacy films John

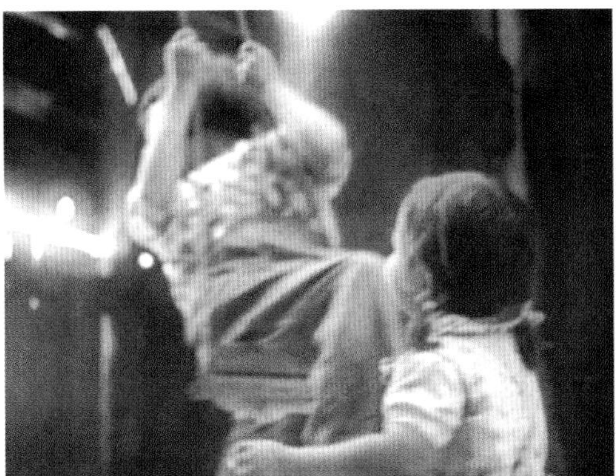
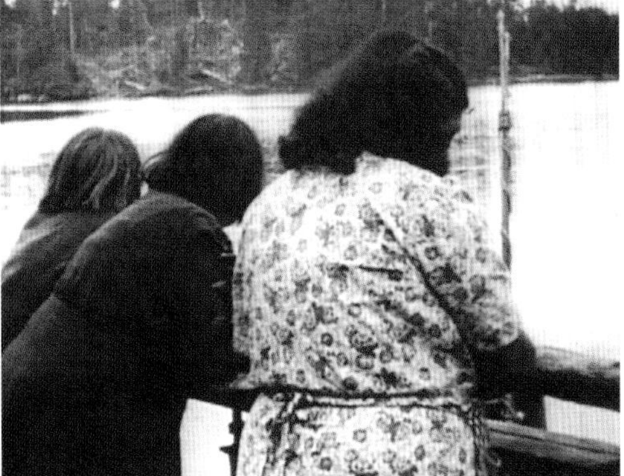
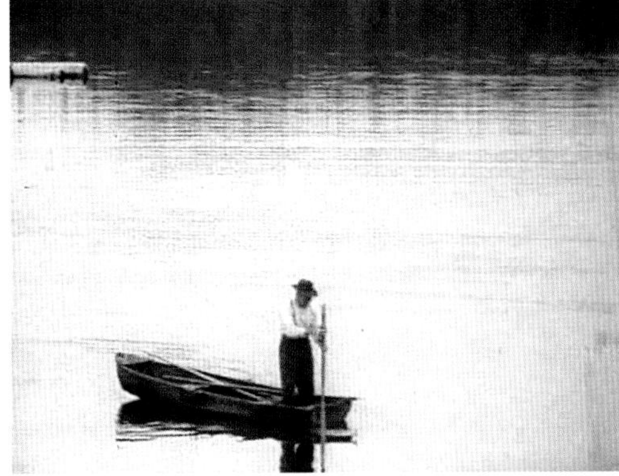
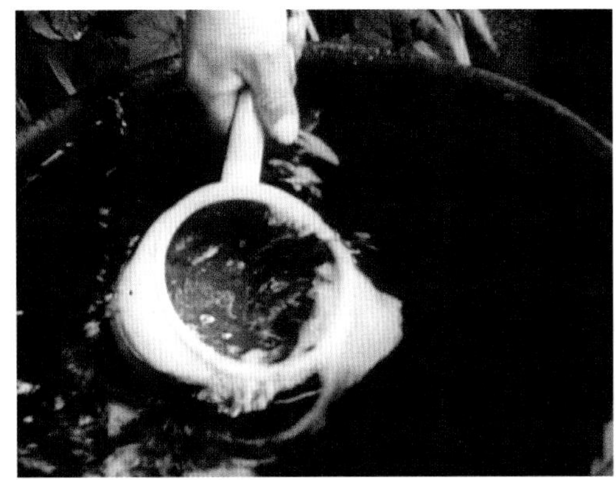

a b
c d

Grierson championed in the 1930s that foregrounded a particular problem or issue. By not directing the audience as to who these people are from a Western perspective, but using their own foundation narrative and their song, the film tries to bring us into the mythic time of its people. All people have myths, and they are what anthropologist Bronislaw Malinowski calls a people's charter, the way they have come to know who they are and explain themselves to each other and the world. Gardner wants to bring us into the Kwakiutl myth rather than into rational explanation of these people. There is a kind of universality to myths that helps to transcend difference and move toward engagement. They both point toward what all humans have in common—foundational myths—and what is distinct among various groups—each foundational myth is different. Anthropologist filmmaker Bob Ascher, who made animated films of myths from four different cultures, finds a strong relationship between myths, dreams, and films and says that "At the heart of the myth-dream relationship is the setting aside of everyday logic."[24] Like Ascher's work, the early films of Gardner set aside realist rationalities and attempt to adhere to strict observation and reportage in favor of poetic artistry.

Another of Gardner's early works, *Mark Tobey* (1952), about the artist then living and working in Seattle, features even more experimentation in sound/image combinations than *Blunden Harbour*, and seems a manifesto about the unique vision of the artist and his alienation from a world that may not understand him. Perhaps Gardner is trying to tell us something about his own impulse to use poetic techniques in what people might expect to be conventional documentary. The film has dramatic handheld cinematography, and voice-over from Gardner and Tobey elaborating on the role of the

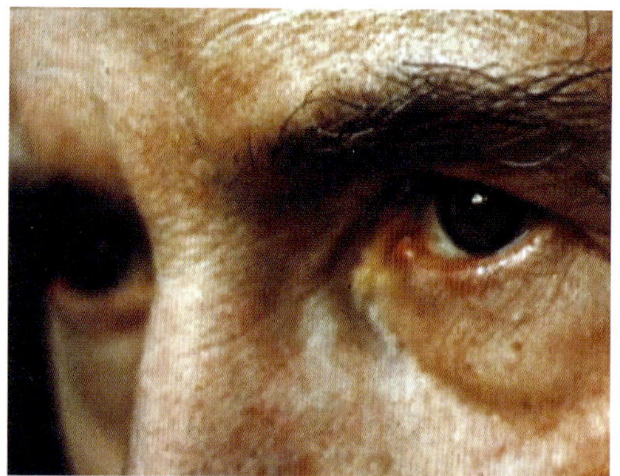

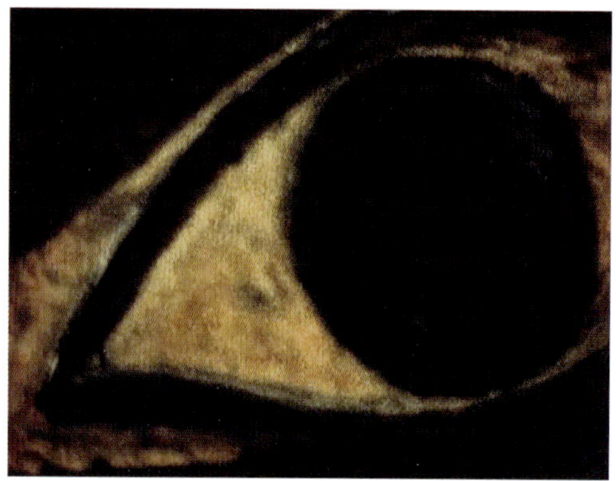

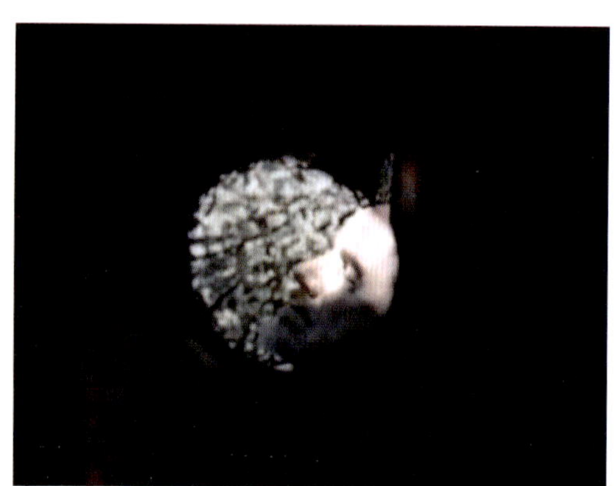

artist in the world and the difference of the artist's vision. It begins in a gallery of Tobey's work; we hear various voices of imagined patrons describing his work or their impressions of him. After this two-minute introductory sequence, a 180-degree pan reveals Tobey emerging from his home, with Gardner intoning, "Why are you artist?" Throughout the film Gardner and Tobey exchange speaking parts. Their words poetically philosophize about art, the role of the artist in society, the artist's vision, and other topics. After the initial gallery sequence in which we see several paintings, the body of the film follows Tobey through the city of Seattle, the Pike Place market, and back home to his studio. These sequences are at times intercut with close-ups of his paintings. Close-ups of Tobey's eyes are often featured and intercut with close-ups of eyes from Kwakiutl masks.

There are occasional superimpositions, and bursts of music composed by Tobey. The end of the film pictures Tobey lying on a hammock, seen through the eye of a mask, as Gardner summarizes, "Is this the end? Mark Tobey is still painting. A picture, a poem, a symphony is the beginning. It is never complete. It is made to be entered by all who chance upon it. It is an opening through which it is possible to reach an experience which is art."

During this time Gardner co-owned a production company, Orbit Films, with avant-garde film pioneer Sidney Peterson, who at that time had already made *Potted Psalm* (1946) and *The Cage* (1947) among other films. Peterson was, for Gardner, a direct connection to the emerging American avant-garde of the period and though their partnership didn't last for long, it happened at a foundational moment in Gardner's development as a filmmaker and he maintained a strong interest in experimental cinema throughout his career.

This interest in the cinematic avant-garde was something Gardner explored in his 1970s television series *Screening Room*, with such guests as Stan Brakhage, Hollis Frampton, James Broughton, and Sidney Peterson. In his dialogues with filmmakers and anthropologists it is possible to see his great interest in a variety of filmmaking strategies from documentary, to experimental, to animation, and to understand even further how this wide interest might have influenced him to try a variety of techniques in his own work.[25] During Brakhage's 1973 appearance on the program, he and Gardner talk about the use of language in film. With the exception of the titles, there is no voice-over or text in Brakhage's films. He says that he wishes he had been a poet, but he was not. They speak of Jean Cocteau, and Brakhage faults him for using poetry in film. "Film has a poetry all of its own," he says, and Gardner remarks, "One shouldn't lyricize the film by putting lyrics with the film." This statement and Gardner's films of the 1960s and 1970s are evidence of his move away from using poetic voice-over in cinema and a move toward a visual poetics of cinema favoring visual and acoustic exploration and experimentation and poetics over language.

After Gardner's experiments of the 1950s came his first feature-length film, *Dead Birds* (1963), shot among the Dani of Papua New Guinea. This film, beautifully and sensually shot, is dominated by Gardner's voice-over interpreting the action and forging a narrative over what is pictured on screen. Gardner told Scott MacDonald that he was not altogether happy with his "performance" of the narration.[26] He was working out of Harvard's Film Study Center at a time when John Marshall, also based there, had achieved success with his 1958 film, *The Hunters*. This film features a rather deterministic voice-over by the maker as we observe the subjects hunting a giraffe. Although *Dead Birds*, too, has a voice-over about the action on screen, Gardner is also making a meta-commentary on the human condition and his propensity toward unending war, as exemplified by the Dani and their ritual warfare, as opposed to Marshall's film's more straightforward narrative concerning a giraffe hunt. Gardner has the more romantic and poetic soul, it would seem, and he is already an extraordinary cinematographer. His opening 36-second shot of a bird in flight is glorious and makes the viewer think not so much of a bird, but of the efforts of human beings to transcend their mortal coil, their earthbound condition. Think of Icarus. But here the voice-over can work against the poetry and sensuality of the images because it moves the viewer toward a specific meaning. In using voice-over Gardner is conforming to expectations for ethnographic films of the time, but as he develops his style he moves away from narration.

In *Rivers of Sand*, about the Hamar of southern Ethiopia, Gardner's voice-over is spare. Again, this film is gorgeously shot with extended sequences that beautifully explore the landscape and characters' way of life. In a departure from Gardner's more cinema-verité camera work, a Hamar woman addresses the camera directly and speaks, fully subtitled, about her experience as a woman living in this culture. Although direct address was fairly common in social issue documentaries from as far back as *Housing Problems* (Edgar Antsey et al., 1935), it was just finding purchase among anthropological filmmakers as they responded to critiques suggesting that their informants should speak for themselves on film. The woman's testimony is interspersed with men in repose talking, hunting in groups, and engaging in ritualized feats of masculinity such as cattle jumping while the women are seen to work at many tasks and engage in a ritualized act of submission by being whipped. In a move that heralds his films to come, Gardner's voice-over in this piece is much more spare than in *Dead Birds*, giving the barest of direction to the viewer. Both the direct address and the attempts to eliminate voice-over appear to be something that Gardner is experimenting with as he continues to develop his filmmaking style.

As Gardner progressed, he seemed less and less willing to present voice-over, and instead allowed the films to function purely, or mostly, cinematically—without resort to either subtitles or narration. Obviously, this has a different effect depending on whether one is fluent in the language of the persons in the films, but for the most part Gardner made films with a Western viewer as the intended audience. Gardner was not as fluent in the language of his informants as the anthropologists who accompanied him in the field and so he relied on his experience *as a visual artist* to guide him in both filming and editing. This has two consequences: one, his films invite a broader, more empathetic and personal response from the viewer, and two, his films are embraced by a broader arts audience who do not feel that they are missing something because they don't speak the language of the filmed subjects. To return to the central claim of this essay, like other anthropologists, albeit ones who produced their research in texts, not in films, Gardner was throughout the 1970s and 1980s moving toward a more embodied and poetic practice that privileged the senses of the filmmaker over linguistic comprehension.

To return to the discussion cited earlier between Brakhage and Gardner while watching *Forest of Bliss*, at some point, Brakhage comments, "This is how I received this film, a wonderful series of metaphors." Although there is much spoken language in the film, none of it is translated or subtitled, so the metaphors of which Brakhage speaks are all visual or aural. The viewer must employ other senses, other ways of knowing than the linguistic, to interpret this film. It is not that it isn't "saying" anything about Benares, it is just not saying anything in spoken or written English. Much like complex experimental films, *Forest of Bliss* requires a different kind of interpretive effort by the viewer. Even the title and title sequence are both instructive and elliptical. Most anthropologists have chosen to name their films in a descriptive way, such as *An Argument about a Marriage* (John Marshall, 1969) or *Bathing Babies in Three Cultures* (Margaret Mead, 1954), but Gardner chose to use an English translation of the Sanskrit name for the city as eulogized in certain religious texts. Benares, also known as Varanasi or Kashi, is the spiritual capital of Hindu India and the funeral and purification rites that Gardner observes along the Ganges River are some of the most sacred in Hinduism.

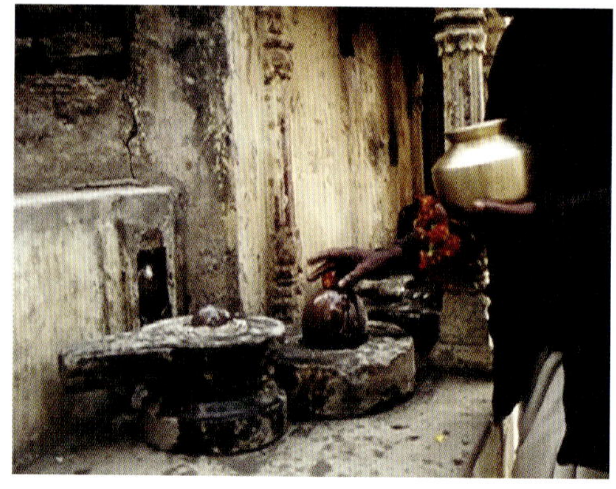

The single piece of text in the film that directs the viewer is: "Everything in this world is eater or eaten. The seed is food and the fire is eater. – W.B. Yeats (from the Upanishads)." This is from a translation of the central Hindu philosophical texts, by the symbolist poet William Butler Yeats. Thus the only text besides the title of the film itself is a translation of a sacred Hindu text by an English-language poet. This text gives us direction as to how to view the film, but it is also analogous to the actions of the filmmaker: he, too, is translating the sacred and the profane, only he is doing so in images and sounds. What the characters say is not as important as the tone in which they say it, the way they move their bodies, the objects they have in their hands and what they do with them. As the old man near the beginning waters and places magnolias on small lingam (phallic) shrines, he says "Baba," which means father, over and over again.

Brakhage says over this footage of the old man, "If you tried to dramatize this it would seem embarrassingly symbolic, but it isn't dramatized." Gardner: "It is what he does everyday of his long, long life." And later, "Mystery and ambiguity are accompanying me and the viewer of this film the whole time." Real life is often more dramatic than dramatic fiction. A symbolic act in recreation will seem hollow but when experienced seems both deeply meaningful and mysterious. Instead of translating action and language (attempting to give the viewer a sense that they *know* what is going on) Gardner allows the audience for this film to experience.

Kinesic anthropologist Ray Birdwhistell claimed that no more than 30 to 35 percent of communication is carried out by words. To complicate matters further, ritual language is often metaphoric and would not be understood by a viewer in direct translation. Gardner's impulse against translation, against strict linguistic comprehension, left him open to the other 70 percent of communication. By refusing translation and leaving precise language to the side, his films allow the viewer to use other ways of knowing. Although Gardner has had his detractors, many audiences, particularly those in Europe and in the art world everywhere, have been open to his work, and his profound influence can be traced to both contemporary filmmakers who are inspired by him and film audiences who embrace the kind of ethnographic nonfiction that moves between art and the experience of life. One such contemporary film artist, Ben Russell, acknowledges a debt to Gardner. In a recent personal exchange he cited *Forest of Bliss* as being "a cinema that vacillates between subjective and objective address, that includes the viewer in the production of meaning and privileges understanding over knowledge." Russell said that for him and his friend Ben Rivers (the 2013 winner of the Robert Gardner film prize) Gardner laid an important foundation. Russell stated, "Although Ben [Rivers] and I come from art backgrounds, [and] Gardner came from anthropology, we somehow end up in the same in-between area, trying if anything to break away from work that can only be read in one particular context."[27]

Ben Russell began making films during his tour with the Peace Corps in Suriname in the 1990s. His first short film *Daumé* (2000), edited when he returned, featured himself and his local friend performing for the camera with a mask and other spare props from their environs. Most of Russell's early work was made in Suriname with his friends from the area and from the very beginning he resisted subtitling his work. Russell says that he has a distrust of language in cinema, or rather the translation of language, as a pathway to knowledge about the filmed subject.[28] Instead, he opts for scenes without translation, or in the case of his *Tjúba Tén* (aka *The Wet Season*, co-directed with Brigid McCaffrey, 2008) translates the audio over black leader as he is setting up a scene with his subjects, and then stops translating when the camera begins shooting. The first time I saw this film I thought of Jean Rouch's comment that subtitles are a scar on the image. And I thought how clever it was to give the audience something that provides some context to read the image. I understand from conversations with Russell that this approach was a compromise with his co-filmmaker McCaffrey, who would have preferred to translate more of the voices in the film. No matter how it came about, or what its intention, for me it is a wonderful compromise between those viewers who feel the need to "know" through language (as in translated dialogue, if not explanatory voice-over) and those who are happy, or prefer, to experience cinema, the *moving image*, in a more sensorial fashion. When voice is not translated, we "read" the image and the subject for gesture, tone, and context. Reading translations below the image gets in the way of these other means of interpretation.

Russell, like Gardner before him, also has a strong sense of how myths can be a way into an experiential or embodied viewing experience that does not require rational explication of the action being viewed. In his feature *Let Each One Go Where He May* (2009) two brothers retrace in reverse the steps their African ancestors took as they escaped the

Dutch three hundred years prior. Like Gardner's *Forest of Bliss*, Russell begins the film with a piece of text, and from there on out there is no language that is understandable to a non-Saramaccan-speaking audience. The text is a translation of a clip from an interview and reads as follows:

> This is how we've heard it:
> During slavery, there was hardly anything to eat.
> They would whip you until your ass was burning,
> then they would give you a bit of plain rice in a
> bowl. And the gods said, they said that is no
> way for human beings to live. The gods would
> help them.
> "Let each one go where he may."
> So they ran.
>
> —Lántífáya, 1978
> Masiáíki, Suriname

What follows are thirteen unedited extremely long takes (each somewhere between nine and eleven minutes) shot in 16mm with a steadicam rig. Many have compared the work of Russell to that of Jean Rouch and there is some truth to the comparisons between *Let Each One Go Where He May* and Rouch's *Jaguar* (1967) in that both are road movies exorcising the history of a people through the individual journey of a man or men. But there are also strands of Gardner in these long takes that follow movement through space, leaving space for gesture, glance, and ritual to provide the viewer with meaning as opposed to telling them what to feel or think.

Russell's films have been widely viewed in film festivals and at art house cinemas. Although he comes out of experimental or artist cinema, with an MFA from the Art Institute of Chicago, his work is widely viewed, particularly in Europe, in anthropological and documentary venues. Most recently, he and Ben Rivers collaborated on a feature film, *A Spell to Ward off the Darkness* (2013) that follows artist-musician Robert A.A. Lowe as he explores three alternative situations: a commune, the Finnish wilderness, and fronting a black metal band. The film is both real and performed and investigates an interest among all its participants to explore a pagan or pre-Christian way of living. Like Gardner, Russell and Rivers are interested in exploring human experience and creating in their film portraits an immersive experience for the viewer.

A final group of contemporary filmmakers whose work seems indebted to Gardner are those working out of the Sensory Ethnography Lab at Harvard University. This interdisciplinary program between the Visual and Environmental Studies Department and the Department of Anthropology engages students to produce work in visual and audio media that takes the sensory world as its subject and eschews verbal or written explanation in the work. The lab is directed by anthropologist and filmmaker Lucien Castaing-Taylor. His recent film, *Leviathan* (2012), made with Véréna Paravel, takes the proscription to be immersive to an extreme, shooting on a fishing boat on the high seas, mainly at night. The filmmakers used small digital cameras that could be easily attached to capture extraordinary angles. The film is not so much about the experience of the men fishing as about the way the boat cuts through the water, how birds follow the boat to pick off the refuse, what a fish might see as it waits in a bin to be gutted, and so on. It has the kind of visceral quality that *Forest of Bliss* evoked with its unflinching shots. Interestingly, *Leviathan* has evoked critiques similar to those leveled at Gardner years prior, with Jay Ruby responding: "Lucien Castaing-Taylor has become the first anthropologist to become a well-regarded avant-garde filmmaker. For me the art world's gain is visual anthropology's loss."[29]

Whether Castaing-Taylor is considered an avant-garde filmmaker or not is immaterial. What is extraordinary is that this work and the work of other recent graduates and fellows of the Sensory Ethnography Lab such as J.P. Sniadecki and Pacho Velez, along with filmmakers Ben Russell and Ben Rivers, have completely transcended the barriers between artist cinema and ethnography. They are following a path laid down first by Maya Deren but charted by Robert Gardner.

By maneuvering between the sites of exhibition and discussion reserved for documentary or ethnographic film (the anthropology classroom, the ethnographic film festival, the monograph on ethnographic film) and the sites occupied by art and experimental cinema (also the classroom, although for a different subject, and the film history and theory books as well as festivals), Gardner opened up or at least helped to widen and deepen a space, an interest, and a productive dialogue for works made with *artistic intent* that feature subjects and spaces conventionally reserved for the anthropologist or the documentarian whose work had the intent of advocacy, scientific discovery, or at the very least some kind of positivist realism. Gardner and his work resisted that intention, bringing the worlds of art cinema and anthropology closer through his interest in both.

Notes

1. Peter Loizos, "A Filmmaker's Journal: An Appreciation of Robert Gardner's *The Impulse to Preserve: Reflections of a Filmmaker*," *Anthropology Today* 24, no. 2 (April 1, 2008), 13.
2. See, for example, Jay Ruby, *Picturing Culture: Explorations of Film & Anthropology* (Chicago: University of Chicago Press, 2000); Jean Lydall and Ivo Strecker, "A Critique of Lionel Bender's Review of *Rivers of Sand*," *American Anthropologist* 80 (1978): 945–946; and Alexander Moore, "The Limitations of Imagist Documentary: A Review of Robert Gardner's *Forest of Bliss*," *Society for Visual Anthropology Newsletter* 4.2 (1988): 1–3.
3. See Paul Friedrich, *Language, Context, and the Imagination* (Stanford, CA: Stanford University Press, 1979); Dell Hymes, "Anthropology and Poetry," in *Dialectical Anthropology* 11 (1986), 407–410; and Stephen S. Tyler, "The Poetic Turn in Postmodern Anthropology: The Poetry of Paul Friedrich," in *American Anthropologist*, New Series, vol. 86, no. 2 (June 1984) 328–336.
4. See Paul Stoller, *Sensuous Scholarship* (Philadelphia: University of Pennsylvania Press, 1997) and Sarah Pink, *Doing Sensory Ethnography* (London: SAGE, 2009).
5. See Arnd Schneider and Christopher Wright, eds., *Contemporary Art and Anthropology* (Oxford: Berg, 2006); *Between Art and Anthropology: Contemporary Ethnographic Practice* (Oxford: Berg, 2010); and *Anthropology and Art Practice* (London:Bloomsbury, 2013).
6. Although the films of Ben Russell and Ben Rivers are often categorized as experimental or experimental documentary, they defy the categories of either. Russell has insisted in private conversation that he is not an experimental filmmaker but an artist who works in film. With this rather convoluted sentence I am trying to communicate that these filmmakers make their films

in places that have traditionally been the province of anthropologists and yet screen their work in venues that have traditionally shown experimental or avant-garde work. Whether he intended to or not, Robert Gardner set the precedent for this.

7. There is significant disagreement over what to call the films and the communities of filmmakers who make experimental film. Historically, filmmakers have sought a variety of terms including personal films, alternative cinema, and avant-garde film. Filmmakers have also resisted the categorization of "experimental film" as a genre like the western or film noir. The visual artist Linda Lai summarizes this: "Experimental film is not a genre, nor the name of a historical moment often called the avant-garde. I prefer to think about experimentation as a continuous, tactical incentive, and the necessity of all conscientious image-artists to find his/her own mode to be 'avant-garde' in specific circumstances" (Lai, "An Interview on 'Door Games Window Frames: Near Drama' [single-Chanel Video Version] with EXiS | Silent Speeches of Linda Lai." Accessed December 24, 2013. http://silentspeecheslai.blogspot.com/2012/10/an-interview-on-door-games-window.html).

8. Ruby has exhorted anthropologists working in moving images to both explore experimental film for its stylistic differences from documentary but also for the ways in which some experimental filmmakers make films that engage with specific theoretical or aesthetic concepts. He has discussed these ideas in many published and online essays including his book *Picturing Culture.* In 2013, on anthropologist Kerim Friedman's blog *Savage Minds*, Ruby wrote: "I would argue that because anthropology is more akin to surrealism than realism, anthropologists should be free to explore the whole of cinema to find ways to communicate anthropological ideas pictorially."

9. For a discussion by Gardner of the influence of Wright and Deren, see his essay "Fixing Time" in his book *The Impulse to Preserve: Reflections of a Filmmaker* (New York: Other Press, 2006). In this essay he articulates how the discipline of anthropology inspired his filmmaking because of its grounding in "moral philosophy" but fell short of providing him with a proscriptive practice. He also articulates how he found Grierson and his social realism grim and "evangelical" and was inspired to make something meaningful and culturally relevant that "lifted up the spirit."

10. *Picturing Culture*, 111.

11. Ibid., 109.

12. Kathryn Ramey, "Productive Dissonance and Sensuous Image-making: Visual Anthropology and Experimental Film," in *Made to be Seen: Perspectives on the History of Visual Anthropology*, eds. Marcus Banks and Jay Ruby (Chicago: University of Chicago Press, 2011).

13. Robert Gardner, "The Fiction of Non-Fiction Film," *Cilect Review*, vol. 2, no. 1. November 1986, 23, 24. In the digital age with cell phones capable of digital photography that can instantly be uploaded to the web, filmmaking is accessible to more people than ever. But the process of actually making a complete film and getting it widely exhibited or broadcast is still limited to a subset of individuals in industrialized countries and elites in emerging ones.

14. Johannes Fabian, "Presence and Representation: The Other and Anthropological Writing," *Critical Inquiry* 16, no. 4 (July 1, 1990), 754.

15. *The Impulse to Preserve*, 337.

16. Martin Heidegger, *The Question Concerning Technology, and Other Essays* (New York: Harper & Row, 1977), 10.

17. Positivism in a very reductive sense was the idea that social phenomena could be observed and reduced to a series of identifiable characteristics that would follow certain structures or laws. For a critique of positivism in cultural anthropology and sociology see Anthony Giddens, *New Rules of Sociological Method: A Positive Critique of Interpretive Sociologies* (London: Hutchinson, 1975).

18. For those unfamiliar with the term, the "crisis in anthropology" was the discipline coming to terms over the second half of the twentieth century with aspects of its history that were intertwined with colonialist, racist, sexist, and imperialist practices and ideologies. It was a time when anthropology was rethinking itself as a scientific discipline and beginning to develop methodologies and practices that were more interpretive and creative, in both research and write-up. The discipline was under significant attack from without as postcolonial scholars,

feminists, and others questioned its legitimacy to speak for and about "others." Notable books from this period include *Writing Culture: the Poetics and Politics of Ethnography*, eds. James Clifford and George Marcus (Berkeley and Los Angeles: University of California Press, 1986), and *Women Writing Culture*, eds. Ruth Behar and Deborah Gordon (Berkeley and Los Angeles: University of California Press, 1995), among others. For the purposes of this essay, what is important to know is that the later part of the twentieth century, especially the last two decades, saw a great expansion in acceptable ways of rendering anthropological knowledge, many of them engaging in creative and highly aestheticized presentation (mostly writing) in ways that were unprecedented in the discipline. Unfortunately, this poetic, creative, lyrical, embodied engagement has yet to be truly accepted as a relevant epistemological strategy *outside* of writing—in performance, moving images, and other visual/aural presentations. The yearly conference *Ethnographic Terminalia* that runs concurrent with the American Anthropological Association annual meetings is a notable exception to this.

19. Tyler, "The Poetic Turn in Postmodern Anthropology," 330.

20. Bill Nichols, ed., *Maya Deren and the American Avant-Garde* (Los Angeles: University of California Press, 2001), 64.

21. Gardner struggled with how best to use voice-over, if at all. In two of his earliest films, *Blunden Harbor* and *Mark Tobey*, the voice-over is elliptical and poetic. Later films such as *Dead Birds* and *Rivers of Sand* use voice-over in a more conventional explanatory sense. This reflects both changes in documentary and ethnographic film practice over the years and his various experiments with *how* to work poetically in *film*. Even within literature on poetics in experimental film there are very different approaches with writing that concerns only films that explicitly translate poems into images (often using the text aurally) to those that exhibit a visual poetics. In looking at Gardner's oeuvre it would appear that he moved from the former to the latter.

22. Peter Loizos, *Innovation in Ethnographic Film: From Innocence to Self-Consciousness, 1955–85* (Chicago: University of Chicago Press, 1993), 140.

23. Stoller, *Sensuous Scholarship*, 209.

24. Robert Ascher, "Myth Into Film," in *Anthropological Film and Video in the 1990's*, ed. Jack Rollwagen (New York: Institute Press, 1993), 71.

25. Gardner's recorded dialogues with filmmakers are considerable. From his *Screening Room* series in which he interviews documentary and experimental filmmakers as well as animators to his dialogue with Brakhage on the DVD that accompanies the *Forest of Bliss* book to his published conversations with anthropologist Akos Östör in the same book. This is where his very best analysis of the films of others as well as reflections on his own can be found.

26. Scott MacDonald, *American Ethnographic Film and Personal Documentary: The Cambridge Turn* (Los Angeles: University of California Press, 2013), 71.

27. Conversation with the author.

28. I have known Ben Russell for more than ten years and have included his work in previous considerations of the interconnections between experimental and anthropological cinema. This particular comment is a distillation of conversations we had in Paris in late 2012 when I was there to present at a festival and he was living there and continued at the 2013 Flaherty Film Seminar where we were both in attendance.

29. Jay Ruby, "Or Would You Rather Be a Fish?," *New York Times*, March 3, 2013.

Chapter 9

A Revolution in Favor of Television: WCVB-TV and Robert Gardner's *Screening Room*

Brian L. Frye

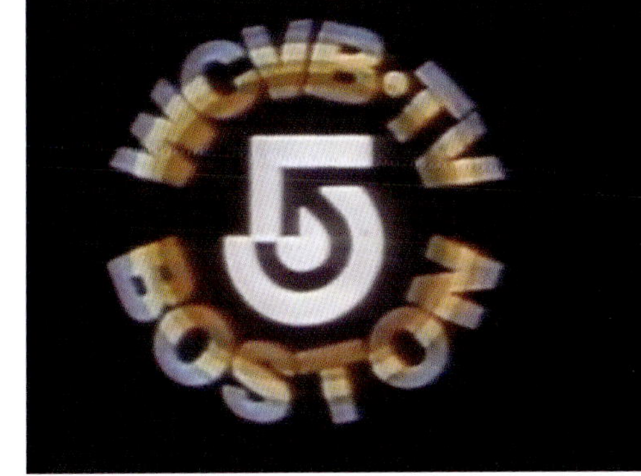

The original WCVB-TV logo

What is good television? Today, that is essentially a normative question. Cable television and the Internet effectively provide a free market in television programs, so revealed preferences tell us what kind of television people want to watch. Good television can only mean the kind of television that people should be watching, whether or not they actually choose to watch it.

But until recently, it was also an empirical question. The supply of television programs was limited by broadcast monopolies, which were vulnerable to market failures. With limited competition, broadcasters had little incentive to innovate, and did not necessarily provide the kind of television programs that people actually wanted to watch. It was an open question whether people wanted something different and better.

In 1963, a group of academics and community leaders decided to test the proposition that people wanted better television. They formed Boston Broadcasters, Inc. (BBI) and applied for the license to operate VHF Channel 5 Boston, intending to operate a commercial television station in the public interest. In 1972, after almost a decade of litigation, they won the license and started broadcasting as WCVB-TV.

During the ten years that BBI owned WCVB, it produced many innovative and unusual programs. Among them was Robert Gardner's *Screening Room*, one of the most delightfully unlikely programs ever aired on a network television station. Essentially, *Screening Room* was a talk show about independent filmmaking. Once a week, Gardner invited an independent filmmaker to show and discuss a selection of films or film clips. But *Screening Room* wasn't just a showcase for independent film. It also introduced a network television audience to intellectual film critics like Rudolf Arnheim and Stanley Cavell, in a uniquely accessible and entertaining way. In any case, it was quite unlike anything one expects to see on network television, then or now.

How was a program like *Screening Room* possible, and what can it tell us about the history of television? Obviously, *Screening Room* couldn't have existed without Gardner, who created and produced the program. But it also couldn't have existed on any station but WCVB. So the story of *Screening Room* begins with the long fight for the Channel 5 license and the creation of WCVB.

The Battle for VHF Channel 5 Boston

WHDH-TV

In 1954, the FCC decided to issue a license for VHF Channel 5 Boston. It received applications from WHDH, Inc. (WHDH), Greater Boston Television Corporation (Greater Boston), Massachusetts Bay Telecasters, Inc. (MBT), Allen B. DuMont Laboratories, Inc. (DuMont), Columbia Broadcasting System, Inc. (CBS), and The Post Publishing Company (Post).[1]

The FCC held a comparative hearing, and the hearing examiner awarded the license to Greater Boston.[2] The hearing examiner also disqualified WHDH because it already held licenses to operate WHDH-AM 850 and WHDH-FM 94.5 in Boston, and was owned by the Herald Traveler Corporation, which published the *Boston Herald* and the *Boston Traveler*, and would decrease the diversification of control of communications media.[3]

WHDH, MBT, and DuMont appealed the decision, and the FCC reversed the hearing examiner, awarding the license to WHDH based on its "strong showing on all of the local factors" and its "past broadcast record."[4] Greater Boston and MBT appealed the FCC's decision to the D.C. Circuit, and WHDH-TV began broadcasting on November 26, 1957.[5]

The "Million Dollar Lunch"

In the meantime, the House Subcommittee on Legislative Oversight launched an investigation of the FCC.[6] On April 2, 1958, it heard the testimony of George C. McConnaughey, the former Chairman of the FCC. Among other things, the Subcommittee asked him whether Robert B. Choate of the Herald Traveler Corporation had ever invited him to lunch. McConnaughey admitted that he had, and that he had accepted. "We met and talked about various things. He did not say anything about his application except to say that his group had an application pending, and that they were very capable people and he just wanted to tell me that. That's all."[7]

That lunch ultimately caused WHDH to lose its television license, and led to the creation of WCVB. Many people assumed that Choate had bribed McConnaughey to award the

Channel 5 license to WHDH.[8] And in 1961, the D.C. Circuit remanded the case for a new hearing, finding that Choate had attempted to improperly influence the FCC.[9]

The Second Comparative Hearing

In 1962, the FCC gave WHDH a temporary license, and a demerit for bad behavior.[10] WHDH immediately filed a renewal application, expecting to receive a permanent license after a perfunctory hearing. So it was surprised when the FCC invited competing applications. Greater Boston, Charles River Civic Television, Inc. (Charles River), and Boston Broadcasters, Inc. (BBI) filed applications, so the FCC scheduled a comparative hearing.[11]

BBI was formed by a group of professionals and community leaders in order to apply for the Channel 5 license.[12] It proposed to use the resources of a commercial station to provide the quality programming of a noncommercial station. Its goal was "to create a different kind of TV station," one that was relevant to "the needs, problems, and tastes of the community: One that brings the best of Boston's unique local resources as well as those of the nation to television audiences, not by a scattering of programs specifically labeled 'educational,' but by infusing the whole schedule with more exciting and meaningful material."[13]

One of the investors in BBI was Robert Gardner, the founding director of Harvard's Film Study Center. Gardner helped develop BBI's proposed programming, based on surveys, demographic studies, committee reports, and interviews.[14] One of the programs BBI proposed was *Screening Room*, which would be hosted by Gardner, and would "provide a showplace for a wide variety of filmed and taped programs which otherwise have no television audience, many of which are produced by students of television and related fields and others experimenting in the art."[15]

In 1969, the hearing examiner awarded the license to WHDH, "not because it is an applicant for renewal but because it has an operating record and its very existence as a functioning, manned station to advance against its opponents, whose promises, after all, are as yet just so much talk."[16] The hearing examiner also accused BBI of overreaching, criticizing its "exaggerated integration proposal," its "extravagant local live proposal," and its "impracticable proposed 24-hour operation," and commenting, "its promises are permeated by an exuberance which makes one doubtful of their fulfillment."[17] BBI, Charles River, and Greater Boston appealed the hearing examiner's decision.[18]

In 1969, the FCC reversed the hearing examiner and narrowly awarded the license to BBI. It found that WHDH's record of past performance was merely average, and awarded the license to BBI in order to increase the diversification of ownership and the integration of ownership and management.[19] After twenty-five years of litigation, the FCC had finally awarded the Channel 5 license.[20]

WCVB-TV

BBI immediately started raising capital, and by 1971, it had about $5 million.[21] WHDH refused to sell its antenna and studio, so BBI rented an antenna from WBZ-TV Boston, and built a studio in a former International Harvester dealership in Needham,

Massachusetts.[22] While WHDH was a CBS affiliate, BBI became an ABC affiliate, because CBS limited local programming. The FCC assigned BBI the call sign WCVB and held that WCVB's authority to operate Channel 5 would begin at 3 a.m. on March 19, 1972.[23]

On March 19, 1972, at 1 a.m., WHDH signed off for the last time, and at 3 a.m., WCVB greeted its viewers with the following message:

> William James once wrote: "If things are ever to move upward someone must take the first step and assume the risk of it." The men and women who comprise Boston Broadcasters Incorporated, and the management and staff of WCVB-TV, now take the first step on a journey in responsible broadcasting that has been nine and a half years in preparation.[24]

In the 1960s and 1970s, most commercial television stations relied on their monopolies to generate profits. They had no incentive to produce innovative local programs, because they could turn a profit by showing network programs. But BBI promised to use its commercial television station to provide public interest television, and it delivered on that promise. The FCC defined public interest television as original educational programs. From the beginning, WCVB presented an unprecedented number of these, including programs on health, the law, and minority issues, and it presented more every year.

At its peak, WCVB showed about sixty-two hours of local programs per week, far more than any other network affiliate.[25] It presented local news programs five times a day, and spent $650,000 producing a series of Saturday morning children's programs.[26] And in 1973, it introduced *Good Morning!*, a news program filmed in the community, rather than the studio, which inspired ABC's *Good Morning America*.[27]

WCVB's station identification proclaimed, "We want what you want. Good television." The television industry approved, as WCVB was widely considered the best commercial television station in the country. And so did the public, as WCVB was wildly profitable. As the *New York Times* noted, "Since shortly after it was founded nine years ago, WCVB, the privately owned ABC affiliate in Boston, has been winning awards and accolades for its programming. The quality, quantity and diversity of its local programs have prompted people ranging from producer Norman Lear to ABC News President Roone Arledge to suggest that WCVB may be the best commercial television station in America. And in the past several years, it has begun to generate impressive profits as well."[28]

But WCVB was still a commercial television station, as well as an ABC affiliate. While it focused on local programs, it also showed many network programs, including soap operas, talk shows, sporting events, and sitcoms. In fact, WCVB showed twice as many network programs as local programs.

Essentially, WCVB was a hybrid of a commercial television station and a public television station. Network programs attracted new viewers and enabled it to experiment on local programs. Local programs helped retain viewers, and enabled it to reach niche audiences. In other words, WCVB's network programs subsidized its innovative local programs, which in turn helped distinguish its brand.

WCVB also focused on identifying and serving public demands. For example, as soon as it started broadcasting, WCVB realized that the public wanted late-night television. Most television stations stopped broadcasting at 1 a.m., when the ratings services stopped measuring viewers. But WCVB got a lot of mail from viewers who wanted to watch television after 1 a.m. So, as an experiment, on September 15, 1972, it introduced twenty-four-hour broadcasting on Friday nights. The experiment was popular, so it was expanded. Soon, WCVB was one of the first twenty-four-hour television stations.

Ironically, while WCVB dramatically increased the availability and diversity of local television programs, it indirectly decreased the availability and diversity of local newspapers. The Herald-Traveler Corporation used the profits from WHDH to support its unprofitable newspapers, the *Boston Herald* and *Boston Traveler*. When it lost WHDH, it couldn't afford to publish the newspapers. It immediately stopped publishing the *Traveler*, and sold the *Herald* to its rival the Hearst Corporation, which published the *Boston Record American*.[29] As a result, Boston gained a first-rate television station, but lost two mediocre newspapers.

Robert Gardner's Screening Room

One of the most interesting and unusual local programs produced by WCVB was *Screening Room*, a 90-minute late-night talk show hosted by Robert Gardner, in which independent filmmakers presented and discussed their films.[30] *Screening Room* hosted a wide range of filmmakers, including documentary filmmakers, animators, and avant-garde artists. The only common element was that the films were aesthetically interesting and not widely available. The purpose of *Screening Room* was to introduce the general public to new forms of filmmaking, by presenting independent films in a context that would enable people to understand and appreciate their significance. It exemplifies the innovative programs created by WCVB, and its success suggests that other commercial television stations were not satisfying consumer demand.

The Origins of Screening Room

Between 1972 and 1982, WCVB produced eight seasons of *Screening Room*, each season consisting of thirteen 90-minute episodes.[31] *Screening Room* was one of WCVB's first late-night programs. Initially, it aired on Saturday from 1:05 a.m. to 2:35 a.m., and then it moved to the same time slot on Sunday.[32] Ultimately, WCVB produced more than a hundred episodes of *Screening Room*, a few of which never aired.

Screening Room was recorded in the WCVB studio and adopted a conventional talk show format. Gardner would introduce the guest, usually a filmmaker, but occasionally a film theorist or critic. Then he would introduce a film or film clip, and ask the guest to provide some context. After showing the film or clip, Gardner and the guest would discuss how and why it was made, what it meant, and how it related to the filmmaker's other work. They would show and discuss additional films or clips for the remainder of the program. And then Gardner would make closing remarks.

Screening Room was unique to WCVB because no other commercial television station could have produced a similar program; while its format was conventional, its content was not. Other stations produced talk shows about commercial films playing in commercial theaters, but only WCVB would present a talk show about independent films, which most viewers would not otherwise be able to see.

Gardner was the creative force behind *Screening Room*. WCVB produced the program because Gardner was an investor in BBI and a director of WCVB. But *Screening Room* reflected his background as a documentary filmmaker and the director of Harvard's Carpenter Center for the Visual Arts. *Screening Room* not only hosted independent filmmakers and showed independent films, but also insisted on serious discussion of those films. Gardner demonstrated how to read a film critically, by carefully articulating his own experience of the films he showed, and challenging the filmmakers to explain their decisions and intentions.

The Structure of Screening Room

The content of a *Screening Room* episode was quite flexible, depending on the films presented and the direction in which the interview proceeded. But the FCC indirectly required Gardner to devote the majority of each episode to discussion. BBI promised the FCC that WCVB would provide an extraordinary number of local programs, and *Screening Room* was considered a local program because it was produced by WCVB. But the FCC rules stipulated that showing a film produced by a third party was not local programming. WCVB probably could have distinguished the films shown on *Screening Room*, but in an excess of caution, it required the majority of each episode to consist of talk.

The discussion-heavy format of *Screening Room* was an enormous advantage, which has proven historically important. Most of the films shown on *Screening Room* were quite unusual and difficult for the general audience to appreciate and understand. Having the filmmakers available to discuss how and why they made the films helped television audiences to understand and appreciate the goals of the filmmakers. In addition, many of the *Screening Room* programs have acquired substantial historical significance, as one of the few instances in which particular filmmakers were recorded discussing their films in detail.

Furthermore, many early episodes of *Screening Room* included film scholars and critics, in addition to the filmmaker. For example, Gardner invited Vladimir Petric, Stanley Cavell, Gerald O'Grady, and Rudolf Arnheim to participate in *Screening Room* discussions. Gardner also invited Octavio Paz and William Alfred to discuss his own film, *Dead Birds*.

However, Gardner eventually stopped inviting guests other than the filmmaker, finding that conversations generally developed more naturally between two people.[33]

Unlike a typical television interviewer, Gardner avoids flip or trivial questions. While his interviews are relaxed, they are not casual conversations. He works hard to engage with each film and to understand the filmmaker's purpose. In some cases, one can feel him struggle to appreciate the merits of a film. On occasion, he even implicitly challenges a filmmaker's choices. For example, Gardner admits that he did not understand the aesthetic and purpose of Yvonne Rainer's films when she was a guest on *Screening Room*, and that it affected his ability to engage with her work.[34]

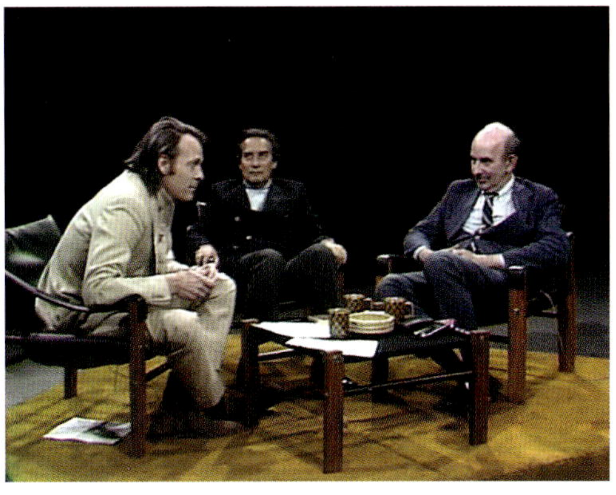

Robert Gardner with Octavio Paz and William Alfred on *Screening Room*

In addition, *Screening Room* materially contributed to the production of independent films, by providing filmmakers with much needed cash. While the budget of *Screening Room* was miniscule by broadcast standards, it was quite substantial for the world of independent film. Most independent filmmakers struggled to make ends meet and many venues paid little or nothing for screenings and appearances. The *Screening Room* budget enabled Gardner to pay his guests about $1,000 to appear on the program, as well as a rental fee for the films they showed. Often, the filmmakers would make as much as $1,500 or $2,000 for their appearance on *Screening Room*, which was quite a substantial amount at the time.[35] In addition, they received invaluable exposure to a different and much larger audience than the one to which they were accustomed.

Screening Room *Programs*

The remarkable range of *Screening Room* guests and films can only be appreciated in context. Gardner was fearless in deciding whom he invited and what they could show. The first *Screening Room* program was taped on December 1, 1972, and aired on January 12, 1973. The guest was John Whitney Sr., an experimental animator best known today for his work on the iconic title sequence of Alfred Hitchcock's *Vertigo*. But Gardner soon interviewed much more controversial filmmakers.

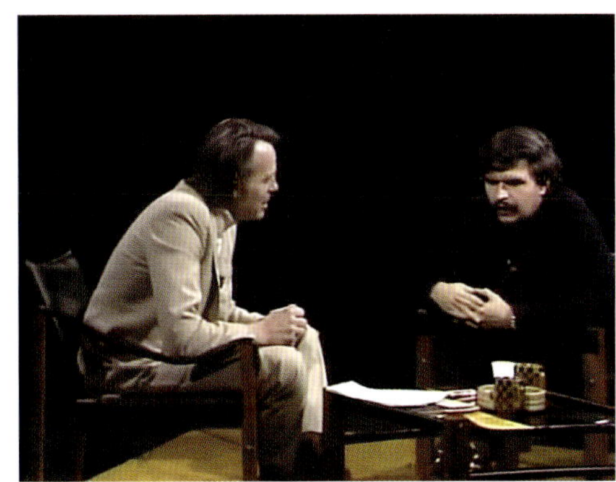

Robert Gardner with Stan Brakhage on *Screening Room*

On May 18, 1973, Gardner interviewed seminal avant-garde filmmaker Stan Brakhage for a *Screening Room* episode that aired on June 22, 1973.

Among other things, Brakhage presented his seminal short film *Window Water Baby Moving* (1959), in which he documented the birth of one of his children. *Window Water Baby Moving* is a silent film, in which Brakhage uses unusual visual effects in an attempt to convey the experience of childbirth. Notably, the film presents detailed close-ups of Jane Brakhage's vagina as she delivered the baby. Gardner insisted on broadcasting the film in its entirety, including the graphic images of childbirth; even today, it is unlikely any network station would broadcast this kind of explicit material, no matter the context.

On March 17, 1977, Gardner interviewed Canadian avant-garde filmmaker Michael Snow for a *Screening Room* program that aired on September 26, 1977. Among other things, Snow presented an excerpt from his film *Rameau's Nephew by Diderot (Thanx to Dennis Young) by Wilma Schoen* (1974). The excerpt that Snow chose to show includes a shot in which a man and a woman urinate into buckets. After the program was taped, the station manager called Gardner to object to the inclusion of the excerpt. When the program aired, the excerpt remained, albeit with a black box superimposed over the genitalia of the actors. Nevertheless, one could still hear the sound of the urination.[36]

And on July 9, 1980, Gardner interviewed French anthropologist and documentary filmmaker Jean Rouch for a *Screening Room* program that aired on November 12, 1980. Among other things, Rouch presented an excerpt from his short film, *Les maîtres fous* (1955), which documents the Hauka movement, widespread in West Africa from the 1920s to the 1950s. Hauka members participated in rituals in which they went into trances, often foaming at the mouth, and performed ceremonial processions that mocked their colonial rulers. *Les maîtres fous* documents a Hauka trance ritual, and has always been controversial because of its shocking imagery. Among other things, it shows the Hauka killing and eating a dog. Gardner's conversation with Rouch is especially rich, given their shared backgrounds as anthropologists and poetic filmmaking styles. For example, Rouch and Gardner have a long discussion about Dogon cosmology and mythology, in relation to one of Rouch's films.

While *Screening Room* presented many films with radical content for commercial television, in another respect the most revolutionary aspect of *Screening Room* was Gardner's willingness to show and discuss non-narrative, formally unusual films that challenged the expectations of television audiences. The most interesting and unique aspect of *Screening Room* was its total independence from and disregard of conventional assumptions about the tastes of television audiences. Gardner presented whatever he considered interesting or important, and assumed that his audience would also be interested.

The Importance of Screening Room

Screening Room was important because of the films it presented and because of how it presented them. Obviously, it introduced a large, popular audience to films that they would not have otherwise known existed and would not have had an opportunity to see. For many people, *Screening Room* offered the closest thing available to a seminar class in independent film, taught by a first-rate professor.

Screening Room also pushed the boundaries of television. Images of childbirth, nudity, and ritual violence all violated FCC guidelines, but Gardner showed them anyway, justifying his decision based on the context in which they were presented. It helped that they were shown in the middle of the night, when more sensitive viewers were less likely to be watching. Still, there was always a risk of repercussions, which thankfully never materialized. The threat of censorship may have indirectly affected Gardner's programming decisions. Several episodes of *Screening Room* were taped, but never aired. In some cases, the decision not to air a program may have been influenced by a concern that the risk of sanctions was too high.

But *Screening Room* was also important because of how it presented films. Gardner modeled a method of hosting a television show that was both conversational and intellectual. He showed that commercial television stations could appeal to real, popular audiences by offering them thoughtful, reflective discussions of art and culture. In other words, *Screening Room* was intentionally and explicitly pedagogical, unlike other commercial television programs. And its success showed that there was real consumer demand for intellectually challenging programs. That lesson of *Screening Room* went largely ignored for many years, until the fragmentation of mass media gradually lowered the fixed costs of providing video content to the public.

The Reception of Screening Room

Almost immediately, *Screening Room* attracted a great deal of critical interest. Shortly after WCVB introduced twenty-four-hour broadcasting, Bruce McCabe of the *Boston Globe* singled out *Screening Room* as an exemplary late-night program. "The all-night shows are a mixed bag of movies, recycled syndicated offerings and daytime repeats, but two original ideas have developed. One is 'Screening Room,' a weekly showing of avant-garde films from 1:05 a.m. to 2:35 a.m. Saturdays, hosted by Robert Gardner."[37]

A few months later, Cary Wasserman of the *Boston Globe* enthused, "No modern art has been more widely misunderstood than modern filmmaking. Robert Gardner's 'Screening Room' (WCVB-TV, Friday nights at 1:05) offers one of the few possibilities in the Boston area for seeing significant work of non-commercial filmmakers, and this week will present Stan Brakhage to show and discuss his films."[38]

Wasserman provided a carefully elliptical description of the content of Brakhage's films. "A Brakhage film almost never relies on traditionally-composed images. Rather there are colors that flash across the screen, novel juxtapositions, images that possess their own subconscious logic ('Window Water Baby Moving') and an underlining of the effect of light and vision on the mind."[39] Wasserman pointedly neglected to mention that *Window Water Baby Moving* graphically documents the birth of a child.

Wasserman also commented on the wide range of unusual and important films and filmmakers that Gardner featured on *Screening Room*. "For an audience, Brakhage's films are a chance to see life through new eyes, and hopefully to be forced to define the nature of vision. It should be added that other programs offer highly diverse work ranging from Yugoslavian animation to cinema verite, all characterized by the risk-taking one associates with the non-commercial cinema."[40]

Unfortunately, there is no hard data on the size of the *Screening Room* audience, because the ratings services stopped operating at 1 a.m., but circumstantial evidence suggests that it was substantial.[41] WCVB introduced and expanded all-night programming on the basis of mail response, showing high demand.[42] And late-night viewers had few other options. Anecdotal evidence suggests that *Screening Room* may have had as many as 250,000 viewers.[43]

Gardner's Other Contributions to WCVB

In addition to hosting *Screening Room*, Gardner contributed to WCVB in many other ways. As a director, he participated in the governance of the station. But he also created a great deal of original television content. Most notably, he conceived of and created many so-called noncommercials for WCVB. As defined by Gardner, a noncommercial was a one-minute short film in a lyrical style that documented a person's life or experience, without selling or advocating anything, or even expressing an explicit point of view.

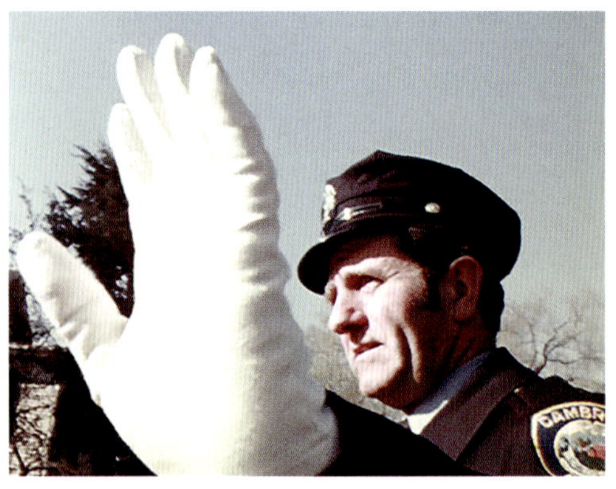

Gardner's noncommercials for WCVB generally documented residents of the greater Boston area as they did their jobs or otherwise engaged in everyday activities. For example, in *Policeman* (1973), a white-gloved Cambridge police officer directs traffic and shepherds children across the street, rhythmically waving his hands, as if dancing to the blues harmonica soundtrack.

In *Lobsterman* (1973), a young lobster fisherman hauls up a lobster pot, pulls out a lobster, replaces the bait, and moves on to the next trap. And in *Farmer* (1973), a grizzled farmer mows long grass with a scythe, pauses to sharpen the scythe, and then returns to mowing.

On regular occasions, WCVB would air one of Gardner's noncommercials during a commercial break, rather than a commercial advertisement. In theory, a noncommercial was like a public service announcement without an express purpose. In practice, the television audience must have found them quite puzzling. One can only imagine people wondering what they were intended to sell. In any case, many contemporary advertisements have adopted the oblique, lyrical style of Gardner's noncommercials.

Gardner also produced several programs for WCVB. In 1977, he produced *The Psychic Parrot*, a thirty-minute short comedy directed by Derek Lamb, an Oscar-winning British animator, who later directed animated segments for *Sesame Street*. *The Psychic Parrot* is a parody, set in the living room of a cartoonishly excitable couple watching television as a psychic parrot predicts the end of the world. It combines live-action and stop-motion cutout animation sequences, and ends with a comedic twist. In 1979, Gardner produced *Cost of Living*, a documentary directed by Richard P. Rogers, in which people from different parts of the community and different social classes were asked to discuss the meaning of money. Gardner also produced Rogers's short film *Anthem*, a three-minute collage of images of the American flag, which was intended to be used by WCVB as its sign-off.

The Legacy of Screening Room

Gardner produced more than a hundred episodes of *Screening Room*, most of which were broadcast. Unfortunately, he destroyed the tapes of several episodes, a decision he later regretted. "In the end I felt that some of them just didn't deserve to exist, and so I destroyed them. I should never have done that."[44]

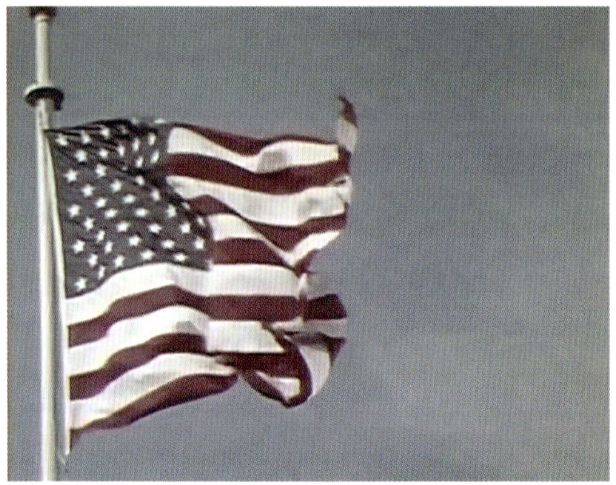

Thankfully, Gardner preserved most of the tapes, and eventually decided to release many episodes on DVD. "I held out maybe thirty, about a third of the ones that I'd done, as being worthy of archiving, and that's what we've got."[45] According to Gardner, the DVD releases "were edited under my supervision by Grace Fitzpatrick, a very nice woman who understood the project and knew what was worth cutting and what was important to keep.

Basically, she just cut out all the commercials and all the interruptions of the program by the station. Plus there were a few places in the programs when something really dumb was said or when something happened that marred the flow. I don't know whether notes were kept of what was eliminated, but we have the original and we have the result of Fitzpatrick's editing."[46]

The End of WCVB-TV

On July 22, 1981, Metromedia, Inc. announced that it had reached an agreement with BBI to purchase WCVB-TV for $220 million, more than twice the highest price previously paid for a television station.[47] At that time, WCVB-TV was producing sixty-two hours of original programs every week, more than any other network affiliate station.[48] In 1980, WCVB-TV had about $20 million in earnings on about $50 million in revenues.[49] Robert Bennett, the chief executive of WCVB-TV, was a former employee of Metromedia.[50] BBI agreed to sell WCVB-TV to Metromedia in large part because many of its investors were elderly and wanted to receive a return on their investments.[51] Ultimately, BBI's shareholders received a return of about 120 times their initial investment.[52]

The sale of WCVB-TV to Metromedia was completed on May 18, 1982.[53] After the sale, BBI's public mission persisted for a while. In fact, Metromedia purchased WCVB-TV in large part because it valued its innovative programming.[54] Much of WCVB-TV's staff, including Bennett, remained and the programming did not immediately change.

However, WCVB gradually reduced its noncommercial programming and became more and more commercial. In 1986, Metromedia sold its television stations, including WCVB-TV, to the News Corporation and 20th Century Fox. WCVB-TV was spun-off and purchased by the Hearst Corporation. Today, WCVB's programming is little different from any other network affiliate station.

The history of WCVB and of *Screening Room* reflects changes in the regulation and consumption of television. BBI won its broadcast license because a court quixotically tried to enforce the requirement that commercial broadcasters serve the public interest. The remarkable commercial success of WCVB and its ability to produce unique programs like *Screening Room* suggest that the court had identified a real market failure. Presumably, WCVB succeeded financially and critically at least in part because its competitors were failing to adequately serve the public interest in unconventional television. *Screening Room* exemplified the kind of program that only a commercial station dedicated to the public interest like WCVB could provide.

WCVB was unusual because its ownership and management included artists and academics like Robert Gardner, who participated extensively in its programming. They helped WCVB achieve its goal of providing good television by ensuring that it took creative risks and produced programs like *Screening Room* and Gardner's noncommercials. The example of WCVB suggests that bringing creative and intellectual voices inside the management of a commercial station may help promote both financial success and the public interest.

Screening Room *Program List—In Order of Broadcast*

Available on DVD from Documentary Educational Resources:
John H. Whitney and Eric Martin, 1973
Standish Lawder with Stanley Cavell, 1973
Les Blank with Peter Guralnick, 1973
Hilary Harris, 1973 and 1979 (same disc)
Jan Lenica with Jerzwy Soltan, 1973
Bruce Baillie with Gerald O'Grady, 1973
Robert Fulton, 1973 and 1979 (same disc)
John Hubley and Faith Hubley, 1973
Derek Lamb, 1973 and 1980 (same disc)
Emile de Antonio with Edmund Carpenter, 1973
Ricky Leacock with Al Mecklenberg and Jon Rosenfeld, 1973
Stan Brakhage, 1973 and 1980 (same disc)
Dick Rogers, 1975
Suzan Pitt-Kraning, 1975
Ed Emshwiller, 1975
Alan Lomax, 1977
Caroline Leaf and Mary Beams, 1977
George Griffin, 1976
Robert Breer, 1976
Hollis Frampton, 1977
Peter Hutton, 1977
Michael Snow, 1977
Yvonne Rainer with Deac Rossel, 1977
James Broughton, 1977
Jean Rouch, 1980
Jonas Mekas, 1981
John Marshall with James Vorenburg and Frank Kessler, 1973
(not released on DVD; inquire with DER)

Available for Research in the Harvard Film Archive's Robert Gardner Collection:
"The Films of the Zagreb Studio" with Zeleimir Matko, 1973
Vlatko Gilic with Vlada Petric, 1973
Ed Pincus, 1973
Claudia Weill and Eliot Noyes Jr., 1973
"Hungarian Films" with Yvette Biro, Gyorgy Kepes, Thomas Renyi, 1973
Jean Pigozzi with Erich Segal, 1973
"Homage to Eisenstein: Part I—Dynamics of the Silent Image" with Vlada Petric, 1973
"Homage to Eisenstein: Part II—Picture, Sound and Color" with Vlada Petric, 1973
"A Film by Robert Gardner: *Dead Birds*" with Robert Gardner, Octavio Paz, William Alfred, 1973
Robert Nelson, 1973*
Alfred Guzzeti, 1975*
Douglas Davis, 1975*
Dušan Makaveyev, 1975*

Peter Chermayeff, 1977
Pat O'Neill, 1977
"D.W. Griffith Retrospective," 1977
"*Rivers of Sand*" with Robert Gardner, 1977
"Maya Deren Retrospective," 1977
Joan Churchill and Nick Broomfield, 1977
"*The Nuer*" with Robert Gardner, 1977
Midge MacKenzie, 1977
Kathy Rose and John Rubin, 1977
Wendy Clarke, 1979
Thomas Harlan, 1979
John Haugse, 1980
Juan Downey, 1980
Michael Rubbo, 1979*
William Geddes, 1980
Polish Animation, 1980*
Dennis Pies, 1980*
Srđan Karonovic, 1981*
Willard Van Dyke and Amelie Rothschild, 1981*
Sidney Peterson, 1981*

Unavailable, Considered Lost:
"Student Films" with George Bluestone, Ted Spagna, Lois Tupper, Maureen McCue, 1973
Clarke Worswick, 1973
Tony Ganz and Rhoden Streeter, 1973
Eila Hershon and Roberto Guerra, 1973
Ann Hersey, 1975*
Teri McLuhan, 1975*
Derek Lamb, 1975*, 1977 (with Grant Munro), 1981
Johannes Manong, 1977
Marz Marzenski and Scott Sorenson, 1977
Dennis Piana with Rufus Seder, 1979
Vlada Petric, 1979*
"Yugoslavian Animation," 1980
Ken Griffith, 1980
Len Gittleman, 1981*
Frank Mouris and Caroline Mouris, 1981*

*recorded but airdate unknown (may not have aired)

Notes

1. In Re Applications of WHDH, Inc., 22 F.C.C. 767 (1957).
2. CBS asked the FCC to dismiss its application before the hearing began, and Post withdrew its application before the FCC decided the case. Massachusetts Bay Telecasters, Inc. v. F.C.C., 261 F.2d 55, 57 & n.1 (D.C. Cir. 1958).
3. In Re Applications of WHDH, Inc., 22 F.C.C. 767, 770 (1957).

4. Ibid. 767 (1957). Four Commissioners voted for WHDH, one abstained, and two dissented.
5. Massachusetts Bay Telecasters, Inc. v. F.C.C., 261 F.2d 55, 65–66 (D.C. Cir. 1958); Greater Boston Television Corp. v. F.C.C., 334 F.2d 552, 554 (D.C. Cir. 1964).
6. Sterling Quinlan, *The Hundred Million Dollar Lunch* (Chicago: O'Hara, 1974), 5.
7. Massachusetts Bay Telecasters, Inc. v. F.C.C., 261 F.2d 55, 66 (D.C. Cir. 1958). Quinlan, 5–6.
8. In Re Applications of WHDH, Inc., 22 F.C.C. 767, 771 (1957); Interview with Dr. Leo Leroy Beranek by William Lang at Cambridge, Massachusetts, October 28, 1989, at https://www.aip.org/history-programs/niels-bohr-library/oral-histories. (Why were they permitting new applicants? They discovered in 1962 that it looked as though WHDH had put on the fix, as they kept putting it—that is, a bribe to the chairman of the FCC to get their license. His name was McConnaughy.)
9. Massachusetts Bay Telecasters, Inc. v. F.C.C., 295 F.2d 131, 132 (D.C. Cir. 1961).
10. In the Matter of WHDH, Inc., Boston, Mass. Greater Boston Television Corp., Boston, Mass. Massachusetts Bay Telecasters, Inc., Boston, Mass., 33 F.C.C. 449 (1962).
11. In the Matter of WHDH, Inc., 16 F.C.C.2d 29, 30 (1966). Greater Boston Television Corp. v. F.C.C., 444 F.2d 841, 845 (D.C. Cir. 1970). Greater Boston appealed the FCC's decision to give WHDH a temporary license, but when Choate died on December 21, 1963, the D.C. Circuit remanded the entire case to the FCC. Greater Boston Television Corp. v. F.C.C., 334 F.2d 552, 554 (D.C. Cir. 1964); In the Matter of WHDH, Inc., Boston, Mass., 16 F.C.C.2d 1, 3 (1969).
12. In the Matter of WHDH, Inc., 16 F.C.C.2d 29, 165–70 (1966).
13. Leo Beranek, *Riding the Waves: A Life in Sound, Science, and Industry*, 167 (2008).
14. In the Matter of WHDH, Inc., 16 F.C.C.2d 29, 167 (1966).
15. Ibid. 29, 203 (1966).
16. In the Matter of WHDH, Inc., Boston, Mass., 16 F.C.C.2d 1, 8 (1969).
17. Beranek,169–170.
18. In the Matter of WHDH, Inc., Boston, Mass., 16 F.C.C.2d 1, 4 (1969).
19. Ibid. 1, 13–15 (1969).
20. Leo Beranek, the president of BBI, compared the proceedings to "Dickens's satires of the worst meanderings of the English legal system during Victorian times." Beranek, 174.
21. Tony Schwartz, "Metromedia Seeks TV Station," *New York Times*, July 23, 1981, at D2; Beranek, 173.
22. Ibid.
23. Beranek, 179; In Re Applications of WHDH, Inc., Boston, Mass. for Renewal of License, 33 F.C.C.2d 432, 434 (1972).
24. Gary Fogelson and Michael Hutcherson, "Change the Channel: WCVB-TV 1972–1982," installation, Apex Art, New York (2011).
25. Tony Schwartz, "Some Say This Is America's Best TV Station," *New York Times*, February 15, 1981, at D1.
26. Ibid.
27. Ibid.
28. Ibid.
29. Dudley Clendinen, "Sales of 2 Boston TV Stations Are Making History and Millionaires," *New York Times*, May 22, 1982, at 11.

30. Tom Cooper, "Screening Room" (DVD Review), *Film Quarterly* 73 (Fall 2005), 59.
31. Scott MacDonald, *Avant-Doc: Intersections of Documentary and Avant-Garde Cinema* (2014), 65–71.
32. Bruce McCabe, "C&W Smasheroo," Boston Globe, February 18, 1973, at B21; Bud Laughton, "Highlights," *Boston Globe*, July 1, 1973, at B7.
33. MacDonald.
34. Ibid.
35. Ibid.
36. Ibid.
37. McCabe.
38. Cary Wasserman, "The Films of Stan Brakhage," *Boston Globe,* June 21, 1973, at 66.
39. Ibid.
40. Ibid.
41. McCabe.
42. Ibid.
43. MacDonald.
44. Ibid.
45. Ibid.
46. Ibid.
47. Tony Schwartz, "Metromedia Takes Control of Station," *New York Times*, May 19, 1982, at D4.
48. Ibid.
49. Ibid.
50. Ibid.
51. Ibid.
52. Clendinen.
53. Schwartz.
54. Ibid.

Chapter 10

On Shamanism and Other Encounters: A Conversation with Robert Gardner in Mexico

Carlos Y. Flores and Antonio Zirión

Until fairly recently both the films and the written work of Robert Gardner were practically unknown in Mexico and Latin America (LA). And although the practice of anthropological or ethnographic film has been present for decades in LA, theoretical debates about what is known as visual anthropology have come to the region only lately. In some European countries and the United States, specialized postgraduate programs and an extensive theoretical literature on visual anthropology have existed for a long time. However, in Mexico and LA there have been few places where it has been possible to study and discuss the debates and approaches—in general this has been limited to isolated courses within undergraduate degree programs in social anthropology, or rare debates in seminars or at conferences. In such a context, Robert Gardner's visit represented a significant catalyst for the development of visual anthropology and ethnographic cinema in Mexico. Gardner came to Mexico in October 2008 to

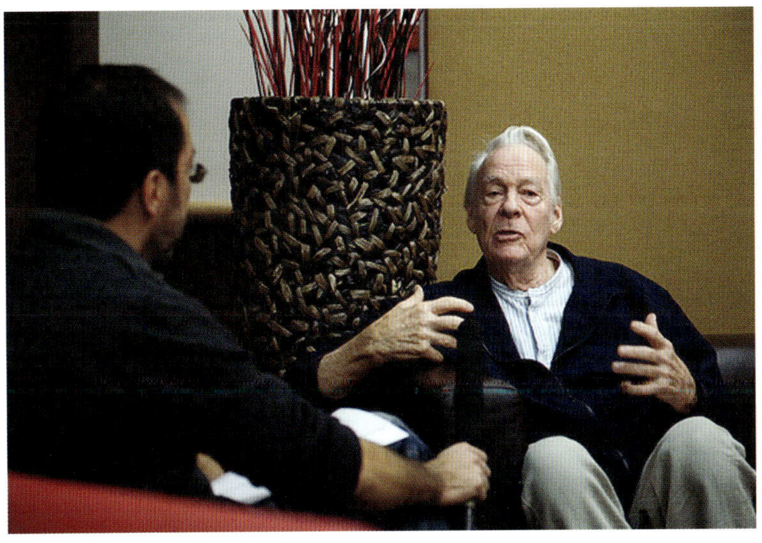

Carlos Flores and Robert Gardner

attend a retrospective of his films organized by the Visual Anthropology Seminar, within the International Documentary Film Festival of Mexico City (DocsDF), held at the Cineteca Nacional. This was the first of a series of retrospectives on ethnographic filmmakers—including Jorge Prelorán, Kim Longinotto, Trinh Minh-ha, Vincent Carelli, and John Marshall—that have been organized recently in Mexico.

In this conversation Gardner talks about his films and the projects he never completed. He discusses the great masters who influenced him, such as Luis Buñuel and Robert Flaherty; also the work of other ethnographic filmmakers such as Jean Rouch and his cinema verité, and the pioneers of North American Direct Cinema. He reflects on philosophical questions related to documentary cinema, principally to do with ethics and epistemology, such as the problem of representation of reality, the blurry division between fiction and nonfiction, and the importance of aesthetic experience as a form of knowledge. He also relates his relationship with important Latin American figures such as Octavio Paz, Nicolás Echevarría, and Jorge Prelorán.

One of the most interesting features of this conversation is the way in which this filmmaker's anthropological dimension is revealed. Gardner reflects on postmodern anthropology and the relationship between the anthropologist-documentary maker, his subject-characters, and his audience. He touches on the issues of suffering, the human condition, and cinema as a therapeutic activity that has allowed him to live in the world and confront its different problems. Finally, Gardner speaks of new tendencies and the future of visual anthropology and ethnographic cinema. At one point in the interview, the theme of shamanism is revealed as a source of inspiration for Gardner.

Julia Yezbick served as videographer for this interview. At one point, as indicated below, she asks a question from behind the camera.

Carlos Flores (C.F.): Jean Rouch said once that filmmakers regarded him as an anthropologist, while anthropologists regarded him as a filmmaker. Does this happen to you as well? Or where would you locate your work?

Robert Gardner (R.G.): I think that is very true of Jean Rouch, an old pal. He was definitely both, although I feel some of his work is more distinctly on the side of anthropology. I think that he felt film was more a tool for anthropology, than anthropology was a tool for film. And so, if I were to make any distinction between us, it might be that I regarded anthropology more as a tool for my filmmaking. I always wanted to use what I could of anthropology's methods and intentions to further my filmmaking, to give me a context to work within.

Antonio Zirión (A.Z.): Being a filmmaker, how did you become interested in anthropology? How did you start making this connection between anthropology and cinema?

R.G.: I actually entered the realm of anthropology through literature; when I was on the Northwest coast of North America I read a book by a very fine anthropologist, now deceased, named Ruth Benedict, who was also a poet. She was not only poetic in her writing but she also wrote poetry. In her book *Patterns of Culture* (1934) there is a chapter about the Kwakiutl, a remnant North West Coast American group of Indians. I became interested in what she was saying about the pattern of their culture and specifically about the life that they used to have, because when I was reading the book, of course, much of that life had passed into history and was no longer functioning. But there were small groups of Kwakiutl people who were still living in small villages in British Columbia, and I found a group and I went and made two little films. That was really my start in what you are calling "visual anthropology." I tried to be not only respectful but also factual. I mean, I didn't impose a story. These were the films *Blunden Harbour* (1951) and *Dances of the Kwakiutl* (1951).

I was also drawn to the writing of exceptionally observant travelers such as Doughty on the Arabs, Melville on Melanesians, and Lévi-Strauss on the Bororo. These and many other authors opened my eyes to hitherto unknown places and people.

A.Z.: Whom do you consider as your main influences?

R.G.: I could cite a number of people whom I have admired and even attempted to be like ever since my childhood. But it was probably not until I had reached adulthood, or thereabouts, that certain people began influencing me in major ways. These earliest influences were related to a time when I realized, with their help, that I was in serious need of examining my own life and even making some major changes in it. Most importantly were those who were unsparing in their view that I was basically illiterate. I needed to read and to look carefully at what mankind had made, at architecture, painting, sculpture, films. Important in these matters were the poet Ted Roethke and the painter Mark Tobey, whom I met as a young person in Seattle early in the '50s.

When I moved to Cambridge I met the poet Robert Lowell and was immediately introduced to a number of writers and artists including Ted Hughes, with whom I eventually developed a film treatment. Josep Lluís Sert was a Cambridge architect who opened doors to his Spanish circle, allowing me to meet a number of wonderful artists including Luis Buñuel, who invited me to watch him make a film in Mexico. I was already in his permanent debt for his having made *Tierra Sin Pan* (1932) and *Los Olvidados* (1950). In those years I also met Octavio Paz, who almost more than anyone else put me in touch with the universe of shamans and gurus. He was, I suspect, the most intelligent person I have ever had the gift of knowing.

There were also strong influences on me exercised by people I never met, great filmmakers like Vigo and Tarkovsky and writers like Melville and Conrad. There were and still are contemporary figures that inspire and influence me. Here I would put Stan Brakhage, Duŝan Makavejev, Christian Boltanski, Sean Scully. The list is long.

A.Z.: You once mentioned that you think of Luis Buñuel as your cinematographic father. Could you talk further on this?

R.G.: Well, I think I was not putting it well. I don't think that his way of making films was the way I was going to do it. Except and unless we just took *Tierra Sin Pan* or *Los Olvidados*, which dealt with both actuality and fiction. I mean, if we stop his career there, then he is much more of a father than when he began to do elaborate story films. One should not discuss actuality filmmaking without speaking of his earliest films, including *Un Chien Andalou* (1929). I think that was where he began getting interested in the experimental or abstract. And I think those elements were important for what I was trying to do in the beginning. But I also want people to know that he once said to me: "you know, this is not the best of all possible worlds." What I think he meant was that we have to be aware of the fact that what is told in fiction films does not wholly or responsibly tell us the true story, because the true story is that there is an awful lot of pain in the world to be seen that such films never show. And he could cite *Tierra Sin Pan* as an example of showing it as well as many other films I'm sure that he saw and liked. So in that sense he is a father for me. I mean, he is somebody to believe in. And he was also such a prolific figure . . . he could do no wrong.

C.F.: We would like to hear more about your connection with Latin America. For example, you worked with Jorge Prelorán. I like his work, particularly because he proposed a new approach to his subjects, using what he called "ethnobiography" as a method in the '60s. Could you tell us more about this?

R.G.: I got to know him when he was involved in making his film *Imaginero* (1967). I liked him very much. He was sent to me by Alan Lomax, the celebrated American musicologist who wrote about jazz, and invented something called "choreometrics," "cantometrics," and so forth. He became a social scientist as well as a great artist. He thought Prelorán might profit by asking me to help him finish this film. I loved the film. I think it was charming in many ways and very lyrical in some ways, historical, responsible, reliable, all the good things. He was a conscientious person. Our paths ultimately diverged when he went to the West Coast, which is a long way from the East Coast. I never really saw him again after that film.

C.F.: You mentioned that Octavio Paz somehow introduced you to shamanism. . . .

R.G.: I think that's fair. I mean, his mind was so capacious, so enormous in terms of his appetite for sensation, the world, facts, history and archaeology . . . everything. There is a little piece of film where he reads the *I Ching*.[1] It is my *I Ching* in that I ask a question and throw the dice, which is quite engaging. But he was deeply interested in John Cage, the musician, composer, mushroom eater, a fantastic person who believed passionately that randomness and chance determine much of what happens in life. Sometimes he wouldn't undertake anything without rolling the dice first to see if he should or should not do it.

But your question I think had more to do with what Octavio Paz's specific interest in shamanism meant to me, and how I used it or abused it, or a bit of both. Well, Castaneda was riding high at the time and Don Juan was a big figure in the intellectual lives of those of us who were somehow marginal or inhabiting parts of the anthropological profession that were not central to its classic purposes. We were interested in the margins of societies, including our own, and in ways of navigating in that realm, which might include shamanism as one of the ways to explore the world of imagination, invention, and so on.

Well, I shamelessly conflated a lot of things, such as thinking that Octavio Paz really was a shaman, even if he wasn't capable of magical flight, which I think is Mircea Eliade's definition of true shamanism. He was close to being able to fly, by sheer willpower, or to move in space and time using his mind, which was so immense.

I was always searching for a way to explore the world of shamanism, and that was what gave rise to my interest in the Ika of Colombia, who I regret didn't actually have true shamans in the classic sense but had priests, a wonderfully educated and imaginative priesthood that did some of the things that real shamans might have done. They were trained for a long time. They had an immense store of knowledge. In my film *Ika Hands* (1988) I featured a *Mama*, as they call a priest.

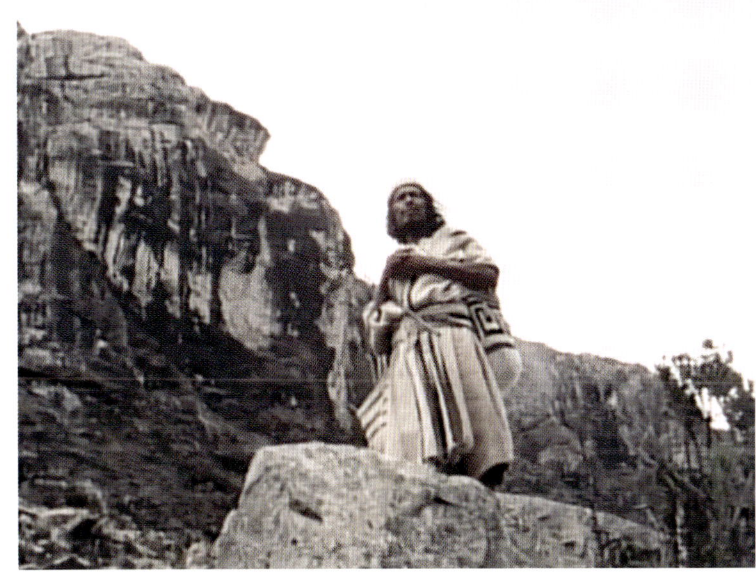

I and a dear friend, Robert Fulton, flew to the Ika in my own aircraft and landed at an old strip made by a Luftwaffe pilot who had fled Europe after the Second World War to escape punishment or his own guilt. He set up this little airfield, which I found and used. I persuaded the *Mama*, the priest, to come with me in the airplane, to go and collect shells on the coast far from where we were in the mountains. I asked him to fly the airplane, because I felt that if he could fly the plane I would have made some progress in the connection between magical flight and shamanism, and so on. It was a very bad idea. . . . It was not such a bad filmic idea; it was a bad intellectual idea. It was just stupid! But it made for a piece of business that I don't regret or think damaged the film particularly. I just feel I got nowhere doing it.

That's about the extent of it as far as Octavio's influence on me regarding shamanism. His influence on me regarding many other things is greater: literature, art, painting, this painter or that painter, this poet or that poet.

C.F.: You know the work of Nicolás Echevarría. Would you like to comment on it?

R.G.: Nicolás Echevarría. . . . I met him years ago when I came down to visit with the Pazes. It was at a party that we met. He said he'd looked at my films and I didn't know how he'd done that, but he apparently had. I mean maybe he had seen them in the United States or maybe he'd seen them in Mexico, I'm not sure. Nico is an exceptional person, so gifted, visually. I just visited a wonderful show of his paintings . . . it is really wonderful. As for his love of actuality filmmaking, one only needs to have seen *Niño Fidencio* (1981) and *María Sabina* (1979), to mention the ones that come vividly to mind; and then consider his frustrating but truly exceptional efforts to make fiction films. All these things I think set him apart as a real innovator and a wonderful spirit to have in the Mexican film movement.

A.Z.: Going back to your particular context, what was your connection with the Direct Cinema movement in America? How come you were not involved in it, why did you stay out? Because I imagine that it was very influential back in the '60s.

R.G.: Good question. By direct cinema you must be referring to cinema verité?

A.Z.: Well, the North American version . . . Leacock, Drew, Wiseman, Pennebaker, the Maysles, et cetera.

R.G.: Oh, the observationalists . . . Well, they are all friends. I know all these people extremely well. We all began our lives as filmmakers more or less at the same time. Maybe Ricky Leacock was ahead of us by about ten years. Actually, as a forerunner of the Direct Cinema movement, he originally had a background in fiction film, working with Robert Flaherty. Although some people might say that Robert Flaherty was a documentary filmmaker, he was also a feature filmmaker, in the sense of caring about the story, and such issues.

As for my start . . . it came after Ricky's but about the same time as the Maysles. It could be said that it all began in experimental film. My early interest in film came about through a familiarity and friendship with some experimental filmmakers, but also through an immersion in classic documentary filmmaking. By this I mean the work of Eisenstein, Riefenstahl, Joris Ivens, who were some of the figures who made these early and magnificent actuality films. They turned me into a person interested in a lyrical approach to the other worlds that I wanted to enter, like the Kwakiutl of the Northwest Coast, which I did before cinema verité really got established. When cinema verité got going it was at about the time I left for New Guinea to make *Dead Birds* (1963). I sort of missed the sound-synch "boat" (as we used to say). Because, you know, although Ricky had developed a method, and Pennebaker used it in various ways, I was still thinking [about] lyrical actuality filmmaking. So *Dead Birds* never either profited or was damaged by the Direct Cinema approach because it was all done with a camera that we used to call wild—it was sound by itself and picture by itself.

C.F.: Yes, but suddenly you had synch-sound and smaller equipment. . . . Did it mean any change for you to have these technological possibilities, in the type of narrative, in the type of approach that you had with your subjects?

R.G.: Not if I understand your question to be about the miniaturization of the technology, putting everything in one package. I did not see that as an advantage. In fact, I found more freedom in being able to work with a camera that was not connected by a cable, or some radio device, to another person. With Direct Cinema you are very much dependent and even physically linked to another whole set of sensibilities, those of the sound person.

I grew to think there was a more productive way of working than being harnessed to an audio world directly connected with the picture. I wanted these two worlds to be separate. I wanted to be able to work on the sound world and the visual world separately, bringing them together from time to time, of course, but not in a constrained synchronized way, but in a more contrapuntal way, where one worked against the other, or worked for the other.

For example, Wiseman didn't shoot but took sound. I mean, he actually carried a sound recorder around and he would direct the film by pointing with his microphone at what he wanted the camera to do. So the camera was subordinated to the intentions of the sound person, who happened in this case to be the director of the film. Out of that came this directly linked together product of cinema verité.

I suppose that was very exciting for a while, but it wasn't truth twenty-four times a second, as Godard said. It was another kind of rendering of reality, that's all. And I just found the opportunities of bringing things to life pictorially more productively done with a camera that was not linked so dependently to the sound.

C.F.: We are interested in knowing how you approach your subjects. Do you have a team working before you go there? Or what about the issue of language, for example? I imagine it is different depending on each film.

R.G.: Well, you put your finger on it, really. It varies depending on where I hope to do something. It may mean having prior knowledge of one kind or another. For example, I made a film with a man named Hilary Harris, a great friend and a wonderful filmmaker, whom I persuaded to go to Africa to make a film on the Nuer. Now the Nuer are, as you know, a classic group of people about whom fine work was done by Evans-Pritchard, a great British anthropologist who wrote a book called *The Nuer* (1940). Then along I came, having read that as a graduate student, and being impressed by it, really impressed. It is literature and it is an evocation of Nuer life. Not irrelevantly we called the film, *The Nuer* (1971).

And so, that was an occasion when I already knew a lot. Now, it didn't necessarily mean that I was familiar with the situation where I was going, because Evans-Pritchard wrote during the '30s. And I was there in the '70s. So things had changed, but even so enough was the same so that I could find evidence of what he was writing about in my much later encounter with the Nuer. So I profited from Evans-Pritchard, of course. But there was nobody who went out in front of me as part of an advanced team or anything.

Let's take another example: *Ika Hands*, which is not a big film in my view. It is not a feature film, but is an hour, or nearly an hour, about a hardly known part of Colombia, South America. But there had already been a wonderfully informed and gifted anthropologist who had written about them, and so I was able to get a little, again I emphasize a little, knowledge of these people before I went. But in the end it was largely an encounter with the unknown. I had to make my way largely by myself.

C.F.: In this sense, as a filmmaker whose stories are you telling? Are they your stories, your subjects' stories, or maybe a communion of both?

R.G.: Well, I have tried to get away with saying that my films were stories in the sense that they had beginnings, middles, and ends. There was a day when I started the film about Benares and a day when I ended it, but I always hoped it had a certain unity, a story unity. The same is true of *Dead Birds*. It is less true maybe of *Rivers of Sand* (1974), which is more *collagist* than linear story making. *Passenger* (1988) is linear storytelling, because it starts with an empty canvas and ends with a finished canvas, which is a story, the story of that canvas, plus being the story of that man's making certain kinds of marks to come to the end of a particular painting.

Now, whether they are my stories or whether they are somebody else's, let's just take an example. In *Passenger* what happened was that Sean Scully, the painter, started his work and I followed him, I recorded what he did. But then in the editing I also altered enormously the sequencing of what he was doing. I went back and forth in time, I repeated passages, I slowed them down and sped them up. I had the tools to do a lot of manipulation of the reality that was out there, and which was seemingly very simple: a studio, nobody in it except me, Sean Scully, and one other person, Bob Fulton, and light coming through a few windows, the canvas up on the wall . . . it was very simple. But it is also not so simple because to make something out of it is a complex matter and it doesn't happen automatically, or if it does then it's not really thoughtful. So, the story came from the circumstances, which were what I described as an empty studio with a painter in it, chance, which was whatever happened to affect what was happening in front of my eyes or in front of the camera, and my intentions, which had to do with examining how an artist's feelings and talent were brought to bear to make a mark, and not just a mark but a set of marks, which became a painting.

I did a book about nonfiction film (*Making* Forest of Bliss: *Intention, Circumstance, and Chance in Nonfiction Filmmaking,* 2001) in which those elements are just things that you have to deal with as a filmmaker, with all three of them, all the time.

C.F.: When you are in the process of making a film, do you think about your potential audience?

R.G.: No, I don't think about the audience, I honestly don't. I'm very selfish in that regard. I really only think about what I can live with afterward. What I can enjoy as having been a successful time, rather than a bad time. I've had lots of bad times making films. I have a lot of films, three, four, five films that I started and never finished. I am now, as a matter of fact, working to complete some of these unfinished pieces. I'm sure there are other filmmakers in the same spot, independent filmmakers. I'm not talking of people in the commercial world, because they have to finish something, and if they don't finish them they don't get paid. But, if I don't finish one, I just put it on the shelf and it doesn't matter to anybody whether I do it or not. I'm not being paid by the meter or anything like that. In these experiences that are now on shelves, old reels of film that I haven't finished putting together as an ultimate object, there are possibilities for new films. Something can come out of it still. It is there. Somebody said: "it is part of the past"; it is not part of the present, it is not part of the future, certainly. No photograph, no image of a photographic nature, including film, is part of the present. Always, once done, it becomes part of the past. And so I'm always dealing with the past, but I don't find any problem with that. It is just the nature of things. Time moves on and film doesn't keep up.

C.F.: The so-called anthropological turn, or the crisis of representation in the late '70s and '80s, began to critically examine issues such as authorship, the shared construction of knowledge, the silencing of subjects in many anthropological texts. These currents arose within anthropology after your first films were made, but have they influenced you in any way or made you reflect on issues of representation regarding your own work?

R.G.: I don't know anybody who showed me better how important observation was, how important representation was, whether it is by words, by photography, or by film, or any other representational means, than Clifford Geertz. His work on cockfighting in Bali seems to me a wonderfully clear proof of how much we can learn by using our eyes. Of course, he put it in an interesting literary manner, into an article, a book. So, the representation is in the words, but the observation, of course, is visual. He couldn't have done that work without having eyesight. I've always tried to imagine a blind anthropology, what would they be doing all day, would it be possible? I suppose ears could be made to hear things that ordinary people don't. But anthropologists should be able to see things that ordinary people don't.

I think that anything I've tried to do in terms of reducing the crisis that there might be in representation is to find in the language of film means for seeing things in an improved or in a more provocative, suggestive, and informative way. If I can find by intuitive devices or by reasonable, objective, observational methods, something that people hadn't noticed or hadn't realized was as important as it is, and I can put that into a context of a larger representation of some part of a culture or some subculture, then I think visual anthropology has proven its value. We need not be so doubtful about the authenticity of representational means. What else do we have? I think all that anthropologists really have are their sensibilities. What do I have except my failing eyesight, my ears, my sensibilities, my prejudices, everything? There is no way to manage any progress in this game of trying to find one's feet, as has been said of anthropology, than to use one's sensibilities. One's sensibilities are inevitably subjective, along with being intuitively promising or correct even, or being imaginatively suggestive, which is also promising.

A.Z.: In this regard, in which ways can cinema contribute to the knowledge of other cultures and humankind in general?

R.G.: Basically, I think, through the ability of audiences to enter into and almost become a part of what is revealed to them on a motion picture screen. For example, Robert Flaherty makes motion pictures of Eskimos and tells a story about them, which is seen and absorbed by his audiences. People see the humanity in what they are shown and begin to understand there is a connection between those they see as shadows and themselves. This wonderfully heightened capacity of film to generate such responses in its viewers is nearly unique in the arts. It nevertheless is not automatic in gaining such access to people's feelings and thoughts. The filmmaking must be of a kind that makes the humanity of others accessible. In other words, it takes visual talents of a particular kind, a kind that depends as much on empathy as craft.

C.F.: There is a piece of film where you and Octavio Paz are watching *Ika Hands*. There is one sentence that you posed to him: "I know a lot about a culture just from seeing." I suppose you were talking about a sort of intuition. Sometimes you don't need to know a language, or at least a verbal language, a rational language, in order to understand certain things. Could you talk further about this?

R.G.: Well, that's an enormous claim to make. Just because I'm looking at something, I'm understanding it? I'm understanding it maybe in limited ways. The very title of the film, *Ika Hands*, actually gives away what I saw/found, what seemed to me a quite important insight. What seemed important was the way they shaped things with their hands, and how they used their hands to communicate.

I think the fact of being an onlooker, not a participant, does require some intuitive judgment, an intuitive sensibility to find meaningful—that's a terrible word— suggestive, evocative evidence of a culture's nature. I feel it happened frequently in India (while filming *Forest of Bliss*, 1986), when I saw/found the importance of marigolds, of bamboo, and other such things. But simple as they may be, they all are intricately involved in the deepest and most intense, ritually intense, and holy aspects of their lives. These simple materials are ways to get into something far more complex.

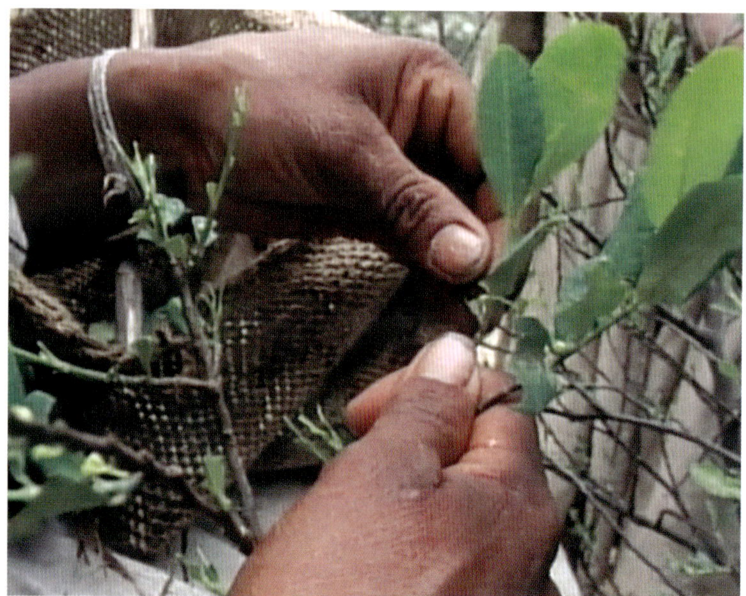

C.F.: In visual anthropology, sometimes we find problems between narratives, languages, styles, ways of doing things, because it involves notions such as science, objectivity, subjectivity, art, et cetera. What do you think are the main tensions between academic anthropology and filmmaking?

R.G.: Well, I don't think there is any special difficulty between academia and filmmaking that doesn't also pertain to literature or painting and academia. I don't think that there is an inevitable clash between these two approaches to revealing human life. I mean you need knowledge and you need visual or verbal talent of some kind.

A.Z.: In this sense, what is the role of aesthetics in anthropology, in ethnographic cinema? How important is it in your own work?

R.G.: If by aesthetics you mean considerations of art in its various forms, it is clear to me there is an important place for it in anthropology. Anthropology claims to seek out the meaning of human life by closely observing it and, ultimately, putting into words (or pictures) what it finds. This is an activity that depends for its best results on a discerning mind and an expressive capability. These are essential elements of any art, whether playing the piano or shooting film. If the goal of anthropology is to try to reveal the meanings of our behavior, how can it dispense with the aesthetic dimension? I sometimes feel as though critics on warring sides of these matters make the mistake of thinking science is opposed to or incompatible with art and vice versa. In my view, they coexist with no difficulty at all. I would submit my own work as examples of why aesthetics should not be ignored.

Julia Yezbick: I liked the way that you described actuality or nonfiction filmmaking, in the way that you do it, as lyrical. Maybe you could talk a little bit about that as an approach, as opposed to trying to really capture truth, what that can do, and what you think nonfiction film, in that kind of vein, what the purpose of it is.

R.G.: I think lyrical is not such a great word and I don't think I should go around using it as much as I do. What I wanted to say is that there is poetry in film. That film can make poetry of its own kind. I suppose any time a film is made about a culture, one is transposing actuality by means of artistic expression. That was what interested me about it early on and still interests me today. It is actually a way—a use of one's sensibility—that has wonderful results. Finding facts is a much harder thing to do . . . well, not harder, but different and maybe harder . . . because I don't think it's ever possible to regard anything as truth. It is OK to see it as an approach, or as an example, or as an approximation. But I think you would be very frustrated as a filmmaker, if you felt you had to bring back the truth. I think that the only truth may be what resides in your experience of that which is out there in the world in front of you.

Primo Levi was the man who wrote *Survival in Auschwitz* (1958), after having gone through the experience of surviving in Auschwitz. He once said (I hope I'm quoting him correctly): "one must be wary of the truthfulness of documentary evidence." Now, what an amazing thing for such a man to say, that anything, even a photograph that you make of a concentration camp, has doubtful documentary value. What he meant, and I'm quite sure of this because he goes on to say the only truth is your own experience, is that you live something and then it becomes something you can call real, something you could even call truth. This had huge meaning for me because I began to look at representations of the world using various kinds of filmmaking and writing, with a little more suspicion.

C.F.: We wanted to ask you about suffering, human suffering, and what this suffering means to you as a filmmaker. For example, you have been in the middle of warfare and you have witnessed injustice. . . . Has filming these situations changed you somehow, existentially?

R.G.: Oh, I think it has absolutely changed me. I've become very attached to people who are suffering, to people who are undergoing pain of one kind or another. I had a title originally for the film that I did on the Hamar [*Rivers of Sand*], which was *Creatures of Pain*.[2] Now, in English there is a subtle meaning to the word "creature," we are all creatures, but the word also means, for me at least, that we make something happen in us, we create something in us. I think when we create a condition of pain we become victims and have to be regarded as creatures of pain. I don't know of any society in the world that doesn't have to deal with the presence of pain in their life, either pain which is imposed on them or pain which is imposed by themselves on themselves. So it is a contemporary issue, but also a dimension of humanity's expression of itself that is I think important to understanding one of the most important elements of the condition that we are in. The human condition is determined by pain, either of our own making or a result of our passive involvement.

But I think I've been able to stay out of crisis by keeping on filmmaking. The filmmaking has steadied me in some manner. I have no idea what I would have become otherwise. I was not going to be a painter, I have no musical talent, except maybe a sense of rhythm, which one needs to be an editor of film. But the excitement of being able to express my feelings about other people and other situations, superficially very dissimilar to my own, but fundamentally the same as my own, was always enough to keep me going. There were times in New Guinea during that big effort to make my first long film when I became so involved in certain of those people's lives that it seemed inconceivable to not be there and participating with them in their experiences. But the only way I could participate was by filming and that was the way I could understand them, or begin to understand them.

A.Z.: What do you think are the most important tendencies in the evolution of actuality filmmaking in the last decades? How do you imagine the future of visual anthropology and ethnographic filmmaking?

R.G.: I think the tendency to relax about such an unhelpful issue as "authenticity" has been positive. The lines that have blurred between fiction and (so-called) nonfiction are essential to the freeing of cinema from its doctrinal prison. I would like to think the future of ethnographic filmmaking would include the abandonment of retaining a category of "ethnographic" that hinders efforts to inquire cinematically into the human condition. Using this term benefits only the dogmatists who prefer to ignore the fact that we are all members of one humanity.

C.F.: Any regrets? Something that you would have liked to do and you didn't do, or something that you did that you rather wouldn't do.

R.G.: Oh, there are. There have been four projects that I put together to do a fiction film. They were fiction films that had very strong affinities to nonfiction. One was from a book called *Cooper's Creek* (1963), which was the story, in the early nineteenth century, of the explorers who went across Australia, from I think Melbourne to the Arafoera Sea on the North Coast of Australia. They set off across the continent and there is this magnificent story of their attempt to do that. Here were some wholly unprepared and ill-suited Europeans unable to relate to an unfamiliar landscape. It was to be a film about the contact between these adventurers who wanted to cross the continent, and the indigenous population, which was, of course, completely at home in this amazing environment. It was these encounters as they made this fateful and tragic attempt at something they had no hope of doing that interested me. It was seeing the relations they had with the indigenous, the aboriginal people of Australia, dancing around them as they tried to pull an ox cart across Australia.

I also was going to make a film about an execution on a French island off Nova Scotia. A man had killed a companion on a drunken New Year's Eve in the late nineteenth century and confessed his crime. He was ultimately beheaded for reasons of a justice imposed by Paris, because the island was under the jurisdiction of France. French justice required that he be executed by guillotine. It is a marvelous story.

Then there is another project I wanted to do, which is a story by John Coetzee, the South African who wrote a book called *Waiting for the Barbarians* (1982). It is a wonderful story about an outpost in some imagined time on a frontier between civilization and barbarians, people who lived beyond the sphere of influence of civilization. I got as far, actually, as getting a producer who funded it and we were building sets to shoot interiors in Marrakech, when word came from the agent of one of the main actors saying his client was having to drop out of the project because his wife might take all his money in a divorce settlement. The actor was Tommy Lee Jones, and Tommy Lee Jones was meant to be my friend because we both had gone to Harvard. I never had a contract. Tommy Lee just shook hands and said he would come and do the job. Well, the moment his lawyer called saying that he couldn't, this immense house of cards just collapsed. So, I never did it. I regret that. There were maybe one or two other situations like that, but no, mostly I don't have much to regret.

C.F.: Lastly, any final comments? Something that you would like to add?

R.G.: I would like to ask you, Julia and Antonio, to put your best efforts and talents into being observers of the world we are in and to make work that can inspire and instruct in as poetic terms as possible, to find solutions for the many difficulties we are in, that humanity is in. I don't mean that the Mexican economy is in or that American politics are in. I mean, things that affect all people in the struggle to survive. You must find ways of expressing the necessity of helping them by making beautiful films.

Few film festivals in my long acquaintance with them have left me more exhilarated or more confident that the future of actuality filmmaking is in the hands of inspired and intelligent young men and women. It could also be noted that Margaret Mead once suggested that we should not underestimate the possibility that a small group of inspired young people can change the world. I am hoping my encounter with such people as yourselves here in Mexico will prove her right.

Notes

1. Gardner includes this material in *Glimpses of Octavio Paz* (2008). For availability, see the Studio7Arts website. —Editors' note
2. Gardner later used this title for one of the *Forsaken Fragments* (2013), filmed in Nigeria, about which he states, "I had gone to Nigeria to watch a ceremony in which young men exhibited their indifference to pain by allowing themselves to be severely beaten by their peers." —Editors

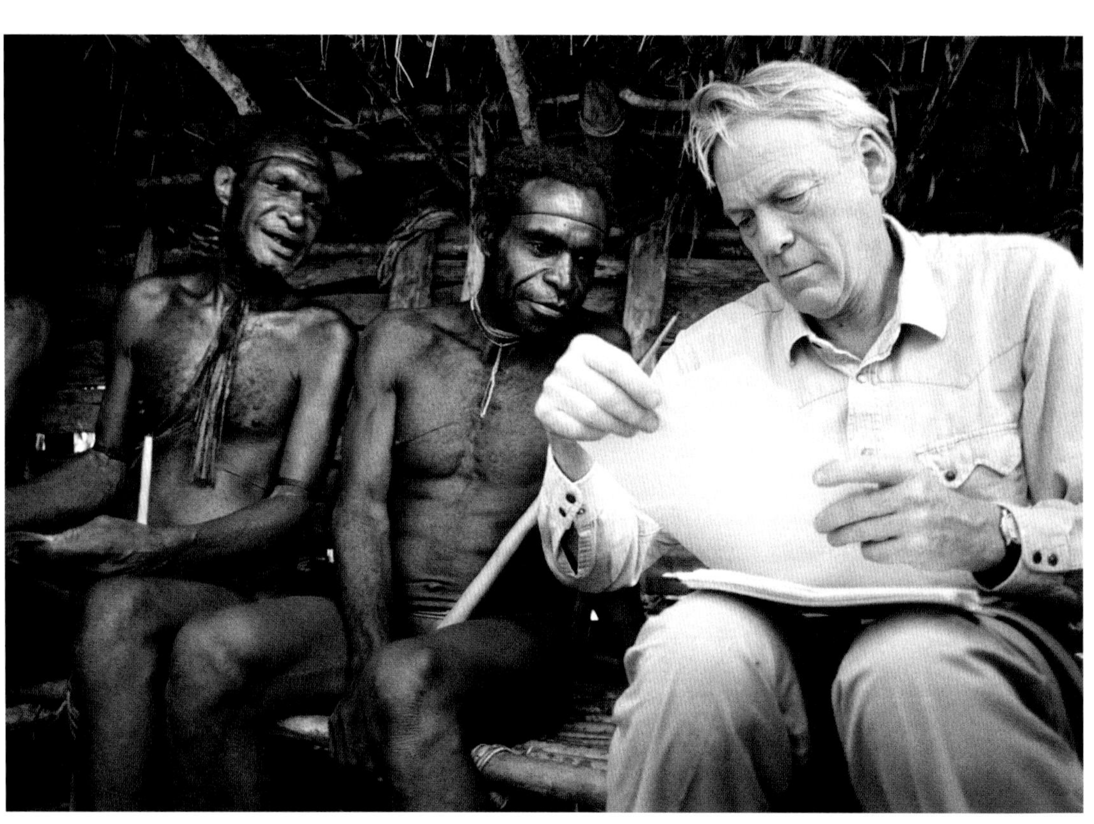

Chapter 11

Returning with Robert Gardner to the Baliem Valley, 1988–89

Susan Meiselas

In the winter of 1988–89 I traveled with Robert Gardner, Richard Rogers, and Robert Fulton to New Guinea for Gardner's first visit there since the filming of *Dead Birds* in 1961. When Bob decided to go back to the Baliem Valley with us, he had no idea what to expect, but wondered who he would find there and how the Dani would remember him. Some Dani had seen the images he had made for his book *Gardens of War* (1967), which came to the Valley along with piles of tourists passing through their gardens. But for most, the photographic prints were a complete surprise, and seeing them, seeing themselves, is what this series captures . . . the sheer delight, both theirs and his, in that moment of first sharing, from Bob's hands finally giving the images back to the Dani, nearly thirty years later.

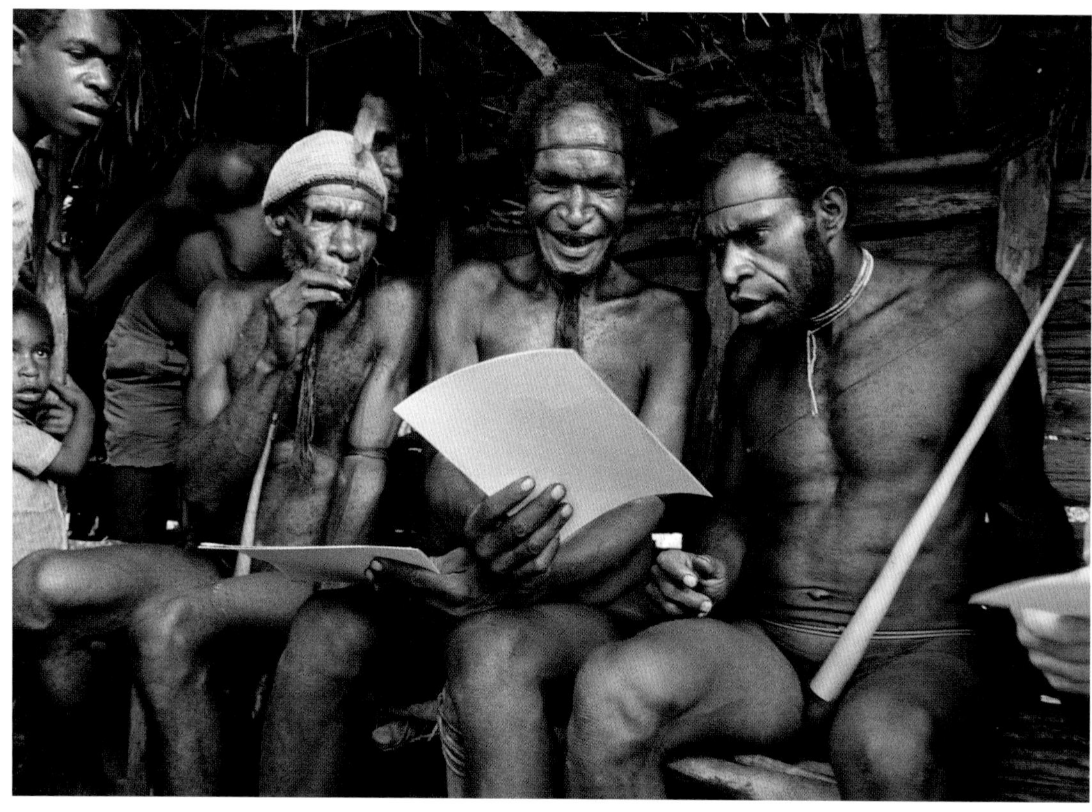

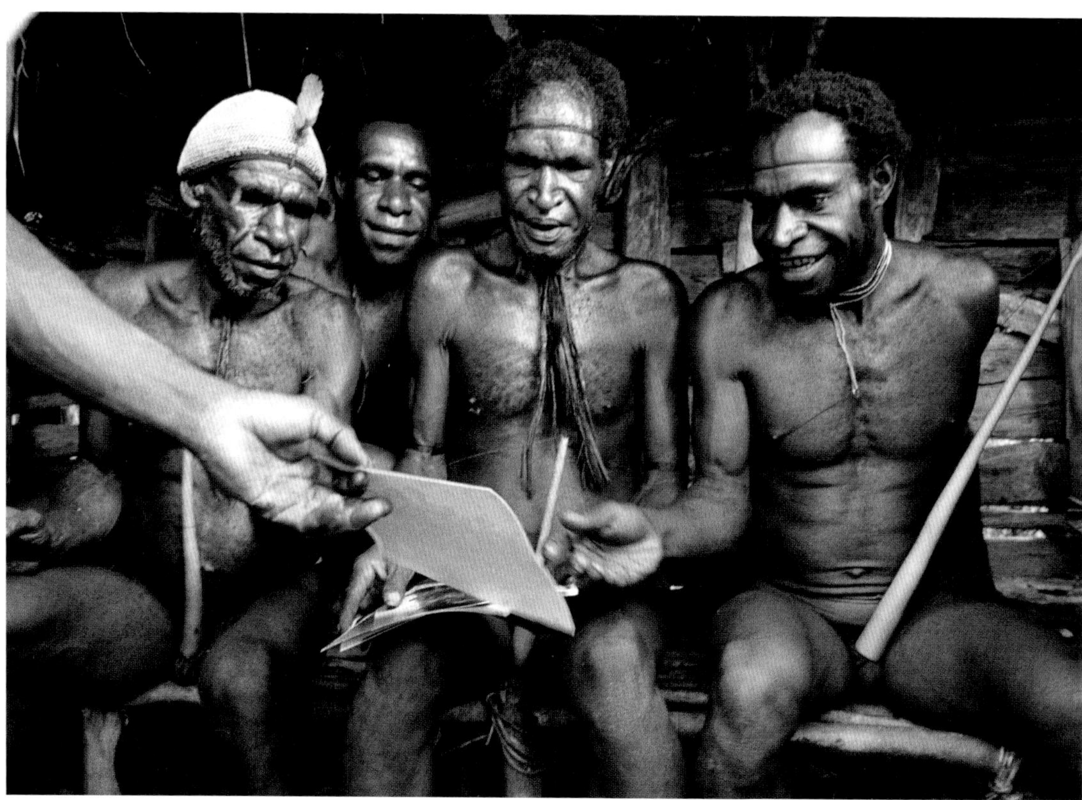

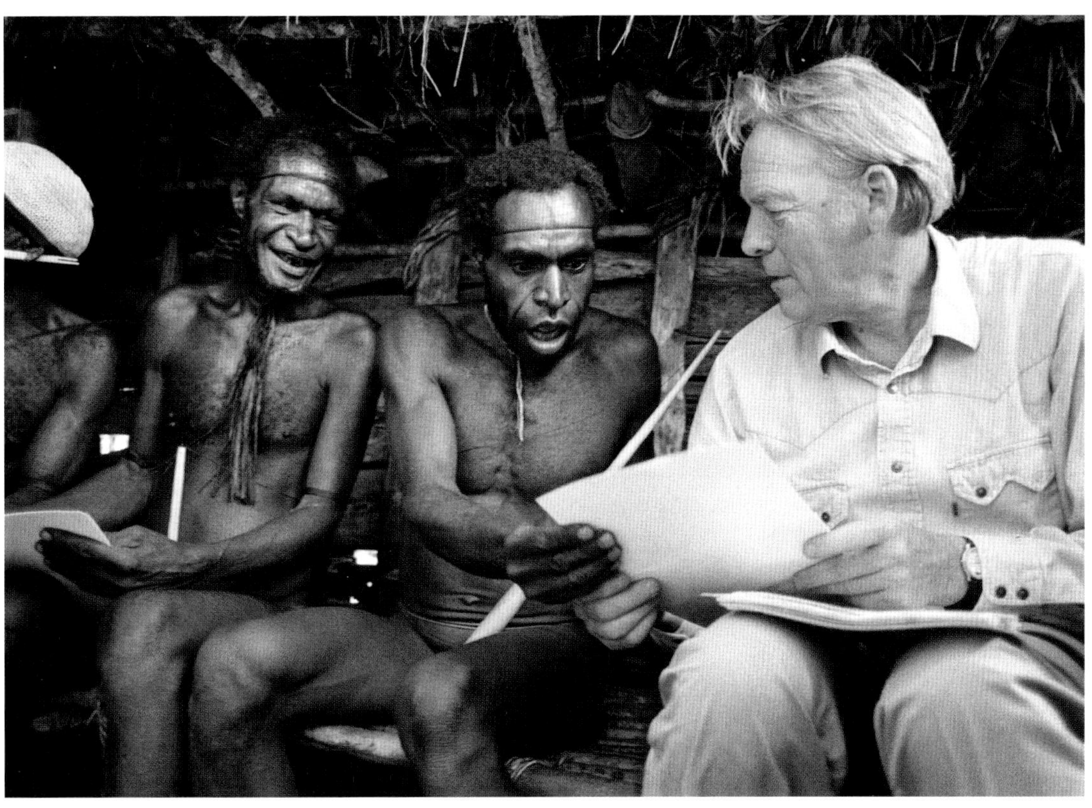

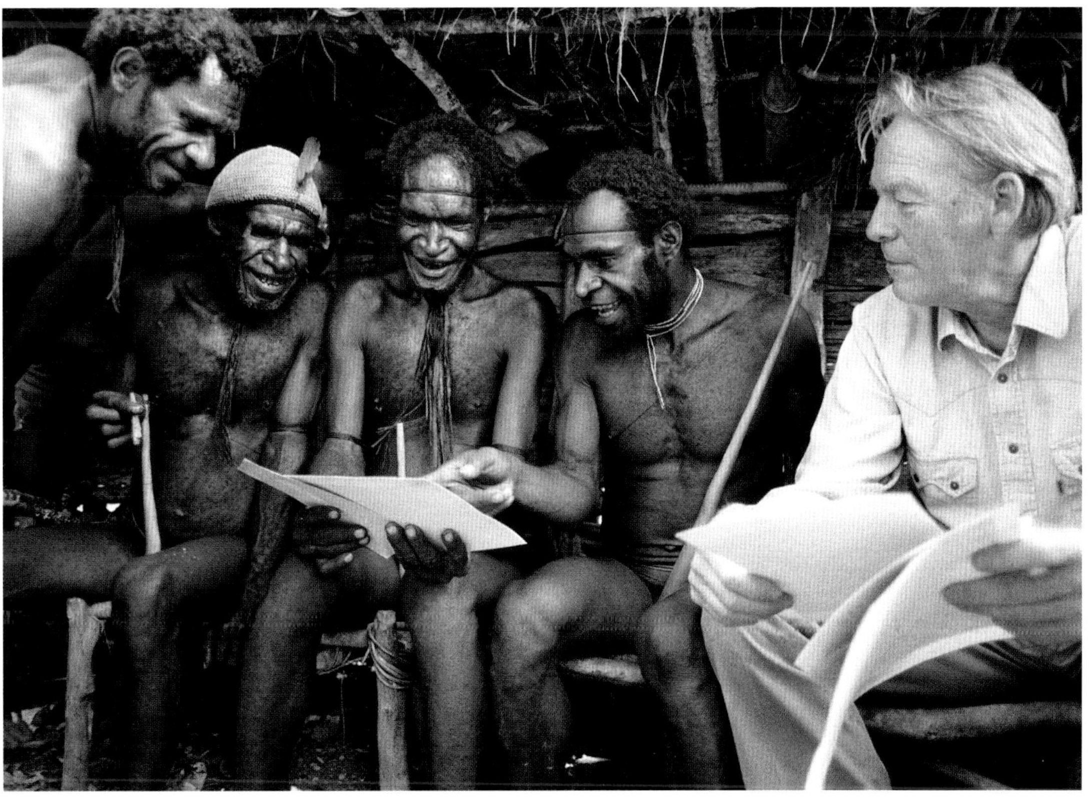

Part II
Looking at Individual Films

Chapter 12

First Encounters: An Essay on *Dead Birds* and Robert Gardner

Charles Musser

One makes a film for its own sake—less as a message than as a testament to what one has seen and what one cares about. Sometimes it is enough to know that the connections are there in the body of the work, available to those who may someday discover them.

—David MacDougall

Nothing is more important than learning to think crudely.

—Bertolt Brecht

The vast majority of films we see only once—or not at all; however, we also find ourselves having repeated and often deepening encounters with a much smaller number over time. Such has been the case for me with Robert Gardner's *Dead Birds* (1963)—even as the documentary itself has accumulated an odd combination of criticism and kudos that have produced its somewhat peculiar canonical status. Its June 2014 Wikipedia page is exemplary. The Internet encyclopedia notes that the Library of Congress selected the picture for the National Film Registry in 1998, follows this information with a brief synopsis, and concludes with a more lengthy detailing of the film's apparent shortcomings.[1] In general, analyses of *Dead Birds* fail to provide adequate historical context. Nor do they explore the film's positive achievements by integrating a sympathetic approach with one that is also critically engaged. With this need for critical sympathy in mind, I offer an investigation of *Dead Birds* and its maker through a series of first encounters, which serve as useful markers for what needs to be said.

Jay Leyda's Film Course

My first film course was a Yale seminar taught by Jay Leyda in the fall of 1970. It was a graduate offering in American studies, entitled "Problems and Methods in American Film History." I was an interloping undergraduate—an impressionable sophomore whose initial interest in cinema came from designing posters and then projecting films for the Yale Film Society.[2] In a small basement screening room, Jay showed us an eclectic array of motion pictures that were designed to challenge our assumptions about cinema and its history. I don't remember if he consistently paired films in counterpoint, but one memorable duo was Pierre-Dominique Gaisseau's *The Sky Above—The Mud Below* (English-Language version of *Le Ciel et la boue*, 1961) and Robert Gardner's *Dead Birds*. Both films were shot in Dutch New Guinea (now West Papua, Indonesia) within a short time of each other. Although my classmates and I were all novice film students, we were immersed in political turmoil both on and off campus, and at least in this instance fully capable of some basic crude thinking. Superficial similarities underscored profound differences. Gardner's documentary left us deeply impressed by its originality, respectful immersion in Dani culture, and relevance to our immediate political climate.

If those classroom screenings involved my first encounter with one of Gardner's documentaries, they were my last encounter with anything by Pierre-Dominique Gaisseau until I decided that it was finally time to revisit this pairing for this essay.[3] Where might that moment of crude thinking take us if reexamined today? *The Sky Above—The Mud Below* was a presentation by Joseph E. Levine, Hollywood's master of movie exploitation, and he doubtless played a crucial role in engineering the picture's 1962 Academy Award for the best documentary. A theatrical release soon followed, and the picture was enthusiastically received by reviewers in the daily press. *New York Times* critic Bosley Crowther hailed the feature as "an exciting account of an expedition into previously unexplored wilds of Netherlands New Guinea," remarking that "Watching its real-life illustration of rugged white men in long dugout canoes, propelled by naked black natives, pushing up a muddy river into the heart of an unmapped tropical region populated by stone-age savages, brings upon one a bold awareness of the incongruities of this world in which we live."[4] John L. Scott of the *Los Angeles Times* found it "without question one of the best film documents of its kind ever made."[5]

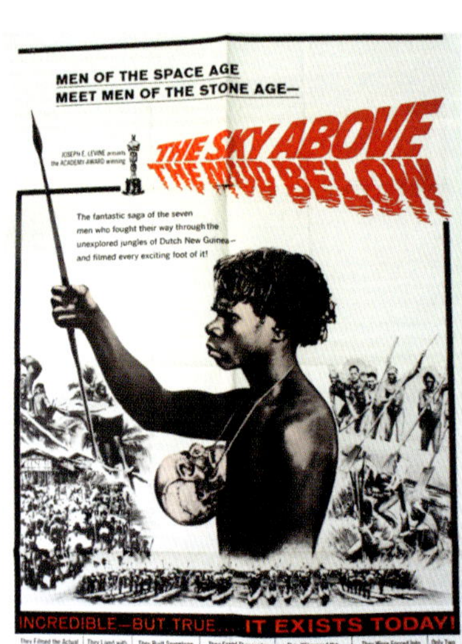

Leyda showed us *The Sky Above—The Mud Below* at the very moment that D.A. Pennebaker's *Don't Look Back* (1967) and Albert and David Maysles' *Salesman* (1968) were the kind of documentaries that were then being shown by Yale's many undergraduate film societies. *The Sky Above* was shot in 35mm color but without synch-sound. Nevertheless, it was not the film's retrograde technology that disturbed us so much as its retrograde genre. It seemed a direct continuation of safari-adventure films such as Osa and Martin Johnson's *Congorilla* (1932) and *Baboona* (1935). In fact, the Johnsons began their motion picture career with the documentary *Among the Cannibal Isles of the South Pacific* (1918). Levine's movie presentation also possessed the sensibility of the Italian "shock documentary" *Mondo*

Cane (*A Dog's World*, 1962), which appeared on the heels of *The Sky Above* and recycled some footage from Gaisseau's success.[6]

Immersed in a Vietnam-era assessment of First-World/Third World power relations, our seminar found *The Sky Above—The Mud Below* to be infuriating and easily critiqued. As Europe's colonial empires are collapsing around them, seven French and Dutch men fly over the Arctic and ultimately land in primitive New Guinea in search of adventure. The filmmakers hire sixty-three Muyu porters to carry their food and heavy equipment through the unknown jungles and across the rivers of their journey. Before journey's end, their thirst for adventure causes the deaths of three porters. Our European protagonists are constantly surrounded by savages, many of whom—it is emphasized—are headhunters, cannibals, and/or pygmies. Gaisseau's narration constantly emphasizes the bizarre and horrifying customs of these people who "live in the stone age," as his crew witnesses terrifying rituals never before seen by the white man. Through camera work, editing, and narration, the filmmakers emphasize their own vulnerability and the natives' collective barbarity—concocting a delicious nightmare that momentarily intrudes into our cinematic dreams.

Not surprisingly, *The Sky Above—The Mud Below* essentially dropped out of motion picture history. It goes unmentioned in Erik Barnouw's *Documentary: A History of Nonfiction Film* (1974) and similar historical overviews.[7] Books and articles on ethnographic film mention it only in passing if at all. Karl Heider remarks that many of the scenes were obviously staged, reducing their value as documents.[8] His limited critique further underscores the film's disturbing politics and hypocrisies. Purportedly dangerous savages were in fact more or less cooperative actors. And yet, when the film had its premiere at the Cannes Film Festival in May 1961, *Variety*'s Gene Moskowitz, who ran the trade journal's Paris office, concluded his rave review, "this subject can take its place among the many outstanding documentaries in filmic history."[9]

Although a comparative viewing of *The Sky Above—The Mud Below* and *Dead Birds* was an experience Leyda's students shared with other moviegoers, we gave little thought to the relationship between the two documentaries in terms of their production.[10] Nor was this an obvious oversight, because Gardner was in New Guinea well before the Cannes premiere of *The Sky Above*. The Gardner expedition may have been aware of Gaisseau's effort (the number of filming expeditions in Netherlands New Guinea was obviously small), but one could safely assume that Gardner did not see the film until his return. Except that this assumption proves to be wrong. In a recent publication, Gardner reveals that,

> *The Sky Above, the Mud Below* (*Le ciel et la boue*) burst upon my consciousness late in 1960, when I saw it prior to its release in 1961, just as I was planning the trip I would make to New Guinea (now West Papua) to study and film an indigenous group of people. For me, and for its time, *Le ciel et La boue* was an amazing visual account of a journey on foot from the southern to the northern coast of New Guinea, with special attention paid to coming-of-age ceremonies practiced by people living on the Asmat Coast in the south. I was tempted to abandon everything, journey forth, and start making a film.

> I had never seen anything quite like this work by Domenic [sic] Gaisseau. What it showed me remains vividly present and real—despite the fact that roofs of houses were removed to provide light for interior shooting. . . .It was simply and impressively riveting in the way movies can be, and it is how all filmmakers hope their films will turn out.[11]

The strong connection was easier to accept than Gardner's enthusiasm, given the profound differences in approach evidenced by the two films. This may not be quite such a mystery if we remember that *The Sky Above* has two sections: in the first, Gaisseau visits the Asmat. Here we see the disconcerting spectacle of men wearing human skulls as ornaments, but Gaisseau also shows more conventional art work, which fascinated Gardner, as one might expect given his two previous films, *Blunden Harbour* (1951), about the Kwakiutl of British Columbia (more accurately known as the Kwakwaka'wakw) who were once famous for their elaborate woodworking and weaving, and *Mark Tobey* (1952), a portrait of the painter.[12] From today's perspective the basis for such interest can be readily grasped by flipping through the museum catalog *Asmat: Perception of Life in Art* (2002).[13] This portion of *The Sky Above* had a powerful enough effect on Gardner that he made a visit to the Asmat and seriously considered filming there before traveling to the Baliem Valley and meeting with the Dani. When I questioned Gardner about *The Sky Above*'s second section, involving the trek through the Central Highlands, he acknowledged something he had left unmentioned in the introduction to his "Asmat Journal" entries: that "I was very distressed by his film. A very high price was paid when he under-dressed or didn't dress his porters for highland travel. It was a thoughtless set of arrangements."[14]

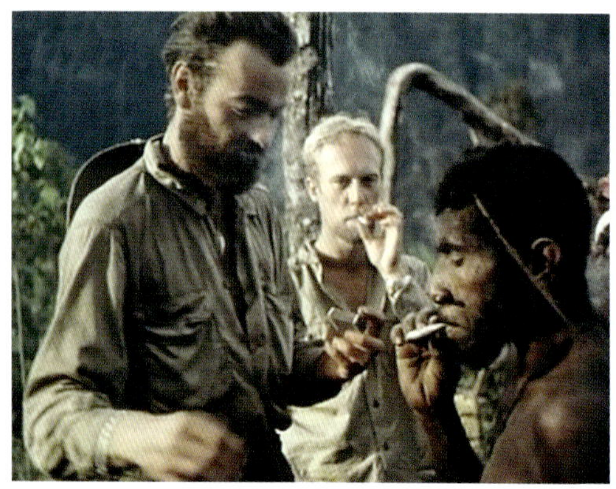

Pierre-Dominique Gaisseau

Pierre-Dominique Gaisseau

My assessment of *The Sky Above—The Mud Below* (with my classmates in 1970 and again more recently) is so at odds with its reception at the time that it demands further explication. Who is this Pierre-Dominique Gaisseau? And how did Gardner come to see an early preview of the film? Answering the second question helps to answer the first one. Gardner had fostered a relationship with Alan Lomax, who would later appear as a guest on his television program *Screening Room* in August 1975.[15] Gaisseau was also a longtime friend of Lomax and "left in Lomax's research collection many unpublished films and sound recordings he had made on his expeditions to unknown and little known parts of the world."[16] *The Sky Above* was edited in the U.S., and when there was a New York screening Lomax alerted Gardner, who came down. In the process the two met.[17]

In the mid-1950s, Gaisseau was described as "a professional adventurer and explorer."[18] Born in 1923 to a well-to-do French family living near the Belgian border, Gaisseau fled to southwest France as the Germans invaded. According to the Gaisseau biography on the Lomax foundation website,

> His arrival more or less coincided with the spectacular discovery of the prehistoric cave paintings at nearby Lascaux by four teen-age boys and their dog on September 12, 1940. One of the boys, Marcel Ravidat, lived next door to Pierre and gave him an unauthorized tour of the caves. The following year, Gaisseau assisted Collège de France professor l'Abbé Breuil in his researches at the site. It was the formative experience of Gaisseau's life: the revelation of a prehistoric world sparked a lifelong interest in ethnography and man's origins that he would later explore more fully in Africa, South America, and New Guinea. Also, it was while working at Lascaux that he met the people who started him on his career as filmmaker.[19]

After the war, Gaisseau worked as a cameraman on an expedition to the Congo sponsored by the Musée de l'Homme and then as a key member of Alain Gheerbrant's team, which explored the origins of the Amazon River, and produced a descriptive study, a photo-book, and a 93-minute documentary, *Des Hommes qu'on appelle sauvages*, directed by Jean Richter, Gaisseau's brother-in-law, which debuted in Paris theaters on July 25, 1952.[20] The phenomenon of multiple products generated by this expedition was hardly new: explorers and adventurers such as Robert Flaherty, Osa and Martin Johnson, and Ernest Shackleton had done this before the war. Norwegian Thor Heyerdahl, of *Kon Tiki* fame, had continued the tradition in the postwar era. It would continue to be characteristic of future documentation efforts by Gaisseau—and the Harvard Peabody expedition to New Guinea.

The prestige of the Gheerbrant expedition gave Gaisseau the opportunity to generate his own. As Susan Tobin recounts, "In 1951, Pierre Gaisseau was the first recipient of the Prize of the Société des Explorateurs et des Voyageurs Français. That year he traveled to Guinea, Africa."[21] Jean Rouch saw Gaisseau as a notable member of a French "school of film making Africanists":

> Pierre-Dominique Gaisseau made a series of ethnographic films on the Toma, Bassari and Nalou peoples; entitled respectively *The Sacred Forest* (first version 1953), *Pays Bassari* and *Naloutai.* Thereafter, Gaisseau again went out with two European companions and all three were initiated into the secret society of the Tomas. The full-length version of *The Sacred Forest* tells the story of their exploits, their gradual acceptance by the members of the Tomas' society, their tattooing, their retreat into the forest and the purification rites, and their final failure to enter the sacred forest, after which, ill and discouraged they gave up. This film, to which a number of ethnologists objected (on the grounds that initiation was the surest way of losing the objectivity required for scientific observation) nevertheless presented something entirely new: for the first time on the screen, we witnessed an attempt, hopeless perhaps but testifying to unbounded respect, to penetrate to the very heart of an African culture.[22]

The initial documentary short, *Forêt sacrée* (1953), won first prize at the 1953 Basel Film Festival. For the film's expanded version Gaisseau returned with painter and poet André Virel, Jean Richter—serving as cinematographer and soundman—and French photographer Tony Saulnier. Released in July 1955, it was endorsed by André Bazin among other French critics.[23] In fact, *Forêt sacrée* (1955) and Jean Rouch's *Mâitres Fous* (1955) offer an interesting pairing even though their filmmaking methods are quite different.

A sixty-four-minute English-language version of *Forêt sacrée*, released in the United States as *Gri-Gri* (1956), was poorly received.[24] Nevertheless, it played intermittently in theaters, as the second half of a double bill, into 1959. It even appeared briefly at Boston's Trans-Lux Theater in 1957.[25] Gardner, then working on *The Hunters*, might have gone to see it "on a lark."[26] Gaisseau also wrote *Forêt sacrée: Magie et rites secrets des Toma* (Albin Michel, 1953): Saulnier provided most of the photographs for the book, which was quickly translated and published in English.

On his next adventure, Gaisseau traveled as a duo with Saulnier to Australian New Guinea, arriving there in January 1955. They were commissioned by *Paris Match* and other magazines for potential photo essays, but their main achievements were once again a book and a short film. Gaisseau's book *Visa pour la préhistoric* (1957), accompanied by Saulnier's illustrations, was quickly translated into English as *Visa to the Prehistoric World* (1957). Like *Sacred Forest*, it is a personal, almost diaristic account of their encounters with the local peoples and their ways of living. Eager to strike out beyond areas of European influence and government control, Gaisseau became interested in the fighting between neighboring tribes and its resonances with modern-day conflict:

> We did not attempt to take part in an actual battle, and had no expectations of ever witnessing scenes such as those described by the interpreters: two rows of warriors standing face to face some distance apart, and hurling insults until their anger has reached a homicidal intensity.
>
> Apart from these essential verbal preliminaries, the underlying causes of their battle are the same as the reasons for war everywhere else, struggles for property and for riches, which in these parts are as basic as their weapons of destruction: a patch of land, a pig or a woman. Only a few millennia separate their wars from ours, and as soon as we have taught them how to reduce the infant mortality rate and extend their lifespan, we shall doubtless find them only too keen to learn about the blessings of nuclear fission and fusion.[27]

The accompanying documentary, Gaisseau's *Survivants de la préhistoire* (*Survivors of Prehistory*), is a nineteen-minute color short that won a first prize at the 1956 Venice Film Festival.[28] Again, much of the film seems carefully orchestrated. In the opening scene the men are dressed in their most elaborate and barbaric finery. They are shown preparing for ritual warfare and running to meet the enemy, but warfare itself is not shown. In many respects Olivia Cooper Hadjian, a reviewer for Kritikat.com, prefers it to Gaisseau's Oscar-winning counterpart, noting: "His more moderate flamboyance and sensationalism make it a less uncomfortable vision. It is however still not anthropology itself."[29]

The success of *Visa to the Prehistoric World* and *Survivants de la préhistoire* precipitated an entirely new full-length feature as producer René Lafuite of Adrennes Films funded a return to New Guinea. Gaisseau, Saulnier, and four other Europeans embarked on a new adventure, and the result was Gaisseau's documentary *Le Ciel et la boue*. Better funding, a longer length, and a larger crew created pressures to produce something more sensational—something that would justify the costs. In fact, costs soon exceeded their resources, and the production company went bankrupt. Arthur Cohn, who worked with Joseph Levine, acquired the international rights. Meanwhile, Saulnier also authored the photo book *Les Papous Coupeurs De Têtes; 167 Jours Dans La Préhistoire* (1961). Its English-language edition, *Headhunters of Papua* (1963), is an elaborately illustrated book that integrates photos (many in color) with text in roughly equal proportions. Saulnier offers a first-person account of their horrific ordeal, in which natural elements rather than the local headhunters proved to be the real antagonists. (In this respect, his storytelling was similar to the accounts of expeditions by Ernest Shackelton, Robert Scott, and Gaisseau among the Toma, in which explorers' sufferings more than actual discoveries serve as the basis for their heroism.) While Saulnier notes that "we never met any Papuans who were not pleasant to us," the reverse cannot be said. Saulnier and Gaisseau had been in the highlands of New Guinea before and had experienced frigid weather firsthand. Did financial difficulties lead to unjustified cost cutting? One way or the other, as Robert Gardner has noted, they did not properly clothe their sixty-three porters. Three of them died as a result—and it is on this note that Saulnier concludes his elegant photo book.

The specter of death did not entirely escape the Gardner expedition, either. In focusing on ritual warfare and the killings that resulted, death pervades *Dead Birds.* Some Christian missionaries thought it was the responsibility of the Harvard Peabody Expedition to stop the warfare, not film it.[30] Yet it was not these Dani deaths that garnered international attention. One member of the Harvard Peabody expedition was recent Harvard undergraduate Michael Rockefeller. Like Gardner (and Gaisseau), Rockefeller became fascinated with the Asmat and their art: after the expedition concluded and he returned to Cambridge, Rockefeller embarked on his own journey to New Guinea, where he died when his boat overturned and he tried to swim for shore.[31] Many associated this tragic accident with the Gardner expedition, including Joseph E. Levine. He became interested in *Dead Birds* as a theatrical documentary that could be sensationalized and made suitable for commercial exploitation by incorporating Rockefeller's participation and subsequent death as part of the film. This was something Gardner unequivocally rejected even though it meant that screenings of the film would be primarily limited to nontheatrical venues. Nevertheless, *Dead Birds* and the death of Rockefeller were often conflated: *Variety*'s review of the film begins "Excellent documentary, in the making of which Michael Rockefeller lost his life."[32]

When Robert Gardner Finally Came to Yale

Even before I completed my undergraduate degree, I moved to New York City and began working in the film industry, eventually making two of my own documentaries. I also pursued a PhD in film studies and began teaching. After returning to Yale as an assistant professor in 1992, I waited patiently for Yale's Department of Anthropology to bring Robert Gardner to campus. When this failed to materialize, I finally extended an invitation

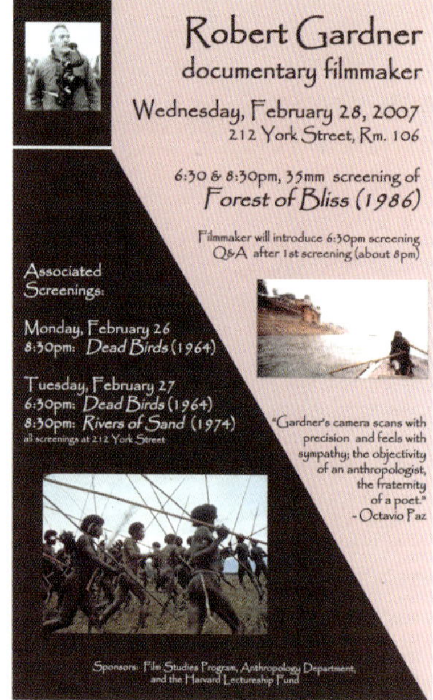

for Gardner to screen three of his documentaries in February 2007: *Dead Birds*, *Rivers of Sand* (1974), and *Forest of Bliss* (1986). I wanted to acknowledge a certain debt as well as give students an experience parallel to my own from earlier days. This proved to be another first encounter: the first time Gardner had been invited to show his films at Yale.

The Yale-Harvard rivalry is well known, but normally relegated to the football field. Although academic interactions are typically more friendly, I gave little further thought to this mild case of bad manners until very recently when I had a chance encounter with Leopold J. Pospisil, professor emeritus In Yale's Department of Anthropology.

Now in his nineties, Pospisil wandered into the film studies program office just as I was beginning work on this chapter. He had shot some film in Netherlands New Guinea and was interested in preserving it. I soon learned that my emeritus colleague had lived with the Kapauku Papuans for a year in 1954–1955, during which he shot a substantial amount of footage. His research was for a dissertation, completed in 1956 and then published in 1958 as *Kapauku Papuans and Their Law*. Pospisil has been known for "his insistence upon an extensive knowledge of the language of the culture, his incomparable fieldwork, his holistic approach and his attention to definition and detail."[33] His initial study takes a rigorously descriptive, scientifically oriented approach, analyzing a wide range of Kapauku behavior including marriage practices, precipitants of frequent warfare, the treatment of elderly and the dead, as well as the nature of good and evil.

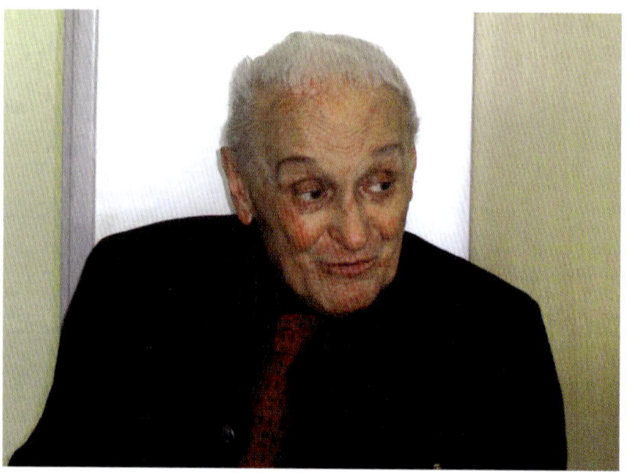

Leopold J. Pospisil

Despite Pospisil's interest in visual materials, his book contains only eight pages of photographs relegated to an appendix. These images seem a useful but modest supplement to his efforts at detailed, objective analysis, which is evident in his initial description of the Kapaukuans:

> The males average 151.2 cm., while the average female stands 142.1 cm high. Their heads are brachycephalic, the average index being 80 for males and 81 for females. Their faces are broad (facial index for males 78; facial index for females 76) and their bodies are well proportioned. Heavy brow ridges as well as deeply depressed roots of broad noses with straight bridges and depressed tips lend to the males a fierce look.
>
> This is even more accentuated by the wreath of black beard left growing on the peripheries of the massive jaw and on the angulated zygomatic arches (PL 7, bottom).[34]

Pospisil brought a 35mm still camera and a 16mm silent Bell & Howell motion picture camera with him on his 1954–1955 expedition and shot Kodachrome II color film in both.[35] The anthropologist used this material for his classroom lectures and for public presentations in the illustrated lecture tradition, including screenings in Washington, DC, New York City, and at Harvard, where Gardner saw them. Gardner's document-based account of the making of *Dead Birds* begins with an exchange of letters about Pospisil with Harold Coolidge of the Pacific Science Board, National Research Council. Coolidge expressed his admiration for Pospisil's monograph and then added,

> I understand that he is returning to New Guinea, and I find myself wishing that you, or someone with the kind of knowledge of film technology which you have developed, might accompany him and make a parallel record of primitive Papuans to the one that has been made of Kalahari Bushmen [John Marshall's *The Hunters*, 1957, which Gardner helped edit]. Pospisil, with very limited funds, has made a film of a war between two stone-age villages, which is a unique anthropological record.[36]

Gardner quickly responded to Coolidge:

> I met [Pospisil] about two years ago just after he had returned from New Guinea and saw his war film. It was a valiant effort and is no doubt a valuable document, but there were so many things wrong with it technically that it can never become a film. I don't mean he didn't approach his subject with feeling and knowledge, I mean he used a camera as if it were a flashlight, pointing it in every direction at once, going at the wrong speed, filming subjects at the wrong distance, most everything scrambled and out of focus. It is one of countless instances of a totally unprepared person taking it upon himself to do a complex piece of work.[37]

Gardner may have seen Pospisil's Kapauku films before they were tidied up—and the battle footage condensed. I recently viewed two reels of his now-standard lecture material, which includes scenes shot in 1959 as well as 1954–1955. Much of it focuses on agriculture, but there is footage of food preparation, dances, and a marriage ceremony. The bow and arrow is widely used to kill chickens, pigs—and in warfare. Indeed, the scenes of warfare are highly dynamic as opposing groups stalk their enemy, shoot, and dodge deadly shafts. This fighting does not appear to be staged for the camera and is caught with remarkable intimacy. The film material focuses on the Kapauku; unlike *The Sky Above—The Mud Below*, it is not about Pospisil and his own ordeals or his relationship to the Kapauku. He is invisible in the films, while he or his camera appears in only a few slides. This might seem unsurprising, but like Flaherty, Pospisil taught his subjects how to use the camera and they did at least some of the filming. His presentation of this material lacks a storyline: narrative progression is limited to several opening establishing shots and concluding scenes of his departure by a pontoon plane.

Coolidge's suggestion that Gardner join Pospisil was apparently pursued. Although the experienced anthropologist was initially agreeable, this potential alliance did not materialize for a variety of reasons.[38] One may have been timing. Pospisil returned to New Guinea in the summer of 1959—perhaps sooner than Gardner was ready to depart. But the idea was fundamentally a bad one. The Kapaukus were part of Pospisil's world. Any filmmaking that happened there would necessarily be on his terms. Gardner had already found a similar arrangement to be awkward when, after completion of *The Hunters*, he went with the Marshalls to the Kalahari Desert in 1958 to do more filming of the Ju/'hoansi. It seems unlikely that Gardner would have repeated this mistake. Likewise Pospisil must have been concerned about introducing a number of outsiders into Kapaukuan culture and its impact on his long-term research. He also saw himself as a veteran anthropologist who knew how to survive in primitive and often dangerous conditions, in part due to his wartime experience as a leader in the Czech resistance.[39] From his perspective, he would have been responsible for a group of young, wealthy, inexperienced amateurs who would not respect his authority. Surely they would get into trouble, and he would be blamed. From Gardner's perspective, Pospisil was also a hopeless amateur—an inexperienced, even inept filmmaker.[40]

After ten years working in different capacities as a filmmaker, the thirty-five-year-old Gardner had accumulated substantial experience and was eagerly putting together his own organization, modeled to some extent on the Marshalls' expedition.[41] In Karl Heider he found a Harvard graduate student in anthropology eager to study the Dani, much as Pospisil had studied the Kapauku. This would be a formative experience for both; they would collaborate and work in tandem for years. Undertakings such as theirs are never without risk and are often considered premature or ill-conceived by those who have already gone through similar efforts. Pospisil advised Gardner on what to bring on this expedition, but that was all.[42]

Pospisil's reservations were not confined to the members of the Harvard Peabody expedition. He also had an encounter with Pierre-Dominique Gaisseau, who was interested in using some of his Kapauku footage for *The Sky Above*.[43] This included a scene showing protracted struggle over the marriage of a young girl. The unhappy girl resists the arrangement, but her eager mother insists. Pospisil's reel follows this sequence with his impressive footage of ritual warfare. Gaisseau was accompanied by a colleague with whom he conversed in French, wrongly assuming Pospisil would not understand. Gaisseau envisioned the marriage kerfuffle as the catalyst for subsequent warfare, though the two sequences were unrelated. Pospisil found their private plans to misuse his footage to be profoundly dishonest: thereafter he would have nothing to do with the man.[44]

Pospisil had learned the Kapauku language and become "best friends" with many of the men. Yet his study of the Kapauku involved a high degree of depersonalization and scientific objectification. In this respect he saw Gardner as an amateur anthropologist who refused to submit to the dictates of the discipline.[45] Pospisil's attitude would seem to echo that of Jay Ruby, who has longed for an ethnographic cinema made by anthropologists who had gone through the ordeal of fieldwork and writing a dissertation monograph.[46] Or as Gardner saw these differences in the 1950s:

> Humanistic tendencies. . .were considered soft and were embraced only by an embattled minority. The pursuit of prediction and similar ways of arriving at certainties was just much more appealing. Such, at least, was the prevailing mood those days and, from the start, I struggled to fall in line.[47]

Gardner believed in a practice of anthropology that "revealed the meaning of one's own life as well as or even better than, the meaning of the lives of 'others.'"[48] For Ruby this meant that Gardner's "humanist desire to provide a meditation about mortality clearly took precedence over the need to articulate the details of Dani culture or to adhere to what was actually knowable about the people."[49] Although Ruby seems to have been unacquainted with Pospisil's work with motion pictures, he was doing very much what Ruby had in mind. And yet the Yale anthropologist's publications in the 1960s indicate that he was less and less concerned with visual documentation.[50]

In the end, Gardner chose to live and film not with the Asmat (Gaisseau) and not with the Kapauku (Pospisil), but with the Dani of the Baliem Valley. All three men shot film in the highlands of Western New Guinea within a few years of each other. In making *Dead Birds*, Gardner was reacting against the others' approaches, despite some attraction to them. In this sense they helped to shape his distinctive voice. Documentary history benefits by seeing these three filmmakers together rather than focusing solely on *Dead Birds*. Yet even this context requires still further expansion: as Thomas Elsaesser has remarked, "Papua New Guinea has long been a favorite among anthropologists. . . . From Margaret Mead (*Growing Up in New Guinea*) to Jared Diamond (*The World Until Yesterday*), they have used New Guinea as a foil against which to measure their own cultural pessimism about our civilization's decline."[51] And not only anthropologists but journalists, explorers, adventurers, and political theorists. A fascination with ritual warfare and a characterization of these Papuans as prehistoric or stone-age people were established tropes—not assumptions that were newly created by the Harvard Peabody expedition.

A framework for understanding *Dead Birds* needs to look inward as well—to the multifaceted outpouring of work by the Harvard Peabody Expedition to the Baliem Valley. Peter Matthiessen's book *Under the Mountain Wall: A Chronicle of Two Seasons in the Stone Age* (1962) was the first major product of that expedition and provided a preexisting context for a viewing of *Dead Birds*.[52] The two works share many of the same characters: Weyak is called Weaklekek in the book. A sustained critical comparison has yet to be pursued, although the book provides a much more chaotic picture of diffused violence and constantly changing alliances among clans and even within households. For *Dead Birds*, Gardner focused on the binary opposition between the two warring factions in ways that spoke to Cold War circumstances. The principle behind the Harvard Peabody Expedition was to generate diverse, overlapping points of view—as opposed to a single perspective as was typical with anthropological work done by Pospisil and others. Gardner's and Heider's heavily illustrated *Gardens of War: Life and Death in the New Guinea Stone Age* (1968) was followed by Heider's *The Dugum Dani. A Papuan Culture in the Highlands of West New Guinea* (1970), Heider's study guide: *The Dani of*

West Irian. An Ethnographic Companion to the Film Dead Birds (1972), as well as Heider's two short films *Dani Sweet Potatoes* (1974) and *Dani Houses* (1974).

My First Encounter with Robert Gardner

I first met Robert Gardner when I was invited to give a job talk (my first) at Harvard's Department of Visual and Environmental Studies. It was 1987 to 1988, soon after I had finished my PhD, and I was frankly petrified. In the process, I had a brief exchange with Gardner, who was on the search committee. Did I gauchely confess to him that it was my first visit to the Harvard Film Study Center and Harvard Film Archive? Knowing my own ability to say the awkward thing at the wrong time, I probably did. Although I had done research in other collections at Harvard, this was my first glimpse of the institutional structure where Gardner had worked on a variety of projects over the years, beginning with John Marshall on *The Hunters* and then *Dead Birds*.

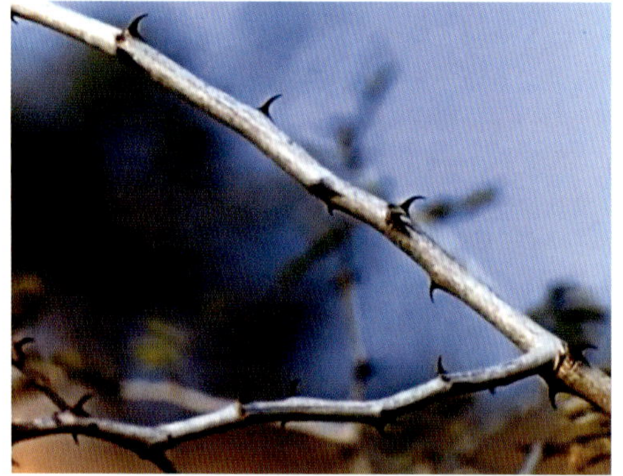

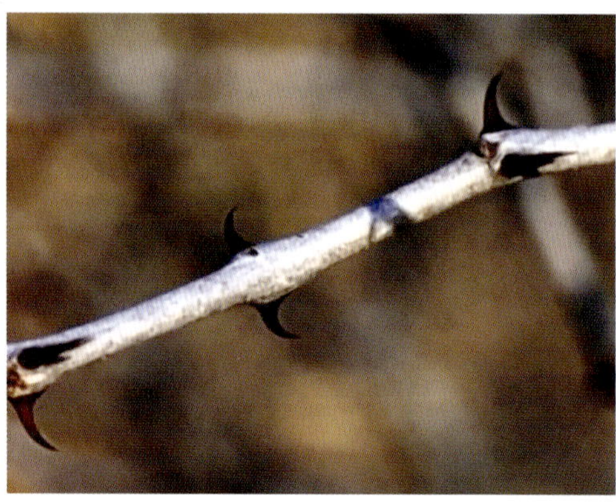

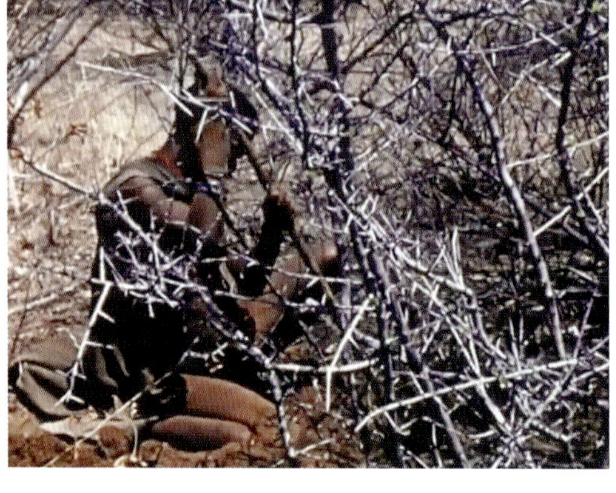

Gardner's work on *The Hunters* is generally seen as the immediate precursor and prime influence on *Dead Birds*.[53] Although there are notable similarities between the two films, there are also significant differences. His collaboration on the postproduction of *The Hunters* was an important learning experience for Gardner, but it was also a project that he subsequently worked against in ways not entirely dissimilar from the ways he worked against *Sky Above* and Pospisil's footage of ritual warfare, though his familiarity with *The Hunters* was far more extended and intimate. Both Gardner's and Marshall's films use voice-overs written and delivered by the principal filmmaker. However, there is no narration during the opening three-minute sequence of *The Hunters*—a series of brief shots depicting the northern Kalahari Desert in Southwest Africa, showing its flora and fauna—including five shots of birds and four shots of !Kung hunters. Relatively banal, perhaps intentionally so, they set the scene but do not construct a spatial-temporal unity. The soundtrack alternates between silence and !Kung music taken on location. Marshall's narration only begins after two transitional shots: first, a dissolve to a simple head title; second, an animated map of Southwest Africa, a long-established convention in documentary that is used to establish the location of a distant, primitive people. When the narration finally begins, it provides straightforward information about the !Kung and how they live. The language is expressive and reflects judgments based on observation: for instance, "It is a bitter land where all the trees have thorns." The correspondence between image and narration is quite literal. The comment about thorns on trees is recited over the third and fourth close-ups of small branches with thorns on them.

These are followed by an establishing shot of a woman who is digging amidst some thorny bushes over which the second piece of narration is delivered: "From the ceaseless labors of women packing and tugging at the land comes most of the people's food."

In many respects, *The Hunters* is an illustrated lecture consolidated and standardized as a sound film—close in some respects to what Leopold Pospisil did with his illustrated lecture. (And yet the absence of opening commentary also distinguishes the film from an illustrated lecture.)

The opening of *Dead Birds* is the antithesis of *The Hunters*. The pretitle sequence is one long 37-second panning shot that follows a bird of prey, taken from above, as it flies over the rain forest canopy and some thatched huts (in contrast to the many shots—including those of a hawk-like bird taken from below—in *The Hunters*). This initial shot is accompanied by location sound of the forest and a bird's cawing. Over the course of this opening the filmmaker tells us, "There is a fable told by a mountain people living in the ancient Highlands of New Guinea about a race between a snake and a bird. It tells of a contest which decided if men should be like birds and die, or be like snakes, which shed their skins and have eternal life. The bird won, and from that time all men, like birds, must die." Gardner starts with narration, while Marshall began his film in comparative silence. And unlike *The Hunters*' narration when it begins, Gardner's opening narration is only indirectly and associatively about what is shown (the bird). From this ethereal shot, Gardner cuts to a Dani funeral and the sounds of mourning. The shift in sound from the cry of a bird to the cries of people is emotionally powerful, and we are immediately immersed into the world of a people very different from us.

In retelling this Dani fable about a bird and a snake, Gardner makes it his own fable as well. Fables are, according to one source, "a form of imaginative literature or spoken utterance constructed in such a way that readers or listeners are encouraged to look for meanings hidden beneath the literal surface of the fiction."[54] We might ask: What new layer of allegory is added in Gardner's retelling of the fable—that is, in his film overall? His point, made quite clearly through the film, is that we viewers are like the Dani. Most obviously: not only like the Dani will we die, but we Americans (and Westerners more generally) engage in our own kind of seemingly perpetual warfare that is little different from that of the Dani.[55]

Both *The Hunters* and *Dead Birds* tell stories (the stories of the giraffe hunt and of the major Dani battle we see are both famously composites), but *Dead Birds* is more artistically ambitious. *Dead Birds*' opening shot sequence of the bird and the parable can resonate with the opening sequence of *The Hunters* with its three shots of a bird of prey: (1) the bird sitting on a barren tree, (2) the bird takes flight, and (3) a panning shot follows the bird in flight. This bird of prey is arguably like the !Kung men whom we see on the prowl looking for food. Both use their wits to survive in this harsh land. (In fact, the hunters will lose one of their kills to vultures later in the film.) The viewer can find an analogy between the men and the birds of prey, but it is more mundane and specific than Gardner's analogy between human beings and birds.

Like *The Hunters*, *Dead Birds* has a title sequence of two shots. The complete title appears over the first shot of the funeral as the men move a dead man's body to its leafy shroud.[56] The next shot shows a stricken-looking man standing behind and perhaps bracing the dead man, who now is in a sitting position. Over this second shot is the title "A film by Robert Gardner." So in place of the map of the Kalahari, Gardner's name appears. Being by Gardner, it is also about him. Importantly, this credit does not appear against a black background—we see through or beyond Gardner's name to the Dani. In short, he establishes that this film shows the Dani through his point of view. With admirable modesty, John Marshall does not give himself credit until the end of the film. As the opening map suggests, *The Hunters* is about a specific people located in a particular place. (In this regard, it is fitting that Marshall after completion of *The Hunters* went to study anthropology at Yale, where Pospisil had begun to teach.) *Dead Birds* is about the human condition, about what the film's creator has in common with the Dani.

Gardner's First Film: Blunden Harbour

Gardner's first serious encounter with the making of motion pictures resulted in *Blunden Harbour* (1951), a portrait of a small village on the coast of British Columbia inhabited by Kwakiutl Indians and the home of a school of artists, in particular mask-maker Willie Seaweed.[57] *Blunden Harbour* establishes the daily lives of the village residents, who feed themselves from the sea. Kathryn Bunn-Marcuse, one of the few people to write about the film, has suggested that it offers an ahistorical treatment and "an eternal ethnographic present"; but this hardly seems the case.[58] As she notes, the people wear contemporary clothing and use modern-day utensils. Likewise, two men are seine fishing from a small motor-powered boat. As the narration remarks, "Old methods with new tools, old tools with new methods." It gradually becomes apparent that *Blunden Harbour* is about a community of art makers and their art. A scene of women scooping steamed clams from their shells leads to that of a man scraping out the insides of a piece of wood: he is carving a toy boat for a young boy, who then plays with it in the sea. Art emerges out of everyday life. Later we see Willie Seaweed painting a mask. The transition from mask painting to ceremonial dancing with masks is made with a final voice-over: "A way of life, a way of death, a way of dreams, and a way to remember." Thus Gardner indicates a crucial role for art in human culture, one in which the creative efforts revealed by the film speak to Gardner's own efforts at a way of life, a way of dreams, and a way to remember. Twenty-five years later I made my own first film, entitled *An American Potter* (1976)—like Gardner I was also twenty-six years old. In both cases, we used our position as filmmakers to watch more closely and better understand someone who had already found his way in a parallel art. Seaweed and studio potter Gerry Williams had found ways to integrate their artwork into the everyday such that the art itself was neither overly intellectualized nor a direct response to modernity and a sense of alienation in the spirit of modern art. Rather, these artists affirmed a continuity with the past.[59] They were both quiet innovators working out of a long tradition where craft meets art. Making a film about such people was a conscious form of apprenticeship even though we were working in a different artistic modality.

In *Blunden Harbour*, Gardner was concerned with "a way of death," and this was something he returned to again in *Dead Birds*. Indeed the poetically inflected voice-over and cinematic strategies utilized in *Blunden Harbour* would be reworked and refined in

Dead Birds. The opening narration, which recounts a myth or fable about the founding of Blunden Harbour, is a case in point. Gardner uses 140 words in *Blunden Harbour* to tell this story, which is somewhat hard to follow. Gardner tightened the corresponding myth of origins in *Dead Birds* to its essentials, using only sixty-three words. In making *Dead Birds*, Gardner undertook a complex work that far exceeded *Blunden Harbour* in ambition and rigor and yet in important ways also remained faithful to many of its essential elements, in some cases with the well-known edict that "less is more."

Other first encounters and crossings in the year 1951 might be mentioned. This was the year that Gardner's first child, Stewart Gardner, was born (as was I, meaning Gardner has been making films as long as I have been alive). For Gardner, filmmaking and fatherhood coincided—a fact that would inflect many aspects of *Dead Birds*. Interestingly, Robert Flaherty died in 1951, which means that Gardner launched his filmmaking career at the very moment that Flaherty's had forever ended. Gardner never met Flaherty, but has often acknowledged him as an inspiration and influence. However, Flaherty's influence on *Dead Birds* must strike us as complex, particularly when one considers not just *Nanook of the North* (1922), *Moana* (1926), and *Man of Aran* (1934)—documentary studies of various ways of life, with a personal and philosophical inflection—but also his fictional/documentary hybrid *Louisiana Story* (1948), made just three years before *Blunden Harbour*.

Some critics have complained that Gardner is engaged in a problematic pursuit of salvage anthropology, putting *Dead Birds* in a category with *Nanook of the North* and *Man of Aran*, for which Flaherty has been often criticized. Yet the differences between *Dead Birds* and these Flaherty films are essential. Gardner did not revive ritual warfare among the Dani as Flaherty revived the hunting of basking sharks among the Aran islanders. Nor did he convince the Dani to put aside guns and use traditional weapons to kill each other, as Nanook put aside his gun for the harpoon during a walrus hunt. Nor were the Dani asked to revert to anachronistic clothing. Gardner was seeking to document a culture before its sustained encounter with the West. By trading cowrie shells rather than T-shirts for Dani assistance and excluding his crew from the camera frame, he easily maintained this kind of separation. (It is worth recalling that Gardner did not pursue "salvage anthropology" in *Blunden Harbour*, either.) These overstated criticisms overlook the deeper reasons for the separation strategy. By keeping the Dani world in front of the camera separate from the modern world behind it, *Dead Birds* enables allegory and constructs analogies between these two worlds. *Dead Birds* offers a mirror to Western viewers who, witnessing the ritual warfare in New Guinea as presented by Gardner, cannot help but see it in relation to the Cold War and its various local manifestations of violence and mayhem. As Scott MacDonald has commented, "Gardner's focus in *Dead Birds* involves a kind of double consciousness: he is committed to representing the Dani as distinct and separate from his own world—paradoxically so that he can suggest general parallels between their lives and ours."[60] Such unsettling parallels force us to ask what civilization has achieved in terms of our ability to co-exist and live peaceably with our neighbors. If *Nanook of the North* focuses on man's struggle with nature, it is only to implicitly congratulate contemporary civilization on its apparent ability to tame the natural world. The impulse behind *Dead Birds* is quite the opposite.

Dead Birds has a more dynamic relationship with *Louisiana Story*. Both feature a young boy vulnerable to the dangers of his environment, along with an adult male figure. Birds, animals, and nature figure in both films and take on symbolic force. Nevertheless, the two films differ in their depiction of encroaching modernity. The oil company intrudes into the Louisiana Bayou, disrupts nature but also somehow co-exists with it while improving the lives of the local family. Missionaries or the Dutch colonial representatives may be the nearest equivalent in the Baliem Valley. Although Gardner mentions them in extra-textual commentary, seeing them as destructive of the Dani way of life, they had yet to make significant inroads in the area where he worked, and found no role in Gardner's film.[61] In *Louisiana Story* Flaherty explores the encounter between modernity and a more traditional way of life, though his honesty or insight into its long-term impact must be questioned. *Dead Birds* is interested in a traditional way of life before modernity, and while Gardner was personally skeptical of its potential benefits, its arrival would only occur after the filmmaking.

The Critical Landscape

David MacDougall begins his remarkable engagement with Gardner's *Forest of Bliss* (1986) with the observation, "What we lack are more commentaries on the intellectual underpinnings and creative processes by which films are made."[62] Gardner has suggested that his film work owes an intellectual debt to important contributions of Western thought, ranging from Sigmund Freud's *Psychopathology of Everyday Life* (1901) to Ruth Benedict's *Patterns of Culture* (1934) and Clyde Kluckhohn's *Mirror for Man* (1944). Scott MacDonald has helpfully touched on the influence of William James and John Dewey on the methods of Gardner and his associates.[63] Charles Warren, in his chapter for this volume, discusses a more proximate philosophical influence: Stanley Cavell, Gardner's friend and long-time Harvard colleague. My task here has not been to devalue or avoid these factors but rather to focus on a network of influential films and filmmakers against which, or in dialogue with, Gardner made *Dead Birds*.

Unlike my own first encounter with *Dead Birds* in 1970, today's film scholar confronts a plethora of commentaries on the film. Certainly there have been laudatory reviews; but for a documentary that won many awards and is generally recognized as a "classic," the critical landscape is surprisingly, even shockingly negative. The principle defender of the film has probably been Gardner himself, through various comments and his book *Making* Dead Birds*: Chronicle of a Film* (2007). (Interestingly, detractors often find ways to use his statements against the film.) More recently Scott MacDonald has offered a more positive assessment but one that still seeks to balance pros and cons. The problem is that this balance occurs within an unbalanced framework. Visual anthropologist Jay Ruby, Gardner's most persistent and influential critic, has set out the terms of the debate and identified the cast of characters in a Manichean universe where some are found to be ethically progressive (John Marshall, Jean Rouch) while others (Gardner) are mired in darkness. Ruby's nonfiction melodrama has been picked up by others such as Sharon Sherman and Craig Mishler. The sky above and the mud below, indeed!

Ruby remarks:

> At the time Gardner was planning *Dead Birds*, a number of documentary and ethnographic filmmakers were voicing their discontent with the limitations imposed upon them by their equipment and the dominant tradition of dramatic documentaries that imitated Hollywood features. . . .In other words, direct cinema and cinema vérité were being invented at the same time Robert Gardner chose to employ a traditional and, for some filmmakers, an outmoded approach to filming and documentary dramatic structure.[64]

Ruby believes that Gardner should have been more attuned to the state of documentary filmmaking and embraced the latest technological innovations being adopted by Drew Associates at Time-Life and elsewhere. Here Ruby seems to conflate two somewhat distinct issues: first, the use of synchronous location sound; second, the relationship between filmmaker and subject.

It is true that portable synch-sound equipment was beginning to be used before Gardner left for New Guinea, but it was at an extremely early stage of development. The equipment that was needed to support and so implement this emergent method was experimental and imperfect.[65] *Primary*, which follows the contest between Hubert Humphrey and John F. Kennedy, was shot in May 1960, and first televised on Friday evening, July 8 as a run-up to the broadcast of the Democratic Convention.[66] By then Gardner had purchased a Nagra tape recorder for the expedition, about which he was quite protective.[67] By the time that *Primary* received the Robert Flaherty Award in late March 1961, Gardner had been ensconced in New Guinea for over a month.[68]

Ruby's anachronistic criticism of *Dead Birds* may gain the appearance of credibility due to the documentary's postproduction, distribution, and exhibition histories. Although the footage was shot in the course of 1961, the film was only finished in December 1963 and began playing in nontheatrical venues in early 1964. It was not reviewed by *Variety* until March 1965, and even then Gardner lacked a 35mm blow up that would produce the print required for screenings in most commercial theaters.[69] Although synchronous filming had become much more common by then, the technical strategies of *Dead Birds* were not a problem for critics or festival judges (it received the Robert Flaherty Award, the Grand Prize at the Florence Film Festival, and other recognition).

Ruby also criticizes Gardner for post-syncing his sound, which seems ungenerous given the state of film/sound technology in 1961. A close examination of *Primary*, for instance, will quickly reveal the severe limits of synchronous sound at that time. Much of it was "post-synced" as well. In any case, documentary sound is almost never unprocessed and generally mixes synch-sound, which is typically filtered, with various kinds of ambient sound. That is, documentary sound is always constructed and the question is: to what purposes and effect. One of Michael Rockefeller's roles was to take location sound, which was added to the sound track and synchronized to the extent that this was possible to generate a sense of embodied space quite different than the sound in either *Blunden Harbour* or *The Hunters*. From the first shot of the bird cawing, to the funeral with sounds of mourning, and Weyak humming as he weaves, Gardner enables the viewer to more fully enter into the world of the Dani as we hear sounds that accompany their lives. That is, Gardner uses sound to provide an audio counterpart to the visuals.

If the issue of appropriating a "traditional style" is to be taken seriously, one might productively contrast *Dead Birds* to Flaherty's *Louisiana Story* (1948), which could be seen as an American neo-realist film and not what we would now consider a documentary. *Louisiana Story* was shot in 35mm black and white and most shots were preplanned (i.e., "directed"). The film's family members were, in fact, not related. Such techniques continued to be used in later documentaries such as Lionel Rogosin's *On The Bowery* (1957) and *Come Back Africa* (1959). In an early "director's statement," Gardner emphasized that "the action was followed, not directed."[70] This would suggest that he shot *Dead Birds* in a cinema verité, observational style even though he lacked synch-sound capabilities. It is true that he shot color while the early Drew films were in black and white. Moreover, he avoided the wobbly camera that is often associated with early American cinema verité. Nevertheless, from a genealogical perspective, as a director/cinematographer, Gardner was working alongside the cinema verité movement rather than in disregard of or opposition to it.

Dead Birds does rely on extensive narration, which cinema verité was reacting against and largely avoiding. However, unlike Gaisseau, Gardner not only wrote the narration, he used his own voice rather than hire a professional narrator. And unlike Pospisil, his narration was carefully constructed and recorded. Given the personal nature of this film, it seems odd to argue, as Jay Ruby has done, that Gardner was following the conventions of Hollywood cinema and had a "need to erase the author and make the narrative structure seamless," showing a "lack of reflexivity."[71] Note that *The Sky Above* is a highly reflexive film: Gaisseau and his film crew are in front of the camera a very large percentage of the time. Gardner's radical act was to remain behind the camera and so make the film about the Dani while not pretending to some elusive objectivity.

Critics of *Dead Birds* too often posit some hypothetical alternative and then demonstrate how Gardner's film falls short of it. Craig Mishler, for instance, feels *Dead Birds* contains "so many subtle fictional pretensions and artistic ornamentations that it has surrendered most of its usefulness as a socially significant document."[72] He focuses considerable attention on the fable of the bird and the snake that Gardner provides in his opening narration. Citing Karl Heider on the subject, he notes that among the Dugum Dani whom Gardner filmed, the conflict between the bird and the snake actually takes the form of an argument rather than a race—though the race version is told by other Dani in the valley. Fair enough. The idea of a race certainly works well with the image of a graceful, fast-moving bird in flight. Gardner makes his choice, for a purpose. Mishler also complains that this opening fable was stripped of its complexity, while, as already suggested, one might with equal justice laud its concision. These are disputes over nuance, and the implied conclusion is that Heider, who spent much more time among the Dani after the filming, learned more about the Dani. One would hope. Need one add that a documentary film and a written text generally do different things—or do different things well?

What Mishler sees as a damning flaw, one could simply find interesting. Filmmakers, ethnographers, and cultural historians are all imperfect constructors of meaning. Their narratives—and our critical insights—can never fully transcend the historical limitations of time, place, and circumstance. Mishler, like Heider, offers worthwhile footnotes to the film, even if Mishler's are made in an ungenerous spirit.

Given that *Dead Birds* appeared at a time when voice-over narration was out of fashion, it is hardly surprising that this element of the film has been frequently criticized. Mishler complains, "There is virtually nothing in the voice-over of *Dead Birds* that is not contained in Heider's ethnography except Gardner's own philosophizing."[73] Filmmakers are not untouched by critical pressures, as Gardner revealed in a 1999 interview in which he confessed to certain reservations about both the text and his reading of it:

> I don't think for a moment that my reading is what I most hoped for the text of *Dead Birds* or for the film for that matter. In fact, in recent years I have been greatly tempted to both rewrite the text and "re-voice" the narration. I have gotten nowhere in accomplishing this task but the desire has not abated.[74]

Few documentary filmmakers like the sound of their own voice, and a reasonable man must be willing to accept some criticisms. Scott MacDonald, an obvious admirer of Gardner's work, picks up on this self-doubt to question the narration in *Dead Birds*, and finds the narration "both awkward and a bit too rote."[75] Going against apparent consensus, I find the documentary's narration to be elegantly written, while Gardner's voicing of this material is perfectly pitched to his images and location sound.[76]

Probing the presumed inadequacies of Gardner's voice-over in *Dead Birds* can nevertheless foster more critically productive efforts, starting with the basic question: "How can we make sense of this film, particularly given Gardner's narration?" Simply put, *Dead Birds* can be seen as a landmark "essay film"—a term that Gardner has increasingly applied to his documentaries and one that Charles Warren also discusses in relation to *Dead Birds* in this collection. Admittedly, the essay film is in many respects a fraught category or genre: what is or is not an essay film depends on the criteria employed and how one approaches the film in question.[77] Certainly the essay film and the documentary overlap substantially. Scott MacDonald shares some of my own hesitations about the term, only using it in passing at the end of *American Ethnographic Film and Personal Documentary* and not applying it to the work of Gardner or the other filmmakers who are his principal concern. As he explains in a footnote:

> The "essay film" has emerged as the newest category of documentary—or at least a newly popular term for certain types of films roughly analogous to the personal essay in literature. . . .Whereas the information in traditional documentaries is often presented by "voice-of-god narrators" who draw clear and definitive conclusions, essay films tend to rely on the filmmaker's personal observations and ruminations on the topic at hand and are less involved with drawing conclusions or creating a sense of resolution than traditional documentaries.[78]

Ruby and Sharon Sherman criticize *Dead Birds* for employing a "voice of god" narration, even though the film's head titles state that this is "a film by Robert Gardner" and the narration is written and spoken by the man who not only shot and edited the film but organized the expedition. Clearly it is a film that seeks to communicate the understandings and insights Gardner gained from his immersion in the life of the Dani over a sustained period of time. The filmmaker's narration differs from the "voice of god" narration in such documentary classics as Frank Capra's *Prelude to War* (1942), Henry Solomon's *Victory at Sea* (1952–1953), or Roman Kroitor and Colin Low's *Universe* (1960).

The essay film can be contrasted to documentaries that seek to maintain an objective, scientific, or impersonal approach to their subject—whether or not this is actually possible. In "The Essay as Form," T.W. Adorno reflects on the way the essay is a hybrid that is often attacked by those who "react to the situation by fencing up art as a preserve for the irrational, identifying knowledge with organized science and excluding as impure anything that does not fit this antithesis."[79] This observation anticipates complaints that have been leveled against *Dead Birds:* that it involves too much art and not enough ethnography, is too personal and so insufficiently objective and scientific. As Sherman writes, despite her sense of the narration as being of the objective, voice of god type, "Believing his responsibility was to reveal his own interpretation, Gardner viewed the Dani as vehicles for his own philosophical interests and thus violated one of the major ethical concerns of fieldworkers—that of treating others as unique and valuable human beings."[80] Sherman seems to suggest that Gardner's insights into Dani life did the Dani a disservice. As she adds, "In determining what he believed was significant for an audience to see, Gardner structured and edited his footage to make a statement that was not necessarily the same statement that the Dani might have made about their own culture."[81] Sherman is insisting on an imaginary objectivity, an absence of personal expressivity that is ultimately an illusion. In any case it is impossible for an outsider—whether Gardner, Pospisil, or someone else—to make a statement about the Dani that the Dani would themselves make.

The essayistic can also be contrasted with the impulse of many documentary filmmakers to tell a story.[82] Storytelling tends to move us away from the essayistic; and here again, there are complaints that Gardner is just telling a story and "makes the narrative seamless" in the style of Hollywood.[83] *Dead Birds* certainly differs from Pospisil's film presentations, which lack a clear storyline or chronology. (Pospisil's illustrated lecture offers an inventory or cataloging of significant features in Kapauka life.) On the other hand, *Dead Birds* certainly lacks the kind of storyline that structures *The Sky Above*—a group of European men involved in a dangerous quest. Although *Dead Birds* unfolds over time, following a certain logic that often involves cause and effect, little actually changes. The body of the film follows a cycle of violence: as the film begins, the Dugum Dani are one-up when it comes to their murderous rivalry, then with the death of a young boy they are in deficit, until they catch a rival Dani stealing a pig and kill him, returning to a net positive that the enemy will in turn seek to reverse. Gardner uses cross-cutting to propel this narrative forward, interweaving scenes of Weyak with scenes of Pua, scenes of Dani men with Dani women, and the Dani with birds. If the narrative structure is seamless, it is also cyclical and so in some sense static.[84]

The film, moreover, exceeds this circular story in various ways. It is essential to consider the opening and the closing scenes, which frame the unfolding of events. The briefly shown Dani funeral in the two shots of the title sequence is not a proleptic scene of the boy's funeral but that of an adult man—totally unrelated to subsequent events. The final narration, which echoes the opening fable, reflects on Gardner's experiences with the Dani but also what he has been thinking about since, at least, his encounter with the Kwakiutl in *Blunden Harbour*:

> Soon both men and birds will surrender to the night. They'll rest for the life and death of days to come. For each, both awaits, but with the difference that men, having foreknowledge of their doom, bring a special passion to their life. They will not simply wait for death, nor will they bear it lightly when it comes. Instead, they will try with measured violence to fashion fate themselves. They kill to save their souls and, perhaps, to ease the burden of knowing what birds will never know and what they as men, who have forever killed each other, cannot forget.

In fact, the body of the film has explored struggles of life and death among the Dani in ways that exceed the simple narrative unfolding of events. This essayist impulse is not only evident in moments of Gardner's commentary, but also at times in the unorthodox images he offers. For instance, immediately after the title sequence, his commentary introduces Weyak over a twenty-nine-second close-up of Weyak's thigh and a pile of bark string he is using to weave his funeral band. Other short sequences of shots avoid conventional audiovisual matchings, as when Gardner first discusses the towers that guard the frontier while showing images of birds, towers, and trees. There is cross-cutting, but not always in the conventional manner.

In his book-length study of the essay film, Timothy Corrigan characterizes essayist thinking as "a conceptual, figural, phenomenological and representational remaking of a self as it encounters, tests, and experiences some version of the real as a public 'elsewhere.'"[85] This seems consistent with Gardner's purpose: "I seized the opportunity of speaking to certain fundamental issues in human life," he writes. "The Dani were less important to me than those issues. . . .My responsibility was as much to my own situation as a thinking person as to the Dani as also thinking people. I never thought this reflective or value-oriented approach was inconsistent either with my training as a social scientist or [with] my goals as the author of a film. I thought this was especially true as long as I was diligent in the gathering of evidence."[86] As he concludes this short essay, "The film attempts to say something about how we all, as humans, meet our animal fate."[87]

The nature of Gardner's experience and how it is communicated is often criticized from two seemingly contradictory positions. Sherman invokes ethnographic filmmaker Jorge Preloran's assertion that "Gardner didn't like those people [the Dani]; you can tell in his narration."[88] David MacDougall remarks, "It is fair to say that Gardner is not particularly interested in the subjective experience of the Dani for its own sake," even as he goes on to add "although there are moments of intense personal sympathy."[89]

On the other hand, considerable criticism has suggested that Gardner is too interested in the subjective experience of his subjects, particularly in those moments when he tells us what Weyak and Pua are thinking. For instance, in the wake of Weyaké's death, for which Weyak feels some responsibility, "Weyak wonders not only about what he didn't do, but also what he did and why the magic that he made when Puakoloba was strengthened didn't work." Or as men are breaking the soil for a new garden, Pua "watches, thinking of the day when he himself would be a farmer." Ruby protests, saying, "most anthropologists then would have objected to attributing thoughts to the subjects of their studies, as would most anthropologists today."[90] How could Gardner know what Weyak and Pua are thinking at these moments? The answer seems obvious: Gardner spent considerable time with both Weyak and Pua. Through direct questioning, through intermediaries, and by observation, he would have learned what Weyak felt and how Pua imagined his future.

In the end, Gardner's use of interior monologue became an act of creative imagining. When Gardner and the Harvard Peabody expedition arrived in the Baliem Valley, the Dani were Other: alien, potentially dangerous, and inscrutable. Gardner's chosen task was to overcome these estrangements, first for himself and his film, then for his audience. His readiness to speak their thoughts and explain their motivations is only one aspect of his efforts to facilitate a sense of intimacy and even identification for his audience. As already noted, his use of sound to create an embodied space brings the viewer into the world of the Dani. Their world becomes our world. Gardner also uses close-ups. He treats the Dani as fellow human beings. They are not inferior or "primitive" in the negative sense of the term. As Gardner remarked:

> I wanted to make a film about certain particular individuals through whose lives and situations the film's themes and narrative threads could be developed. This was a decision of the most basic kind. Among other things, it meant that the camera would not be used for passive observation but as an active agent in disclosing the identities and recounting the experiences of some individuals but not others. I wanted to see all I possibly could of the context within which these individuals existed. . . .I was interested in entering the lives of some very real and particular people. I was not at all interested in making a film about abstractions like society, culture and personality, or about items on somebody's ethnographic laundry list.[91]

Weyak is Gardner's counterpart in the film. There is a deep connection between the two men—a kind of mutual identity and respect. Both are in charge of small groups of men, while Weyak's funeral band and Gardner's film both commemorate individual deaths and affirm a way of life.[92] Likewise, Gardner became Pua's surrogate father. Pua recalls Gardner's own son—and since Pua's father had died (he only has a stepfather), this connection came about naturally.[93] There is a lovely moment in the film, easily misconstrued, when Gardner is filming Weyak measuring the fiber band he has been weaving. The voice-over notes, "Pua, who has come to visit with a friend, helps him lay it out." Some have tried to see this as an effort to create a contrived father-son relationship between Weyak and Pua.[94] This is not the case: Gardner is that friend.[95] There is a real father-son relationship between Pua and Gardner, rather than an artificially constructed one between Pua and Weyak. When I asked about his relationship to Pua, Gardner responded, "his father had died, from causes unknown to me, and I did become a surrogate parent, which was a pleasure I enjoyed all his and my life."[96] Their reunion in *Dead Birds Re-Encountered* (2013) movingly confirms this, as William Rothman's essay in this volume demonstrates.

David MacDougall further complicates the picture when he argues that Weyaké, the boy who is killed and whose funeral we see, becomes Pua's surrogate self in *Dead Birds*. I would argue, however, that Weyaké was a surrogate for someone else: Michael Rockefeller. Weyak feels immensely guilty for the death of Weyaké, even though everyone knows it was not his fault. Weyaké should never have gone to the unguarded frontier to get a drink at the river. Gardner must have felt very much the same way vis-à-vis Michael Rockefeller, who went off on his own after the Peabody expedition. Rockefeller also made a bad decision, and it cost him his life. Although Rockefeller's tragic death did not happen on Gardner's watch, that did not prevent him from feeling crushed, guilty, devastated. It is not surprising then that Gardner's narration, written after Rockefeller's death, emphasizes Weyak's sense of failure and responsibility. One can only imagine that Gardner knew all too well what Weyak was feeling.

The relationship between the ritual warfare of the Dani and the Cold War, particularly at a time of rising brutality in the Vietnam War, has been frequently noted. For some, given the controlled nature of Dani violence, there were ways in which their system appeared more civilized than our own.[97] Further, in presenting a people who had not yet felt the weight of the modern world—the political, economic, and cultural subservience to a more powerful center that would soon arrive—*Dead Birds* also invited speculation about a world that was undergoing a process of decolonization. Additionally, *Dead Birds* spoke to the changing world of U.S. race relations in the Civil Rights era, at least metaphorically. In its quiet insistence on equality and intimacy across profoundly different races and cultures, the film suggested possibilities for racial understanding and cross-racial intimacy at home. In this sense, *Dead Birds* strikes me as a film that resonates with Robert Young and Michael Roemer's *Nothing But a Man* (1965). To appreciate this, it helps to see the film repeatedly and over time. The Dani become less strange and ever more familiar. Once again, I reencounter that old friend Weyak guarding the frontier. As I get older, I have come to appreciate his manly bearing and well-toned torso—as well as his patient weaving of the belt.

Aldous Huxley has noted, "Essays belong to a literary species whose extreme variability can be studied most effectively within a three-poled frame of reference. There is the pole of the personal and the autobiographical; there is the pole of the objective, the factual, the concrete-particular; and there is the pole of the abstract-universal. . . .The most richly satisfying essays are those which make the best not of one, not of two but of all the three worlds in which it is possible for the essay to exist."[98] Somewhere in this constellation, I would put *Dead Birds*.

Notes

1. Following the submission of this chapter, I plan to update the Wikipedia page for *Dead Birds.*
2. I now teach a similar graduate course—"Historical Methods in Film Study."
3. Many thanks to Charles Warren in particular, who encouraged me to grapple with this pairing. Also to Melanie Honma for research contributions. In recent years, I have found myself haunted by memories of Jay Leyda, in particular various passing remarks that he made to me (and others), which were underappreciated at the time—and his programing choices, such as this one.
4. Bosley Crowther, "Screen: 'The Sky Above'," *New York Times,* June 20, 1962, 40.
5. John L. Scott, "'Sky, Mud' Fine Film Document," *Los Angeles Times*, August 23, 1962, 26. Brendan Gill of the *New Yorker* offered a somewhat ironic perspective on the film, noting, "it is certainly a chance to study curiosities of custom and dress that outdo one's fondest recollections of these treasures of unself-conscious nakedness which, in a primmer time, gave the *National Geographic* so vital a place in the coming of age of American boys" ("Suburban Savages," *New Yorker*, June 30, 1962, 68).
6. Susan Tobin, "Pierre Gaisseau," www.culturalequity.org/alanlomax/ce_alanlomax_profile_gaisseau.php
7. Jack C. Ellis, *The Documentary Idea: A Critical History of English-Language Documentary Film and Video* (Englewood Cliffs, NJ: Prentice Hall, 1989); Betsy A. McLane, *A New History of Documentary Film*, 2nd ed. (New York: Continuum, 2012); Ian Aitken, ed., *Encyclopedia of Documentary Film*, 3 vols. (New York: Routledge, 2006). There is a parallel history of documentary in the United States, which could be chronicled through Academy Award winners. Unlike Barnouw's influential and impressive study, Ellis and McLane fail to include Robert Gardner's work as well.
8. Karl Heider, *The Ethnographic Film*, rev. ed. (Austin: University of Texas, 2006), 94.
9. Gene Moskowitz (Mosk), "Le Ciel et La Boue," *Variety*, May 10, 1961.
10. The review of *Dead Birds* in *Variety*, for instance, briefly compares the two films ("Dead Birds," *Variety*, March 10, 1965).
11. Robert Gardner, *Just Representations* (Cambridge, MA: Studio7Arts & Peabody Museum Press, 2010), 32.
12. See Robert Gardner, *Making* Dead Birds*: Chronicle of a Film* (Cambridge: Peabody Museum Press, 2007), 45.
13. Ursula Konrad, Alphonse Sowada, and Gunter Konrad, eds. *Asmat: Perception of Life in Art* (Mönchengladbach: B. Kühlen, 2002).
14. Gardner to author, October 25, 2013.
15. "Screening Room with Alan Lomax," Documentary Educational Resources. www.der.org/films/screening-room-alan-lomax.html
16. Susan Tobin, "Pierre Gaisseau." www.culturalequity.org/alanlomax/ce_alanlomax_profile_gaisseau.php
17. Robert Gardner, phone conversation, September 25, 2013. It is not entirely surprising therefore that the only substantive biography of Gaisseau is provided by the Association for Cultural Equity (ACE), a nonprofit founded by Alan Lomax. ACE is "dedicated to explore and preserve the world's expressive traditions with humanistic commitment and scientific engagement" (Association for Cultural Equity, www.culturalequity.org/ace/ce_ace_index.php).
18. Dust jacket, Pierre-Dominique Gaisseau, *The Sacred Forest: Magic and Secret Rites in French Guinea* (New York: Knopf, 1954).
19. Susan Tobin, "Pierre Gaisseau."
20. Alain Gheerbrant, *L'expédition Orénoque-Amazone, 1948–1950* (Paris: Gallimard 1952), translated into English as *The Impossible Adventure: Journey to the Far Amazon* (London,

Gollancz 1953). Gheerbrant's photo book, *Des Hommes qu'on appelle sauvages* (Paris: R. Marin 1952), was a complement to the film. A forty-minute television version, produced by David Attenborough, was shown on the BBC in December 1953.

21. Susan Tobin, "Pierre Gaisseau."

22. Jean Rouch, *The Cinema in Africa—Present Position and Current Trends* (Paris: United Nations Educational, Scientific and Cultural Organization, July 2, 1962), 12.

23. André Bazin, *Forêt Sacrée*," *L'Observateur*, July 4, 1954, 29.

24. The *Los Angeles Times* reviewer remarked that the documentary "makes no attempt at delicacy. . . .Neither does it make an attempt at understanding although its narrator insists that it does" ("Novel Film Presented," *Los Angeles Times*, April 6, 1956, 19). See also "Unilluminating Documentary on Africa," *New York Times*, September 29, 1956, 12. For length see: http://movies.msn.com/movies/movie-synopsis/gri-gri/

25. "Entertainment Timetable for Boston and Vicinity," *Christian Science Monitor*, October 5, 1957, 10.

26. Gardner to Musser, phone conversation, January 2014.

27. Pierre-Dominique Gaisseau, *Visa to the Prehistoric World* (London: Muller, 1957), 129.

28. The film has become available as an extra on a French DVD with *Le Ciel et la boue.*

29. Olivia Cooper Hadjian, "Tintin in New Guinea: *Heaven and Mud*—DVD Edition," www.critikat.com/Le-Ciel-et-la-Boue-edition-DVD.html

30. Leopold Pospisil to Charles Musser, February 4, 2014. Gardner, *Making* Dead Birds, 26, 71.

31. A book by Carl Hoffman, *Savage Harvest: A Tale of Cannibals, Colonialism, and Michael Rockefeller's Tragic Quest for Primitive Art* (New York: Morrow, 2014) rather sensationally reopens this story, asserting that Rockefeller was killed and eaten by cannibals.

32. "Dead Birds," *Variety*, March 10, 1965.

33. Rebecca R. French, "Leopold J. Pospisil and the Anthropology of Law," *PoLAR: Political and Legal Anthropology Review* 16:2 (June 1993), 1.

34. Leopold Pospisil, *Kapauku Papuans and Their Law* (New Haven, CT: Yale University Publications in Anthropology, 1958), 13.

35. Leopold Pospisil to Charles Musser, January 17, 2014. His film training was indebted to Yale's audiovisual department.

36. Harold Coolidge to Robert Gardner, January 27, 1959, in Robert Gardner, *Making* Dead Birds*: Chronicle of a Film* (Cambridge, MA: Peabody Museum Press, 2007), 12.

37. Gardner to Coolidge, January 29, 1959, in Gardner, *Making* Dead Birds*,* 12.

38. Pospisil to Musser, January 17, 2014.

39. Not a member of the Communist underground, Pospisil was imprisoned by the postwar Czech government, which sought to discredit him as a Nazi collaborator. Detained for more than a year, he eventually proved his innocence in court. Freed, he soon came to the U.S. See Benjamin Frommer, *National Cleansing: Retribution Against Nazi Collaborators in Postwar Czechoslovakia* (Cambridge: Cambridge University Press, 2004), 125–126.

40. In our discussions, Pospisil repeatedly cited the death of Michael Rockefeller as confirmation of his assessment—repeating the conflation that appears in the *Variety* review of *Dead Birds* and no doubt elsewhere.

41. Gardner was also aware of the Archbold zoological expeditions to West New Guinea's Baliem Valley, which had begun in the early 1930s and continued after World War II.

42. Robert Gardner, "Memorandum of Conversations with Leopold Pospisil, Eliot Elisofon, Margaret Mead, Michael Rockefeller," May 19, 1960, in *Making* Dead Birds, 21.

43. Brian Meacham and I recorded Pospisil as he screened two reels of footage and provided accompanying commentary on March 12, 2014. The material he showed Gaisseau is in the more dynamic second reel, which Pospisil sometimes screens by itself (i.e., dispensing with the more mundane first reel).

44. Pospisil to Musser, January 17, 2014.

45. Pospisil criticized Gardner for not learning the Dani language. On his part, Pospisil mastered Kapauku to the point where, he claims, it became his most fluent language and he wrote his field notes in it (Pospisil to Musser, March 12, 2014).

46. Ruby puts forth a fantasy of an anthropological cinema "designed by anthropologists to communicate anthropological insights about the human condition." Ruby, "An Anthropological Critique of the Films of Robert Gardner," *Journal of Film and Video*, vol. 43, no. 4 (Winter 1991), 3.

47. Gardner, *Making* Dead Birds, 4.

48. Gardner, *Making* Dead Birds, 5.

49. Ruby, "An Anthropological Critique of the Films of Robert Gardner," 7.

50. Pospisil's ongoing work in anthropology pursued issues of much broader scope. See Pospisil, *Anthropology of Law: A Comparative Theory* (New York: Harper & Row, 1971).

51. Elsaesser, "Kobarweng," October 2013, http://thomas-elsaesser.com/index.php?option=com_content&view=article&id=91%3Aneuer-berliner-kunstverein&catid=39%3Ablog-category-01&Itemid=70&limitstart=3 é. Other groups and anthropologists were in Dutch New Guinea in this period. The Star Mountains Expedition (1959) included cultural anthropologist Dr. J. Pouwer (www.papua-insects.nl/history/Starmountains%20exp/Starmountains1959.htm). Gottfried Oosterwal was an anthropologist and Seventh Day Adventist who published *People of the Tor: A Cultural-anthropological Study on the Tribes of the Tor Territory* (Northern Netherlands New-Guinea) (Assen: Van Gorcum 1961), while John-Erik Elmberg published "Field Notes on the Mejbrat People in the Ajamaru District of the Bird's Head (Vogelkop), Western New Guinea," *Ethnos* 20 (1955), 2–102, and "Further notes on the northern Mejbrats (Vogelkop, Western New Guinea)," *Ethnos*: *Journal of Anthropology*, 24:1–2 (1959), 70–80. Roy Rappaport, who received his PhD from Columbia University in 1966, did fieldwork among the Tsembaga Maring in New Guinea in the early 1960s. His dissertation became *Pigs for the Ancestors: Ritual in the Ecology of a New Guinea People* (New Haven: Yale University Press, 1968).

52. Loren Eiseley, "Miniatures of Ourselves," *New York Times*, November 18, 1962.

53. Scott MacDonald, *American Ethnographic Film and Personal Documentary: The Cambridge Turn* (Berkeley: University of California Press, 2013), 68–72.

54. "Fable, Parable, and Allegory, *Encyclopædia Britannica, Academic Edition*, www.britannica.com/EBchecked/topic/1457283/fable-parable-and-allegory.

55. As Jonathan Kahana observes, "The power of social documentary comes from its allegorical displacement of particular details onto the plane of general significance." *Intelligence Work: The Politics of American Documentary* (New York: Columbia University Press, 2008), 26.

56. The second word of the title—"Birds"—appears first at the end of the shot of the flying bird. The word "Dead," and so the full title, appears with the cut to the funeral. This emphasizes the metaphorical equivalence of dead birds with dead humans.

57. "Blunden Harbour," Wikipedia. Blunden Harbour is on the Canadian mainland, not Vancouver Island as many descriptions of Gardner's film suggest.

58. Kathryn Bunn-Marcuse, "Kwakwaka'wakw on Film," in *Walking a Tightrope: Aboriginal People and Their Representations*, eds. Ute Lischke and David T. McNab (Waterloo, Canada: Wilfrid Laurier University Press, 2005), 318–319.

59. Gerry Williams explicitly associated himself with the early-American potter Daniel Clark as Seaweed does with his ancestors. Nevertheless, both must be seen as innovators rather than simply stuck in a past that is rapidly receding.

60. MacDonald, *American Ethnographic Film*, 71.

61. Gardner, *Making* Dead Birds, 26, 71. One might imagine a hypothetical documentary in which Gardner followed missionaries or Dutch representatives as they settled a new area and began to "civilize" or otherwise "improve" the local inhabitants' way of life.

62. David MacDougall, "Gardner's Bliss," in *The Cinema of Robert Gardner*, eds. Ilisa Barbash and Lucien Taylor, (Oxford: Berg, 2007), 153.

63. MacDonald, *American Ethnographic Film*, 7–9.

64. Ruby, "An Anthropological Critique," 8.

65. The scope and cost of equipment needed for cinema verité filmmaking is too often minimized. That these new practices were introduced through Time-Life is not incidental. Time-Life had the resources and the New York location had the infrastructure that could effectively support this innovation.

66. "Television Programs: Wednesday Through Saturday," *New York Times*, July 3, 1960, X13. It was shown on Channel 11, WPIX, an independent television station.

67. Gardner, *Making* Dead Birds, 25. Gardner has also addressed this issue quite directly, remarking:

> Nineteen-sixty was the precise moment in the history of cinema when workable and lightweight synchronous sound and film equipment was being developed and tested. I had made some trials of my own as early as 1957 when I accompanied John Marshall to the Kalahari and brought a small, soundproofed camera that would run at a constant speed, but it seemed an impossibly awkward and ponderous way to make films. So I chose a camera designed for straightforward image making. . . .In New Guinea I was adequately but modestly equipped. (Robert Gardner, "The Impulse to Preserve," in Charles Warren, ed., *Beyond Document: Essays on Nonfiction Film* (Hanover, NH: Wesleyan University Press, 1996), 175.)

68. "Film On Politics Cited for Prize," *New York Times*, March 29, 1961, 28.

69. Ernest Callenbach's review in *Film Quarterly* came out in 19:3 (Spring 1966), 56–58. The film may have had its New York City debut at Donnell Library in May, 1964.

70. Film note: "Dead Birds," University of Minnesota Film Society, April 27, 1964, CineFiles, University of California-Berkeley Art Museum and Pacific Film Archive.

71. Ruby, *Picturing Culture*, 101.

72. Craig Mishler, "Narrativity and Metaphor in Ethnographic Film: A Critique of Robert Gardner's *Dead Birds*," *American Anthropologist*, New Series, vol. 87: 3 (September 1985), 669.

73. Mishler, "Narrativity and Metaphor in Ethnographic Film," 670.

74. Ilisa Barbash, "Out of Words: A Conversation with Robert Gardner," in *The Cinema of Robert Gardner*, 102.

75. MacDonald, *American Ethnographic Film*, 71.

76. Gardner's *Forest of Bliss* (1985) officially debuted in the same month as Mishler's article criticizing Gardner's narration for *Dead Birds*. *Forest of Bliss* not only has no narration, it lacks inter-titles or subtitles, so that even verbal utterances go untranslated. This involves a certain irony because that film made many of the same critics and anthropologists equally unhappy. See David MacDougall, "Gardner's Bliss," in Barbash and Taylor, *The Cinema of Robert Gardner,* 155.

77. Timothy Corrigan, for instance, considers Vertov's *Man with a Movie Camera* (1929) to be an essay film. See Corrigan, *The Essay Film: From Montaigne, After Marker* (Oxford: Oxford University Press, 2011), 51–52.

78. MacDonald, *American Ethnographic Film*, 392.

79. T.W. Adorno, "The Essay as Form" (1958), trans. Bob Hullot-Kentor and Frederic Will, *New German Critique* 32 (Spring–Summer 1984), 151.

80. Sherman, *Documenting Ourselves*, 42.

81. Ibid., 43. Sherman also cites Karl Heider to suggest that Gardner was wrong to focus on ritual warfare as an "'essential quality' of Dani life" because they seemed to have adapted to peace under Dutch pacification with little difficulty. In fact, given the pervasiveness of ritual warfare and other forms of violence among the Dani, its cessation might readily have been felt as a relief. Other anthropologists who studied Papuans in the Central Highlands indicate the ways in which warfare was a pervasive aspect of these groups.

82. Sheila Curran Bernard, *Documentary Storytelling: Creative Nonfiction on Screen*, 3rd ed. (Burlington, MA: Focal Press, 2007).

83. Ruby, *Picturing Culture*, 101. Catherine Russell characterizes *Dead Birds* as "psychological narrativity" in *Experimental Ethnography* (Durham, NC: Duke University Press, 1999), 14, 190.

84. This structural element makes it that much easier to accuse Gardner of showing the Dani as operating outside of history.

85. Corrigan, *The Essay Film*, 35.

86. Robert Gardner, "On the Making of *Dead Birds,*" in *The Dani of West Irian: An Ethnographic Companion to the Film* Dead Birds, ed. Karl G. Heider (Andover, MA: Warner Modular; Module 2, 1972), 34.

87. Ibid., 35.

88. Sherman, *Documenting Ourselves*, 171.

89. MacDougall, *Transcultural Cinema*, 109.

90. Ruby, *Picturing Culture*, 101.

91. Gardner, "The Impulse to Preserve," 175–176.

92. Scott MacDonald suggests a parallel between Weyak weaving a long bark fiber band and Gardner making his strip of film. The connection is there, but I would argue it is deeper.

93. Gardner does not provide any equivalent connection to females. Only with Weyak's wife are we briefly allowed a similar kind of intimacy. While this is certainly one of the film's limitations, *Making* Dead Birds shows it to have been a necessary one. The women were reclusive and difficult to film.

94. See MacDougall, 108.

95. Although the depictions of Weyak and Pua can be compared to those of ≠Oma Tsamkxao and his son Tsamkxao in *The Hunters*, the two individuals are much more developed in *Dead Birds*: Weyak and Pua are introduced immediately after the head titles and have an ongoing prominence thereafter.

96. Gardner email correspondence, April 14, 2014.

97. Ernest Callenbach, "*Dead Birds* by Robert Gardner," *Film Quarterly*, 19:3 (Spring 1966), 56–58. Although *Dead Birds* suggests that this violence might be characterized as "controlled," Matthiessen's *Under the Mountain Wall* gives a different sense—that the violence was pervasive and often unpredictable.

98. Aldous Huxley, "Preface to *Collected Essays*," quoted in Corrigan, *The Essay Film*, 14.

Chapter 13
Allegory and Gender Representation in *Rivers of Sand*

Mauro Bucci

Translated from the Italian by Zakiya Hanafi and the author

Rivers of Sand is a 1974 documentary about the Hamar people, filmed by Robert Gardner in southwestern Ethiopia. Like his first feature film, *Dead Birds* (1963), the documentary is a reflection on the human condition—one that moves away from conventional forms of storytelling, however, in order to experiment with image and audio techniques—techniques that come to full expression about a decade later in *Forest of Bliss* (1986). As is frequently the case in his cinema, in *Rivers of Sand* Gardner develops a strong central theme around which he builds the portrait of indigenous life. While dealing with what are often ordinary, everyday matters, the film's exploration of the relationship between the male and female genders arrives at reflections of an existential character. In particular, *Rivers of Sand* focuses on the inequalities between Hamar men and women: the system of violence and oppression that regulates the life of women is the lens through which Gardner looks in order to describe the local culture. This theme determines the aesthetic choices and modes of expression that he employs. Gardner is primarily interested in communicating his own point of view, not in conducting strictly scientific research. The film was shot at different times, in 1968 and 1971; starting with the second period of filming, Gardner collaborated with the anthropologists Jean Lydall and Ivo Strecker, especially. However, the different position that the two scholars took on the type of documentary to be made led them to view Gardner's work in a negative, polemical light: in short, they complained that he misunderstood and distorted the indigenous reality.[1] In the view of Peter Loizos, Lydall and Strecker's criticism stemmed from their more conventional ideas about film, because they apparently expected *Rivers of Sand* to provide a realistic, descriptive representation of Hamar culture, a conception that is quite far from the more personal, elaborate work created by Gardner.[2]

In *Rivers of Sand*, Gardner uses the technique of the interview with subtitled translation to give voice to a native woman named Omali Inda. Through her words, we are given a picture of the restrictions and violence to which Hamar women are routinely subjected. Omali Inda's point of view guides the film, which comes across as more than simply a portrait of the indigenous culture. In her account there resonates another story—one about the status of women in the West in the 1970s, a period when the role and identity of women were being redefined under the influence of feminist thought. In *Rivers of Sand* the representation of life as a Hamar woman overlaps with experiences and emotions relating to all women and, at a more general level, to all people. This issue is intertwined with the exploration of the mutual adaptation between the genders, ultimately leading to an important theme of Gardner's ethnographic cinema: the constraints that culture inevitably and sometimes painfully imposes on each person—on the place or role that tradition reserves for individuals in society.

After some words from Omali Inda, the scrolling text that introduces the film suggests the universal value of the Hamar experience by talking about "divisions and conflicts which are familiar to men and women everywhere." This aspect of the film can be understood as more than simply a creative choice made by the filmmaker. *Rivers of Sand* appeals to that deep layer of shared humanity that allows Western viewers to gain familiarity with the value of cultural facts very different from their own. The description of the indigenous culture acquires meaning according to the model of what, in written anthropology, James Clifford calls "ethnographic allegory."[3] We make use of this concept to examine the themes and modes of expression of Gardner's representation and the particular perspective adopted in *Rivers of Sand*. We see how the allegorical function is reflected in the description of the culture achieved by this film, in terms of both content and form.

Clifford writes, "Allegory prompts us to say of any cultural description not 'this represents, or symbolizes, that' but rather, 'this is a (morally charged) story about that.'"[4] He argues that allegory does not simply add another meaning to the cultural description; rather, it is an indispensable means for the structuring of the text that renders unfamiliar realities intelligible. For Clifford, this double structure is intrinsic to all ethnographic accounts of other cultures, implying that they are not, therefore, "neutral" representations. Instead, they are inevitably partial points of view that allow particular traits of the culture to be grasped according to the allegorical register through which the text is constructed or read. This is the case whether the double structure is made evident—by asserting the allegorical value of the research; or left hidden—by presenting the text as a purely realistic account of the observed culture. Referring to the beginning of *Nisa: The Life and Words of a !Kung Woman*[5] by Marjorie Shostak, which gives an evocative account of a !Kung woman giving birth, Clifford writes: "the story of an occurrence somewhere in the Kalahari Desert cannot remain just that. It implies both local cultural meanings and a general story of birth. A difference is posited and transcended."[6]

Allegorical discourse is particularly important in the films of Gardner, in which the representation of the indigenous world touches on topics that are highly relevant to the experience of Western viewers. Significantly, speaking at a 1977 conference, Gardner stated that every one of his films is "a kind of extended metaphor": for example, *Dead Birds* "is a metaphor about death, its inevitability, and our need to confront it."[7] This is a filmic gaze, then, that goes beyond a specific ethnographic description to address questions of a much broader scope. In *Rivers of Sand*, the resources of cinematographic language are used to express a vision that becomes an allegory for the Western society of the film's time and beyond. The ethnographic description given by the film transcends the Hamar reality, allowing viewers to engage with a different society by means of interpretive categories that are familiar to them. These allow viewers to gain an understanding of the other culture and to be emotionally involved in the indigenous life, while at the same time prompting reflection on the values of their own society. This was especially the case at a time when individuals were confronted by new social dynamics that questioned traditional male and female roles.

The Image of Women in the Early 1970s

During the time *Rivers of Sand* was made, the women's movement had a strong voice in the United States. In the film world, documentaries began to investigate issues regarding the status of women in society through stories told from the woman's point of view. As Patricia Erens observes, "By eliminating the omniscient male narrator, women could speak in their own voices and validate their experiences."[8] These female "portraits," which were also made possible by the diffusion of new technologies for synchronous sound recording, gave space to everyday problems, social discrimination, situations of oppression, and so forth, that had previously remained in the shadows, in order to make the claim for a different idea about women and a new position for them in society and in Western history.[9] In the 1970s, the change in the cultural climate left its mark in the social sciences, which, for the purposes of this paper, saw the development of a feminist anthropology that was particularly attentive to studying the concept of gender and examining women's conditions of subordination. In ethnographic documentaries of the period, the subject investigated often appears in the title. For example, *Masai Women* (Chris Curling, 1974), made for Granada Television's *Disappearing World* series, includes interviews with indigenous women conducted by anthropologist Melissa Llewelyn-Davies that describe the position of women in institutions such as the family or marriage. The film addresses the iniquity of social customs and rules for the women, particularly regarding the ownership of animals. Other examples are some short films in the AUFS *Faces of Change* series, which give voice to women from different societies, using interviews, commentaries, and recordings of conversations between natives. *Afghan Women* (Josephine Powell, Nancy Hatch Dupree, 1974) investigates the role of women in relation to work, family, marriage, and schooling; while *Andean Women* (Hubert Smith, 1974) also looks into the issue of gender disparities, describing male oppression and idleness at certain moments, and the denigration and subjugation of women in spite of the important productive role they play in society.

In *Rivers of Sand* the emphasis given to a female character who resolutely describes the meaning of being a woman in her culture, the account she gives of the inequalities between the sexes and the violence and social pressures that affect the female gender, can be partly attributed to the new awareness and mode of representation of women in this period.[10] *Rivers of Sand* is more critical toward indigenous traditions than any other of Gardner's films. He himself states that he did not want to exclude his personal judgment in the description of Hamar culture.[11] *Dead Birds* also deals with issues concerning the link between culture and violence—"difficult" ones for Western observers, such as the partial amputation of fingers that Dani women are subjected to as a harsh mourning practice. However, unlike the way Hamar customs are portrayed in *Rivers of Sand*, this film avoids a negative characterization of these traditions. In *Rivers of Sand*, the comments that Omali Inda makes directly disclose the harsh existence of Hamar women. Unlike previous documentaries about exotic communities, the complementarity between the genders does not appear to be the result of a balanced and harmonious order; instead, mutual adaptation leads to oppression and endurance. The difficult living conditions are due not only to the constant struggle to survive in a hostile, semi-arid environment, but also to the problematic coexistence of men and women; in other words, to causes that are internal to the community.

***Gender Dualism in* Rivers of Sand**

Rivers of Sand represents the two genders mainly through the activities of daily life and the division of labor in their society. Parallel editing shows the menial or heavy chores such as cleaning activities, collecting water, or grinding sorghum performed by women, intercut with the seemingly less-demanding occupations that the men devote themselves to—such as hunting or the care and decoration of the body. Special importance is given to creating elaborate hairstyles using clay and colored substances. Cattle raising stands out as one of the productive activities that the film shows men engaged in. The fulcrum of the description of female subjugation lies in Omali Inda's account of the violence and iniquities that women are subjected to or that they submit themselves to in accordance with social practices, especially after marrying. *Rivers of Sand* describes the power of men over women, legitimized by a cultural tradition.

The theme of social inequalities between males and females is developed both by juxtaposing situations and practices, and through associations of a symbolic nature. The film represents behavior, customs, and sensations of Hamar life, creating continual friction between the different activities and living conditions of the two genders. We see women undergoing whippings, scarification practices, tooth extractions, the application of metal rings to the body, and almost incessantly at work. Through the editing, their situation is compared to the condition of animals, who are also destined to suffer at the hands of Hamar men. By contrast, the men are often shown resting, taking care of their bodies, practicing divination, and pronouncing ritualized blessings. The difficult social condition also extends to the men, however: because of the position of power that they enjoy, they are afflicted with "wasted energies, idle spirits, and self-doubt," as Gardner's voice-over informs us. The viewer is taken on a dark journey into the Hamar culture, an often claustrophobic world, especially for the women, where, as Charles Warren notes, the camera "moves restlessly over distances with people and domestic animals, seeking meaning, as if seeking escape."[12] Actions, sounds, objects, and comments converge to create a totalizing description aimed at closing the female experience within a state of stifling social oppression.

This negative view of the indigenous culture is corroborated by Gardner's voice-over commentary, which, as Loizos notes, instead of using "neutral" words, uses terms that imply a value judgment against aspects of Hamar society associated with the gender relationship.[13] Although at various times we are shown the natives in good spirits, *Rivers of Sand* gives us a hard, pessimistic picture of the indigenous Hamar world. The images of cruelty toward people and animals; the bitter testimony of the protagonist; the feeling of suffocating rules impossible to escape—further reified by the funeral of a woman whose corpse is followed by the camera until it is slid into an arid pit—all add deeper significance to the first words spoken by Gardner in the film: "A day begins in the dark for the Hamar." This statement refers equally to the chores that people do every day before dawn and, as William Rothman points out, to the fact that "the satisfactions that gladden their hearts emerge from the suffering they endure and inflict."[14]

The rain and the rushing river in flood after the funeral suddenly break the feeling of this prison of sand and stones, offering a cathartic moment in the representation of indigenous life. The change is illusory, however. Only a few hours later, the water dwindles and disappears to make way once again for the dry river bed and the inhospitable environment that reflect the stasis in the emotional sphere and moral fiber of Hamar society.

What is expressed in this emblematic representation of the landscape is an interior dimension, belonging to the personality of the natives. These stretches of sand continue, invisibly, to maintain "the possibility of life," since the water remains below ground even when the rivers run dry.[15] The life to which the river is brought back for an intense but fleeting moment expresses the fragility and transience of existence; it suggests the need for people to fight for survival and then cling to their fellow human beings. In *Rivers of Sand*, the forms of culture that give rise to oppression and violence are in dramatic tension with the deepest sentiments of human nature. In the words of Rothman, "The human need for love, which is the other face of the human avoidance of love, is a deep subject of all of Gardner's films."[16]

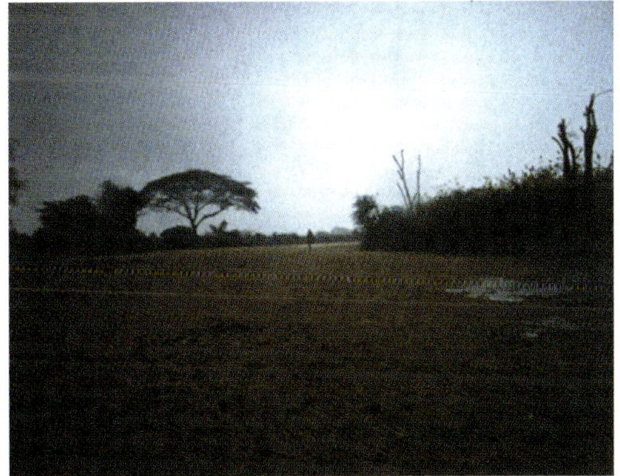

The Themes and Rhetoric of Omali Inda's Account

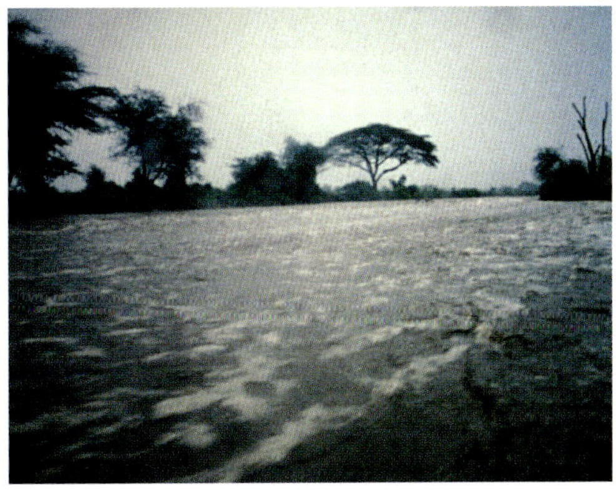

In *Rivers of Sand*, scenes showing the harvesting and grinding of grain, hunting, livestock raising, ritual dances, body decoration techniques, and so on, follow each other, alternate, or repeat. The film does not develop along a classical narrative line, like *Dead Birds*, although such a structure does come into play when Hamar life is presented to the viewer by the narrating character, Omali Inda.[17] Her introductory remarks have a beginning, a development, and an end—a tripartite structure, in other words, that gives rise to a dramatic problem. They suggest the interpretation of the film, which can be considered a development of the concepts expressed in her opening words. *Rivers of Sand* begins by addressing an important rite of passage in the life of a Hamar woman. It is an inevitable, recurring moment, presented as the beginning of a journey: "a time comes when a Hamar woman leaves her father's house to live with her husband." In the continuation of these opening remarks on marriage, Omali Inda touches on all the key points that will be highlighted in the film: the inequality between genders, the contrast between the indolence of the men and the industriousness of the women, the physical and psychological discomfort experienced by the women, and the control exercised over them by the men in their lives. The female condition is immediately illustrated using a metaphor that the film returns to over and over again: that of the quartz that slowly but surely smoothes down the grindstone, just as the lives of the women are shaped by the supremacy of the men ("the quartz is his hand, his whip, and you are beaten and beaten"). This image represents the difficult but seemingly necessary adaptation between the genders. At times, Omali Inda's monologue is accompanied by shots of women's bodies at work and of stones beaten with quartz—the visual equivalent of the issues explored.

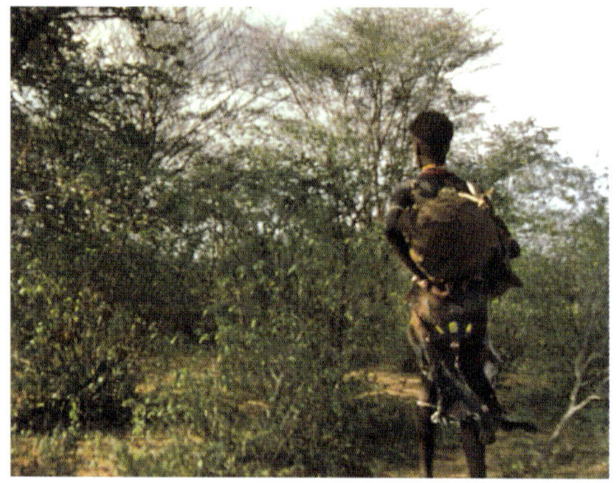

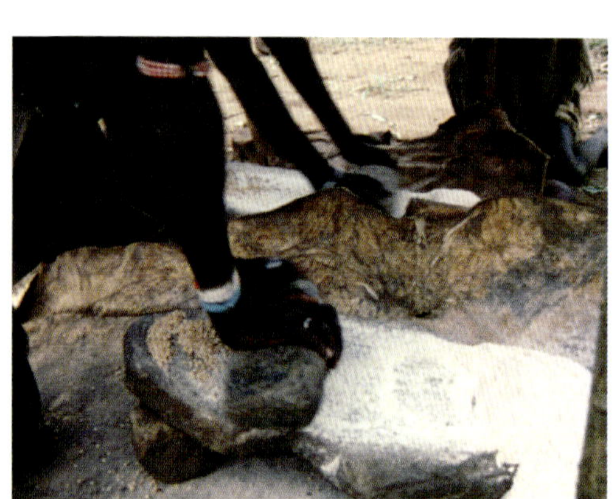

The course the Hamar woman follows involves both a spatial change (from her father's house to that of her husband), and an inner transformation that leads her to resign herself to an inevitable fate—to fit in, that is, with the social norms. Although this conflict in a woman's life cannot be settled, it can at least be resolved through acceptance. In effect, at the end of this first speech, talking about the Hamar husband, Omali Inda says: "you get used to him, you become one of his people. You become reconciled to stay. And that is that."

No matter how different indigenous traditions may be from those of Western viewers, this experience of Hamar women evokes a widely shared human reality. It points to the tensions between men and women, to the difficulties in adapting to a new life and to a shared existence with another person following marriage; to the need for both genders to establish an equilibrium together or some form of coexistence. Through this story of the relationship between genders in Hamar society, the film allegorically addresses the world of the viewer, especially that of female viewers.

The story of Omali Inda seems familiar not only because of the issues examined but also because of the rhetorical methods adopted. Comments on the film sometimes misunderstand the fact that Omali Inda does not relate personal experiences in her monologue—she almost never uses the first person—because the subject is the Hamar woman in an abstract sense. The story takes on an impersonal slant, and the generalization thus more easily alludes to the experiences of the public. Also, as we read in the subtitles, her monologue often employs the second person. Although Omali Inda refers to the Hamar woman as a category, the "you" spoken as she turns her gaze toward the camera emphatically calls the viewer into question. The message thus becomes more direct and persuasive, and has the effect of more deeply involving the public in the interpretation given of her own culture, as well as provoking the public to think of their own. This is reinforced by the intimacy and intensity of the close-ups of her face.

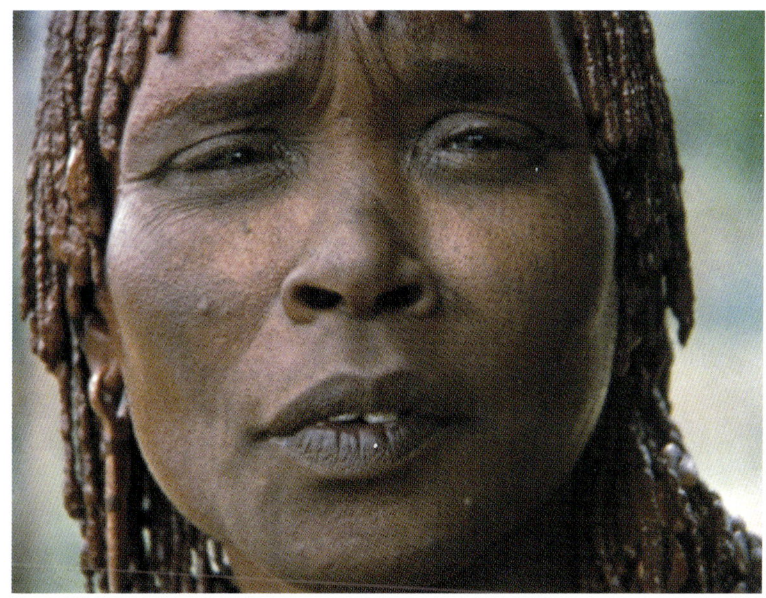

According to Omali Inda's initial account, for Hamar women marriage means learning about a new reality and coming to a different understanding of women's lives. This initiatory path takes on the quality of a journey, a teleological form of narrative in which events are arranged according to a progression that starts from a beginning and ends by arriving at a destination. This is an ethical route, a type of story familiar to the Western viewer, one aimed at reaching an end toward which, in this case, the life of the Hamar woman is directed. By presenting the story of female experience based on the allegory of the journey, the viewer is introduced to the knowledge of another culture through an easily recognizable form. Visually, this idea is evoked in the film by the various images of women walking, often on their way to perform strenuous tasks. Significantly, shots of a girl walking as she holds up a full calabash next to her legs are among the first and last images of the film.

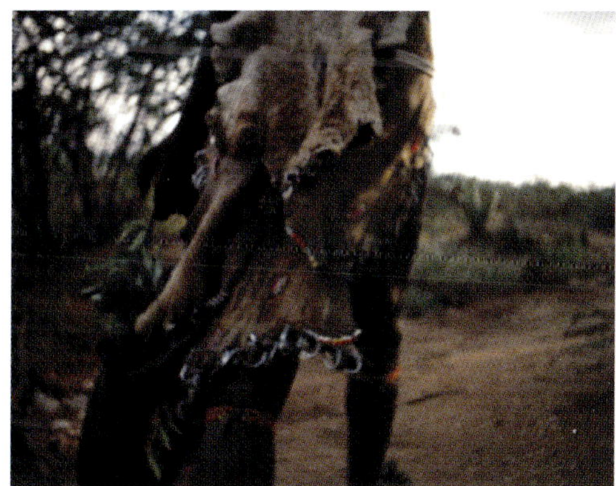

The life course followed by Hamar women is also symbolically sealed by the image of a man filmed in long shot at the beginning and end of the documentary: he first walks toward the camera, holding a stick, then later in the opposite direction, swinging the stick in his hand.

When audible, the sound of his steps is amplified. In the opening sequence, Omali Inda talks about the difficulties at the beginning of married life, and at the end of the film she returns to the subject of women's resignation and acceptance of their condition, which leads to a slackening of the husband's control. These different situations are represented symbolically by the movement of this man in relation to the camera position and, consequently, in relation to the viewer's point of view, thus suggesting the beginning and end of a process of submission. This idea gains support at the conclusion of the film from the women's singing combined with the sound of the grindstone, whose rhetorical meaning—the physical and psychological wearing down of women—is a recurring aspect of the film.

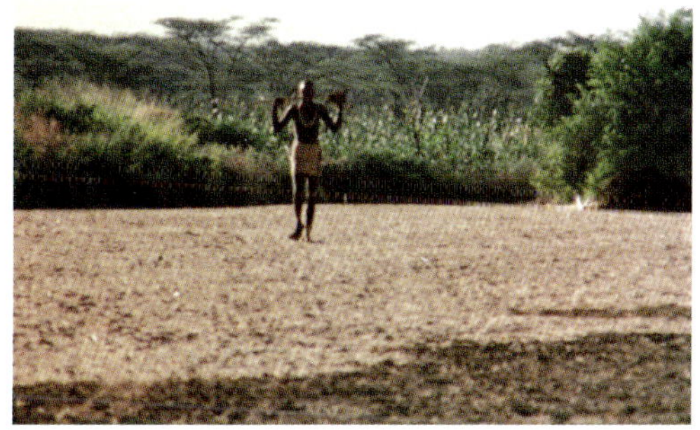

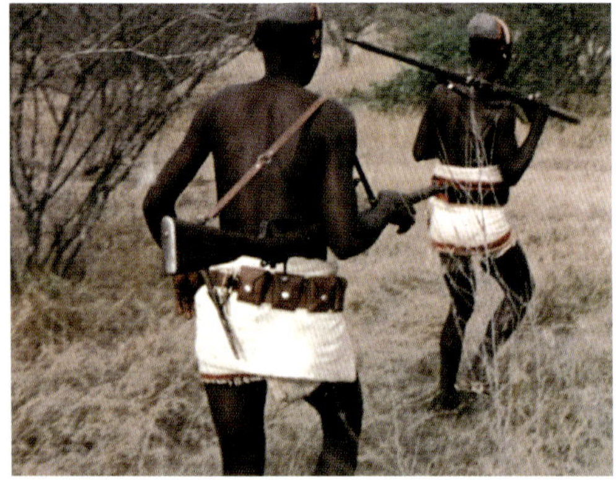

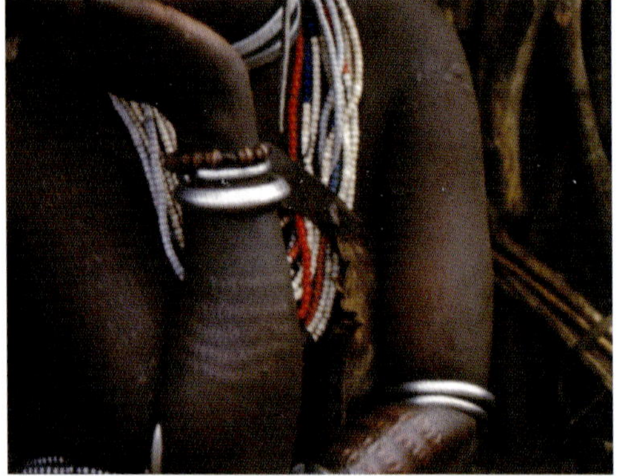

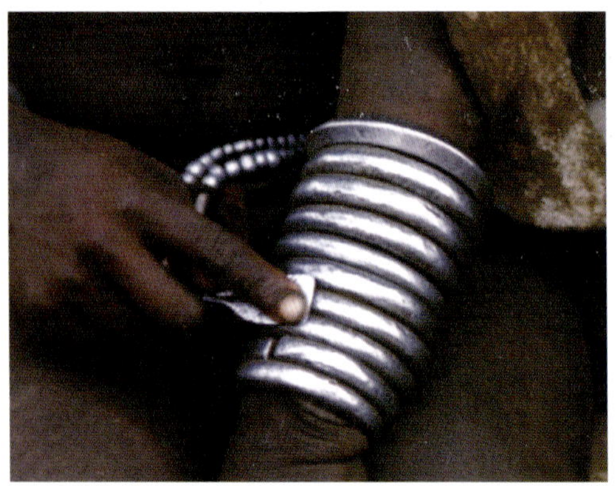

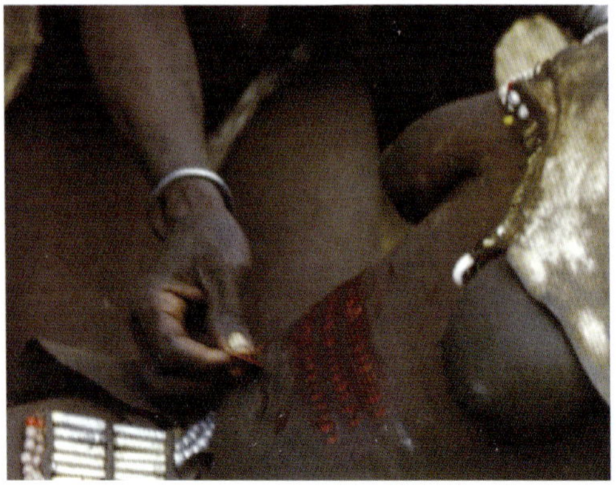

Objects, Bodies, and Indigenous Identity

Elements of the material culture of the Hamar are used to represent the genders and their different social status. From Omali Inda's account, we know that the grindstone is smoothed down by the quartz, and sorghum is ground on the stone, just as the wills of the new wives are gradually worn down by the oppressive Hamar customs that enslave women to their husbands. This material practice is a powerful leitmotif of the film. The hard work and constant physical movement that grinding sorghum requires is contrasted to the much less demanding use of other objects by the opposite sex. Among these, the rifle is particularly important: a recurring tool in the film, it is reserved exclusively for men, becoming a symbol of their power. For Loizos the rifles underwrite the identity of these people as men, while according to Gardner, guns are inextricably tied to the ego of the Hamar male.[18]

Not limited to reflecting a symbolic meaning, the grindstone and the rifle are tools that appear closely linked to the bodies that use them and evoke a strong sense of touch. The grindstone and the quartz become extensions of the female body: these tools are almost never shown as inert, independent objects, but primarily in relation to a body that is bent over, moving, and hard at work. The grindstone acquires a metonymic value: subjected to constant wear and modeling, it is a tool that represents woman; but at the same time it consumes her body, its energies, by the constant physical effort it requires. The images and sounds often evoke the tactile sensation of this practice: the rough quality of the stone surface that conforms to the quartz, in the same way that the woman's body adapts to the man and is molded by culture. This representation conveys an impression of strong physicality. In portraying women, the camera lingers on bodies bent over work, on backs marked by whip lashes, on skin furrowed by ornamental cuts, and in one scene on a young girl's front teeth being extracted. The shots are often intimate. The female body is fragmented into close-ups of hands, backs, shoulders, ankles, and so forth, that show the repetitive grain grinding movements, the tactile character of scars, the limbs encircled by rings that are loudly rubbed, and the blood and pain of body modification practices.

The inhospitable environment where the Hamar live, made of "rivers of sand" and "thorn scrub," as the text informs us, is also imprinted on the women's bodies when the thorns of the plants are used to pierce and lift the skin during scarification. The metal blade used in this operation, the rings that imprison the limbs and neck, the knife used for extracting teeth, and the whips wielded by the men are all objects that construct the female body. They show it, that is, to be

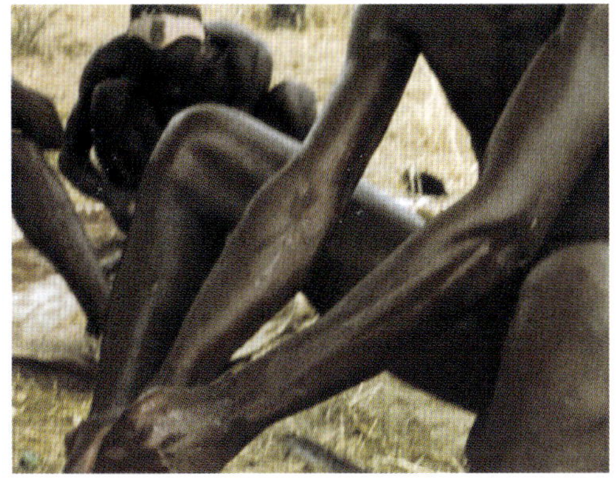

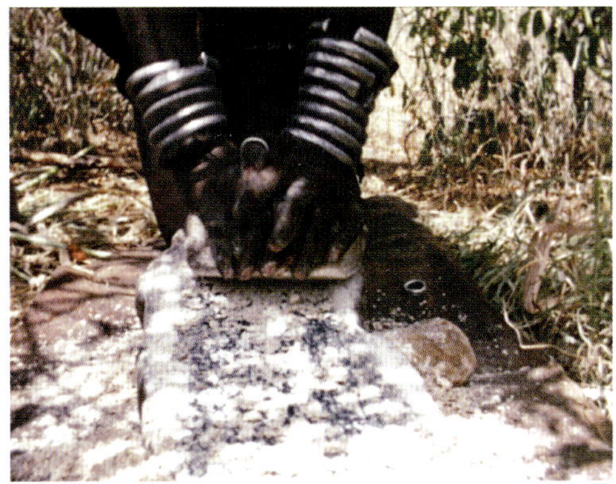

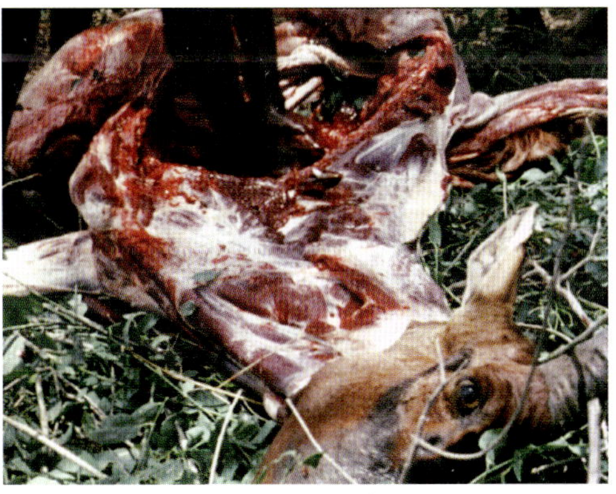

the culture's privileged locus of inscription. While the grindstone takes on corporeal connotations, the Hamar woman is conversely represented as an object: in Omali Inda's account, she is deprived of decision-making power because she is almost always under the influence of her husband or other male figures.

By contrast, the bodies of men are shown as perfectly smooth, with practically no scars and free from constraints. Often in resting positions, lying down or sitting, the male bodies are repeatedly the objects of care and attention. The gaze of the camera sometimes slips over completely naked male forms. In *Rivers of Sand* we see men covering their skin with white clay, rubbing their arms or their whole body with water, and carefully decorating their hair. The film captures the sensuality of these bodies and their gestures, as well as calling attention to male vanity. In contrast to the grindstone, which we see almost exclusively in use, the rifle receives attention similar to that given to the bodies of men: it is caressed and cared for by male hands, taking on bodily qualities itself. In addition, the smoothness produced by male hands that slide along the weapon or their own body is opposed to the roughness evoked by the women's grindstone or the ribbed surfaces of their scarified skin.

Hands and the work they perform take on special significance, as they do in several other films by Gardner. In his view, hands are very important because, along with eyes, they define the human being.[19] In the first minutes of *Rivers of Sand*, for example, the shot showing the hands of a woman at the grindstone, followed by one of a man dipping his hands in the blood of an antelope carcass, do more than just inform us about the different activities performed by the two genders. The first image expresses the hard work and subjugation of women, while the second transmits the power and violence that characterize male identity in the film. The similarity of the hand movements further suggests that in their different roles men and women participate in the same culture.

Another object appears at different times in the film: a crescent-shape stool made of wood, whose use is reserved exclusively for men. We see it while it is being carved, carried around, and used to rest. It is an instrument in *Rivers of Sand* that represents masculine privilege, and the use of it is often contrasted to images of women at work. As we know from Omali Inda, women can only sit on the ground, in their skirts, maintaining a respectful attitude toward social customs.

The male body is characterized by an unusual lightness. This is conveyed to us in shots of the male figure silhouetted against the sky; in the images of hunters framed between ostrich feathers at the end of a hunt; and in the ukuli ceremony, where young men soar in the air as they jump over cows.

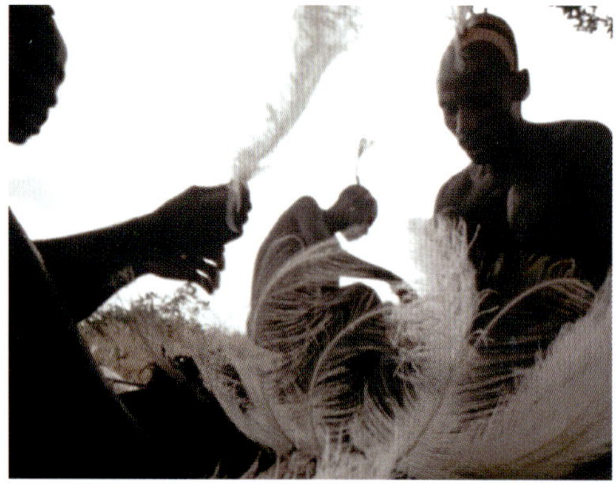

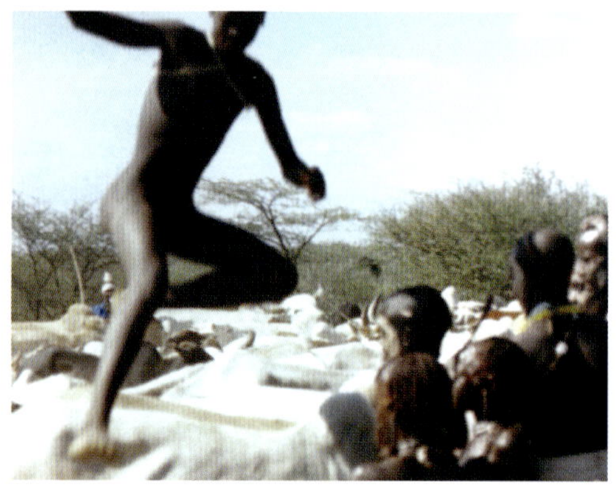

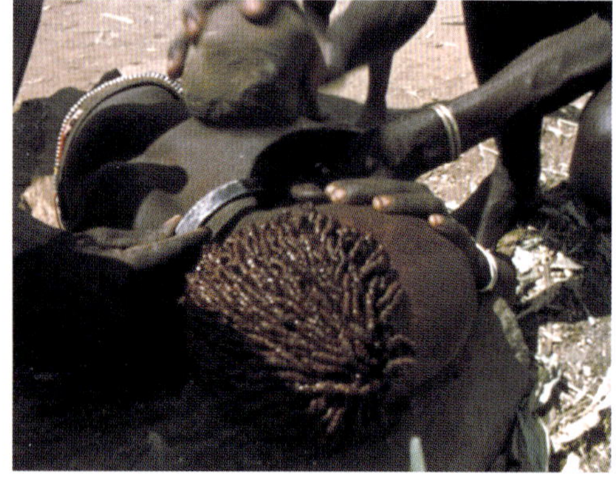

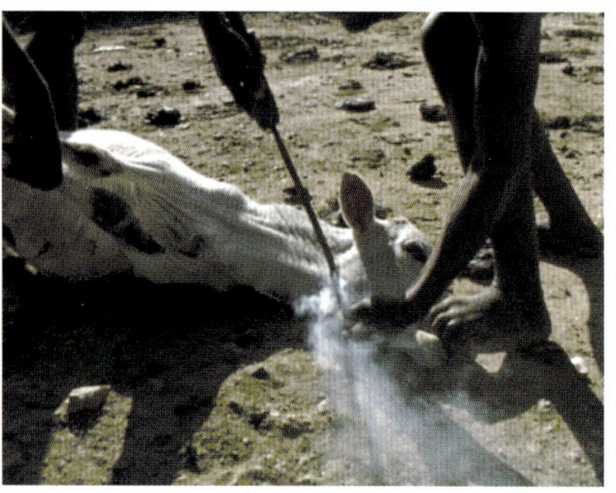

In addition, some shots of birds flying in the sky are accompanied by male songs that are markers of male identity in the film. This depiction is in contrast to the heaviness of the female condition. Women's bodies are portrayed, at various times, walking while loaded with objects and bent over on the ground as they work. They are inextricably linked to the grindstone, to the stones placed on the grave of a woman who died in childbirth, and to the stones used to pound and tighten the metal rings that weigh down women's necks and arms. Men and women live in real and conceptual spaces that are often separate. A similar representation of genders, understood as different "worlds," also appears in *Dead Birds*, where, Gardner notes in commenting on a scene, the men are symbolically associated with the sky while the women are connected to the earth.[20] In *Rivers of Sand*, the difference between genders is above all a difference of bodies that the culture constructs and treats in different or opposite ways.

Representation of the Animal World, the Use of Sound, and Children

The reality of oppression and pain experienced by Hamar women is also conveyed by a parallel with the domination and violence inflicted by men on domestic or hunted animals. At the beginning of the film, for example, shots of women as they dance with heavy anklets are alternated with shots showing the killing of an antelope; or the whipping of a woman by a man is preceded by the shot of a donkey and accompanied in the background by its braying. The ritual whippings performed on the women represent male supremacy. The amplified sound of the lashings, with the action shown at times in slow motion, makes them some of the most tension-filled images of the film. In a particularly striking sequence, using parallel editing, the image of a girl around whose neck a pair of ornamental rings are being tightened is juxtaposed to that of a calf being branded twice on the same spot.

This filmic procedure, a feature of the Soviet montage school, creates an analogy between images from different contexts, guiding the viewer's interpretation and more powerfully communicating certain concepts. In this case, the juxtaposition is used to suggest that the treatment of Hamar women is akin to the treatment of animals. What is communicated, then, is the dehumanization of women resulting from male domination and control. The scene is framed by shots of a pile of sorghum with a branch from the baraza tree on top of it. The voice-over tells us this is a sign that the harvest is "domesticated, stabilized, controlled." The connection to the situation being shown and the allusion to the female condition become obvious. In addition, in the funeral scene shown previously, butter and branches of the baraza tree, which the voice-over tells us are also used to make the whips, are left on the gravestones of a woman in order "to protect and control the dead."

As for sound, in a particularly dramatic scene showing the extraction of a girl's front teeth to make her look more attractive, in addition to a woman singing, we hear the rubbing of the grindstone, and the metallic sound of rings, indicative of constriction or oppression. Throughout the film, nondiegetic women's singing usually appears as a counterpoint to scenes of pain, endurance, or oppression experienced by Hamar women, thus communicating the close relationship between these situations and Hamar female existence in general—and, in some cases, their seraphic, dignified acceptance. Despite the hard labor, women do not show signs of fatigue or resentment of their condition and they often appear to be smiling.[21] Similarly, male singing is repeatedly used to give significance to the activities that distinguish the identity or nature of the men. These practices include decorating the body, collecting honey, and the cow jumping that takes place during the ukuli ceremony. In the scene showing the killing and preparation of an ostrich, Loizos notes that the symbolic value of hunting is communicated by introducing nondiegetic songs into the film that emphasize how ceremonial, celebratory, and expressive of Hamar virility this experience is: the film thus allows us to understand an aspect of this activity that a pragmatic representation would have obscured.[22] The songs of women and the sound of the grindstone still predominate, however, because the film focuses on the theme of women's oppression. These sounds are to be heard even in the final images of the documentary.

The use of sounds is therefore very important in *Rivers of Sand* and is not intended to simply provide a realistic description of the Hamar world. The sounds are in some cases accentuated or used separately from the sources that produce them, to deepen the significance of what we see. In addition, as Thomas Cooper states, throughout the film "there is a luscious sensuousness of sound—routine effects eventually become melodic instrumental motifs."[23] The sounds of the objects, the environment, the male voices, and the women's songs combine with the careful editing of the images and, in some cases, with the use of freeze frames and slow motion, to give the film an extraordinary musical rhythm, something beyond the literal recording of the Hamar world.[24]

Hamar customs and power dynamics are further revealed through children's games. In one scene we see men whipping animals to maintain control, and immediately afterward a child is playing with stones, gathering them together like animals inside a small "fence" made of earth. Obviously, the child is mimicking the behavior of the adults. Play activity through which children become familiar with their future role in the community is a conventional scene in the filming of other cultures. We find it in *Nanook of the North* (Robert Flaherty, 1922), *The Hunters* (John Marshall, 1957), and *Dead Birds*, for example. However, in *Rivers of Sand* it takes on even more significance because of the value invested in the representation of animals. Not only will cattle raising continue, these images imply, but so will the forms of power over women, which are destined to be handed down from one generation to the next. The shot that follows, showing women working at the grindstone, which represents the condition of women and the adaptation between genders, corroborates this view. The transmission of customs is one of the themes talked about in Omali Inda's account. However, in this scene it is communicated at a purely visual level. Elsewhere in the film, the idea is recalled by short shots of children handling small whips or sticks.

Omali Inda tells us that the oppressive social system is accepted by the Hamar wives primarily to raise and take care of the children: "it's for the children that I stay and struggle on. It has always been this way for women." This idea also gets expressed through images. In one scene, a baby goat shown alone in a fenced-in area seems to be threatened by a vulture that gets closer to it in every new shot. Shortly afterward we see that it is safe, protected by an adult goat that we imagine to be its mother. This scene is interspersed, moreover, with shots of a pregnant woman working at the grindstone, and a man handling a gun. Thanks to the juxtaposition of these images, without any verbal explanation, the situation of the animals becomes a metaphor for the role of women in Hamar society. What is communicated is how important it is for mothers to raise and protect their children and, by implication, to accept the difficult conditions of life imposed by male domination. The last images of the scene are accompanied by women's songs that, as we know, give emphasis to the female situation. *Rivers of Sand* deals with the material culture of the Hamar, but also with their immaterial culture, such as the quality of the relationship between male and female, and the transmission of customs and values.[25]

Conclusion

Although we often see men and women in different situations in *Rivers of Sand*, at times they are also represented in joint activities, such as in the dance scenes for the ukuli ceremony, toward the end of the documentary. For the young males, this is a rite of initiation into adulthood, an event that sublimates the eroticism and sexual tension that permeate the entire film. For Octavio Paz, the dance provides a time when men and women express their union in *Rivers of Sand*: a ritual event of reconciliation between male and female, an abolition of differences, and at the same time a metaphor for the act of copulation.[26]

Although the dances convey a sense of communion, the traits that distinguish the depiction of the sexes and their hierarchy during the rest of the film are maintained in the ukuli. At different stages of the ritual, for example, the camera lingers on the anklets and the backs of the women marked by scars. Some images of their hard labor at the grindstone are also inserted between the shots of the dances. The men appear in positions of power, filmed from a low angle or in the act of whipping. The women submit to the ritual, however, and, in some cases, respond provocatively.

As we have seen through Omali Inda's words, the images and editing, the voice-over commentary, and other elements, *Rivers of Sand* launches a critique against the social oppression of women. The question has different facets, however. The domination of men over women is not the only thing to be described: in certain cases, the women actually seem to encourage or choose to submit to some of the customs—such as whippings or tooth extraction—in spite of the painful endurance these practices demand. Women are often shown happy and smiling in the film, as we have noted. In *Rivers of Sand*, the paradox of customs that are violent and painful but at the same time asked for by the women can be explained by taking into account an important theme explored by the film: namely, the strength of social norms in deeply shaping the lives of individuals, not only through coercion but also through the process of enculturation. The values expressed by the Hamar community are internalized and accepted by its members, even though the tradition gives rise to constraints and afflictions. For example, in spite of the iniquities of female life that Omali Inda often emphasizes in her self-aware account, her words also express the necessary acceptance of conditions because they are part of Hamar social customs. They are practices handed down from generation to generation: "your grandmother and mother were beaten and you will be, too. It was always this way," "beating is our custom—we were born with it. Our ancestors were made by it—our mothers were born with it," and so on. Gardner says, "*Rivers of Sand*, like many of my films, is in important ways about the tension between individual will and cultural imperatives."[27] The film shows the power of culture to shape desires, needs, and behavior; to define, that is, the identity of the person.

Rivers of Sand examines how adaptation between men and women is socially constructed: the practices of the Hamar are a specific cultural response to universal needs and problems. In his exploration of the relationship between the two genders, and of the condition of women in particular, Gardner's film dialogues with the world of the viewer: it goes beyond the description of the local culture, allowing us to recognize a common *human* experience.

Speaking about the beginning of *Rivers of Sand*, the filmmaker Sandra Nichols describes the impact, despite the exotic customs of the natives, that the film's protagonist and her words (spoken into the camera and translated in the subtitles) had on her:

> I was knocked out to discover that she was talking about something any woman can identify with: her nervousness at getting married and moving in with her new husband. Hearing her voice up full and understanding what she was saying was for me a direct line to her feelings, and into her heart. It was a powerful moment of connection: she was no longer a distant "other," instead for a moment she was my sister.[28]

The commentary at the end of *Rivers of Sand* addresses the issue of vanishing customs, stating that the Hamar are destined to enter modernity and, to some extent, to lose their own peculiar ways and traditions. However, Gardner concludes by stating,

> What may not change is what already makes them most unexceptional—the painful difference between what they must and what they might want to be—as men and as women, for themselves and for each other.

The situation described in *Rivers of Sand* ultimately concerns not only the Hamar, but every person: the film alludes to the difficult relations between genders, and the link between the individual and society. *Rivers of Sand* allows us to draw a moral from the representation of Hamar life: it invites us to become aware of the constraints imposed by social standards and the inequalities that roles can give rise to—the way they seem obvious and inevitable because of their deep roots in everybody's life. The knowledge that the existence of the individual is not shaped by immutable or natural laws, but, rather, by cultural patterns—that is, possible options in the way human beings live, as Gardner reminds us in his film *Ika Hands* (1988)—allows us to confront the restrictions imposed by social models with a more critical attitude, and to consider them amenable to change. The theme of the constraints imposed by culture is also present in *Dead Birds* and *Deep Hearts* (Gardner, 1981); however, in *Rivers of Sand* the subject is examined in a less contemplative and far more critical manner. This documentary does not prompt the public to take action for social change in an explicit or pedagogical fashion. That said, its clear denunciation of the difficult situation of Hamar women encourages viewers to share the film's negative assessment of the indigenous women's state of subordination and, because of the allegorical value of the representation, invites them also to reject the inequalities between genders present in their own society, regardless of whether these customs form a cornerstone of the status quo. Finally, the film speaks to the fundamental need of a life in common that concerns all individuals as human beings. *Rivers of Sand* expresses an important feature of Gardner's poetics. As he says:

> Films like mine, I have hoped, would act in some manner or other, as a mirror of the viewer's own soul, that is to say, life experience. To the extent this occurs, I am confident that a viewer will examine his or her own life, which seems to me the most desirable goal of all.[29]

Notes

1. Jean Lydall and Ivo Strecker, "A Critique of Lionel Bender's Review of *Rivers of Sand,*" *American Anthropologist*, vol. 80, no. 4, 1978, 945–946, and Ivo Strecker, "Filming Among the Hamar," *Visual Anthropology*, vol. 1, no. 3, 1988, 369–378.
2. Peter Loizos, *Innovation in Ethnographic Film–From Innocence to Self-Consciousness 1955–1985* (Chicago: University of Chicago Press, 1993), 152–153.
3. James Clifford, "On Ethnographic Allegory," in *Writing Culture—The Poetics and Politics of Ethnography*, eds. Clifford and George E. Marcus (Berkeley/Los Angeles/London: University of California Press, 1986), 98–121.
4. Ibid., 100.
5. In his essay on allegory, Clifford uses the ethnographic description given in this 1981 book as a case study. Some of the aspects of Nisa analyzed by Clifford refer, like *Rivers of Sand*, to feminism and the meaning of being a woman.
6. Clifford, "On Ethnographic Allegory," 99.
7. Gardner, quoted in Craig Mishler, "Narrativity and Metaphor in Ethnographic Film: A Critique of Robert Gardner's *Dead Birds*," *American Anthropologist*, vol. 87, no. 3, 1985, 670.
8. Patricia Erens, "Women's Documentary Filmmaking: The Personal is Political," *New Challenges for Documentary*, ed. Alan Rosenthal (Berkeley/Los Angeles/London: University of California Press, 1988), 554–565.
9. In anthropological filmmaking, the development of audiovisual equipment made it possible to more effectively investigate aspects of immaterial culture. Claudine de France notes that thanks to it, ethnographic films could add direct verbal expression to the images, and thus report the emotions, experiences, and interpretations of the filmed subjects: this allowed them to confront issues that were previously the prerogatives of ethnographic writing. ("Filmic Anthropology: A Difficult But Promising Birth," *Visual Anthropology*, 6:1, 1993, 8.)

10. In addition to the feminist movement, a few other factors that Gardner acknowledges as having influenced the perspective adopted in *Rivers of Sand* include criticisms about the excessive importance given to men in *Dead Birds*, and the difficult personal circumstances that the filmmaker was experiencing as his marriage to his first wife was coming to an end. (See Gardner in Ilisa Barbash, "Out of Words: The Æsthesodic Cine-Eye of Robert Gardner—An Exegesis and Interview," *Visual Anthropology*, vol. 14, no. 4, 2001, 399–400.)

11. Ibid. Peter Loizos observes that during the early 1970s, the impact of feminism challenged the tendency of anthropologists to avoid expressions that implied value judgments about other cultures. (Peter Loizos, "Robert Gardner's *Rivers of Sand*—Toward a Reappraisal," *Fields of Vision—Essays in Film Studies, Visual Anthropology, and Photography*, eds. Leslie Devereaux and Roger Hillman (Berkeley/Los Angeles/London: University of California Press, 1995, 318.) Moreover, Gardner added to his own statement: "I don't think anthropology is doing its job by being value free, I honestly don't. I think it's just avoiding its responsibility to find larger truths" (Gardner in Ilisa Barbash, "Out of Words," 400). Jean Lydall's response (to Gardner's comments and to *Rivers of Sand*) became the starting point for further discussion on the role in anthropology of the values and opinions of natives and of the ethnographer and of generalizations about the human condition. (Jean Lydall, "Whipping Scars and 'Larger Truths'—Response to Loizos on Gardner," *Anthropology Today*, vol. 24, no. 4, 2008, 28–29.) The debate, appearing in *Social Anthropology*, involved Lydall and João de Pina-Cabral and followed on his article there entitled "Larger Truths and Deeper Understandings" (*Social Anthropology*, vol. 16, no. 3, 2008, 346–348).

12. Charles Warren, "The Music of Robert Gardner," in *The Cinema of Robert Gardner*, Ilisa Barbash and Lucien Taylor, eds., (Oxford: Berg, 2007), 24.

13. Loizos, *Innovation in Ethnographic Film*, 153–154.

14. William Rothman, "Dancing with Gardner," in *The Cinema of Robert Gardner*, eds. Ilisa Barbash and Lucien Taylor (Oxford/New York: Berg, 2007), 138.

15. Gardner, *The Impulse to Preserve—Reflections of a Filmmaker* (New York: Other Press, 2006), 139.

16. Rothman, "Dancing with Gardner," 138.

17. The interview with Omali Inda in *Rivers of Sand* is the result of questions asked by Gardner with a rough translation made in the field by Strecker. Subsequently, Gardner asked for a literal English translation of the interview for the editing; he then "reworked" the text to put it in a form that could be used in the film. He says: "The way I worked in *Rivers of Sand* meant that I could interpret what Omali Inda was saying by putting her words through the filter of my own sensibilities. It might be more correct to say we were co-authors with a significant assist from Ivo Strecker" (Gardner quoted in Ilisa Barbash, "Out of Words," 394). The question of the translations is addressed by Barbash (Ibid. I, 393–395), Jean Lydall ("Filming The Women Who Smile," *Ethnographic Film Aesthetics and Narrative Traditions*—Proceedings from NAFA 2, eds. Peter Ian Crawford, Jan Ketil Simonsen, Aarhus, Denmark: Intervention Press, 1992, 147), and in Gardner's commentary to *Rivers of Sand* (included in the 2008 DVD edition).

18. Loizos, "Robert Gardner's *Rivers of Sand*," 320.

19. Commentary by Robert Gardner and Ross McElwee for *Dead Birds* Special Edition DVD, Film Study Center, 2004.

20. Ibid.

21. "Robert Gardner's *Rivers of Sand*," 319–320.

22. Ibid., 320.

23. Thomas W. Cooper, *Natural Rhythms: The Indigenous World of Robert Gardner* (New York: Anthology Film Archives, 1995), 59.

24. The role of sound is also discussed by Gardner and Robert Fenz in the commentary included on the *Rivers of Sand* DVD (2008). Gardner recognizes the importance of using sounds for their musical qualities, because of the way they can affect the viewers' senses and describe the indigenous space. He claims that he is dissatisfied by a purely realistic recording of sound, preferring to work on it to derive a more meaningful representation from it. Fenz points to the particularly rhythmic quality that the combination of sounds and images gives to *Rivers of Sand*.

25. As Karl Heider states, with the film on Hamar society Gardner explores an ambitious theme, given the difficulty of representing an abstract subject like the female role. In *Rivers of Sand* "Gardner has attempted to move ethnographic film closer to the real concerns of anthropology. That is, more anthropologists are concerned with describing cultural attitudes and values than are trying to describe warfare or housebuilding" (Karl Heider, *Ethnographic Film: Revised Edition* [Austin: University of Texas Press, 2006], 41–42).

26. Octavio Paz, "The Feather and the Grindstone," *Harvard Magazine*, vol. 77, 1974, 48–50.

27. Gardner, *The Impulse to Preserve*, 269.

28. Sandra Nichols, quoted in Peter Loizos, *Innovation in Ethnographic Film*, 158.

29. Gardner, personal communication, June 28, 2011.

Chapter 14
Word against Flesh in *Rivers of Sand*

Irina Leimbacher

Ambiguity is a cardinal fact of life. All that I think I can hope to do with words or with images is to make that ambiguity more discernible and the mysteries more accessible

—Robert Gardner

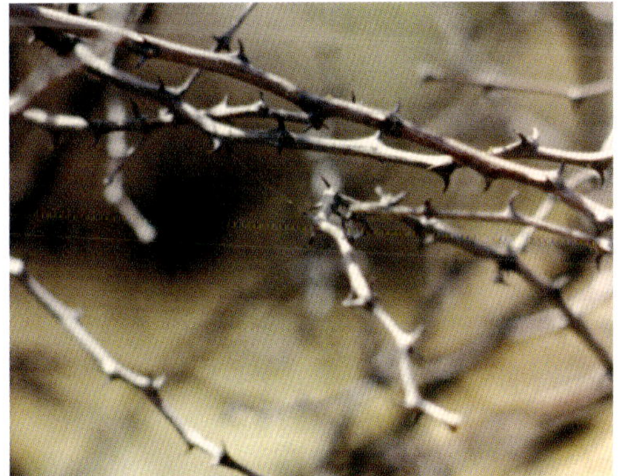

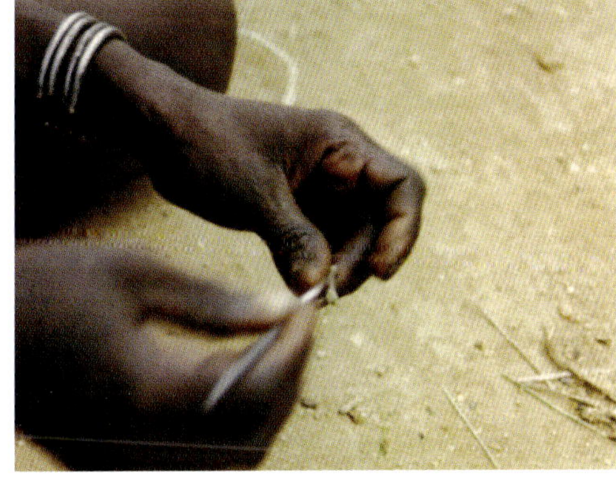

First just a bush, a thorn bush. Next a woman's hands pick some thorns from a branch. We hear the sound of repeated scraping accompanied by images of the up and down motion of a hand. Something is being rhythmically brushed against the metal leg rings adorning a woman's ankle and calf. Later, it is revealed to be a small blade being sharpened against the rings' rippled surface. Among the group of seated women, a smiling young woman appears, gestures, then lies down, her torso bare. The thorn that had been plucked from the bush is used to pull up a bit of flesh in the area above her belly and the now-sharp blade to make a small incision in her skin. Then another, and another. Each pull of the skin with the thorn is followed by a nick of the blade, and a geometric pattern of cuts appears on the woman's torso. Close-ups of the blade, of multiple arms and torsos, are seen next to the woman whose skin is pulled and nicked again and again. She is lying on the ground with her arm slung back and over her face, so we cannot see her expression. When the area above her belly is gently wiped, blood from the numerous cuts rises to create a flat red liquid surface. A woman spits on her blade then brushes

a b
c d
e f
g

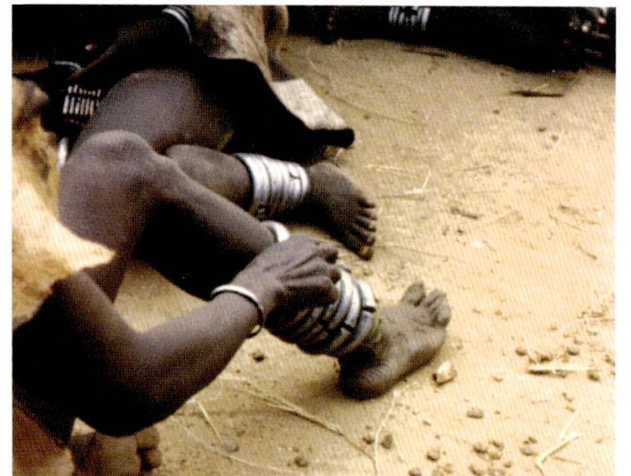

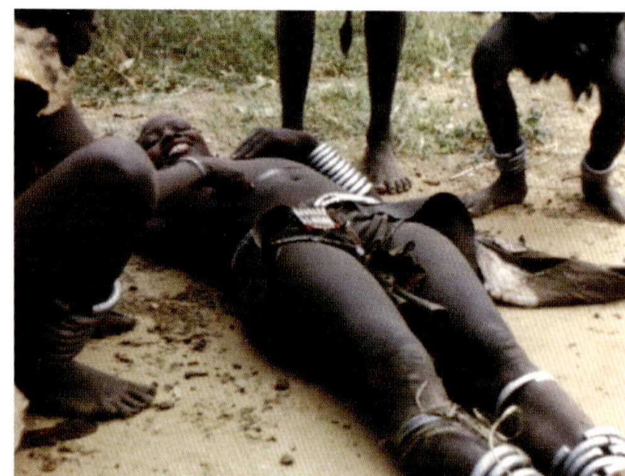

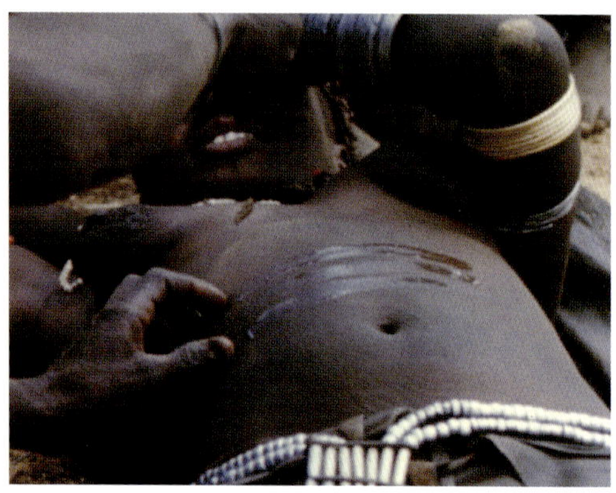

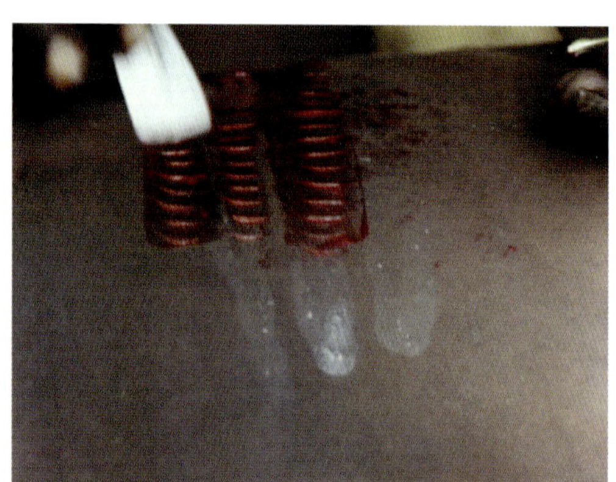

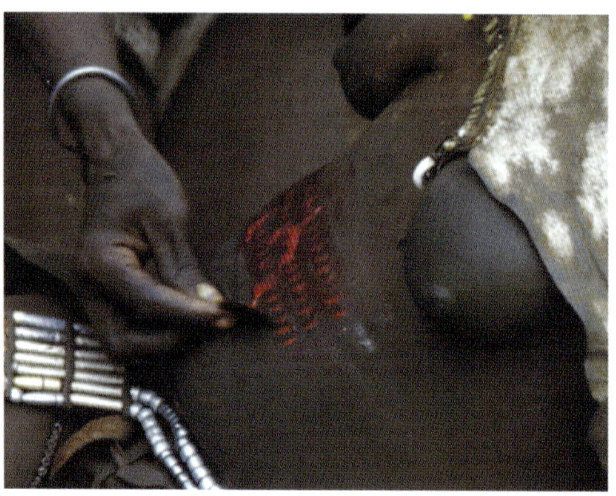

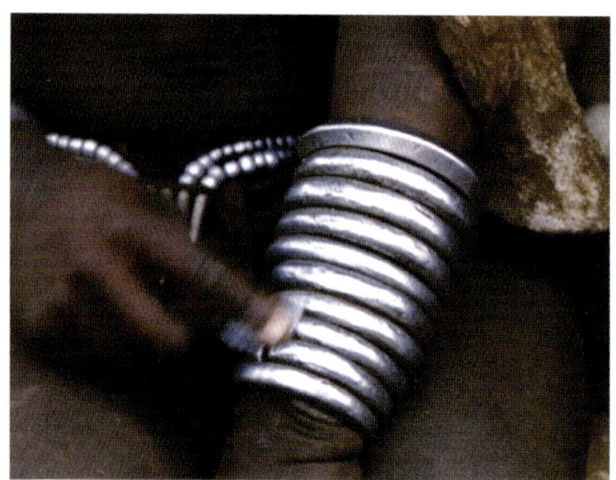

it up and down her leg with the same repetitive motion as earlier. The camera pans ever so slightly to reveal a baby nursing at her breast.

Watching Robert Gardner's *Rivers of Sand* (1974), shot among the Hamar in Southern Ethiopia, is an unsettling experience. It is a film one does not, and cannot, forget. Despite most characterizations of the film as being

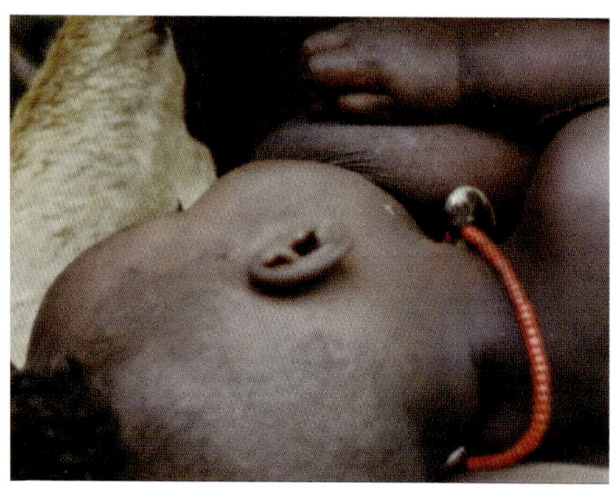

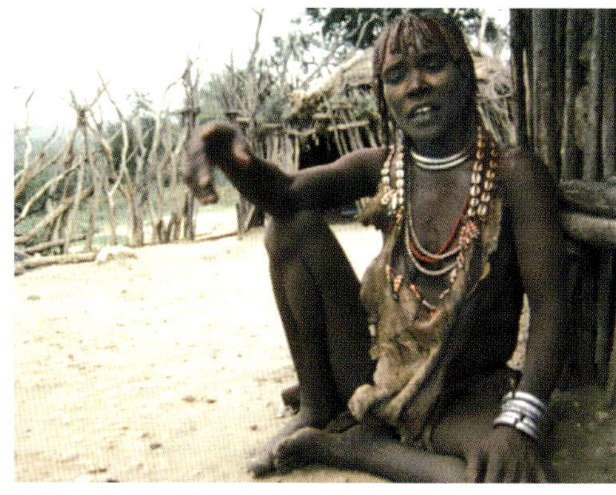

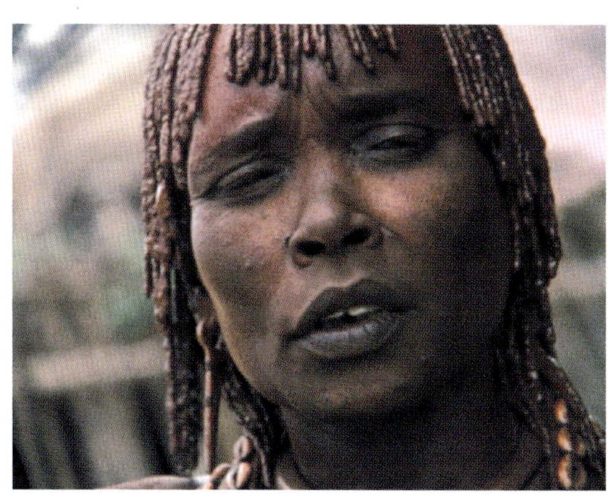

about gender inequality among the Hamar, the visceral power of *Rivers of Sand* extends far beyond the categories and binaries often used to describe it. Its ethical and affective force does not, I believe, lie in a particular message or critique of Hamar culture, but rather in Gardner's dynamically shot and edited images of people's lives as depicted primarily through bodily actions and practices. With his camera focused on Hamar bodies and gestures, Gardner also inserts *his own* body into the process of seeing by way of highly kinesthetic camerawork and editing. We, too, are then compelled to insert our bodies into the experience of viewing and listening to the film.

"[I]t was exotic, it was bloody, and it was painful," Gardner says in his commentary track on the DER release of *Rivers of Sand* by way of explaining why he wanted to shoot the aforementioned scene. He could have said something similar about a number of scenes in this film. He then adds: "and pain unites us all." I want to suggest that it is not pain per se that "unites" us humans in this case (presumably Gardner's "us" here refers to those on opposite sides of the camera and projection screen), but rather a visceral and empathic engagement with the experiences of others. I believe this is what Gardner was after. The question then is how is such an engagement produced and encouraged, especially cross-culturally? How can film provoke such engagement? And why does Gardner constantly emphasize pain when discussing his depiction of Hamar life?[1]

One of the many striking aspects of *Rivers of Sand* is Gardner's use of an eloquent and photogenic Hamar woman to frame and repeatedly contextualize his images and sounds. Although we never learn her name in the film, she is referred to in commentaries as Omali Inda or Omaleinda.[2] She speaks almost exclusively about the different roles of men and women in Hamar culture. Omali Inda's dominant presence in the film and the role Gardner creates for her—that of a spokes*woman* for the Hamar—was remarkable at the time the film was made. Addressing us directly and looking at the camera most of the time that she speaks, she not only appears throughout the film but opens and closes it, thus creating a frame for all that comes between. Because she is given far more screen time than any other figure in the film and is the only person to physically address us, it is easy to assume that the film is "hers," and that she speaks for it. However, Omali Inda's is only one voice among many that together comprise the more complex "voice" of the film.[3]

Visceral, frequently ambiguous, and sometimes contradictory, *Rivers of Sand* "speaks" *not* primarily through Omali Inda's or even Gardner's occasional words, but as, or even more, powerfully through the flesh—that of the Hamar women and men we see and respond to, but also that of Gardner's cinema, its intensities and plasticity. These spoken words and embodied flesh neither wholly collude nor are they in opposition. Instead the two rub up against each other and create friction, like the woman's blade against her leg rings. While Omali Inda's words shape and channel our understanding of the bodies and events in the images, Gardner's images sharpen, intensify, or complicate her (and his own, rather sparse) words. Neither can contain nor adequately explain the other. Rather it is the ambiguity and tension between the words we hear and the flesh we see that create the force—and ultimately the voice—of the film. Here I examine Gardner's use of Omali Inda's words, his camerawork, and his editing as three elements that play alongside and against each other. As the film moves forward, the mounting sense of words' incapacity to contain what we see of the Hamar world on the screen keeps us actively receptive to Gardner's physically dynamic, aesthetically rich, and conceptually challenging images and sounds.

Whether it is interpreted as a "realist" film, a "symbolist" film, or an "allegorical" film,[4] discussions of *Rivers of Sand* almost always focus on the question of Gardner's representation of and attitudes toward Hamar gender inequality. In fact, the controversies it provoked were concerned on the one hand with Gardner's aesthetic vision and on the other with his alleged misinterpretation and misrepresentation of gender relations among the Hamar. For some anthropologists, Gardner's portrayal of Hamar men and women was "haughty," "crude," and "unenlightening"[5]; for others it was simply not meant to be taken so literally. Instead, the depiction of inequality as a product of culture was envisioned as a reflection on the intransigence of gender roles in general as well as in Gardner's own personal life.[6] Nevertheless, the description of *Rivers of Sand* that appears on both Gardner's and his distributor's website includes the unqualified statement: "Hamar men are masters and their women are slaves. The film tries to disclose the effect on mood and behavior of lives governed by the idea of sexual inequality." Categorical statements like this, whether made by critics, advocates, or Gardner himself, only do a disservice to the film. They reduce its extraordinary visceral power to the question of proving or illustrating a point.

With its fluid and sensual camerawork, assertive editing style, minimal explanatory voice-over, and direct address by one of the film's subjects, *Rivers of Sand* marked a new stage in Gardner's filmmaking. If his overall filmmaking trajectory embodies a slow but sure "withdrawal from language," as Ilisa Barbash has suggested,[7] *Rivers of Sand* lies at a pivotal juncture in this movement. Although Gardner contributed to a number of films in the interim, his own previous ethnographic film was *Dead Birds* (1963), and it is interesting to compare the two. *Dead Birds*' beginning-to-end voice-over not only explains the culture of the Dani but narrates (in Gardner's voice) the inner lives of his two male "main characters." In *Rivers of Sand* omniscient voice-over recedes to make room for the more emphatic presence of the voice of Omali Inda who is here given the primary role of commenting on cultural norms. While *Dead Birds*' camerawork uses wide establishing shots, a frequently steady camera, and only occasional intimations of the fluid "moving toward" and "following" that would become central to Gardner's later camera style, *Rivers of Sand* presents us with few if any establishing shots and a highly mobile camera often cleaving to the surface of things. The close-ups and extreme close-ups engage viewers in a highly tactile and haptic vision. It is as if we are enmeshed, for the brief time of the film, in the world that we see. *Rivers of Sand*'s editing style is also distinct from *Dead Birds* and from other ethnographic work of its day. With minimal focus on discrete events, it adheres to a looser montage aesthetic motivated by thematic concerns.[8] In doing so, it abandons the narrative structure created for films such as John

Marshall's *The Hunters* (Gardner participated in the editing) and his own *Dead Birds* and eschews both real and invented chronology. It is organized more like a visual essay on specific aspects of Hamar life. Yet it is an essay carefully framed by the compelling and authenticating voice of a local woman.

In the 1970s ethnographic filmmaking was thriving but also hotly debated among anthropologists, and *Rivers of Sand* was the subject of much controversy. Unabashedly ignoring any of the "rules" of observational ethnographic filmmaking—such as those published by Gardner's former colleague in New Guinea, anthropologist Karl Heider[9]—the film also pays no heed to the reflexive or participatory experiments as practiced by Jean Rouch and David and Judith MacDougall in the 1960s and 1970s.[10] Out of sync with the trends of the day, it was—and is—criticized variously for its allegedly incorrect portrayal of the Hamar, its "bad" ethnography, its lack of reflexivity, and its aestheticizing qualities. One of the film's critics, anthropologist Ivo Strecker, was invited by Gardner to work with him among the Hamar. After the film was completed he and fellow anthropologist Jean Lydall (who accompanied Strecker and their children to Ethiopia) accused Gardner of misunderstanding Omali Inda and misrepresenting Hamar culture. Frustrated by what they argue is a misuse of Omali Inda's words and specious editing on Gardner's part, Lydall and Strecker went so far as to call *Rivers of Sand* an "ethnographic farce."[11] Anthropologist Jay Ruby, who made Gardner his whipping boy for several decades, had more general criticisms, claiming that Gardner was not a professional anthropologist, practiced salvage ethnography, put aesthetics above all else, and was unconcerned with revealing the material or intellectual processes of his production.[12] Gardner has been defended by other anthropologists, most notably Peter Loizos,[13] who makes the case that Gardner's own aims and interests have little to do with those of Lydall and Strecker or Ruby. This is substantiated by Gardner's own declaration that he was neither an anthropologist nor a maker of ethnographic film. Indeed, in response to such criticism he once dryly commented: "the emptiness of this hapless genre is perpetuated in endless, solemn debate by social scientists, arguing, finally, for nothing other than a cinema bereft of aesthetic concerns."[14]

There is no question that Gardner's own cinema explicitly and ecstatically embraces its aesthetic concerns. In fact, *Rivers of Sand* was motivated by an artistic vision he had even before reaching southern Ethiopia. As Gardner discusses in his filmmaking journal, he was eager to depict a culture that held interest for him "pictorially" and that was not "yet another example of waning traditional life."[15] This aesthetic concern led to the exclusion of certain aspects of contemporary Hamar life from the film, for example, the Hamar passion for Western clothing that Gardner repeatedly remarks on, despairingly and disparagingly, in the journal.[16] Thus, to a certain degree one can concur with Ruby that the film is a work of salvage ethnography, artificially "salvaging" a version of a culture that no longer exists. Gardner also excluded any reflection on the process of production in the film itself, a reflexivity that Ruby and others at the time thought was necessary to critique the political and discursive power structures inherent in documentary cinema. However, Gardner later made available a number of paratexts including the complete version of his extant filmmaking journals and a commentary track with journal excerpts on the DER DVD release.[17] In these journals he is disarmingly forthright, concealing neither his often fraught (and occasionally politically incorrect) attitude to others nor his persistent self-doubts.

Indeed, Gardner's writings and interviews suggest insightful self-criticism and constant reflection on the creative process. He seems to feel no need to dissimulate his all-too-human emotions, expectations, and ambivalence while in southern Ethiopia. Covering most of two trips he made to the area in 1968 and 1971, the journals reveal someone alternately frustrated with, appreciative of, and profoundly ambivalent about his interlocutors. We read that Gardner was looking for an aesthetically pleasing and untainted (by Western values) culture to fix on celluloid, and he was repeatedly disappointed by the Hamar. Even having made his commitment to work among them, he is still full of doubts and frequently expresses unabashed irritation with the men, whom he describes as self-important, insecure, and narcissistic.[18] Although Gardner's irritation and judgment are discernable at times in the film, I argue that as a whole *Rivers of Sand* transcends this or any single conclusive attitude to the world he depicts.

Because much of the criticism leveled against the film concerns how Gardner uses or misuses the speech of Omali Inda, I would like to look at her role more closely. Incorporating synch-sound speech of any extended duration was still difficult in ethnographic films, especially when Gardner began shooting in 1968. Translation becomes a complex process, as it involves translating simultaneously from one cultural context to another, one language to another, and also from one medium (oral) to another (written), with lengthy spoken language transformed into brief subtitles for the screen.[19] Although Gardner had recorded interview footage for Hilary Harris's *The Nuer* (1971), it was only at the end of his second and final stay in southern Ethiopia that he conducted this interview with Omali Inda. Edited and then deployed to create an overall structure for the film, her speech is striking for many reasons: it is lengthy, it is used throughout the film, and it is a woman who speaks from and about what seems to be a male-dominated world. Shot frontally in medium close-up or close-up, Omali Inda sits on the ground and addresses us through Gardner's camera as she speaks. Her powerful aural and visual presence easily governs our experience of *Rivers of Sand* because this is the rhetorical position Gardner has created for her. Yet it is important to remember that all filmed interviews are highly constructed and that it is a mistake to equate a voice solicited, edited, and carefully deployed in a film with the voice *of* a film.

The interview is a dialogic process, and words are uttered in response to a solicitation as part of an exchange between two people. As mentioned earlier, Gardner interviewed Omali Inda at the very end of his time in the field. His shooting journal suggests that he had developed an empathic relation to Hamar women and an unsympathetic, even occasionally disdainful, perception of Hamar men by this time. This is the context in which the interview or conversations with Omali Inda took place. As is common in many filmed interviews, we never hear Gardner's (nor his translator's) side of the dialogue, and there is no reference to his role in eliciting Omali Inda's words. In fact, naive viewers might read her speech as an autonomous declaration, as a form of testimony about the condition of Hamar women for the world. However, if one listens closely, it is clear that she is responding to specific, and probably quite pointed, questions. Indeed, her eloquent and vivid statements are *for* Gardner who is soliciting her opinions about men and women's roles in Hamar culture.

Describing *Rivers of Sand*, Karl Heider writes that Omali Inda "speaks at great length about her life."[20] Lydall and Strecker also believe audiences will assume this. They accuse Gardner of misusing her words as if they were "factual" when they are actually "a conventionalized story of womanhood" and claim that Omali Inda herself was never beaten though she speaks at length about beatings.[21] But if one listens to Omali Inda—or as in most of our cases, reads the subtitles that Gardner used to translate her speech—nowhere does she speak as if she is presenting a biography. She speaks about "women," "a woman," "you" (as used in English when equivalent to the impersonal "one"). Only infrequently are the words "I" or "me" used, and even then she usually appears to be speaking about Hamar women, not herself as an individual. In fact, we learn nothing conclusive about any details of her own life—whether she is now married, has children, lives with her husband's family, and so on. It seems quite obvious that she is offering Gardner a generalized description of what it means to be a woman in the Hamar world in response to his inquiries. She speaks not about herself but about her vision of "the life of a woman." This is not a first-person narrative but a third-person narration: Omali Inda's idiosyncratic perspective in dialogue with Gardner's interests, assertions, and undisclosed questions. Thus her function in the documentary is much closer to that of the local "expert" who can provide insight, than to the subject of a portrait documentary. While we can only guess at his questions, Gardner clearly was seeking an insider's perspective on the gender dynamics that he himself found so problematic during his two stays among the Hamar. The assumption by anthropologists (or the viewers they imagine) that Omali Inda is speaking for herself, mainly about herself, or even speaking literally, seems to emerge from a prejudicial belief that members of small rural societies do not generalize, do not use metaphor, and that they can *only* speak about themselves!

On the other hand, Gardner occasionally places her words, ostensibly more "authentic" than his or any outsider's, as if they could or should be a surrogate for his own. He seems to want her to stand in for and confirm his negative impressions of gender dynamics among the Hamar. Indeed, his images complement her words at several moments in the film. Yet, even when Omali Inda appears to speak for the film, with visuals didactically confirming her words, it is the other way around. Filmmakers select, cut, reorganize, and control the individual voices they choose to deploy. Any filmed interview is a work of co-authorship given the crucial role of the filmmaker in each phase of the pre-, post-, and production process. And, as mentioned earlier, makers of ethnographic documentaries also control a nonlocal audience's access to meaning through translation and subtitling. Gardner is forthright about this latter process. Both in his DVD commentary and in his interview with Ilisa Barbash, he notes that he had Omali Inda's words translated literally, and then he personally retranslated them as one would do with a literary work, "putting her words through the filter of my own sensibilities."[22] "I'm partly a director, in the way I film her, translate her answers, put words in her mouth. I have altered them somewhat,"[23] he says. He acknowledges that he and she were co-authors of the text, but that—possibly unfairly, according to him—he "did [his] part without asking Omali Inda's permission."[24] Like all filmmakers, Gardner used what he wanted of his subject's words and translated her speech into subtitles with a language, rhythm, and emphasis that fit his conceptual and aesthetic aims.

A simple but revealing example of the impact of Gardner's translation on our reading of the film can be found in the references that Omali Inda makes to Hamar women's leg ornaments. These rings are an element of fascination for Gardner's camera; there is a repeated focus on them throughout the film. Indeed, the two visual and aural leitmotifs associated with women are the grindstone on which the women grind their sorghum, and the leg rings that adorn them. These bands of metal worn by most of the young women—it is worth noting that Omali Inda does *not* have any at the time of her interview, but we are never told how and why they would be taken off—are alternately translated in the subtitles as "leg irons" or as "leg rings." Yet the two terms have quite different connotations and resonances for English speakers: "irons" connote shackles, restraint, possibly slavery, while "rings" are associated with personal adornment and jewelry. The first time Omali Inda refers to them, they are translated as "leg irons," whereas later "leg rings" and "leg irons" are interchanged in the same passage, with "rings" being used more frequently. In her initial comment on them, Omali Inda is contrasting how children are gendered and says (according to the subtitles): "When a son is born, his father gives him a gun. When a girl is born, leg irons are her gun."[25]

In and of itself, the meaning of the contrast expressed here is ambiguous. Gardner lets us hear these latter lines soon after a passage in which Omali Inda speaks about women being beaten that concludes, "it's for the children that I stay and struggle on. It has always been this way for women."[26] Gardner's placement of this remark and his choice of the term leg irons *seems* to suggest that while boys are given tools to go out and hunt, women are given irons that enslave or imprison them. However, one could also interpret this passage, especially in light of some of the things that Omali Inda says later, as asserting that while boys are given weapons to manifest their power over nature and bring the meat necessary to the community's nourishment, girls are given adornments of beauty and seduction to manifest a different power. The film clearly shows that leg rings are objects of cultural value and indicative of a certain status. Indeed, later in the film, Omali Inda speaks about how they add to a woman's beauty. Without them she is considered drab and immature—"but with leg rings she goes with a clang, clang. Who is that with iron things?"[27]

As we see elsewhere in the film, the leg rings, in addition to being visually ornamental and a sign of "having things" according to Omali Inda,[28] can be employed for practical functions, for instance, as a surface on which one can sharpen a blade. They also serve, perhaps most importantly, as an aural mark of presence and a medium of musical expression. In each of the dance scenes, Gardner emphasizes the movements of women's legs, with their rings, through visual and aural close-ups. These rings clang percussively as the women move and rhythmically bring their calves together. Watching these sequences through Gardner's framing and cutting, we feel the metal surface of those rings on flesh, and we feel their weight. But we also feel and hear—perhaps more intensely—their power, as their allure for Gardner's camera and microphone attests. They become a visually and aurally emphatic expression of female presence (both singular and communal) that the men do not have.

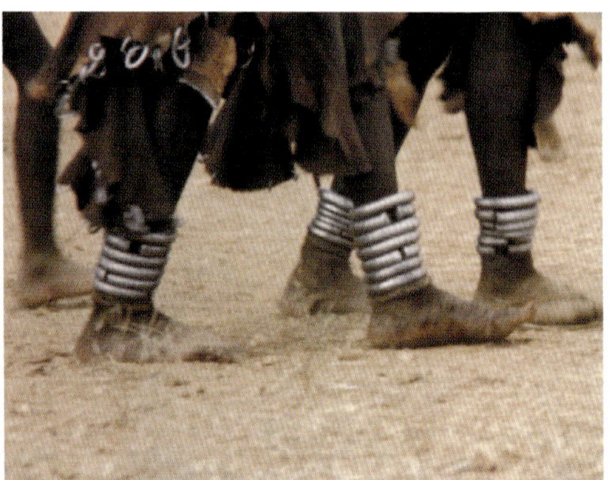

Nothing is without its quotient of ambiguity in this film. If Omali Inda and Gardner appear to be damning the role women are forced to play in Hamar culture in some instances, Omali Inda expresses affection and pride in women's roles elsewhere. Gardner deliberately lets inconclusive, ambivalent, and sometimes enigmatic meanings seep out from her words as he also does with his own images. And Gardner's camerawork constantly emits a fascination with both women and men undergoing various beautification practices, whether or not he might want to condemn some of these practices morally (as he suggests in his descriptions and discussions of the film). Indeed, the contributions of his cinematography and editing against and alongside the words are fundamental to the complex polyphony of Gardner's film. In *Rivers of Sand* the camera becomes immersed in and moves *through* spaces: the dry river bed, the thick ripening fields of sorghum, the cattle pen, the thorny scrubland where ostriches are sought, killed, and eaten. This camera observes and follows people, focusing on gait, gesture, and the repeated motions of daily labor and personal adornment, both of women and men.[29] With the world quite often in close-up, sometimes even extreme close-up, as viewers we are thrust into the life and world we see. One physically feels the body and the eye of the filmmaker in these cinematic gestures. The environment becomes palpable. We feel the rhythmic grinding of the grain (also accentuated through the sound design), we feel the effort and contractions of the women's muscles in our own bodies, we can touch the ripe stalks of sorghum that brush against the camera lens, the multitude of tiny grains as they are winnowed and fill the entire world on view. We can also feel the incisions in flesh, the arm that smarts and jerks back from a heavy blow to close a metal bracelet, a lower front tooth being cut, sawed, and finally wrenched out of a young girl's mouth as a sign of her courage and beauty.

It is rare that an ethnographic film, or any film for that matter, is capable of creating such a sensory and vivid experience of life. Gardner writes that film "has a way of *heightening* the life it portrays, owing to the kind of mediation it performs."[30] Film is never neutral, and camerawork—Gardner's in particular—is an immensely expressive and persuasive tool. We (viewers) don't just see it, but we see, and feel, *according to* it, as Merleau-Ponty said of painting.[31] In *Rivers of Sand* it is the bodily gestures we see and, as importantly, Gardner's cinematic gestures *according to which* we see them, that provoke an intense embodied engagement and response. This potential of film, or other art, to engage directly with bodily sensation and awareness has been discussed by many thinkers, especially those working in the tradition of phenomenology or the discipline of neuroscience. The automatic physical response that we have when attentively watching others partake in physical actions or perform expressive gestures has been equated by neuroscientists with empathy, defined by the latter as a "matching between what the other is expressing by means of ostensive behavior and what we would feel were we expressing those affective states ourselves."[32] While actions or expressions that suggest pain are particularly forceful in provoking such embodied responses (we feel what we see taking place in or on another's body in our own body), any gesture that evokes strong physical sensation can have a powerful impact on the entire sensorium of the viewer. *Rivers of Sand* is full of such actions and gestures, not just those that draw blood, but also those that convey the impact of motion, weight, touch, and texture on the body; those that highlight interactions between people and their physically palpable environment; and those that are emphatically rhythmic and repetitive. Gardner's mobile camera and dynamic editing accentuate the already highly kinesthetic and visceral aspects of what he chooses to film. Yes, Hamar women endure physical pain, but Hamar communities also work, grieve, produce and procure food, adorn themselves, and exuberantly participate in rituals of collective life. Under the immersive, tactile guidance of Gardner's camera-eye, all of these arouse an intuitively embodied engagement in us.

Filmmaker David MacDougall has written at length about what he calls "visual knowledge" and its importance to anthropology. Neither conceptual nor propositional, it cannot be reduced to words. It is "stubborn and opaque, but with a capacity for the finest detail."[33] Different than knowledge obtained through words, it needs to be approached, understood, and evaluated differently from words as well. Images are not description, explanation, or analysis; they are nothing like declarative statements. Instead they,

> make use of principles of implication, visual resonance, identification and shifting perspective that differ radically from the principles of most anthropological writing. They involve the viewer in heuristic processes and meaning-creation quite different from verbal statement, linkage, theory-formation, and speculation. . . . Above all, the visual media allow us to construct knowledge not by "description" (to borrow Bertrand Russell's terms) but by a form of "acquaintance."[34]

For MacDougall, the power of images and visual media is that they allow documentarians "to construct works that give a richer sense of how culture permeates and patterns social experience."[35] In this process, the body—of the person on screen, the filmmaker, and the viewer—plays a prominent and productive role, because film can create "affinities with bodies other than our own."[36] The viewer reacts not only to the bodies seen on film but also to the filmmaker's body whose gestural traces remain in the work. In this way, "the bodies of the subject, the filmmaker, and the viewer become interconnected."[37] This sensory and synesthetic engagement with the body states of others occurs independently of and parallel to any verbal communication—it is provoked by and through the flesh. Thus the verbal address of Omali Inda—and Gardner's occasional distant philosophizing words—rub up against the visual and aural sensations, without one able to contain the other.

According to MacDougall, one of the reasons anthropologists who work in the medium of writing are wary of the visual is the potential "excess" of visual meanings. Strong and palpable images defy containment or absorption into either expository discourse or narrative structure. They can suggest multiple associations and interpretations that exceed the intellectual edifice or proclaimed intention of the work that contains them. It is this "threat of undisciplined interpretation" that has resulted in many conventional ethnographic films being reduced to illustrated lectures, according to MacDougall.[38] Gardner's work, with its gradual exclusion of language over the course of his career, is open to and encourages multiple and complex readings of his visual materials. As made clear by his anthropologist critics, however, this is not always appreciated. Excess of meaning produces ambiguity and uncertainty. While Gardner, as cited in the opening of this essay, holds that ambiguity is a crucial fact of life, others find it disconcerting.

In *Rivers of Sand*, however, Gardner sometimes seems to do battle with himself in this regard. At times he proceeds as if he wants to, at least temporarily, rein ambiguity in. One way to do so without language is through associative or contrastive editing. Editing provides a means of progressively contextualizing visual and aural material, augmenting or restricting its meanings. In *Rivers of Sand* Gardner's editing is both more dynamic and occasionally more dogmatic than in any of his other ethnographic works. Because the film is structured as an essay and not as a chronological narrative or an expository analysis, the editing plays a crucial role in determining the energy and meanings of individual sequences. Overall *Rivers of Sand*'s structure suggests a contrast between women's lives and men's lives in what Gardner depicts as a largely segregated society. Aside from a few scenes—dancing, the funeral, one instance of hairdressing, a young woman getting her tooth cut out and another having a ring pounded together by men—most of the film takes place either in an exclusively female or exclusively male world. The rhythm of the film goes back and forth between women and men, with women shown collecting water, harvesting and grinding grain, shooting slingshots at birds, and getting adorned in ways that seem particularly painful to a Western audience. Men, on the other hand, are shown drinking and spitting coffee, saying blessings, seeking advice from a sandal oracle, carving and relaxing on their stools, going hunting and eating their catch, getting honey, and adorning themselves in ways that seem pleasurable and indulgent. This structure is reinforced by Omali Inda's comments (again, always in response to Gardner whom we cannot hear) consistently contrasting the upbringing and roles of women with those of men.

Writing about Gardner's strategies in the later *Forest of Bliss* (1986), Roderick Coover notes that Gardner creates a kind of synesthesia through his repetitions of sound and image and that his editing suggests associations through a montage of dialogics rather than one of dialectics.[39] We can see the beginnings of this development already in parts of *Rivers of Sand*, with the aural/visual synesthesia created by a powerful soundtrack that occasionally functions like a piece of musique concrète with the grindstone as a key instrument. However, with regard to editing, some segments in the film use montage as "dialectically" and heavy-handedly as Eisenstein's slaughter sequence in *Strike* (1924). Eisenstein's theory of the "montage of attractions" combined strong, often corporeal, images into montage sequences "that subject[ed] the audience to emotional or psychological influence . . . calculated to produce specific emotional shocks."[40] *Rivers of Sand*'s often remarked-on sequence in which images of a girl having a neck ring pounded on alternate with a cow's neck being branded, is a case in point. Jean Lydall has written about this as an especially egregious example of Gardner's deliberate and uninformed cultural misinterpretation.[41] However, one needn't read this montage as it is commonly read—montage always maintains *some* ambiguity, because the relationship of parts is never singular. It may be, as interpreted by most critics, that Gardner is dogmatically imposing a value judgment—in other words, saying: "you see, men treat women just like men brand cows." Yet the intercutting of the cow that cringes under the branding iron also adds to our bodily engagement with the woman whose facial expression we cannot see (we only see her neck and a hand pounding the metal closed). Just as Eisenstein's close-up slaughterhouse shots create a visceral engagement with the strikers' less visually explicit fate, the Hamar cow gives a bodily impression of pain that then extends to our perception of the woman, without necessarily being equated with her. In other words, the image of the cow recoiling may provoke, or heighten, a gut-level perception of the woman's physical experience—or Gardner's interpretation of the woman's experience. Whatever Gardner's intent, the multiple possibilities and meanings generated by this intercutting extend beyond any single reading.

Another example of Gardner's potentially heavy-handed editing occurs in one of the most distressing (for non-Hamar viewers) segments in the film: a young girl getting her tooth excised. Here we are privy to the physically arduous process of the girl's tooth being literally sawed out of her bleeding gums by an older man. We also see her facial expressions, suggesting pain but also stoicism. After the procedure is complete she sits with her head down with the blood from her mouth staining the ground in front of her.

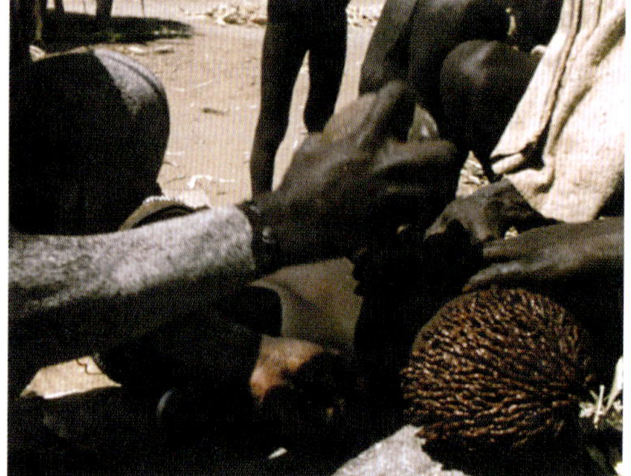

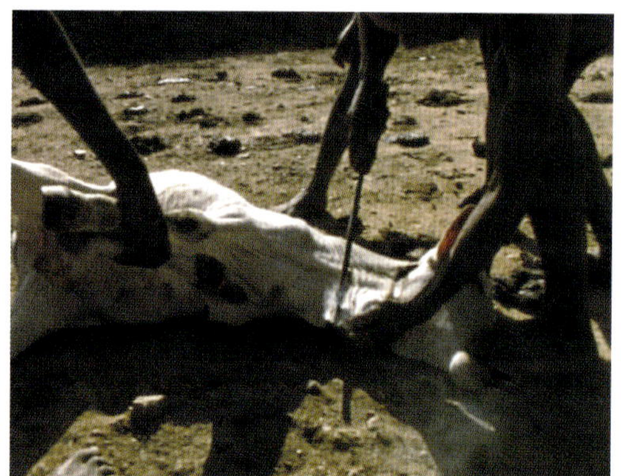

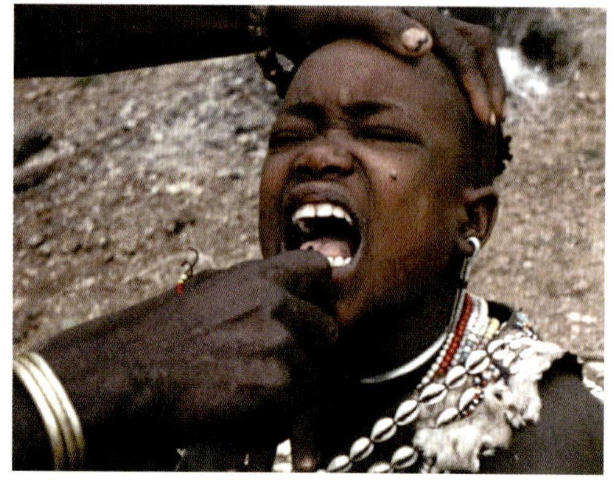

Unlike in other scenes, in this one we are given Omali Inda's explanation of the act and its cultural and aesthetic significance *before* we see it. In fact we also see what appears to be the same young girl with her tooth already out playing near Omali Inda (the girl is highlighted by an awkward, if brief, freeze frame). After Omali Inda speaks about the practice of removing a front tooth, she turns (obviously responding to a question we do not hear) to the reasons for and meaning of this practice. Not everyone has a lower tooth excised. Only those who are brave do so, and it is a sign of courage and beauty. Those who aren't brave are nicknamed the "ones who chew," she adds, since chewing is easier for them. Immediately following this explanation the film cuts to the scene of the girl's painful excision. But the images of the bleeding child are abruptly, and somewhat shockingly, intercut with three short shots of men in close-up biting into large chunks of bloody meat.

Gardner's rhetorical set up and heavy-handed editing of the scene suggest that he wants us first to read this as another of the painful adornments undergone by women and administered by men, and second, to realize that men maintain the pleasure of eating meat while women who have had a lower front tooth brutally removed do not. It is the men who chew, not the women or the girl. However, if one takes a closer look throughout the film, we can see that many men also have a missing lower front tooth. The film overall contradicts the simplistic judgment that Gardner's editing seems to make in this sequence. If one carefully examines the earlier scene of the three hungry ostrich hunters observed by Gardner's camera at quite some length as they dine and adorn themselves after their kill—all have a tooth missing. In fact, missing front teeth (I'm guessing here) may have a functional role in the practice of repeated spitting both in the ritualized blessings and in recycling of water for washing hands and body. Gardner's insertion of the montage of men and bloody meat into the sequence seems to stubbornly insist, in the face of ever more ambiguity, on the repeated opposition of female pain and the male pleasures (here chewing meat) ostensibly inaccessible to them. Yet this binary interpretative framework is repeatedly challenged by the more complicated realities suggested by the carefully observed images and sounds taken as a whole.

Rivers of Sand calls for close viewing and close listening. Gardner's own emotional responses to certain aspects of Hamar culture are embedded in the film, in his commentary, in the camerawork, and in his editing strategies. Yet I believe he allows, and even encourages, the film as a whole to transcend any single point of view and ultimately resist any, including his own, moralizing interpretation. This is the film's great power. In Gardner's arresting and deeply engaged images and sounds, one experiences an unsettled and unsettling mixture of awe, admiration, condemnation, fascination, and the desire *and failure* to comprehend what one sees. As much as Gardner may be personally concerned with a specific gender dynamic, the final *film* seems open to a broader depiction of the Hamar approach to living, their aesthetic vision, and their appreciation of beauty as created through collective rituals and often painful practices of bodily adornment. This strong aesthetic vision links the Hamar culture with Gardner's own quest.

While Omali Inda's solicited and edited statements about gender divisions, the power of men, and the resignation of women are crucial to our experience of *Rivers of Sand*, they also secrete a similar excess and ambiguity of meaning as they brush against each other and Gardner's images. In fact, the images, tonalities, and intonation patterns of Omali Inda's strong presence and voice speak to us as forcefully as do her translated words. *That* she is there, a woman, addressing Gardner and us directly, is at least as important as *what* she says. As the film proceeds we become less and less certain of any absolute or definitive statements about the Hamar and more and more open to the ambiguities and aesthetic resonances of their culture and the film. At the outset we might interpret Omali Inda's comments as decrying the horror of a husband's beating qua taming of a newlywed wife. By the end she seems to be saying that the beating of wives is simply a part of life, and gender divisions are necessary. Indeed, we are never actually sure what she means by "beating," because a husband can "beat without beating" (according to the translation). As importantly, she never mentions or explains the ritual whipping that Gardner so emphatically portrays using slow motion and accentuated sound. And at the same time, we never see in Gardner's images the kind of marital beatings she describes. Gardner's images suggest, instead, that the ritualized whipping involves flirtation, play, and seduction as well as any implicit and explicit physical domination. Just as the multiple leg adornments of the women may be "irons" of servitude, they may also be the "rings" of beauty, prosperity, and feminine sensual power. The scarring of skin and the excision of lower front teeth are painful and bloody, but they are also proof of physical endurance and courage and the expression of a resilient aesthetic vision.

"I do often feel entangled in my thoughts" Gardner once said, commenting on George Eliot's line that "we all get our thought entangled in metaphors."[42] A powerful, unresolved, and emotionally and philosophically entangled engagement with Hamar life emerges, very forcefully, from his film *Rivers of Sand*. Despite Gardner's occasional deprecatory comments about Hamar men, his statement that Hamar women are slaves, or the static, binary model of gender dynamics that occasionally surfaces, the world as conveyed through the flesh—of the Hamar, of the audience, and of Gardner's embodied cinematography—repeatedly defies such limited reading. It is not when a film explains, understands, or judges its subjects that it is inherently ethical, but, as Sarah Cooper has suggested, when a film and its viewers realize that people *cannot* be explained by the filmmaker or by us. The viewer's recognition of subjects who "resist reduction to the vision of the filmmaker who fashions them" is paramount to an ethical engagement with others.[43] While *Rivers of Sand* on the one hand seems to make a (potentially contestable) statement about the oppression of Hamar women by Hamar men (and gender inequalities in general), the film is more potent as a riveting portrait of a people and a culture that exceed the filmmaker's (and our) ability to grasp them. Gardner repeatedly allows such excess to come through in the ample and evocative energy of his tactile camerawork as it comes in contact with the more restraining, but also ambiguous, force of Omali Inda's and his own words, as well as some of his seemingly didactic montage sequences. This multiplicity of voices and modes of engagement never wholly concurs; no conclusive response to the Hamar world nor to Gardner's film is to be had. We are left to grapple with the enigmas, paradoxes, and questions that the film eloquently raises. As suggested by Gardner's words at the beginning of this essay, in making *Rivers of Sand* he has made the extraordinary Hamar mysteries more accessible to the rest of the world, but he has also made their complexity and ambiguity much more discernable.

Notes

1. In writings, interviews, and the DER DVD commentary, Gardner repeatedly says that he originally intended to name the film *Creatures of Pain* but was dissuaded by colleagues. See, for instance, "*Rivers of Sand*," *Harvard Magazine*, October 1974, 43.
2. For the sake of consistency I use Gardner's transliteration of Omali Inda here and not that used by other anthropologists. This should also make it clear that I am speaking of the character that Gardner constructs in and for his film.
3. In speaking about the "voice" of the film, I refer to Bill Nichols' seminal essay in which he defines the voice of documentary as not merely dialogue or spoken commentary but "that which conveys to us a sense of a text's social point of view, of how it is speaking to us and how it is organizing the materials it is presenting to us." Nichols, "The Voice of Documentary," *Film Quarterly* 36:3 (1983), 18.
4. Peter Loizos has suggested that *Rivers of Sand* is misread when considered (by Jean Lydall, Ivo Strecker, and others) to be a "realist" film and claims that Gardner should more appropriately be understood as working in a "symbolist" tradition, likening some of his work to that of the painter Paul Gauguin. See Loizos, "Robert Gardner in Tahiti, or the Rejection of Realism" in *Innovation in Ethnographic Film: From Innocence to Self-Consciousness 1955–1985* (Chicago: University of Chicago Press, 1993), 140, 166. Mauro Bucci, on the other hand, refers to the film as "allegorical" ("Allegory and Gender Representation in *Rivers of Sand*," this volume).
5. Jean Lydall, "Whipping Scars and 'Larger Truths,'" *Anthropology Today* 24:4 (August 2008), 28–29.
6. Gardner makes reference to the end of his first marriage and its significance to his attitude to Hamar gender dynamics both in a 1989 letter to Peter Loizos and in a 1999 interview with Ilisa Barbash. "Letter to Peter Loizos," in *Just Representations*, ed. Charles Warren (Cambridge, MA: Studio7Arts & Peabody Museum Press, 2010), 269. Barbash, "Out of Words: A Conversation with Robert Gardner," in *The Cinema of Robert Gardner*, ed. Ilisa Barbash and Lucien Taylor (Oxford: Berg, 2007), 107.

7. Barbash, 100.

8. Loizos, who discusses the thematic concerns and strategies of *Rivers of Sand*, goes so far as to call it "flamboyantly a montage film" in "Robert Gardner's *Rivers of Sand*: Toward a Reappraisal," in *Fields of Vision: Essays in Film Studies, Visual Anthropology, and Photography,* ed. Leslie Devereaux and Roger Hillman (Berkeley: University of California Press, 1995), 317.

9. Karl G. Heider, *Ethnographic Film* (Austin: University of Texas, 1976). Although Heider has nothing but praise when writing specifically about Gardner, his former colleague, his rules for ethnographic filmmaking include "Whole Bodies and Whole People in Whole Acts," and he criticizes Hilary Harris' *The Nuer*, on which Gardner worked, for its "poorly understood fragments of behavior" (108). He argues that "entire bodies of people at work or play or rest are more revealing and interesting than body fragments. Events should be shown from beginning to end" (125). *Rivers of Sand* clearly does not comply and in fact embodies the antithesis of Heider's model.

10. Such experiments include Rouch's works of ethno-fiction like *Jaguar* (1967), *Moi*, *un noir* (1958), and *Petit à petit* (1970) as well as his cinema verité experiment with Edgar Morin, *Chronicle of a Summer* (1961). The MacDougalls also experimented with reflexive strategies in their films shot among the Turkana; for instance *The Wedding Camels* (1974/77) includes lengthy segments in which the subjects film the filmmakers and are asked what they feel should be included in the film about them.

11. Jean Lydall and Ivo Strecker, "A Critique of Lionel Bender's Review of *Rivers of Sand*," *American Anthropologist* 80 (1978), 945.

12. See especially Ruby's chapter on Gardner in *Picturing Culture: Explorations of Film and Anthropology* (Chicago: University of Chicago Press, 2000), 95–113.

13. In Loizos' chapter on Gardner in *Innovations in Ethnographic Film* cited above and in his reappraisal of *Rivers of Sand* in *Fields of Vision*, 311–328.

14. "Letter to Dr. Harry Tomicek, May 1990," *Just Representations*, 274.

15. Gardner, *The Impulse to Preserve: Reflections of a Filmmaker* (New York: Other Press, 2006), 111, 116. Elsewhere in the journal Gardner suggests that he had hoped to find a community that would "disclose to my camera the fascinating details of a life hitherto scarcely imaginable and certainly not yet fixed in particles of silver nitrate" (129).

16. See *The Impulse to Preserve*, 116, 131, 134, and 141.

17. These journals are published in *The Impulse to Preserve*.

18. See *The Impulse to Preserve*, 133, 143, 157.

19. See MacDougall's important and detailed discussion about the problems of subtitling in ethnographic films of this period in *Transcultural Cinema*, ed. Lucien Taylor (Princeton: Princeton University Press, 1998), 165ff.

20. Heider, 35.

21. Lydall and Strecker, 945.

22. Barbash, 102.

23. Gardner, DVD commentary on *Rivers of Sand*.

24. Barbash, 102.

25. Gardner, "*Rivers of Sand* Commentary," *Just Representations*, 220.

26. Ibid.

27. Ibid., 221.

28. Ibid.

29. Gardner's highly mobile cinematography in *Rivers of Sand* feels as if it has been influenced by his friend and later collaborator Robert Fulton, whose work he knew and admired and with whom he would shoot *Mark Tobey Abroad* in 1971–1972 and *Deep Hearts* in 1981.

30. Gardner in a 1980 talk published as "The Moral Nature of Film, with a Response by Robert Fulton," *Just Representations*, 244.

31. Maurice Merleau-Ponty, "Eye and Mind," in *The Merleau-Ponty Aesthetics Reader*, ed. Galen A. Johnson (Evanston, IL: Northwestern University Press, 1993), 26.

32. Gallese, Vittorio, "Commentary on 'Toward a Neuroscience of Empathy: Integrating Affective and Cognitive Perspectives,'" *Neuropsychoanalysis: An Interdisciplinary Journal for Psychoanalysis and the Neurosciences* 9:2 (2007), 147.

33. MacDougall, David, *The Corporeal Image: Film, Anthropology, and the Senses* (Princeton: Princeton University Press, 2005), 21.

34. Ibid., 311.

35. Ibid., 314.

36. Ibid., 32.

37. Ibid., 51.

38. Ibid., 316.

39. Roderick Coover, "Worldmaking, Metaphors and Montage in the Representation of Cultures: Cross-Cultural Filmmaking and the Poetics of Robert Gardner's *Forest of Bliss*," *Visual Anthropology* 14 (2001), 415, 428, 431.

40. Sergei Eisenstein, "The Montage of Attractions (1923)," in *Selected Works Volume I: Writings 1922–1934*, ed. Richard Taylor (Bloomington: Indiana University Press, 1988), 34.

41. Lydall and Strecker (945) believe that Gardner blatantly misuses these images to reinforce his erroneous and misleading vision of oppressed Hamar women. They write that the ornamentation was requested by the woman and is performed by her brother while the burning was a medical treatment for a sick cow.

42. Cited in Thomas W. Cooper, *Natural Rhythms: The Indigenous World of Robert Gardner* (New York: Anthology Film Archives, 1995), 92.

43. Sarah Cooper, *Selfless Cinema? Ethics and French Documentary* (London: Maney, 2006), 5.

Chapter 15
Look At Me!
Deep Hearts and the Vertiginous Self

Murray Pomerance

There comes a time—I believe we are in such a time—when civilization has to be renewed by the discovery of new mysteries, by the undemocratic but sovereign power of the imagination, by the undemocratic power which makes poets the unacknowledged legislators of mankind, the power which makes all things new.

—Norman O. Brown, May 1960

I am going to write about Robert Gardner's *Deep Hearts* (1981), a film he made with his "closest friend and soulmate" Robert Fulton, "who flew his plane into a thunderstorm" (Warren communication). But exactly in the way the film shows an act that is circular and in its fashion unending—*eine unendiliche geschichte,* as it were—I feel in respecting, absorbing, and reflecting it the need to lapse into circularity myself; that is, to begin a long way from the beginning, so that I will travel the long journey to the proper end. As Edward Albee had Jerry say in *The Zoo Story*, "Sometimes a person has to go a very long distance out of his way to come back a short distance correctly."

Andante

For the space of a year, around the time John Fitzgerald Kennedy abruptly ceased being President of the United States, three social scientists worked in nine high schools across the country to engage in a study of student values and, by implication, the adolescent experience in mass society.[1] Carl Nordstrom and Hilary Gold worked at this with Edgar Z. Friedenberg, then at the University of California, Davis, who discussed some of the findings in his landmark 1965 volume *Coming of Age in America: Growth and Acquiescence*. The central device of the study was a set of six fabular tales of high school life, for each of which the selected students, having read it, were to choose, from a set of nine cards, the three best, three worst, single best, and single worst fictive "high school students" who fitted the context of the given story problem. Intensive interviews were conducted to solicit information about how and why students made the choices they did. The book itself, surely among the most profound treatises on education, civil behavior, American culture, and Schelerian ressentiment ever published, is less my concern here than one of the test stories and the way students responded to it. These were, after all, young unmarried people of sexual maturity, shaped by their culture and environment.

In "The King's Visit," the monarch of a country "not unlike Denmark" is to visit the area and would like to meet some "spirited young people." The subjects are given nine choices and asked to rank them as to their suitability for selection to meet the King. The top two choices made consistently across all nine schools—accounting for 69 percent of the decisions—were: (1) Karen Clarke, who is described on the test card as being, among other things, "always well groomed and polite" and "completely in command of herself in any situation"; and (2) Elfrieda Eubanks, "so sweet you couldn't help liking her. . .tall, slender, and very graceful" (54–55). Interestingly, the worst-liked characters were these: Scott Cowen, who is "supposed to be a genius" but whose work "does tend to be sloppy. He's sloppy also in the way he dresses"; and Johnny Adams, "something of an enigma," who "runs around with what are called beatniks. . . .No one would ever call him good-looking, he has a sort of squeaky voice, and most of the time he could use a haircut and shave" (64–65). As Friedenberg concluded, "Scott and Johnny were perceived as security risks, unstable, and unpredictable. . . .It seemed far more likely to [our subjects] that Johnny would appear before the King unkempt and unshaven, cracking insults in jive-talk" (67). I have chosen this story from the half-dozen administered to the subjects because of its implications about impression management, self-styling, status consciousness, self-regard, and the passage to adulthood, the character of the visiting King operating as a kind of notably expectant and meritorious audience in front of whom, presumably, the best possible picture of the school population should be presented in an ideal light. What students are being asked to decide about here, it seems to me, is not only school and its structure but also the process of constructing and keeping up certain forms of appearance. Karen Clarke and Elfrieda Eubanks are, for the tenth, eleventh, and twelfth graders who chose them, ideal subjects indeed, "well groomed" and "graceful," girls who are, respectively, "in command" and "so sweet you couldn't help liking her." The failures are quirky boys, unpolished, unattuned to the principal value of being impressive in social situations, indeed "sloppy" and "unkempt." For a clear majority of adolescent subjects, then, looking good was in many ways a central value of their experience. One need hardly emphasize that in this respect nothing has changed.

The young people in American high schools, both in the early 1960s and today, reflect in their concern with suitably crafted appearance a sense of competition and a keen awareness of the power of external judgment, as related to achievement, career success, and interpersonal popularity. By and large, as they dress up to make themselves look "good" or "beautiful," they are not propelled by the prospect of mating (which I take to be distinct, especially nowadays here, from sexual connection). To the extent that the boys, eschewing the behavior of earlier models like Scott and Johnny, work to beautify themselves, it is not typically in the name of finding a wife among the high school cohort. Looking good is more likely, as they calculate it, to make them superior in a hunt for jobs, friends, and fame.

Among the Wodaabe of Niger,[2] a culture as complex and enduring as that of America, there is a ritual celebration of male beauty that would stagger the "Scott Cowens" and "Johnny Adamses" on the other side of the world. The Wodaabe are strictly nomadic, and leaving "no trace of their passage from encampment to encampment" move through their territory in strict rejection of "all efforts made to change their precarious way of life," which, they believe, is "the only one for them because it is the way of tradition."[3] Annually, at the end of the rainy season, groups from competitive lineages meet in a clearing to celebrate together, for a virtually uninterrupted period of seven days, the *Gerewol*. This extended male dance is both beauty contest and endurance test, culminating with a moment in which three young women from the nondancing lineage make their choice of the most beautiful male dancers: this is a kind of symbolic mating, suggesting a pattern through which members of the two groups might conjoin. These dancers are a few years older than the American teens, and yet, like those teens, neither children nor fully and commitedly adults in their defining culture. In a way, their dance is the route to a full manifestation of the dancers' investment in themselves as adults; they literally seem to dance themselves into growth. After the choice is made by the selection committee, the *Gerewol* is done, and the encampment is broken up, the camels loaded, and a voyage begun again toward the future.

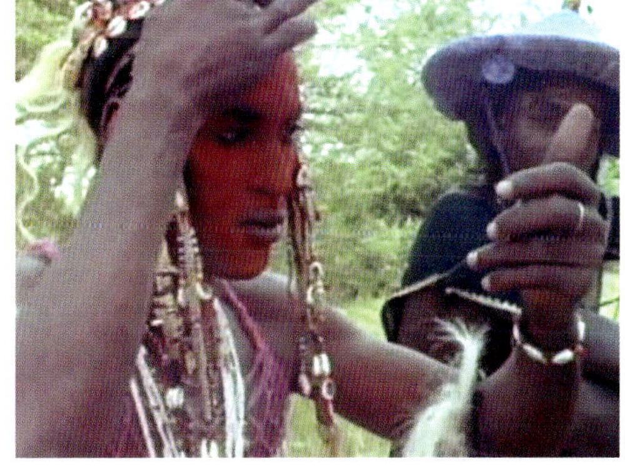

Central to the dance form is the body styling engaged by the young men who will compete against one another. Tall and slender, they mask over their bronze skin with makeup (pigment mixed with fat), elaborating both the basal facial tone (with a yellow color for lightening) and extensions of the face (a straight line down the bridge of the nose, to suggest length; kohl on the lips and around the eyes to accentuate the eye whites and the white of the teeth) and marking ornamentations on the torso, cheeks, and forehead (with circular or dot patterns). They shave the hairline to extend the forehead vertically. They garb themselves fabulously.

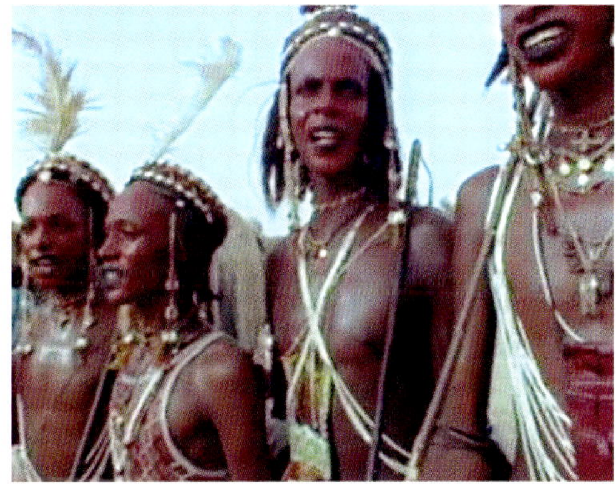

From wrapping the turban to final inspection in a handheld mirror, dancers give painstaking care to every detail. Their women have spent months embroidering the tunics they wear. Beautifully crafted knives, spears, swords, leather purses, and silver ornaments have been purchased from Tuareg smiths. Leather talismans are worn to ensure beauty, guard against jealousy, heighten appeal. Shiny objects such as zippers and locks, watchbands, and empty cartridges are incorporated into costumes.[4] Further, the dancer ties a woman's wrapper snugly around the hips and constrains the knees, so that his steps will have to be short—a further elongation of his already slender frame. Gesticulations and patterned movements are aimed to produce a sense of undying frenetic energy, the eyes playing a particularly dramatic role as they are opened very wide while the dancer turns his gaze in all directions. The use of "zippers and locks" and other objects taken from technologically advanced cultures bespeaks an attitude of incorporation and utilitarianism, as one finds in cargo culture and in the imitation of Western artists who use found materials (Picasso, Arman, Tony Duquette, James Hampton with his "Throne of the Third Heaven of the Nations' Millennium General Assembly"). Every conceivable article to hand is put to use toward the realization of a beautiful effect. Every visible node of the body is examined, corrected, refined, polished, decorated, painted, displayed through movement and pose. In the brief moments of repose between sessions, the dancers repair to privacy, often in pairs, and help each other touch up or refresh their makeup, the better to magnify grimacing, grinning, gawking, and generally groping rhythmically for the glittering prize of attentiveness.

It is hardly true in America, where youth are confined in the social structure of adolescence that sequesters them from the freedoms of childhood while denying them the powers and responsibilities of adulthood, that the quest for personal beauty is a deeply serious matter, since triumphing in it results only in status. But among the Wodaabe, as with other tribal peoples, adolescence as we know it is nonexistent; and the young bodies dancing for success are experiencing all the desperation and yearning associated with major life decisions. This is, after all, an attempt on the part of each youth to attain what members of his culture would call full manhood. The dance is an existential commitment, not an entertainment. The making up of the body, its maintenance of energy, the festive and astonishing garb (ostrich plumes in the headdress), and the pulsing, repetitive, exhausting, disorienting, transcendental, charging effect of the continuous dance constitute together a splendid agon, a deep personal and realized struggle for survival in and through one's self.

It was while studying the Bushmen of the Kalahari in the mid-1950s along with John Marshall that Robert Gardner, now plunged thoroughly into the practice of visual anthropology, founded the Film Study Center (FSC) at Harvard (where he presided, gently and authoritatively, for forty years). "It is almost a commonplace," he wrote, "that sight is a selective process and that we see as much what we wish to see as what is held before our gaze. If it is necessary, for the sake of conducting anthropology, to depend on such an inexact means of access to information, it is worth considering possibilities for giving it some corrective support." At the FSC, he hoped, assistance could be provided "to the seeing of human life."[5] While photographs—even arresting high-quality photographs such as we see in the Wodaabe work of Carol Beckwith—might typify human behavior and cultural form, might instantiate the interpretable pose, it remained true for Gardner that "cinematic recordings of human life are unchanging documents providing detailed information on the behavioral characteristics of man."[6] To be emphasized here, I believe, is the observation that cinema is recording human life; life, not cultural moment; life, not abstracted form. In front of the camera the subject moves through both space and time, and because of this, in the case of the *Gerewol*, for instance, we have not only the decodable appurtenances of costume and makeup but the vivacious use, through appreciable dance, of color, body, space, and materials. Furthermore, "If the film narrative is uncompromisingly real and sufficiently expressive of the significance of the experience it portrays, the audience will, at the very least, be made more deeply aware of the validity of what they witness. The audience's humanity will be confirmed" by means of a direct act of witnessing.[7] It is real, meaningful, and ennobling for us precisely as, and to the extent that, we see it.

The danger in photographing Gardner saw plainly enough. The "bizarre or exotic" might easily distract and overwhelm the observer's senses, so that he would find himself "beclouded by difference."[8] What needed to be achieved was a certain clairvoyance, the ability to respond to the visible without the clutter and gravitation of one's own cultural heritage and predisposition, thereby gaining access to "an entirely believable humanity in the unfamiliar" (244). With a goal such as this, Gardner was working in a tradition exemplified also by (among others) Kurt Wolff, whose anthropology often fixated on the challenge of "surrender"; by Sol Worth and John Adair, confronted by the challenge of seeing 16mm motion pictures made for them by their Navajo subjects without being bound by the conventions of Western cinematography; and by Gregory Bateson, who in an argument with Margaret Mead offered the conjecture that art, not science, was the root of the deepest anthropological vision.[9] Mead appears to have had a lot of trouble accepting the artistic engagement of an anthropologist's relatively intrusive camera (a camera like Gardner's, or like Bateson's), complaining,

> The only real information that [Robert Gardner's] *Dead Birds* gives anybody are things like the thing that my imagination had never really encompassed, and that's the effect of cutting off the joints of fingers. You remember? The women cut off a joint for every death that they mourn for, and they start when they're little girls, so that by the time they're grown women, they have no fingers. . .I knew about it, I had read about it, it had no meaning to me until I saw those pictures. There are lots of things that can be conveyed by this quasi-artistic film.[10]

Yet it is difficult not to suspect that for her, in deeper truth, *Dead Birds* is overloaded with "things that had no meaning" until she saw the pictures. If indeed we are to presume that beyond the fingers Gardner's film, for Mead, really does not convey information—and one could surely find the same basis for starchy complaint with *Deep Hearts*, in which the *Gerewol* spins out with broadening frenzy and deepening conviction, yet so fully alive to the eye that "information" might, yes, be lost—yet we must wonder what this "information" is that Mead and the empiricists find so valuable, that the participatory or engaged camera can fail to collect since, presumably, the photographer is too avidly seeing what he wants to see?

When he went with John Marshall to study the Bushmen in 1958, Gardner informs us, he decided to keep a journal. Reflecting on that practice more than fifty years later, he notes:

> Like other such efforts to register thoughts and feelings about what I see and hear, these journal entries have a personal and subjective dimension that frequently stands in rather stark rejection of strictures regarding objectivity and precision. It was a time when I was increasingly frustrated with the ascendant emphasis in social science on value-free thinking and anthropology's growing infatuation with the allure of hard science.[11]

In the context of this way of seeing and understanding the world—in the late 1960s it came under the rubric of "humanism"—information, of the sort that the distanced, locked-down camera could offer, was an inorganic abstraction from the complex flow of actual life, which is to say, actuality. Information advertises itself as unbiased, unattached to the elements of a scene, and thus removable to a safe distance where rational analysis and comparison may be undertaken by students unaffected by—in the deepest sense, unobservant of—the experience under study. Jean Rouch (who gave extensive consideration to the state of filmmaking, narrative and documentary, in Africa in the 1940s and 1950s)[12] wrote about the practice of visual anthropology, however, that "The observer's presence can never be neutral. Whether he wishes it or not, the observer himself is integral to the general movement of things and his most minute reactions are interpreted within the context of the particular system of thought that surrounds him."[13]

Information would purport to diminish the observer, yet it also manages to diminish the people or things under observation, because it is universally true that what cannot be reduced cannot be informative. Gardner's films, and particularly his *Deep Hearts* and *Forest of Bliss* (1986), are stunningly uninformative in the sense required by Mead. They convey life directly to the senses, and thus confront the viewer with the challenge of accepting the strange and unfamiliar as coherent and logical unto itself.

Lento

How convenient and informative it can be to consider as symbolic communication only what is generated by human beings or their artifacts, reserving for the wind, the trees, the rivers, the animals, and the clouds a category called "nature," which does not "tell."[14] *Deep Hearts* utterly confounds our sense of what does or does not, might or might not, add meaning to our experience of watching. The vivid, sunburn color, the throbbing dance, the intoxicating sounds of repetitive stomping and drumming and breathing, are both involving and disorienting. Charles Warren suggests a ritual of gender play in which dancing young men "dress and behave as women, with the aim that one of the men be chosen as exemplar by a woman, who may be acting at the behest of still other men" and points to "freeing," "ambiguity," and "letting go."[15] I found myself unconfused about gender while watching the film, or perhaps unconcerned, yet the endurance aspect of the *Gerewol* became exhausting and exhilarating for me, since the dance and its encompassing rituals of makeup and preparation were couched in a troubling and delicious contradiction, the one between showing the self and avoiding the gaze of the other's eyes. "The Bororo are worried about consumption by others' eyes," writes Warren, thinking, too, of the camera and the way it can contain and assimilate by recording an image;[16] William Rothman echoes:

> In *Deep Hearts*, Gardner all but forgoes narration, apart from his putting into his own words what he tells us is a Bororo's greatest fear: "to be devoured by another person's eyes or mouth, by the way they might look, or the words they might speak." From this fear follows the desirability, as a Bororo understands it, of having a "deep heart." When

> Gardner adds, "If their heart is deep, no one can see what it contains," he is speaking as an anthropologist, relaying to us what such "others" believe. But he is also speaking as a man who knows firsthand, as we all do, about such a belief or fantasy.[17]

It is not atypical in visual anthropology to find researchers (cultivated by Western habits of viewing) in positions of surprise or wonder when confronting their subjects' fear of, or disinclination toward, facial display, looking into other people's faces, or facial close-ups. Studying the Navajo through participant filmmaking, for example, Worth and Adair were initially taken aback by their subjects' refusal of some Western conventions of facial gazing and expression.[18]

Whether or not the Bororo male youths Gardner portrays are attempting to simulate the presentational styles of Bororo females, as Warren sees it; whether they are acting out a deeply structured cultural gender confusion or a principled commitment to the universality of gendered singularity, unmistakable it remains that they are devoted to adorning themselves in meticulous and energetic fashion. The camera lingers near them as they paint and examine themselves, work in dyads to check out face decoration, stretch and preen themselves (my words), slide into the dance, keep themselves going, produce the smiles that will make visible, thus appraisable, the teeth, and so on. They are showing off not only their individual makeup and sartorial creativity but also their inherited physical aspects, their long bodies, their sharply defined noses, their penetratingly dark eyes, in this way pointing to the fact that our body cultures provide broadly accessible avenues to exhibition and draw into featured status the bodies that are our own.

The adornment is complexly associated with the self of the persons we see dancing onscreen. Indeed, the film is a constantly traveling, constantly throbbing commitment to the pictorialization of this Bororo self, at one and the same time continuously obsessed with presentation and continuously hiding. The "deep heart" or true heart—that cannot be seen because of the makeup—is at once ineffably present, and moving with the dance and its aspiration; and absent, because the stranger's (the camera's) vision of the exterior obscures it, prevents intelligent passage to its boundaries. "If their heart is deep, no one can see what it contains." But this with, and in, the same burst of energy that makes the individual dancer radiant in uniqueness among the crowd, shimmeringly visible. The more successfully each dancer manages to adorn himself, the more he can be seen hiding his heart. Although at the conclusion of the film, when the females step forward to choose the winner of the contest, it is not explicitly stated that they are operating according to this principle in doing their "tasteful" work, it remains apparent that the most magnificent persona covers the deepest heart.

What the Bororo culture holds in common with our own, and with European culture in general, quite beyond the Western-style trinkets that the nomads have collected on their journeys during the past year and now utilize functionally to ornament their bodies, is a commitment to the myth of a buried self. The treasure, which contains the seeds of the greatest truth, is tucked away—Ali Baba's cave, the Bororo heart—and it is only by way of some rite of passage that bona fide members of the culture have access to it. In the *Gerewol*, it is by patiently and devotedly observing every hop and step of the dance, every gesture of every body, that the “deep heart” may be located through its ceremonial garb. The dance is a kind of expression that flows out of the deeply situated reservoir of this heart. By this laminated structure—a motor or furnace of intent beneath a chassis of personability and style—one is reminded of Erving Goffman’s “Doctrine of Natural Expression,” which points to a widely diffused “appeal to the nature of the beast” that informs our thinking about culture, form, and behavior:

> It is, of course, hardly possible to imagine a society whose members do not routinely read from what is available to the senses something larger, distal, or hidden. Survival is unthinkable without it. Correspondingly, there is a very deep belief in our society, as presumably there is in others, that an object produces signs that are informing about it. Objects are thought to structure the environment immediately around themselves; they cast a shadow, heat up the surround, strew indications, leave an imprint; they impress a part picture of themselves, a portrait that is unintended and not dependent on being attended, yet informing nonetheless whoever is properly placed, trained, and inclined.[19]

Consider, regarding the Bororo themselves, the heart as a quintessential sign-producing object; the manifest dance as its shadow cast out (by day and by firelight); the meeting place in its growing frenzy as Goffman’s surround heated up; the decor of the body as the imprint or part picture; and the persons informed by all of this, properly placed, trained, and inclined, embodied in the women for whom the dance is executed. From the point of view of the film, however, the informed subject is Gardner’s camera, which is to say, Gardner. So very properly placed is he that we often have the glimmering suspicion he is Bororo himself, and has danced this dance.[20]

Scherzo

It may be said that two “games” are played by *Deep Hearts* in the presence of its audience, one of them self-reflexive and incisive about cinema and its powers; the second illuminating and invoking a certain euphoria of being and viewing (if, even through the agency of its necessary distance from action, viewing can be thought different from being). First comes a kind of celebration of presence, produced by the interminable action of a camera that works through its own mute commitment. It is quite another thing, after all, to be told about the operation of a culture—one is bombarded by strange words that point to disorientating configurations of space and embodiment, temporal distensions and compactments—even by a resource one can trust as knowledgeable and on the inside. All tellings are heard through the veil of the teller’s personality and investments, angle of approach, sense of memory and aspiration. Further, all tellings ultimately (or swiftly) become narrative, thus thematic. Thematism is blinding. What is shown by Gardner’s camera—the voice behind it modest and diminished almost to silence—is the working and outplaying of the Bororo group spirit directly, as it is happening, without the interference of a logic of assembly and an “informing” perspective. To have access to another culture in this blunt and in some ways overwhelming fashion is to be uplifted, uprooted, to fly across intercultural space in an unmeasurable fraction of a second. Thus, *Deep Hearts* invigorates and also stuns its audience with a presence that challenges with its very directness.

But once we are "inside" the culture it becomes impossible not to detect a stunning contradiction, come alive and put in full rhythmic (even hypnotic) play throughout the excursion. First, just as is specified by Roger Caillois, the dancers behave as though following the central dictum: "One plays only if and when one wishes to. In this sense, play is free activity."[21] Beyond this, however, the dance seems to belong at once to more than one of Caillois's "classes" of game. It exemplifies agôn in its breathtaking competitiveness, its testing endurance, its demands on the dancers to keep up both the rhythm of the music and the sparkle of their appearance through a grueling passage of time. But it also exemplifies the chance game, alea, because the target of the activity is snatching the glance from a judgmental female; the females' eyes are roving, and so, to some real degree it is a matter of happenstance when they fall upon a particular dancer. It exemplifies mimicry in that no single one of the dancers would claim that the face he sports inside the *Gerewol* is practically his own, his own in the everyday sense for all intents and purposes. And it exemplifies ilinx ("a state of dizziness and disorder"[22]) because once the rhythm has caught one's freedom and spun it, once the dancers have become intoxicated (as it were) by their repetitions, it happens that their sense of space and time is warped and turned on its head. There is vertigo in this final game component, loss of orientation, loss of being, in the furnace of experience. And it is a good thing that the dance lasts seven days only, because there is a point past which vertiginous repetition ceases to be pleasurable and starts to imprison.

A still deeper vertigo is inspired and implied by this film. The young men dance and act in a kind of glorious self-contradiction. Their deepest hearts are persistently invisible and interior, thus beneath what we are given to see, or behind it, or inside it, in a living sanctuary of truth. Yet at the same time it is true for each of them at each instant that his experience and interactional presence is called up entirely, and wholly, by the elaborate surface appearance (an appearance produced by each one at substantial cost) that he wears. As they dance, then, these young men present a self to be looked at and also searched for, a self that is, upon every beat, both present and absent. I think one could say—and Gardner's roving, circling camera seems to see it this way—that they circle rapidly from a locus of inward focus and secrecy to a locus of outward focus and publicity. And in this rapid circling, or alternation—an alternation in their consciousness as they focus on their looks but also on the depth of their hearts, and on the connection between the two; yet also an alternation in the way they present their society to the strange viewer through the magic of this camera, present it as being both obscure and brilliantly visible—a vertiginous escape from the everyday is achieved. This escape is sacred, certainly; but what is vital about it is less its sanctity than its vertiginousness, that the way out is by flickering back and forth between two bound, yet also contradictory, states of thought.

"The sociologist [Georg] Simmel sees showing and hiding, secrecy and publicity, as two poles, like yin and yang," wrote Norman O. Brown, "between which societies oscillate in their historical development. I sometimes think I see that civilizations originate in the disclosure of some mystery, some secret; and expand with the progressive publication of the secret; and end in exhaustion when there is no longer any secret, when the mystery has been divulged, that is to say, profaned."[23]

a	b
c	d
e	f

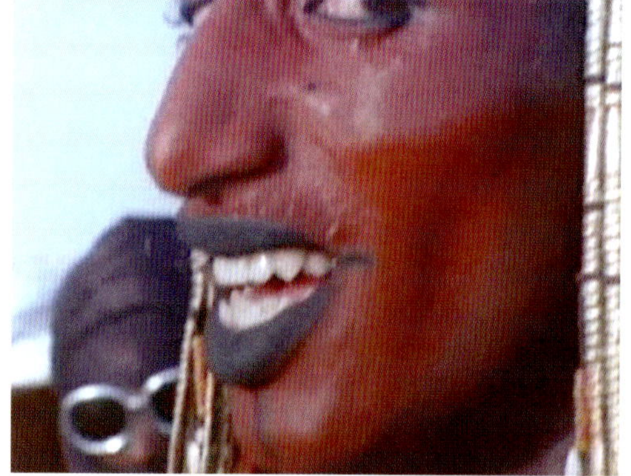
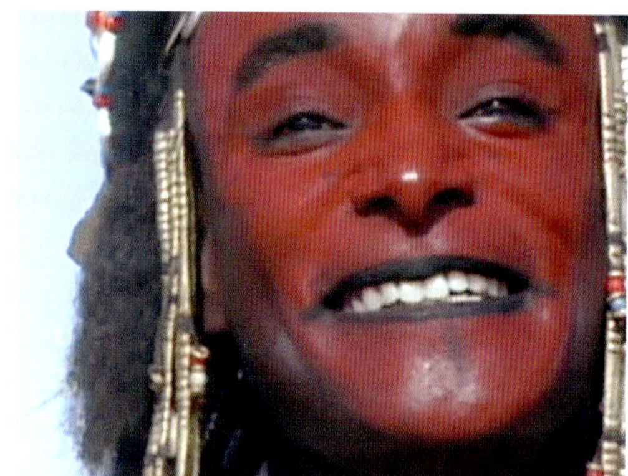
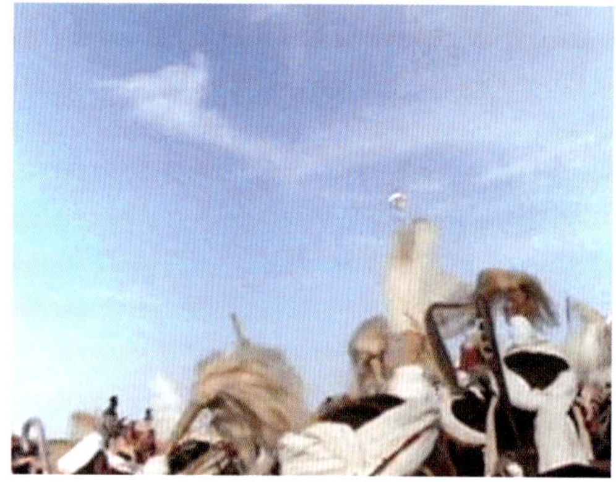
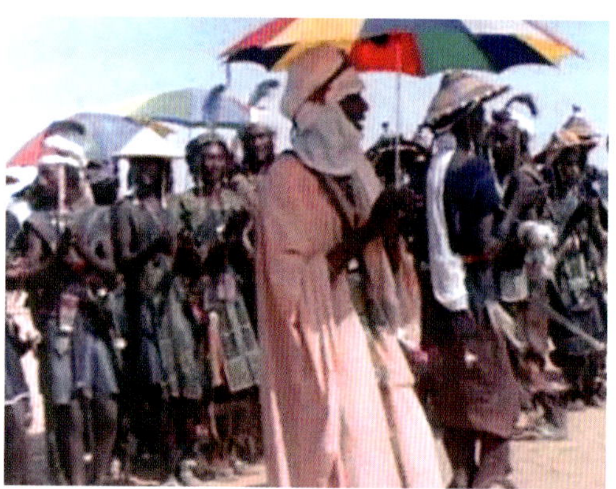
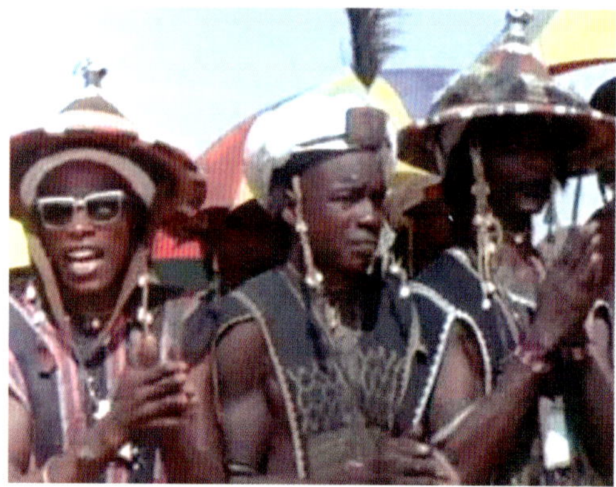
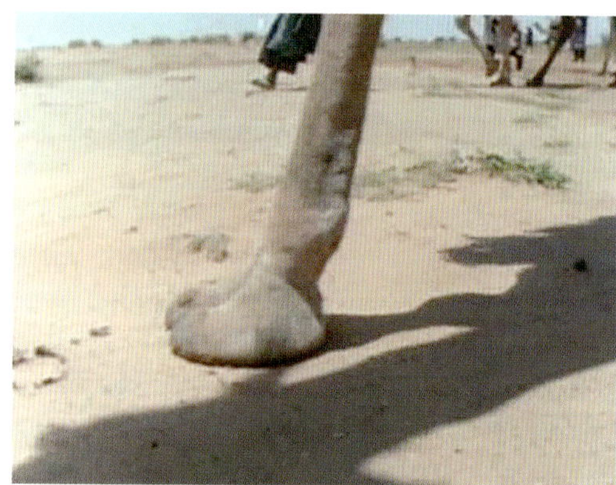

Day and night and night and day. The purple sky and the green sky. The bodies singing "Aiahhhhhhhhh." The hands gesticulating, speaking to space. The lips pulled back and marked, the flashing teeth. The flashing eyes. The thrusting torsos, lifting and relaxing feet, the plumes ascending and dropping, yellow plumes, gray plumes, the high grasses, the women bearing baskets on their heads in a straight line across the horizon, the lumbering wildebeest, the rains, the sharp teeth, the beads dropping from the woven hair, the dry earth, the grassy earth, the bowls of milk, the cheeks painted (actors applying makeup), the yellowed face, the old lady weaving a basket, the older men showing the younger men how to make a look, fingers applying paint to the lips, the long line kicking up dust, the dark and delicate feet, the fabric upon the hips, the patient camels, the camels attendant, a face painted oxblood red, the long line, the blue sky, fingers touching up the eyebrows, a face as orange as yams, the blue burnoose, the blue sky, the long line, the smile of victory, the sharp teeth, the prize teeth, the blue sky, the multicolored umbrella. The hands, the clapping hands, the open hands, the trading hands, the open hands, the camels' feet sliding away.

Notes

1. Edgar Z. Friedenberg, *Coming of Age in America: Growth and Acquiescence* (New York: Vintage, 1965), ix–xii.
2. The Wodaabe ("People of the Taboo"), sometimes referred to as the Bororo, wander with their cattle through Niger, Nigeria, Cameroon, and the Central African Republic. They do not write.
3. Carol Beckwith with Marion Van Offelen, *Nomads of Niger* (New York: Abrams, 1983), 17.
4. Ibid., 186.
5. Robert Gardner, *Just Representations* (Cambridge, MA: Studio7Arts and Peabody Museum Press, 2010), 228.
6. Ibid., 229.
7. Ibid.
8. Ibid., 244.
9. See Kurt H. Wolff, *Surrender and Catch: Experience and Inquiry Today* (Dordrecht: Reidel, 1976); Sol Worth and John Adair, *Through Navajo Eyes: An Exploration in Film Communication and Anthropology* (Bloomington: Indiana University Press, 1972); and "Margaret Mead and Gregory Bateson on the Use of the Camera in Anthropology," *Studies in the Anthropology of Visual Communication* 4: 2 (Winter 1977), 78–80.
10. "Margaret Mead and Gregory Bateson on the Use of the Camera in Anthropology," 80.
11. Gardner, *Just Representations*, 4.
12. See Jean Rouch, "The Situation and Tendencies of the Cinema in Africa," *Studies in the Anthropology of Visual Communication* 2: 2 (Fall 1975), 112–121.
13. Rouch, "On the Vicissitudes of the Self: The Possessed Dancer, the Magician, the Sorcerer, the Filmmaker, and the Ethnographer," *Studies in the Anthropology of Visual Communication* 5: 1 (Fall 1978), 7.
14. Larry Gross, "Sol Worth and the Study of Visual Communication," *Studies in Visual Communication* 6: 3 (Fall 1980), 13.
15. Charles Warren, "The Music of Robert Gardner," in *The Cinema of Robert Gardner*, eds. Ilisa Barbash and Lucien Taylor (Oxford: Berg, 2007), 27.
16. Ibid.
17. William Rothman, "Dancing with Gardner," in *The Cinema of Robert Gardner*, eds. Ilisa Barbash and Lucien Taylor (Oxford: Berg, 2007), 27.
18. See Sol Worth and John Adair, *Through Navajo Eyes*, 156 ff.
19. Erving Goffman, *Gender Advertisements* (New York: Harper, 1976), 6.
20. Charles Warren, "The Music of Robert Gardner," 17–31.
21. Roger Caillois, *Man, Play and Games*. Trans. Meyer Barash (Urbana: University of Illinois Press, 2001), 7.
22. Ibid., 12.
23. Norman O. Brown, "Apocalypse: The Place of Mystery in the Life of the Mind," in *Apocalypse and/or Metamorphosis* (Berkeley: University of California Press, 1991), 4.

Chapter 16

Nomadic Metrosexuals: Framing Beauty, Editing Ritual, and Exhibiting Masculinity in *Deep Hearts*

Ricardo E. Zulueta

What I am doing. . . is to not just register the world in optical terms, cinematic terms, but to inquire into it as a writer might call it to do an essay of a kind that attempts to find a meaning or many meanings that lie within these actualities. And if that can be called philosophy, I'm happy to know that; if it can be called poetry, I'm happy to know that, because I think poetry is one of the most penetrating ways of representing the world. If it is called art as a kind of overarching endeavor, I welcome that as well. It is not that I am against science, I am hoping that science itself is a kind of art and that art is what we are all attempting in some way or other, whether painters or poets or filmmakers or photographers or anything else. And so there you have my credo.

—Robert Gardner

When viewing *Deep Hearts* (1981), one encounters the mesmerizing cinematic poetry of Robert Gardner. Far from a sterile and distanced look at the "other," Gardner's experimental documentary offers spectators a unique, immersive, and deeply moving film experience. *Deep Hearts* has been described by Charles Warren as Gardner's "most lighthearted" work.[1] Yet this seemingly unassuming film yields insight into a complex tribal society that strangely echoes our own Western culture in its negotiation of gender roles, obsession with beauty and body image, and preoccupation with status and fashion. Through the extensive use of close-ups, dramatic camera angles, jump cuts, freeze frames, step-printed slow motion, and visual metaphors, with only minimal voice-over narration, Gardner's film emerges, in Sarah Pink's terms, as "embodied and sensory."[2]

In her 2006 book *The Future of Visual Anthropology*, Pink writes in regard to contemporary ethnographic films, "This work is concerned with reflexivity and ethnographers' self-awareness of the sensory experiences through which they [ethnographers] come to comprehend other people's lives and experiences. Here [in recently produced ethnographic films] comparison comes by reflecting on one's own sensory experience and expectations."[3] Gardner's approach was ahead of its time, insofar as *Deep Hearts* functions very aptly within the parameters Pink sets out to characterize ethnographic documentaries made more than two decades later. However, characterizing Gardner's films about other cultures simply as "ethnographic documentaries," no matter how advanced in approach, would fail to acknowledge their personal dimensions. In films such as *Deep Hearts*, Gardner creates, as William Rothman writes, "intimate, mysterious relationships between the camera and the camera's 'subjects,'" an emotional connection to his subjects; he is truly able to explore his own humanity by capturing and reflecting on the humanity of the people he films.[4]

As *Deep Hearts* opens, Gardner does not employ an opening title, establishing shot, or voice-over narration to introduce viewers to the film's world. As the sun rises, a group of almost imperceptible silhouettes are noticed leaping up and down in unison, a sort of coordinated dance shot in slow motion, in the foreground of the frame. We are transported to the midst of the action—the *Gerewol* ceremony—a weeklong male beauty contest of the Wodaabe (or Bororo, a subgroup of the Fulani), which takes place in the sub-Saharan Sahel at the end of the rainy season. A jump cut to a low angle shot reveals svelte dancers in flux, aligned perfectly in a row. This shot showcases the men's lanky, statuesque bodies as they tower over us, emphasizing their imposing regal presence and simultaneously conveying the sensation that we are now among the tribe.

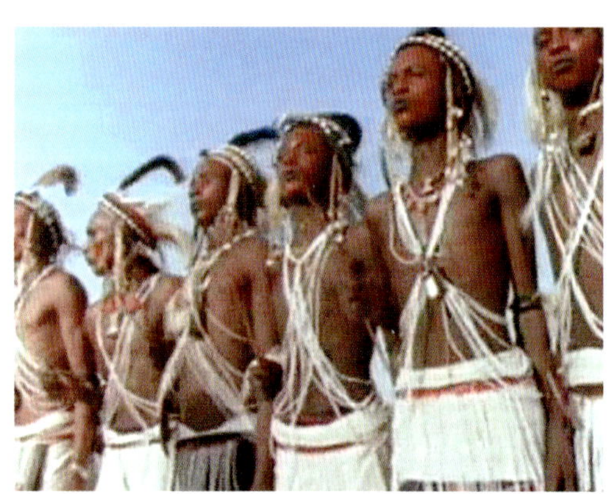

The camera then pans across the line of young men, filming them at eye level and presenting us with a closer view of their Modiglianiesque faces contorting into exaggerated theatrical expressions. Their eyes open wide, flashing huge smiles that reveal brilliant white teeth, the Wodaabe men engage us in a public spectacle showcasing their culture's version of charm.

Gardner's camera's undulating, panning movement comes to a halt at the sight of one striking young man. It lingers for a few seconds on his graceful gestures. Unlike all the other performers, who ignore the camera's presence even though it appears to be very close to them, this man acknowledges the camera by momentarily making eye contact with it. As he catches Gardner's attention, his act of turning his eyes to the camera makes clear that Gardner has caught his attention, too. By freezing this frame, the way Truffaut freezes the final shot of his protagonist in *The 400 Blows* (1959), Gardner creates a moment of stasis within a film that is a whirlwind of almost constant movement. This enables us fully to register not only this young man's magnificently chiseled features, but also the vulnerability—and the power—his shining eyes reveal. When his eyes meet the gaze of Gardner's camera, they pierce the facade of his decorated face-turned-mask, transforming it from a spectacle into a picture of a human soul. And when Gardner finds himself moved to linger on this face, the man's eyes, windows to his soul, become a mirror in which the filmmaker finds his own humanity reflected. By following this freeze frame directly with the title "DEEP HEARTS," Gardner underscores the significance of this revelation, especially powerful when he negotiates the tension between stasis and camera movement.

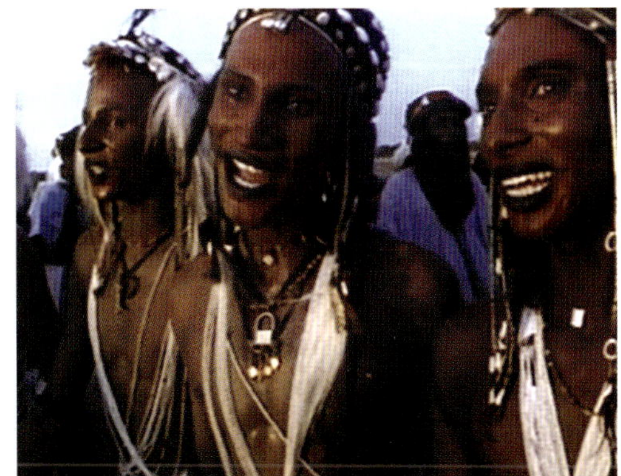

After this compelling opening, Gardner cuts abruptly to a long shot of Wodaabe women walking across the desert carrying bowls of milk on top of their heads. He abruptly cuts again, this time to a shot of bulls running across a field. This conjunction of images anticipates the culmination of the *Gerewol*, when women will choose the winner—the most beautiful man referred to as the "bull." But Gardner's juxtapositions of shots are also unfailingly aesthetically satisfying and emotionally expressive.

"Uniquely," write Ilisa Barbash and Lucien Taylor, Gardner's film work "displays at once a radical commitment to depicting the world as he apprehends it, unfettered by any of the strains of moralism that lie behind the didactic dogmatism that mars much 'educational' filmmaking, and also a commitment to experimenting with cinematic style that stems from an avant-garde tradition."[5] In ways reminiscent of Maya Deren or Stan Brakhage, Gardner often blurs the line between reality and imagination, communicating mainly through dream-like sequences in which the few words he speaks in voice-over are more poetic than literally informative, as when he speaks the words, "Each year [. .] the Bororo Fulani and their beloved cattle converge in great numbers of temporary ponds which catch the uncertain rain between endless dead dunes." Gardner's films feel very intimate, as they not only bring us closer to the world of his camera's subjects, but also to his own feelings. When he dissolves from a shot of raindrops falling into a puddle of water to an extreme close-up of a man's face painted in *doobal* (white dots on face), the combination of the amplified soundtrack of the raindrops with the visual effect of the montage dissolve evokes a haunting melancholy—Gardner's own. It is as if *Deep Hearts* grants us access to the world of the Wodaabe through a continuous subjective point-of-view shot that not only captures what the man behind the camera sees, but also his mood as he is seeing it.

And yet, the camera itself seems to have its own autonomy as it moves, flirts, and dances with the Wodaabe. Gardner's close friend Robert Fulton, who filmed some of the shots in *Deep Hearts*, asserted during an interview in 1973 on Gardner's television program, *Screening Room*, that his camera is an extension of his body and thus it rotates the same way his arm is naturally able to rotate. In doing so, he becomes one with the world he records with his Bolex camera thereby allowing for smooth movements that come naturally to his body. David MacDougall writes in reference to Robert Flaherty and Dziga Vertov, "In their attempts to take the viewer closer to the world of the subject, films had to become part of a larger, three-dimensional imaginative conception, instead of objects to be inspected or windows to be looked through. One of the consequences of this was to acknowledge the importance of the camera's shifts in point of view, in contrast to the ideally static and objective stance of scientific observation."[6]

Gardner's camera assimilates events it films into experiences. In weaving these experiences into a poetic reality, Gardner employs an almost sculptural approach, which gives the illusion of a three-dimensional space in which the camera can freely move. For instance, in one particular *Gerewol* sequence, Gardner's handheld camera moves back and forth between the dancers. Without resorting to editing, this long take makes us feel that we are looking through the filmmaker's eyes. Seven contestants gather and form a line in the center of the surrounding crowd in order to better display themselves. Gardner, who seems to be standing a few inches away from the dancers, rotates his camera in order to offer a panoramic view. It is at this instance that we realize Gardner is encircled by dancers, as well as the Wodaabe observing the performance. The visual contrast between the overwhelming presence of the contestants in the foreground and the figures in the background enhances the illusion of depth.

Gardner's camera flows in rhythm with the nomads' footsteps; it roams as if floating freely, spontaneously, in the air, in a way anticipating Terrence Malick's restless camera in *The Tree of Life* (2011). Even the most ostensibly quotidian activities are presented to us as *tableaux vivants* of intense beauty. The subtlest details are magnified in overwhelming close-ups that reveal these people and their culture in ways words cannot.

Some of the most powerful close-ups in *Deep Hearts* detail the laborious grooming the Wodaabe men go through in preparation for their performances in the *Gerewol*. Gardner's camera does not simply record these preparations; it beholds, inspects, and examines their behavior as they epilate their faces and paint them with *makkara* (saffron colored powder) and *kooya* (red powder). Pampering and above all admiring themselves in tiny pocket mirrors, their gaze fixed on their own reflection, they forget that the camera is observing them.

These brief yet powerful shots vividly convey that these men are insecure and apprehensive as they strive to turn their human faces into beautiful masks. They are psychologically complex individuals with their own "inner lives"—subjects, not mere objects, to Gardner's camera.

We begin to understand from the close-ups that in the *Gerewol*, more than physical beauty is at stake. And it is at this point in the film that Gardner breaks his long silence and says, in voice-over,

> The Bororo invest their remarkable looks with the mystique of beauty and at their rainy season gathering create a spectacle called "*Gerewol*" in which they display themselves and compete for approval as physical and moral specimens. It is known from childhood that they belong

> to an exclusive group and this realization engenders both excessive self-regard and a fear of losing what they have learned to prize. On this account they fall easy prey to envy, which they try to control with a deep heart. They say if their heart is deep, no one can see what it contains and in it they can preserve both their love for themselves and their envy of others.

Hiding their true selves under the mélange of jewelry, accessories, make-up, and exaggerated facial expressions, the Wodaabe endeavor to bury within their "deep hearts" their love of themselves, their envy of others, and their fear of being "devoured" by the mouths and eyes of those around them. And yet, by capturing the suspicious sidewise glances they stealthily shoot each other, as well as the admiring looks they cast at their own images in the mirror, Gardner demonstrates that his camera has the power—and that he harbors the wish—to reveal what they keep hidden in their deep hearts.

In "The Language of Personal Adornment," Mary Ellen Roach and Joanne Bubolz Eicher write:

> Reactions to the three-dimensional, and mobile, presentation of body and dress on the basis of its aesthetic qualities alone are almost impossible; for as human beings receive stimuli they continually process and respond to these stimuli attributing meaning to them. Thus, what is seen may stimulate an aesthetic response, but it also carries a number of other messages, frequently of social and psychological significance.[7]

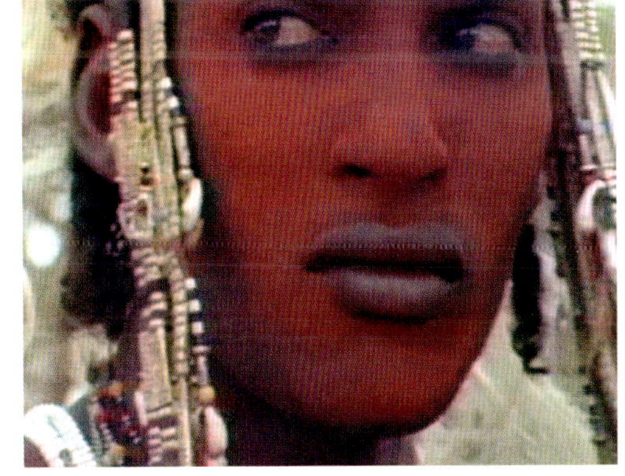

The Wodaabe of Niger consider themselves to be the most beautiful people on earth.[8] The concept of beauty is at the very core of their society. Mette Bovin notes in her book *Nomads Who Cultivate Beauty* that in the Wodaabe language, "*wodi* means beautiful and *woodi* means 'there is, it exists' [. . .] 'to be pretty' and 'to exist' are closely related conditions."[9] Much like consumers in Western society, the Wodaabe are obsessed with their physical appearance. Tom Ferguson wrote for the *Sunday Telegraph*, "[Wodaabe men] spend more time on make-up than Michael Jackson."[10]

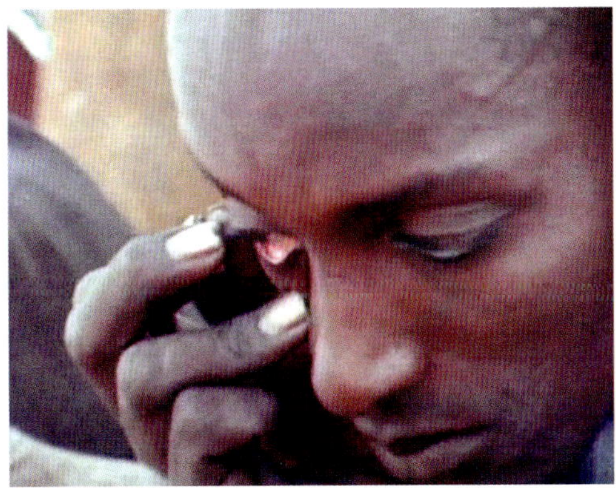

In true Western "metrosexual" form, these men spend several hours every morning in front of the mirror making sure that their mascara (black kohl) is applied perfectly symmetrically—especially surprising given that the Wodaabe earn their livelihood as rustic herders.[11]

In fact, some of Gardner's close-ups of the men resemble fashion spreads featuring men wearing make-up, as in recent print advertisements for Jean Paul Gaultier's *Le Beau Male* make-up collection or other marketing campaigns promoting male cosmetic products.[12]

The Wodaabe believe it is males who are endowed with true beauty much like we regard the male peacock or cardinal as possessors of the most impressive, colorful plumage. According to David Coad, metrosexual men share common denominators that he outlines as narcissism, fetishism, and exhibitionism.[13] The Wodaabe possess all of these characteristics. However, as Peter McAllister notes, "Metrosexuals are renowned for applying traditionally feminine notions of beauty to men; the Wodaabe, by contrast, actually invert them. They consider men, not women, to embody human beauty."[14] Unlike Western standards of masculinity, the Wodaabe culture considers hair, makeup, jewelry, fashion, and other adornment to be male symbols of beauty. Thus, they do not appropriate "feminine notions of beauty," because to them beauty is a masculine concept to begin with.

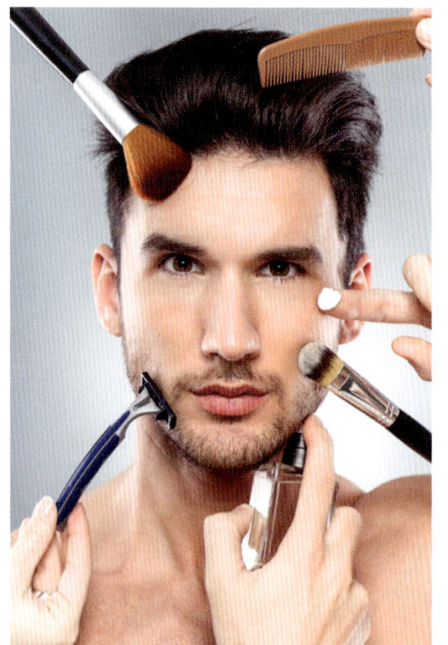

David Buchbinder writes, "Despite the evident belief of many that masculinity and femininity are unchanging and inevitable properties of male and female bodies, respectively, these attributes are in fact culturally specific and historically conditioned. If this were not so men and women could be expected to behave identically everywhere, in all cultures and at all times; but this is not the case, as much historical, anthropological, and sociological research indicates."[15] The Wodaabe are a prime example of the principle that gender may be fluid, an example that has the potential of playing a beneficial role in the ongoing Western discourse on masculinity.

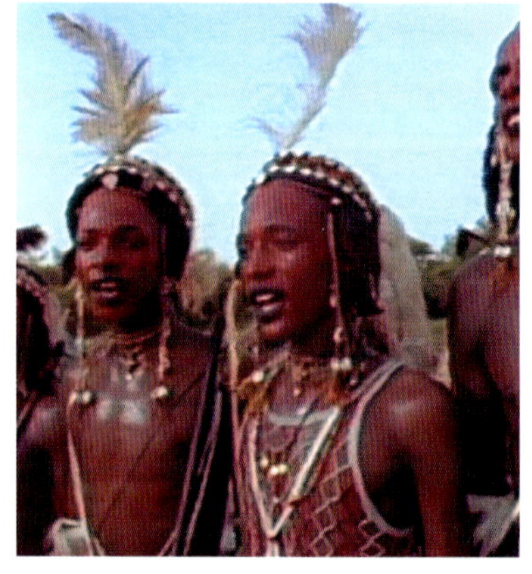

In *Deep Hearts*, the fluid definition and dynamic representation of masculinity are highlighted through the men's fashion. I use the term "fashion" rather than "costume" here to differentiate between clothing and accessories that are adapted according to personal style and taste, and a traditional garment that is historically fixed. As is evident when comparing footage of the Wodaabe's consumption patterns across different decades, their fashions change and evolve over time, much like cyclical Western fashion trends.[16] In general, though, the garb of the dancers in the *Gerewol* could be described as gender-bending, as it incorporates signifiers of both femininity and masculinity. In *Deep Hearts*, the men are wearing long skirts made from women's cloth and adorn themselves with cowrie shells (which symbolically represent the female sexual organs) that are incorporated into their long braided hair.[17] In contrast, their masculine chests are bare and they wear an erect ostrich feather in the middle of their turbans, as if it were a symbol of phallic potency.

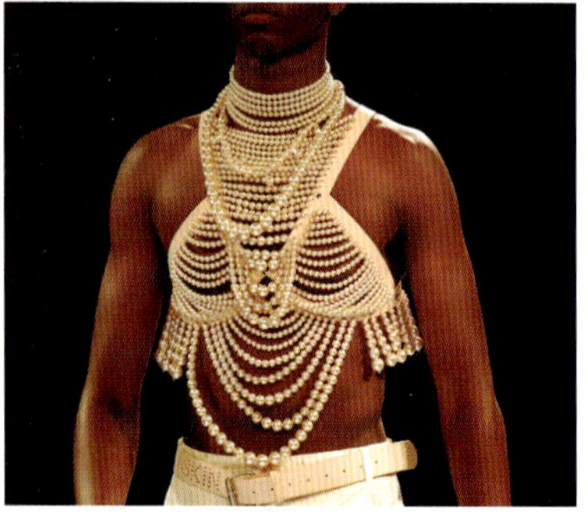

The men's intricate, distinctive style has had an impact on contemporary European and American men's and women's fashion. Recently, Belgian fashion designer Walter Van Beirendonck's Spring/Summer 2012 menswear collection featured a model of African descent wearing a vest made out of strings of white pearls—an androgynous look reminiscent of *Gerewol* garb.[18]

French *haute couture* designer Jean Paul Gaultier also fashioned looks inspired by the Wodaabe men's ornamentation featuring accessories and

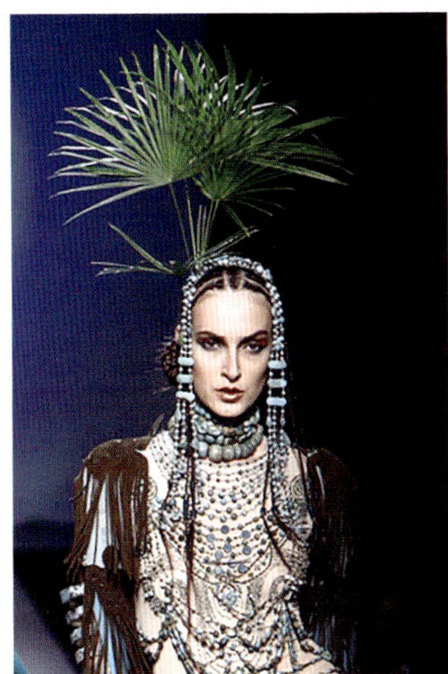

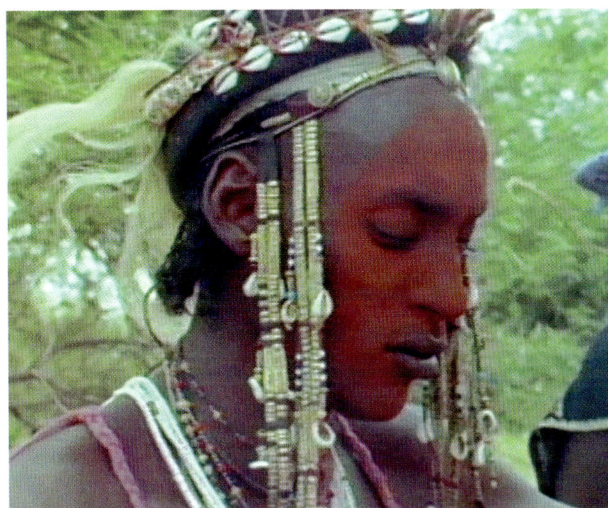

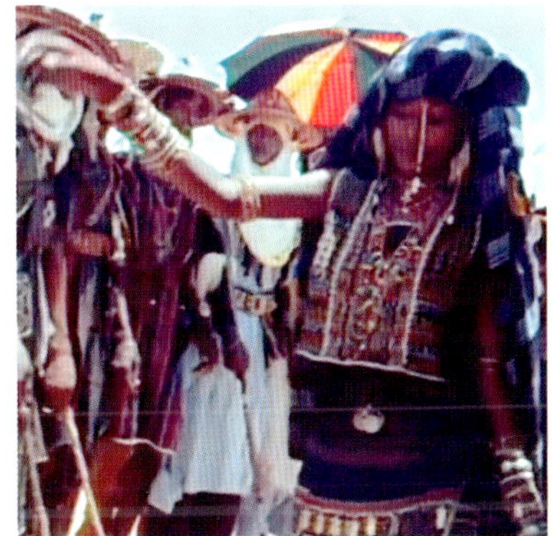

hairstyles, but substituted palm tree leaves for the ostrich plumes. He displayed the African tribal-inspired look during his Spring 2010 women's collection.[19]

Even the renowned *maison de couture* Chanel adapted the *Gerewol* look for their Fall 2011 women's wear collection, drawing inspiration from the multilayered beading effect and head pieces showcased at the ceremonies.

The Wodaabe men, however, are not the only ones gaining the attention of the fashion industry; the women have also become muses to some of the most *au courant* designers. For instance, Nigerian-born fashion designer Duro Olowu (now based in London) drew inspiration from and reinterpreted the oversized, bouffant silhouettes and other tribal motifs of Wodaabe women for his 2011 Spring collection.

While this community of nomads, resented for their hubris by the rest of the Fulani, rejects modern ways of living, its members in many ways behave like conspicuous consumers. Beads, custom jewelry, and embroidered clothes are fetishized commodities that are coveted and venerated, not only as tools of seduction but also to ensure the affirmation of their rank among the Bororo. Much as Westerners assert their social status by donning designer outfits by Louis Vuitton or Gucci, with their emblematic designer initials etched into eyeglasses or buttons and monogrammed into luxury purses, the Wodaabe attempt to gain the admiration of others by paying a great deal of attention to accessorizing their clothing with details as varied as zippers, belt buckles, safety pins, faceless watches, glass beads, and buttons that they acquire when roaming through cities in Niger.[20] These acquisitions are charged objects that can serve a vital purpose for the less physically fortunate. A Wodaabe man who does not meet the tribe's strict standards of beauty can make up for his "ugliness" by having *toggu* (charm). Charm can trump beauty for the Wodaabe.[21] And *toggu* can be achieved by customizing one's looks with accessories.

For the full week of *Gerewol*, the young men dance to display their beauty, charm, and physical prowess. Gardner's handheld camera dances rhythmically with the dancers' footsteps. His dynamic lens moves in and out, pivots, pans across the line of contestants, and provides oblique camera angles that succeed in conveying the physicality of the performance. Sometimes Gardner frames the men in long shots where the contestants are seen standing in rows shoulder-to-shoulder. Across the globe, bodybuilders exhibit their muscular toned bodies at a *Mr. Universe* competition, to demonstrate that they embody the perfect male physical specimen.[22]

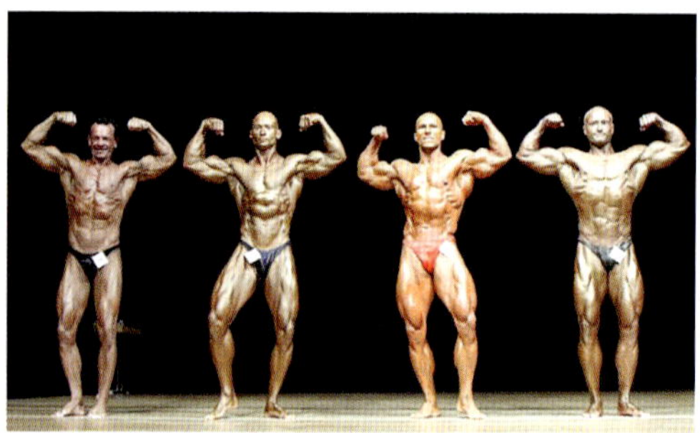

Woodabe dancers show off their masculinity as they jump up and down and raise their herder sticks in the air to display their phallic virility. And unlike the bodybuilders' bulky aesthetic, the ideal Wodaabe male is tall, slim, and symmetrical, with an aquiline nose, large eyes, long hair, thin lips, and white teeth.

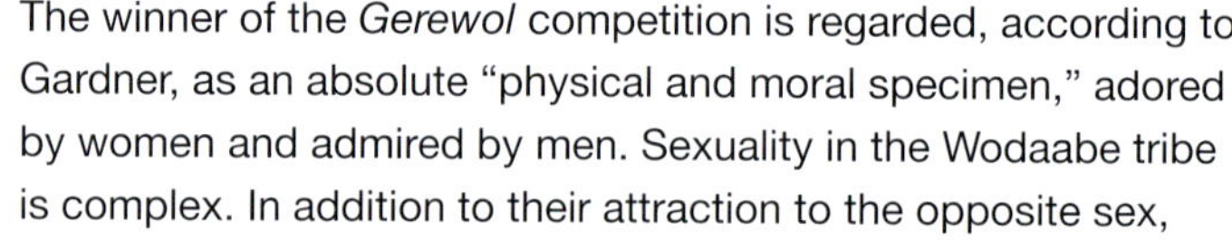

The winner of the *Gerewol* competition is regarded, according to Gardner, as an absolute "physical and moral specimen," adored by women and admired by men. Sexuality in the Wodaabe tribe is complex. In addition to their attraction to the opposite sex, there exists a homoerotic fascination at play within their male-to-male physical idolization. According to Mette Bovin, "Wodaabe teenagers have a relatively free sexual life before marriage [. . .] Cousins [of the same-sex] often sit very close together, on the same mat, arm in arm, and even knee to knee, or lie down close to one another on the mat."[23] Because only unmarried young men are permitted to participate in the *Gerewol*, the ritual can be seen as a transitional rite of passage in which same-sex and heterosexual desire converge. In Western culture, this sort of homosocial desire, propelled by an appreciation of male beauty by men, shades into the homoerotic as well, and can be traced back to ancient Greece. Peter McAllister writes,

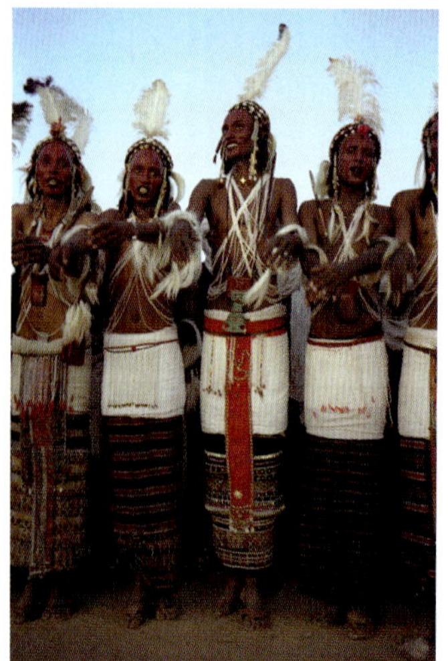

> Athletes were worshipped sexually to such a degree, in fact, that some sportsmen attracted hordes of love-struck gay groupies. Socrates, for example, described the chaos when the handsome young athlete Charmides attended the gymnasium: "Amazement and confusion reigned when he entered; and a troop of lovers followed him."[24]

The homoerotic admiration for male athletes is still at play today, as is evident by the proliferation of men's magazine covers and provocative underwear advertisements featuring David Beckham directed toward male consumers. Beckham can be perceived as the European equivalent to the Wodaabe "bull," as his public persona is glorified and admired by men, not only for his athletic accomplishment but for his physical appeal.[25]

In *Black Looks*, bell hooks claims that the contemporary drag balls in Jennie Livingston's documentary *Paris is Burning* (1990) "have the aura of sports events."[26] Livingston's documentary may seem at first to be representing a culture the polar opposite of that in Gardner's film. However, some commonalities exist between them that are worth exploring.

Paris is Burning chronicles the drag ball culture of New York City in which the African American and Latino LGBT community engage in a competition of "fierceness" (including charm) and "realness" (beauty). Much like the *Gerewol*, in which two rival clans compete over beauty, the drag balls involve two dueling "houses" (also called "families") that face off against each other in front of their community with the hope of winning the coveted ball trophy and becoming "legendary" in their "tribe." This American subculture competes based on physical agility, beauty, and attitude in categories that fluctuate between established norms of masculinity and femininity. For instance, entries such as "Butch Queen Vogue Femme," "Butch Queen in Pumps," or even "Masculine Executive Realness" are listed in the evening's competition program. Men may "walk" the ballroom runway dressed as business executives, while swinging their hips like fashion models on the catwalk, while others may "act macho" while wearing six-inch Manolo Blahnik stiletto heels. Similar to the Bororo at whom the other Fulani look askance—they are social outcasts in a sense—ball culture's accoutrements and customs propose that the *masculine* can be *feminine* and vice versa. Makeup, skirts, and jewelry then become genderless.

Ballroom contestants prance, pose, and dance in order to "battle it out" in front of their community, displaying their extravagant fashions. This impulse parallels the Wodaabe's competitive rituals where dance is like war, or a ritual battle.[27] "Voguing," a pacific form of "throwing shade" (fighting) in which dancers contort and pose with attitude, as if modeling for the cover of a fashion magazine, is the ritual dance of the "houses." (This dance genre became a mainstream phenomenon when Madonna appropriated it for her video *Vogue*.) Livingston's camera follows the fierce competitors as they walk across the stage, twirl, and sashay away. Both the Woodabe dancers and the ballroom competitors line up and await the final verdict at the end of the competition. Unlike the Wodaabe men, who may be rewarded with a bride and tribal acknowledgment, the prize awarded to ball dancers is an ornate sporting trophy and street credibility.

While *Paris is Burning*'s subject matter resonates with that of *Deep Hearts*, the two differ significantly in that Livingston does not allow her own subjectivity to be perceived as an influence in the shaping of her film. bell hooks claims,

> Jennie Livingston approaches her subject matter as an outsider looking in. Since her presence as white woman/lesbian filmmaker is "absent" from *Paris is Burning,* it is easy for viewers to imagine that they are watching an ethnographic film documenting the life of black gay "natives" and not recognize that they are watching a work shaped and formed by a perspective and standpoint specific to Livingston.[28]

Gardner's presence, on the other hand, is strongly felt throughout his film, as the camera seems to translate what he is feeling. Livingston's close-up shots in the ballroom sequences might be comparable to the *Gerewol* sequences, but they lack the sense of intimacy Gardner's camera engenders. While *Deep Hearts* features a multitude of full-frontal close-ups, *Paris is Burning*'s close-ups are mainly framed as profile views of the performers. Livingston's side-view close-ups never grant us access to her subjects' deep hearts. Because most of these close-ups occur during the ballroom scenes, where the contestants are performing

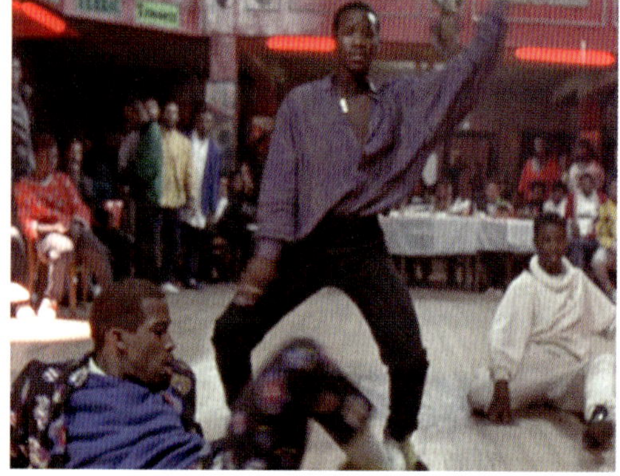

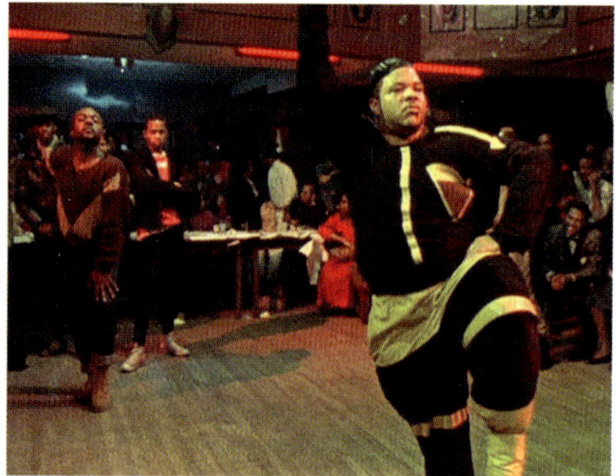

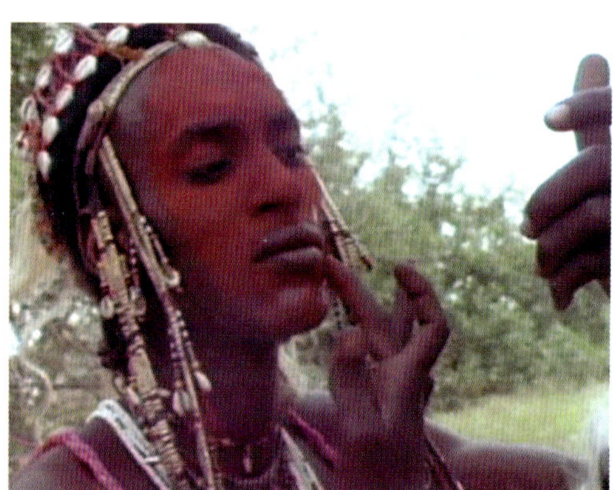

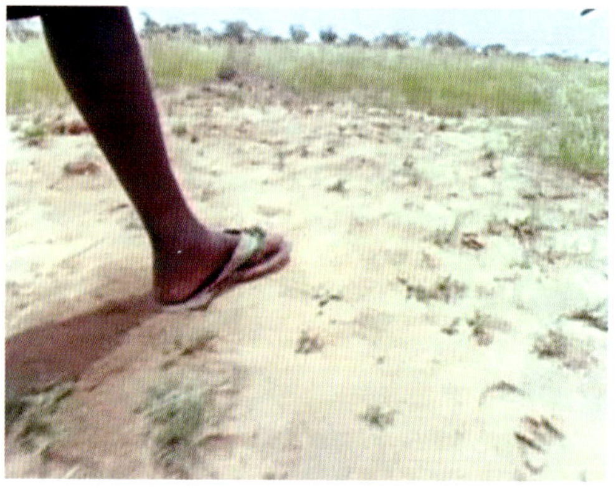

realness, a version of others' realities, Livingston's film creates barriers between the spectator and the world of the film, whereas Gardner's film breaks down such barriers.

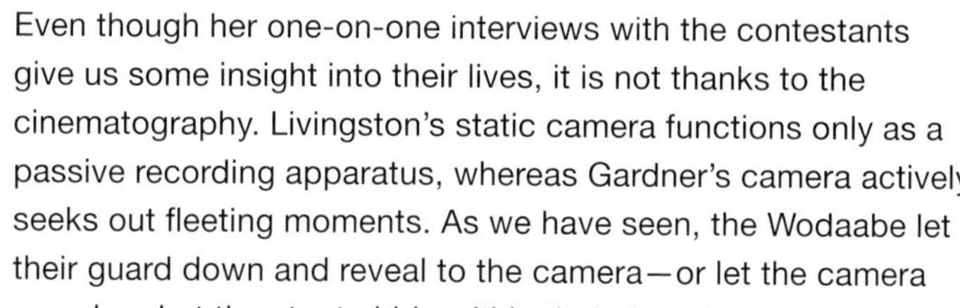

Even though her one-on-one interviews with the contestants give us some insight into their lives, it is not thanks to the cinematography. Livingston's static camera functions only as a passive recording apparatus, whereas Gardner's camera actively seeks out fleeting moments. As we have seen, the Wodaabe let their guard down and reveal to the camera—or let the camera reveal—what they try to hide within their deep hearts.

Deep Hearts is not a detached ethnographic film, but a personal film. In fact, it is, in Rothman's words, Gardner's "humanity, what he has in common with the 'others' he films and with us, that gives him standing to speak."[29] Gardner manifests his empathy, for example, when filming the Woodabe women. He often intercuts shots of the men grooming themselves with shots of women working. The women are seen milking cows, cooking, cleaning, and transporting milk and water to refresh the dancers. The camera follows them as they go about their quotidian chores. Gardner films these scenes with a certain heaviness that emphasizes the hardship of the women's diurnal labor. Gardner films the women in real time, utilizing long takes. With great patience, his camera follows every small, arduous step until they reach their destination. For added emphasis, Gardner points his camera directly toward the sun, giving us a sense of the debilitating extreme heat these women have to endure in performing tasks that nurture their families.

During the *Gerewol* ceremony, however, the mood shifts as the women prepare to take charge of their own destinies by choosing the man they deem to be the most perfect mate. Gardner changes the tone and alters the pace by using quicker cuts to convey the growing excitement of the *suboybe* ("choosers"), each about to decide whether she will go on a romantic escapade with a man of her choice or even leave her present husband to marry the man she finds more beautiful.[30]

Gardner frames the finale of the *Gerewol* ceremony with dramatic camera angles that reinforce the intensity associated with picking the winner of this weeklong contest. Three striking young women selected to choose the "bull" are presented to us in a low angle profile shot. Their right arms swinging in the direction of the row of dancers, one by one the *suboybe* slowly approach their preferred mate. In the next shot, one of the *suboybe* is shown in the foreground as she faces the line of men in the background. The woman is shown on the left side of the frame, occupying a larger portion of the screen than the men. She appears taller and in control of the selection ritual, in a position of dominance as, indeed, she is.

When the next *suboybe* approaches the contestants, Gardner provides us with a close shot of her arm swaying back and forth toward the men. It is as if the camera has become one with this woman. Just as she is about to make her final selection, Gardner noticeably slows down the speed of frames per second, to emphasize this charged moment.

a	b
c	d
e	f

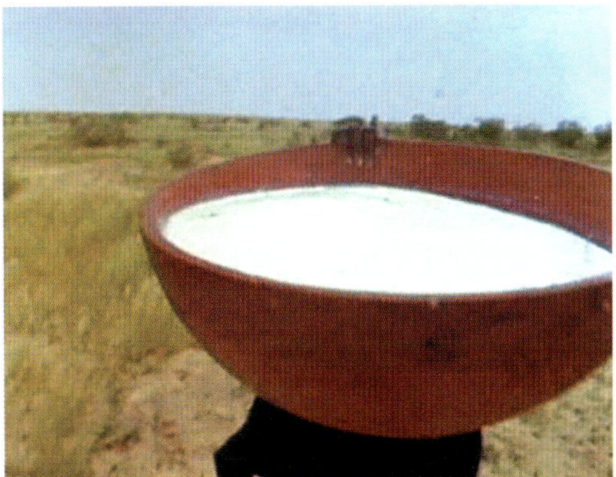

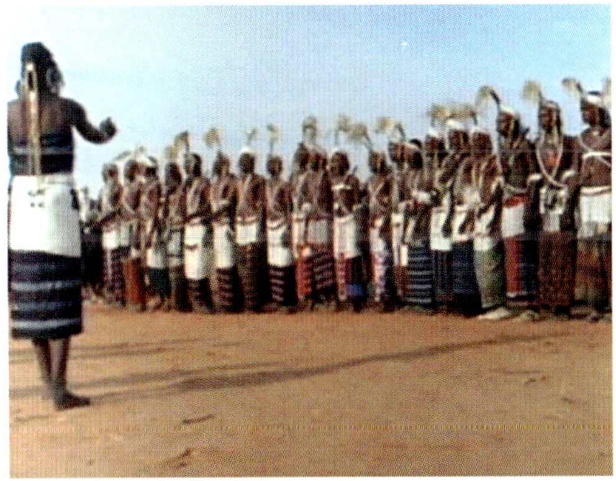

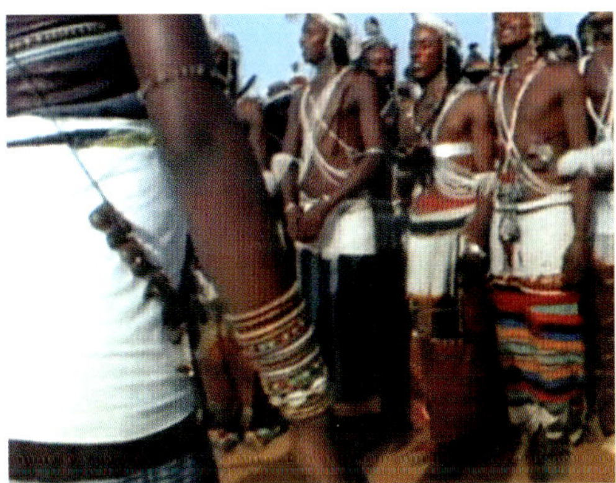

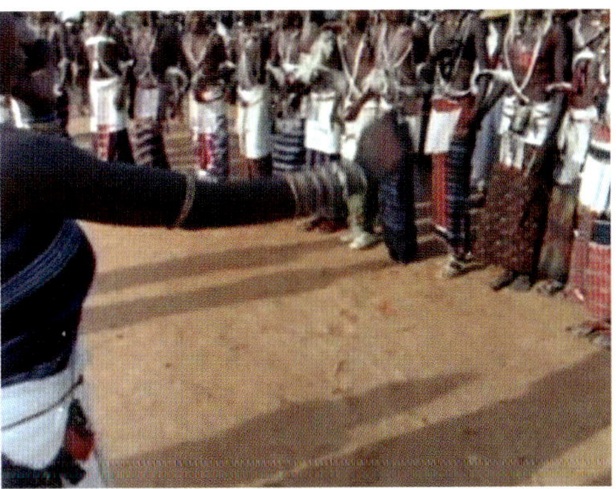

Once the winner is selected, the camera singles him out, and Gardner reprises the freeze-frame effect he employed in the film's opening, as jubilant chanting and shouts of victory are heard in the background. Without warning, Gardner now cuts abruptly to a slow-motion

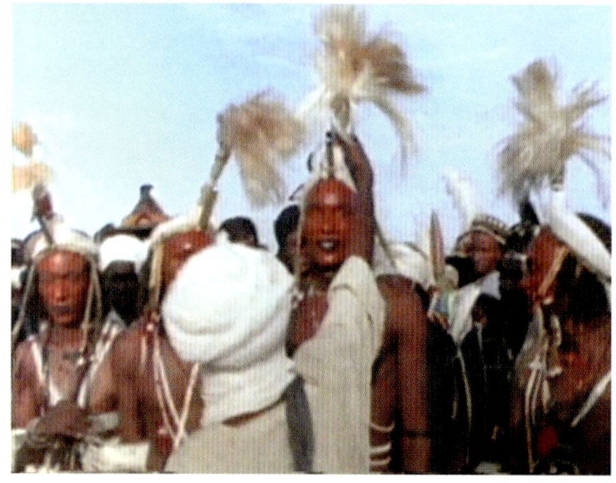

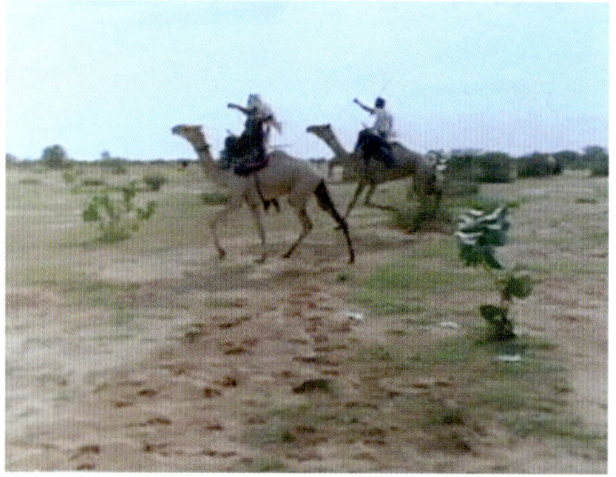

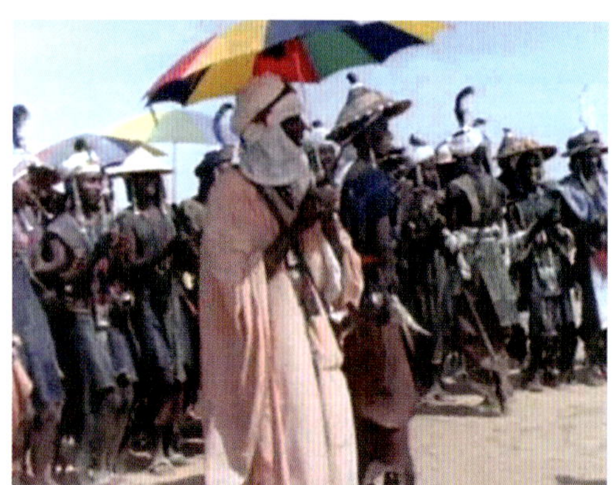

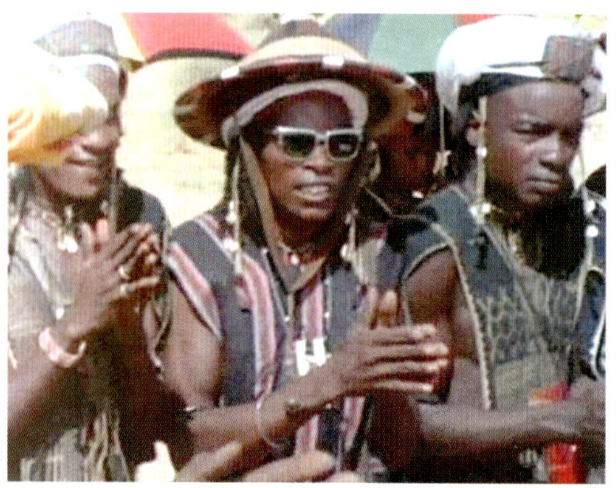

extreme long shot of nomads riding camels into the desert. No sounds at all accompany the shot. Yet this silence carries the same intensity as the chants in the previous scene. This very brief moment transcends reality, or makes reality itself appear unreal, as if we are seeing a world suspended in time. It seems at first that this radical cut from such a jubilant celebration must be a mistake. However, the sharp contrast demands our attention, punctuating the significance of the ceremony by contrasting it with the stillness of the silence.

As the Wodaabe clans bid farewell to each other, Gardner takes one last look at them. He moves his handheld camera back and forth noticing the men's garments. The shaky movements seem random at first, but then it becomes clear that the camera is singling out, one after another, particular possessions of the Wodaabe: sunglasses, manufactured rubber shoes, plastic rings, colorful umbrellas. By emphasizing such material possessions, Gardner is subtly making the point that even the Wodaabe, a people deeply rooted in their traditions and cultural heritage, have succumbed to the allure of mass-produced artifacts of our material culture that signal the by-products of globalization, emphasizing that in the global macrocosm, there is no "other."

Culturally, Robert Gardner could hardly be more different from the Wodaabe. And yet, as a descendant of a wealthy "Boston Brahmin" family, he could almost have been considered an honorary Wodaabe, insofar as he possesses similar strong tribal connections to his own clan. What we imagine to be a proper New England upbringing, where pride and ostentation are frowned on, however, stands in opposition to the self-indulgent social rituals of the Wodaabe. It is because of this stark contrast between the filmmaker and his subject that, after viewing *Deep Hearts*, we find ourselves wondering who Robert Gardner really was. Through the process of filmmaking, I believe Gardner attempts to answer this question for himself. The introspective process of making films allowed him to observe, analyze, and discover how he felt about the world and his place and role in it.

The intuitive fluidity with which he and his camera lovingly, sensitively, and fiercely interacted with the Wodaabe, suggests that he felt an intimate kinship with them. Perhaps Gardner's own "natural" reserve is a facade, like their painted faces and exaggerated expressions, to keep others from looking into his deep heart, the metaphysical space in which he hid his true feelings, as they do, from the eyes of those he feared might devour him—figuratively speaking. And perhaps when he was hidden behind the camera, filming these men, he could safely reveal his true feelings by opening his own deep heart—and theirs—without fear of being devoured.

Notes

1. Charles Warren, "The Music of Robert Gardner," in *The Cinema of Robert Gardner*, eds. Ilisa Barbash and Lucien Taylor (Oxford: Berg, 2007), 17.
2. Sarah Pink, *The Future of Visual Anthropology: Engaging the Senses* (London and New York: Routledge, 2006), 46.
3. Ibid.
4. William Rothman, *The "I" of the Camera: Essays in Film Criticism, History, and Aesthetics, Second Edition*, Cambridge Studies in Film. (Cambridge and New York: Cambridge University Press, 2004), xx.
5. *The Cinema of Robert Gardner*, 8.
6. David MacDougall, *The Corporeal Image: Film, Ethnography, and the Senses* (Princeton, NJ: Princeton University Press, 2006), 238.
7. Mary Ellen Roach and Joanne Bubolz Eicher, "The Language of Personal Adornment," in *The Fabrics of Culture: The Anthropology of Clothing and Adornment*, eds. Justine M. Cordwell and Ronald A. Schwarz (The Hague and New York: Mouton, 1973), 8.
8. Mette Bovin, *Nomads Who Cultivate Beauty: Wodaabe Dances and Visual Arts in Niger* (Uppsala, Sweden: Nordiska Afrikainstitutet, 2001), 15.
9. Ibid.
10. Tom Ferguson, "Out TV Choice this Week," *Sunday Telegraph*, July 24, 1988.
11. Ibid.
12. Getty images. Reproduced by permission of IStock Photo.
13. David Coad, *The Metrosexual: Gender, Sexuality, and Sport* (Albany: State University of New York Press, 2008).
14. Peter McAllister, *Manthropology: The Science of the Inadequate Modern Male* (Sydney: Hachette, 2009), 194.
15. David Buchbinder, *Studying Men and Masculinities* (London and New York: Routledge, 2012), 4.
16. *Nomads Who Cultivate Beauty*, 35.
17. Ibid., 41.
18. Walter Van Beirendonck Spring–Summer 2012 "Read My Skin Collection," Dan Lecca.
19. Jean Paul Gaultier Spring–Summer 2010 Collection. Photo used by permission of Jelka Music.
20. Bovin, *Nomads Who Cultivate Beauty*, 69.
21. Ibid., 39, 42.
22. Bodybuilding *Mr. Universe* Competition (public domain).
23. Ibid., 69.
24. McAllister, *Manthropology*, 210.
25. Ibid., 187–218.
26. bell hooks, *Black Looks: Race and Representation* (Boston: South End Press, 1992), 148.
27. *Nomads Who Cultivate Beauty*, 69.
28. *Black Looks*, 151.
29. Rothman, "Dancing with Gardner," in *The Cinema of Robert Gardner*, 137.
30. Bovin, *Nomads Who Cultivate Beauty*, 48.

Chapter 17
Film, Matter, and Spirit: *Forest of Bliss*

Richard Allen

Everything in the world is eater or eaten, the seed is food and fire is eater.

—W. B. Yeats

Forest of Bliss (1986) is a documentary film that takes place within the holy city of Varanasi (formerly Benares) and, more specifically, on the *ghats* of the city, the steps that lead down to the water on the banks of the river Ganges. There, we see how the bodies of the dead, dressed in fresh cloth and bedecked with flowers, are brought to the Ganges for purification before being cremated in the holy fire that will help the soul on its way into the next stage of life's journey in rebirth. Gardner "documents" some of these ritual practices and the specific kinds of labor they involve. He also takes special care to show the labor that allows them to exist, such as the cutting, transportation, and weighing of firewood; the creation of bamboo "ladders" that support the transportation of corpses; the passage of bodies through the streets; the gathering, sorting, and transportation of marigolds; the acts of worship, devotion, and purification that make possible the passage of the soul; as well as the more banal and venal aspects of corpse disposal.

However, Gardner's intention in *Forest of Bliss* is far from that of orthodox ethnography that seeks to explain to the audience what it is we see and hear. There is no voice-over narration in the film nor is there any translation of the isolated instances of conversation the camera records. Gardner's camera is obviously highly selective in what it chooses to show and not show. The film focuses on only three individuals at any length, and only one of these is directly associated with the activities of cremation and burial. The actions of the central figure in the film, whom Gardner later revealed in his book *Making of Forest of Bliss* to be a faith healer, Mithai Lal, are often inscrutable and opaque to the viewer.[1]

Gardner seems purposively mystifying and elliptical in revealing the physical and social landscape, showing us only fragments of activities, and forcing us to try to infer what is taking place on screen.

At the same time, in *Forest of Bliss*, events and incidents that might seem to be peripheral to any sober ethnography of burial rituals take on great significance or weight. The sounds and images of boats moving on the water are prominent in the film. The sequences involving wood barges are partially justified by the theme, but their prominence is not immediately explicable. Most mysterious are the images of boats that are collecting and transporting dirt or sand. Searching for an explanation, we might initially think this sand is the residue of cremation, yet the size and scope of the activity defies such an explanation. We are simply watching the transportation of sand from one side of the river to the other. Other activities that are depicted are merely those that take place in the vicinity. For example, we return periodically to images of kites, kite flying, and to the children who play with them. Their activities have nothing directly to do with the subject matter at hand. Special attention is paid to animals: oxen, stray dogs, and birds. Most controversially, perhaps, the film contains a lexicon of sometimes savage images of death, putrefaction, dirt and feces, both animal and human, which seem to give an unseemly and arbitrary weight to the most unpleasant aspect of the environment.

All these motifs of the film were subject to criticism on the film's release, which fell broadly into two sometimes overlapping camps. Anthropologists censured the film for its explanatory opacity, selectivity, and apparent arbitrariness. The film was deemed to fail an implied set of professional standards of objectivity required of the "ethnographic film."[2] For others, such as Jay Ruby, the criticism was more directly moral and political: the film rendered its subject mystifying and exotic, determinedly "other" in the manner of the orientalizing gaze criticized by Edward Said.[3] However, it seems to me that if we are to analyze the film's limitations, we must first grasp its achievements, which, by and large, its army of detractors determinedly failed to do. Thus, one of Gardner's most vociferous critics, Jay Ruby, dismisses the film as "a jumble of incomprehensible vignettes that are apparently made to be savored for their formal content."[4] In this chapter, I set out to understand *Forest of Bliss* on its own terms. I argue that *Forest of Bliss* is a profound work of documentary art in the way that its form and style express its meaning. Gardner's film brings to bear the full stylistic arsenal of film upon elements of actuality in order to create an experience for the spectator that is akin to ritual, where banal facts of quotidian life are perceived as expressions of spirit, or of a higher transcendent time. In this way, as a film, *Forest of Bliss* enacts the ways of being that it strives to represent.

Form and Structure

In formal terms, *Forest of Bliss* is structured as a day in the life of a city, along the lines of "City Symphony" films like *Berlin: Symphony of the City* (1927) or *A Bronx Morning* (1931). This is a very loose template on which to organize the events we see. In Gardner's film the sun rising and setting frames the narration. Some events that begin the film clearly take place in the morning, such as the ritual bathing in the Ganges and morning *puja*. Other events, echoing the film's opening, clearly take place toward the end of the day, such as the evening prayers. However, other than these clear-cut markers, what we see and when in the film takes place according to an indirect mode of narration that gradually reveals to the viewer, and then only partially, the character and nature of ritual cremation activities that take place on the banks of the river. The various activities that make the cremation possible—collection and transportation of wood and marigolds, weighing wood on scales, the making of the bamboo biers, and the transportation of bodies through the streets—while elliptically introduced, are gradually shown to converge on the ghats themselves and what takes place there. Gardner has rationalized this strategy as having the audience "find their feet" in the environment in a manner that is akin to what an anthropologist is required to do: "Why all this ambiguity and mystery about these things called simple elements?" Gardner asks. "I thought the audience would not simply wait for the mysteries to be dispelled but would come up with their own solutions, supply their own answers, and so, in that way, they would be doing their own anthropology." He goes on to say, "I would be content if they merely registered the facts: fires, scales, boys, kites, thermals. I'm confident they would then, at some level of their imagination, work out their meaning."[5]

In the middle section of the film, a series of events on the river's banks that are given extended treatment situates us more concretely. We visit a hospice for the dying where the elderly are blessed with holy water. A body on a bamboo ladder is carefully dressed for cremation with a brightly colored pink sheet and marigolds, after a stone courtyard has been cleaned and purified with water from the Ganges. On the ghat where the cremations take place, corpses arrive for burial on bamboo biers overseen by the owner of the ghat. A boat is blessed with an elaborate *puja* ceremony as, in the background, a corpse is brought down to the river. Finally, having been introduced to the burning corpses elliptically and only in the background of shots, we directly perceive an open cremation 68 minutes into the film. This shot forms a dramatic climax to the work. It is followed by a series of scenes that anticipate a sense of closure. Jewelry remnants taken from the corpses are sorted in the evening light, water is broken on the fires, embers slowly die, boats drift on the water, mysterious prayerful incantations are performed to the mother goddess in half light, children fly kites and play, and finally an evening *puja* is offered to the Ganges.

Further unity is given to the work through the appearance of three people who are introduced in the opening sequences and recur throughout the work, though they are not identified by name in the film. All three characters are filmed by the River Ganges and help to give that location a preeminent place in the film through the personal connection they forge with it. Furthermore, all three characters have a self-conscious sense of themselves as engaged in a public performance: they are all figures who preside over rituals within the film. Since they are also all, in their different ways, clearly conscious of their role in front of the camera and because their presence pervades the film, they also seem to preside over the film in a manner that contributes to our sense that *Forest of Bliss* is a film that participates in the rituals it depicts.

One of these characters is Mithai Lal, a stooped, wizened old man, whom we are first introduced to as he walks gingerly down the steps of a ghat to do his morning *puja* for the mother goddess. Gardner amplifies the sound of his grunting, coughing, and belching in a manner that gives us a distinctive sense of intimacy with the character's physical existence, his mortality. Twice in the film, Gardner juxtaposes him with human corpses floating in the river, and Mithai Lal seems to inhabit the twilight and dark recesses within the world of the film. Mithai Lal is a "low" earthy character, playful, perhaps even cunning, whose charisma is evident in later scenes that depict, in a darkened cave-like interior, what seem to be *puja* rituals and incantations to the mother goddess in front of a rapt largely female audience. In fact, he is a faith healer who allows himself to be possessed by the goddess Ganga in order to intercede with her on behalf of his clients.[6] Mithai Lal's possession appears as a kind of performance that is manifest in his intense and seemingly random bursts of laughter that Gardner refers to as his "cosmic cackle."[7] Gardner augments our apprehension of Mithai Lal's possession-performance by depicting his looming, leering shadow on the wall in the half-light, like a playful demon or a trickster, who compels us, like the audience within the film, with his strange fascination.

The second character is an uncouth, obese man, identified by Gardner in his book as the Dom Raja, whom we initially peer at through the darkened opening of his house as he lies on his belly smoking a cigarette while a woman in the interior massages his back. Later, we see him entertaining potential clients as they huddle in front of him at a respectful distance. During the course of the film, it emerges that he is in charge of a ghat where the cremations are performed and extracts payments from his clients, argues with mourners, and most disconcertingly, through his minions, garners jewelry and remnants of personal effects from the burned corpses. He is evidently a relatively rich man with an overweening sense of self-importance. He squats, eating, in his pavilion overlooking the ghat, attentively observing the goings on, like a feudal lord surveying his kingdom. His mortality, too, is registered as we watch in discomfort as he receives his daily injection. As with Mithai Lal, though more so, our perception of the Dom Raja is framed by Gardner's camera. He is introduced via the pealing of bells that announce the morning *puja*, and, equally, announce his entry into the film. His house is introduced by the low angle shot of a statue of a tiger circled by birds of prey, and accompanied by the sound of a barking dog. Later, he is surrounded by caged birds. In the context of the imagery that defines the film, he is framed as a predator.[8]

The final character is less sharply defined. He is evidently a pandit, identified by Gardner in his book as Ragul Pandit, and a figure of some gravitas and authority whom we initially perceive saying his morning prayers by the banks of the Ganges. Late in the film, we see him carefully, ritually, dressing himself against the light of the setting sun in preparation for evening *puja*. Lean and erect, there is an evident self-possession and self-control about this man, a sense of calm authority, and Gardner treats his actions with a certain respectful detachment, as if seeking to bestow on his own work the qualities he admires in the person he films. The pandit tends to be filmed from the side and from behind rather than from the front. As befits his status as a pandit, he is a figure who is associated with light rather than darkness, thereby forming both a parallel and contrast to Mithai Lal. Toward the conclusion of the film, Ragul Pandit is compared to an animal; an erect white dog calmly observes its surroundings as the pandit wraps himself in his white loin cloth. And the pandit, too, is revealed as vulnerable, mortal, as the sun shining through the translucent cloth reveals to the audience his skin and his genitals.

Sound and Montage

As my comments on form and character already suggest, stylistically speaking, *Forest of Bliss* is constructed as a cinematic montage that attends to every element of shot style, mise-en-scène, and sound whether discovered or imposed, and to the way in which shots and sounds are combined through editing, in order to create meaning and expressive significance from the assembled elements. However, the art of *Forest of Bliss* resides not simply in a set of formal and stylistic operations through which meaning is created or expressivity is engendered, as if these elements were added on as a supplement to "actuality," as ornament is attached to a building. If we are to get to the heart of this film, we need to understand how what the film is about, its subject matter, actually comes to be expressed through its form and style. Initially, rather than characterize this achievement in summary form, I examine in detail the first eleven shots of the film, which form a prologue. These shots not only cue us to the representational and expressive role of montage, but to the distinctive imagery that governs the film, in a manner that serves to frame the way in which we receive and understand the film's more conventional sequences of dramatic action, including the representation of the film's three central characters.

Gardner's use of sound is central to the aesthetic achievement of *Forest of Bliss* and indicative of his overall approach to cinematic montage. Customary sound-practice organizes our perception of sound relative to what we see in the image, such that distant objects sound softer and near objects sound louder. However, in the opening shot of the film this hierarchy, which subordinates sound to image, is purposely undercut. In a hazy brown and beige telephoto image the camera tracks left to right a scrawny dog trotting along the sandy wasteland in front of some birds.

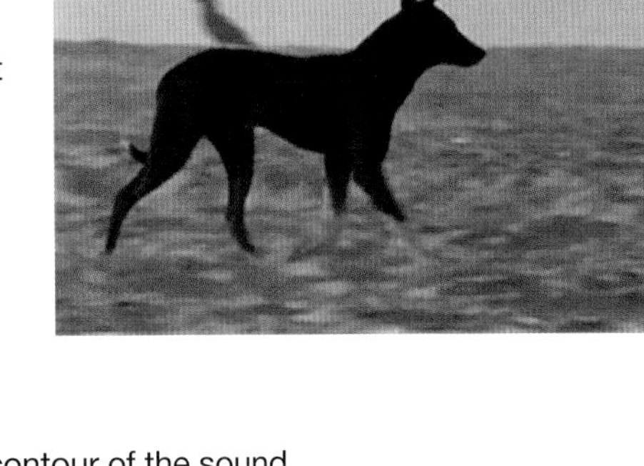

The telephoto shot registers a distance that is uncannily compounded when the dog turns its head as if in response to the camera's gaze, of which it cannot be aware. Even before seeing this dog, we hear the cawing of a bird and the sound of bells, which we might intimate to be ritual bells, and then as the dog emerges into view, we hear, very loudly, the pat-pat-pat of its feet on the sand in counterpoint to the sound of the bells.

Through the manipulation of shot distance relative to sound in this opening shot, Gardner declares his strategy of amplifying sound into an "aural close-up." While a visual close-up brings the object nearer, the effect of an aural close-up is to make the sound contour itself more "present" to the ear. Rather than simply naturalizing the sound in what it is we see, we attend to the aural contour of the sound itself, its texture, timbre, and rhythm, as a sensory variable, a sound-entity.[9] The way we hear the "pat-pat-pat" of the dog's feet as the crunching of sand granules evokes a sense of tactile immediacy, a sensory immersion in the world of matter.

At the same time, through the amplification of sound, we are required to attend to the relationship that sound bears to the image as an independent variable in an audiovisual montage. The sound of the dog's feet appears to be partly, like the bells, added to the image. Our immersion in the actuality of sound is thus equally an immersion into the imaginative world of the film in its expressive and representational registers. The sound of the bells enters into semantic conflict with the image, the sublime versus the banal, the spiritual versus the material, that helps bestow on this opening shot an aura of profound melancholy. But the sound of the bells, the crunching sand, and the image of the dog also form a unified sound-image, where the sublime appears co-extensive with the quotidian banality of matter. This opposition in unity is precisely made possible by film, in its capacity to render actuality mediated by thought—here embodied in Gardner's sound-montage.

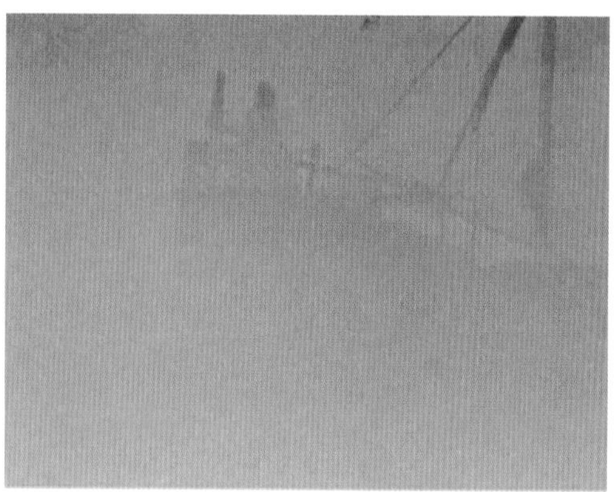

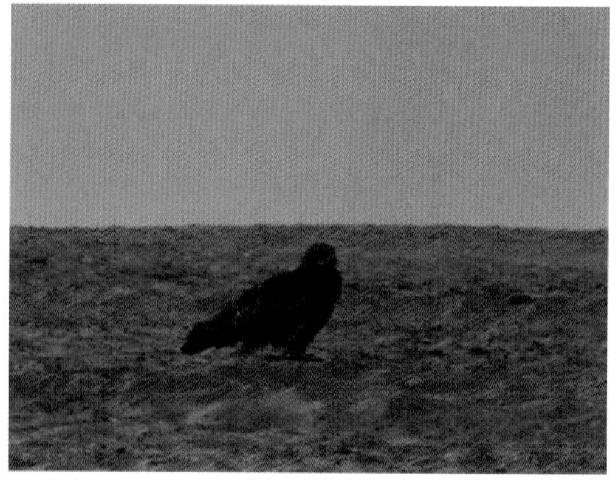

In the second shot, which is echoed in the fourth shot, we perceive through telephoto, in a misty blue haze, a boat on the Ganges moving left to right, its oars loudly and rhythmically dipping in the water.

The mist, here and elsewhere, conveys in a rather obvious way a sense of mystery: our attempt to decipher what we see through the mist prompts our reflection on the effort of understanding that this film is going to invite from the spectator. Between the bluish shots of the boat, in beige, we see a large bird on the sand, perhaps a bird of prey—linked to the earlier image of the dog (itself preceded by the cawing of a bird) in the way the shot is composed, including the brief look that the bird makes toward the camera.

Here, the montage construction of the opening sound-image is carried over to the juxtaposition of images themselves. The image montage suggests beige versus blue, soil versus sky, the concrete versus the ethereal. The contrast further suggests the juxtaposition of the earthly, the animalistic and predatory, with the sublime, the spiritual, and the eternal, as the ethereal boats effortlessly glide on the flowing water of the Ganges. This connotation is underscored by the continuing sound of bells, now accompanied by the calm lapping of the oars in the water, all contributing to a sense of transcendent serenity. Birds are a pervasive, though not intrusive, presence in the opening sequence on land, and then fluttering about the sky around the boats, and heard alongside the bells on the sound track. They suggest here, as elsewhere in the film, a figure of mediation between earth and air, the predatory and the transcendent. The direction of the gaze of both bird and dog, together with the movement of animals and boats from left to right, gives a unity and a forward momentum to the sequence, underscored by the continuity of tempo that is marked by the pat-pat-pat of the dog's feet and the rhythmic movement of the oars in the water.

With the sound of bells and birds continuing in the background, the sound of oars dipping in water forms a bridge between the shot of the boat gliding in the blue haze to an earthy beige image, in long telephoto shot, of men in the foreground carrying what appears to be sand from boats moored behind them. Gardner then cuts to a shot, bathed in blue, of a boy holding a kite that we don't see.

The image of the boy gazing upward to the heavens is thus linked stylistically to the hazy shots of the boats. But when he starts running across the sand, the pat-pat-pat o zf his feet on the ground echoes the early sounds of the dog, and links him back to the earth and the animal. Via a sound-bridge of the pat-pat-pat of the boy's feet, Gardner then cuts to the sun, as if through montage the boy, in a God-like gesture, pulls a red sun up out of the haze, thereby bringing into being the life-cycle of the day as the narrator brings into being the life-cycle of the film. The sun-kite floats in the sky like the boats on the river, evoking a holistic universe.

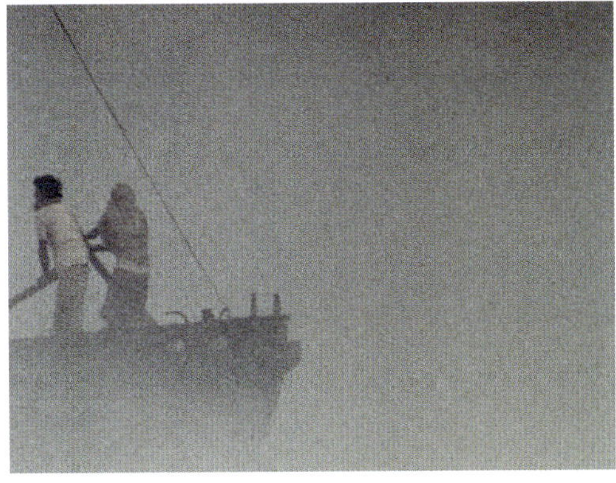

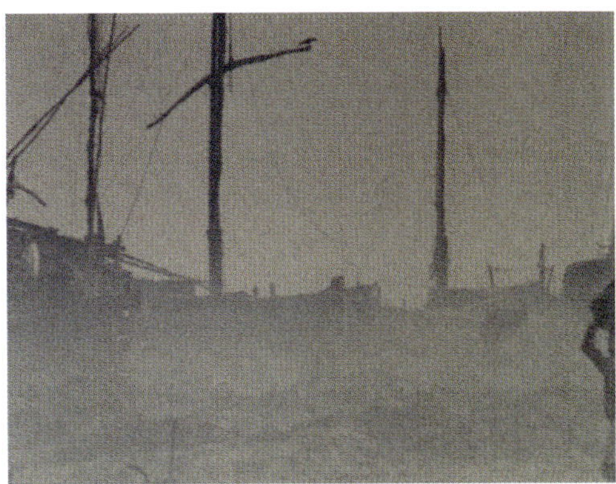

a	b
c	d
	e

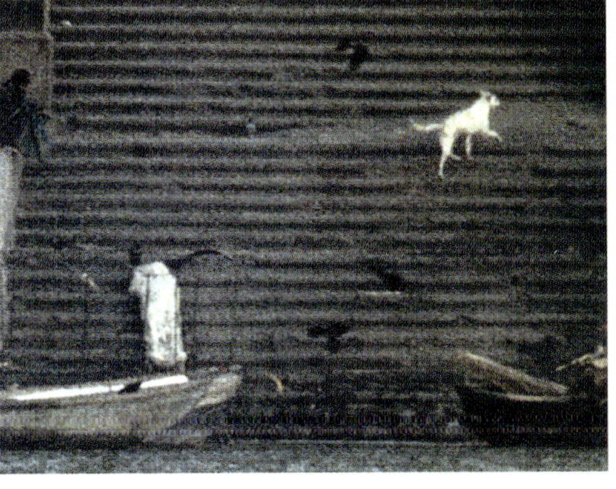

Gardner then cuts to a long telephoto beige z shot of an ancient worn ghat speckled with birds, on which there is a low mound of dirt.

The lines of the steps are bisected left to right and bottom to top by the movement of a white dog, who climbs up toward the pile of sand or dirt. This movement uncannily echoes the movement of the sun rising from the haze, again linking the banal and the transcendent via the omnipresent background sound of bells. Meanwhile, in the bottom right we see what we—at least retrospectively—can understand to be a corpse covered in a white sheet, overlooked by a boat moored in the foreground. The white-sheeted corpse seems mysteriously linked to the white dog, as if the dog embodies a spirit that has arisen from it. Human and animal appear intimately connected to each other, here, in a continuum of life and death, as they are throughout the film. Meanwhile, a human figure seated above the corpse wears a turquoise garment that echoes the earlier serene turquoise-blues of water and sky. This shot again connects land and water, but now through the emphatic architectural element of the steps. They become, in the film, the central passageway between life and death, between the material and the transcendent or spiritual. The steps are, as it were, the stairway to heaven. However, this is a stairway whose spatial coordinates are crucially inverted; it is a path *down to* transcendence that takes us back into matter and to the goddess who is a river, rather than away from matter into some ethereal realm.

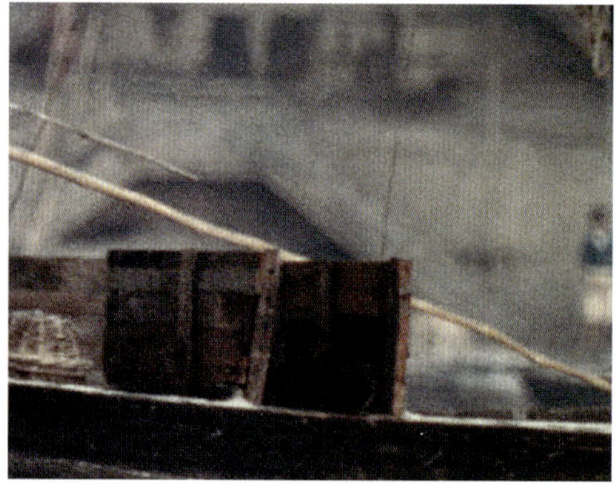

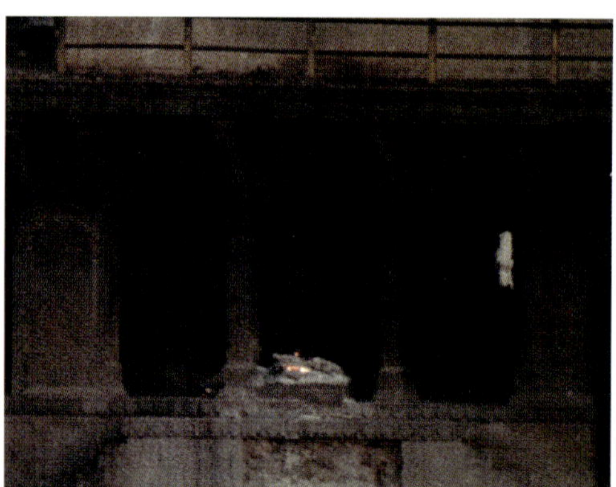

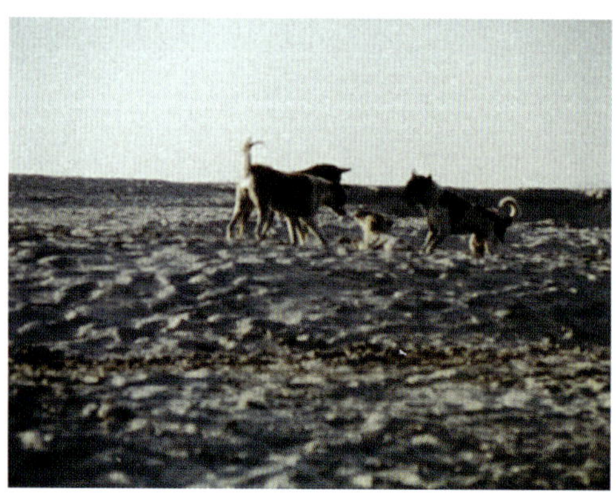

Following the movement of the dog into off-screen space, again in telephoto image, a boat crosses our line of vision (left to right) in front of an out-of-focus ghat, where, again, we perceive a human figure as a bluish mass.

The boat reflects on its surface the red glow of the rising sun. So now three central motifs are combined in the same image: the ethereal, languid movement of boats (earlier connected with the turquoise-blue of water and mist), the beige-brown of sand and now the ghats, and the red fire of the sun. The movement of the boat leads us to the penultimate shot in this sequence, where we see what we come to understand in the film as the source fire for funeral pyres. Its redness echoes the red flame of the sun, whose power, at once destructive yet life-giving, is echoed and answered by the flames of the sacred fire in which the body is burned and the soul thereby released.

The architectural elements of the shot here are suggestive of a temple and, in the upper right, in an extraordinary visual gesture, hangs a white rag of cloth, echoing the white shroud of the corpse, as if suggesting the remnant of the material life that has been given up. Finally, while this shot is in view, and still in the aural presence of bells and birds, we hear the extremely loud and disturbing sounds of dogs fighting to the death. Gardner cuts to an image of two feral dogs on the beige sand in the morning light tearing to pieces another dog, that screams in pain, as a bystander in the far right background walks by seemingly uncaring or unawares.

This sound-image is shocking, for it points to the brutality of nature's cycle of life and death in the way that only film can, that is, by allowing us to actually witness the temporality of death at work. The image receives its echo in the quotation from Yeats's translation of the *Upanishads*: "Everything in the world is eater or eaten, the seed is food and fire is eater," which now appears as a title and begins the film's short title sequence.

The Ritual of the Film

Forest of Bliss takes as its central subject the rituals that enable the passage of life into death to be conceived as part of a spiritual cycle of death and rebirth. In many of these rituals the holy water of the Ganges plays a central role in realizing the incorporation of matter into spirit. Human beings, living and dead, as well as deities are ritually cleansed by the water of the Ganges. Holy water is given to the dying and spread on the floor of a courtyard after a corpse has been laid there. Rituals are performative actions that are constitutive of the state of affairs that they refer to. They are actions performed for their own sake, and they are repeated actions that in their timeless repetition make reference to a higher time that transcends or makes relative ordinary time. Here, the banal brute fact of life being rendered inert and disintegrating into dust is transformed by ritual into a liberation of the spirit through the alchemy of holy water, fire, and prayerful incantation. But how can the fact or meaning of ritual be depicted? This is a problem Gardner confronted throughout his career: the filmmaker is always outside holy space, either invisible or intrusive. His answer in *Forest of Bliss*, I believe, is to create a work that participates in a meditation on the relationship between matter and spirit. *Forest of Bliss* allows us to perceive the banal reality of secular, finite, mortal time as a reflection of transcendent, cyclical, spiritual time; the matter of life as the expression of spirit. *Forest of Bliss* is a visionary film that enacts the ritual it represents both through choice of subject matter and the way that subject matter is shot and composed.

What is immediately striking, perhaps shocking, about many of the rituals we see in the film is that they are rituals of purification by water that take place in the midst of banal materiality marked by dirt, putrefaction, and pollution. Gardner deliberately draws attention to this by cutting from Mithai Lal purifying himself in the waters of the Ganges and performing *puja* to the shot of a chalky looking, decaying corpse floating in the water.

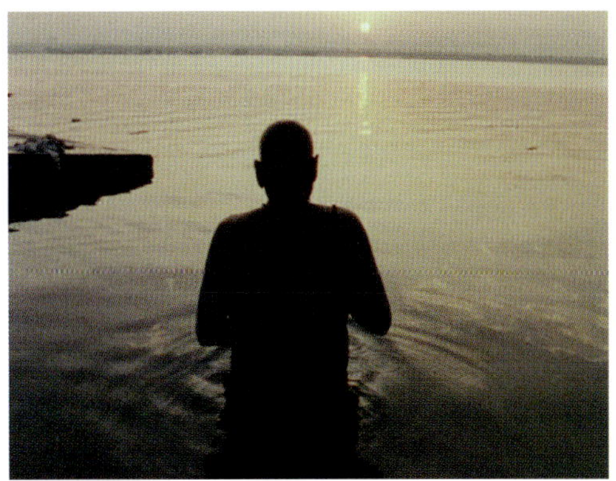

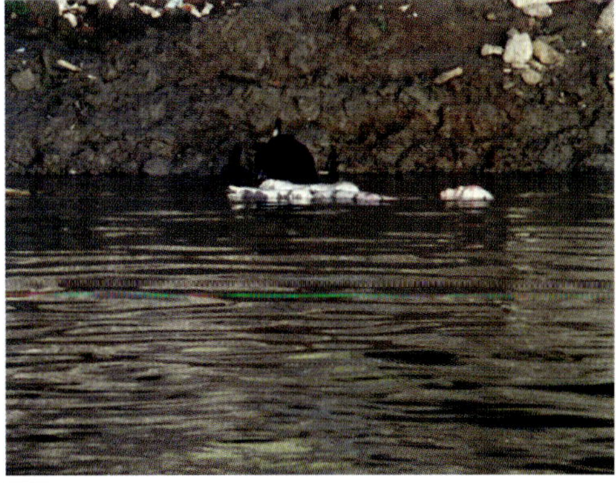

The point here is not, I think, primarily to show us how polluted the Ganges is, nor is it to show us how foolish the healer is by bathing in polluted waters; the cut between Mithai Lal and the floating corpse is there to highlight the way the sacred, ritual nature of the healer's practice transcends the space, time, and banality of material causality, even as it informs it. We shouid note here that the healer's bathing is itself not simply a purifying practice but a morning exercise in which he shows off his prowess. His improvised *puja* is also a form of play, like a child playing in bathwater. However, many of the activities depicted in the film are not themselves obviously rituals, though they have a purpose related to ritual, such as the cutting, gathering, and transportation of the wood for the fire; other signal actions like the gathering and transportation of sand on barges have no salient purpose at all. However, I think Gardner's intention here, in the larger scheme of the film, is to render these actions, too, from the standpoint of ritual, as actions that are both repeated from time immemorial and repeated in the cyclical time of the film, and therefore viewed from the aspect of higher time even as all are concrete acts of mortal labor.

Gardner, here, is clearly vulnerable to the charge of deploying a romanticized Western gaze on his subject, which from the perspective of a distracted modern world in flight from death, seeks to essentialize the material labor of the subjects he depicts in timeless immanence. In a similar way, as Jyotsna Kapur points out, by using the everyday facts of putrefaction and pollution in Benares to serve as an argument about the banality of matter and its transcendence, the film tends to obscure a more situated, concrete, historical understanding of pollution and its effects.[10] However, by the same token, this central blind spot of the film also yields its deepest insight. "Actuality" is instrumentalized by Gardner to serve the poetic depiction of a way of being that is deeply congruent with the forms of religious life existing in the holy city of Varanasi. The truths the film yields are not more important than those a historically situated documentary might yield (they may for some be less important). However, they are metaphysically profound truths that are of great importance to many within the culture the film depicts and rendered compelling, for any receptive spectator, through Gardner's audiovisual poetry.[11]

Human life in *Forest of Bliss* is one of many forms of life that are subject to destruction and rebirth. The title of the film is "Forest of Bliss," *anandavana* in Sanskrit, a term that describes the mythical forest of retreat, meditation, and enlightenment in the *Puranas* that was imagined to be located on the Rajghat plateau where the city of Varanasi grew up.[12] As this title emerges against a black background, after the opening montage and the quotation from Yeats, we hear the dull, resonant, "knocking" sound of wood being cut and then the crash of a tree being felled, accompanied by the cry of a man that takes on a kind of mythological or universal significance through the amplification of sound and the absence of source image. This sound is echoed later in the dull, resonant sound of giant logs of wood being dumped into boats or onto the ghats, as we watch these actions. We also see and hear the sound of wood burning on the sacred fires by the water's edge. Here, the "life-cycle" of wood becomes both contiguous with and expressive of the passage of human life. Just as the burning wood is reduced to embers, so, too, are the human corpses dissolving in the flames reduced to an undifferentiated pile of ashes. The burning pyres are associated by contiguity with the great river itself in which bodies are bathed prior to cremation. Water like fire contributes to physical decay and putrefaction, as manifest by the human

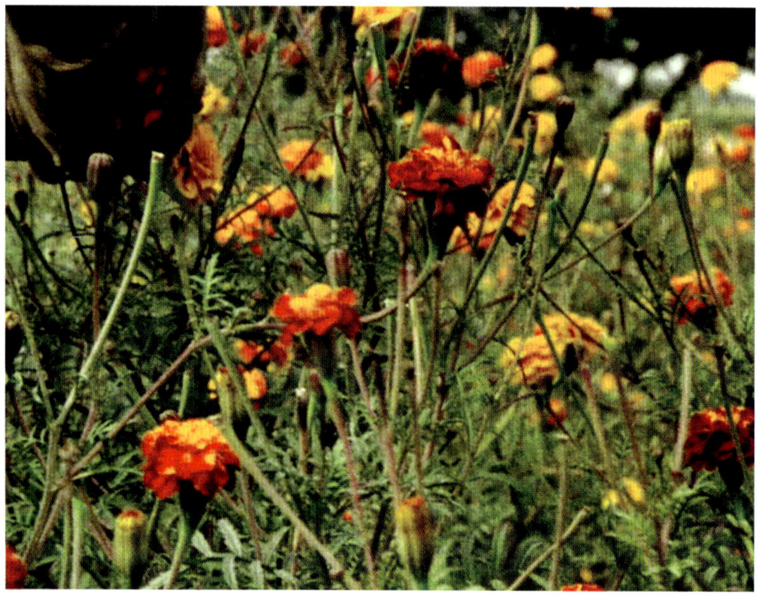

corpses floating in the water, and Gardner poetically connects this decay—dust to dust, ashes to ashes—with the movement of the river, which seems, as it were, to deposit the material residue of life on its opposite bank, from where it is mysteriously recycled again for some unknown purpose in the sand boats.

The image of a living forest given life by the waters of the Ganges is provided by the lush growth of marigold plantations that is introduced 16 minutes into the film. This veritable "forest of bliss" is pictured as a forest by Gardner's tight, low-angled close up, which renders palpable the thick texture of the leaves and stems and the brilliant, saturated saffrons of the marigold heads.

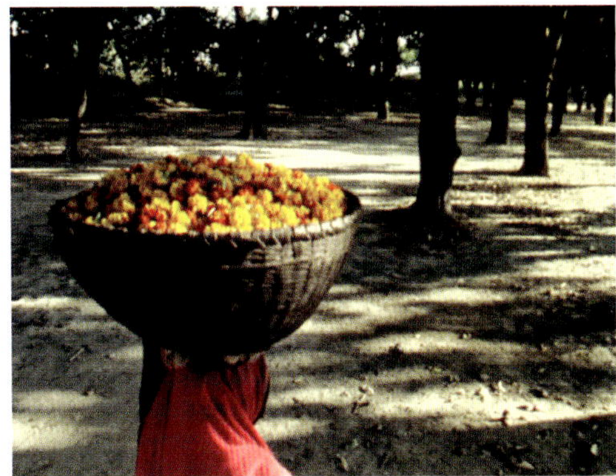

Here, again, the life cycle of nature is brutally manifest as the heads of the marigolds, in their prime, are dexterously picked off by a wizened old laborer, each beheading amplified, almost comically, by a dull thud of sound.[13] But this execution is not in vain; it is the prelude for rebirth. In the next shots we perceive the marigolds carried by a woman in a glorious basket of color, as if she is carrying the sun itself.

Her labor is in turn associatively linked to the transportation of wood from the forest by the men. Marigolds play a ubiquitous role in the *puja* ceremonies depicted in the film, as individual heads set out on the water on flaming lotus leaves, and as garlands bedecking deities, boats, and corpses. They are also scattered across the gray and beige images of Gardner's film like little suns. But the saffron flame of the marigolds, too, must be extinguished like the setting sun, crushed under foot, melted by water, consumed by fire, or chewed on by oxen or other animals, in a series of shots that are distributed throughout the film.

Like the marigold heads, the wood of the forest is equally repurposed or given a new life. Wood is used to create bamboo frames for transporting the dead. Initially, we see these frames being carefully constructed by an old man from individual pieces of bamboo as we hear the magnified sounds of his adze, chisel, and mallet on the wood. We might initially conclude from the appearance of these frames that they are ladders, until we realize that they are used for transporting the dead. At this stage our understanding of the frames as "ladders" takes on a metaphorical connotation that links them to the image of the steps on the banks of the Ganges, to which the bodies themselves are born and ultimately burned. After their use for transportation it appears that these frames are disassembled, and later we see the bamboo canes gathered en masse at the house of the Dom Raja—perhaps as part of a payment or tribute—and for some as yet unknown use.

Wood is also repurposed in the form of the boats that ply the Ganges. Gardner explicitly enacts a metaphor of rebirth in a long sequence where we see a newly refurbished boat being "blessed" in a *puja* ceremony in preparation for its launch in the river, while in the background a cortege bears a corpse down to the river for blessing prior to cremation. The sides of the boat are tapped with a mallet and decorated with yellow and saffron handprints that echo the color of the marigolds that are used to decorate the prow. This

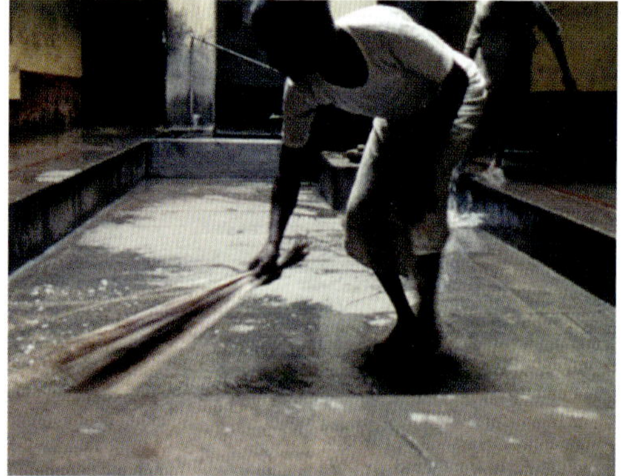

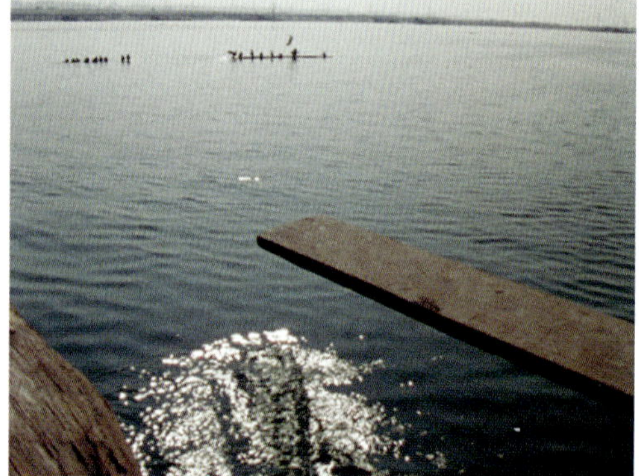

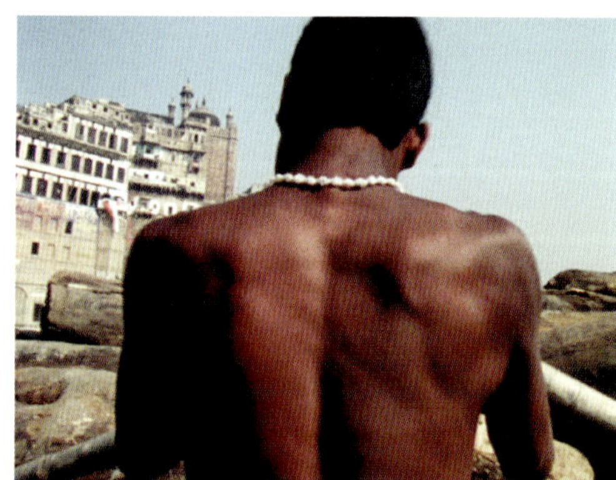

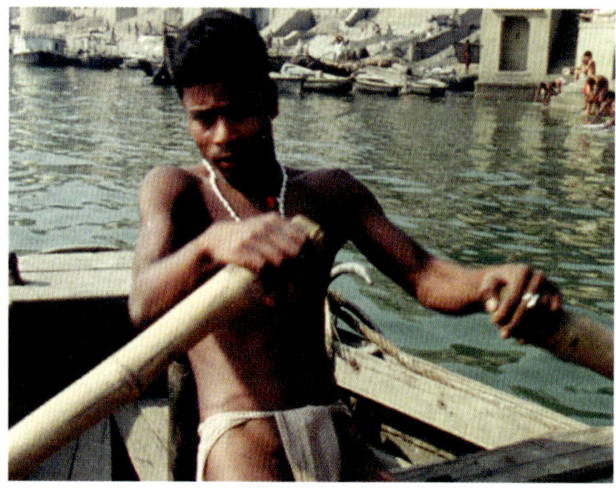

particular ceremony, which might seem peripheral to the central concern of depicting funerary rites on the Ganges, is given lavish and detailed attention by Gardner. This is because the figure of the boat and the boatman is arguably the central conceit in *Forest of Bliss*. The parallel that is drawn here between the initiation of the boat and the offering of the body of a newly dead person to the river intimates the sense that the body being born to the water is about to be launched like the boat into the continuation of life's journey in death, having been blessed with the water of the Ganges. Indeed, as Ákos Östör points out, Gardner intercuts the boat with a shot of a corpse on the funeral pyre in a manner that suggests the pyre itself is a boat-like structure.[14] We might also think in the context of this parallelism that the bamboo "ladders" are themselves like boats that bear the corpses to the river. But what is the purpose of this boat that in its individuation seems to stand for all the boats in the film? What will it carry? Throughout the film we see boats carrying wood, sand, and, sometimes, human corpses on the river, as we hear the rhythmic sound of creaking oarlocks and the lapping of paddles on the water. In some mysterious way it seems that all the boats on the Ganges in *Forest of Bliss* are bearing loads that traverse the passage between life and death.

The River Ganges and the River Styx

In *Forest of Bliss*, it is as if, for Gardner, the murky, polluted waters of the Ganges are the waters of the Styx, bearing passengers on the journey of death. In the most literal rendering of this analogy, the underworld, in Gardner's imagination, lies on the far side of the river, the side that is not sacred and is uninhabited, the wasteland where all life ends up reduced to dust and where the film begins.[15] This conceit contributes to our sense that the prosaic, everyday, and timeless labor on the waters of the Ganges takes on the quality of a ritual that is equal to the rituals surrounding the use of the holy water in the purification of the dead, for every boatman is figuratively like Charon, who enables the dead to pass onward in their journey. The feral dog who imperiously stalks the wasteland at the beginning of the film, and those who hunt and scavenge later, take part in this myth as representatives of the fearsome Cerberus who guards the gates of the underworld.

Gardner's syncretic combination of Greek mythology and the Hindu idea of rebirth has certain precedents in the highly syncretic Indic tradition where Eastern and Western forms of religious practice have been combined.[16] However, in the context of this documentary about Benares, the idea of the Ganges as Stygian water is a purely imaginative poetic construction. For the film's subjects (as far as we can tell), there is no symbolic meaning to crossing the river, and no underworld on its far bank. In this respect, Gardner's use of this metaphor as an organizing principle of the film, which some may see as a distorting or disfiguring lens, is a way of declaring his hand: *Forest of Bliss* is the rendition of what the director sees and hears into forms he can understand. Just as the quotation from the *Upanishads* is announced at the beginning of the film as Yeats' translation of the sacred Hindu text, so, too, does *Forest of Bliss* creatively interpret the events that take place on the banks of the Ganges under the imaginative, though informed, gaze of an outsider.

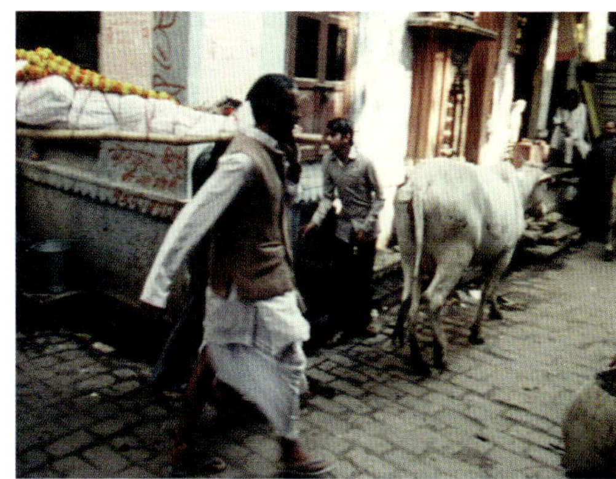

The manner in which the Stygian metaphor informs the film and helps to organize the choice and organization of sound-images within it is exemplified in an audiovisual montage midway through the film [shots 207–224] that occurs shortly before the boat initiation sequence. We have seen a body being prepared for cremation in a courtyard and the space then physically cleansed and spiritually purified with the water of the Ganges to the sounds of incantation.

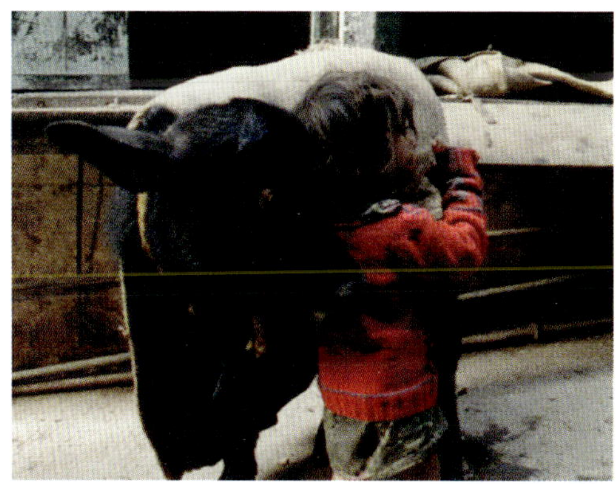

Subsequently, Gardner cuts to three different images of a young oarsman transporting heavy logs of wood to the sound of creaking oarlocks, juxtaposing the weighty inertness of matter with youthful labor. Then, continuing the movement of the boatman, we see bearers carrying a body through the streets on a bamboo ladder, ritualistically chanting *Ram nam satya hai* ("the name of Ram is truth").

A little girl looks back, through a montage, at the disappearing cortege and forward, as it were, to an almost extinct funeral pyre by the river.

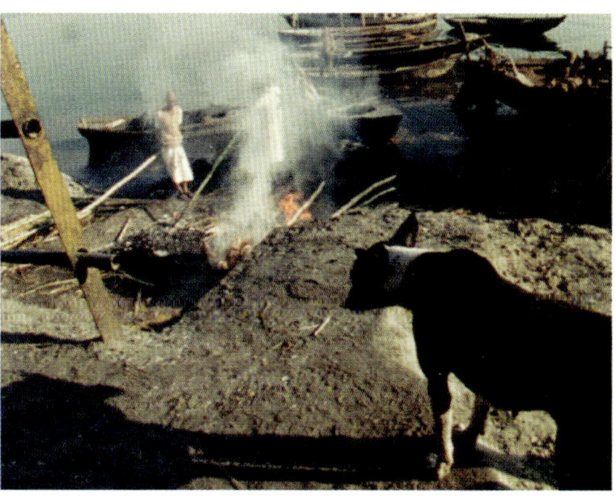

The narrow, downward sloping alleyways with the bearers flowing through them take on the appearance of riverlets. Gardner himself speaks at one point of "a stream of death going down toward the *Manikarnika* [ghat]."[17] This image helps crystallize the thought of the frame bearing the corpses as a kind of boat. The sacred city is thereby rendered, through Gardner's imaginative projection, as a metaphorical extension of the Ganges herself. But if those streams are Stygian waters bearing the dead, we are also invited to think of them as following the gullies of the nourishing rivers that flowed from the Rajghat plateau down to the Ganges in the mythical forest of bliss: death and transcendence are thus combined in their movement.

a	b
c	d
e	f
g	h

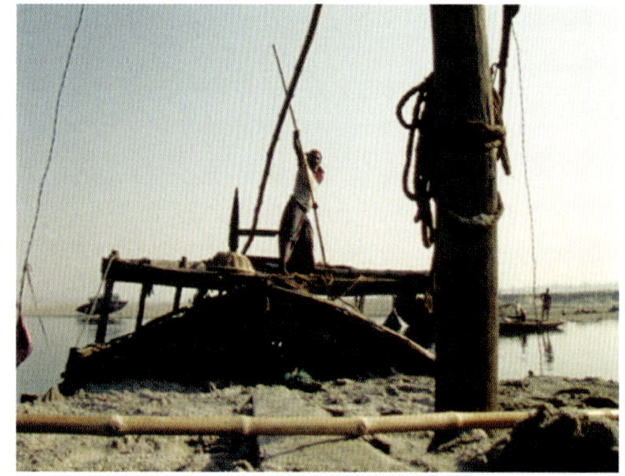
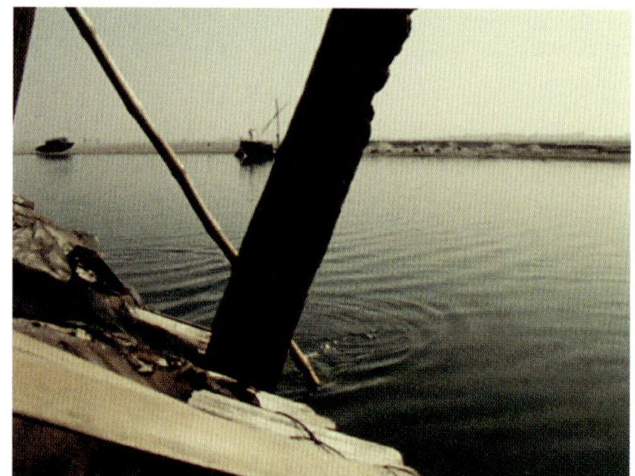
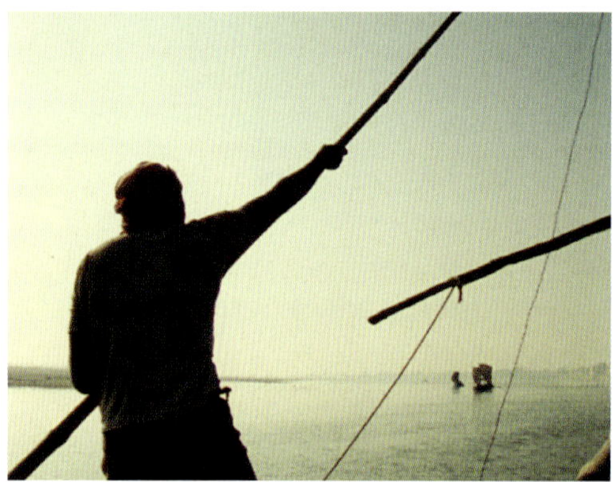
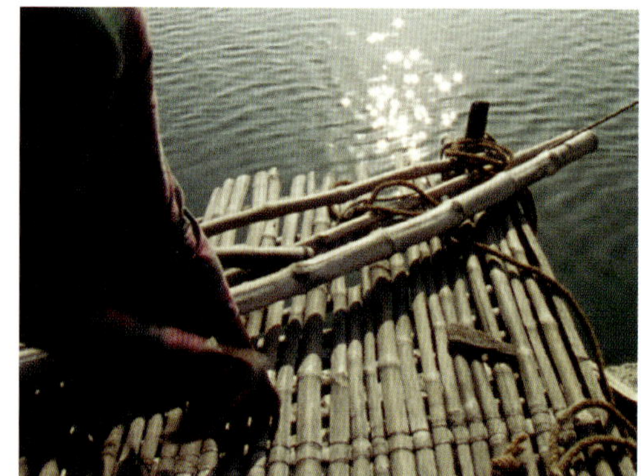
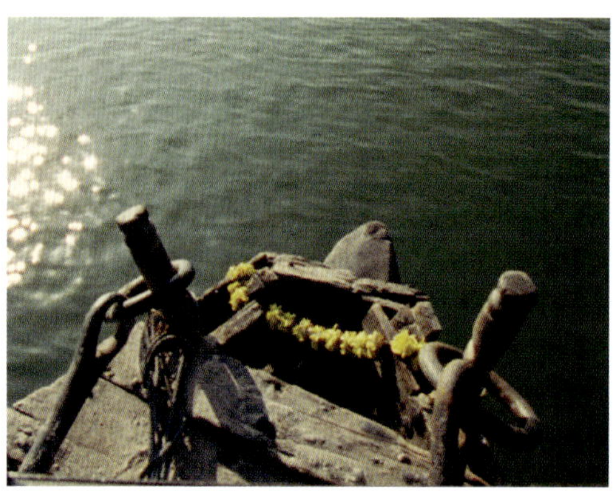
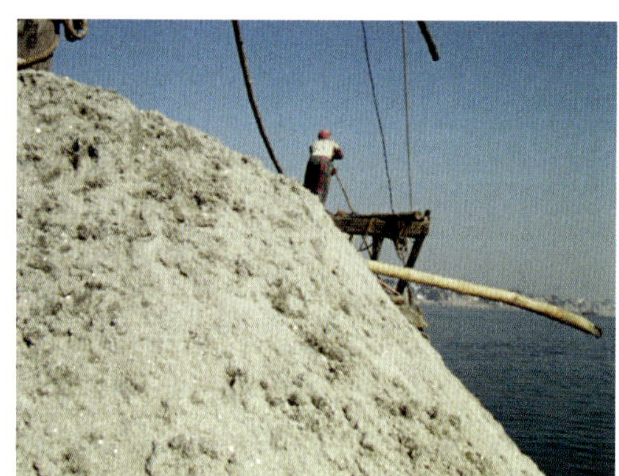
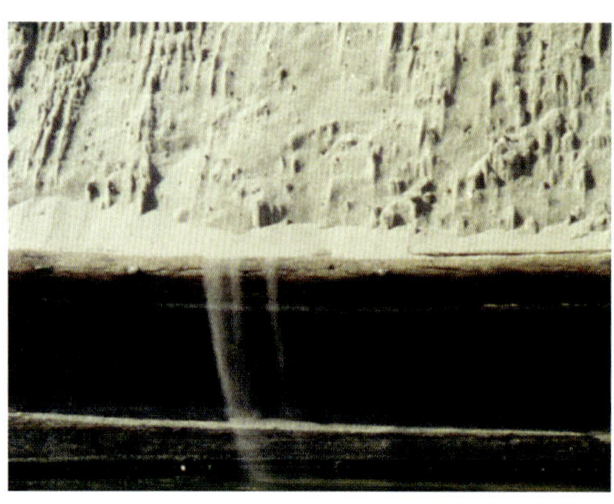
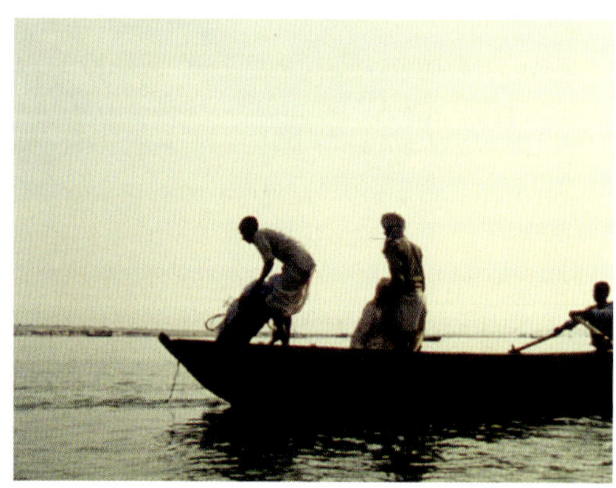

Gardner returns the viewer to the Ganges, where we see and hear an aging boatman punting sand down the river on a large barge, whose prow is laced with marigolds, in an exquisite series of seven sound-images accompanied by the creaking sound of the bamboo platform on which the man walks (thematically linked to the bamboo ladders) and by the lapping sound of his pole in the water.

Here old Charon is more strongly evoked. These images of the sand boats are again expressive of the weighty deadness of matter, but now the relationship with death is made explicit, through context and juxtaposition. In the final shot of the sequence, which is accompanied by the evocative sound of children's voices wholly disconnected in real space from the movement of the boat on the water, we watch as wisps of sand fall from the side of the boat, giving the appearance of ashes being scattered on the water. In the very next shot, a group of men in a boat on gently lapping water release a sheeted corpse into the water, echoing the movement of the wisps of sand—dust to dust, ashes to ashes.[18]

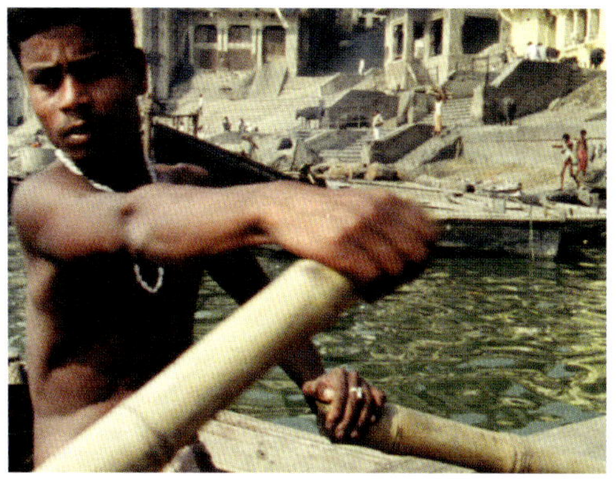

Finally, we return to an image of a young oarsman dipping his oar in the water in the evening light, as a porpoise in the distance rises and falls like a creature from the underworld, suggesting an attunement between the rhythms of the human and the natural worlds.

In medium shot, the oarsman approaches a ghat, wearing a bright red carnation head unmistakably attached to his white beads. He looks screen right, and through creative geography Gardner links his gaze to an empty funeral pyre that is framed through a weighing scale that is now empty of wood.

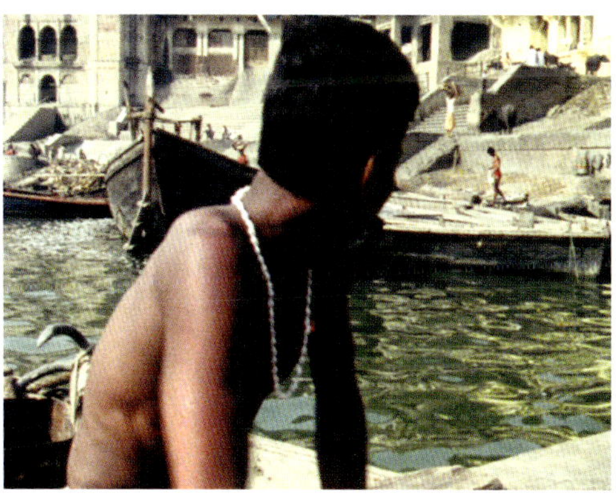

Death is evoked as absence. We finally realize the destination of the wood and the purpose of the boatman who carries it.

The Metaphor of the Kite

In representing the passage from earth to sky, from matter to spirit, the metaphor of the kite, as announced in the opening sequence featuring the kite-sun, is a pivotal one in the film. Because the figuration of the kite also features prominently in the film's own summation, I conclude by examining the role of this motif in more detail. In a two-shot montage that occurs moments after the sequence I described, an ox on the shore of the river chews a marigold head, against the background of a boat full of logs, and then moves up the riverbank with a nimbleness that belies its cumbersome size, while behind it steam rises up from a large pile of dying embers as we hear the cries of children.

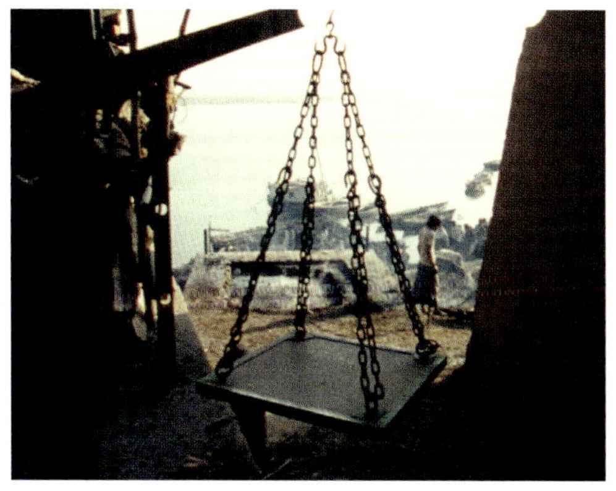

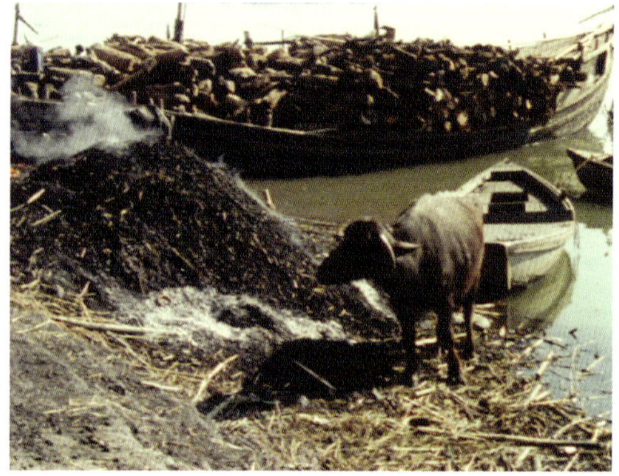

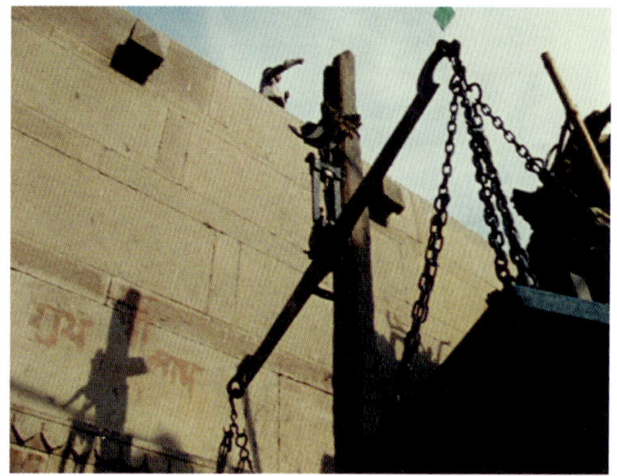

A sense is conveyed of life rising up from the river (recall the image of the dog in the opening montage). In the subsequent shot, taken from a low angle, we look from underneath empty scales at a wall, again suggesting death as absence, where, up above, a boy flies a green kite as the sound of children's voices is intensified.

The right to left movement from the previous shot is continued in the upward sweep, in this low angled shot, from bottom right to top left. Throughout the film kite flying is shown to be an everyday activity around the ghats; indeed, the rising air of the thermals from the cremation sites forms an ideal playground for kite flying. Yet supervening on this reality is the thought, conveyed through mise-en-scène and montage, that a kite lifted in the thermals expresses the aspiration to transcendence and that, in the connection between the high-flying kites and the young boys on the ground who guide them, this transcendence is also a form of rebirth.

Gardner admits it was harder to introduce the imagery of the kite in the film than to represent other objects: "There were not as many kite-image possibilities as marigold ones."[19] The first time we see an actual kite is a full fifteen minutes into the film. As Mithai Lal walks from adorning lingams with marigolds, he passes by a colorful kite on the ground without seeing it. In what is clearly an unplanned moment in the filming, the camera pivots to observe it lying in tatters on the ground, a discarded piece of refuse, a dead kite, as it were, which establishes a kinship between the kite and the ubiquitous marigolds that lie scattered across the ground after their use. Later, we see a brief shot of kite sellers organizing their kites, not unlike the women who thread the marigolds. Then after the low angle shot of the kite in the thermal, we return to images of a kite being flown and then pulled down from the sky in the twilight, in a shot that evokes in reverse the film's opening where the kite-sun is pulled up into the sky. The shot is preceded by the image of a sailboat moving gently across the city backdrop accompanied by cawing birds that makes explicit a connection, intimated but not cemented in the opening sequence, between the kite-sun and the sailboats on the water, and the birds; all are figurations of the lighter, transcendent aspects of the cyclical passage of spirit through matter that counterpoint the images of dust, death, and putrefaction.

A final kite montage, pivotal in expressing the vision of the film as a whole, takes place soon after this. From early on in the shooting, Gardner was obsessed with the idea of filming a kite falling into the water: "There was some obscure feeling that kites drifting off towards the far shore and sometimes falling into the river has a larger meaning. They are wonderful inventions: so frail, so lively, and so urgent. Then there is the string that both guides and attaches them but can also break and release them."[20] The sequence is introduced by a shot of three men on a boat with a white shroud about to leave dockside. Gardner cuts to a boy vigorously and with great concentration flying a kite to the sound of children's voices. Then, in an image of austere beauty in the twilight calm of the evening, accompanied by the sound of children's voices and pealing bells, the boat moves into view near the sandy banks on the far shore of the river. With a deftness of gesture, which is intercut with the shot of a red kite being hauled in, one of the men slips the shrouded corpse, perhaps of a child, into the water. Then, in a felicitous moment for the filmmaker, in the very same shot, behind the boat, one red kite, then another, floats gently behind the boat toward the surface of the water. It is an image that presents the idea of death as a kind of weightlessness. To be sure, the physical corpse that slips into the water will end up as dust on the far shore of the river, and yet, too, the spirit in the form of the kite floats free of its material tether, the sense of freedom it evokes underscored by the random nature of an image that cohered by chance. In the film's final kite image, which helps brings closure to the film, transcendence in death is once more evoked as a symphony of flying kites plays against the image of the setting sun that silhouettes the city with its glow.

Forest of Bliss is a work whose own aestheticized ritual in space and time is expressive of the rituals that mark the passage of the spirit into death that it seeks to represent. The act of representation in *Forest of Bliss* is one in which the factual evidence presented by the camera of the events that take place on and near the Ganges in Benares is filtered through the creative gaze of the filmmaker, who selects, records, and edits. The result is a work of art that seeks to uncover the kind of meaning in events and things that those who practice the rituals within the film might think about and feel. Although these meanings, as they are represented in the film, are not inherent to the objects and events depicted, they are made to appear inherent, because the representational capacities of film are such as to render thought and "reality" co-extensive. The film thus succeeds in evoking for the spectator an experience of the world as an enchanted place. To be sure, in *Forest of Bliss*, the world is rendered in all its messy physical and moral existence; the brutal facts of physical decay and disintegration, in particular, are laid bare in such a manner that they give grounds for despair. At the same time, it is the very fact of death at work everywhere that, under the transformative gaze of Gardner's camera, leads to an experience of re-enchantment for viewers who are receptive to its imaginative power.

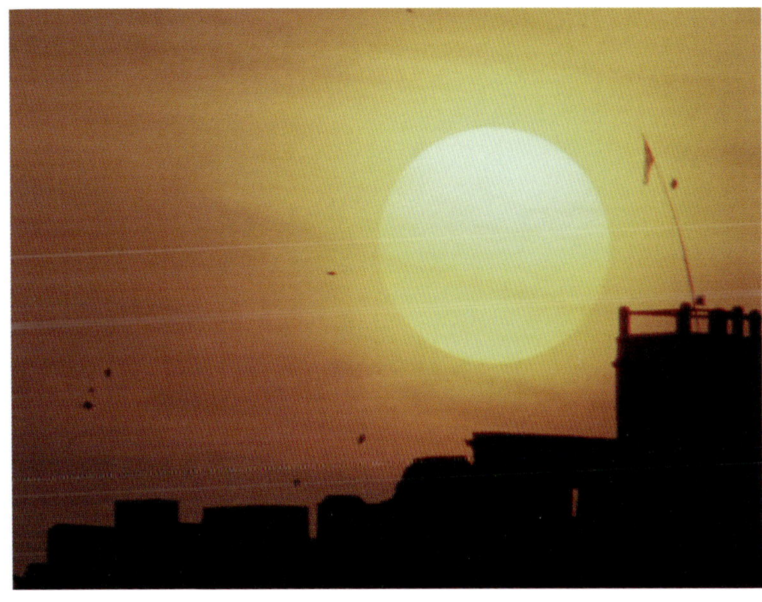

Notes

1. Robert Gardner and Ákos Östör, *Making* Forest of Bliss*: Intention, Circumstance, and Chance in Nonfiction Film* (Boston: Harvard Film Archive, 2001), 26.
2. See Alexander Moore, "The Limitations of Imagist Documentary," *Society for Visual Anthropology Newsletter*, 4:2 (Fall 1988), 1–3, and Jonathan P. Parry, "Comment on Robert Gardner's *Forest of Bliss*," *Society for Visual Anthropology Newsletter*, 4:2 (Fall 1988), 4–7.

3. See Jay Ruby, "An Anthropological Critique of the Films of Robert Gardner," *Journal of Film and Video* 43:4 (Winter 1991), 13.

4. Ruby, "The Emperor and His Clothes," *Society for Visual Anthropology Newsletter*, 5:1 (Spring 1989), 11.

5. *Making* Forest of Bliss, 78 and 83.

6. The nature of Mithai Lal's activities as a faith healer was described in detail by anthropologist Jonathan Parry in his early critical review of the film. See Parry, "Comment on Robert Gardner's *Forest of Bliss*," 6.

7. *Making* Forest of Bliss, 103.

8. Gardner's critical framing of the Dom Raja may be criticized on ethical grounds. Speaking of the sequence in which the Dom Raja argues angrily with mourners, which casts him in a negative light, Ákos Östör emphasizes that he consented to be filmed while he did not consent to other sequences. Gardner further points out that the inflated ego he manifests is part of his own self-presentation. See *Making* Forest of Bliss, 99–100. At the same time, the Dom Raja could obviously not be fully cognizant of the way he was being framed. This is an ethical dilemma posed by all documentary filmmaking and portraiture more generally.

9. Pierre Shaeffer, inventor of *musique concrete*, coined the term "acousmatic" sound to refer to this idea of the sound-contour in *Traitée des objets musicaux* (Paris: Seuil, 1967), 91–99.

10. See Jyotsna Kapur, "The Art of Ethnographic Film and the Politics of Protesting Modernity: Robert Gardner's *Forest of Bliss*," *Visual Anthropology* 9 (1997), 167–185.

11. For an early, sympathetic evocation of the work, see Radikha Chopra, "Robert Gardner's *Forest of Bliss*—A Review," *Society for Visual Anthropology Newsletter*, 5:1 (Spring 1989), 2–3.

12. See Diana Eck, *Banaras, City of Light* (New York: Columbia University Press, 1999), 29–31.

13. Gardner speaks of "the life cycle of the marigold" in *Making* Forest of Bliss, 54.

14. Ibid., 88.

15. Ibid., 17.

16. I am thinking here of the influential syncretic doctrines developed within the Brahmo Samaj, especially the attempt by Keshab Chandra Sen (1838–1884) to combine Hinduism with Christianity. See also the religious universalism preached by the influential Bengali guru Ramakrishna (1836–1886).

17. *Making* Forest of Bliss, 91.

18. Gardner reports: "There are two scenes where, after trying very hard, I managed to get sand spilling off this boat into the river. I suspect these are the images that call up the idea of ashes. They were certainly intended to say something about both mortality and the cyclical nature of existence." *Making* Forest of Bliss, 67.

19. Ibid., 70.

20. Ibid., 110.

Chapter 18
The Same Thing from Different Angles: Resituating *Forest of Bliss*

Julia Yezbick

The allegation is false that a fact taken from life, when recorded by the camera, loses the right to be called a fact if its name, date, place, and number are not inscribed on the film.

—Dziga Vertov, "The Same Thing from Different Angles"

In the short 1926 essay enigmatically entitled "The Same Thing From Different Angles," Dziga Vertov describes what he terms *film-facts*—the bits of life "caught unawares" by a camera that remain visible facts despite lack of contextual or extra-diegetic information. While much has been made of the notion of the camera's ability to capture life "as it is" since his 1926 essay, this is an apt starting point for revisiting a film that some have claimed revived the City Symphony genre, of which Vertov was a pioneer.

In the past quarter of a century since its release, Robert Gardner's *Forest of Bliss* (1986) has elicited more anthropological discourse—both praise and vitriol—than perhaps any other film. Today, epistemological shifts in anthropology proffer new angles from which to look at this "same thing" (Gardner's *Forest of Bliss*). As Ilisa Barbash and Lucien Taylor have suggested, the sensorial shift in anthropology has opened up the realm of anthropological knowledge beyond the traditional coupling of meaning and naming, signification and language.[1] Contemporaneous to this sensorial shift have been new provocations about the relationship between art and anthropology. A number of scholars now encourage an increased attention to the crucial consonances and dissonances between artistic and anthropological modes of interaction with and communication about the world.[2] In this essay, I situate Gardner's *Forest of Bliss* within these shifting epistemological tides. I do this by looking at *Forest of Bliss* from three "angles": from within anthropology's historical relationship to art and expressive ethnographic forms; second, from within the cinematic genre of City Symphonies (in particular in relation to Vertov's *Man With a Movie Camera,* 1929); and finally, tracing Gardner's influence forward to look at the ways it resonates with Lucien Castaing-Taylor and Véréna Paravel's *Leviathan* (2012) and other works being produced at Harvard's Sensory Ethnography Lab.

These "angles" expose a focus on the senses, aesthetics, and the body, and place Gardner's film as a crucial pivot between the efforts of early City Symphonies to convey a quintessential sense of a particular modern city and the films that are today depicting place with immersive, embodied, and sensual filmic styles.[3] Although we may never be able to see through another's eyes, we certainly can look *with* another, as the title of the present volume suggests. We might ask what it means to *look, listen, and feel* with and alongside another. As a nonfiction filmmaker myself, embarking on an urban project, I take this opportunity to rethink the meanings of place, its significance for those present in it, its conveyance, and the possibilities for ethnographic films' productive borrowings from other expressive forms.

Angle 1—Words and Beyond: Art, Film, and Anthropology

Art has been studied as an integral part of the anthropological project since the Victorian era.[4] Though historically focused on non-Western objects and artifacts (i.e., baskets, masks, pottery, textiles), many recent publications are once again addressing the parameters of the anthropological study of art, and calling for increased attention to Western art and for "critical ethnographic studies of contemporary art worlds."[5] These scholars often assert the need to address both the complicated social worlds within which art is made, and the power that it yields (spiritually, economically, socially, affectively, or otherwise), as well as the creative processes, formal aesthetic qualities, and values in which it trades. Furthermore, recent trends in contemporary art have renewed discussions about the convergences and divergences between art and anthropology, presenting new incitements to think about their similar and disparate intentions, methodologies, audiences, content, and forms.[6]

Although anthropologists are increasingly adopting practices and methodologies from contemporary art, these remain largely acts of experimentation and provocation. These provocations have again brought to the fore the constructed nature of ethnographic products and the slippages and overlaps between what anthropologists produce and the products of aesthetic or artistic endeavors. While such practices and skill-based borrowings are certainly not unprecedented, Gardner's work, and ethnographic filmmaking more generally, has perhaps pushed the agenda from one of borrowing methods and skills to one of elevating the aesthetics of the finished product onto equal ground with the intended accuracy of its content. In 2005, I helped a friend and colleague, Antonio Zirión, interview Gardner at a retrospective of his work in Mexico City. When Antonio asked him about the role of aesthetics in anthropology, Gardner responded candidly: "If the goal of anthropology is to try to reveal the meanings of our behavior, how can it dispense with the aesthetic dimension? I sometimes feel as though critics on warring sides of these matters make the mistake of thinking science is opposed to or incompatible with art and *vice versa*. In my view they coexist with no difficulty at all" (hence this volume).

While some readers may find Gardner's sentiments easily agreeable today, it is important to remember that *Forest of Bliss* was released at a moment in anthropology's history that Marcus and Fischer deemed a "crisis of representation," in which they identified a general "uncertainty about adequate means of describing social reality."[7] The anthropological community's response to *Forest of Bliss* at the time of its release was, in short, contentious. The debates that arose around *Forest of Bliss* were no doubt riding on the wave of discourse following the publication of another seminal text, Clifford and Marcus's *Writing Culture*.[8] This text brought to the fore the recognition that ethnographic description transforms or translates the field experience into literary conventions.

Long before the "crisis of representation" in written anthropological discourse, anthropological filmmakers had grappled with the constructed nature of their films. The inherent reflexivity of filmic images belies the processes that produce them. They are at once both a record and an expression and bear the indelible marks of their making. An editor's cut, though it may feel seamless, cannot be entirely hidden from the viewer. An unwanted object in a shot cannot be deleted like a word on a page. In this way, filmmaking is a subtractive process, whereas writing is additive. This not only necessitated that ethnographic filmmakers address their role in sculpting the ethnographic product but also prompted them to borrow methodologies from the direct cinema movement, cinema verité, and even fiction and avant-garde film. Despite these borrowings, anthropology's "iconophobia" appeared to be rampant as "ethnographic filmmakers were often reluctant to depart from a narrow range of realist conventions."[9] Gardner's *Forest of Bliss* is not only an important exception to the epidemic of "iconophobia;" the academy's response to it also marks this work as a milestone in the exploration of aesthetic possibilities for anthropological film and media-based scholarship more broadly.

Forest of Bliss challenged ethnographic writing as the *sine qua non* of anthropological knowledge production, and through filmic means put into practice the expressiveness and evocative capabilities espoused by Stephen Tyler and others in *Writing Culture*. Yet, to some of the more staid members of the anthropological community, Gardner's brazen aesthetics came to represent the potential harm that was possible if ethnographers took the argument of *Writing Culture* to its logical end. Jay Ruby noted that Gardner's film was released at a time when many anthropologists were grappling with the ethical and political implications of their work, and he saw *Forest of Bliss* as a particularly insensitive instantiation of a "nineteenth-century notion of artistic license."[10] Though accusations of artistic liberties were not the harshest of Ruby's critiques leveled at Gardner, this points to a broader epistemological divide in anthropologists' approach to film and creative expression at the time. Though critically advocated by the authors of *Writing Culture*, expressiveness and evocation were for many in diametrical opposition to objectivity and accuracy, and the aims of aesthetic considerations in opposition to scientific ethnography (visual or written), whose goals should be to present and interpret empirical evidence. It is this divide that *Forest of Bliss* unsettled.

Forest of Bliss was not, however, made with the intention of disturbing the ethnographic film canon, as it did not claim to be such a film. *Forest of Bliss*, Gardner said, is a "personal film, not an ethnographic one."[11] Nevertheless, in the United Kingdom, the film won a prize as the best ethnographic film of the past two years. Nonfiction films that resist conventional categorizations as "ethnographic" or "experimental" or "avant-garde" often default to definition by context, the difference in venue determining their categorical status.[12] Other scholars have looked to funding sources or commonalities in distribution or reception for clues to the underlying nature of a seemingly uncategorizable film.[13] Categorical quandaries aside, how to evaluate such work remains a problem for many anthropologists.[14]

David MacDougall notes that the "crisis of representation" effected a shift toward greater emphasis on experiential perspectives (as opposed to schematic descriptions). This shift, he argues, elicited new interest in the potential of film, suggesting that "knowledge of the kind conveyed by film may have renewed anthropological validity."[15] The evocative and affective potentials of film have led an increasing number of scholars working at the boundaries of art, anthropology, and film, to call for an epistemological and methodological push to go "beyond the narrow concerns of ocularity to investigate ways of knowing located in the body and in the senses."[16] These renewed provocations and expansions advocate an extension of representation that fundamentally shifts the relationship between experience and expression that traditionally structured and defined the ethnographic project. Discussing the work of Judith Okley and Roanna Heller, Grimshaw and Ravetz add that we might "begin to think of disciplinary identities and objects in [terms of] performance," thus expanding an art-anthropological praxis beyond the limitations of the notion of the "text"-as-art-object and expanding such praxis beyond the semiotic.[17] Perhaps the recent confluence of interests in the anthropology of art, visual anthropology, and sensory ethnography has opened up a space for anthropologists to revisit *Forest of Bliss* as a work of art and to locate its provocations as contributing to anthropological practice *and* theory.

In the last ten years, several universities have begun offering courses in "sensory ethnography" to attend to a more wholly sensorial engagement with the world and with various media to express it.[18] In an attempt to make sense of the many meanings of "sensory ethnography," Karen Nakamura describes one orientation of this trend as "aesthetic-sensual ethnography," which she associates almost exclusively with the work being produced at Harvard's Sensory Ethnography Lab (SEL), which operates alongside the Film Study Center founded by Gardner in 1957. Nakamura distills two main features of this work: the move beyond a discipline of words, and an integration of the aesthetic arts and ethnography.[19] This "aesthetic-sensual" mode of ethnography is epitomized by Gardner's later work, particularly *Forest of Bliss*.

Recalling the process of shooting *Forest of Bliss*, Gardner often emphasizes this observational aspect of the work and the importance of developing "a sensitivity to the way things unfold in actuality."[20] He describes watching and waiting for certain things to happen—for the workers at the Mukti Bhavan to clean the floor after washing and removing a corpse, or for a kite to fall into the river, and being ever-vigilant and ready with his camera. He configures himself in his environment in a "state of elevated readiness in which one's eyes are open to all the relationships possible between visible entities."[21] This trance-like state, Gardner writes, is "essential in order to see the connectedness of events not only as elements in the physical space they occupy but in their significance as phenomena linked by meaning."[22] In an interview with Ilisa Barbash, Gardner describes a demonstration he saw by Len Lye in which he dropped an unfolded piece of paper to the ground, asking the audience to watch it glide and dip on its journey to the ground. "What I take from this," remarked Gardner, "is that in film experience we kinesthetically incorporate actuality or its fictional equivalent and almost relive it in the process. Maybe new and different understanding arises from these felt experiences."[23]

Angle 2—City Symphonies and the Corporeal Image

"Films, like ghost stories," writes David MacDougall, "are littered with bodies, and although these bodies are in one sense ghostly and evanescent, they are also in many ways, to our senses, corporeal."[24] MacDougall asserts that art provides a link between our own bodies and something else physical: the material traces of another work or, in films, the testament to bodies that were present before the camera. *Forest of Bliss* is a deeply corporeal film and demonstrates MacDougall's full sense of the term in that it testifies to the bodies both before and behind the camera. This quality positions it interestingly within the genre of City Symphonies, and also as a crucial pivot in the exploration of the sensorial shift in ethnographic and nonfiction filmmaking.

In the 1920s, films such as Dziga Vertov's *Man with a Movie Camera* and Walther Ruttman's *Berlin: Symphony of the City* (1927) took as their subject the modern city, in both its utopic and more frightening instantiations. While City Symphonies have varied considerably in the decades since these first films, certain characteristics bind them together. City Symphonies generally have relatively quick cuts, they are often structured around the diurnal cycle (or "a day in the life" of a city), and they tend to foreground patterned movements and rhythms of a particular place. The city itself—its structures, bridges, sidewalks, streets, and subways—is often the main focus of the film, sometimes yielding metaphorical parallels, as in "the city as machine," or the "city as body" or "organism" (as in the case of Hillary Harris's 1975 film *Organism*). This genre varies widely, however, in its relationship to and depiction of the human subject, and the extent to which the camera is embodied (i.e., giving human-scale perspectives) or privileged (giving bird's-eye, or extra-human views). Many City Symphonies oscillate between the depiction of humans *en masse* as a swarm of beings (as in *Organism*), and the rendering of experiences of one or two individuals. Occasionally, a character might serve as an unassuming tour guide, as the camera follows him or her through the streets or at different engagements throughout the day. However, generally the viewer identifies with the perspective of the filmmaker or the apparatus itself, rather than a personality or "character," per se. In *Man with a Movie Camera*, Vertov inserts his brother and cameraman, Mikhail Kaufman, into the film to make literal (or rather figural) this identification. We see Mikhail throwing himself under moving vehicles, balancing on the edge of a moving car while filming, and even, through trick photography, inside a sudsy beer stein with his tripod and camera at his side. Seeing him so often reminds us that everything we see, from far and near perspectives, is the view of the filmmaker or apparatus (which itself takes on human-like qualities when, through stop-motion photography, the tripod walks on its own and the camera comes out of its box and attaches itself as the Cyclops head).

Many times throughout the film we see Mikhail in a precarious place or position with his camera. This is generally followed by a shot from the camera's perspective, emphasizing the point that these two perspectives are different; one is that of the apparatus (a presentation) and the other is that of cinema (a representation). Throughout the film, the persistent criss-crossing of gazes, both human and extra-human, and between diegetic spectators, cinema-goers, and ourselves as viewers watching others watch, foregrounds what Vertov saw as the potential for a truly visual cinema made possible through the perfection of machines.

Like many filmmakers before him, Vertov used the camera to reveal things that would otherwise be obscured to the human eye. His "kino-eye" is a mechanical prosthetic, extending and enhancing human visual capability, but not mimicking it. It was his mission to put forth a cinema not encumbered by the limits of human perception, but wholly different and more perfect than anything to which our fallible senses could aspire. The kino-eye, as espoused by Vertov and his colleagues, the *Kinoks*, could show the world as only it (the apparatus) can see it. In his "Variant of a Manifesto," Vertov writes, "The main and essential thing is: The sensory exploration of the world through film. We therefore take as the point of departure the use of the camera as a kino-eye, more perfect than the human eye, for the exploration of the chaos of the visual phenomena that fills space."[25] Vertov's filmic innovation was not to reveal the formerly obscure, but to link this capability—endowed by the camera—to his revolutionary ideals, thus asserting a connection between the ideal citizen enhanced with modern technology and an ideal city and society.

Man with a Movie Camera is a composite, idealized, Soviet city stitched together with everyday scenes from Moscow, Kiev, and Odessa. The film opens with a shot of a large camera and a small cameraman superimposed on top of it. The opening montage shows the city and a young woman waking from slumber. The young woman stretches and blinks her eyes, and the blinds in her room flutter and flicker like her eyelids. We see a shot of the camera's aperture opening that establishes the metaphor: this is a new way of seeing.

The film continues as a reeling assemblage of industry, labor, people, and transportation; but if there is any human subject advanced by the editing, it is the cameraman, and he plays a supporting role to that of the camera itself. In the last quarter of the film, the human body is made into a specimen on which to demonstrate the rigors of the mechanical eye. This segment is dominated by shots of people exercising and playing sports (throwing shot-put, high-jumping, hurdling, swimming, diving, horseback-riding, playing volleyball and soccer, and so on). Yet, despite the beauty of their sculpted bodies, the camera upstages them, rendering all these human movements in slow motion—something no human eye can accomplish. Additionally, there are allusions to the mechanical extension of the human ear through radio. A radio speaker is shown with images of an accordion, a piano, and a singing mouth superimposed on it. A woman riding on a carousel is juxtaposed with riders swirling along a track on motorbikes, a form of mechanical horses. These scenes depict the ideals of the Kinok's manifesto: "Our path leads through the poetry of machines, from the bungling citizen to the perfect electric man."[26]

The magic of the filmic medium is exposed in a reflexive manner through scenes of the film editor cutting and splicing the film and reanimating the people within the frame. This makes transparent both a technologically enhanced sensorial immersion in place as well as the artifice of such an experience. Vertov, nevertheless, maintained that this type of cinema would proffer *film-facts* through the magic made possible by the camera and such editing techniques.

Vertov chose not to use intertitles, which were common at the time to simulate dialogue and add other contextualizing information to a scene, preferring to highlight the new language of the visual made possible through his camera. Described as a camera operator's diary, the opening titles of the film explain its mission: "Attention Viewers: this film is an experiment in cinematic communication of real events without the help of intertitles, without the help of a story, without the help of theatre. This experimental work aims at creating a truly international language of cinema based on its absolute separation from the language of theatre and literature." In this abandonment of exposition, we can see a similar intention between Vertov's experiment and that of Gardner's *Forest of Bliss*.

While Vertov depicts an idealized and generalized Soviet city constructed by the "perfect electric man," Gardner uses the particularities of one city to comment on universal human conditions. Vertov's man was made perfect through mechanical enhancement, while Gardner sets the inherent impermanence of the human body as his literal and figural focus. Centered on the cremation ghats of the holy city of Benares, now Varanasi, India, Gardner takes us through the city whose main industry is comprised of the various services rendered for the ritual and pragmatic care for the dying and the deceased. This focus highlights the materiality and the ephemerality of the human body. The film begins with a dog running on sand, seemingly on the hunt. This opening shot coupled with a gruesome sequence of a dog fight and the epigraph, taken from a translation of the *Upanishads*—"Everything in this world is eater or eaten. The seed is food and the fire is eater"—sets the sober tone of the film. The bodies that we subsequently see, some of whom become familiar to the viewer over the course of the film, are archetypal and unnamed—a priest, a pyre attendant, a bamboo litter-maker, a marigold-picker, and so on. There are three prominent figures who emerge over the course of the film: Mithai Lal, a healer, Ragul Pandit, a Hindu priest, and the Dom Raja, the overseer of the great cremation ground of Manikarnika Ghat. We do not learn their names in the film, but observe as they attend to their daily tasks. Some of the bodies we see are no longer living; carried through the streets on their way to the funeral pyre for their prompt release from this world, or floating in the holy Ganges becoming food for carrion crows or dogs. Though the treatment of human subjects in *Forest of Bliss* does not depart dramatically from earlier City Symphonies in that the main identification of the viewer remains with the filmmaker, rather than an on-screen human subject, it does give a much more embodied perspective to the life and industry of the city.

Gardner's camera in *Forest of Bliss* is embodied and grounded, such that we see what Gardner sees, from his height and perspective. There are moments in the film when we see the concrete steps of the ghats from a low vantage point or are looking down on a bushel of marigolds being carried on the head of a woman, but these remain within the scale of embodied human perception.

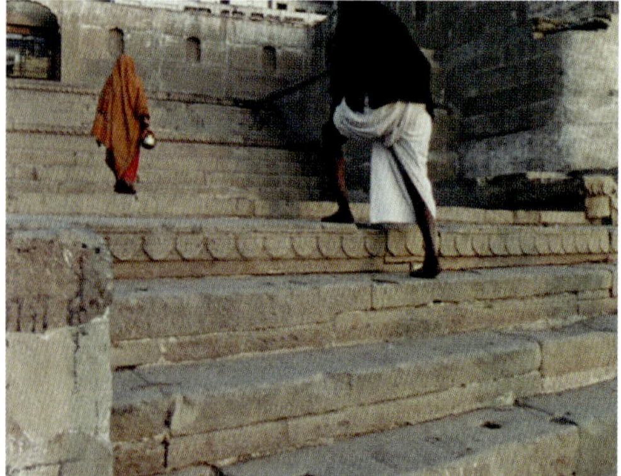

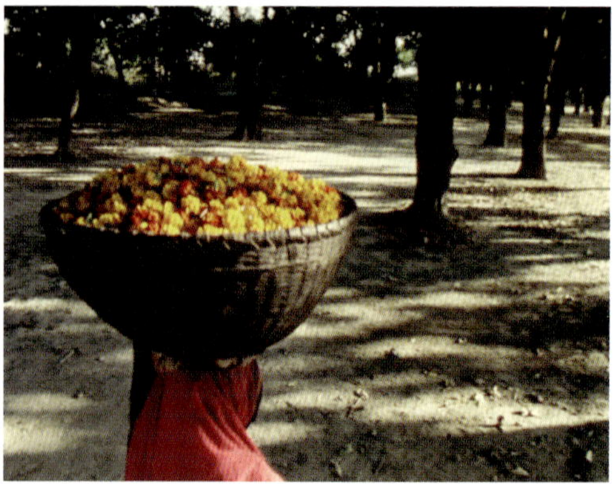

There are no bird's-eye views, or perspectives from underneath moving vehicles. In this way, Gardner's body becomes a "residue" in the work, adding a visceral layer to the more overt bodies on the screen and allowing us to see and hear with and alongside him.[27] Beyond camera angles and techniques, *Forest of Bliss* builds a corporeal resonance in more evanescent and experiential ways. The images and sounds build in a coalescing manner such that the viewer gains a sense of being in the city, among the people, animals, wood, marigolds, and boats.

MacDougall points out that the celebrations of a mobile camera as an extension of our own bodies and perceptual capabilities are equally evident in Vertov's extra-human camera perspectives, as in the ecstatic, even erotic pleasures described by other filmmakers. For Gardner, filming is as "close to cinematic orgasm as [he'll] get."[28] Through Gardner's deft ability to convey the physicality and texture of place, we come to share in this erotic pleasure. To feel the smoothness of the stone streets in Varanasi, or the stiff resistance of the oar in the oarlock is to follow his sensual journey. The Varanasi that he presents to us is clearly not the "city as machine"—it is a profoundly human and visceral city, a city with a complex sensorial ecology organized around the cycles of death, ritual, and rebirth. Indeed, Scott MacDonald points out that the daily cycles evoked in City Symphonies highlight the fact that cities necessitate a ritualization of their chaos to render them comprehensible and foreground their productive order. He writes, "In other words, Benares itself is a daily ritual, and the only way in which it differs from other cities [. . .] is that its primary industry is (or at least in *Forest of Bliss* seems to be) a continual direct confrontation with the materiality of death itself."[29]

The experiential register and the sensorial immersion it elicits in its audience are not wholly unique to *Forest of Bliss* among either City Symphonies or "ethnographic" films. Beattie notes that it was common for "showing" to take precedence over "telling" in City Symphonies.[30] Certainly other films of the ethnographic avant-garde (such as Jean Rouch's *Les maître fous*, 1955, and Maya Deren's posthumously completed *Divine Horsemen*, 1985) have used the camera to convey a sense of the embodied experience of the event or place in which they were filmed. But *Forest of Bliss* may represent a breakthrough in displaying sensorial and affective intensity to such a degree, perhaps affording the viewer a sense of participating in the ritual of the city itself. The absence of spoken dialogue, voice-over, and subtitles not only further locates us in Gardner's perspective as a foreigner who did not speak the language, but it also serves to plunge the viewer into the textures, rhythms, and smells of Varanasi.[31] The lack of linguistic exposition on the part of the filmmaker or the subjects in the film wrought much of the criticism from the anthropological community at the time of its release. In preceding decades the advent of synchronous sound, and the ability to subtitle indigenous subjects' speech were hailed as ways to "give voice to the people," which was, for a time, taken as an ethical necessity of ethnographic film. However, Gardner's personal

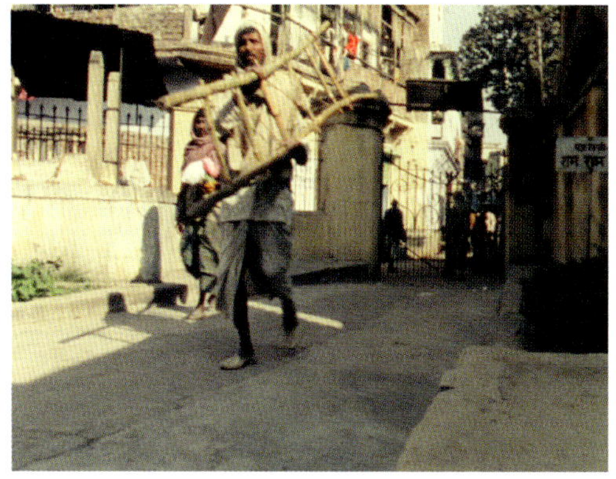

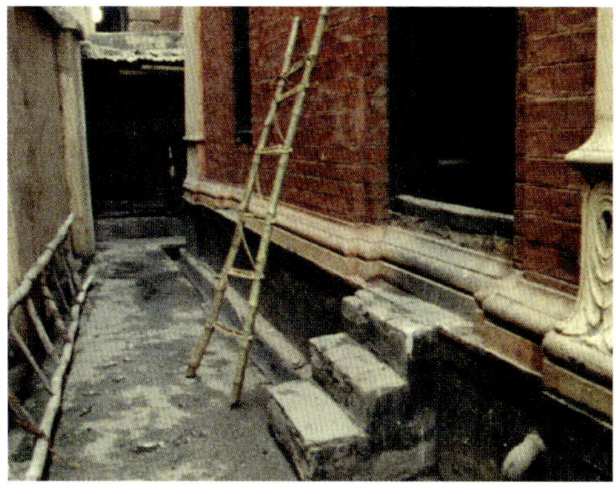

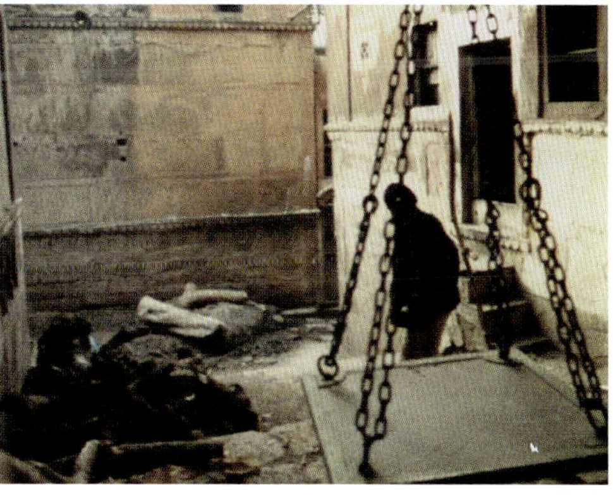

trajectory, which moves progressively away from a "discipline of words," pushed forward into a nonexpository space and into a more sensual, immersive cinema, implicitly asserting that ways of knowing exist beyond those rendered by words alone.

Rather than a measured representation of cultural truths, or a didactic account of ritual performances, Gardner's film presents a sensory ecology of the ghats and lanes of Varanasi, a visceral world of tactile, olfactory, and emotional engagements with his surroundings. Gardner is not concerned with expounding the interpretations that local inhabitants of Varanasi might attach to the rituals presented and the objects followed. Rather, his aim is a somatic, material, and metaphoric one. The entangled images and sounds of sand, water, fire, marigolds, kites, bamboo, and wood slowly weave together into networks of people, spaces, and events. We see the metal harvested from the funeral pyre and laid at the feet of the Dom Raja, displaying a complex material economy of death. We see marigold farms and the irrigating, picking, stringing, and transporting of this ubiquitous flower, which is charged with a sacred power in one scene, and eaten by a cow in the next. Qualitative perceptions here come across with a unique intensity. We do not learn how many pounds of wood are used in each pyre, only that they equal the amount of time and energy to burn one human body.

David MacDougall describes the "composite" characteristic of the visual whereby "we grasp objects and events in their complexes and continuities, and it is the interrelationships of these that are often more important than the components of the images taken separately."[32] This offers a way of exploring connections in the social world—not only arrangements of material objects but also "the relations between objects and actions, and the interplay between actions occurring simultaneously or in close combination."[33] Images and sounds afford a poetic implication through juxtaposition that builds a palimpsest of potential meanings both literal and metaphorical. Objects are selected from their reeling and relentless reality, composed and framed. They are heightened for our observation and placed in relation to other objects and events, creating a composite of things taken together as a complex sensory ecology. As McDougall states, "In *Forest of Bliss*, Gardner is committed to bringing us into a closer communication with wordless things and the networks of associations, by no means fixed, that may surround them."[34] Meaning that arises through such composite image-sound assemblages requires the viewer's active participation. The viewer's eyes, ears, and mind fill in the gaps to create a coherent space and meaning over the course of the film. When one first sees the bamboo litters that are used to carry the deceased to the ghats, one can only guess at their usage. Are they ladders? Scaffolding? A pile of wood beside an empty hanging scale seems incidental as we watch Mithai Lal, a local healer, walk past it on his way to the Ganges for his morning bath. Only later do we learn of their significance and as the film unfolds we come to realize the interconnections between these seemingly unrelated objects and actions.

Sound also plays a crucial role in constructing the sensorial ecology of Varanasi. In addition to recording synchronous sound on location, Gardner added some sounds in postproduction. This serves to heighten certain effects, at times making things sound closer than they appear and at other times denying us the sounds of things that appear to be nearby. The opening shot of a dog running across the sandy shore is recorded at the end of a long zoom lens, as is apparent by the foreshortened perspective, yet we hear its footsteps as if it were nearly within reach. The viewer, then, has a sense of being attuned to a specificity of texture and density, a tactility or "haptic" engagement with the images on the screen. The sound of Mithai Lal's grunting as he descends the steps to the ghats conveys the restrictions and struggles of his aging body. At other times, the audio conveys dryness and wetness, pliability and rigidity of materials. Scratchy, rattling voices, and clear shrill chimes of a bell give a sense of the humidity or crispness of the air and the surfaces of the built environment off which it ricochets. A particular crunch of a marigold tells you something about the porosity of its inner structure. The audio also conveys the rigidity of bamboo when a ladder/litter is disassembled, and the weight of a clay pot as it falls and breaks on the ground.

Much of the audio in *Forest of Bliss* does not gesture to the profilmic so much as it focuses the viewer intently on what is on the screen—the very embodied "here"-ness of the camera. To be sure, one hears the sounds of bells and chanting in the distance throughout the film, but the closeness of most of the audio hones and directs one's attention to an almost pinpoint acuity, to such an extent that each scene seems dominated by the friction of foot on step, mallet on bell, hammer on wood, tooth on marigold, oar in oarlock. This sensorial relationality thrusts the viewer into the space of Varanasi. All the more so, then, at the moments when the audio seems to miss its visual target, and our perceptual world slips, one feels the dreaminess of reality and the ephemerality of our bodies.

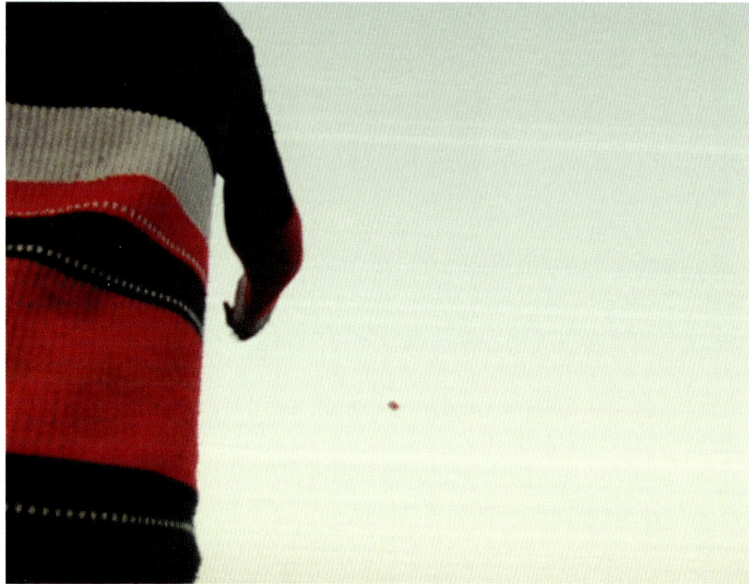

Gardner's deft ability to push and pull our attention between the sensorial immediacy of place, on the one hand, and a reflective consciousness of our own impermanence and frailty, on the other, is partly due to the ways he selects and highlights specific sonic elements. In one symbolically laden shot near the end of the film, a kite flits and falls into the water behind a boat in which two adults are depositing a small corpse into the watery mire.[35] Just before this shot we see a young boy flying a kite.

With him, we hear the sound of the paper kite being tugged and rustling in the wind over the river. We do not hear the sound of his arm brushing against his sweater, or his breath. Our focus, like his, is fixed on the paper kite high in the sky. Yet, in the shot that follows, we do not hear the sound of the body or the kite falling into the river. Rather, the sound of bells chiming in the distance carries through this cut from the living boy flying his kite to the boat divesting itself of its once living cargo. The bells here signal the pervasive gaze toward the "other side" of life, their sound traveling upward and across the river. The disjuncture of audio and image here resonates profoundly. We can sense the immanence of death, yet we also feel the liveliness of the children's kites, no matter the perilous nature of their journeys. This moment of reflection on the transiency of life is disrupted by the next cut, where we find ourselves walking closely beside a water buffalo whose beastly breath reaffirms our animal nature and our commonality as living beings that cannot escape death.

In the next five minutes of the film there are other instances of Gardner's use of a selective audition. Amid the bustling temple, we see a man prostrating himself on smoldering embers. We hear the sounds of temple bells loudly clanging and the soft whispers of devotees; but we do not hear the sound of the man's bare chest hitting the coals as he thrusts his body downward or the crackling sound of his torso rolling over the embers. Immediately after this shot, we see a girl drawing with chalk on the ground. The sun is getting low in the sky and we feel the film, too, reaching its dusk. The sound of chalk on stone is crisp and keen and we hear children playing nearby. As the girl throws her rock and leaves the frame, Gardner cuts to the only slow motion shot in the entire film—that of the girl playing hopscotch and skipping away from the camera, turning around and skipping back toward the camera.

In this shot we do not hear the sound of her feet hitting the ground, but rather the continued din of the sonic surround. Again, this selective auditory composition casts the viewer into a moment of reflection, but the metaphorical magnitude of the shot is not what Gardner wishes to convey in any pragmatic or expository way. In the video conversation *Looking at Forest of Bliss* (2000), Gardner explains to Stan Brakhage, "Hopscotch is the way to get to heaven. Heaven is the last square, isn't it? Yeah. And this is why I put it in, but I don't want anybody to list to that kind of arcane instruction. They have to feel it here, you know, with this child." The auditory and image compositions of the film exemplify the ways in which intersubjectivity is attuned to the senses—we, as viewers, can hear, and in some way sense, what others felt as we allow Gardner to guide and focus our attention.[36]

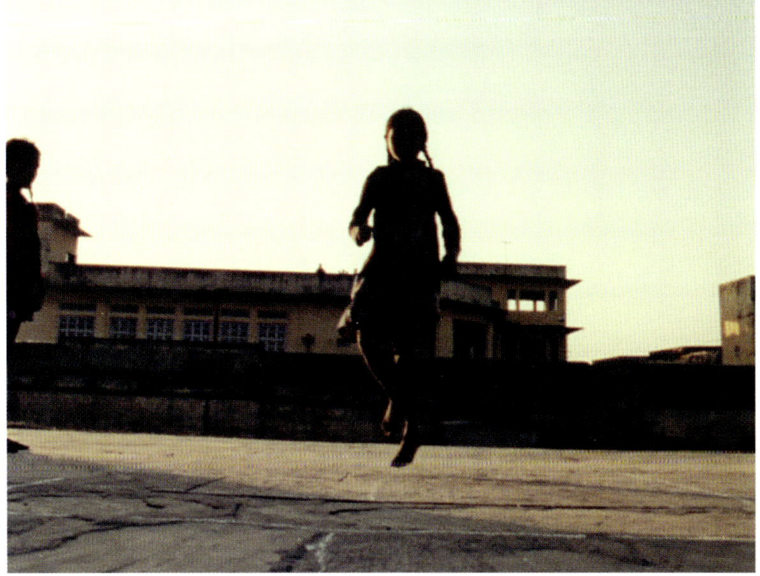

Angle 3—Immersion and "Aesthetic-sensual Ethnography"

The "sensory turn" and the resistance to *linguifying* films expands the scope of possibility within anthropological expression. The creative rendering of sensorial immersion in a place and time grounds us as viewers in our perceptual selves as we look, listen, and feel with and alongside Gardner. The cognitive gaps that emerge as questions in the viewer's mind—*Why are they doing that? What is the significance of the boats, the marigolds, the wood?*—are temporarily bracketed as we take in the material and temporal flow of images, trusting that unresolved ambiguities will proffer productive questions rather than didactic answers. In an interview with Ilisa Barbash, Gardner discusses the abandonment of voice-over in *Forest of Bliss*: "I did this in part because I mistrusted the authority of voice-over but I also wanted to allow mystery and ambiguity to play a part in the larger understanding of what I was putting in the film."[37]

Sensory immersion necessitates a relinquishing of any intention on the part of the filmmaker to achieve the holism espoused by Karl Heider's vision of ethnographic film as "whole people, whole bodies and whole acts."[38] In postproduction, the composition of a film is determined in part by its trajectory of disclosure. In this way, mystery becomes as important as revelation. The "slow disclosure" or "slow reveal" allows the viewer to put the pieces together, to discover connections between things, people, places, and events. In *Looking at Forest of Bliss*, Gardner describes the importance of the heavy mist that shrouds a galleon on the Ganges in the opening sequence of *Forest of Bliss*. He explains that he didn't "want the confusion of a city yet" nor to fully disclose the meaning of people carrying baskets of sand, but rather, to maintain "a little bit of mystery."

The capacity of image and sound to immerse its viewers in another sensory world—to plunge them into the overflowing of categories and flashes of recognition—has been demonstrated by a recent film produced in Harvard's Sensory Ethnography Lab. Though not a *city* symphony, Lucien Castaing-Taylor and Véréna Paravel's *Leviathan* submerges the viewer into the sensory world of a commercial fishing boat trolling the waters off New Bedford, Massachusetts in a way that resonates with the musical editing structures of the City Symphonies. City Symphonies largely equated life and vitality with modern industry and mechanization. In *Forest of Bliss*, the industry is one of death and shows little of the "modern" world.[39] *Leviathan* seems to take another direction by seeing death and the struggle for life—both of the fish and the fishermen whose livelihoods depend on this work—within one modern industry (that of the commercial fishing industry). Many early reviewers have noted that to describe *Leviathan* as a film *about* the commercial fishing industry is both accurate and deceptive.[40] The "about" is subverted by the film's commitment to immersion over explanation, to sensory saturation over verbal analysis or context. Much like *Forest of Bliss*, this film refrains from voice-over or extra-diegetic exposition and plunges the viewer into a reeling environment where fish, sea, fishermen, seagulls, and boat are embroiled in an epic struggle for existence.

The more structural or programmatic similarities between *Leviathan* and *Forest of Bliss* —such as the opening scriptural epigraphs[41]—are minor in comparison to the powerful immersive qualities that each executes. The embodied camera in *Leviathan* extends Gardner's subjective gaze (which in turn was a rehumanization of Vertov's mechanized *kino-eye*) by affixing the camera directly to the bodies of fishermen. Yet *Leviathan* in many ways is also a return to Vertovian cinematic tropes. Small waterproof cameras that were attached to the end of a pole afford us views of sea and air that extend the human eye and embodied perception. The swift arcs of cameras flying into the air amid ravenous seagulls and seamlessly plunging into the hoary waters of the Atlantic are truly Vertovian in impulse.

"Aesthetic-sensual ethnography," to use Nakamura's term, describes a sense of being there brought about by the elaboration of sensorial and temporal experience of a place. *Forest of Bliss* brings a sense of immersion to the City Symphony genre by giving the viewer a human-scaled look into the streets, ghats, and boats of a city. Left to slowly untangle the images and affects of this strange city, viewers are rewarded with a powerful sense of being inside this complex place. *Leviathan* continues this aspiration by tossing the viewer—tenuously tethered to any sense of up, down, night or day—into the perceptual worlds of commercial fishermen. Like Gardner's three main characters, *Leviathan*'s fishermen are unidentified and their speech is not subtitled or otherwise made comprehensible, thus accentuating a sense of being on the fishing boat over the development of individual personalities or a didactic explanation of events and processes.

The almost excruciating din of *Leviathan*'s soundtrack also plays a critical role in the sense of being aboard the commercial fishing vessel. Mixed by the Sensory Ethnography Lab's Ernst Karel (and then mastered by Jacob Ribicoff), the grating audio invades our ears, propelling us into the overwhelming sonic seascape. The clashing and clanging of chains reeling the nets up from the sea, the squawking of seagulls, and the rush of crashing water against the sides of the boat are exhausting to endure and elicit a felt empathy with the captain whom we witness falling asleep in the galley while the television drums onward, ironically playing the fishing show, *The Deadliest Catch*.

Many reviewers have noted that *Leviathan* is and is not a "documentary," a veritable "merger of academia and art house."[42] While the praise garnered by *Forest of Bliss* did not save it from the acerbic criticism of some anthropologists, a reception of *Leviathan* by the academic community has yet to occur. A review in *The Village Voice* states that *Leviathan* "explodes the antiquated paradigm of the documentary or ethnographic film" and plunges the viewer into "full, relentless, estranging immersion."[43] Additionally, the paracinematic materials (still frames and gallery installations) accompanying *Leviathan* align it with the growing body of works that are forging new paths in the spaces of overlap between art and anthropology. Paracinematic materials, such as Castaing-Taylor's digital audio-video installations *Coom Biddy* (2012) and *Hell Roaring Creek* (2010), grew out of his production (together with Ilisa Barbash) of *Sweetgrass* (2010). *Leviathan* has also spawned a gallery installation, *He Maketh A Path To Shine After Him; One Would Think The Deep To Be Hoary* (2013), which reworks the footage of the feature film into a single-channel silent video. As media continue to spill over from their original formats and into galleries, photography books, and web platforms, these expand the traditional audience of anthropological materials and reach across disciplinary boundaries in new ways. Discussing the gallery-based work of Eva Stefani, David MacDougall, and Barbash and Castaing-Taylor, Grimshaw and Ravetz note, "Understood as experiments in a phenomenological anthropology, they propose new ways of presenting human experience. The radical nature of the challenge follows from pushing further into the real—not seeking to more effectively represent it."[44]

Gardner's *Forest of Bliss* provided a catalyst for renewed efforts to extend anthropology beyond a discipline of words and inspired a new generation of filmmakers to explore the possibilities of sensual and immersive filmmaking. Gardner's intellectual progeny can be traced through the filmmakers active in Harvard's Film Study Center and Sensory Ethnography Lab, particularly films by recent alums Stephanie Spray and J.P. Sniadecki. Together with Libbie Cohn, Sniadecki made *People's Park* (2012), a 78-minute single shot of an urban park in Chengdu, China. In this film, the camera floats, almost supernaturally, through throngs of people dancing, singing karaoke, dining, and sitting and chatting on benches. Cohn, who was holding the camera, sat in a wheelchair as Sniadecki slowly pushed her through the crowd. This positioned the camera at waist level and gives the film a sense of bodily movement that is uncanny, affording a specific viewing of the park. *People's Park* documents the passing moments of encounter with strangers—the quizzical glances and fleeting expressions of the pedestrians as well as the frequent acts of performance displayed at times with an explicit acknowledgment of the camera. The reflexivity inscribed in these performative encounters foregrounds what Taylor describes as "the active engagement between filmmaker and filmed in the production of cinematic meaning," where the medium's ability and "particularly its use of experience, make it. . . at once subject and object to itself."[45]

As we slowly move through the park, each encounter reveals new boundaries of familiarity or foreignness, exhibition or concealment, and the cacophony and mingling of amplified sound adds a sense of being in this public space, witnessing and being confounded by the many simultaneous ways in which it is used.

Far from the frenzy and din of *Leviathan*, *Manakamana* (2013) by Stephanie Spray and Pacho Velez is a meditative, 118-minute film shot entirely from inside a small cable car going up the side of a mountain to the Manakamana temple in Nepal. Comprised of eleven 10-minute shots (the length of one 400-foot reel of film), this film immerses the viewer in a space that exceeds its small physical confines. One's attention drifts from the passing landscape to the people as they move through various states of contemplation and anticipation along their pilgrimage to the holy site. Rather than an embodied camera that belies the corporeality of the filmmakers, in *Manakamana* the camera is likened to the apparatus of the cable car itself. The duration of one trip up the mountain roughly equals the length of time on one reel of film, providing a structural element that draws a parallel between these two mechanized cycles of time. Shot on the same Aaton 7 LTR camera that Gardner used to shoot *Forest of Bliss*, Spray remarks in an interview with producers Lucien Castaing-Taylor and Véréna Paravel that she and Velez were well aware of the legacy of *Forest of Bliss* and the fact that both films were shot at popular pilgrimage sites. In addition to the similarity of sites, Gardner's influence can be seen in the foregrounding of the experience of place and the patient and careful observation of these filmmakers. Speaking about her work, Spray states, "I hope that, if my previous films are about anything, they are about something basic about experience itself, what it feels like to linger in a place with people over time. For this reason, I favored rambling conversations to interviews, and shots that loiter with their subjects, allowing the shots to develop internally as well as within in the larger structure of the film."[46]

By foregrounding the temporal and material experiences of a place, these films recuperate a radical empiricism that subverts the tendency within anthropological epistemology to distrust perceptual surfaces and seek out what lies beneath, behind, or under. Webb Keane notes that certain assumptions are built into a Western intellectual heritage that tend to "divide attention between things and ideas," where things are taken to be the material surfaces in and through which we interact with the world, whereas ideas are taken to be isomorphic with interiors, thoughts, meanings. Western associations of depth with profundity deny the many attributes that are gleaned by our sensory perception, desiring a deeper "about-ness" at the expense of surface detail and apprehension. Rey Chow notes that this focus on depth, profundity, and interiority exudes its preference for a "*somethingness* in representation," whether on the screen or in a book.[47] Yet, the affect/effect of sensory immersion in film is paradoxically about the limits of experience. We see and look with another, from another's subjective perspective (mediated through the camera, projector, screen and the "filter" of the recordist). The limits of perception are perhaps the defining characteristic of being, for it is these limitations that ground us in our own bodies. Following Wittgenstein, if we recognize the subject as the *condition* of experience—as at once both the limit of experience and the experience of limits—the relation of the subject to the world is one of shifting limits of perception and apperception. It is in this profilmic space—a space that exists in relation to, and which lies at the boundaries of, our field of vision/experience—that we can detect the existence of things beyond our grasp.

To look at the same thing from different angles is at the heart of observational practices—a triangulation of ways of seeing and ways of knowing. Gardner's *Forest of Bliss* is just one angle from which to look at Varanasi, ritual, and death. MacDougall writes, "Whether one would prefer a more 'ethnographic' Benares, or a Benares more situated in contemporary Indian history and politics—Gardner's way of seeing social and cultural interconnections can still be productive for anthropology [. . .] he is interested in integrating fragments of experience into a thematic reality—a 'film truth' which can never be the truth of other methods."[48]

Though MacDougall's sentiment is not the totalizing quest of Vertov's *kino-pravda* ("film-truth"), which sought to make "the invisible visible, the unclear clear, the hidden manifest, the disguised overt,"[49] both acknowledge that these film-truths, or film-facts, are part of a different way of knowing and expressing the human condition; that these truths offer something distinct to our search for knowledge, and that they exceed singular interpretations of *about-ness,* or the "name, date, place, and number" of a "fact taken from life." Indeed, they not only offer something distinct *to* our search for knowledge, but also distinct *from* it. As both an *about* and an *of*, films inherently present and represent; they are both a composition and a record of a filmmaker's engagement with the found materials, sensations, and rhythms of a place. Beyond meaning and the pragmatic significance of events, Gardner brings to bear ways of being in the world that exceed our quests for knowledge.

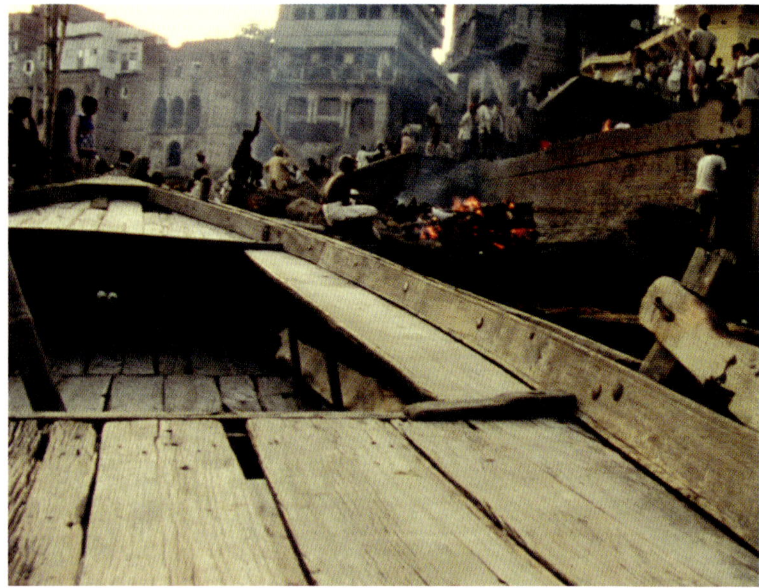

In *Looking at Forest of Bliss,* Gardner points to the corner of the frame and says, "See way up at the right there is the circumambulation of the corpse with the sacred fire. That I know because I was there, but it is not important to the feelings that I want engendered by the scene. It is not that particular piece of sacred duty that is important; it's the color and the gesture which are important."

Taylor writes, "Once one allows the possibility that film could make a scientific statement about the world, we can step outside the seductive myth system that would have us believe that it is only a crass copy of it."[50] While we may have been trying to step out of this "seductive myth" since Vertov's 1926 manifesto, I remain hopeful that recent provocations in the relationship between art and anthropology and the expansion of anthropological knowledge beyond the traditional coupling of meaning and naming will continue to open up new spaces of exploration for nonfiction filmmaking.

Notes

1. Ilisa Barbash and Lucien Taylor, eds., *The Cinema of Robert Gardner* (New York and Oxford: Berg, 2007), 9.
2. See, for example, Arnd Schneider and Christopher Wright, eds., *Contemporary Art and Anthropology* (New York: Berg, 2006) and *Between Art and Anthropology: Contemporary Ethnographic Practice* (New York: Berg, 2010); Anna Grimshaw and Amanda Ravetz, eds. *Visualizing Anthropology* (Bristol, UK: Intellect, 2005) and *Observational Cinema: Anthropology, Film and the Exploration of Social Life* (Bloomington and Indianapolis: Indiana University Press, 2009); and Howard Morphy and Morgan Perkins, eds. *The Anthropology of Art: A Reader* (Oxford: Blackwell, 2006).
3. In addition to the concept of aesthetics elaborated by Kant and Baumgarten, I take this term to include the more expansive, Aristotelian notion of *aesthesis*, understood as "our total sensory experience of the world and our sensitive knowledge of it" (Jojada Verrips, "Aesthesis and An-aesthetesia." *Ethnologia Europaea*, vol. 35, no. 2, 2006, 27–33).
4. For a wonderful history of this era of anthropology, see George Stocking, *Victorian Anthropology* (New York: Free Press, 1991). See also Elizabeth Edwards and Chris Morton, *Photography, Anthropology and History* (Aldershot: Ashgate, 2009).
5. George E. Marcus and Fred Myers, *The Traffic in Culture: Refiguring Art and Anthropology* (Berkeley: University of California Press, 1995), 27.
6. See, for example, Claire Bishop, *Artificial Hells: Participatory Art and the Politics of Spectatorship* (New York: Verso, 2012).
7. George E. Marcus and Michael M.J. Fischer, *Anthropology as Cultural Critique: An Experimental Moment in the Human Sciences* (Chicago: University of Chicago Press, 1986), 8.

8. The debate about *Forest of Bliss* largely concerned its "ethnographic-ness" and the nature of "ethnographic film" and was hashed out in the *Society for Visual Anthropology Newsletter* in the late 1980s and in the *Visual Anthropology Review* in the 1990s. A few notable articles include: David MacDougall, "Gifts of Circumstance," *Visual Anthropology Review*, vol. 17, no. 1, Spring/Summer 2001, 68–85; Jay Ruby, "The Emperor and His Critics," *SVA Newsletter*, Spring 1990, 9–11; Andrew Moore, "The Limitations of Imagist Documentary: A Review of Robert Gardner's *Forest of Bliss*," *SVA Newsletter*, Fall 1988, vol. 4, no. 2, 1–3.

9. *Visualizing Anthropology*, 3.

10. Jay Ruby, "The Emperor and His Clothes: A Comment," *SVA Newsletter*, vol. 5, issue 1, March 1989, 10.

11. Heidi Larson, "Gardner's Forest Fires: Hindu Bliss," *Anthropology and Humanism Quarterly*, 12 (3 and 4), 1987, 98.

12. See Christopher Wright, "In the Thick of It: Notes on Observation and Context," in *Between Art and Anthropology: Contemporary Ethnographic Practice*, eds. Wright and Arndt Schneider (New York and Oxford: Berg, 2010). Recent works, such as those coming out of the Sensory Ethnography Lab at Harvard University, are showing at film festivals that are not explicitly concerned with "ethnographic" film, as well as being reworked for gallery settings, for example, Lucien Castaing-Taylor and Ilisa Barbash's *Sweetgrass* (2010) and *Sheep Rushes* (2010), as well as Castaing-Taylor and Véréna Paravel's *Leviathan* (2012).

13. Kathryn Ramey, "Productive Dissonance and Sensuous Image-making: Visual Anthropology and Experimental Film," in *Made to be Seen: Perspectives on the History of Visual Anthropology*, eds. Marcus Banks and Jay Ruby (Chicago: University of Chicago Press, 2011), 258. Ramey suggests that the work of Chick Strand, for example, has managed to elude anthropological film canons despite her anthropological training and self-identification as an ethnographic filmmaker because it did not circulate in anthropological circuits. (Ibid., 268.)

14. David MacDougall and others have argued for the development of a filmic, visual, or sensorial anthropology distinct from its written rubrics—one that does not take the sensorial as an illustrative supplement to the anthropological text, but takes seriously the forms of knowledge that emerge "from the very grain of the filmmaking." MacDougall, *Transcultural Cinema* (Princeton: Princeton University Press, 1998), 76.

15. Ibid., 137.

16. *Visualizing Anthropology*, 2.

17. Ibid., 13.

18. McGill University, Tufts University, and others have offered courses addressing "sensory ethnography" as a way to explore a broader sensorial spectrum of human experience from taste and foodways to sound and audition. Harvard's Sensory Ethnography Lab and the University of Manchester's Granada Centre for Visual Anthropology have offered more developed programs in "sensory ethnography" or "sensory media" since the mid-2000s.

19. Karen Nakamura, "Making Sense of Sensory Ethnography: The Sensual and the Multisensory," *American Anthropologist*, vol. 115, no. 1, 2013, 133.

20. Robert Gardner and Ákos Östör, *Making* Forest of Bliss*: Intention, Circumstance, and Chance in Nonfiction Film* (Cambridge, MA: Harvard Film Archive, 2001), 37.

21. Ibid., 180.

22. Ibid.

23. *The Cinema of Robert Gardner*, 98.

24. David MacDougall, *The Corporeal Image: Film, Ethnography, and the Senses* (Princeton: Princeton University Press, 2006), 13.

25. Dziga Vertov, *Kino-eye: The Writings of Dziga Vertov*, ed. Annette Michelson, trans. Kevin O'Brien (Berkeley: University of California Press, 1984), 14–15.

26. Ibid., 8.

27. *The Corporeal Image*, 26.

28. Ibid., 27.

29. Scott MacDonald, *American Ethnographic Film and Personal Documentary: The Cambridge Turn* (Berkeley: University of California Press, 2013), 94.

30. Keirh Beattie, *Documentary Display: Re-Viewing Nonfiction Film and Video* (London: Wallflower Press, 2008), 52.

31. For excellent discussions of the absence of words in *Forest of Bliss,* see *The Cinema of Robert Gardner*; Ilisa Barbash, "Out of words: The aesthesodic cine-eye of Robert Gardner: An Exegesis and Interview," *Visual Anthropology* 14:4, 2008, 369–413; and *Documentary Display*.

32. *The Corporeal Image*, 37.

33. Ibid., 38.

34. *The Cinema of Robert Gardner*, 157.

35. In *Looking at Forest of Bliss*, a 2000 video conversation with Stan Brakhage, Gardner describes this scene, saying: "The kite is a very frail object at the end of a very frail tether, you know, it's like, for me, metaphorically speaking, a life at the end of a thread that can break at any time." The Gardner/Brakhage conversation is included on the *Forest of Bliss* DVD produced by Studio7Arts, 2008.

36. For a lovely description of the effects of listening to a soundscape, see Michael D. Jackson, "Reflections on Copenhagen: Listening with Steve." *Sensate* (2011), http://sensatejournal.com/2011/03/michael-jackson-reflections-on-copenhagen/

37. *The Cinema of Robert Gardner*, 101.

38. Karl Heider, *The Principles of Visual Anthropology* (Berlin: Walter de Gruyter GmbH, 1974), 75.

39. Gardner was criticized for depicting the traditional and enduring aspects of Varanasi to the denial of the "modern." See Jyotsna Kapur, "The Art of Ethnographic Film and the Politics of Protesting Modernity: Robert Gardner's *Forest of Bliss*," *Visual Anthropology*, 9:2, 1997, 167–185.

40. A.O. Scott. "Or Would You Rather Be a Fish? 'Leviathan' From Lucien Castaing-Taylor and Véréna Paravel," *New York Times*, February 28, 2013.

41. The opening epigraph of *Leviathan* is taken from the Biblical book of Job: "He makes the depths churn like a boiling cauldron and stirs up the sea like a pot of ointment."

42. Dennis Lim, "The Merger of Academia and Art House: Harvard Filmmakers' Messy World," review of *Leviathan* by Lucien Castaing-Taylor and Véréna Paravel, *New York Times*, August 31, 2012. See also Pat Dowell, "'Leviathan': The Fishing Life, From 360 Degrees," National Public Radio, March 16, 2013.

43. Melissa Anderson, "Steel Yourself for Leviathan, A Watery Knockout," *Village Voice*, February 27, 2013.

44. Ravetz, *Visualizing Anthropology*, 142.

45. Lucien Taylor, "Iconophobia," *Transition*, no. 69, 1996, 79.

46. From an interview published on the film's official website, http://manakamanafilm.com/director-qa/

47. Rey Chow, *Primitive Passions: Visuality, Sexuality, Ethnography, and Contemporary Chinese Cinema* (New York: Columbia University Press, 1995), 154.

48. MacDougall, "Gifts of Circumstance."

49. Vertov, 41.

50. Taylor, "Iconophobia," 82.

Chapter 19
Hand Eye Coordination: Robert Gardner's Artist Films

Richard Deming

At the opening of his essay "The Film Sense and the Painting Sense," Parker Tyler insists, "There has always been commerce, more or less conscious, between painting and the film."[1] The idea may be broadly stated, but it is useful to have this claim hovering in order to begin thinking about the issues that certain films of Robert Gardner's take on in relation to the exchanges—both latent and active—between painting and film. If how Gardner represents the people and things on which he trains his camera has long been a fascinating and provocative aspect of his films, the issue is perhaps even more complex when his work represents the very processes of representation itself.

Within his oeuvre, the artist films are not an afterthought—Gardner's cinematic engagement with artists is present from the very beginning of his body of work, with his first film about the Abstract Expressionist Mark Tobey appearing in 1952. One could see Gardner's artist films as being part—however distinct—of his ethnographic corpus. Built into that classification, however, would lie the claim that artists are somehow a group set apart from the rest of culture—that the life and thinking of artists is separate from the lives of people watching the films. The implication is that art is not a part of life, that art is somehow exotic or otherworldly. It would also place Gardner himself at a remove from his subject when actually he tends to blur the distance between what he is doing with his camera and what the people before his lens are doing. With the artist films, Gardner locates the filmed behavior as specific in terms of the art practices depicted, but this behavior is not separate from the world inhabited either by Gardner or by the potential viewers of the film. Gardner's artist films collapse distance between the activity of art and the viewer.

There is a biographical context for Gardner's interest in artists. The filmmaker's father was the favorite nephew of Isabella Stewart Gardner, one of the preeminent collectors in the history of American art, who left her house and collection as a museum in Boston, where Robert Gardner grew up. Furthermore, beginning in 1949, before turning so resolutely to the practice of making films, Gardner spent time teaching medieval art and history at the College of Puget Sound. As a young man he worked restoring mosaics at the Chora Church in Istanbul. We can safely say that aesthetic concerns about representation always played a role in Gardner's thinking—they were a part of his cultural DNA. In telling ways, Gardner's world was that of an artist. His very mode of perception was that of an artist, and so the world he lived in was determined by its capability to be art, and was thus constituted by his aesthetic responses.

Moreover—and this is important—such artistic perception was predicated on the sense that the phenomenal world makes moral claims upon our attention. "I propose that in film's very nature," Gardner has written, "somewhere embedded in its formal attributes as a mediator of the phenomenal world, there arises a capacity for evoking moral responses in those who come in contact with it."[2] Such a formulation suggests that in his role as filmmaker, he was the shaper of a moral possibility occurring in response to—indeed, as part of—aesthetic experience. This is what I mean when I say Gardner thought like an artist rather than as merely an observer or documenter of human behavior.

There are others who have more expertise and more at stake than I do in wanting to discuss the ways that Gardner's films extend the boundaries of anthropology. Surely it is possible that something could be both anthropology and art. I simply want to underline the fact that Gardner thought like an artist in regard to film. He placed the emphasis not on the content, but on the form, on the medium itself. In "The Fiction of Nonfiction Film," Gardner wrote, "All filmmaking consists in shaping something in such a way and with such materials and devices that it becomes an object, an object that is always an invention: another item of culture with form and content."[3] Gardner said in his interview with Ilisa Barbash that one of film's unique qualities is that it appeals "to our kinesthetic natures, especially our capacity for empathy."[4] He extended this idea, positing, "in film experience we kinesthetically incorporate actuality or its fictional equivalent and almost relive it in the process. Maybe new and different understanding arises from these felt experiences." How the imagination coalesces around attempts to articulate the experience was Gardner's subject; it is his own aesthetic, ethical response that asks viewers to draw near and take part in a shared imagination of how to imagine possibility, for these possibilities are found in what we do to make them.

If art creates the capacity for moral response, what happens if the filmmaker's art and its responses overlie the painter's art? Gardner's artist films seek to reveal the poetics and behavior and rites that are all part of the work of a work of art. That is to say, in Gardner's films the art is inseparable from the artist in the act of creating it, and in the end inseparable from Gardner and his active art as filmmaker, and inseparable from us as viewers—if we will engage with what we see.

In *Mark Tobey* (1952), Gardner's second film, he tried a poetic approach to his subject. Tobey was an important Abstract Expressionist, though he is often placed at the edges of the group of artists to whom that label applies, largely because he left New York and lived for many years in Seattle, before moving in the last part of his life to Basel, Switzerland. Despite his being outside of the artistic nexus of New York, Tobey remained quite influential, and in 1958 he was awarded the City of Venice painting prize at the Venice Biennale, becoming only the second American to have won a prize there since the Biennale began in 1895. Steven Naifeh and Gregory White, in their much-lauded biography *Jackson Pollock: An American Saga*, suggest that a 1944 New York show of Tobey's work made an impression on the much younger Pollock, who at that time was just coming into his own and shared a similar sense of abstraction with the older painter.[5]

Tobey's work is often characterized by a dense network of threads and loops of strokes often calligraphic in nature and appearing over a layer of paint. Writing in his 1962 monograph about the artist, William Seitz describes the work this way: "Mark Tobey's paintings are seldom large, and many are smaller than this page. They are usually rendered in tempera and watercolor rather than oil, in unassertive colors. His surfaces are worked with brush strokes that can be explosively bold, but are more often as delicate as strands of a spider web or as ephemeral as smoke arising from a cigarette."[6] In a review of a retrospective of Tobey's work in Paris in 1961, originally published in the international edition of the *New York Herald Tribune*, John Ashbery suggested that Tobey's reputation had never been as great as that of Pollock or Franz Kline because Tobey's work was always much smaller in size and dimension, subtler in its strokes, and more understated in its use of colors. Ashbery felt that because it isn't monumental the size of Tobey's work produces a recognizably human scale. "In a time when everything is measured by the inhuman figures of megaton and billion, Tobey's work strikes a note of hope. For it implies that no matter how vast and foreign are the spaces that surround us, there is nothing so unlike man that it cannot be comprehended and translated into human terms by the artist."[7] These methods of recognition—comprehension, translation—work throughout Gardner's filmic portrait of Tobey. In fact, what Ashbery says here could describe Gardner's work as well.

Mark Tobey, *Canticle,* 1954

Mark Tobey is comprised of various scenes—Tobey at a gallery, Tobey working, and Tobey moving through Seattle gathering material. There is no exposition or historical context provided. The film opens as a silhouette walks slowly past a sign on a wall with letters spelling out "Mark Tobey," clearly indicating an exhibition. Gardner's camera cuts to various paintings hanging, while we hear on the ambient soundtrack the sort of banal (sometimes apt, sometimes inane) observations one overhears at any art opening. "It's a new space alright, but why does he have to be so derivative?" a woman's voice drawls; "tangles, cobwebs, spaghetti," three different voices offer; a person interjects off-screen: "intersubjectivist." The voices speed up and blur into the sound of cackling chickens. Onscreen the paintings are interspersed with glimpses of Tobey talking to people, while also there is a shot of him wearing a strange mask while looking at a painting and then turning to the camera. When the voices give way to chickens squawking, we see Tobey standing in a formal pose between two paintings, and the scene dissolves to some other part of the city.

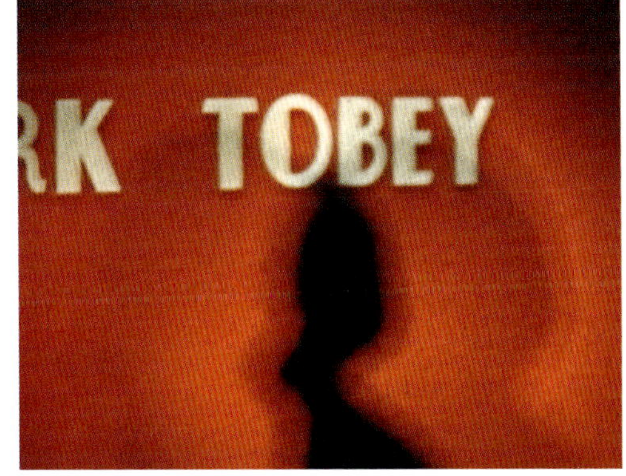

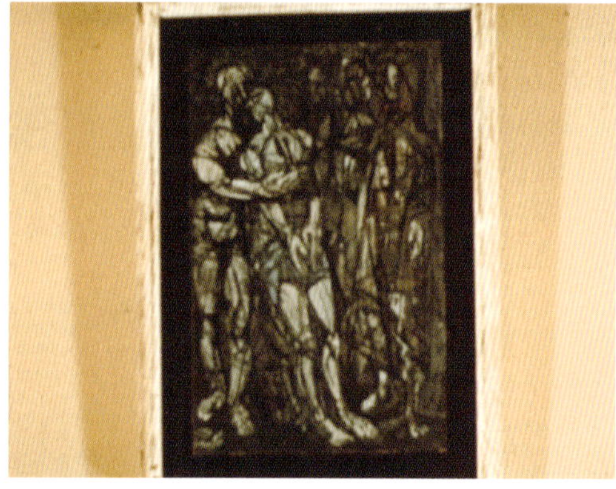

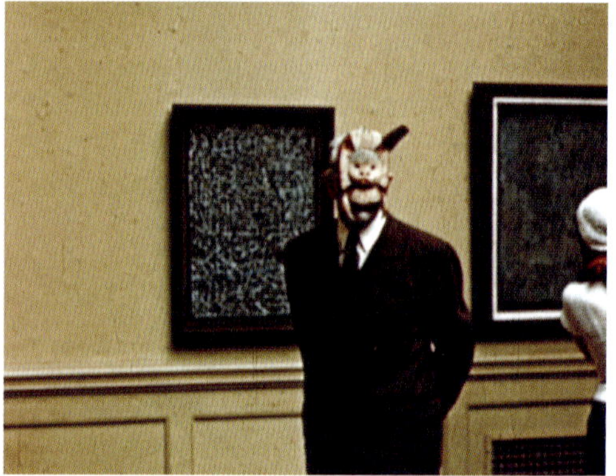

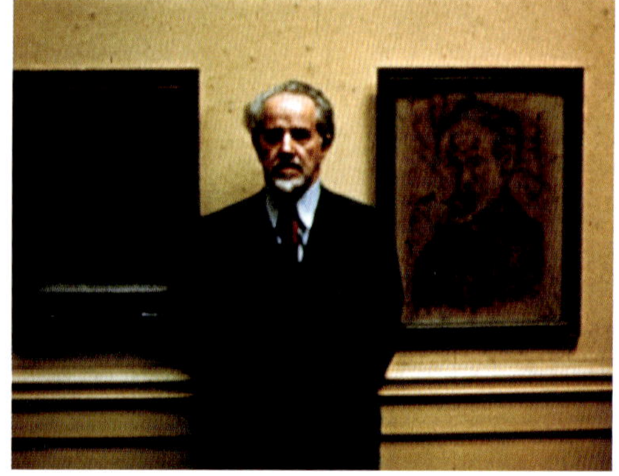

This seems to be Tobey's home, and as he steps out, we hear a voice that is much more focused and authoritative than the party conversation. Throughout the film Gardner provides only a poetic voice-over, not directive narration. The first thing we hear from this voice is, "*Why* are you artist? Why the chasm between us? Your beard gives me the willies." The third sentence is largely facetious, of course, and it makes us wonder whether the first two questions are in earnest or if they are meant to be part of the mocking tone of the introductory scene at the art opening. The film won't go on to answer the first question, but it does seem that Gardner takes the second question seriously—indeed all his artist films will try to address the gap that exists between artists and viewers and show that art both separates and brings people into contact.

In many ways, the film's narration doesn't have the elegance that marks so much of Gardner's work after this point, but it is the visuals, appropriately enough, that are the true power of *Mark Tobey* and its portrait of the artist. The film makes use of several avant-garde techniques—from its ironizing of the voices in the gallery and the surreal image of Tobey in a mask, to the lack of exposition that creates some alienation, to the radical juxtapositions of images—and these require viewers to actively engage with what they see. After establishing at the beginning of the film what Tobey's paintings look like, Gardner finds countless real-world correlatives that reveal Tobey's forms and figures are not wholly mental but are derived from patterns that are everywhere around us. Gardner does this by showing Tobey walking down a street as the camera stays at a slight remove. We're meant to follow him into his way of seeing things. The scene then jumps to various close-ups of the wires and cables of street cars, which immediately recalls the dense crossing lines of Tobey's paintings. Gardner had already foreshadowed the way his camera would provide analogues: in the opening sequence, the crossed wires of a heating vent appear amid the shots of paintings. At that point, it seemed just to provide a sense of the specifics of the gallery, but now the viewer recalls that moment and links it to the art.

At one point Gardner's film offers what amounts to an enactment of the first paragraph of a 1951 essay by Tobey entitled "Reminiscence and Reverie," in which the painter writes:

> On the third floor of Manning's Coffee Shop in the Farmer's Market in Seattle confronting the Sound, the windows are opaque with fog. Sitting here in the long deserted room, I feel suspended enveloped by a white silence.
>
> Two floors below, the farmers are bending over their long rows of fruit and vegetables; washing and arranging their produce under intense lights shaded by circular green shades. Above, where I sit, the world

> seems obliterated from all save memory; abstracted without the feeling of being divorced from one's roots.
>
> My eye keeps focusing upon the opaque windows. Suddenly the vision is disturbed by the shape of a gull floating silently across the width of the window. Then space again.[8]

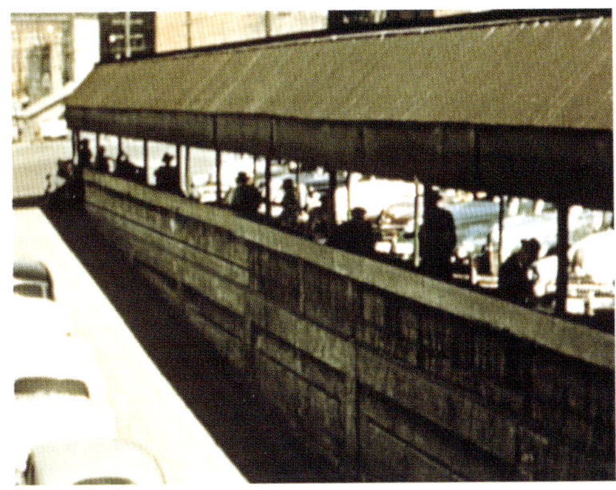

Gardner, through his use of montage, makes visible the associative jumps Tobey describes here. Placing images drawn from ordinary aspects of life—a market, a street, the dump—and Tobey's paintings next to one another, and sometimes using dissolves to let the images briefly overlap, and by using the camera to blur and reshape what we see.

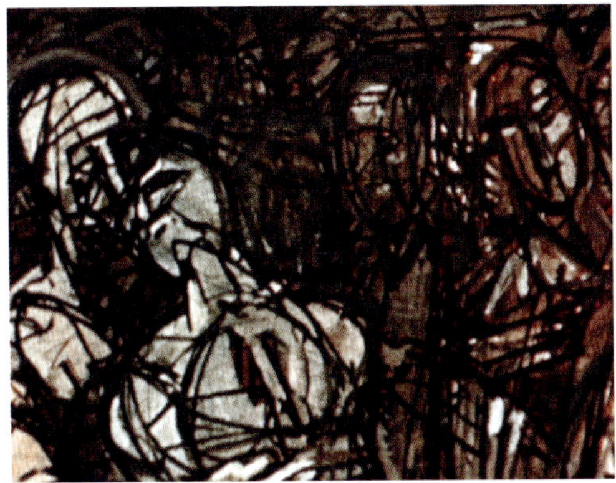

Gardner's experimental techniques attempt to render vision as a complicated perceptual process that is never stable and is also always informed by levels of abstraction. We are now primed to see that even as Gardner teaches us to see Tobey's work as shapes abstracted from, but still recalling, the world, the paintings are meant to teach us how to see in the world its particular possibilities for aesthetic experience—in the angles of apartment building windows or the facade of a train station or bundles of wire fencing at the city dump. Every line and angle of the urban space seems to become full of possibilities for response, for reading how the sheer fact of objects and things act upon us. And because Gardner shows Tobey interacting with people all over the city, the film suggests that abstraction is not only *not* separate from life, it is always shot through with a sense of human interaction.

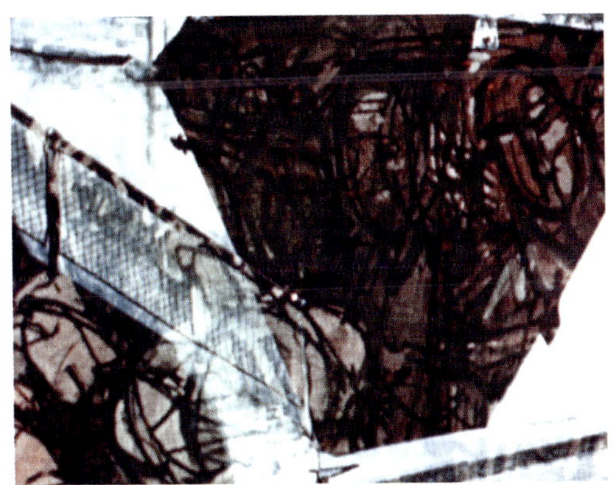

In providing correlatives for Tobey's aesthetics, Gardner's own artistic processes become part of the audience's experience. In part, this means that Gardner's filmic techniques interpose, and so we are never directly exposed to Tobey's work. What the filmmaker offers are interpretations and visual descriptions of Tobey's work and his aesthetic sensibility. The readings are comprised of images rather than words. Furthermore, in the ways it trains the viewer's eye, the film acknowledges its "commerce" with painting, which, as we have seen, Tyler describes as an intrinsic aspect of cinema. Because we are familiar with abstract painting, we know how to derive the interconnections Gardner is suggesting through the angles and perspectives he frames with his camera. *Mark Tobey* is more than an exposure to a particular artist—it serves essentially as an exercise in vision, and this is underscored by the fact that the voice (whose monologue is a combination of a meditation on art by Gardner and lines from

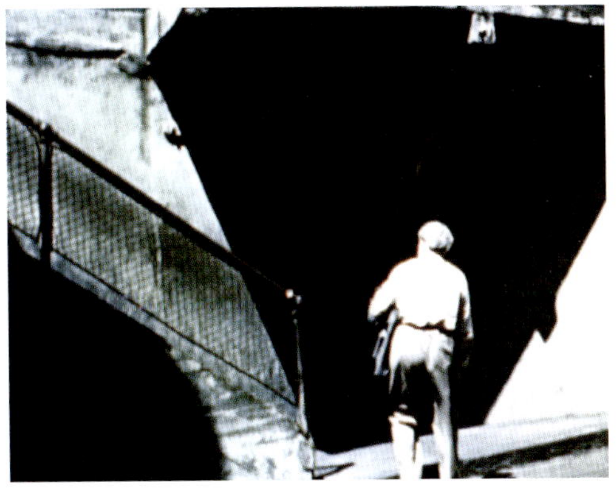

poems by Tobey) keeps coming back to the trope of the eye and seeing. The film becomes a vision of another's way of envisioning.

Twenty years later, in *Mark Tobey Abroad* (1973), Gardner returns to offer another portrait of the abstract painter, now in his eighties, who by that time was living in Basel. The second film has elements in common with the first. Again, we see Tobey moving around the city and interacting with the locals. Again, Gardner points his camera at cobblestone streets and ripples on the face of the river, to show that abstract patterns are always surrounding the painter. With the later film, Gardner dispenses with voice-over and instead we hear Tobey speaking: he reminisces about his work (often candidly and critically) as he flips through prints and thumbs through catalogues, and assesses figures such as Pablo Picasso, Alexander Calder, and others (even more critically and candidly). There is now a fragility to the view of Tobey—call it "Portrait of the Artist as an Old Man"—and Tobey would die just a few years after Gardner's visit.

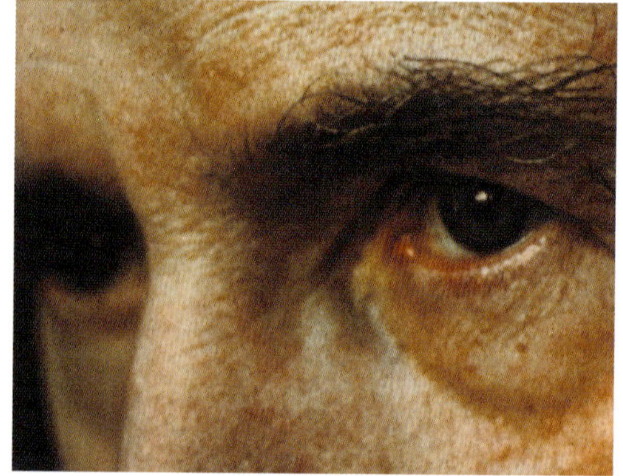

The intimacy comes with a relaxing of some of the more robustly experimental moves of the original film, and in the later one we hear Gardner, off camera, prompting Tobey with questions and comments. Tobey isn't isolated from the filmmaker as he had been in the original film. The new film has some of the ease that we associate with home movies, and the relationship between Gardner and Tobey seems filial now, whereas with the earlier film it seemed more like a student's wonderment regarding a striking teacher. The later film, like the earlier one, has no didactic point or argument, though once again an implicit argument arises from the way that Gardner composes his images. What particularities Gardner chooses to linger over visually helps determine the viewer's sense of Tobey and his work.

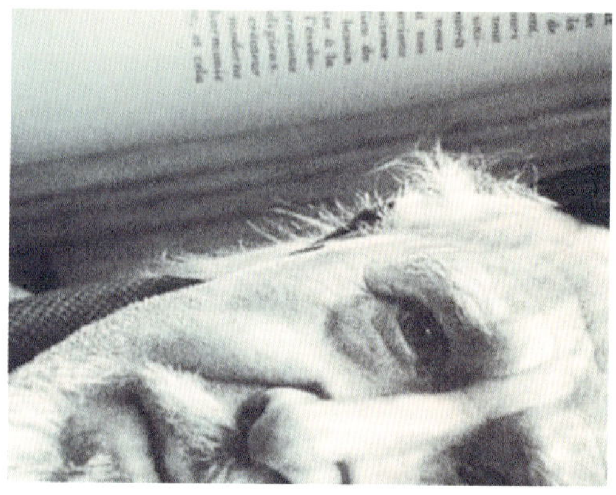

In notes that he kept during the filming of *Mark Tobey Abroad*, the filmmaker mentions that he had gained a new insight into Tobey's work. "I'm thinking about visual motifs, and one of them is Mark's hands. In my earlier film about Mark, it was the eye and the line, and I didn't do much with the hand. But now I think his hands are the most eloquent part of him."[9] Throughout the film, the camera follows the hands as they gesticulate, point, prepare tea, rub the painter's eyes—they are lit from above as Tobey plays his own composition on the piano.

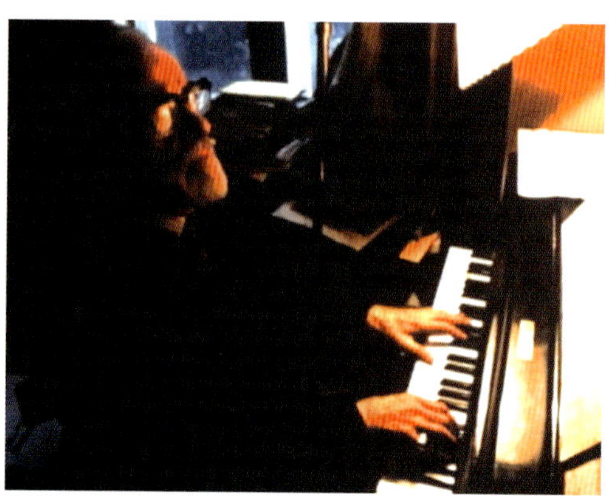

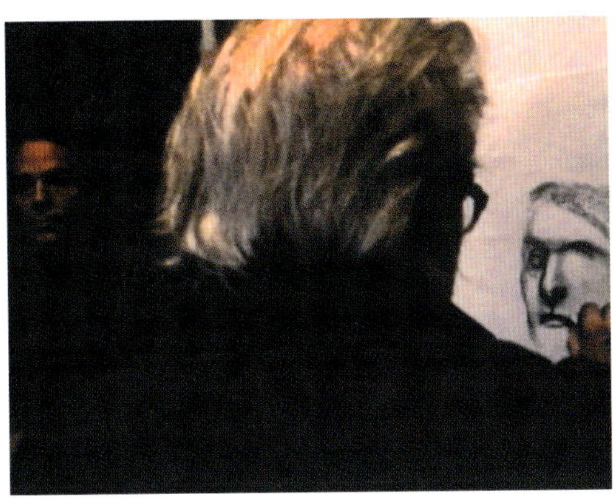

Perhaps most importantly, we see Tobey's hands as he sketches Gardner, who enters into the film as a subject of a charcoal portrait. He sits, posing, next to the sketch as Tobey works, and the perspectives start to fold over one another: the viewer watching as Gardner's film watches Tobey looking at Gardner, as from this looking the painter creates something.

So, too, does Gardner's film work this way, creating something out of looking. And so, by extension, the viewer creates as well—he or she determines meaning out of the visual materials, and by keeping the eyes trained on the screen the viewer, too, has an aesthetic experience that offers the possibilities of judgment.

In his artist films, it would not be accurate to say that Gardner tries to *capture* on film the artists' processes so as to demystify them, nor to romanticize them. *Capture* implies there is some stable object that gets placed, unchanged, on film. As filmmaker, Gardner attempts instead to represent artistic processes intimately, personally, and in such a way as to create a cinematic dialogue between his work and the work with which the artists onscreen are engaged. The films enact a dialogue between the arts while also indicating that the artists (on either side) don't disappear into the work—the work traces their movements at every turn. In the later Tobey film, Gardner builds his interpretation around the hand, the movement of which the camera can follow, as it cannot follow vision itself. Vision can only be approached by analogue. The hands' movements leave traces in the work and as the work.

In his more recent work, Gardner continued to explore the idea of the hand as site of articulation for an artist. The argument is at its widest metaphoric scope in Gardner's recent film *Deus ex Boltanski* (2010). With this piece, Gardner bears witness to the installation at Paris's Grand Palais of a monumental work by French artist Christian T. Boltanksi: *Personnes*, consisting of sixty tons of clothes and discarded items arranged in dozens of rectangular piles, with an immense pyramid of clothes several meters high at the center. Gardner shows the progress—and thus process—of the installation, which is designed to remind us of the people to whom the clothes and items belonged and to foreground their absence. "To choose some thing, to look at somebody, is to give them life," Boltanski says in the film, indicating that choice and attention are the ways that we forge a relationship to things, or people, in a form of engagement or even cathexis. Again, it is hard not to think of the way that Gardner has chosen the artist, and of the way his camera's gaze forges a connection between the perceived and the perceiver. But this connection isn't solely between the filmmaker and the subject. The viewer also exercises the choice to look at the film. The intersubjectivity that a film makes possible flows in two directions—toward the subject and toward the viewer.

Even though Boltanski's installation is primarily conceptual in nature, Gardner finds himself centering the camera on the massive hydraulic claw hanging above the pyramid. Again and again the claw reaches down and adds new items to the pile—a gesture of the hand, even if this time the hand is mechanical. The claw serves as a surrogate for Boltanski, and its movements and gestures connect metonymically to the materialization of his vision and imagination. With this trope connecting the mechanical claw with the artist's hand, we are free to see, given the reflexivity of the films made by an artist about an artist, that in Gardner's work the handheld, moving camera has the capacity to register gestures as well, in the ways that it signals small and large movements of the person holding the camera. The movements of the hand translate as movements of the lens, and the viewer can see the results of these movements, reminding one that the film is being made by a human being, *Homo Faber,* and not simply by a machine. The technology, rather than displacing the presence of the artist, is the extension of an aesthetic process that is the measure of the human capacity to imagine and create.

The identification of the artist with gesture recurs in the three films Gardner made with Sean Scully, the Dublin-born contemporary abstract painter. *Passenger* (1998), *Scully in Malaga* (1998), and *Testigos* (2007) were all undertaken during a visit Gardner had with the artist in Barcelona in the summer of 1997 (though the last of the trilogy would not be completed until years later) and in conjunction with an exhibition of Scully's work created between 1987 and 1997. Scully had befriended Gardner in the early 1970s when a John Knox Fellowship brought him to Harvard from England.[10] As an artist, Scully has always walked a line between minimalism and abstract expressionism in that his painting generally draws upon geometric shapes, checkerboard squares, and vertical and horizontal stripes, which might suggest a minimalist sensibility. Yet, the edges in his work reveal a degree of abstraction, a legible presence of the artist's hand, and the whims of decisions made through the act of painting, its motions and movements of a brush being dragged across canvas or linen. "Paint strokes are very crucial to an understanding my work," Scully has written.

> [The strokes] do not simply describe the form in my work; they affirm the human spirit. What is particularly moving to me about this idea, and what is also very dynamic about it, is that a paint stroke that describes a form *also* describes a gesture. That means that it stands outside technological development and can never be subjected to mechanization or technology. It is always about renewing the primitive impulse in order to make the gesture.[11]

The gesture, no matter how subtle, is the measure of the human presence as it deals with the materiality of paint, brush, canvas in the attempt to realize design.

Sean Scully, *Maesta,* 1983

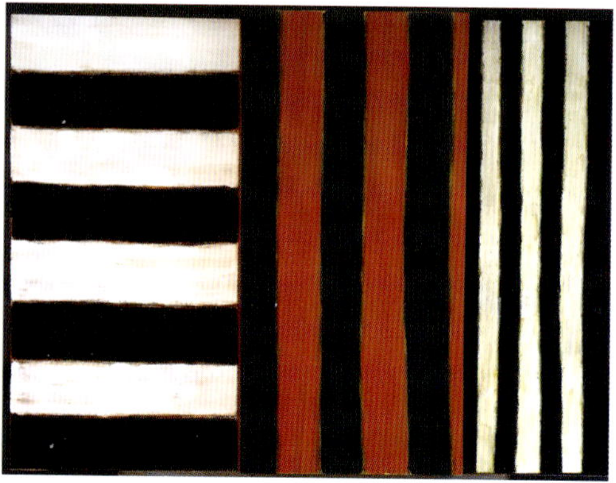

When one considers Scully within the spectrum of a second generation of New York School painters, the inheritance he has drawn from Mark Rothko and Barnet Newman becomes evident, since Scully shares with those older artists an investment in the spiritual dimensions of art. Scully, in an interview with Robert Enright, describes his paintings as "a kind of simmering truce, a point where emotion and structure, beauty and difficulty, light and darkness, rising and falling are somehow at a point of resolution."[12] Rather than a testament to the precision of geometric shapes and stripes, as would be the case if the work were indeed more conventionally minimalist, Scully's paintings instead measure the personal in response to the perceived fixities of the shapes that the work employs. The brushstrokes are visible enough at the edges and across the surface so that Scully's movements remain within the frame of what we see, as traces. The brushstrokes become the visible evidence of a body no longer there.

Two of the films in Gardner's series focus on the painter at work. The third, *Scully in Malaga*, deals with the mounting of an exhibition at Malaga's Salas del Palacio Episcopal. Along with the actual work of installation, Gardner's film includes scenes of the painter caring for an injured bird, as well as shots of Scully's elderly parents arriving and dancing an elegant *paso doble* in traditional Spanish dress.

The most important of the three Gardner films is *Passenger*, which focuses on Scully creating his painting of that name. Scully's piece involves a large canvas that has a rectangle cut out of it and that serves as a second surface for an "inset." The large canvas and the smaller one are painted separately. The large one alternates two light and two dark horizontal swaths of paint, while the smaller has three stripes each of more muted colors. The smaller rectangle is positioned, somewhat seamlessly, within the larger work. In that way, the inset is a kind of passenger accompanying the larger context.

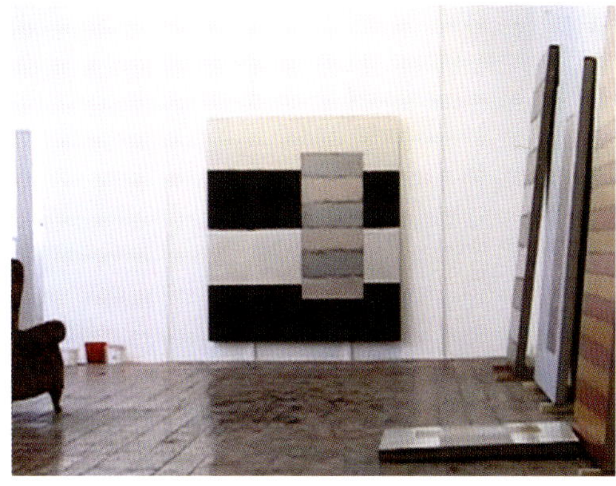

Final shot of *Passenger*

It is hard not to think of this interdependent relationship of the two parts of the painting extending to the film and Scully's painting. The context of Gardner's film generates an additional frame. We could see the film as suggesting, though not so insightfully, that Gardner (and thus the viewer) is a passenger on Scully's quest to create his work. We could also push the idea, however, and realize that the film and the painting inhabit one another—Scully's *Passenger* sits within, is carried along by, Gardner's *Passenger*, yet we would not have the film were it not for the painting. And, arguably, given Gardner's appearance within the environment of the studio, the presence of the filmmaker affects the painter, who is trying to strike that "simmering truce" of forces that can offer some kind of resolution.

In some way Gardner's presence must affect the process, and therefore, the painting, which is both the result of the process, and, in a sense, the record of it. The film, too, is both process and record. Both the painting and the film become the evidence of the real work of the art: the making of the painting and the film entails the action of human beings attempting to express a struggle with abstraction and materiality.

One useful touchstone for thinking about the parameters of a genre that includes Gardner's *Passenger* might be the photographer Hans Namuth's short film about the seminal American action painter Jackson Pollock, entitled *Pollock '51*. In both films a filmmaker enters a painter's studio to present the development of a painting or series of paintings within that space.[13] Namuth's film does offer a somewhat leaden voice-over from Pollock himself—in Gardner's film there is no such exposition; in fact there is absolutely no dialogue—but the visuals are focused on the painter moving over the horizontal canvas, crouching and lunging, dripping and flinging paint in ways that seem almost balletic despite the hyper-masculinity of Pollock's posture: a cigarette dangling from his lips, his dungarees and work boots crusted with layers of old paint. At times,

Namuth shows only Pollock's hunched-over silhouette cast against a white wall (which doesn't actually seem to be one of the walls of Pollock's studio) and then cuts to extreme close-ups of the chaotic patterns of paint—mainly black and white with some accents of red appearing periodically—clinging fast to the visible texture of the canvas.

Certainly, this film romanticizes the process of painting, but the challenge for Namuth is obvious: how to depict the action of action painting in a way that communicates the interior struggles of the painter, his desire to present on canvas the gestures that signal an authentic self. This was the goal of so many of the New York School painters, and, it should be said, remains a goal for someone such as Sean Scully.

Harold Rosenberg characterizes the abstract work of the 1940s and '50s, arguing,

> At a certain moment the canvas began to appear to one American painter after another as an arena in which to act—rather than as a space in which to reproduce, re-design, analyze or "express" an object, actual or imagined. What was to go on the canvas was not a picture but an event.
>
> The painter no longer approached his easel with an image in his mind; he went up to it with material in his hand to do something to that other piece of material in front of him. The image would be the result of this encounter.[14]

Namuth, then, needed to convey some of the essence of Abstract Expressionism by finding a way to render the process of painting *as* an event, and Pollock, who was no stranger to drama, was able to comply.[15] In *Pollock '51* the painter *doesn't* approach an easel; he has laid his canvas on the ground or floor. Throughout the ten-minute film, and contributing to the dramatic performance unfolding visually, we hear on the soundtrack the composer Morton Feldman's "Jackson Pollock," an often-discordant score for two cellos written for the film upon the painter's request.[16] Every element of *Pollock '51* is arranged to make painting into an event, and it becomes hard to tell if the filming isn't also part of its being an event.

In the second part of Namuth's film, Pollock begins painting on a sheet of glass beneath which the camera is placed, so that the viewer is looking up through the "arena in which [Pollock] acts." Although this allows us to look at Pollock's face and hands as he works, as if that reveals some secret, it does raise the odd question of what it means to have a point of view centered by the camera at the locus of the art, and from the position of the object in the process of being made. Does that perspective offer some hidden insight into the process because we are afforded a view—primarily the artist's face—usually obscured from us? Perhaps it is enough that there is a kind of intimacy that we gain in being able to look unblinkingly into the eyes of a serious artist working at his painting. It literalizes the idea that in looking at art we are encountering the artist.

In the Scully films, Gardner varies from Namuth's approach, even as there are some resemblances. In *Passenger* and *Testigos*, Gardner doesn't employ a score that is meant to direct and guide emotional responses to the visual. The only soundtrack is comprised of the tracks that Scully plays while he is painting—and these tend toward rock and roll and folk by such artists as REM, Neil Young, and others. Even though in that way Gardner doesn't orchestrate responses, the movement of the camera often draws attention to itself because it is not smooth, elegant, and effortless. The camera's sometimes hectic movements insist on how what we see, the way we see it, and in what order we see it, is determined by the filmmaker, not the audience. I say "hectic" because small moves of a cameraman's hand have a tendency to make the lens jump. However, these movements are imperfections that reveal the presence of a human being operating the camera and reflect the way that the unsteadiness of Scully's hand makes the crucial difference between minimalism and a robustly humanist Abstract Expressionism. In this way, Gardner, in formal terms, doubles with the camera what is being done on Scully's canvases and their gestures of Abstract Expressionism.

The filming (actually video) is largely handheld, but it also shifts between the camera Gardner is operating and another, static, camera set up near the back of the studio that offers what constitute master shots. These wide-angle views sometimes show Gardner standing near or even directly over Scully as he paints.

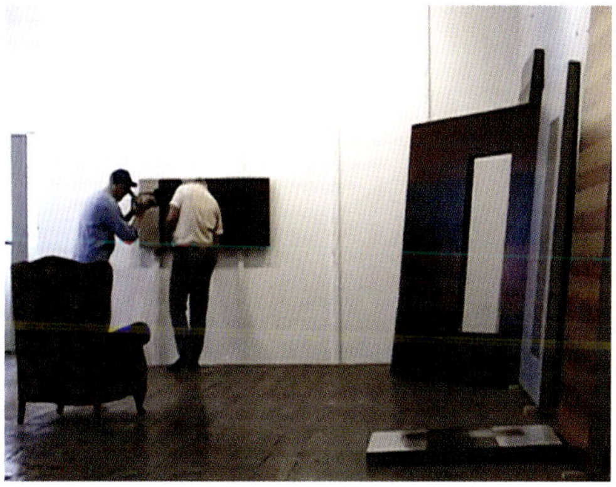

The film keeps reminding us of the presence—let us not call it an intrusion—of the filmmaker in the studio. This also represents one of the few times in his career that Gardner lets himself be viewed in his work. To call the film *Passenger* a recording of the process of painting *Passenger* would be to ignore the fact that what the viewer has is not a direct experience of the painting. The painting comes by way of the film. How we look at the painting is guided by the camera. The painting itself is not incidental—it is an event, as the film is.

For Gardner, film heightens reality. He explains, "Film is not simply a mirror recording our physicality, but a medium achieving a transfiguration of our ordinariness."[17] Gardner's artist films go a step further into this situation than his other work, as they provide a figure for transfiguration in the art being filmed. In these films cinema, as an art, *encounters* art, and the results, as Gardner suggests, have ethical implications because they are the intertwining of personal responses, which viewers must then respond to.

There is a larger context for thinking about artist films, especially because a number of titans in the field of film criticism and theory—Siegfried Kracauer, Parker Tyler, André Bazin—have looked at intersections of art and film in the form of artists films, while never quite resolving arguments about what such films accomplish. The touchstone for these thinkers, and perhaps Gardner himself, is *The Mystery of Picasso* by Henri-Georges Clouzot, which appeared in 1956 and won the *Prix du Jury* at that year's Cannes Film Festival. Gardner has indicated that he had this film in mind when he was making his films about Sean Scully, *Passenger* and *Testigos*.[18] Clouzot, director of French thrillers such as *Diabolique* (1955) and *Wages of Fear* (1953), here created not quite a documentary, perhaps, but a creative nonfiction film. Avoiding didacticism,

Clouzot's film also keeps exposition to a minimum as viewers are presented just with Picasso creating sketches, drawings, and paintings over the course of seventy-five minutes. (In 1956 Picasso was the most influential painter in the world—indeed the century seemed to belong to him—and so there really wasn't much explanation or introduction that was necessary.)

In essence, Clouzot adopted an approach similar to Namuth's, insofar as he saw the value of being able to create a reverse-shot perspective of Picasso at work. The director devised a setup by which Picasso used a kind of ink that bled through translucent canvas, while the director positioned his camera on the opposite side so that what it sees are simply the lines appearing on the white screen, one after the other.

As revealing as the film might be in terms of Picasso's technique, it does, as Namuth's film does as well, self-consciously reaffirm the most familiar stereotypes of the heroic painter. This attempt at mythologizing is suggested in Gardner's Tobey films in the way that the figure of the painter is presented in Romantic terms as heroically transforming the world into art. In the Scully films, aesthetically stripped down as they are, Gardner chooses instead to focus wholly on the process of making paintings and minimizes the perceived gap between artist and audience.

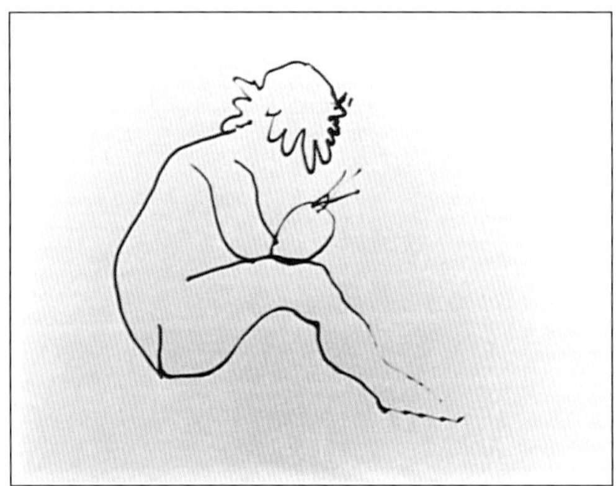

One crucial difference between *Pollock '51* and *The Mystery of Picasso* is that instead of going to Picasso's studio, the director had the famous artist work on a very bare set. Using a spartanly appointed studio allowed Clouzot to control the environment and set the lights in order to obtain the best shots he could of Picasso at work. The result is that the film, though quite minimal, remains quite professional looking. That is also is its limitation: the film does not represent the actual process of making art, since Clouzot more or less sets up a kind of laboratory situation or, perhaps more appropriately described, a kind of exhibition of the activity of painting. The viewer is provided a simulation of the artist at work, one made seemingly all the more authentic because that artist is the most significant painter of the time. Although one might say that Picasso wasn't an Abstract Expressionist and therefore he wouldn't necessarily worry about whether he was "really" making art or just going through the motions for a camera crew, in fact Picasso destroyed all the work that he created during the filming. That destruction indicates some aesthetic disassociation between the work he was making for the film and what he created when not in front of a camera.

The title of Clouzot's film, with its emphasis on *mystery*, indicates the dilemma that the filmmaker confronts. That is, despite being able to watch Picasso create, viewers are no closer to understanding the inner workings that produce the art itself. And Clouzot's film further distances the viewer since with every frame the director exerts his control over the *mise en scène*. What a viewer experiences is not so different from what we see in Namuth's or Gardner's films, in that all three insist on the camera and mediation. But the artifice of Clouzot's work reveals how shaped that version is to the very extent it tries to minimize those elements that would bring attention to the fact that it is cinema and not direct experience. If Picasso's painting is depicted as spontaneous, Clouzot's film shows a radical, even ironic tension in the fact that it is so carefully composed and thus the very opposite of spontaneous.

After Namuth and Clouzot, what a viewer recognizes with Gardner's *Testigos* and *Passenger* is a different sense of the relationship of cinema to painting because the sense of form is markedly different. Gardner's two films don't represent the work and its process, they reproduce it in formal terms. This is something different from merely mimicking the style of the art, which would entail more frenetic forms of visual abstraction, as of the sort one might see in later work by Stan Brakhage (himself an admirer of Gardner's oeuvre), who in *Dante Quartet* (1987) painted directly onto 35 and 70 mm film stock and scraped away at the images of the found footage he used (including material culled from Billy Wilder's *Irma La Douce*). One cannot help but think of Abstract Expressionists when watching *Dante Quartet* and other related films by Brakhage, such as *Untitled (For Marilyn)* (1992), *Blue Value* (1996), or *Lovesong* (2001), as loops, swoops, and threads of paint move across the screen animatedly, the paint not hemmed in by the frames of film since it is layered on the stock and not actually photographed.

Gardner doesn't take on such painterly methodologies, and the result is that there is a much subtler connection between the film and the art it is trying to approach. Any attempt at mere imitation would not bring Gardner closer to either Scully or Mark Tobey. Gardner's work doesn't abandon its ties to direct representation, yet it does not pretend that no abstraction or perceptual reordering takes place. What Gardner offers in his films is a camera (and thus a filmmaker) trying to approach its subject—the poetics of that approach, that desire to draw near, is what he is after. And the subject shapes the approach even as the approach determines how the viewer perceives and experiences the subject. This is the way to keep the mystery of art a living thing and not something just to explain or to further mystify.

André Bazin, in "A Bergsonian Film: *The Picasso Mystery*," argues that the real value of Clouzot's film is that it identifies the spectacle of the coming to be of the painting in terms of duration. A viewer experiences the way that a work develops over time, and we experience that time as it transpires—even if that duration is shaped by editing and effects such as speeding up the film. In fact, the shaping the filmmaker does serves to help the viewer experience the time *as* time rather than getting absorbed by sequence or plot or narration. Bazin says that the experience isn't merely pleasing, merely showing in instructional terms how the painting comes to be an object. The parts of the process of painting as an activity, the work, is where the film's interest and meaning lie and not, rather, with the *result* of the process. Bazin insists, "Film here is not the mere moving photography of an a priori, external reality. It is intimately and legitimately organized in aesthetic symbiosis with the events pictured."[19] Thus, neither film nor painting stands subordinate, as they are intertwined collaborations: the process of the painting occurs through time, just as the frames passing over the projected light are also an experience of time, and the viewer watches as the film keeps attention consistently on process. A clear difference between Clouzot's and Gardner's films is the level of self-consciousness that is present. One can be absorbed in Clouzot's *Mystery of Picasso*, whereas Gardner's more improvised, rawer, even amateur-seeming technique, one drawn from the rich tradition of

American avant-garde and underground cinema, consistently draws attention to itself and its own *poesis*. In any case, however, the painting as an object in space is never wholly subsumed by the mediation—its very materiality is what both the artist and the filmmaker wrestle with.

For Gardner the artist's eyes provide the opportunity for the hand's gestures, and those gestures call forth cinematic responses that are gestures. Gardner's films on artists push outward to the viewer so that we consider the processes that the films' engagement with the painters are undertaking in terms of perception itself. The viewer watches these conflations and collaborations, internalizing them, cognitively and perceptually fashioning a usable meaning, a creative interpretation. These layers of activity and perception are legible gestures of a larger actuality, an actuality that in turn takes an aesthetic intelligence to see—because it cannot be approached in purely empirical or rational terms. The necessary step is to realize that looking at art and cinema is to choose to participate in the ways that human beings articulate their presence not as objects but as events, minds moving so as to take part in an inclusive, sometimes generous, sometimes intractable, always present actuality.

Notes

1. Tyler, *Art Digest*, 28 (1954).
2. Gardner, "The Moral Nature of Film," in *Just Representations*, ed. Charles Warren (Cambridge, MA: Studio 7 Arts and Peabody Museum Press, 2010), 243.
3. *Just Representations*, 249.
4. Ilisa Barbash, "Out of Words: A Conversation with Robert Gardner," in *The Cinema of Robert Gardner*, eds. Barbash and Lucien Taylor (New York: Berg, 2007), 98.
5. See pages 525–526, *Jackson Pollock: An American Saga* (New York: Harper, 1991). Not everyone agrees with this. Evelyn Poynton maintains there is no evidence that Pollock saw Tobey's show that year. *Jackson Pollock* (New Haven: Yale University Press, 2012), 50.
6. *Mark Tobey* (New York: Museum of Modern Art, 1962), 9.
7. "Mark Tobey" in *Reported Sightings: Art Chronicles 1957–1987* (New York: Knopf, 1989), 188–190.
8. *Magazine of Art*, 44, (October 1951), 228.
9. "Mark Tobey Journal," *Just Representations*, 70.
10. It is worth noting that although he was born in Ireland, Scully was raised in England and became a U.S. citizen in 1984. He currently lives in Germany. Part of the reason that he came to the United States was the allure of the New York School and what that generation of painters suggested about the possibilities for aesthetic achievement available in America.
11. "How and Low, or the Sublime and the Ordinary," in *Resistance and Persistence: Selected Writings*, ed. Florence Ingleby (New York: Merrell, 2006), 15.
12. Robert Enright, "A Dark But Vital Light: An Interview with Sean Scully," *Border Crossings* 26, no. 3 (2007), 50–60.

13. The year of Namuth's film is important to note because Gardner had just begun making films himself and within a year would make his own artist film about a major Abstract Expressionist figure, Mark Tobey.

14. "American Action Painters" in *Tradition of the New* (New York: Horizon Press, 1959), 25.

15. Rosenberg's "American Action Painters" first appeared in 1952 in *Art News*. Thus, Namuth would not have had this specific passage in mind when he was making his film; yet, to call the creative processes of abstract painting an event was not wholly original to Rosenberg. I cite his essay largely because it has become so definitive a description.

16. There is some debate about this aspect of the film. Feldman describes the situation as I have, in "Crippled Symmetry," included in *Give My Regards to Eighth Street*; however, David Revill, in his biography of John Cage, *The Roaring Silence* (New York and London: Arcade, 1992), offers a slightly different version. In Revill's account, Lee Krasner, Pollock's wife and herself an accomplished painter, had originally approached Cage about contributing a score. Cage declined, but recommended his friend, the then all but unknown composer Feldman. Pollock specifically had wanted a score by an American composer, and odds are that Cage's score would have been no less dramatic than Feldman's.

17. "The Moral Nature of Film," *Just Representations*, 244.

18. *The Cinema of Robert Gardner*, 115.

19. *Bazin at Work: Major Essays and Reviews from the Forties and the Fifties*, ed. Bert Cardullo, trans. Alain Pette and Bert Cardullo (New York: Routledge, 1997), 216.

Chapter 20
Learning from Catalonia

Bruce Jenkins

An extensive body of critical writing exists that charts the relationships between film and other machine-age technologies such as the locomotive, the automobile, and the airplane. Less well documented is the role that the "machine for living"—to invoke the term that Le Corbusier used to designate residential architecture—has played as both an analogue for and a frequent object of the cinematic gaze. The Lumière brothers turned a fairly routine task of home improvement, the demolition of an old wall, into one of the earliest subjects of their pioneering work in the medium, and among the key scenes in *Nanook of the North* (1921), the first feature-length documentary, was an extended sequence that records the construction of an igloo. Within the commercial cinema of the silent era, architecture became linked to particular genres, ranging from Buster Keaton's precise integration of buildings into his sight gags in comedies like *Steamboat Bill, Jr.* (1927) and *One Week* (1920) to the psychologically overwrought built environments that exude evil and madness in early Expressionist horror and fantasy films. The avant-garde was no less active in turning to the home as a site in which to situate its assaults on the bourgeoisie, as Dalí and Buñuel demonstrated by their ribald injection of peasant culture into the dignified interiors of a Roman villa in *L'Age d'or* (1930).[1]

Perhaps the most generative approach to architecture as a subject for the cinema was marked out by a group of independent filmmakers who seemed to literalize Le Corbusier's metaphor by focusing on the dynamism of the built environment, creating a genre of "City Symphony" films that in deploying the most advanced techniques of the era (Soviet montage, French prismatic effects) would, as Hans Richter noted, "create nature anew."[2] Richter, a German filmmaker of both experimental work and sponsored documentaries, emerged as a major advocate of a socially engaged, poetic practice while railing against "today's ineffective and boring films of culture, nature, and cities."[3] This "other" cinema that Richter advocated has had at best a modest and discontinuous history, episodically embraced by a heterogeneous group of artists beginning in the postwar era with the designers Charles and Ray Eames and finding adherents from among nonfiction filmmakers (Francis Thompson, Chris Marker, Michael Blackwood), avant-gardists (Shirley Clarke, Hilary Harris, Gordon Matta-Clark), and art-film directors (Michelangelo Antonioni, Peter Greenaway, Hiroshi Teshigahara). Architecture and the cinema, although theoretically linked in structural ways, have, on the thematic level, remained situated primarily on parallel tracks, with an occasional light embrace or pas de deux between this most compelling of time-based media and the archetypal spatial medium that is architecture.

Enter Robert Gardner, a filmmaker who in "chasing the chimera of isolated people" has frequently focused his camera on Western artists and third-world artisans.[4] In much of his work, the built environment, while distinctive (Sean Scully's studio in Barcelona, an Ika *concurrua* dwelling in a mountainous region of Colombia), often assumes a secondary role, particularly amid cultures that seem to live out their lives alfresco—the Dani in New Guinea, the Nuer and the Hamar in Ethiopia, the Bororo in the Niger Republic. Indeed, there tends to be more emphasis in his films on what might be called "machines for dying"—the funeral chair in *Dead Birds* (1963), the ladder-like bamboo litter used to bear the dead down to the Ganges in *Forest of Bliss* (1986)—than on abodes for the living. Nevertheless, in *2 Sons of Catalonia: Josep Lluís Sert & Joan Miró* (2013), a recently completed short film that was more than four decades in the making, Gardner openly embraced the practice of architecture and found in one of its key modernist figures a compelling analogue for his own attempts to create works that utilize the aesthetic interplay of space and light to mediate the realms of nature and culture. Because it has been little seen to date, we make an effort to describe the work in some detail here before reflecting on its place in Gardner's cinematic enterprise.

2 Sons of Catalonia

The moving cinematographic recording essentially substitutes for a tour around and through the building.

—Bruno Taut

The cinematic-architectural tour that is *2 Sons of Catalonia* is divided into several parts situated in various Mediterranean locales, beginning and ending with the longest sections, set in Barcelona. The film opens with a scene suggestive of a typical morning routine. After four brief shots including a superimposed title that identifies the locale—the Joan Miró Foundation in Barcelona—Gardner moves his camera from outside the walls of the museum to the inside of the compound, as a groundskeeper appears bearing a bright yellow hose. He sets out not only to water the shrubs and lawn but also to hose down some of the outdoor sculpture—a red stabile that glistens in the light, a black sculpture set above a reflecting pool that has been glimpsed in one of the opening shots. Thus, even before the first words are spoken, the film suggests a sort of symmetry between the natural and the manmade elements in this realm. Another symmetry is quickly sketched out by Gardner's camera, which frames the approaching figure of the Catalan architect Josep Lluís Sert, seen from inside through the glass doors of the museum he designed.

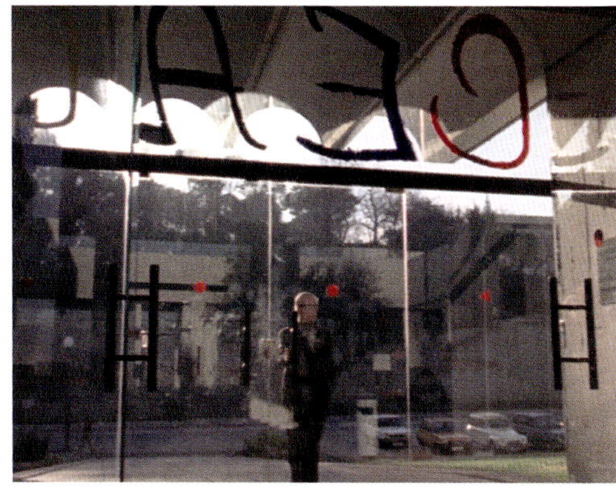

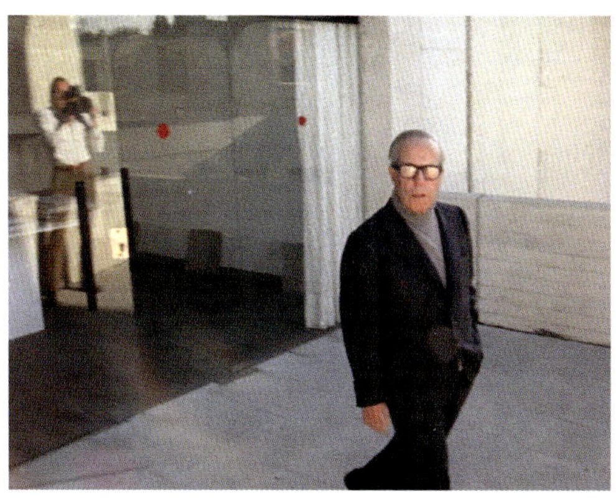

On the soundtrack, Sert describes the openness of the building, while Gardner, for his part, provides a cinematic demonstration of this fluid spatiality in a brief sequence that cuts from the architect's entry to a simple reverse shot that frames him against the matching doors leading out to the building's courtyard and concludes with him standing outside, next to a sculpture and an olive tree, as he describes the importance of displaying Miró's artwork within a natural setting.

As this section develops, Sert reenters the museum and, walking through its galleries, comments on the way that the spaces flow, on the system he devised with ceiling-mounted light traps to produce a diffused illumination for the paintings, and on the overall cloistered feel of the interiors. Continuing on to the sculpture gallery, he climbs a ramp that facilitates viewing work in the round; here he describes the positive effect of more direct lighting on sculpture. We begin to sense that in architecture, as in cinema, lighting is an essential element in directing the perceptual experience. As if to emphasize this relationship between the mediums, as Sert exits the building onto an outside terrace we catch a full reflection of the filmmaker himself, already outside, in the glass door.

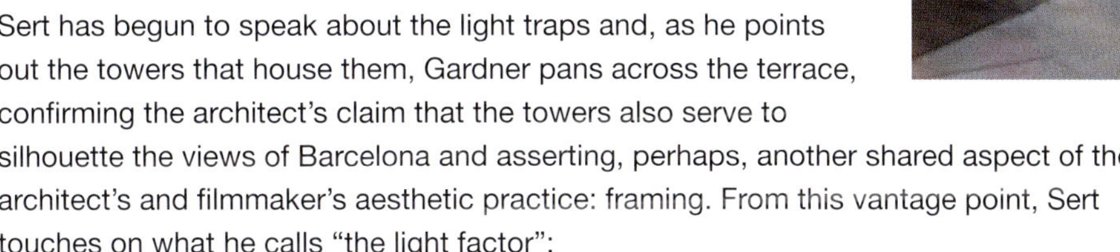

Sert has begun to speak about the light traps and, as he points out the towers that house them, Gardner pans across the terrace, confirming the architect's claim that the towers also serve to silhouette the views of Barcelona and asserting, perhaps, another shared aspect of the architect's and filmmaker's aesthetic practice: framing. From this vantage point, Sert touches on what he calls "the light factor":

> Light is not only important here because, of course, it is necessary, but it is important symbolically. Nothing exists without light; there is no life to sculpture or to painting without light. And here we chose for this building to have natural light and plenty of it. And I believe that this natural light gives the pictures and the sculpture great animation and life.

It is here that the architectural discourse begins fully to resonate with the film that we are viewing, and we are able to glimpse Gardner's larger project—not simply a double portrait of an architect and an artist, the titled "two sons of Catalonia," but, equally, an exploration of two art forms that achieve their poetic force by reframing and illuminating the world.

Returning to the courtyard, Sert sums up for us what Gardner's camera has already made evident—namely, that this is "a simple building with simple forms and rather simple materials that are here exposed and shown." Again addressing concerns that seem equally germane to documentary film, Sert acknowledges his architecture's role in serving as "background to the works of art and to the pictures"—a sort of conduit that brings together art and nature in the architectural ensemble. Gardner concludes this opening part of the film with a nod to his own form of cinematic simplicity: as the architect is seen retracing his steps and exiting the museum through the glass entry doors, Gardner cuts to a single image of the upper

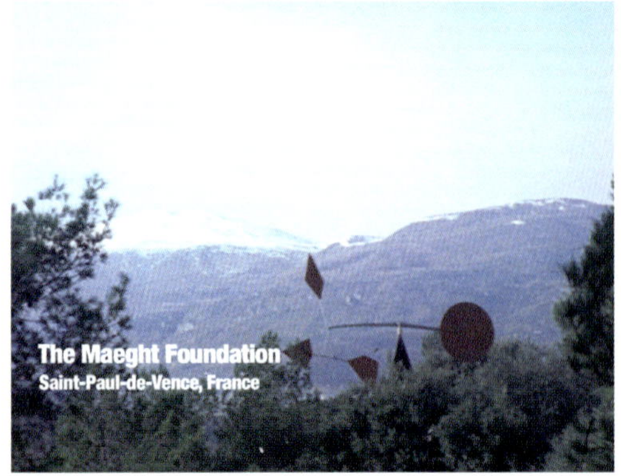

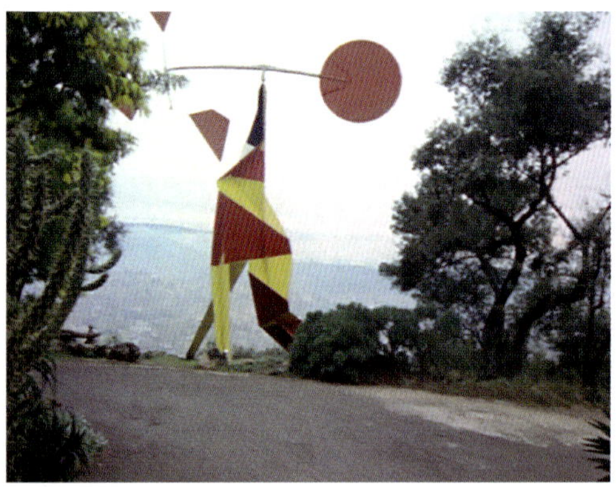

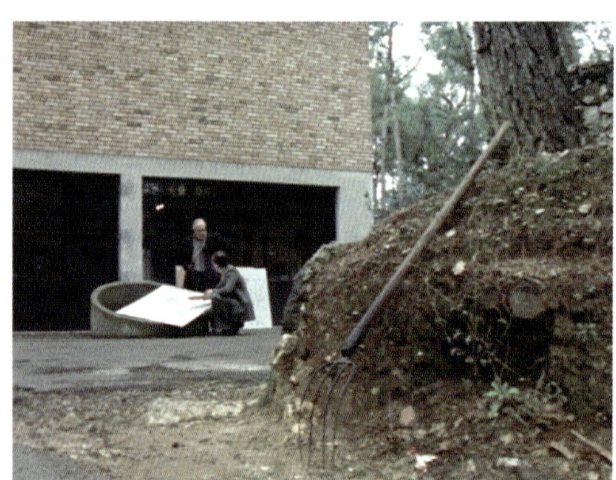

section of the building, which now frames a blue sky bisected by the white stream trailing from a jet crossing over the airspace above the Montjuïc section of Barcelona.

While providing closure, this final image of the first section also carries a certain metonymic force as the scene shifts from Catalonia to Saint-Paul-de-Vence, in the French Maritime Alps. A title—"The Maeght Foundation"—signals the change of venue, as does the opening image of the top of a standing mobile by Calder framed between treetops in the foreground and mountains in the distant field.

Nature and the built environment again interact as Sert is introduced walking down a private drive on a damp, overcast day. As he turns to walk into the compound, Gardner pans past him to reveal the official signage for the Maeght Foundation, with its graphic representing the upturned figure of Sert's signature impluvium roof. We catch up with the architect as he passes a large black Calder stabile near the main entrance. Instead of moving inside the museum, however, Gardner cuts to a terraced garden and a full view of the Calder glimpsed in the opening shot, about which Sert is speaking to his wife, Moncha.

Most of the visit to the Maeght is taken up with a meeting between Sert and the museum's director, Jean-Louis Prat, which begins on an upper terrace of the complex as the two converse, initially in English, about building a new addition. In contrast to the docent-like role he assumed earlier at the Miró Museum, Sert is now engaged in a professional discussion about the proposed architectural project, and it is Gardner who provides a context by panning across the roofline of the adjacent buildings. As they continue the conversation, now in French, the architectural plans for the new wing are shown in close-up, while the camera pulls back to reveal that the architect and his client are now situated outside on the grounds of the art center. Gardner cuts to a long shot of the two men, with a pitchfork laid against the *repoussoir* figure of a tree trunk in the foreground that dramatically frames the scene. The image serves as a subtle allusion to one of the key, but unseen, works that Maeght commissioned Miró to create for the Foundation in 1963—an iron-and-bronze sculpture titled *La Fourche* (The Pitchfork) in which the eponymous object rotates atop the structure, Calder-style.

While Sert, armed with a metal ruler and red pen, and Prat continue their discussion in an interior workspace, Gardner cuts to the exterior of the center. Standing in the Giacometti courtyard is an elegantly attired woman in an ecru dress, fully accessorized with a hat, gold bracelets, light brown pumps, and a matching purse. She is seen from the back with a stylist attending to the final details. As the model begins her walk, Gardner cuts to a long shot that emphasizes the formal similarity between her stride and the posture of the adjacent Giacometti sculptures and reveals a small photography crew at the far end of the courtyard.

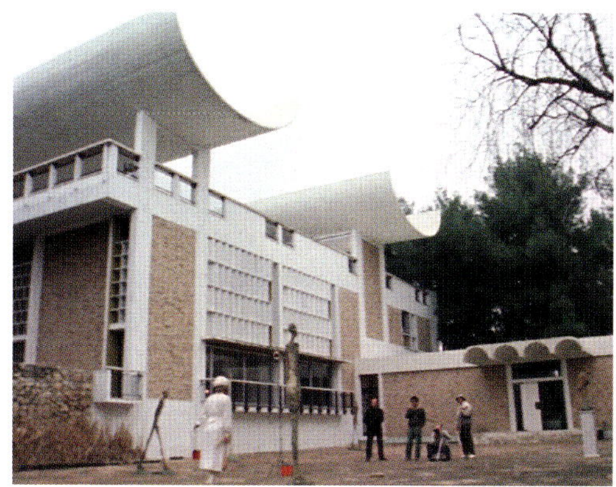

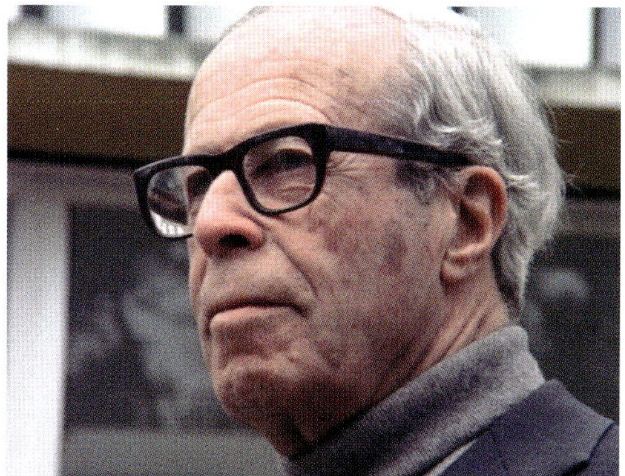

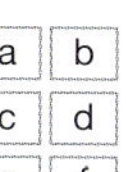

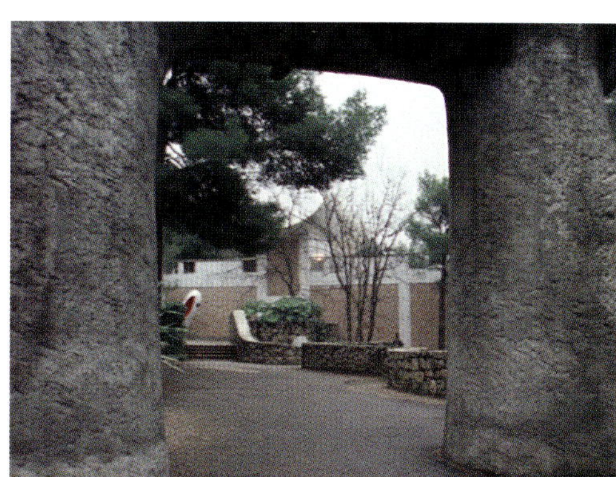

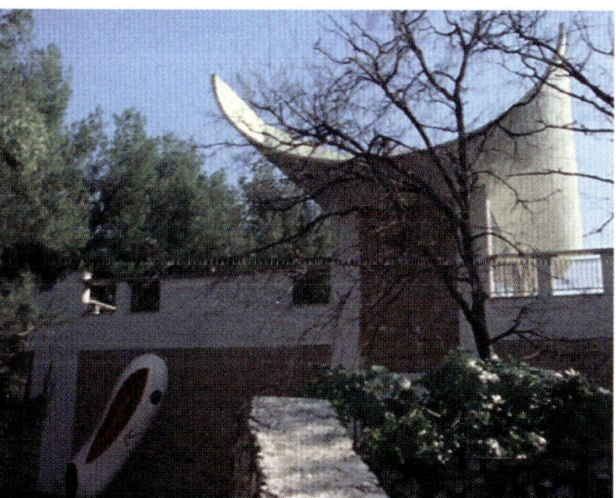

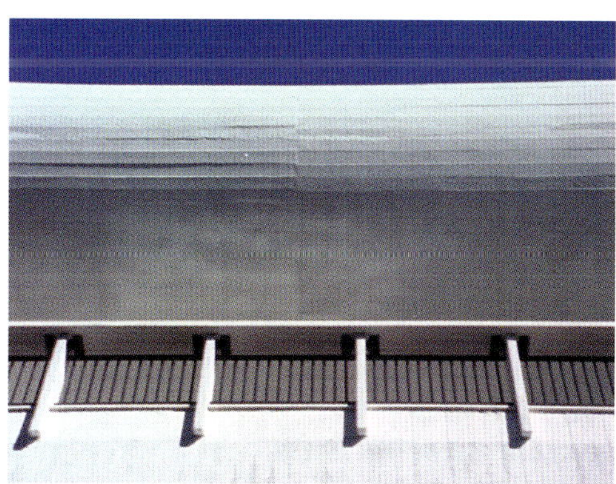

A close-up of Sert in the courtyard serves to link the fashion shoot to a final look at the complex as Gardner expands the single-shot transition used at the close of the Miró Foundation section into an Ozu-like series of six images. He begins with a low-angle shot of the top half of one of the Giacomettis leaning in toward the upturned impluvium roof above a gallery, and advances farther into the complex with an image of a large portico-like cement sculpture—Miró's *L'Arc* (The Arch)—that frames the entrance to the terraced space known as the Labyrinth, designed to display specially commissioned large-scale sculptures by Miró. With a simple pan that moves along the whitewashed top of the Labyrinth's undulating stone terrace wall, the camera brings us into a contemplative space in which the architecture and the artworks seem fully integrated. Nature, too, has a role in this mix, as the next image presents the underside of an impluvium with the subtle reflection of water

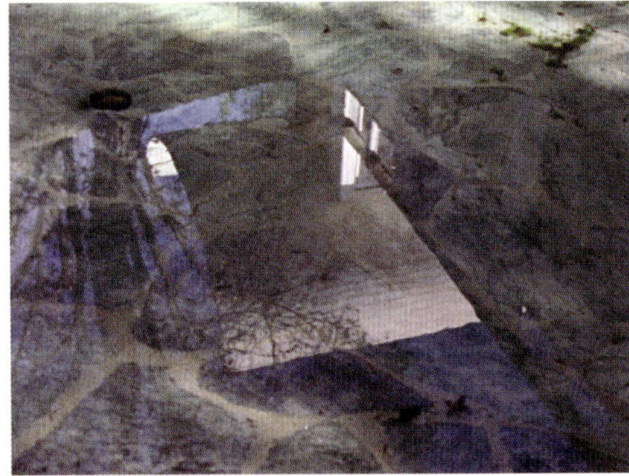

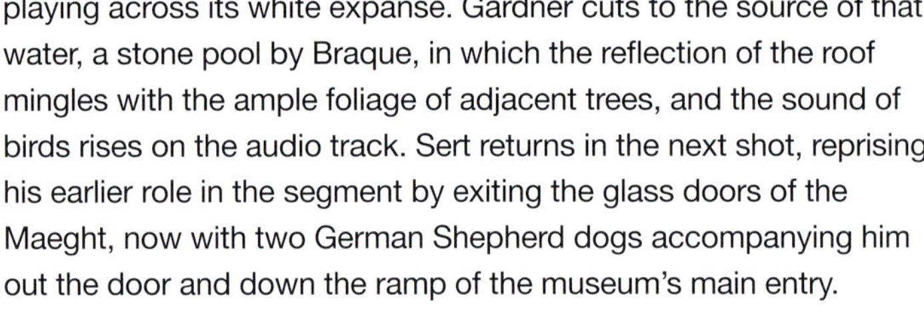

playing across its white expanse. Gardner cuts to the source of that water, a stone pool by Braque, in which the reflection of the roof mingles with the ample foliage of adjacent trees, and the sound of birds rises on the audio track. Sert returns in the next shot, reprising his earlier role in the segment by exiting the glass doors of the Maeght, now with two German Shepherd dogs accompanying him out the door and down the ramp of the museum's main entry.

Sert's exit from the Maeght Foundation is seamlessly matched by the cut to his entry into Joan Miró's studio, across the Mediterranean in Palma de Mallorca.

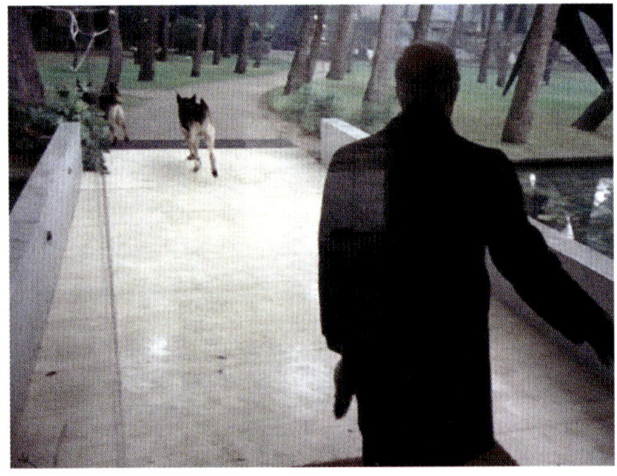

The transition suggests an intimate relationship not only between these two creative personalities but between the two architectural sites as well. They in fact share a significant history, because it was Aimé Maeght's visit in 1957 to Miró's studio that had prompted the celebrated art dealer to contact Sert about designing a center to house his art collection on property in the Maritime Alps, where he maintained his summer home. What impressed him was the way that Sert had responded to his close friend Miró's request for "a very large studio. . . in order to have enough room to hold many canvases, because the more I work the more I want to work."[5] Twenty years later, at the time of the shooting in 1977, the studio remains a catalytic space for the artist, at this point in his eighties.

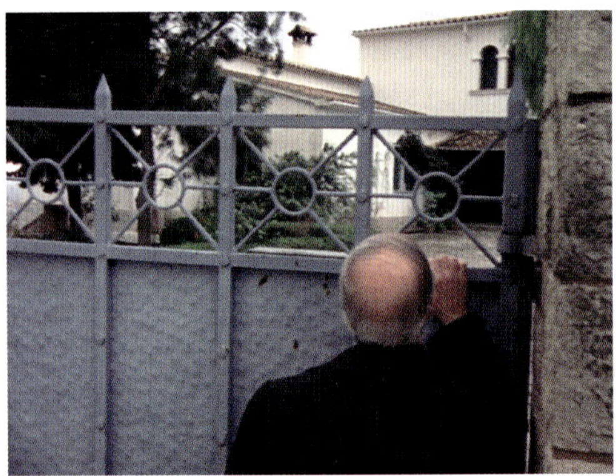

Sert meets Miró standing on a terrace above the studio and speaks in English about the changes in the view and the history of the property as an orchard. Switching to Catalan, he suggests that they go downstairs to the studio, and the artist trails behind him, slightly piqued about the film shoot taking time away from drawings he has left unfinished. The first image of the interior of the large two-story studio is of a film technician, seemingly having nothing to do with Gardner, setting up a light stand in the loft area, somewhat comically framed so that the man's light seems to be illuminating a hanging relief of the sun.

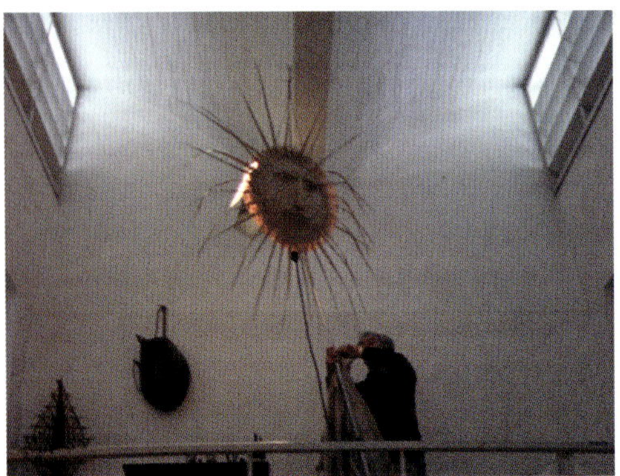

Gardner pans across the studio, which is filled with dozens of paintings and drawings resting on easels, leaning against walls, and lying on the floor, and his camera comes to rest on the figure of Miró, who enters the scene and perches himself on a stool next to the British writer and curator Roland Penrose, who is at work on a television documentary about the artist.

While ostensibly continuing to capture the relationship between these "two sons of Catalonia," the film renders a contrastive portrait of two distinct modes of nonfiction filmmaking as well. Moving out of the way of the film crew, Gardner retreats to the loft to document the production process, beginning with the cameraman and sound man walking behind Miró, who is armed with a very long paintbrush and a dish of paint as he approaches a tall canvas and begins to dab the brush onto the surface of an abstract black figure. The brush is dry, and Gardner cannot resist zooming in to the brush as it encounters the canvas. The moment is subtitled "Miró pretending to paint for the camera crew."[6] Another simulated paint stroke brings the cameraman and soundman back into Gardner's shot; they tower over the artist, who does his best to convey his working method.

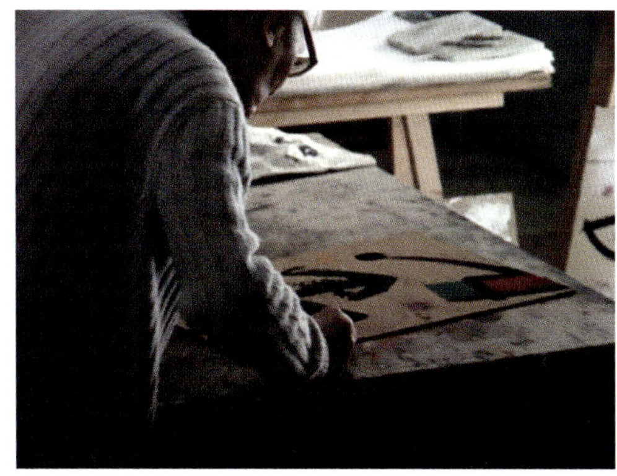

Only when the crew departs is Gardner able to film Miró actually at work in the studio. The scene he captures is not only de-dramatized—here there is no brush, no paint, no simulation—but is shot with the same available light that the artist uses. Wearing his glasses and leaning over a paint-splattered table, Miró carefully inspects a small painting on wood panel as Gardner zooms in to match the painter's own proximity to his work—thereby embedding one mode of observation inside another. If film shares the ambulatory, spatial, and light dimensions of architecture for Gardner, it also maintains the possibility of sharing the observational capacities of the painter.

The section ends with Sert and Miró together on the upper level of the studio, chatting in Catalan and looking out the window. The production team is outside shooting the exteriors, and as the two men wave, Gardner pans his camera to show the kneeling cameraman, Penrose leaning on his walking stick, and three of the crew carrying equipment. Perhaps responding to the recent invasion by multiple filmmakers, the artist and the architect are discussing the issue of access, with Sert reassuring Miró that the studio could be a space for "selected people" to come and see his work. Miró concurs, but he insists that "the important thing here is the work that still has to be done."

Moving a hundred miles or so across the Mediterranean, the film shifts from the Balearic Island town of Palma to Ibiza and, as in the previous transition, Gardner engages in a temporal journey back in time. As the camera tracks Sert down the streets, the architect recalls the early 1930s and his discovery, along with his modernist architectural colleagues, of an enduring form of vernacular Mediterranean architecture. While standing in front of a typical building, he explains that they were seeking "a cleanup of everything that was stylish or tied to academic training," and that what they found there were "these old buildings that were whitewashed and looked like very modern buildings." In an extended shot that employs a highly mobile camera, Gardner visually captures Sert's argument, simultaneously illustrating the claims by panning across the adjacent buildings as the architect describes the essential features of urban spaces drawn from this simple cityscape.

The symmetry between Sert's belief in the importance of spatial continuity and Gardner's use of the temporally continuous single take serves to establish a certain parity between the disciplines, and as this section proceeds, the roles of architect and filmmaker begin to merge. From his position in a medium close-up in front of the camera, Sert not only can speak about the built environment but, in pointing out the key elements of the streetscape, seems even to direct the camera's gaze. As the architect elaborates on the "scale of those houses. . . scaled to human measure" and the harmonious feel of the place created by the way "the windows and the balconies repeat," Gardner pans to reveal the apartment buildings and then begins to walk through the scene. This doubled engagement—at once haptic and kinesthetic—reaches a climax in a low-angle tracking shot that vividly captures the upper stories and balconies of these buildings on both sides of a narrow lane.[7] The scene ends with Sert, again accompanied by his wife, walking away from the camera and passing under an arched portico that leads down a cobblestoned street in the Old Town.

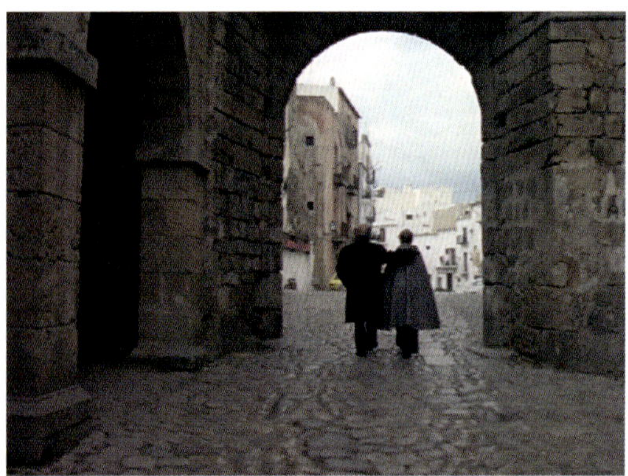

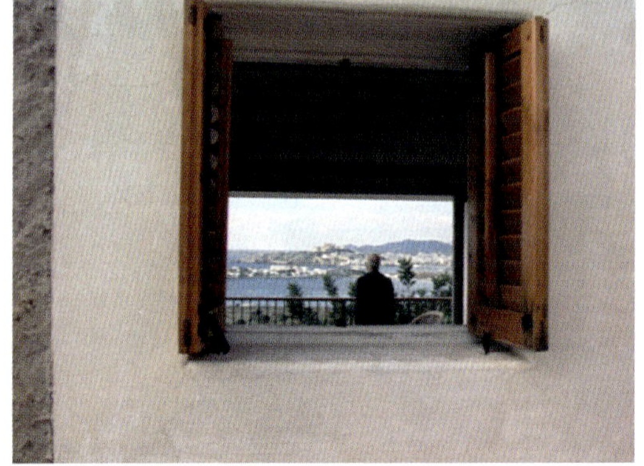

The transition to the next section of the film begins with an almost picture-postcard view of the iconic castle that resides above the harbor of Ibiza, which a cut reveals is being filmed from the interior of a house with a living room and patio that look out on this extraordinary scene. The setting is formally identified in a third shot as Sert, still dressed in his blue suit and gray turtleneck sweater, is seen from above, walking onto the tiled entry and then climbing the steps to his own home in Ibiza. He enters the house by climbing an interior staircase, turns into the front room, and continues out to the patio. Again, the ambulatory exercise involved in the experience of the architectural ensemble is echoed in the camera's journey. Here Gardner completes the series of images of the castle and harbor view by framing the architect through a window with open wooden shutters, as we look in and through at the back of the living room and see Sert as he walks onto the patio terrace leading out from the opposite side of the living room, with its spectacular view—a carefully constructed image that Sert has created through his design and Gardner has re-created through his camera work.

Any touristic notions are quickly dispelled as Gardner joins Sert on the exterior space and captures the architect's story about the property, which, like the land adjacent to Miró's studio, had been terraced for agriculture. The terrace walls had fallen into disrepair, and Sert rebuilt them, painting their tops white like those along the Maeght's Labyrinth, according to the "Ibiza tradition." The house again is "very simple" and was built by peasant laborers from the south of Spain who worked with a "great degree of imposition," resulting in "right angles not exactly ninety degrees" and "lines not too straight." As they had done on the streets of Ibiza, the filmmaker and the architect engage in a cinematic pas de deux as the camera follows Sert's hand gesturing up toward the roofline and describing one of the defining features of the house—a flat roof without eaves or cornices that creates a "light line" against the Mediterranean sky.

As if to demonstrate each element of the traditional mode of construction, Gardner pans across the terrace and tilts up to the unadorned edge of the roof, in effect recapitulating the artisanal methods deployed by the builders through his handheld compositions. From

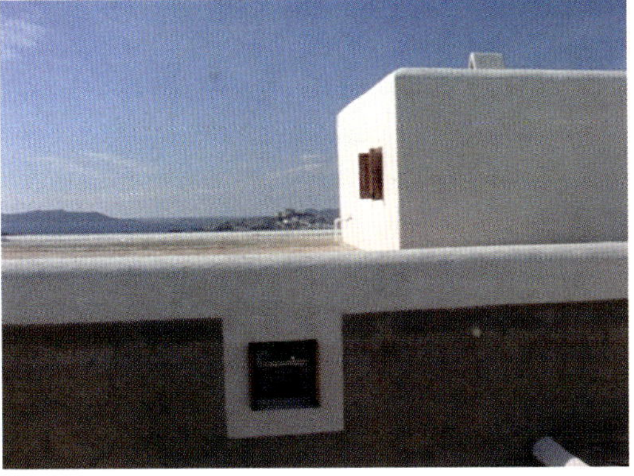

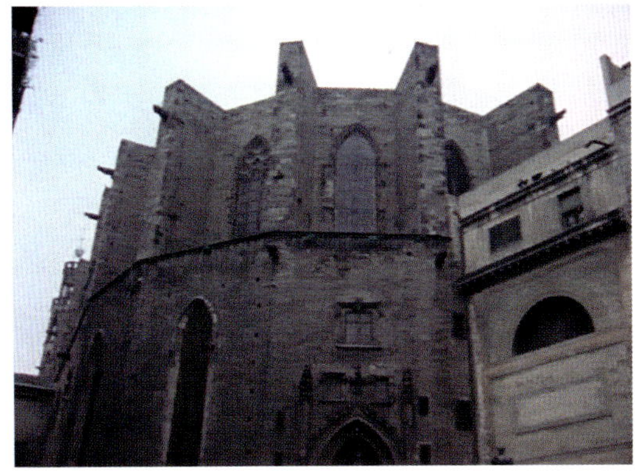

this perspective, Sert's description of the construction of the house begins to serve as a commentary on the filmmaking process itself, which is taking place in the same locale; it is simple, the direct product of improvised means, imperfectly aligned, and of a piece with traditional methods of the past. This said, the section concludes with imagery that seems more in the vein of Antonioni than Flaherty, as the architect ascends sets of stairs to the top of his house and stands in striking isolation against the majestic seascape below. As Sert exits the scene, Gardner holds on the composition, which we can recognize as the same iconic view of the castle and harbor seen earlier.

The final section is the longest and yet begins in medias res, with Sert seated in the back of a car speeding down a busy street and talking about Picasso during his starving-artist days in Barcelona.[8] A title soon confirms that we are back in Barcelona, the architect's birthplace and the heart of both traditional Catalonian architecture and the type of modernist practice in which Sert and his contemporaries were engaged. The Picasso story, about the artist's resorting to trompe l'oeil in order to furnish his apartment, ends with Sert identifying the locale as "near Santa Maria del Mar." One shot later, the architect is out on the streets of the district adjacent to this medieval church and describing it as "the most important architectural monument in Barcelona." As he elaborates on its significance, Gardner's camera pans to a long shot of the semicircular east wall of the church.

Sert notes that "it has the very rare condition of being started and finished in a relatively short period of years," and the clarity of the design suggests to him that it was done by "one hand." Gardner has begun to walk, filming, toward the church and is soon joined by Sert, who describes in some detail the distinctive features of the building: the widely spaced octagonal columns, the symmetry of the aisles, and the distinctive square buttresses. The men are now adjacent to the west wall, with its elaborate entrance and the twin towers that flank either side of the facade.

But the two are not alone. Gardner's tracking shot includes images not only of the impressive rose window and the soaring towers, but also of the area's traffic congestion, where delivery trucks crowd the church's entrance and cars are parked all along the street. He also comes upon a group of school children, some of whom take notes while others sketch the church's exterior, and a hurried businessman who thrusts an inquiring sideways glance directly into the camera lens. As Gardner reaches the church's majestic entrance, he tilts the camera up to capture the geometrically patterned metal doors, the carved religious figures set in a tympanum, the large rose window, and the twin towers.

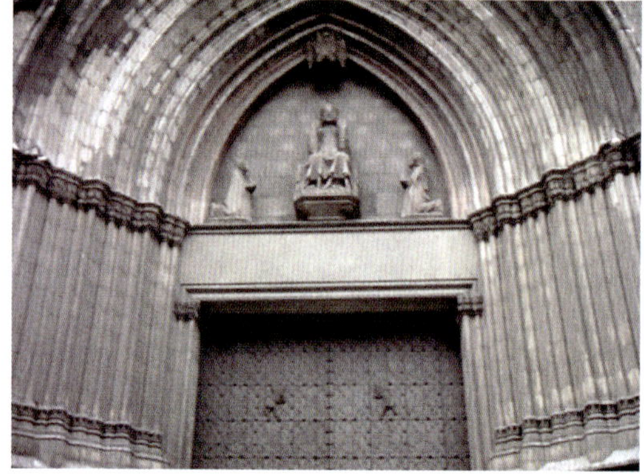

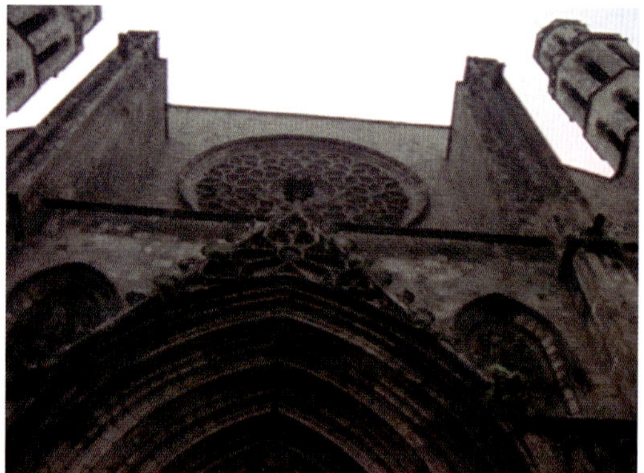

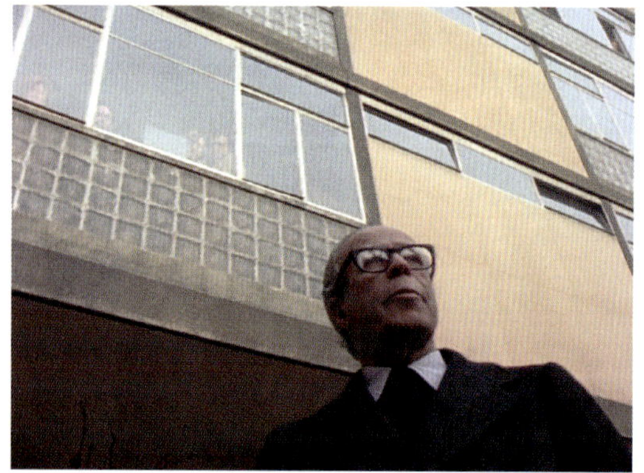

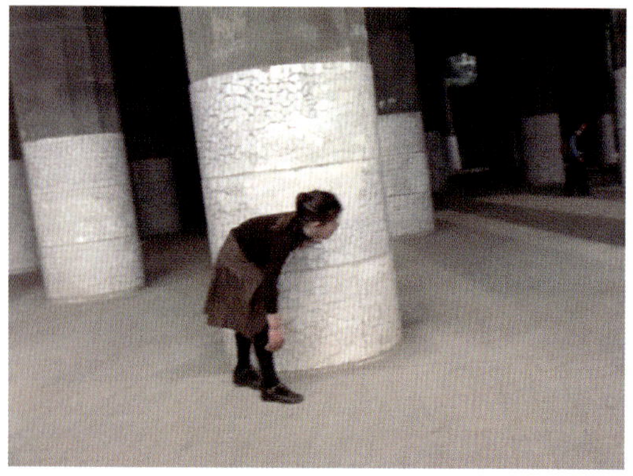

Sert, now off-screen, continues to narrate, but when he comes into view in the next shot he is standing adjacent to the Central Anti-Tuberculosis Clinic, the first large-scale project he designed and the last building he completed in Spain before going into exile during the Civil War, first to Paris, in 1937, and then to the United States two years later.

Sert calls the clinic "a museum," by which he means that, in working for the first time on a major project, he needed to borrow elements from the most innovative work of others, in particular from Le Corbusier. He recalls the French architect's visit to Barcelona in the late 1920s and his unhappiness at having to present a lecture at ten at night. Le Corbusier nevertheless spent a week in Barcelona, at the end of which he invited Sert to work for him in his Paris office. Among the many things that Sert learned from his French mentor at the time was a new appreciation for the work of the Catalonian architect Antoni Gaudí, who had been largely reviled by Sert's generation. Here Gardner shifts locales, and Sert becomes the unlikely guide to the work of this visionary figure as filmmaker and architect together mount the elaborate tiled stairway of the Parc Güell. Like their earlier visit to Santa Maria del Mar, they must share the site with a throng of school children who actively respond to the playfulness of Gaudí's designs. The camera resists the easy pictorial pleasures of the park and reserves its attention for the less ornate market area, which Sert describes, as schoolgirls use the massive columns as hiding spots in a game of tag. Making his way to the top of the park, Sert walks out onto a large terrace surrounded by a serpentine array of tiled benches, and gazes out contemplatively toward the panoramic view of the city below as the girls in the foreground noisily continue their game.

In a nearby café, Sert returns to his stories about the early careers of Catalonian artists, focusing now on Miró, who lived and made his art in a small Barcelona apartment. Sert and Gardner then appear in a small arcaded street, from which the architect points out "the house where Miró lived" and the commemorative plaque that is now attached to the facade of the nineteenth-century building. He mentions Miró's fondness for the small metalwork heads that adorn the neighboring buildings, while Gardner cuts to close-ups of several of these decorative figures.

Looking up at the house again, Sert seems still amazed that the artist could produce large canvases in such small quarters.

Their tour of the city, and the film itself, concludes with visits to two major functionalist buildings: a nineteenth-century market and a military barracks built on the site of a Gothic-era shipyard. The former is a cast-iron and sky-lit structure from 1870 that Sert calls "a rather beautiful shed" and compares to the former Les Halles in Paris, though of smaller scale. The latter provides the first occasion in the film for Sert to speak about the Spanish Civil War, for it was this barracks that the people of Barcelona stormed, in 1936, in loyalty to the Spanish Republic. Sert and Gardner are at the site, however, to attend to another feature of the space, a strikingly arched sky-lit structure that housed a shipbuilding facility dating back to medieval times. For the young Sert and his circle of fellow architecture students, this "simple industrial building" proved that they were "not the first ones. . . to do crazy things": the pared-down approach they advocated had been employed "by practical people many centuries ago."

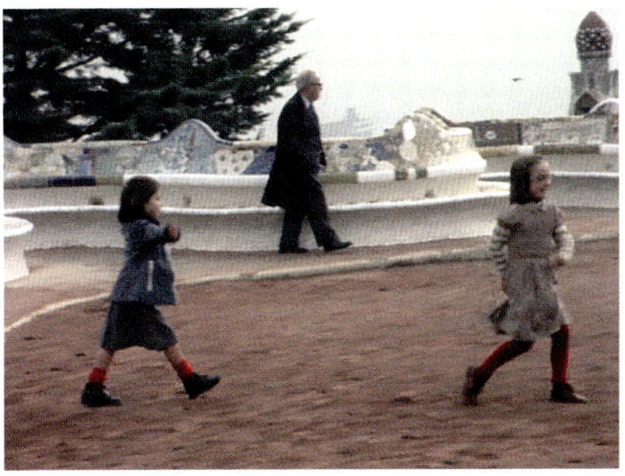

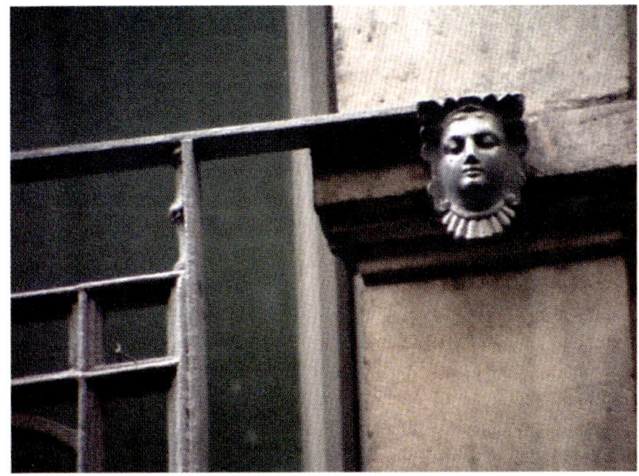

As Sert begins to elaborate on the ways that this kind of building, along with folk architecture, "took into consideration the human scale" as well as human needs, Gardner inserts a sweeping, spinning quasi-abstract image, looking up at the sky-lit ceiling of the market, that evokes the visual tropes of the City Symphony. This departure from the functional relationship of sound and picture signals not only a poetic response to the dynamism of this supposedly functionalist space, but creates a visual metaphor for Sert's mode of enlightened thinking.

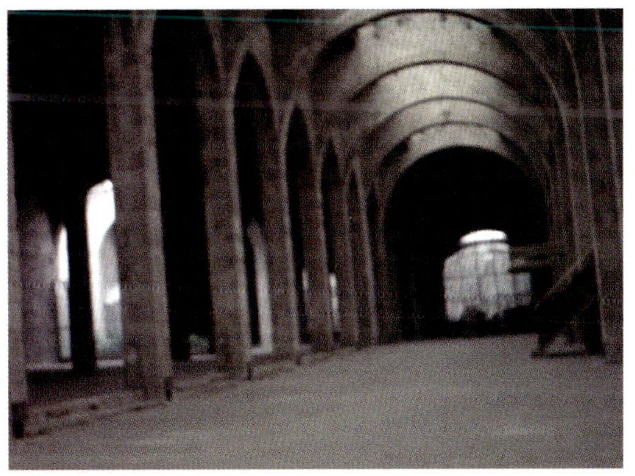

Cutting back to the architect as he walks through the armory, the film draws to an end with Sert's summation of his aesthetic, in which he describes the deeper ambitions of his practice: "Our invention was more of a rational kind of way of building that took into consideration not only the practical function of the building but everything t00hat made architecture architecture, which means give it a spiritual dimension. . . . Beauty can bc done with very simple means and very simple things." A beat later the screen goes dark, and the sound of church bells is heard as the brief credits for the film appear.

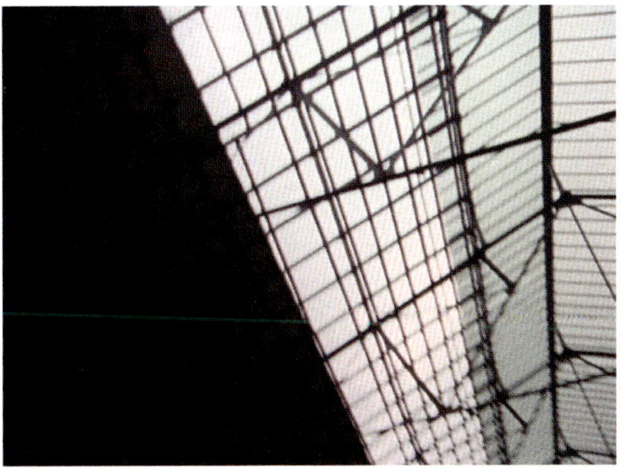

2 Sons of Cambridge

I was concerned from the time I started architecture studies with the relationship between the arts—the places in a modern city where they could come together.

—Josep Lluís Sert

2 Sons of Catalonia utilizes a reverse chronology in accompanying the architect Josep Lluís Sert on a tour of several of his most historically significant Mediterranean projects. It begins with the Miró Museum, completed in 1975, two years before its appearance in the film; moves back in time to the Maeght Foundation from 1964; visits Miró's studio from the mid-1950s, followed by Sert's own home on Ibiza from 1960; and ends with his first major public building, completed in 1937 in Barcelona. Gardner's use of this hysteron-proteron structure subtly reveals the causal links and cultural influences that animate each of these buildings. It is a strategy that privileges the art of Joan Miró while tracing the aesthetic and technical development of a Sertian style as it emerged from under the domination of Le Corbusier into a distinctive form. All of this gives the film a valedictory feel, a palpable sense of looking back at the past, of chronicling the achievements of a lifetime of work and of visually cataloging an architectural legacy. And yet, the two titled protagonists of the film, joined at times by the filmmaker, seem to actively challenge this reading.

This countervailing force to the film's seeming valediction is captured in the image of Miró's irritation at the intrusion of two competing film productions into his studio. "The important thing here," Miró sternly reminds Sert, "is the work that still has to be done." A similar sensibility emerges in the extended sequence devoted to Sert's plans for an addition to the Maeght Foundation; the architect, too, still has work to be done. In these scenes we are shown two men who are unwilling to dwell in the past and are keen instead to focus on the future. Sert was already in his mid-seventies and nearing the end of his professional career when this film was shot, while Miró was a decade older and yet no less keenly determined to continue his work. Joining these "two sons" is a third figure, that of the filmmaker Robert Gardner—a son of Cambridge, where Sert came to settle in 1953, directing the Harvard Graduate School of Design, founding a studio, and setting his mark across three decades on the built environments of Harvard, MIT, and Boston University.

Gardner has always regarded his anthropological projects as pathways to "help me understand myself in more ways than the people I observed."[9] The lengthy genesis of the Catalonia film, which the filmmaker initiated in the mid-1960s yet only completed some four and a half decades later—when, it is interesting to note, Gardner himself attained the age of his former subjects—speaks to both the retrospective aspect of the journey on which Gardner accompanied Sert and his own fierce determination to continue to produce new work—determination such as he had encountered in his two main protagonists. While its footage comes from mid-career, the film itself seems more a work of "late style" in its continual reflexive gaze back on the aesthetic links between architecture and the cinema. But it is not a reflection on just any architecture. What makes the film distinctive is the extraordinary symmetry it displays in portraying a mode of building that, while clearly modernist, is deeply indebted to older, vernacular forms. Much as Sert defined his architectural aesthetic in opposition to the ornateness of Gaudí and the complicated building practices of the late nineteenth century, Gardner long eschewed both the formalities of standard ethnographic practice and the normative modes of nonfiction portrayal. Hence his delight in being able to capture the small-scale, handcrafted practice of Joan Miró that the British producers had bypassed in their focus on the monumental. Gardner equally engages in the revelation of seminal relationships between the streets of Barcelona and the art of the studio in his subtle rhyming of visual forms, such as Miró's *L'Arc* and the archway through which Sert and his wife pass.

In the architect Josep Lluís Sert, Robert Gardner found a brother in arms, an artist working in a seemingly normative field of commissioned work and assembly line processes who, by mining the historical past, discovered a singular pathway forward for his practice. Gardner, too, spent a lifetime exploring the world through moving images, working like Sert with "very simple means and very simple things," and trying to discover the "spiritual dimension" that animates art and life. And like his subjects in this film, he remained focused on the work that still had to be done.

Notes

1. *The Surreal House*, a 2010 exhibition at the Barbican in London, focused on precisely this nexus of architecture, film, and the avant-garde, and included *L'Age d'or* in its opening day of screenings.
2. Hans Richter, "Film von morgen," *Das Werk* 16, no. 9 (1929), cited in *Hans Richter New Living: Architecture, Film, Space*, eds. Andres Janser and Arthur Rüegg (Baden, Switzerland: Lars Müller, 2001), 33.
3. Ibid.
4. Robert Gardner, *The Impulse to Preserve: Reflections of a Filmmaker* (New York: Other Press, 2006), 112.
5. Jan K. Birksted, *Modernism and the Mediterranean: The Maeght Foundation* (Aldershot, England: Ashgate, 2004), 18.
6. This scene may have seemed too contrived to the filmmakers, as it was left out of the finished documentary, *Joan Miró—Theatre of Dreams* (1978).
7. The reference here is to Walter Benjamin and a body of contemporary theory linking film and architecture by scholars such as Giuliana Bruno, Vivian Sobchack, and Juhani Pallasmaa. For an overview, see François Penz, "Museums as Laboratories of Change: The Case for the Moving Image," in *Film, Art, New Media: Museum Without Walls?*, ed. Angela Dalle Vacche (London: Palgrave Macmillan, 2012), 283.
8. As William Rothman has pointed out, the use of Barcelona here resembles the strategy Gardner utilized in *Dancing with Miklos*, his film about the filmmaker Miklós Jancsó, in which the city of Budapest figures significantly.
9. Gardner, *The Impulse to Preserve*, 112.

Chapter 21
Dead Birds Re-Encountered: A Journey of Return

William Rothman

Although failing eyesight kept Robert Gardner from his accustomed place behind a camera, the last few years of his life were an extraordinarily productive period in which, working with previously shot footage, he completed *2 Sons of Catalonia: Josep Luís Sert & Joan Miró* (2013), *Forsaken Fragments* (2010/2011), and *Still Journey On: An Unfinished Examination of Life* (2013), as well as *Dead Birds Re-Encountered* (2013). These late works are important additions to his legacy. *Dead Birds Re-Encountered*, his final work, tells the story of his return to New Guinea in 1989 to re-encounter the people and places he had filmed a quarter of a century earlier; to re-encounter *Dead Birds*, his breakthrough film; and to re-encounter himself as he had once been.

Gardner's best-known films—*Dead Birds* (1963), *Rivers of Sand* (1974), *Deep Hearts* (1981), *Forest of Bliss* (1986)—are typically referred to as "ethnographic." Although these films do achieve and communicate ethnographic knowledge, as Daniel Morgan argues in his chapter for this volume, Gardner thought of himself as an artist, not a scientist. In *Dead Birds Re-Encountered*, the impulse toward ethnography is clearly subordinated, as it is in all his late works. Subordinated to what? One meaningful answer is that the primary concern of these last videos is with—and for—the particular people in them whom he cared about, and who cared about him. They also have an autobiographical dimension; they are concerned with, and for, Gardner himself—as a man and as an artist. In *Dead Birds Re-Encountered*, the filmmaker is a major character.

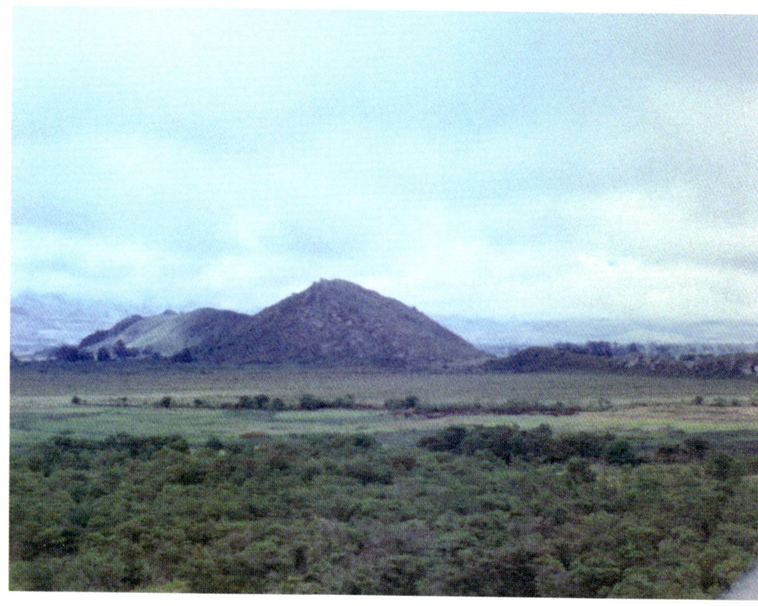

As the film begins, we hear Gardner say in voice-over, "In 1961, I stepped into another world, if not another planet." His narration is much sparser than in *Dead Birds*, and spoken in a voice at times slightly hesitant. This is no surprise, because in 2013 Gardner was eighty-seven years old, although still sharp of mind and in good health. What we see as Gardner speaks this opening line is a pristine landscape—a distant high hill or mountain looming over what he will call, later in the film, a "ravishing valley" as yet unscarred by the road which, in his eyes, has since defiled it.

This opening shot of *Dead Birds Re-Encountered*, shot by his close friend Robert Fulton, employs time-lapse cinematography, a technique that also works beautifully in footage Fulton shot for Gardner's masterpiece *Ika Hands* (1988). It accelerates the movement of the clouds, causing ever-shifting patterns of light and shadow to swirl evocatively over the unchanging mountain. The effect evokes a world that is past. Gone. Yet here it is, unchanged yet ever-changing. Only much later in the film will we be told that this hill is the Warabara, which marks the place where battles, sometimes deadly, were fought. On the words "when I took up residence in a forest of Araucaria trees at the foot of a mountain wall," this vision at once of transience and permanence, yields its place on the screen to a black and white still photograph of a tent amidst trees, viewed from a distance.

The preceding shot returns to the screen as the filmmaker completes his sentence, "in the millennial highlands of West Papua."

Gardner's voice-over continues. "One of the first to greet me"—we see a black-and-white photo of a man dressed (all but undressed) in native garb—"a man named 'Wali,' was

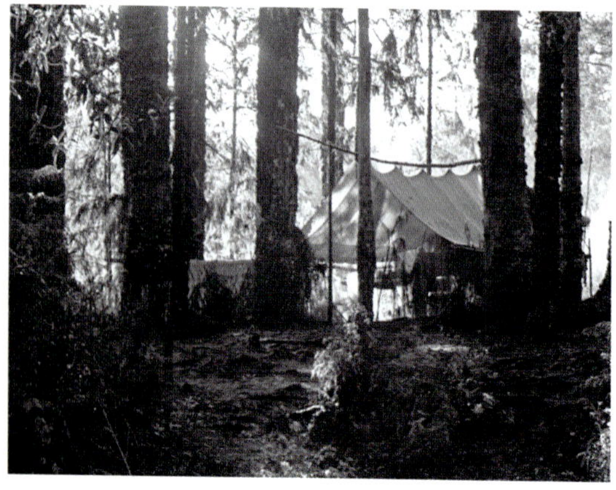

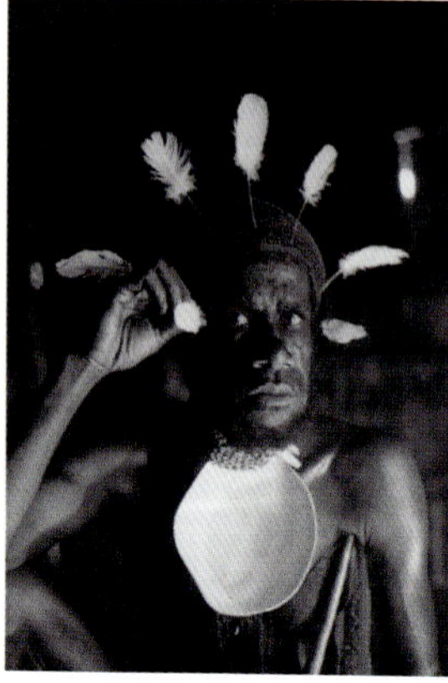

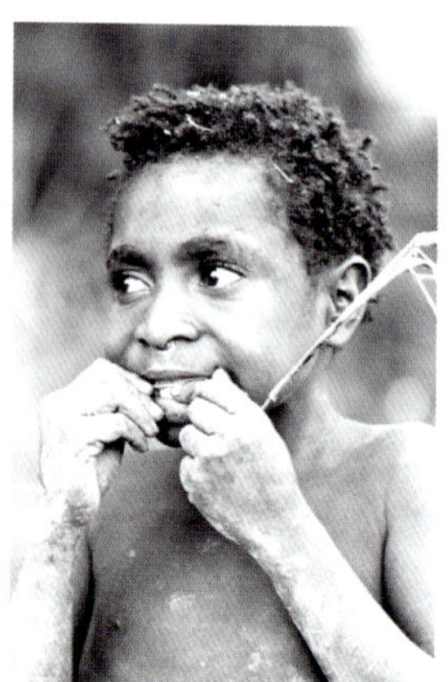

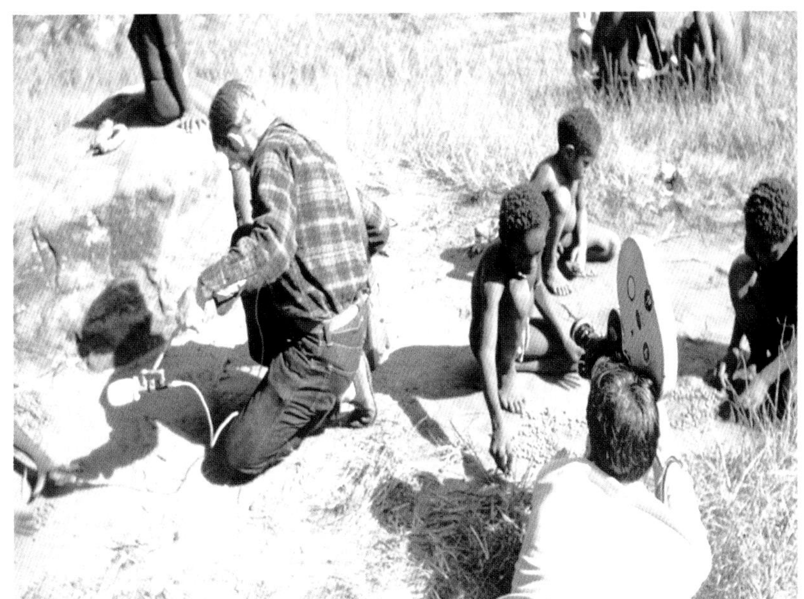

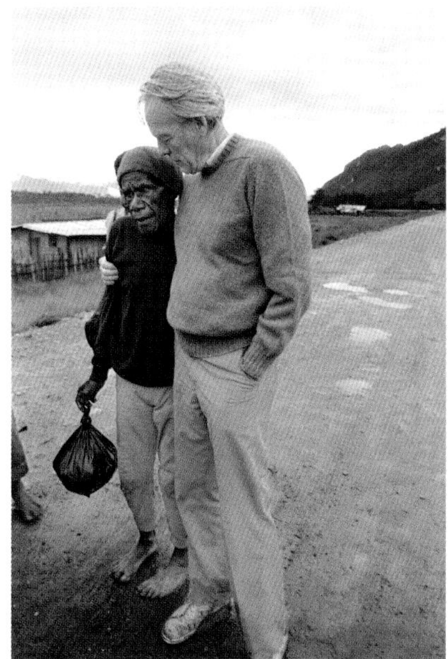

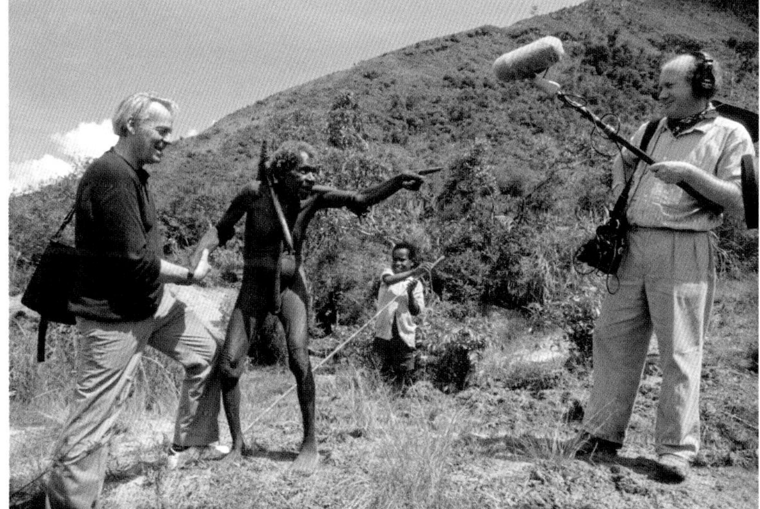

to take me as far as I could go into his world." On the words "And so did a small pig herder, a boy named 'Pua,'" there is a cut to a photo of Pua as a child. "Both were essential to my understanding of their world."

The photo in the next shot is of Gardner himself, filming. At the left of the frame is the late Michael Rockefeller, fussing with sound equipment. "They let me see them through the lenses of my cameras, both still and cine."

There is a reprise of the "mountain/clouds shot," which lingers on the screen. "Out of that scrutiny emerged not only books and articles, but a feature-length film I gave the title 'Dead Birds.' In 1989, the time had come when I could no longer resist. . . ." What we next see is a photo of a gray-haired Gardner, his arm around a visibly aged Wali. The plastic bag Wali is holding, and more so the road on which they were walking when this photograph was taken, establishes that Wali's world has changed as much as he has. ". . . Going back for another look at the people, and places, which had become such important memories."

On the word "memories," the mountain/clouds shot is reprised yet again. "Thus I set off, bringing with me my two dearest friends, Robert Fulton and Richard Rogers. . . ." On these last words, there is a cut to a photo of the gray-haired Gardner, a man greeting him who is dressed in the traditional way, a child, and Richard Rogers with a boom microphone. ". . . who agreed to help me make a film of this journey of return." (The distinguished photojournalist Susan Meiselas, another of Gardner's good friends, was part of the group. This volume benefits greatly by including several of the photographs she took at the time.)

The image fades out, bringing to a close the film's deceptively simple opening sequence.

Ethnography

In his first film, *Blunden Harbour* (1951), Gardner presents all the behavior we view as typical for the people who live in the village. Such everyday behavior is revelatory of how they live, hence of ethnographic interest. *Dead Birds*, like Robert Flaherty's *Nanook of the North* (1922), passes back and forth between what is typical for the Dani and what is particular to Pua and to Weyak. When Gardner tells us that Weyak always pauses on the way to his watchtower, his heart gladdened by the natural beauty of the valley, there is no implication that all or most Dani men do this, that they have Weyak's acute appreciation of beauty, or that the burden of sorrow would weigh as heavily on their conscience as it does on his, so Gardner tells us, if a boy should fall victim to the enemy on their watch. Gardner's narration presents Pua, too, as an individual. When Gardner refers to "the work and love" it takes "to make a boy," he means this to apply to boys in general. Perhaps Gardner could characterize other Dani boys, alone with the pigs they tend, as "waiting for manhood." But not every Dani boy projects the dreaminess, the air of solitary reflection, that Gardner attributes to Pua.

Dead Birds Re-Encountered is not unconcerned with the ways the lives of the Dani in general had changed since Gardner filmed *Dead Birds*. Yet there are only two extended passages centrally concerned with an everyday activity of ethnographic interest. They both involve interactions with tourists. In Pua's village, a group of Europeans is shown a compound with immaculate thatched huts built specifically to impress tourists. For the Dani, who participate in such charades to earn money to buy the Western clothes they never needed before the Indonesian government forced them to abandon so much of their traditional culture, this is an "ordinary" scene, sad to say—one revelatory of their everyday life.

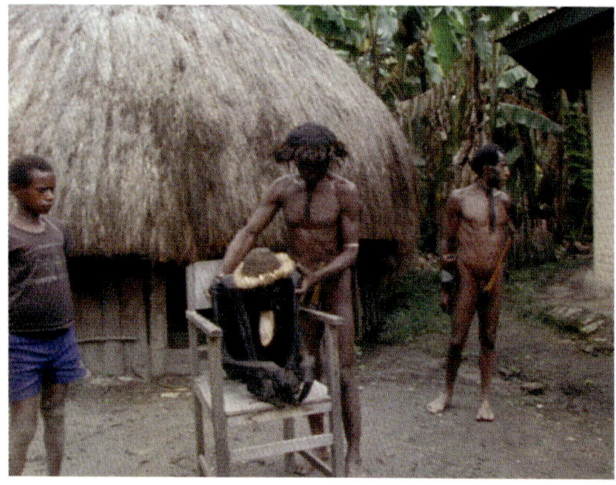

In a sequence set in a nearby village, Gardner's camera dwells on telling details—the haggling over price, the cash changing hands, the protruding pot belly of the man who cracks crude jokes when he tries on the traditional penis gourd, with its phallic appendage, that has to be tied to the testicles. These indignities are complemented by the film's most starkly grotesque moment, when at another tourist site a Dani man goes into a hut and emerges with a mummified human body, pathetically small, which he places on a wooden chair to make it easier for the tourists—and Gardner—to get good shots of it.

There is an ethnographic dimension to this scene insofar as its place in the film hinges on its everydayness, not on any feature that makes this instance different from other instances. But Gardner has no interest in informing us, for example, whether this shriveled mummy is a trophy of war preserved as a token of enmity against the enemy, a revered personage, or perhaps a dead child, originally preserved to keep alive important memories, or out of fear of angering its ghost. His camera is concerned with capturing the attitude of the tourists, who show no sign that it troubles them that they are perhaps being disrespectful of the dead, and that of the impassive Dani participants and observers, who also show no sign of feeling troubled by what is going on.

As Pua, one of the observers in the first of these passages, watches the insensitive tourists snap their photos, so many trophies to take back with them, the film gives us no cause to think that he is any more troubled than the other Dani. Indeed, in his own village, as the film will show us, Pua, too, is actively engaged in exploiting his own "exotic" culture to make money from tourists, as he must if his family is to survive in the brave new world the Indonesian authorities forced the Dani to enter.

The devout Hindus in *Forest of Bliss* treat the dead as sacred. To Gardner, every human life is of value, and unique. As Louise Brooks once put it, "No one's life is a jest." Gardner films and edits these scenes in ways that underscore their grotesque absurdity, but at the same time acknowledge the underlying pathos embodied by the mummy, once a human being with a soul, now reduced to a commodity deprived of all vestiges of dignity.

Wali

Gardner's reunion with Wali—the only one of the three main characters in *Dead Birds Re-Encountered* who did not have a major role in *Dead Birds*—is the first significant "live action" in the film. It is followed, shortly afterward, by an astonishing scene in which Wali delivers a passionate peroration, an uninterrupted torrent of words that lasts fourteen minutes, fully a third the length of the film. After this, Wali plays a less prominent role.

The reunion of Wali and Gardner is preceded by a shot of the road. The camera holds this framing until a truck in the far distance barrels into the foreground and exits the frame, leaving a cloud of dust that hangs heavy over our view of the mountain. The roar of the truck motor segues to an excited yelping, which serves as a kind of sound overlap to the next shot, in which Wali, wearing Western clothes, his extended arm visible at the extreme right, moves left, the camera reframing with him across a picture-perfect thatched hut and a watching child, and finally disclosing Gardner's presence. The intimacy of the camera's attunement to Gardner as well as to Wali testifies to the blessing it was that when the filmmaker chose to step out from behind the camera to be filmed, he had Robert Fulton on hand to film him—a man who was not only one of Gardner's few peers as a cameraman, but who in some ways may have known Gardner better than he knew himself. Similarly the rapport between camera and subjects throughout *Dead Birds Re-Encountered* is enhanced by the precision of the editing, the work of Gardner with what he acknowledges as "the essential collaboration" of Rebecca Meyers.

As the two men embrace in medium shot, Gardner is turned away from the camera; Wali's face is half in shadow. Wali hugs Gardner warmly and repeatedly. Gardner, restrained by upbringing and temperament, pats Wali's back.

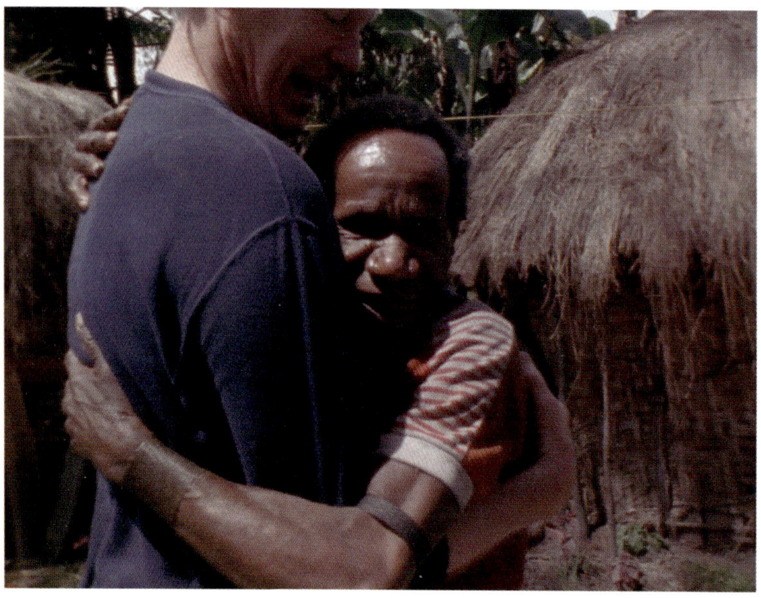

"Where'd you find clothes?" Gardner asks—not a real question, because he knows Wali does not speak English. Over the line "We're both old men now, huh?" there is a cut to both men's legs from the knees down, revealing Wali to be barefoot, before the camera returns to the previous framing. Wali lets out a long, loud sound, somewhere between a chirp and a wail, which Gardner gamely echoes, although not as robustly. There is a brief silence that he breaks by saying, "This was a long time Wali, huh?" There is a cut to an angle that allows us a clear view of Gardner's expression as he responds to Wali's wailing, laughing, hugging, and even kissing by giving his shoulder another affectionate tap. The sheer excess of Wali's warm greeting seems to all but overwhelm Gardner, but also touch and amuse him. And how can we not be touched and amused, too? Gardner's temperament precludes his matching Wali's exuberance, but he appears no less happy to be reunited with his old friend after all these years.

It would take a heart of stone to be unmoved by Wali's infectious exuberance. Perhaps it would take a heart of stone, as well, not to suspect that there might be an admixture of theatricality in his display of warmth. Watching this passage, and the passage that follows it in which Wali delivers an increasingly vehement monologue, I, for one, find myself unable to be sure what, or how deeply, he is really feeling. It isn't clear whether he delivers this monologue to Gardner (whom he knows as "Pom") or to the camera, because it isn't obvious whom or what he is looking at, if anyone or anything, as he speaks. Furthermore, with only four exceptions, during the duration of the sequence's eight long-held, static takes of Wali—illuminated in a pool of light and surrounded by the darkness of his hut—the camera remains fixed in place. This is the only passage in the film in which the camera seems to be running on autopilot, with no one calling the shots.

Wali's monologue, fully subtitled, is fascinating for the direct testimony it gives to one man's take on the traumatic changes to his world and to himself that had taken place over the preceding quarter of a century. Now, he says, he no longer kills or rapes or steals pigs; all he wants is clothes and money; and he is no longer afraid of ghosts, because they no longer frequent the places he goes. Despite its fascinating content, Wali's emotional and not always coherent account of his role in facilitating Gardner's making of *Dead Birds*, and of the changes in his world and his life, has an effect strikingly different from that of Omali Inda's commentary, addressed to the camera, in *Rivers of Sand*. Although she stops short, as Gardner does not, of passing judgment on her society for its pervasive abuse of women, the filmmaker takes her analysis of the treatment of women in her culture to jibe completely with his own. By contrast, partly because of the way Wali is filmed, what we see offers no clue as to how we are to take his tirade. We can't even be sure what his mood is, what he has "inside of him," as the subtitles translate one of his recurring locutions. Is it anger? If so, at whom? Is it guilt? Is he making a pitch for Gardner to give him money or clothes? To what extent is he speaking from the heart, and to what extent is this a theatrical performance? We cannot say. And Gardner does not say, perhaps because he does not know. At the time he must have been even more in the dark than we are, because he was far from fluent enough in Wali's language to have understood more than bits of what he was saying.

Aesthetically, this is far from the strongest sequence in the film. Why, then, didn't Gardner leave it on the cutting room floor? One reason, I believe, has to do with Wali's remarks about ghosts. In *Dead Birds*, Gardner's voice-over has a lot to say about the Dani's fear of ghosts, the fact that Dani men go into battle because they believe that the ghosts of those killed by the enemy demand that their deaths be avenged (although the Dani also fight and kill, Gardner tells us, because they like to). But nothing Gardner says in his voice-over in *Dead Birds* intimates that he, too, might believe in ghosts, or fear their power. (The French DVD of *Dead Birds*, in which Jean Rouch speaks a translation of Gardner's narration, has the mood of a ghost story. Rouch's own films always have this tone, both because he has the perfect voice for ghost stories, and because he believed in the reality of ghosts, as did the Africans he loved to film.) Between 1989 and 2013, Gardner's "journey of return" had taken on new meaning for him. The people in the film he cared most about had died. So had two dear friends who had embarked on this journey with him. For Gardner, the world of *Dead Birds Re-Encountered* had become a world of ghosts.

Here is a fragment of what Wali says about ghosts:

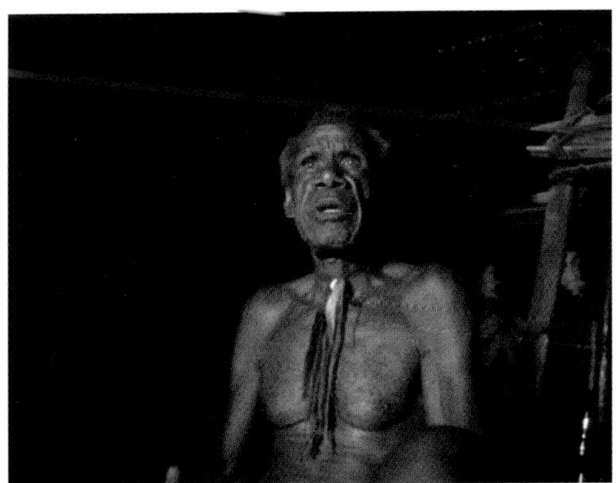

> I say we were afraid of them. There was lots of war in those days and we wanted to keep the ghosts happy. The spirits of the dead, our ancestors' spirits—what if we ran into them in the night? What if we went outside at night to relieve ourselves? This is what made us afraid. But the government came and told us not to fight, and the spirits are no longer around like before. . . . And at night we are not afraid. . . . The ghosts aren't around. We can take a flashlight that you people use, and walk. In the old days when we were killing, we were afraid of the ghosts.

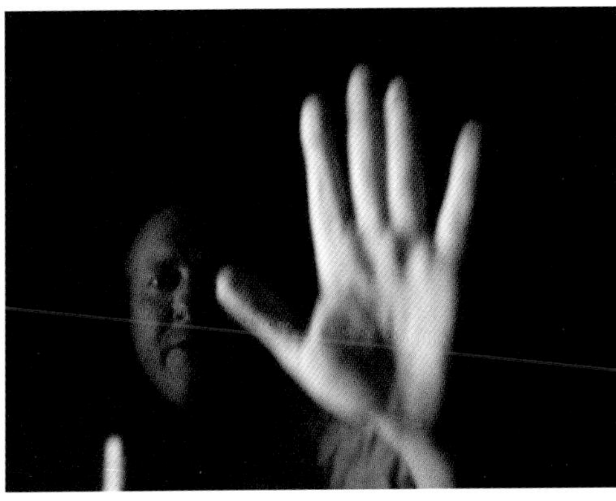

At this point, the camera, so long dormant, pans swiftly and vertiginously to the left. Momentarily, the frame is engulfed in darkness before an uplifted hand, and then a man's face, white as a sheet, bathed in an eerie light, emerges from the shadows. A ghostly apparition, indeed! But then he holds up all five fingers, taps smartly on a microphone, and says, looking directly into the camera, "Take number five." A cut back to Wali makes this "ghost" vanish as suddenly as it had appeared.

Actually, this is the fourth time in the sequence such a thing has happened. But because Wali's monologue drags on so long, the effect is uncanny, hallucinatory, each time. Of course, this is no ghost; it's the man taking sound, Richard Rogers, doing what he has to do to keep sound and image synchronized. But Richard Rogers died in 2001, his life cut short by cancer. To Gardner, this apparition that keeps materializing and vanishing *is* a ghost. How could he leave his dear friend's ghost on the cutting room floor?

Weyak

After this unsettling sequence a shot fades in, of Gardner and Weyak. In *Dead Birds Re-Encountered,* as in *Dead Birds*, Gardner makes clear that Weyak has his complete sympathy. This makes the sequences that revolve around him unsettling in a different way, because this man with a sweet face seems so diminished by the passing years that he cuts a poignant figure.

When they greet, Weyak says in Dani, presumably to an unseen interpreter, "He remembers my name!" With a shy smile, he looks at the camera. "I saw you already and recognized you." Affectionately, Gardner, who towers over Weyak, kisses the top of his head. Weyak says, more or less to the camera, "They told me this man would come, and here he is!"

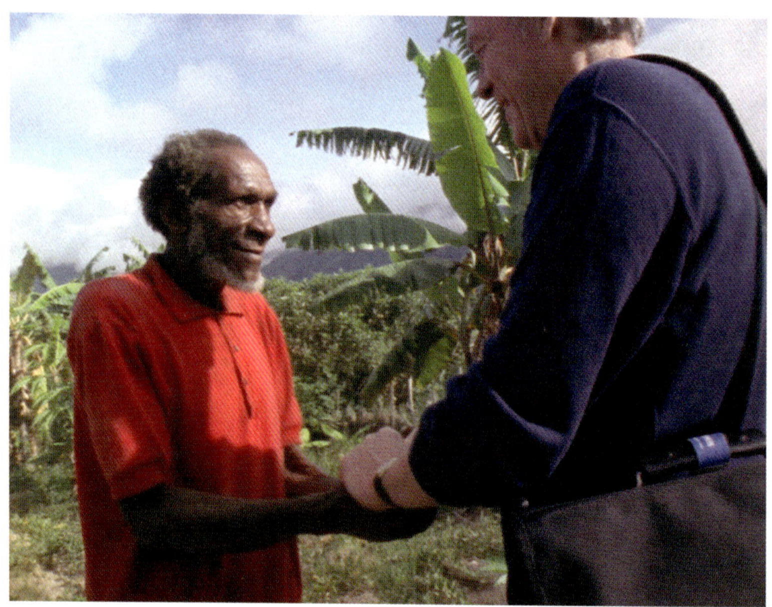

As Weyak begins to lead Gardner somewhere, there is a cut to a time-lapse landscape shot, accompanied by the melancholy sound of wailing wind. This shot provides an expressively apt transition to the passage that follows, which begins with a cut to Gardner and Weyak in a part of the valley that Gardner tells us, addressing the camera, was where Weyak had his watchtower, his reference illustrated by a shot from *Dead Birds*, desaturated to black and white. "The tower was right here," Gardner says, pointing over Weyak's bowed head. As if sensing that Weyak is feeling melancholy, Gardner puts a consoling hand on his shoulder, but Weyak doesn't look up. To me, there is something indescribably beautiful and sad about this slight, bearded man as he appears in this shot. "And he would come every morning from. . .his village. . .and climb the tower, and look out over here towards the Warabaga," Gardner says, his voice steeped in nostalgia as he describes the routine of each day for Weyak in that long lost world.

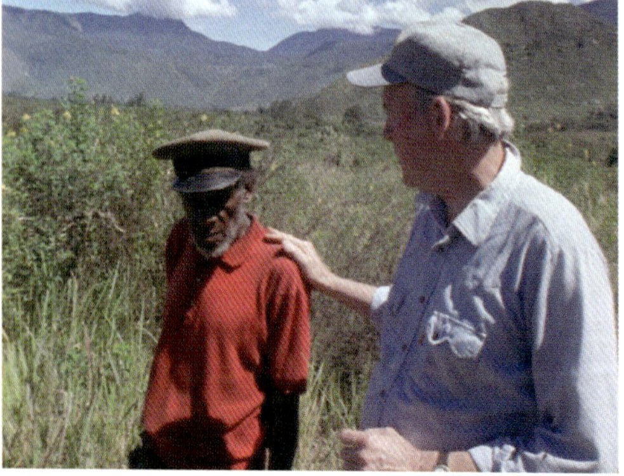

The camera pans in the direction Gardner points, then back, as he says, "That's where the men were fighting. . . . Then he'd come back and make a fire and smoke would go up and Laklokek, his wife, would come out here and start working the garden." Gardner again puts a gentle hand on Weyak's shoulder. "And here he is now today, twenty-eight years later. And there's no tower. And there's no war." Gardner is looking at Weyak, whose head is still bowed, his eyes downcast. "But he's, uh. . ." He pats Weyak on the shoulder. "He's doing fine."

I sense that Gardner senses that Weyak is not "doing fine," at least at this moment. Tactfully, he brings the scene to an early close by saying, "So let's go now to, uh, Homoclep? OK?" He touches Weyak's elbow as a cue to start walking. Weyak gives the most minimal nod in agreement. "Um, OK," Gardner says to the camera, unable to come up with anything positive to add, as he begins to walk off to the right. I have the impression that he is a little sad to find Weyak, always a quiet, introspective man, seeming so withdrawn.

Pua

The mood could not be more different when Pua, eight years old when Gardner first met him, asks "Are you Pom?" and, reassured, shakes his hand, embraces him warmly, and says, looking up at the taller man, "Oh my brother! Oh, I love you my brother. My brother."

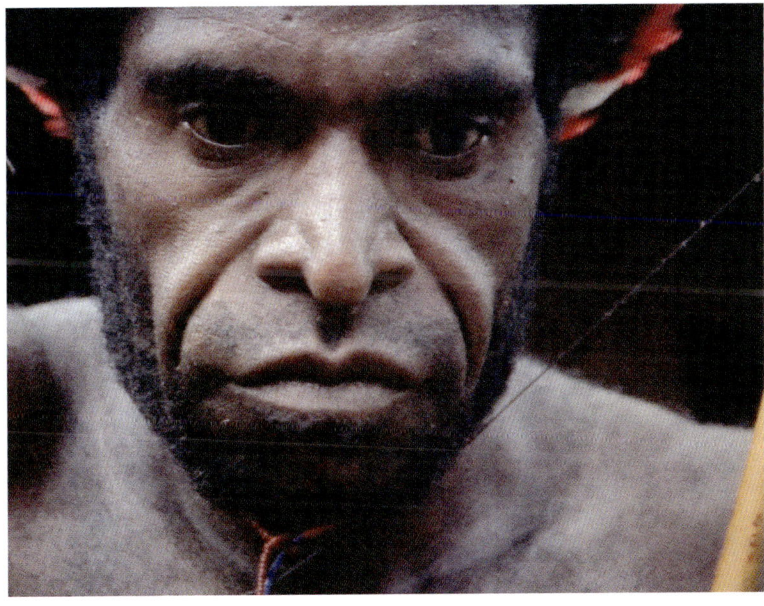

"When I knew Pua," Gardner tells us, "he was a little boy who took care of pigs. That was all he did, take care of his father's pigs." This young man, who spent his childhood days alone with pigs and "waiting for manhood," is no longer alone. A young adult with a wife, a daughter, a number of pigs (the figure varies from one to ten depending on who is asked), and carefully thought-out business plans, Pua is striving to thrive in the modern world, not escape from it. His world is no longer "another planet" from Gardner's. For better or worse, Pua's world is now Gardner's world; it is also our world, the one existing world, as Stanley Cavell likes to say.

One lovely passage perfectly illustrates this. I am thinking of the moment at which the filmmaker, framed with Pua in a two shot, says with Gardner's trademark sage but mischievous smile, "Well, I'm older, that's for sure, but not too old to come to see Pua and, uh, not too old to, you know. . ." Gardner's eyes narrow a bit; he looks up and into the middle distance for a moment as he gropes for a gracious way to end this sentence, ". . . to stay a little while and then come back," he says, his eyes almost closed, before meeting Pua's gaze. (Seven years later, Gardner kept his promise and returned for another visit.) There is now a cut to an intimate, exquisite close-up of Pua, his expression deeply serious, his gaze turned inward.

Over this shot, which captures and casts so powerful a mood, we hear Gardner say—this is not a voice-over; it is something he said then and there—"Pua is a good man, and he will have to find his way." The world in which, as Gardner predicts, Pua will "find his way" is the world in which Gardner himself, another good man, had to find his way. The affection in Gardner's voice is palpable when he adds, "And, and I'm sure he will," and repeats, a bit wistfully, "I'm sure he will."

By the time Gardner was editing *Dead Birds Re-Encountered*, he knew that his hopeful prediction about the young man's future had turned sadly ironic. Cancer cut short Pua's life only a few years after this scene was shot, just as it cut short Richard Rogers' life—facts that Gardner refrains from mentioning—wisely, I think—in his narration. For all his belief in Pua's capability and commitment, the slight stutter with which he says "And, and I'm sure he will" belies a less than complete confidence in his prediction, a shadow of a doubt—in retrospect, a foreshadowing—that Gardner resists acknowledging, indeed tries to erase but only darkens, by repeating, "I'm sure he will."

From one beautiful shot of Pua, deep in thought, Gardner cuts to another. Framed slightly from below, Pua is sitting in what momentarily we realize is a helicopter, as the rotor cuts through the frame, its speed—and accompanying thumping noise—accelerating.

There is a cut to a shot looking out the open door as the helicopter begins to move and Gardner begins the longest voice-over in the film:

> The enormity of cultural change between my first and my 1989 meeting with the Dani can scarcely be exaggerated. Pua was a vulnerable and tender child of about eight years whom I had chosen as one of the principal players in a story I wanted to tell. I hoped to see what I was experiencing through his eyes. On my return, Pua was a mature adult witnessing vast changes to his childhood landscape and society. I asked Pua to join me in a helicopter ride that would reveal his daily surroundings in a new way. I especially wanted him to see the road that left a brutal scar across the soft belly of this ravishing valley. I cannot be sure what he was feeling as he gazed at his familiar surroundings, but it was clear he was given to lengthy thought.

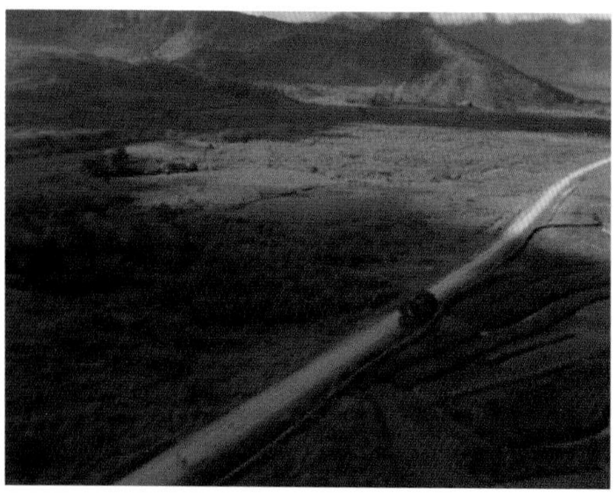

These words are accompanied by views of the valley below, taken from the helicopter, and shots of Pua, in traditional garb, taking in this landscape Gardner wanted him to see the way birds do. (Tom Conley's chapter in this book has much to say about the powers and the limits of aerial views in Gardner's work.) This sequence culminates in an eloquent shot of Pua looking out the window, lost in thought, feathers on his shoulders blowing in the wind.

In *Dead Birds*, Gardner repeatedly tells us what Pua and Weyak are thinking. In later films, he never again arrogates to himself the authority to tell us his camera's subjects' thoughts. Here, Gardner asserts only that it is clear that Pua is "given to lengthy thought,"

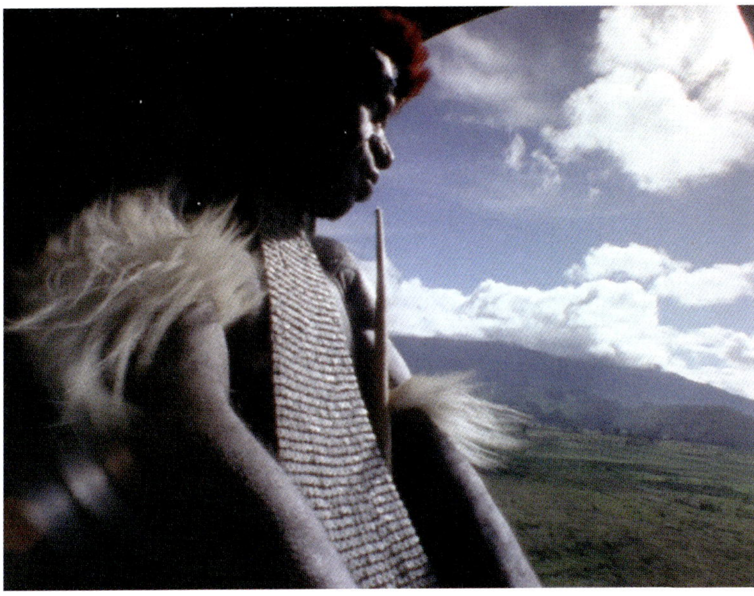

an assertion his camera backs up and which implies no claim to know the young man's private thoughts, which remain his, and his alone. Gardner says about Pua, "I cannot be sure what he was feeling as he gazed at his familiar surroundings." This line comes immediately after "I especially wanted him to see the road that left a brutal scar across the soft belly of this ravishing valley," which leaves no room for doubt as to what Gardner feels about the road. These lines, together, invite us to ask ourselves other questions about Gardner's feelings—questions that his words leave pointedly unanswered. Why did he "especially want" Pua to see this road, and to see it this way? How did he expect Pua to feel about it? Why did he want Pua to feel that way? And how did not knowing what Pua is feeling make Gardner feel? The point I am making is that even though he speaks to us directly, we cannot be sure what *Gardner* was feeling as he gazed through the lens of his camera at Pua. Nor can we be sure what he was feeling, so many years later, when he spoke this voice-over, whether consciously or not, in such a way as to bring home that he, too, had private feelings that were his, and his alone.

This is not the film's only instance of voice-over that invites us to ask ourselves questions that Gardner's words pointedly do not answer. Early in the film, for example, he says this: "In 1989, the time had come when I could no longer resist going back for another look at the people, and places, which had become such important memories." Evidently, for some time he had resisted going back. Why? In 1989, he could no longer resist going back. Why? Why had going back become not only possible, but necessary? Why then? The important memories of the time he spent shooting *Dead Birds* finally compelled him to go back. What memories? Why were they important? What gave them the power to compel him to return? After 1989, those memories must have melded with memories, no less important, of that "journey of return." Why did it take him so many years to complete a film from the footage he had brought back? Evidently, he had resisted going back to this footage to take another look at it. Why? And why, in 2013, did he find himself unable to continue to defer returning to footage that by then had come to be inscribed with more than half a century of important memories?

Why he felt that he could—and had to—complete this film when he did is a part of the film's story Gardner could not have told—could not have known—in 1989. It is a part of the story his narration does not tell, a part of the story the completed film tells only by not telling it, by expressing it cinematically, that is, consigning it to silence. As an artist, Gardner communicates what he wishes known about himself. His private feelings are his and his alone or, rather, in this case, they are a matter between him and the ghosts of those he cared about, and who cared about him—who give the film its life.

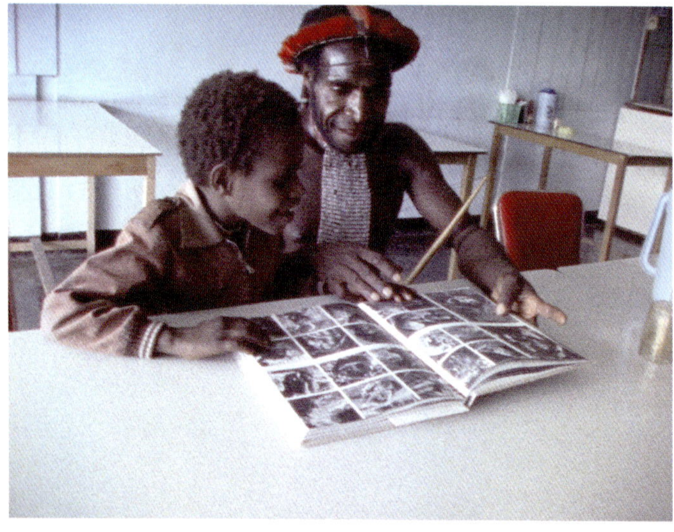

Every Story Has an Ending

In a life-affirming sequence near the end of the film, Pua and his daughter—about the age Pua was in *Dead Birds*—pore through the pages of *Gardens of War*, a book containing photographs taken by Gardner and others during the making of *Dead Birds*.

Pua patiently answers his daughter's questions and makes such comments as "This is Mike [Michael Rockefeller] and Pom"; "Hey, that's Yeke Asuik!"; "Usak's father is here"; "That is this one's father"; "I think that's me in the back"; "Look at this. Wow! Look! Look!"; " "This one has a spear"; and "This looks like the father of Arokop."

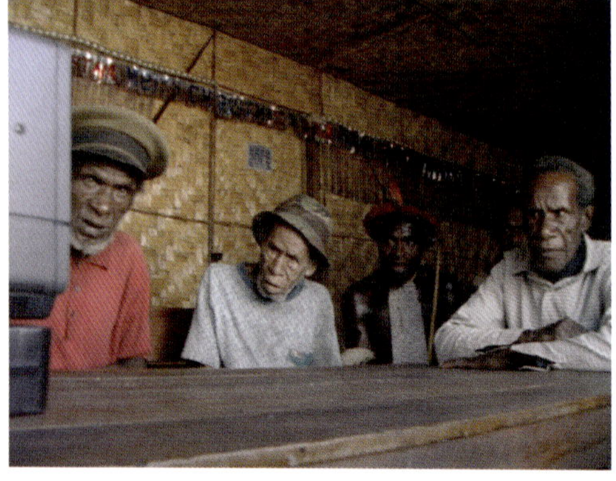

The film draws to its haunting conclusion with two additional scenes also self-evidently set up by Gardner for the purpose of being included in the film he wanted to make. The first of these scenes begins with a shot of Weyak, a man a subtitle will inform us is "Kurelu," Pua and Wali all sitting at a table intently watching a television monitor at the far left of the frame.

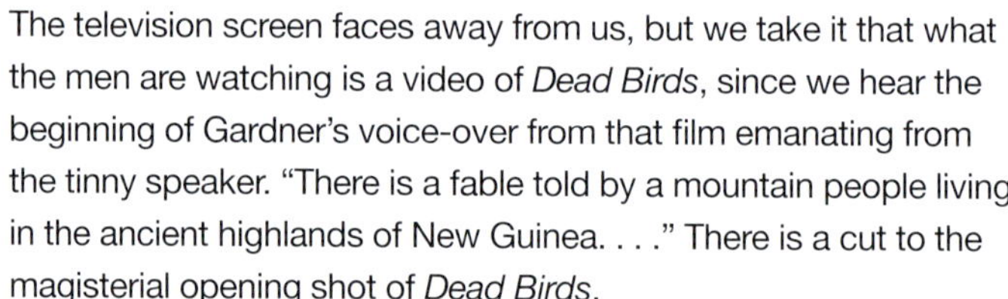

The television screen faces away from us, but we take it that what the men are watching is a video of *Dead Birds*, since we hear the beginning of Gardner's voice-over from that film emanating from the tinny speaker. "There is a fable told by a mountain people living in the ancient highlands of New Guinea. . . ." There is a cut to the magisterial opening shot of *Dead Birds*.

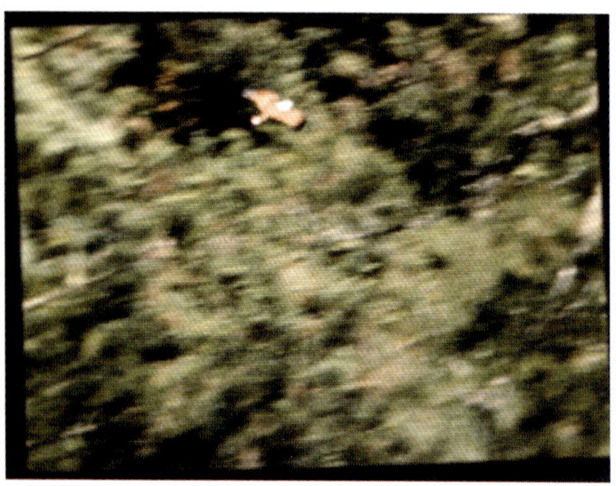

The slightly askew narrow black border that frames the image here, and the visible lines that mark it as a low resolution television image, lead us to "read" this shot as one filmed at the time directly from the monitor screen the men were watching. (For several such shots in this sequence, this is an effect created in postproduction, as Rebecca Meyers explained to me. The shot in *Dead Birds Re-Encountered* was made from a DVD of *Dead Birds* and modified, after the fact, to appear as if it had been taken from the television the men were watching.)

Gardner's voice-over from *Dead Birds* continues: ". . . about a race between a snake and a bird. It tells of a contest to decide whether men would be like birds and die, or be like snakes, which shed their skins and have eternal life. The bird won." At this point in the opening of *Dead Birds*, the word "BIRDS" is superimposed over the image of the soaring bird. "And from that time all men, like birds, must die." Just before these last two words, there is a cut, within the opening of *Dead Birds*, to a shot, accompanied by plaintive wailing, of Dani villagers carrying a boy's dead body. Gardner's camera—as he was shooting this action at the time of filming *Dead Birds*—pans to follow their movement. This shot, over which is superimposed the film's full title, "DEAD BIRDS," ends with a dissolve to a poignant shot of the dead boy, obviously much loved, over which the title "a film by Robert Gardner" becomes superimposed. In the course of these last two shots, Gardner's camera—as he was filming *Dead Birds Re-Encountered*, not *Dead Birds*—begins slowly zooming out. This makes the shot's frame-within-the-frame, and the image it contains, grow steadily smaller, and clearly reveals that we have been viewing a film being shown on a television screen. This movement is interrupted by a shot of Weyak and Kerulu in the "present" (a present that is itself the past), implying that they were watching the same shots from *Dead Birds* that we were watching.

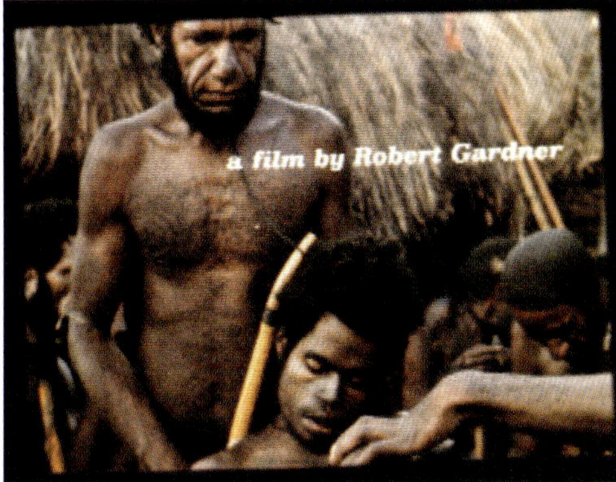

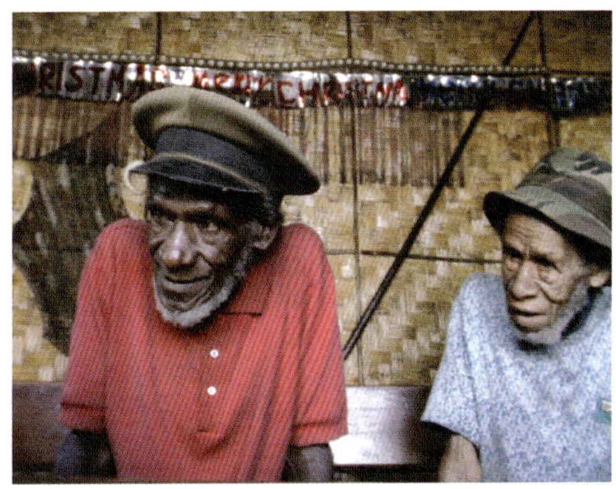

The zooming resumes after a cut back to the monitor screen, on which we see a close-up of a man's hands twisting some kind of thread. Within *Dead Birds*, this shot of weaving, which is alluded to in later shots, serves as a metaphor for the passing of time, as Charles Warren suggests in his essay for this volume, a metaphor enhanced visually, in *Dead Birds Re-Encountered*, by the way the zoom shrinks the image from *Dead Birds*.

As the *Dead Birds* voice-over continues ("Among those who tell why men must die is Weyak"), there is, within the film-within-the-film, a cut to an extreme close-up of Weyak that identifies him as the weaver in the preceding shot. This shot appears to have been made in postproduction from the DVD of *Dead Birds*, not filmed from the monitor screen at the time the men were watching the film. Only the narrow black border added to frame of the image marks this as the world of *Dead Birds*, not the world of *Dead Birds Re-Encountered*. The effect is uncanny when this shot is followed directly by a beautiful shot of the Weyak of the "present" watching the Weyak of the "past," the toll taken on him by the passage of time underscored by the fact that both shots frame him from the same angle.

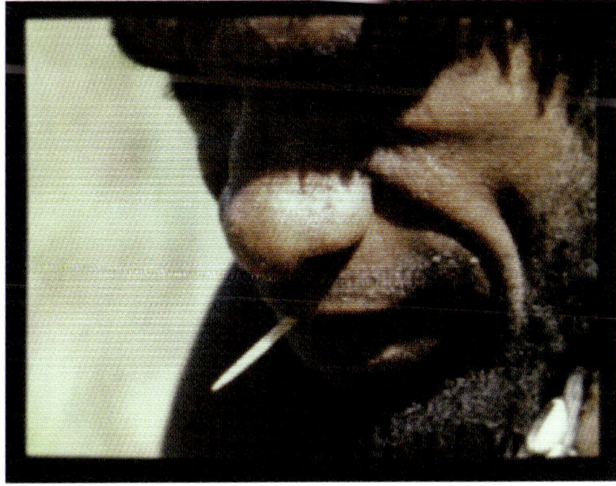

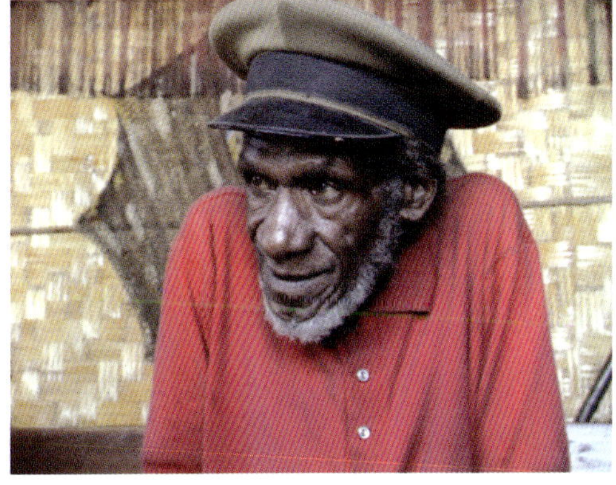

Dead Birds identifies Weyak as one of those who tells the myth that explains why men must die. Indeed, he serves in the film as *the* bearer of this knowledge all human beings possess, the knowledge that we must die. In a way, Gardner's editing of this section of *Dead Birds Re-Encountered*, which distills the story of *Dead Birds* into a handful of sequences that we see the Dani men watching, downplays Pua and brings Weyak to the fore—at once making us aware of the toll the years seem to have taken on him, and underscoring the centrality of death as a theme in both films. As we hear Gardner saying, in his *Dead Birds* voice-over, that Weyak was "neither very rich nor very powerful" but had "the respect of all with whom he lives," the shot of Weyak in

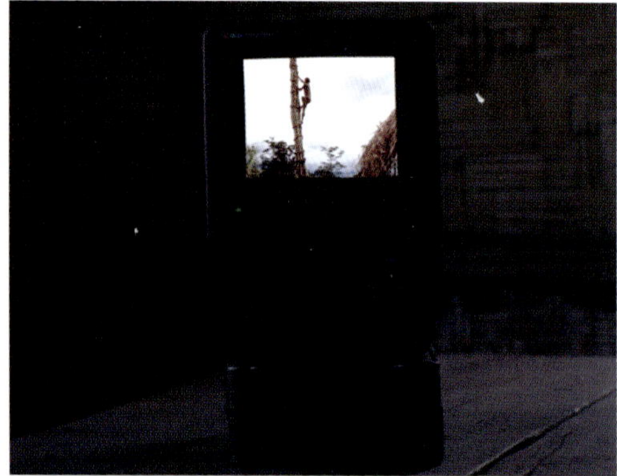

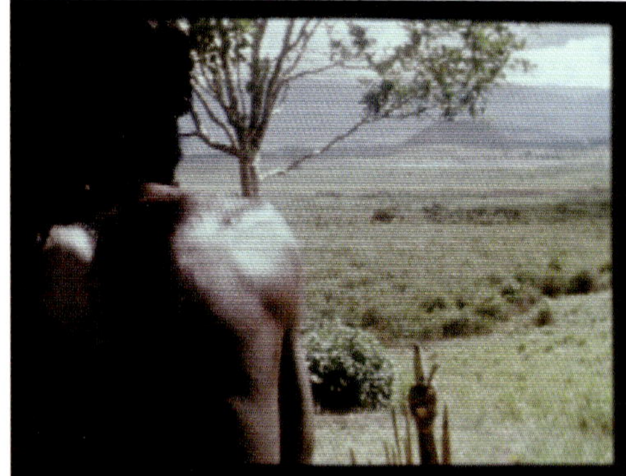

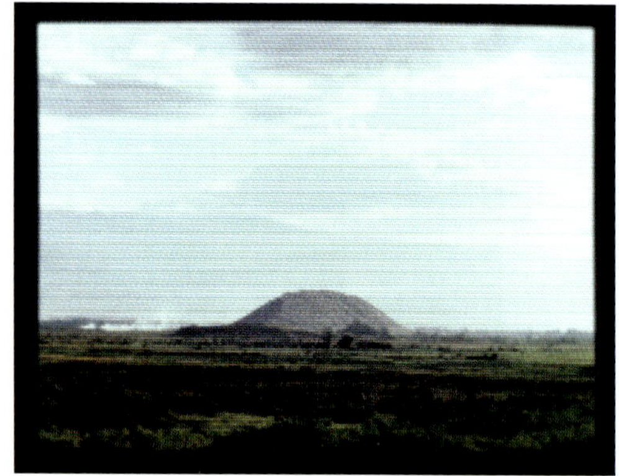

the "present" is followed by a shot of the television, on its screen the image of Weyak climbing his watchtower. Gardner frames this shot from an angle that conveys the impression that it represents Weyak's point of view.

Weyak, watching his own projected image, seems so withdrawn that we do not know what he is thinking, or even whether he is thinking at all about the film or the present situation, a fact ironically underscored by the next line we hear Gardner speak: "Today, Weyak is especially alert, because it is already two weeks since he and all the others of his group celebrated their killing of an enemy warrior." The next shot we see, framed by the telltale black border, is of Weyak-as-he-was, framed in the foreground with his back to the camera, looking into the depths of the frame toward the distant mountain—a viewer, just like us.

The following shot from *Dead Birds*, representing Weyak's point of view, moves Gardner to describe it poetically in his voice-over as a view of "the emptying fields toward the Warabaga, and the twilight which fills with the shapes and sounds of swallows. The sight never fails to please him even when his thoughts concern the enemy and what they must be planning."

Gardner's wording of these sentences links Weyak's appreciation of the beauty of nature, epitomized for him—and for Gardner—by "the shapes and sounds of swallows" in the twilight, with Weyak's status within *Dead Birds* as the bearer of the knowledge that men, like birds, must die. This is why, I take it, Gardner completes his narration's delicate invocation of the act of killing over a shot from *Dead Birds* of the distant mountain viewed as it was in the mountain/clouds shots that appeared in the film's opening, although now it is devoid of the time-lapse motions of clouds and shadows that made those shots metaphors for the passage of time. This shot, which links the world of *Dead Birds* with the world of *Dead Birds Re-Encountered*—the world of the past with the world of the "present," a present that is also past—even as it asserts their separateness, and which is rendered doubly mysterious by its echo of the opening of *this* film, then fades out.

Gardner's first film, *Blunden Harbour*, also begins with a voice-over—written, but not spoken, by Gardner—in which the narrator invokes a myth traditionally told by the people the film is about. This narrator, beginning his recounting of the myth with the words "I think now of," pointedly refrains from identifying who or what his "I" is. We know he cannot be the myth's protagonist, the Whale-Man, weary of ceaselessly wandering, who wants to become a real man and chooses Blunden Harbour as the place to build his house. Rhetorically, the narrator is a figure for the filmmaker himself, just embarking on his life of wandering in search of his own Blunden Harbour—no Whale-Man, to be sure, but a Camera-Man—perhaps another way of not being a "real" man, of being outside the human circle.

In *Dead Birds*, unlike *Blunden Harbour*, Gardner speaks his own narration, but he words it entirely in the third person. In *Dead Birds*, there is no suggestion that the narrator feels a special connection with the people who tell this "fable" other than that he, too, being a man, must die. Gardner invokes the telling of this fable by "mountain people," rather than telling it himself, thus not necessarily endorsing the myth's moral that because human beings are fated to die, they must be incapable of shedding their skin, incapable of a metamorphosis, like that achieved by the Whale-Man, so traumatic as to be tantamount to death and rebirth. Ralph Waldo Emerson says that what in his essay "Circles" he calls the wonderful "way of *life*," the practice his writings champion and strive to exemplify, is by *abandonment*, by letting one's old self die so that a new self can be born.[1] Is *Dead Birds* the skin Gardner's new film must shed for *Dead Birds Re-Encountered* to be born?

The next part of the sequence alternates scenes from *Dead Birds* that depict warfare, and shots that detail the men's reactions to the film they are watching. Perhaps too young to have even witnessed such battles, Pua watches with gleaming eyes. At one point, Wali claps as one of his "team" makes a good move. They all behave like men watching a football game or a soccer match. Accompanying this passage is Gardner's fascinating narration from *Dead Birds* explaining that the enemy feels a sense of urgency—both to appease angry ghosts and to experience the lift to their souls that comes from killing an enemy—to avenge a death their side suffered weeks before. "Until they do, they live in a state of spiritual decline. . . . By contrast, causing the death of an enemy is tonic to the soul."

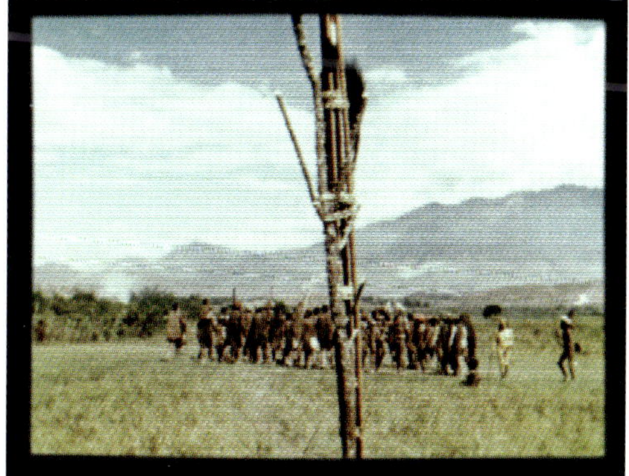

At this point, *Dead Birds Re-Encountered* jumps ahead to later in *Dead Birds*: the funeral of a boy an enemy raiding party killed at the river, thus evening the score. Then it jumps ahead again to the point in *Dead Birds*, close to the ending, when another enemy is killed. "From the place he died," Gardner's 1963 voice-over explains, "the enemy was dragged feet first along a slippery path out to the dance ground, which lies halfway between the mountain wall and the frontier." There is a series of close-ups: Wali; Kurelu; Weyak; Wali again, in an even closer shot. "At dawn, they carried him away to where his friends could claim the body."

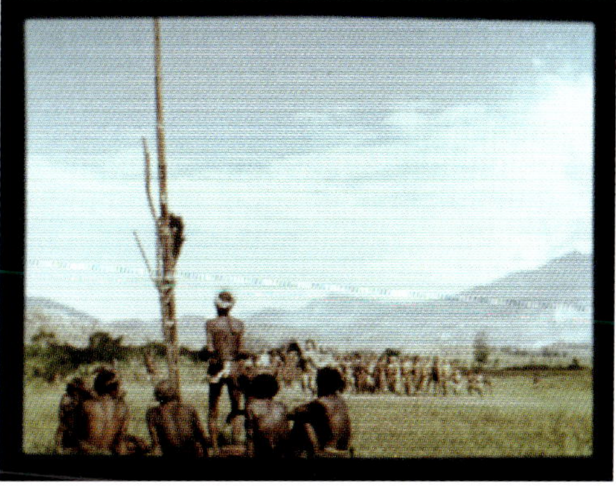

There is a cut to a shot from *Dead Birds* of a watchtower, the camera slowly tilting down. "Captured enemy ornaments and weapons are at the dance ground with an early group of women and some older men who brought them." The camera has tilted all the way down to frame the base of the tower, with dancers in the background and the mountain behind them. This is followed by a deep-focus shot that would have made André Bazin proud: a group of men in the foreground at the base of the tower—one of them is dancing—and dancers in the background, the dance accompanied by loud, rhythmic yelping.

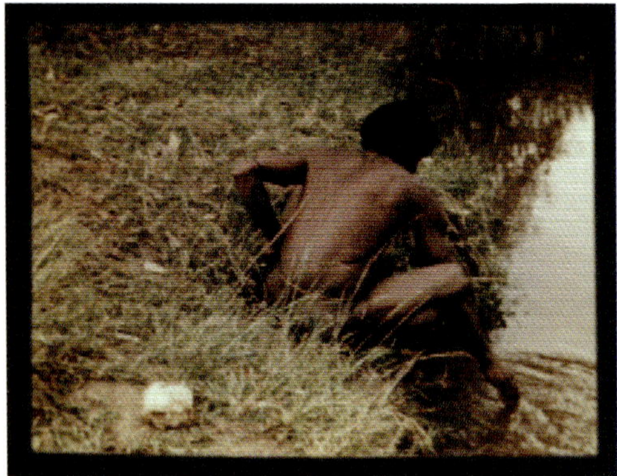

An abrupt cut takes us to a shot with Pua, Wali, and some younger Indonesian men crowding the frame. (These are men who work for the local government and thus represent the authorities who forced the Dani to give up their ritual warfare, wear Western clothing and take part in a society in which they must earn money in order to survive.) "This is what we used to do, my younger brothers," Wali says, taking on the mantle of teacher. Then we hear Gardner's voice, coming from the tinny speaker, saying, "Thirsty, and knowing that today the river is quite safe . . ." "There's Weyak!," Wali exclaims with some excitement. (There is a cut to the shot they are seeing, but taken from the *Dead Birds* DVD, not the television screen.) We see Weyak on the riverbank, stooping down to scoop up water with his hands, followed by a close-up of his cupped hand.

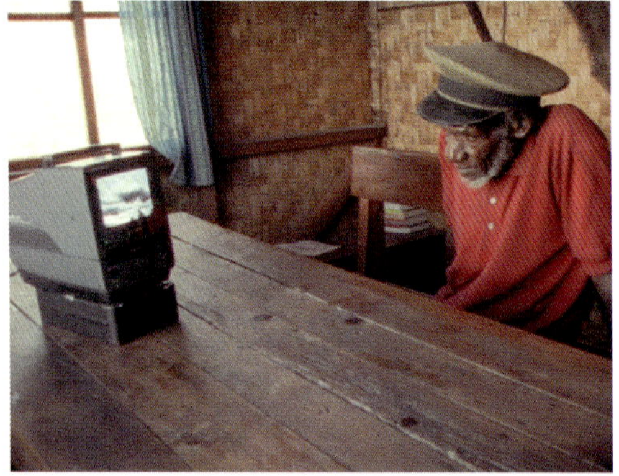

Despite the black border that frames them, these shots are so vivid that the effect is startling when the next cut takes us out of the world of *Dead Birds* to a strikingly composed shot with the television at the left—for the first time, we see how tiny its screen is—and Weyak sitting alone at the right, his body so slumped it is hard to discern whether his eyes are open. On the small screen we can see the dancers whose loud yelping again fills the air.

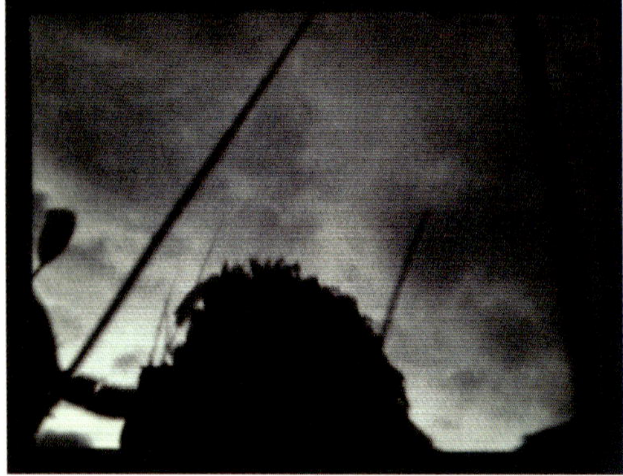

Then there is a cut to Kurelu and Wali, at the other end of the table, with men behind them, their faces cut off by the frame line. Over the line "Soon, both men and birds will surrender to the night" with its double meaning—they'll surrender to *this* night, to awaken in the morning; they'll surrender to death, never to awaken—there is a cut to an extended, breathtaking shot of dancers with spears and feathers, silhouetted against the sky, passing through the frame. "They'll rest for the life and death of days to come. For each, both awaits, but with the difference that men, having foreknowledge of their doom. . . ."

On the word "doom," there is a cut to an extreme close-up of Wali; "bring a special passion"; on the word "passion," a cut to Pua; "to their life."

These moving close-ups are followed by a shot of all the men except Weyak. They don't understand a word of Gardner's narration, yet they all have serious expressions, as they look in the direction of the television off-screen to the left. Gardner's camera holds on this framing almost until the end of the *Dead Birds* narration.

> They will not simply wait for death, nor will they bear it lightly when it comes. Instead, they will try with measured violence to fashion fate themselves. They kill to save their souls and, perhaps, to ease the burden of knowing what birds will never know. . . .

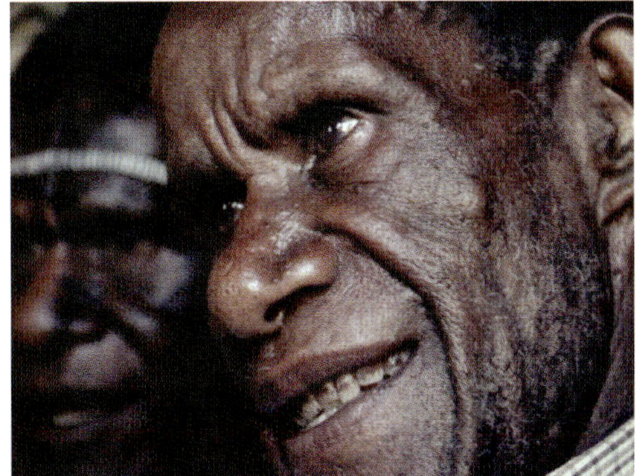

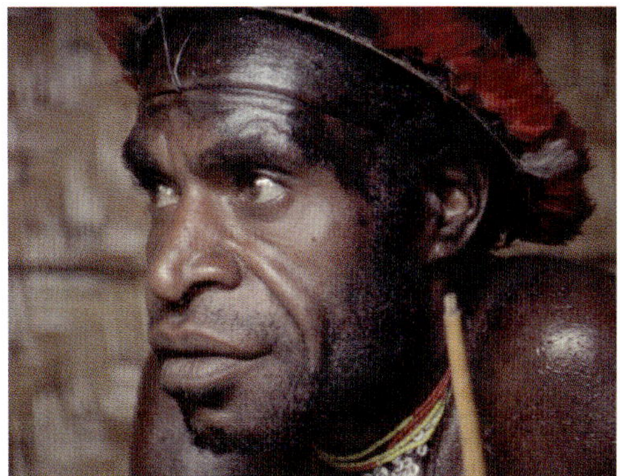

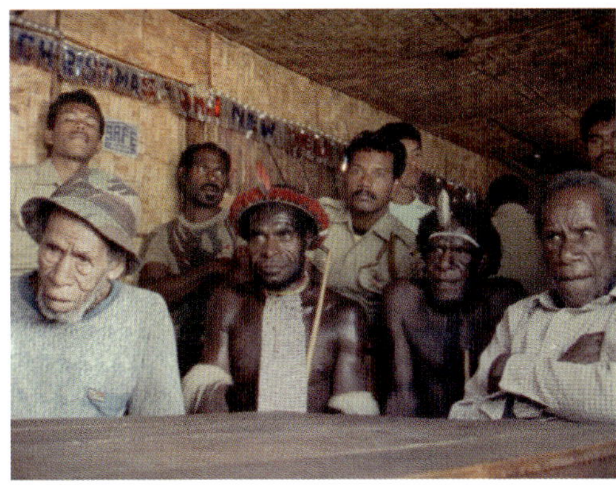

At this point, there is a cut back to the world of *Dead Birds*. We see the flowing river. On the far side we make out, in the twilight, Weyak rising to his feet and walking slowly away from the riverbank. On the soundtrack, the rhythmic yelping of dancers mixes with the squawking of birds as Gardner's voice-over approaches its end, "and what they, as men, who have forever killed each other. . . ." He finishes the line over an even more beautiful shot of the flowing river, "cannot forget." Weyak, a tiny figure silhouetted against the sky, walks away at the top of the ridge on the far shore.

The rhythmic yelps and bird cries fade slowly into silence. The shot does not fade to black, as we might expect, however. Rather, there is a direct cut from the world of *Dead Birds* to the world of *Dead Birds Re-Encountered*. Sitting in broad daylight on the grass of the riverbank, we see Pua, screen left, facing Gardner, who is only partly visible at the opposite edge of the frame. Immediately, the camera zooms out to include Weyak, sitting screen left from Pua, and to bring Gardner fully into the frame.

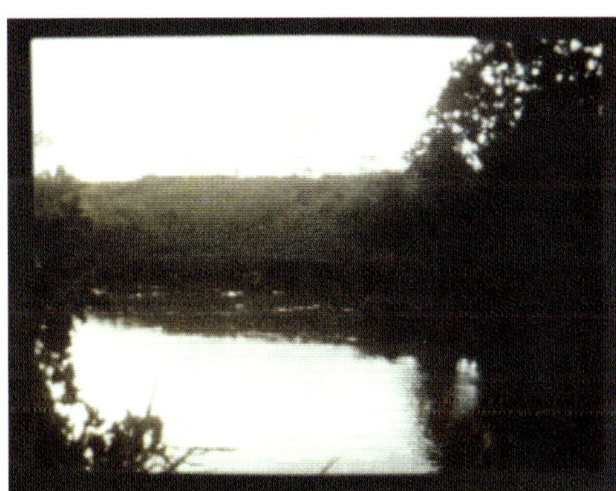

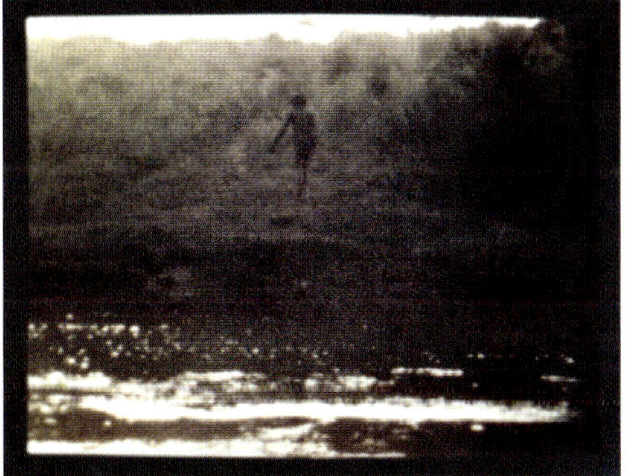

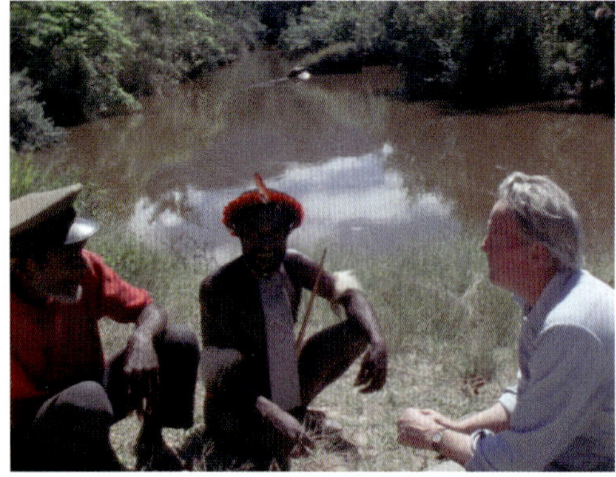

Addressing the camera but only occasionally looking in its direction, Gardner explains that they are in a place Weyak and Pua know very well. In *Dead Birds*, this river, like the Ganges in *Forest of Bliss*, is at once a place of renewal and a place of death. This is where people come to drink. Gardner points out that it's also the place where one of Pua's young friends was killed by the enemy, adding that Weyak "felt very badly" about that death, because his watchtower was just over the hill. "He felt that he should have been here for it, but he wasn't. And that's what happened, and that's what happens, and, uh. . ." His voice trails off.

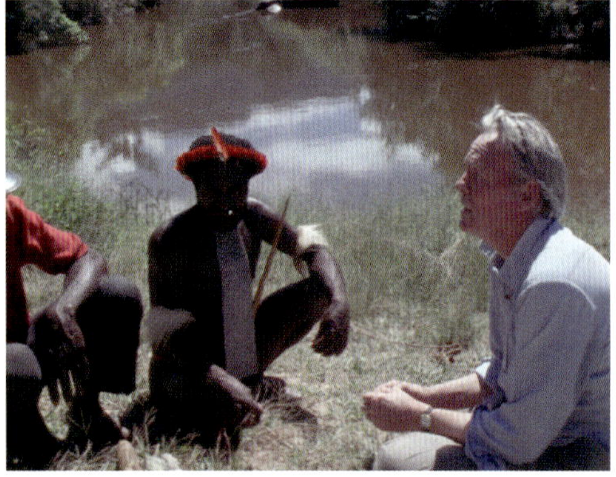

As Gardner is saying all this, he turns now and then to the camera, gesturing with his hands. Robert Fulton, behind the camera, spontaneously reframes the shot so as to give Gardner more prominence. An effect of this, which we may not notice, is that Weyak's face becomes cut off from view. When Gardner, saying to Weyak (in English, a language Weyak does not understand) "You mustn't feel badly about it," spontaneously leans in toward Weyak, and extends his long arm to give him a consoling pat on the knee, the camera reframes with his gesture, causing Weyak's face to reenter the frame, perhaps making us chagrined that we hadn't noticed its absence.

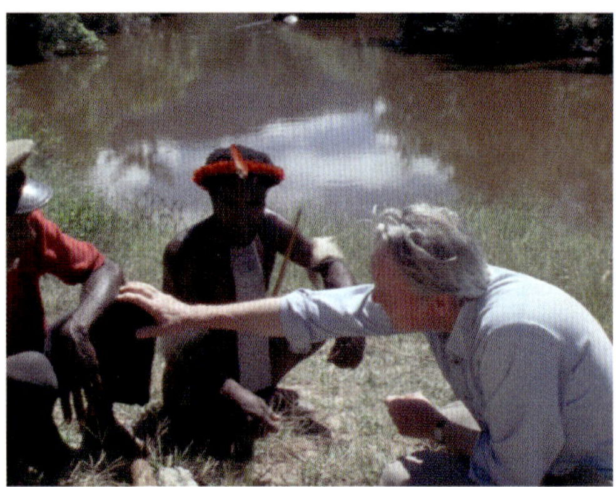

Gardner again addresses the camera to reiterate how upset Weyak was at the time, adding, "He's OK now." He says this not fully convincingly, because the film has given us reason to believe that *Gardner* believes that Weyak never stopped feeling sorrowful about the death for which he holds himself responsible. With a shrug, but without shrugging off his own melancholy mood, or ours, Gardner gestures toward the river and says, "Well, this is where the film ends, really." What film does he mean? The next words he speaks—"The river is still running"—suggest that he is referring to the film he is there to make about his "journey of return." This suggests, in turn, that he is already planning to use this little scene he has set up, in which he is sitting with Weyak and Pua by the river, to provide this film with its ending. But the next thing Gardner says—"And Weyak comes down for a drink. . ."—suggests, rather, that by "the film" he means *Dead Birds*, whose ending is the scene we had just watched, in which Weyak, indeed, "comes down for a drink." He finishes his sentence with words that foreshadow the ending of *both* films: ". . . with the sky full of birds."

In a tone of voice one might expect from a man who had just seen a ghost, Gardner says, "But now, it's very strange to be thinking about these things." He looks up and appears ready to emit a weary sigh. What we hear is too loud to be a sigh, though. It is a sound overlap with the film's final shot, which is also the penultimate shot of *Dead Birds*: the

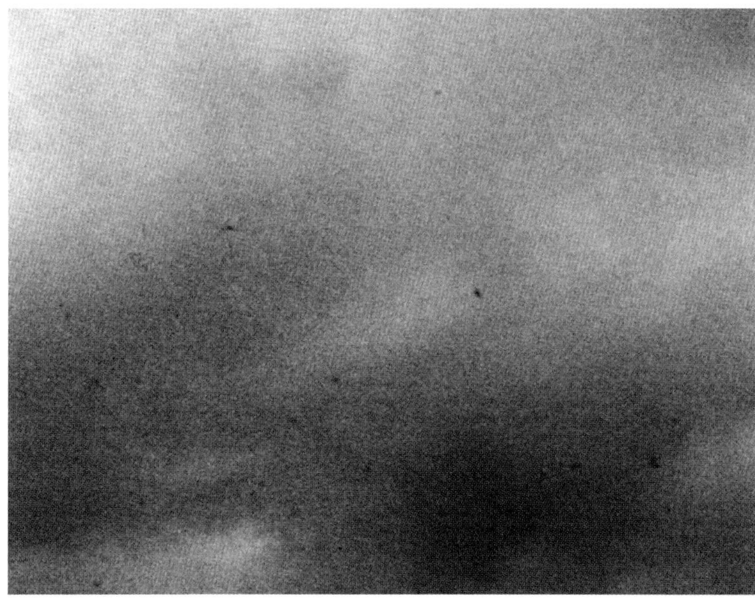

twilight sky filled with "the shapes and sounds of swallows"—so many birds, so high in the transfigured twilight that they are so many dots, so many stars in the firmament, but also so many grains of a film stock pushed to its limits by the gathering darkness. This vision at once of the infinite and the infinitesimal is held for a long time before the screen abruptly becomes black, although the sounds of swallows linger for several seconds.

When the Dani men are viewing *Dead Birds* on a small television screen, our attention is divided between watching what they are watching, and watching them watching. The sequence is edited in such a way that we can always distinguish the film-within-the-film from the film that contains it. Some of the shots from *Dead Birds* were taken from the monitor the Dani were watching. Others were taken from the DVD of the film, but given a black border to underscore that they are shots from the film the men are watching. The final shot of *Dead Birds Re-Encountered* forgoes the black border. What it gives us to view is not contained within a frame-within-the-frame or otherwise set apart formally from the body of the film. The world of *Dead Birds* has *become* the world of *Dead Birds Re-Encountered.* And the world of *Dead Birds Re-Encountered* has *become* the world of *Dead Birds.* The entirety of *Dead Birds Re-Encountered* leads to this moment at which the two fuse, the "present" film returning to the "past" film by incorporating its art and its ending. By transforming Weyak's acceptance of death's necessity into Gardner's anticipation of his own death, *Dead Birds Re-Encountered* draws a circle around the circle the earlier film had drawn, to invoke Emerson's metaphor. To once more invoke the film's own metaphor, *Dead* Birds is the skin that had to be shed to enable *Dead Birds Re-Encountered* to be born. In *Dead Birds Re-Encountered*, Gardner himself, no less than Weyak and Pua, is the subject whose otherness and mystery, and whose power to create art that communicates what he wishes known, Gardner reflects on and—as a true artist—respects.

Dead Birds ends with Weyak at the river, removed from his fellow villagers who are singing and dancing to celebrate the killing of an enemy and to "revive their souls," as Gardner tells us in his voice-over before his voice falls silent. The absence of narration for long stretches of this passage respects the power of the film's images and sounds to capture, and transfigure, the mood cast by the singers and dancers. It is as if the filmmaker, possessed by this mood, allows *his* art to fuse with *theirs*. Only when dusk deepens into night and the pulsating dancers, silhouetted against the Prussian blue sky, verge toward spellbinding visual abstractions, does Gardner begin speaking again, the haunting final words of his narration resonating with the poetry of his cinema.

Dead Birds presents its shot of the twilight sky as from the point of view of Weyak, whose attunement to nature's beauty is inseparable within the film from his solitude and from his status as one who tells why men must die. The shot allows *Dead Birds* its eloquent ending. We take Weyak, looking up at the twilight sky, to be contemplating the dark mysteries of life and death, of permanence and transience, perhaps pondering the unanswerable question: why he is still alive while an innocent boy is dead. This ending confirms that Weyak is the film's exemplar of humanity, haunted by yet accepting of the fact that we are all fated to die. But in being posited as standing in for human beings in general, Weyak represents humanity in the abstract. This makes his vision of death an abstraction as well. For those as young and sprightly of step as Gardner was when he shot *Dead Birds*, death *is* an abstraction.

In *Dead Birds Re-Encountered*, the same shot takes on an altered meaning. We read it as Gardner's own vision, not Weyak's. And Gardner does not raise his eyes to the heavens, as Weyak does at the end of *Dead Birds*, knowing he will be pleased, as the narration tells us this man always is, by "the shapes and sounds of swallows" in the twilight. Gardner fades out the final shot of *Dead Birds Re-Encountered* without telling us how these "shapes and sounds" make him feel. The shot itself, with the bird sounds almost painfully ratcheted up, has an overwhelming visceral impact, as if Gardner, at this moment, feels assaulted, ambushed, by this vision. He does not feel the way Joan of Arc does, in Carl Dreyer's masterpiece, when she looks up and sees the birds wheeling above her, the sun in their wings, knowing that, as Cavell puts it in *The World Viewed*, "They, there, are free. They are waiting, in their freedom, to accompany her soul."[2]

This anticipation of his own death with which Gardner ends *Dead Birds Re-Encountered* is no abstraction. At the age of eighty-seven, as he was when he completed the film, death was too imminent a prospect to be an abstraction. As he was completing the film, death must have felt especially close at hand, not simply because of his advanced age, but also because the film's world had become a world of ghosts to him. He had not finished mourning the premature deaths of the two dear friends who had embarked with him on this "voyage of return." And Pua, no longer a "vulnerable, tender" eight-year-old boy as he appears in *Dead Birds Re-Encountered*, but still vulnerable and still tender, had also been cut down in his prime. Wali and Weyak, too, were dead. Only a few months after the film's premiere screening at Harvard's Carpenter Center, death came to Robert Gardner, too.

"Now, it's very strange to be thinking about these things," Gardner says just before he looks up and receives this climactic vision. He already feels a sense of strangeness, the kind of experience Cavell had in mind when he wrote, in *The World Viewed*, "I think everyone knows odd moments at which it seems uncanny that one should find oneself just here now, that one's life should have come to this verge of time and place, that one's history should have unwound to this room, this road, this promontory." Cavell's passage goes on: "Movies bring home the knowledge, or self-knowledge, that we exist in the condition of myth, that we do not require the gods to show that our lives illustrate a story which escapes us; and it requires no major recognition or reversal to bring its meaning home."[3]

Gardner has often said about *Dead Birds* that it tells a story he wanted to tell, a story he knew, at least in broad outline, while he was filming and even before filming began. Insofar as he went back to New Guinea because he wanted to make a film of his "journey of return," the story

Dead Birds Re-Encountered tells is not—cannot be—a story he already knew—already knew he wanted to tell—when he embarked on that journey. How could he know the story of a chapter of his life before he lived it? How could he know, when he asked his two dearest friends to accompany him, that it would take a quarter of a century to complete the film he had embarked on his "journey of return" to make? How could he know this film's story until it unfolded, revealed itself to him, in the course of the journey? Making a film that tells the story of Gardner's "journey of return"—the story of the film's creation—*was* his journey, or at least part of it.

Only when I had almost finished writing *Documentary Film Classics* (1997) did it dawn on me that all six of the great films I was writing about had the same overall trajectory. In *Nanook of the North*, for example, Nanook and his family, in search of food, penetrate deeper and deeper into the frozen wilderness until they reach the place where the melancholy "spirit of the North" fully reveals itself, and it is upon reaching this geographical and spiritual place that Flaherty's film ends, without envisioning a way back. In *Land without Bread* (1933), a film that made a powerful and lasting impact on Gardner, the narrator and his companions depart from Alberca and cross high mountains into the land of the Hurdanos, then penetrate deeper and deeper into this impoverished region until the horror that is the Hurdanos' existence fully reveals itself. Once the camera arrives at this place, Buñuel ends his film, also without envisioning a way back. Most—perhaps all—of Gardner's films, *Blunden Harbour*, *Rivers of Sand*, *Deep Hearts*, *Ika Hands*, and *Forest of Bliss* among them, follow a similar trajectory. And so do *Dead Birds* and *Dead Birds Re-Encountered*. *Dead Birds* ends at the river—a place of death, but in the end a place of renewal. *Dead Birds Re-Encountered* ends with a return to the same river—a place of renewal, but in the end a place of death. In returning to the river, the film returns to *Dead Birds* as well, re-encountering its ending as the artist's anticipation of his own death, his acknowledgment of its necessity, its finality, its unstoppability. Mythically, death is a necessity if Gardner's last film is to be born.

It is characteristic for a Gardner film to climax cinematically, as *Dead Birds* does, with a passage in which its own art fuses with the art of the subjects he is filming. In *Blunden Harbour* and *Rivers of Sand*, as in *Dead Birds*, Gardner's art fuses with dance. In *Deep Hearts*, it fuses with the performance art, as we might think of it, of the men who are participating in the "beauty contest" with which the film climaxes. In *Ika Hands*, it is the chanting of the man named Mama Marco as he walks into the clouds, the culmination of his meditation, the fusing of song and nothingness at once captured and effected, cinematically, by the camera. *Forest of Bliss* climaxes not with the sequence in which we finally observe a dead body being cremated, but with the subsequent performance of the healer, whose ecstatic chanting at once possesses, and is possessed by, Gardner's rapturous camera.

Not surprisingly, such fusions also occur in Gardner's films about works of art and artists. An example is *Passenger* (1997), the longest of three short films Gardner made about the painter Sean Scully. *Passenger* documents Scully's creation of the painting of that name. He calls his painting "Passenger" because it has a large hole in the middle that is filled by another painting, which is like a passenger riding within it. Gardner's film is about the creation of this painting, but it is also about the creation of the film itself—the eponymous "passenger" being at once the film, which rides within the painting, so to speak, and the painting, which rides within the film. In *Dancing with Miklós* (1993), Gardner's tribute to the art of Miklós Jancsó, it is the great Hungarian director's film *The Blue Danube Waltz* (1992), the making of which is Gardner's subject, with which Gardner's own film fuses—or, in this case, dances. And in *Still Journey On* (2013), which I take to be a lighthearted but deeply felt companion-piece to *Dead Birds Re-Encountered*, Gardner's film fuses with the anthem of the same name, sung with inimitable brio by the great Scottish music hall performer (Sir) Harry Lawder, and with his own solitary dance, accompanied by the last stanza of the song on the soundtrack, which concludes the film:

> Ev'ry road thru' life is a long, long road
> Fill'd with joys and sorrows too,
> As you journey on how your heart will yearn
> For the things most dear to you.
> With wealth and love 'tis so,
> But onward we must go.
> Keep right on to the end of the road,
> Keep right on to the end,
> Tho' the way be long, let your heart be strong,
> Keep right on round the bend.
> Tho' you're tired and weary still journey on,
> Till you come to your happy abode,
> Where all you loved and were dreaming of
> Will be there at the end of the road.

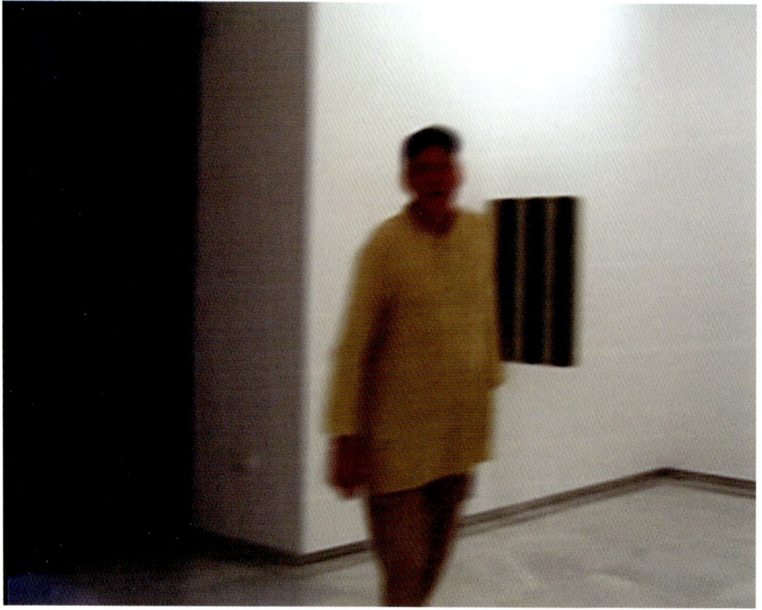

The shot of Gardner dancing was originally taken by Robert Fulton, captured on late 1990s consumer-grade video and in slow motion, at the time of the making of the Scully films, fifteen years before Gardner found this inspired use for it. For *Still Journey On*, he slowed the shot down further in postproduction. Softened by its low resolution and its manipulation of time, the shot is so blurry, Gardner's figure so indistinct, that he can hardly be recognized—a clever but moving way for him to acknowledge the failing eyesight that had robbed him of his ability to view the world through a camera lens, and his refusal to let that keep him from "still journeying on."

Dead Birds Re-Encountered documents Gardner's return to Papua New Guinea to re-encounter the people he had known when he filmed *Dead Birds* there. And yet, the artist's "journey of return" did not end when he brought back from that "other planet" the footage he and Fulton had shot, but only when he finished creating *Dead Birds Re-Encountered* from that footage. The words Gardner speaks in *Dead Birds Re-Encountered*, on screen and off, say what he felt needed saying about this "journey of return." They also consign to silence what he could say only in the cinematic language, only in the poetry of the film's images and sounds. Part of what Gardner's last film is saying is that although he was approaching the end of his "long, long road thro' life," he was still "journeying on." But he was not "journeying on" in the hope that when he reached the "end of the road" he would find "all he loved and was dreaming of" in that "happy abode" from which neither bird nor man has ever returned. He had built his house in the one existing world, the world into which he had been born, the world in which he was fated to die, the world he had devoted his life to filming, the world his films transfigured, the world in which his art will live on. He had built his house in *this* world. This Camera-Man had found his Blunden Harbour—a place where "journeying on" meant returning home.

Notes

1. Ralph Waldo Emerson, "Circles," in *Emerson: Essays and Lectures*, ed. Joel Porte (New York: Library of America, 1983), 414.
2. Stanley Cavell, *The World Viewed: Reflections on the Ontology of Film, Expanded Edition* (Cambridge, MA: Harvard University Press, 1979), 159.
3. Ibid., 147.

Acknowledgments

The editors are very grateful to Dr. Adele Pressman and Studio7Arts for crucial help with the production of this book—among other things, for permission to reproduce still photographs from Robert Gardner's books *In and Out* and the forthcoming *Still Points*. Thanks to Hannah Wild at S7A for assistance in many ways.

Thanks to Documentary Educational Resources for making films available to our contributors for study over the past several years, and especially to Executive Director Alice Apley and Director of Design and Media Frank Aveni for providing us with images from Gardner's films. Eric Masunaga and Modulus Studios kindly provided us with images from *Rivers of Sand* and *Forsaken Fragments*, and Eric has helped greatly in various ways. Haden Guest, Jeremy Rossen, and Mark Johnson at the Harvard Film Archive kindly provided further sources for images.

We are grateful to Barbara Epler and New Directions Publications and to the Harvard Peabody Museum Press and Dr. Pressman for permission to reprint Eliot Weinberger's writing on Gardner.

Thanks to Kate O'Donnell at Harvard Peabody Museum Press for very helpful advice on the book's production.

We thank Peter Blaiwas for his beautiful book design and James Peltz and Laurie Searl and everyone at SUNY Press for their help and advice and good work on the book's production. Murray Pomerance, editor for SUNY's Horizons of Cinema series, took an encouraging early interest in the book and helped see us through its many stages toward completion.

We thank all our writers for their hard work in producing and perfecting the chapters here, and thank Susan Meiselas for her evocative photographs of Gardner and the Dani.

Credits

Robert Gardner film stills appear courtesy of Documentary Educational Resources (DER), Watertown, MA.

Title page (iii) and chapter 11 (138–41) photographs by Susan Meiselas appear courtesy of Magnum Photos.

Pages 8 and 24 photographs by Robert Gardner appear courtesy of Dr. Adele Pressman and Studio7Arts.

Page 8, Coptic headdress [Boy wearing huge crown] copyright © Robert G. Gardner. Courtesy of the Peabody Museum of Archaeology and Ethnology, Harvard University, PM# 2013.3.1.13.15.33.

Page 8, Nuer woman drawing on a wall [Nuer woman painting house] copyright © Robert G. Gardner. Courtesy of the Peabody Museum of Archaeology and Ethnology, Harvard University, PM# 2013.3.1.9.279.22.

Page 13, from Pieter Apian, *Cosmographia*, f. 3 r. Courtesy of the Houghton Library, Harvard University.

Page 220, Man being made up, Getty images. Used courtesy of iStock Photo.

Page 221, African-style vest, Walter Van Beirendonck Spring–Summer 2012 "Read My Skin Collection," photo by Dan Lecca. Used by permission of Walter Van Beirendonck.

Page 221, Costume with palm tree headdress, Jean Paul Gaultier Spring–Summer 2010 Collection. Used by permission of Jelka Music.

Page 267, Mark Tobey, *Canticle*, Smithsonian Museum of American Art. Reproduction authorized for educational or non-commercial purposes.

Page 272, Sean Scully, *Maesta*, Smithsonian Museum of American Art. Reproduction authorized for educational or non-commercial purposes.

Excerpts from "The Camera People," from *Outside Stories, 1987–1991*, copyright © 1987, 1988, 1989, 1990, 1991, 1992 by Eliot Weinberger. Reprinted by permission of New Directions Publishing Corp.

Preface to *Still Points* by Robert Gardner, copyright © 2015 by Eliot Weinberger. Reprinted by permission of the Peabody Museum Press, Harvard University.

Appendices

Robert Gardner Biographical Sketch

Robert Gardner was born in 1925 in Brookline, Massachusetts to an old Boston family. After graduating from Harvard College, he worked on mosaic restorations at the Byzantine Chora Church in Istanbul, then spent time in California and the Northwest, where he taught a history of medieval art at the College of Puget Sound. He read Ruth Benedict's *Patterns of Culture* (1934) and through it became interested in the Kwakiutl of British Columbia, leading to his first film, *Blunden Harbour* (1951) and the nine-minute *Dances of the Kwakiutl* (1951). At the same time, Gardner came to know painter Mark Tobey in Seattle—as well as poet Theodore Roethke—and started on his path of filming artists with his 1952 portrait of Tobey. He was also seeing and becoming excited by West Coast screenings of experimental films brought forward by Amos Vogel's Cinema 16 film society in New York—especially the work of Maya Deren. Gardner became friendly with San Francisco avant-gardist Sidney Peterson, and the two planned a fictional project, never realized, involving the Kwakiutl.[1]

Gardner studied anthropology at the graduate level at Harvard, and founded the Film Study Center in Harvard's Peabody Museum of Archaeology and Ethnology, where he worked with John Marshall to edit *The Hunters* (1957), a breakthrough filmic study of the hunter/gatherer !Kung of southern Africa's Kalahari Desert. The Museum sponsored Gardner's trip to central New Guinea in 1961; there he lived among the virtually stone-age Dani, who were engaged in constant warfare, and filmed what would become *Dead Birds* (1963), which was edited back at the Film Study Center. It was at the point of completing this film that Gardner moved the Film Study Center to Harvard's Carpenter Center for the Visual Arts, where he began teaching filmmaking in a creative arts program. *Dead Birds* itself took final shape after a screening—with much succeeding discussion—not for anthropologists, but for a literary gathering including William Styron (the host), Lillian Hellman, Robert Penn Warren, Terry Southern, and Mike Nichols, as well as Peter Matthiessen, who had been with Gardner in New Guinea.[2]

Gardner made numerous films over the years, shot on location amid premodern cultures in British Columbia, New Guinea, Africa, and South America, or, in the case of India, focusing on immemorial ritual practices—most famously *Dead Birds*, *Rivers of Sand* (1974), *Deep Hearts* (1981), *Forest of Bliss* (1986), and *Ika Hands* (1988). Going back very early, though, he also made films on other subjects, mostly on artists at work—painters Mark Tobey and Sean Scully, sculptor Alexander Calder, film director Miklós Jancsó, multimedia artist Christian Boltanski, architect Josep Lluís Sert and his fellow Catalan Joan Miró. Gardner also planned several fictional projects that did not come to fruition—at one point working with Ted Hughes on a script about a real-life nineteenth-century Australian adventurer, at another time working with J.M. Coetzee on an adaptation of his novel *Waiting for the Barbarians*, and scouting locations for this in North Africa and China.[3]

In Gardner's years at Harvard's Carpenter Center and in its Visual and Environmental Studies Department, he made films that involved travel to and considerable time spent in far-flung places. But it was important to him as well to teach creative nonfiction filmmaking, to befriend and co-teach with Stanley Cavell and make sure that Harvard paid serious attention to film, to found and develop the Harvard Film Archive, and to bring guest filmmakers and teachers to Harvard such as Dušan Makavejev, Jancsó, Raul Ruiz, and Chantal Akerman. Further, in 1972 Gardner and some friends won the broadcasting license of Boston's ABC television affiliate, and Gardner hosted the series *Screening Room* for a dozen years, which brought independent filmmakers to screen and discuss their work (Brian Frye's article here includes a list of all the programs). Gardner also produced films for others in these years—including animated films by Jan Lenica and Derek Lamb and Jancsó's feature *The Blue Danube Waltz* (1992)—and continued to administer the Film Study Center as an entity giving technical and financial support to people making nonfiction films. Following his retirement from Harvard in 1999, he administered Studio7Arts along similar lines, supporting filmmakers, photographers, and book designers.

From early on Gardner engaged in collaborative filmmaking with—most notably— Hilary Harris on *The Nuer* (1971); experimental filmmaker Robert Fulton, who traveled with Gardner in South America and Africa and shot material for *Deep Hearts* and *Ika Hands*; and multifaceted nonfiction filmmaker Richard Rogers, who, along with Fulton and still photographer Susan Meiselas, traveled with Gardner back to New Guinea in 1988–1989 to gather material Gardner would use for *Dead Birds Re-Encountered* (2013).

Throughout his career, Gardner practiced still photography as well as film (Eliot Weinberger and Fanny Howe address that work here). In 1969 Gardner collaborated with Karl Heider to produce *Gardens of War*, a book of photographs of the Dani taken by himself, Heider, Michael Rockefeller, Eliot Elisofon, and others, and for which Gardner wrote extensive reflective essays on Dani culture. Gardner had been an eloquent journal writer since the 1950s, chronicling his travels and film projects. With *Making* Forest of Bliss in 2001, he began to publish books of interviews, journals, essays, and talks, looking back on his career and reflecting on film, anthropology, and other subjects. Robert Gardner died in June of 2014.

Notes

1. Robert Gardner, "Introduction," *Making* Dead Birds: *Chronicle of a Film* (Cambridge, MA: Peabody Museum Press, 2007), 3.
2. *Making* Dead Birds, 124–125.
3. Gardner, "Cooper's Creek" and "Waiting for the Barbarians," in his collection *Just Representations* (Cambridge, MA: Studio7Arts and Peabody Museum Press, 2010), 45–55, 103–137.

Robert Gardner Filmography

(asterisks indicate collaborations)
Blunden Harbour (1951, 22 minutes)
Dances of the Kwakiutl (1951, 9 minutes)
Mark Tobey (1952, 19 minutes)
Dead Birds (1963, 83 minutes)
Marathon (1965, 28 minutes)
People and Particles (1965, 27 minutes) *producer, directed by Barry Ferguson and Michael Butler
The Great Sail (1966, 10 minutes)
Imaginaro (1968, 54 minutes) *producer, directed by Jorge Preloran
The Nuer (1971, 73 minutes) *producer, directed by Hilary Harris and George Breidenbach
Land-divers of Melanesia (1972, 34 minutes) *producer, directed by Kal Muller
Screening Room Series (1972–1981)
Mark Tobey Abroad (1973, 28 minutes)
Rivers of Sand (1974, 85 minutes)
Moving Pictures (1975, 19 minutes) *producer, directed by Richard Rogers
African Carving (1975, 19 minutes) *producer, directed by Thomas Blakeley and Eliot Elisofon
Altar of Fire (1976, 45 minutes) *directed with J.F. Staal
Cost of Living (1975, 55 minutes) *producer, directed by Richard Rogers
The Shepherds of Berneray (1981, 57 minutes) *producer, directed by Allen Moore and Jack Shea
Deep Hearts (1981, 58 minutes)
Sons of Shiva (1985, 29 minutes) *made with Ákos Östör
Serpent Mother (1985, 28 minutes) *producer, directed by Ákos Östör and Allen Moore
Loving Krishna (1985, 55 minutes) *producer, directed by Ákos Östör and Allen Moore
Forest of Bliss (1986, 90 minutes)
Ika Hands (1988, 58 minutes)
Blue Danube Waltz (1991, 90 minutes) *produced with Michael Fitzgerald, directed by Miklós Jancsó
Dancing With Miklos (1993, 28 minutes)
Passenger (1998, 25 minutes)
Scully in Malaga (1998, 7 minutes)
Good To Pull (Bon à Tirer) (2000, 10 minutes)
Testigos (2007, 10 minutes)
Glimpses of Octavio Paz (2009)
Forsaken Fragments (2010–2011, circa 50 minutes)
Deus Ex Boltanski (2011, 11 minutes)
Still Journey On: An Unfinished Examination of Life (2011, 22 minutes)
2 Sons of Catalonia: Josep Luís Sert & Joan Miró (2013, 31 minutes)
Dead Birds Re-Encountered (2013, 45 minutes)

Publications by Robert Gardner

A Human Document: Life and Death in the New Guinea Stone Age (Gehenna Press, 1964)
Gardens of War: Life and Death in the New Guinea Stone Age, with Karl G. Heider. Introduction by Margaret Mead (New York: Random House, 1969)
Making Forest of Bliss*: Intention, Circumstance, and Chance in Nonfiction Film*, with Ákos Östör (Cambridge, MA: Harvard Film Archive, 2002)
The Impulse to Preserve: Reflections of a Filmmaker, ed. Ted Perry (New York: Other Press, 2008)
Making Dead Birds*: Chronicle of a Film*, ed. Charles Warren (Cambridge, MA: Peabody Museum Press, 2008)
Beauty Contest (Cambridge, MA: Studio7Arts, 2009)
In & Out, with Fanny Howe (Cambridge, MA: Studio7Arts, 2009)
Human Documents: Eight Photographers, eds. Kevin Bubriski and Charles Warren (Cambridge, MA: Peabody Museum Press, 2009)
The Story of Umaru Dikko (Cambridge, MA: Studio7Arts, 2009)
Just Representations: Observations of a General Nature, ed. and intr. Charles Warren (Cambridge, MA: Studio7Arts & Peabody Museum Press, 2010)
Still Points (forthcoming from Peabody Museum Press)

Books about Robert Gardner's Work

Barbash, Ilisa, and Lucien Taylor, eds., *The Cinema of Robert Gardner* (Oxford: Berg, 2007)
Cooper, Thomas W., *Natural Rhythms: The Indigenous World of Robert Gardner* (New York: Anthology Film Archives, 1995)
Loizos, Peter, *Innovation in Ethnographic Film: From Innocence to Self-Consciousness, 1955–1985* (Chicago: University of Chicago Press, 1993) (includes a large discussion of Gardner)
MacDonald, Scott, *American Ethnographic Film and Personal Documentary: The Cambridge Turn* (Berkeley and Los Angeles: University of California Press, 2013) (includes a large discussion of Gardner)
MacDonald, Scott, *Avant-Doc: Intersections of Documentary and Avant-Garde Cinema* (Oxford: Oxford University Press, 2014) (includes a significant interview with Gardner)
Peterman, W., R. Thoms, R. Kapfer, eds., *Rituale Von Leben und Tod: Robert Gardner und Seine Filme* (Munich: Trickster Verlag, 1989)
Tomicek, Harry, *Gardner* (Vienna: Österreichisches Film Museum, 1991)

Contributors

Richard Allen is professor of cinema studies at New York University. His books include *Projecting Illusion* (1995) and *Hitchcock's Romantic Irony* (2007), and, as co-editor, *Film Theory and Philosophy* (1997) and *Wittgenstein, Theory, and the Arts* (2001), as well as three anthologies on Hitchcock. Most recently he has turned to Indian Cinema as co-author of *Islamicate Cultures of Bombay Cinema* (2009) and he is working on a book entitled *Double Takes: Bollywood Cinema and the Poetics of Recognition.*

Mauro Bucci studied film in Bologna, with a degree thesis on Robert Gardner, and visual ethnography in Rome. He has published an essay on *Forest of Bliss* (2011) in *Bianco e Nero* as well as an extensive essay on *Dead Birds* (2012) in an Italian volume on anthropology and representation, edited by Adriana Destro. He has also written for the online journal *Visual Ethnography*, which is under the patronage of the University of Basilicata.

Gayatri Chatterjee teaches at the Film and Television Institute of India in Pune. She is the author of the British Film Institute monograph *Mother India* (2002) and *Awara*, a study of the Raj Kapoor film (1993, new edition 2003), as well as many articles. She has taught widely in India and Sri Lanka and at Berkeley, UCLA, Brown, St. Anthony's College, Oxford, and the University of Pennsylvania. Her documentary *Homes for Gods and Mortals* (2013) deals with displacement of villagers near the Khajuraho temples.

Tom Conley is Lowell Professor of Visual and Environmental Studies and of Romance Languages and Literature at Harvard, and a former Guggenheim Fellow. His books include *Film Hieroglyphs* (new edition 2006), *Cartographic Cinema* (2007), *The Self-Made Map: Cartographic Writing in Early Modern France* (new edition 2010), *An Errant Eye: Topography and Poetry in Early Modern France* (2010), and translations of Michel de Certeau and Gilles Deleuze. He has contributed essays to many volumes on film and literature.

Richard Deming is a poet and theorist who teaches in the English Department at Yale, where he is director of creative writing. His books include *Listening on All Sides: Toward an Emersonian Ethics of Reading* (2008) and the collection of poems *Let's Not Call It Consequence* (2008). Winner of the Berlin Prize in 2012, he was recently the John P. Birkelund Fellow at the American Academy in Berlin. He contributes regularly to *Artforum*, *The Boston Review*, and other journals.

Carlos Y. Flores has taught in the MA program in visual anthropology at Goldsmiths College, University of London, and now teaches in the Department of Anthropology at the Autonomous University of the State of Morelos in Mexico. He has published books and articles on visual anthropology, political violence, and processes of community reconstruction and access to law in the Maya region. His most recent collaborations with indigenous community video projects in Guatemala have led to the anthropological documentaries *K'ixba'l* (*Shame*, 2010) and *Two Justices: The Challenge of Interlegal Coordination* (2012).

Brian L. Frye is an assistant professor of law at the University of Kentucky College of Law, whose research focuses on legal issues affecting artists and arts organizations. He is also a filmmaker, who received a master of fine arts in filmmaking from the San Francisco Art Institute. He produced the documentary *Our Nixon* (2013), and his short films have shown at the Whitney Biennial and New York Film Festival, among other places. His writing on film and the arts appears in *October*, *Cineaste*, and other journals.

Fanny Howe has published many books of poetry, fiction, and essays, most recently *Come and See: Poems* (2011) and *Second Childhood* (2014), a finalist for the National Book Award in poetry, *Radical Love: 5 Novels* (2006), and the memoir *The Winter Sun: Notes on a Vocation* (2009). Her *Selected Poems* won the 2001 Lenore Marshall Poetry Prize. In 2009 she was awarded the Ruth Lily Prize of the Poetry Foundation for lifetime achievement. She has taught widely in universities in the United States. She worked with Robert Gardner to produce the book of photographs and meditations, *In and Out* (2009).

Bruce Jenkins is professor of film, video, new media, and animation at the School of the Art Institute of Chicago, and was formerly the Stanley Cavell Curator of the Harvard Film Archive. His recent books include *Gordon Matta-Clark: Conical Intersect* (2011) and, as editor, *On the Camera Arts and Consecutive Matters: The Writings of Hollis Frampton* (2009). Jenkins is at work on the catalogue raisonné of the films of Andy Warhol.

Irina Leimbacher is assistant professor of film studies at Keene State College in New Hampshire, having previously taught ethnographic cinema in the Anthropology Department, University of California, Berkley. She was artistic director of the San Francisco Cinematheque for a decade and guest curator of the Flaherty Film Seminar in 2009. Leimbacher has written several articles on nonfiction and experimental cinema and installation art and is currently working on a book on cinematic testimony.

Susan Meiselas is a documentary photographer who lives and works in New York. She is the author of *Carnival Strippers* (1976), *Nicaragua* (1981), *Kurdistan: In the Shadow of History* (1997), *Pandora's Box* (2001), and *Encounters with the Dani* (2003). She accompanied Robert Gardner to the Baliem Valley in 1989 and 1997. Meiselas has co-edited *El Salvador: Work of Thirty Photographers* (1983) and *Chile from Within* (1990), and co-directed two films about Nicaragua: *Living at Risk* (1985) and *Pictures from a Revolution* (1991) with Richard P. Rogers and Alfred Guzzetti. In 1992 Meiselas was named a MacArthur Fellow. She has served as president of the Magnum Foundation since its founding in 2007.

Rebecca Meyers is the film programmer for Bucknell University's screenings at the historic Campus Theatre in downtown Lewisburg and teaches in Bucknell's Film/Media Studies Program. She has served as director of film programs for ArtsEmerson at Emerson College, Boston, as archive coordinator for the Harvard Film Archive, and as co-director of the Onion City Film and Video Festival in Chicago. She is a filmmaker whose works have screened at venues including Anthology Film Archives and the London, Edinburgh, San Francisco, Toronto, and New York Film Festivals. From 2009 to 2013 she served as Associate Director of Studio7Arts and film editor for Robert Gardner.

Daniel Morgan is associate professor of cinema and media studies at the University of Chicago, having formerly taught at the University of Pittsburgh. He is the author of *Late Godard and the Possibilities of Cinema* (2012) and is at work on books on film and philosophy, with Richard Neer, and on the history and aesthetics of camera movement. His work on André Bazin, Max Ophuls, and Jean Rouch has appeared in *Critical Inquiry* and other journals and anthologies.

Charles Musser is professor of film and media studies at Yale University. He is the author of *The Emergence of Cinema: The American Screen to 1907* (1990), *Edison Motion Pictures, 1890–1900: An Annotated Filmography* (1997), and other books on silent cinema. With Jane Gaines and Pearl Bowser, he co-edited *Oscar Micheaux and His Circle: African American Filmmaking and Race Cinema of the Silent Period* (2001). His articles on documentary have appeared in *Film Quarterly*, *The Moving Image*, *Film History*, and other journals. His own documentary films include *An American Potter* (1976), *Before the Nickelodeon: The Early Cinema of Edwin S. Porter* (1982), and *Errol Morris: A Lightning Sketch* (2014).

Murray Pomerance is professor in the Department of Sociology at Ryerson University, Toronto. His books include *Marnie* (2014), *The Eyes Have It: Cinema and the Reality Effect* (2013), *Alfred Hitchcock's America* (2013), *Michelangelo Red Antonioni Blue* (2011), *The Horse Who Drank the Sky: Film Experience Beyond Narrative and Theory* (2008), *Johnny Depp Starts Here* (2005), *An Eye for Hitchcock* (2004), and many edited anthologies, most recently *The Last Laugh: Strange Humors of Cinema* (2013)

Kathryn Ramey is an anthropologist and filmmaker and associate professor of Visual and Media Arts at Emerson College, Boston. Her scholarly research and many articles focus on the social history of the avant-garde film community, the anthropology of visual communication, and the intersection between avant-garde and ethnographic film. She is the author of *Experimental Filmmaking: BREAK THE MACHINE* (2016). Her award-winning films have screened at the Toronto Film Festival, the TriBeCa Film Festival, L'Alternativa Barcelona, and 25fps Experimental Film Festival in Zagreb, among other venues.

William Rothman is professor of film studies at the University of Miami. His most recent books are *Must We Kill the Thing We Love?: Emersonian Perfectionism and the Films of Alfred Hitchcock* (2014) and the expanded edition of *Hitchcock—The Murderous Gaze* (2013). He is also the author of *Documentary Film Classics* (1997), *The "I" of the Camera: Essays in Film Criticism, History, and Aesthetics* (expanded edition 2004), and, with Marian Keane, *Reading Stanley Cavell's The World Viewed: A Philosophical Perspective on Film* (2000). He has edited two books on nonfiction film, and contributed many essays to books and journals.

Maxime Scheinfeigel is professor of the aesthetics and history of cinema at Université Paul Valéry—Montpelier III, and author of *Les âges du cinéma: trois parcours dans l'évolution des représentations filmiques* (2002), *Cinéma et magie* (2008), *Jean Rouch* (2008), and *Rêves et cauchemars au cinéma* (2012). She has edited six volumes on documentary, the future of cinema, cinema's relation to music and theater, and other topics.

Charles Warren teaches film studies at Boston University and in the Harvard Extension School. He is the author of *T.S. Eliot on Shakespeare* (1987), and edited *Beyond Document: Essays on Nonfiction Film* (1996) and, with Maryel Locke, *Jean-Luc Godard's* Hail Mary*: Women and the Sacred in Film* (1993), as well as several of Robert Gardner's books. He has contributed essays to recent volumes on Stanley Cavell, Jean Rouch, Michael Haneke, and Hitchcock's *Vertigo*, as well as to *The Wiley-Blackwell History of American Film*. He writes on music for the online journal *New York Arts*.

Eliot Weinberger's books of literary essays include *Karmic Traces* (2000), *An Elemental Thing* (2007), and *Oranges & Peanuts for Sale* (2009). His political articles are collected in *What I Heard About Iraq* (2005) and *What Happened Here: Bush Chronicles* (2005). He is the editor of *The New Directions Anthology of Classical Chinese Poetry* (2003), and the general editor of a series, *Calligrams: Writings from and on China*. Among his many translations of Latin American literature are *The Poems of Octavio Paz* (2012) and Jorge Luis Borges' *Selected Non-Fictions* (1999).

Julia Yezbick is a filmmaker, artist, and doctoral candidate in media anthropology and critical media practice at Harvard University. Her work has been screened at international film festivals including the 2015 Berlinale Forum Expanded. She is a member of Harvard's Sensory Ethnography Lab, a Harvard Film Study Center Fellow, the founding editor of *Sensate*, an online journal for experiments in critical media practice, and runs Mothlight Microcinema in Detroit, where she lives and is currently conducting her dissertation research.

Antonio Zirión is professor and head of the Anthropology Department at the Metropolitan Autonomous University, Mexico City. His award-winning documentaries, based on collaborative strategies with urban youth subcultures, include *Voces de la Guerrero* (2004) and *Out of Focus* (2013). He has published two photography books: *Mano de obra* (2013) and *Traspasos* (2014). He was director of the Visual Anthropology Conference at the National School of Anthropology in Mexico from 2005 to 2012, and has been since 2006 curator of Cinema Among Cultures within DocsDF (Mexico City International Documentary Film Festival), and since 2011 film programmer for Ambulante Documentary Film Festival, which tours Mexico.

Ricardo E. Zulueta holds an MFA in visual art and PhD in film studies. He researches and lectures on the interdisciplinary connections between film, media, contemporary art, and fashion studies. Zulueta's award-winning multimedia artworks have been exhibited at such venues as the International Center for Photography, Smithsonian Institution, New Museum of Contemporary Art in New York City, Museo Reina Sofia in Madrid, Steirischer Herbst in Graz, and Museo Alejandro Otero in Caracas. He has published in a number of journals including *Film and History* and *Fashion Theory*. His current book project focuses on the work of artist and filmmaker Ryan Trecartin.

Index